Cinema and Semiotic

Peirce and Film Aesthetics, Narration, and Representation

Johannes Ehrat

UNIVERSITY OF TORONTO PRESS
Toronto Buffalo London

© University of Toronto Press Incorporated 2005
Toronto Buffalo London
Printed in Canada

ISBN 0-8020-3912-X

Printed on acid-free paper

Library and Archives Canada Cataloguing in Publication

Ehrat, Johannes, 1952–
    Cinema and semiotic : Peirce and film aesthetics, narration, and
representation / Johannes Ehrat.

(Toronto studies in semiotics and communication)
Includes bibliographical references and index.
ISBN 0-8020-3912-X

1. Motion pictures – Semiotics.   2. Motion pictures – Aesthetics.
3. Peirce, Charles S. (Charles Sanders), 1839–1914.   I. Title.   II. Series.

PN1995.E397 2005   791.43' 01' 4   C2004-901722-5

University of Toronto Press acknowledges the financial assistance to its
publishing program of the Canada Council and the Ontario Arts Council.

University of Toronto Press acknowledges the financial support for its
publishing activities of the Government of Canada through the Book
Publishing Industry Development Program (BPIDP).

CINEMA AND SEMIOTIC:
PEIRCE AND FILM AESTHETICS, NARRATION,
AND REPRESENTATION

Saint Paul, je crois, disait que l'image aura sa plénitude dans la résurrection
Jean-Luc Godard, quoted in *Ishaghpour* (1986), 297

Contents

Acknowledgments

Cinematography (movement-writing) began as steganography (hidden writing on the wall of the Roman College). Athanasius Kircher, S.J., is credited with the invention of cinema as idea and as apparatus. He called it *steganographia catoptrica* (fol. 912) in his *Ars magna lucis et umbrae in decem libros digesta, quibus admirandae lucis et umbrae in mundo, atque adeo universa natura, vires effectusque uti nova, ita varia novorum reconditiorumque speciminum exhibitione, ad varios mortalium usus, panduntur*; only later it went by its hallmark *laterna magica*. This was in 1646. Fr Kircher was more interested in bringing the hidden truth to light (so much about the seminal 'cinematic apparatus') than in entertaining (even though his demonstrations of the *laterna magica* in the Roman College apparently were also major social events, of which he was perfectly aware when he wrote on the very same fol. 912: 'Notandum & hic literas singulas nescio quo occulto naturae pictricis artificio omni colorum genere depictas videri: quae res uti insolens est, ita & dici vix postest, quantam in spectatoribus admirationem suscitet').

It is my joy to continue humbly – in this same venerable Collegium Romanum (which became the Gregorian University) – the intellectual pursuit of the secrets of light and shadows (also *ad varios mortalium usus & a.m.D.g.*).

My own *admiratio* for cinema kept growing as a result of long study. The ground was laid in particular by a few teachers, to whom I remain grateful and indebted. Marc Gervais, S.J. (Loyola campus, Montreal), taught me everything about cinema and forced me to emphatically see and write (*sans* split infinitives, *clare et distincte*, in plain English) what cinematographic eyes see and not what mind speculates. I owe him all my love for cinema. Enrico Carontini (Université du Québec à Montréal), in his spirited way, introduced me to the thought of C.S. Peirce. He opened for me a new intellectual horizon. Pierre Boudon (Université de Montréal), with rigour and method, introduced me to Aladdin's cave of semionarratology, the work of his teachers A.J. Greimas and Ch. Metz. I owe him Cartesian clarity and decisive encouragement in adversities. To them and all my Roman teachers my profound gratitude.

If my first contact with University of Toronto Press was as pleasant as I could have dreamed, it was due to the fine reception I received from Ron Schoeffel. Len Husband put as editor so much effort into the laborious delivery of this book that I remain greatly indebted. Two anonymous readers have given very encouraging reviews of the manuscript; Reader A, in particular, with his fair and very critical remarks was most helpful by forcing me to rethink a great deal. In fact, thanks to his remarks I clarified a number of important points and rewrote many others, and in some of my opinions I had to yield to the better argument. To whomever it may concern: thanks a lot! I am grateful to Frances Mundy for having assigned Matthew Kudelka to copy edit the manuscript, which he did thoroughly and with a detective's nose for what I could have meant but did not write. I am particularly grateful to M. Way, Westminster University, London, UK, who corrected, criticized, and challenged many of my theses and put them into the Queen's English. I received much personal support and encouragement from my Toronto friends, in particular B. Bulajić (who unwaveringly believed in this book), B. Bulajić (whose Boomerang is returned with this book) and J. Daniel (who helped me read the manuscript).

Finally, teaching a lot of intelligent students from many interesting cultures here, at this university of the nations, also on subjects contained in this book, helped me greatly to probe my thoughts. Kardinal-Bea-Stiftung, Munich, and my community here gave sizable subsidies, which I gratefully acknowledge.

My brother, sisters, and parents have always accompanied me; they alone know how much they deserve my gratitude.

CINEMA AND SEMIOTIC

Introduction

εἰκὼν τοῦ ἀοράτου

(cf. Col 1,15)

This book is about film, not films. The business of film theory is theory, not the interpretation of films.[1] In principle, we must assume film to be a certain kind of meaning, a cognitive conduct. That is, film theory scrutinizes meaning as such, and does so in its cinematic specificity.

Philosophy reflects the possibility and the conditions of meaning and cognition as such. It also contributes to a better understanding of cinema – an understanding that is measured by philosophy's answers to crucial problems of cinematic meaning. One of the most difficult problems is art, including film art. Do aesthetic works cognize something, or do they express mere subjective feelings? The best works of art seem to be creative and to make visible the unimaginable. Thus film aesthetics, as a theory of an elusive object, avers itself to be the touchstone for adequate theorizing. Narration is the next crucial problem of film theory. It would be naive to assume that narratives describe facts. In fact, narration imitates action and provides intentions and future. One has to grasp the nature of time in order to understand how narration manipulates it. Is cinema capable of truth? We can understand this crucial problem only if we leave behind the simplicist, essentialist equation of the photographic image with mundane states of affairs before the lens.

Most film theories apply some sort of philosophical argument. Ours is Semiotic,[2] as far as it has a direct bearing on subjects of concrete cinematic meaning. In a debate with other philosophies of cinema (Deleuze, Cognitivism, semiology), the Semiotic solution I propose here argues for new or different solutions to crucial problems of cinematic meaning.

Do we really need answers to fundamental problems of cinema?[3] Would it be better to confine meaningful theorization to specifics such as 'cinematic metaphors,' 'film-editing conventions according to epochs and national styles,' 'illusionism in cinema,' 'realist essence of cinema,' and so forth? Even assuming that answers to such specific questions are necessary, they are not solvable in themselves. Fundamentals are not optional. Every close examination of specific film problems reveals strong links of presupposition that answer, explicitly or not, crucial fundamental questions about meaning in cinema. The fact is that there is no methodology that is 'native' to film in the same sense that linguistics is native to language. Comprehension of film cannot thrive on borrowed means. Theory suffers when we adopt methods used for other objects on a metaphorical or analogical basis. This is because we constantly risk overstretching the principle of analogy, the metaphorical point of comparison between the two objects. Interpretations based on those analogies in fact jump to conclusions – sometimes even leap – and they cannot but falter once their metaphorical basis is shaken. The reason for this becomes apparent when we take into account what such methodologies postulate in terms of theory of reality. Methods must construct their object within their particular purview, and that purview alone gives being to those objects. For example, language is more than the object of linguistics; in linguistics, language exists in respect to its regular nature. All of this provides us with excellent reasons to investigate the foundations of film theory before that theory becomes a method. This investigation can only be philosophical.[4]

Where is the contribution of Peircean Semiotic? First and foremost, Semiotic does not fit squarely into the eternal canonical debates in film theory;[5] rather it relates to its major points of contention. Fundamentally, it responds to the three basic questions relating to major areas of film theoretical debate:

- *The Question of Truth*: Why and how can film represent objects of another universe? The entire 'realism' debate (Bazin, Pasolini, Eco) had shifted to a seemingly more technical level of cinematic codes of representation; there, it finds itself stuck in the interminable number of codes and in the hopeless complexity of any theoretical attempt to pass from codes to actually perceived meaning. Thus, the question of cinematic representation can still be seen as open. Semiotic will be able to contribute a novel approach.

- *The Question of Narration*: Why and how can film represent time?[6] This second area, cinematic narration, is severed quite deliberately from the first. The two are often lumped together with the representation problem. Yet when we phrase the problem as one of time, we can see where the essential difference must lie, and also that dealing with it involves other theoretical concepts. Neoformalism and Metz's *grande syntagmatique* address this problem, but we must wonder whether they provide an adequate answer to this question: How does film construct narrative time? Again, Semiotic will contribute a novel approach.
- *The Question of Discovery*: Why and how can film induce, beyond representation, the aesthetic processes? Aesthetic is perhaps the most neglected area in film theory. It bespeaks a terminological deflation in this field when the title of Aumont's book promises 'L'esthétique du film,' yet between the covers there is no trace of it. 'Esthétique' is, as if it were a matter of course, translated into the more manageable problems of perception, narration, and code.

Peircean bits and pieces have found their way into various popular film books and into a number of footnotes in film theory books. Mostly, this involves discussions of signs, which are shrunk to sign divisions that do not measure up to classification in Peirce's sense. Generally neglected is his Pragmaticism and his aesthetic. Because this is – like Peircean scholarship in general – a rather new area of philosophical inquiry,[7] it has not yet born fruit for film aesthetics. Here, the absolute (albeit waning) domination of semiology in film studies ('semiotics') has perhaps contributed to the lamentable underestimation of a great thinker. Unfortunately for Peirce, he did not, like Hegel, enjoy the chance during his lifetime to present his thought in an organized fashion or to have his pupils do so. So it should not surprise us that there is no Peircean Ästhetik. Yet Peirce's thought is sufficiently architectonic to allow a faithful concept of his aesthetics as a philosophical science of norms.

The *pointe* of a Semiotic sign theory – even with Peirce's rudimentary reputation in film theory – is far from evident. In some central points, Semiotic contradicts semiology; furthermore, its explanatory power is not limited to conventional signs, or codes. A Semiotic sign theory might at first glance seem quite unintuitive, because its implicit point of reference is not in language. Language – this is intuitive to every speaker. As relational achievements, however, signs are strictly logical and depend on tributary mathematical reasoning. This logic, however, is the logic of Signs, which are there only to be used and whose usage is the only means available to produce meaning in human behaviour (i.e., to control one's actions). Self-controlled behaviour has only one form, the Sign, which is a logical relationship and therefore must comprehend every meaningful action. Meaning can thus not be limited to actual action (or what now is speakable or 'languaged'); besides all existent past and present action, self-controlled behaviour must also comprehend all possible action. Here we are already beyond the realm of speech, because one can speak only what is conceived, or exists as *this* idea. This cannot, however, become the boundary of meaning, so there must be space for the conceivable. Self-controlled behaviour requires a further openness, which also transcends facts and the existing: one might see any number of facts, but not yet understand the one rule which unites them all into one law. There is no limit to cognition, and future cognition is not constrained by our present cognition.

All of this is contained in the Sign form. Signs are not 'just signs,' because everything is a Sign, otherwise it would not be: that is, either possible, or true, or necessary. As a consequence, it is extremely misleading to say, 'This is a sign,' because we would then have to be able to say, 'This is not a sign,' which is wrong. In fact, negation is a relation of existence, and therefore a Sign. An existential relation to objects is just one of three dimensions needed in every sign relation. Semiotic therefore can claim reasonably to be non-reductionist but to grasp all 'phenomena,' or world in its givenness. Whatever there is (for us) is Sign. Other sign theories are limited to language and convention and must explain everything as a function of language.[8] In this study I will attempt, then, to let Semiotic bear its fruit.

One fruit of the Semiotic of truth is a new perspective on representation. The heading chosen for this topic is 'the cinematic object'[9] in the very literal sense of *ob-jectum*, the vis-à-vis of film: How does cinema capture its other? In this way, we do not narrow the question to how cinema produces an illusion. Representation of the other – the entire gamut, including illusion – is one of the fundamental functions of cinema, and every theory of film must arrive at its own answer explaining how this happens. Our Semiotic theory, by making use of the triadic Sign relation, should be capable of grasping the widest possible spectrum of 'objectification.'

Cinema is often equated with narration (it is 'bolted to its body,' as Metz says). In this study I will make a distinction between representing something and narrating something. Narration, of course, makes use of representations, but its point is a completely different one: time. Narratives, with the aid of an appropriate enunciation, give a probabilistic form to time. There is evidently a profound problem in this transformation, since narrative time is not its own source. The source of time, including all further transformations (and narration is merely one of them), is Continuity, which is cognized as an Iconic Sign. Such a theory of time will be able to overcome the traditional split in time theories between physical and psychological time. The idea of Continuity is in itself a difficult one to grasp, but it must be distinguished from time as experienced in an existential now – for instance, in narrating.

It is much more difficult to provide a non-technical general idea of aesthetic. On the premise that it is cognition and, therefore, that it has 'practical consequences,' aesthetic as cognitive conduct has the specific task of relating to normativity. Contrary to certain sociological tenets (Weber, Habermas, the 'Critical' tradition), a norm is not a 'rationality.' Rational behaviour is possible only when one is already in possession of the norm. A norm's invention or constant reinvention is, however, a matter of Iconic Feelings. Norms as feelings are neither experience nor cognition, but they are necessary, as various types of pragmatic guidance, for various types of cognition. The indirect grasp of norms poses a challenge to Semiotic processes connected with it, as well as to aesthetic enunciations aiming at it. We will find that this delicate process of aesthetic cognitive conduct involving non-cognition leads to a specifically cinematic aesthetic,[10] just as there is a specific musical aesthetic. Although it becomes extremely difficult to assign a valid interpretation to an aesthetic sign, in theory such a sign's mode of operation is perfectly clear. However, this is not a licence for arbitrariness.

The result of this Semiotic approach to cinema is a three-part thematic division. First I will prepare the ground with a Semiotic theory of meanings and realities. Then I will consider the cinematic object (representation and truth values), cinematic narration (time production), and cinematic aesthetic (perception). Finally I will consider comprehensively the cinematic production of the different meanings (enunciation). While adhering to a strictly theoretical purview, I will be integrating some film analysis or Interpretation. These integrations, however, will be restricted to the Semiotic dimension concerned.

1 On Signs, Categories, and Reality and How They Relate to Cinema

Peirce in film theory: he is seldom fully integrated, but even when rejected, he seems to be generally known about. Judging from the cursory remarks scattered in film literature, he would have felt misunderstood. Sometimes this misunderstanding has an actual genealogy, one that reflects an interpretation of an (imaginative: Deleuze) interpretation of an (early systematizing: Deledalle) interpretation of Peirce; and Deledalle considers only sign theory. Small wonder that Peirce's signs have become a 'regression à l'infini'[1] and a 'quadrillage universel monté ... autour de la représentation.' Another voice, Peter Wollen's Peircean classification of films through the use of one of the sign trichotomies, has remained largely inconsequential. Only in Deleuze has Peirce found a more conspicuous place in film theory. Deleuze's is among the more fascinating efforts to apply Peirce to the fundamentals of film theory; that said, Deleuze would not have been himself had he not used Peirce in a highly creative and idiosyncratic way. It is fair to assume that Deleuze had his own theory in mind, for which he also found some use for bits and pieces of Peirce's sign classification.

Those in film theory with an antisemiotic attitude – and there are quite a number – most often are actually rejecting semiology and what was developed at the École des Hautes Études and the Centre National de la Recherche Scientifique. Sometimes, Peirce is the baby thrown out with the bathwater of film semiology (aka 'film semiotics'). It is not difficult to show that Peirce plays no part in the logomachy of codes and code systems often improperly identified with semiotics. It is indeed difficult to grasp Peirce if one does not begin with the cornerstone of his thought: his theory of Categories. Peirce's Categories are – deliberately – so abstract that they are often seen as superfluous as well as worthless for film analysis. Yet it is the attempts to bend Peirce to the forms of Saussure's binary arbitrary sign concept that effectively destroy Peirce's usefulness. For Ropars, the 'vertigo of the circle of the system's circulation' a result of Peirce's 'tout est signe.' One could concur easily if signs were Saussurean place values. Yet with regard to Peirce, is there a better way to express a disregard of the logical as well as the metaphysical implications of our categorical way of 'possessing' being?

It seems quite obvious that Peirce is still not being heeded enough in film theory. I admit from the outset that he provides no easily applicable theoretical concepts. His system's architecture is highly complex, and we must consider it carefully and in its entirety if we are to draw useful and meaningful results from it. It has never been and never will be easy to comprehend Peirce. He did not make his system easy to access, and he rarely had an occasion to present his semiotic in a comprehensive way. He had no pupils – only a number of followers who used his heritage for their own purposes.

Owing to the deplorable personal and scholarly fate of Peirce, there have been a number of divergent interpretations of him; his adoption is continuing to evolve. This is quite usual with every great philosopher. William James 'abducted' pragmatism during Peirce's own lifetime. Peirce's early posthumous defenders included Dewey, who inspired Mead. Through Dewey and the Chicago School, Peirce still has a subliminal influence. He was last rediscovered back in the 1950s by Goudge, at which point it became undisputable that he was an important thinker in his own right and not merely the forerunner of pragmatism and Morris. The dispute at the time revolved around whether he was or was not a systematic thinker. His recent fame as a 'proto-semiologist' may, however, be based on a thorough misunderstanding, one that arose when Roman Jakobson was introduced to Peirce by Morris (cf. Liszka 1981; Portis-Winner 1994).

A serious rethinking of Peirce started with Max Fisch and Murray Murphey. To Murphey (1961) we must credit the first genetic view of Peirce's intellectual development. He understood clearly the crucial importance of Peirce's early metaphysics before the New List of Categories appeared in 1867. Also, he was among the first to appreciate how theories of mathematical continuity contributed to Peirce's later evolutionary metaphysics. However, Murphey was criticized for his negative judgment as to how accurately Peirce had understood Kant's *Critique*. From this perspective, Peirce supposedly left four contradictory architectonic systems, and failed because the 'master key' to his system, Continuity, 'eluded him' at the end. Few scholars have followed Murphey in his despondent conclusions; even so, he set the standard reference point of critique. On a re-evaluation of Peirce's discovery of Existential Graphs, it would seem that this 'elusion' of Continuity is not so complete. Murphey in a reprint he 'still holds to most of what [is] said in the original book' (1993:v); even so, he has slightly revised his judgment about Peirce's failure. Since that work, any unhistorical view of Peirce's system architecture (i.e., without considering its development) has been impossible.

Another legacy is that Peirce's development must be seen as closely connected to his advances in formal logic (in particular, his discovery of the irreducibility of the three syllogistic figures), in the logic of relations, and in the logic of quantification (which opened new pathways for modality). Many early studies suffered from the slipshod manner in which Peirce's writings were published (Murphey was among the first to make extensive use of unpublished manuscripts). Burk and Weiss's pioneering edition of Peirce's Collected Papers had a thematic organization that is not especially helpful for gaining an understanding of the progress of Peirce's reflection.

Today it is undisputed that Peirce was a very important thinker.[2] In the field of analytical philosophy, it is possible although admittedly not easy to determine clearly Peirce's lasting presence (cf. Oehler 1993). Russell became acquainted with Peirce's semiotic division of signs through Lady Welby, who showed him her correspondence with Peirce in 1903. It is safe to assume that Peirce is having a pervasive influence in today's 'analytical mainstream.' Furthermore, there is a new interest in Peirce in the wake of the crisis in analytical thinking. In fact, one of the most interesting rediscoveries relating to Peirce concerns the metaphysical strand in his thought. The early non-analytical response was interested in Peirce mainly in his role as the founder of Pragmatism; since then, his clear interest in metaphysics has been coming to the fore. Within the pragmatist tradition we must count Deledalle (1987) and Apel (1975), who inspired much of Habermas's Peirce interpretation. Esposito (1980) and Pape (1982), among others, have contributed to a metaphysical reading of Peirce. All these waves of Peirce interpretation present a complexity of thought and systematic connections; they also exhibit the poverty of some reductive readings.

Peirce and film have a slim history. There is much more to Peirce than what has become a ritual quote[3] in film theory – his famous definition of the sign (2.228). This is not the place to present Peirce's thought in a comprehensive manner; even so, it is worthwhile to apply it to cinema (our chief aim). This, however calls for a succinct summary of the principal elements that I intend to apply later. One of the best summaries with a special orientation toward Semiotic can be found in Peirce's letter to Lady Welby (dated 12 October 1904). One first possible objection or doubt in film theory must be addressed: What profit is there for film theory from those very fundamental epistemological theories such as the Categories? They have more to do with the constitution of reality than with a medium of expression. If it is only for the sake of giving a foundation to signs, what can film semiotic achieve? Unlike theories hinging on the structural paradigm (cf. Deleuze 1973), Semiotic does not by methodological inclination yield a genre classification of film narratives, psychoanalytical viewer constructions, and the like. Instead, it is a method of discovery. This has profound consequences for film theory, and provides an alternative to some of the recent debates on constructivism. It implies that something exists to be discovered and that there is someone who discovers it. It does not imply that everything is already in the conventions and their variations, nor does it imply that the subject is superfluous to a language being able to speak by itself. This is sometimes taken for granted in film theory (or is dealt with as a foreign element such as constructivism adjunct to an otherwise narratological film theory).

Yet why should the film sign not be a discovery instrument for what is outside the mind? The advantage of Peirce is the breadth of his theory, which includes as a necessary part the complex and creative vis-à-vis the cognitive mind and the real, together with the complexities of social and individual cognition. That which usually is retained in the dignity of being object of inquiry, is merely the third element of Semiotic. An inquiry of that sort is unnecessarily restrictive in a Peircean perspective. This is just one aspect (viz., generality) that is beyond the individual act of apprehension and yet is thoroughly involved in it. There is no doubt in Semiotic that general principles are applied to concrete instances when something is cognized as being a case of something general. Usually a word would be the generality that helps the understanding of something happening as an instance of what the word describes. Similarly, conventions of cinematic representation would convey meaningfulness into something apparently fortuitous, casual, singular. A gaze off-screen or off-frame is a convention that creates ('the meaning of') space (to be populated narratively). If cinematic gazes had no conventional rules, they would just be gazes.

It is certainly interesting to investigate the 'vocabulary' of film. Since conventions must be finite in number, one can hope to gather their entirety; this would help us understand the variations of the rule. This is a basic 'figure of thought' in formalism, for instance. From a semiotic perspective, however, it is merely one of three fundamental elements of cognition. For the discovery of the new – the true progress of cognition – this third element is the least important one,[4] albeit necessary. It is through Semiotic that one discovers the 'method of discovery.' Even in cinema (which must be dominated by conventions), there are processes whereby a novel cognition comes to light.

Instead of investigating the cinematic use of conventions and their power to marshal meaning by rules, we should look into the mind-expanding, meaning-creating cognitive processes made possible by cinema we will see that in a Semiotic framework, all creative processes in the mind are related to Iconicity and that cinema has all the attributes that are necessary to contribute to a certain kind of cognitive growth. To anticipate, cinema compares with what Peirce in his later thinking called 'diagrammatic thinking' without being merely a diagram. Diagrams, of course, are not to be taken as the only sites of this thought process. They merely instantiate a type of thinking. In 'How to Make our Ideas Clear' Peirce distinguishes three levels of clarity. Level I could be called the unreflected application of a concept to a manifold; Level II is by way of definitions; only Level III brings clarity into the realm of the Possible. To date, signs have been treated merely as codes and equivalents. How can something function as a sign that is not clearly defined in a positional, binary place-value system of differences? This is unimaginable. If, however, the possible is already sign and thus creates a type of reality, it is no longer feasible to take a differential system as an *explanans* of sign behaviour. Not having sufficiently acknowledged this third form of clarity impairs the adoption of Peirce – see, for instance, the philosophy of signs of Simon (1989). Unfortunately, the latter is limited to the definition type of clarity, that is, the systemic interpretation of signs by other signs. Simon is quite typical in his underestimation of sign functions. All of this suggests why signs as theoretical constructs have been abandoned in film theory.

It must be conceded that cinema as sign is largely non-definitional. In its essence, it depends on the fact that a concept (idea, 'content') is invented or found through behaviour and expectation. Diagrammatic thinking consists exactly of that, and of a mental experimentation with the non-existent but possible. How important it is to include Vagueness has only recently been emphasized in the literature on Peirce. It is crucial for a Semiotic understanding of cinema, as will become clear later. Instead of an impairment of cinematic signification, necessitating its 'syncretistic code cohabitation,' to remain inherently vague is really its truly poetic potential. As a constant and early feature in Peircean thought this insight found its expression in a number of novel concepts: Vagues, Modality, Iconicity, method of discovery. There will be ample occasion to glean its enormous consequences, which will salvage Peirce from 'sign theorists' including Eco (1975) and Deleuze (1985), who 'sign-classify' Peirce back into clarity Levels I and II. As film theory, this central aspect of Peircean thought should open pathways hitherto unconsidered in 'semiotic' film theories. Film semiotics has made little use of Modality. In spite of some conspicuous investigations in 'enunciation theories,' which refer either to Genette's modalities of verbal moods, or to the logic of modalities within a logic of possible worlds such as Hintikka's, outside Peirce modalities have not yet found their way into a theory of signs. As an inevitable consequence, aesthetics (for one) has been starved. It should become clearer from what follows that a truly Peircean approach has much to offer to a genuine understanding of essential cinematic meaning as such, not just to some of its lateral aspects. The master key to this understanding is diagrammatic thinking (and its various forms of expression) at the base of cinematic meaning. We will have to show the cinematic sites of iconicity, once the semiosic nature of iconicity is understood. At any rate, the purpose of semiotic is also this: to clarify mental processes before and beyond rules or conventions.

Peirce himself planned – but never had the occasion – to publish a comprehensive presentation of his thought, which is inherently systemic and architectonic. One of his projects for a *magnum opus*, a kind of *Kritik der reinen Logik*, was rejected by the Carnegie Foundation. We have the 'Syllabus,' a mature and quite dense course outline (first edited in its entirety by Pape 1982), but this is merely the sketch of a cathedral. There have been a number of excellent recent systematic studies, on which we shall rely for our present purposes, but it is still risky to write about Peirce without recourse to his own guideline. As more and more of his manuscripts (80 per cent of them unpublished) become available, it is becoming obvious that these comprise traces of a work in progress rather than the final word of a thinker.

The architectonic nature of Peirce's system would allow many alternative ways to present Semiotic concepts but not all of them equally suit our purpose, which is to develop a basis for understanding of film. We can start with any of the broader questions of philosophy – ontology, the nature of cognition, and unearth Peirce's actual answers to them. Our theory to access film will be through pragmatism, starting with the preconditions of action. Since every theory is based on assumptions, the main task at hand in accessing film is to argue honestly for its assumptions. In this chapter I will begin to do just that. Without systematically addressing problems of film theory, I will suggest how classical questions about cinema can be solved on the basis of a novel theory: a comprehensive theory of meaning, through signs, based on fundamental relations to reality – the 'categories.'

As the natural starting point, which comprehends all meaning, then, we investigate action *in se* – that is, meaningful conduct and everything which makes it possible (§1.2).

To *act* means to possess a formal blueprint of this and all possible actions. Such a universal form of action must be further analyzed, not through the usual approach of subjective intention, but rather by analyzing how acting depends on the real *as it is* – as appearances of different complexity (§1.3, §1.4).

In acting, such dependency entails control, or deliberate efforts to achieve goals guided by values. The perils of postulating an ontological dependency – that acting can only follow what is objectively there – are carefully avoided provided that a proper concept of value is attained. Investigating the relation of action to its different classes of values in behaviour gives a formal idea of every possible meaning in action. Pragmaticism comprehends meaning as relational, and meaning is analyzed in the logic of relations (§1.6).

Only then do signs come into play. Signs are the universal form of meaning, and Semiotic as a process constructs or decomposes meaning. This step will also mark an explicit difference between semiology and Semiotic (§1.4.1).

The clarification of our assumptions is not for its own sake; rather, it is directed toward debate with prevalent film theories and their quite different assumptions: cognitivist or constructivist film theories, semiology, Deleuze. We conclude by revisiting Pragmaticism, not as film pragmatic, but as a pragmatic theory of cinematic meaning (§2). Its purpose is to connect our project to fundamental issues in contemporary film theory.

1.1 The Use of Signs[5]

Film theorists today are not generally fond of signs. Some even seem tired of the profusion of signs, codes, signifieds, signifiers, and the like.

So what is the use of signs? This question is more than legitimate – it is crucial. Does it further the theory of cinema to cast the object of investigation into a semiotic terminology? Unless it is a real advance, casting everything in the terminological 'mould' (Deleuze) of 'sign' will be futile, a mere *modus dicendi*. It is the task of this book to show that our understanding of cinema advances when we conceptualize it as a sign process. This means above all that there must be compelling reasons for us to place the idea of sign in the middle of the spider's web of explanations concerning cinema.

The worth of a concept should manifest itself as we go about identifying and framing a problem. This implies that some way of defining a problem will be more fruitful than other ways. Semiotic will help us understand cinema only if it reflects this.

So where do we start? Before the question becomes unfathomable, we have to agree on a basis that is comprehensive and that excludes nothing. It seems that no one can reasonably deny that film is experience. Furthermore, no one can deny – on reflection – that film as an experience is at least somewhat unique. The premises so far require only that they give rise to meaningful questions about a phenomenon that is seen by all (albeit certainly not by all in the same way). It is not then necessary to take this as a dogma.

This basis to questioning can be stated clearly, and its implications – both positive and negative – can be made explicit. Thus, the field of questioning is more open when the aspects mentioned are treated as possible problems. Conversely, if they are not seen to be problems, the phenomenon will have been artificially oversimplified. Thus:

- When cinema is treated like a normal perception (of world objects), the point of cinematic vision is missed.
- When cinema is treated like a normal experience of time, the peculiarly constraining mode in the serialization of moving images is missed. It is neither a causal chain, nor a constraint of syntactic rules, nor the pure chance of arbitrary world events. Instead, it imposes its own logic of the type *post hoc ergo propter hoc*. It produces the impression of one *time*, but not of one *rule*.
- When cinema is treated like a normal exercise in style – as if in cinema one could use its own sort of stilted language, as if one could use in cinema a level of rhetorical *ornatus* – one misses the point of cinematic beauty.
- When cinema is treated as if it produced a normal dynamic of identity – as if Me, Self, I, or psychoanalytical personality structures were

produced in exactly the same way as in an interpersonal or social context – one misses the point of the particular cinematic way of being vis-à-vis.

This spells out the consequences of our questioning basis and indicates that there can be no *ceteris paribus* film theory. Cinema necessitates a theory that from the start does justice to its peculiarity. Only this can justify the use of a comprehensive theory such as Semiotic. Adequate theories should be no less complex than their object. A theory should not negate the problem itself in order to make a convincing case for its own theoretical explanations. Of course, we cannot exclude the possibility that the object 'cinema' will reveal itself as even more complex than can be grasped with Semiotic. Here it would have to be admitted that the Semiotic paradigm leaves too many questions unanswered and that the phenomenon it is capable of seeing is a simplification. Conversely, however, less complex film theories would leave even more questions open. Simplicity is not a positive attribute for a theory if it leads to a reductive view of the phenomenon being investigated. For example, it would be too simple to lump together perception with film viewing simply because the peculiar nature of perception in cinema cannot be grasped theoretically. If comprehensiveness is claimed for Semiotic, it must certainly embrace this specificity. When demonstrating the usefulness of Semiotic for solving genuine film-theoretical problems, then, we must place Semiotic in a debate with other theories that are vying for the solution of the same problems.

Semiotic claims to be comprehensive, that it can see – and reconstruct theoretically – the cinematic phenomenon in its entirety. What justifies this? Such a claim cannot be based on commonsense assumptions. Ultimately, it amounts to claiming a grasp of all phenomena. Semiotic claims that it conceptualizes (without necessarily knowing) all possible, all existent, and all necessary phenomena. Clearly, this is not possible as a normal cognition in an existent fact's present, nor is it even possible as knowledge and remembrance of past facts. It even exceeds cognition of a law that subsumes all past facts and that projects all future facts. It is even more difficult for comprehensiveness to be reached through what Husserl in his phenomenology called 'natural attitude' – that is, the normal taken-for-granted belief in the existent suchness of the world at hand. For instance, there can be no question of assuming, as often happens, that there is a real-world course of events that only needs to be narrated in truthful order (with or without an artistic 'poetically estranged' style). Nor can it be assumed that our visual perception 'takes in' (or into con-*sider*-ation, i.e., taking it from the 'stars') the world as it is. Film theory need only concern itself with artistic transformation, perhaps thought to be based on the art-typical omission of certain perceptive stimuli. Film theories based on such assumptions already believe too much. There is no basis left, then, for a serious debate with, say, an (apparently outlandish) film theory such as Deleuze's. We have to take cinematic meaning in its most general and widest possible sense; then we must investigate the explanatory potential of Semiotic.

Every film theory has to make some assumptions about the relationship between cinema and reality. At this point it does not matter whether we conceptualize this relationship as totally transparent or as manipulative; it is enough to admit that there is 'something cinematic' in between reality and a perceiving, experiencing mind (cognition, signifying power, or any other receptive instance). As soon as we accept that a factor between seeing and the intentional vis-à-vis is brought to bear – in other words, that film is truly a medium – the question arises as to what exactly happens in and through such a mediation. One can still contend then, that film intrudes little if at all into reality perception and that the real 'estrangement' must be wanted artistically, but that is still to be shown. If, however, we accept the basic horizon of the problem, then in comparison with other theory solutions of this relationship, the first distinctive marks of Semiotic stand out.

1.1.1 Which Approaches Are Available in Film Theory to Relate Cinema with Reality?

A first option for theory – which might be called the 'epistemological solution' – has it that the gulf between (phenomenal) reality and the (solitary) mind is bridged through cognition. For cinema, such a model implies that the mind organizes sensory data so that they make sense; 'sense' falls within the competence of a subject-inherent activity – that is, within its operational rules and acquired internal conventions. However, there is no naturalistic way to cognition. When it comes to film, the conceptual grasp of a cognitive mind is still captured in the Kantian dilemma. If we knew the mind in itself, attempts to escape an aprioristic 'knowledge' of the mind as such would mostly lead to a *petitio principii*. Apparently, cognitive film theory is vaguely aware of this danger and tries to escape it with the help of other knowledge of the mind. In not begging the principle, these film theories often dele-gate the justification of cognition to psychology, sociology, or other factual positive sciences. We will encounter these problems during a later discussion of 'cognitivism in film theory.'

A second option comprises all sorts of psychological solutions (which some film theorists have no difficulty in amalgamating with the first option). The mind's relation to the real is understood in princi-ple as a psychological operation. The 'world horizon' in the natural attitude of an intentional subject is no more than an 'act correlate' of that relationship of intention; strictly speaking, this involves no hypotheses relating to the reality or existence of the physical world itself. A remarkable reconstruction of the film experience on this basis has been proposed by Casebier; however, Mitry had already gone into the same direction in his phenomenology and psychology of film. As it relates in principle to an immanent psychic event, the problem is not merely the reality of the real but, more directly, communication with other subjects. Cinema is located in the realm of pre-given and social forms, which enable the reconstruction of meaning in the subjective psyche.

A third option recasts the relationship space and time. As space, the relationship between the real and the mind consists of divisions among many parts; as time, the same relationship is one whole. The idea behind Deleuze's approach – which was inspired by Bergson – accounts for the two fundamental dimensions in our relation to the real – namely, on the one hand we always see a manifold of different things, and, on the other hand we have a feeling ('intuition') of the unity of one whole. For this film theory, cinema is nothing short of a secular tool for both experiences, which are essentially different. Only the first sort of differentiating experience corresponds to the cognitive approach (similar to the first option). Evidently, the reality of the whole is quite different from the reality of the space full of 'dividual' objects. Thus, the relationship of the mind to the real can be one or the other but not both.

A fourth option can be termed the linguistic solution. Here the rela-tionship to the real is screened by the language system. It is assumed that everything is in language. So these theories can sacrifice both the concept of reality and that of mind. Semiological film theory tends to cast the bipolar relationship into one mould – that of codes. Meaning is created by differentiating operations of a system, which produces codes, and certainly not in subjectivity. This solution tells us just how we experience something in film; however, it does not allow comparison of either the real or the subjective meaning, since all is subsumed by the language system.

The final option, Semiotic, is different in important respects from all of the above. Strictly speaking, there is no epistemology. The laws of thought are not deduced from *a priori* thoughts; rather, they must be observed from the practical exercise of thought (i.e., in behaviour). The replacement of epistemology comes from the theory of the sign process. The single steps, which show how abstract thought is placed in the larger context of acting, are very roughly sketched in the following theses (i.e., everything remains to be proven). It is important to note that this shifts the problem itself to the wider context of action, or behaviour of conduct.[6] The decisive marks of Semiotic distinction – justified in this chapter – can be formulated as an ordinal series of theses:

1 We do not cognize, we *act*. This basic idea gives rise to what will later be called Pragmaticism.
2 Yet we do not act in the manner of a lone, singular mind manipulating mindless objects. Rather, we act *habitually*.
3 We do not acquire habits as stored 'empirical' data from previous actions; rather, our habits are *obtained through rules*.
4 We do not establish arbitrary rules (by sheer convention), rather, the rules of our habits *rely on norms*, which are prior to and transcend every act (even of agreement).
5 We do not deduce norms in an *a priori* way (as a privileged cognition before experience), like gods or as if at the dawn of creation. Rather, we can find norms – the conditions of the possibility of our present acting – only on the basis of experience, grounding their values *on what is true, what is possible, and what is necessary*. Empirical normativity therefore remains grounded on precedent behaviour.
6 We do not have inborn ideas about what is (existent, possible, necessary. Rather, our habit-guiding *norms must be taken from the phenomenal world through its presentation of itself to us, through the way it presents itself, through its requiring from us adequate methods of access*.
7 We do not act habitually because we follow norms immanent to our mind; rather, experiential *behaviour consists in relations to something else*. Such relating is not, however, done in only one way (e.g., factual relation); it can be of different kinds. The phenomenon dictates that we relate not only to facts but also to necessary laws and to merely possible qualities. Each relation then follows its own adequate rules.

8 We do not act (i.e., relate to the phenomenal world) always within
   the constraints of the rule of necessity; however, *if we do relate to the
   phenomenal world under the premiss that it must be as it is, such a relation
   is a sign.* Every sign encompasses an objective fact, a characteristic of
   that fact, and a law. If, however, in our relation there is no dominant
   respect of necessity, we still relate to the phenomenal world in a
   sign, which can then abstract (or relent) from the nature of one or
   two of its components. In the latter signs, cognitions are consequently of lesser logical necessity, their scope is a lesser generality,
   and their validity can range from a contingent to a merely momentary force of law.

   This series illustrates the pragmatic-Semiotic option. It also provides
the outline of Peirce's particular, elaborate version of Pragmatism. At
this stage, it certainly begs more questions than it answers problems. For
our present purposes, we need no more than signposts of this distinctively Semiotic approach. It would be rather foolish to assume that Pragmatism is self-explanatory. On the contrary, a solution that conceives the
relationship of a cognizing mind to the real in a pragmatic manner bur-
dens itself with a cumbersome task. Ontology would perhaps have
offered the easiest solution by equalizing intellect with thing (*adaequatio
intellectus et rei*). The transcendentalist approach, which merely isolates
the necessary elements of the cognitive judgment, would also be relatively simple. Transcendental pragmatic remains an entirely different
moral judgment. Folding cognition into behaviour, however, leaves no
room for a parallel ontological or transcendental universe from which to
reflect at a distance (i.e., apparently safe from begging the question)
regarding the sublunary universe of experience. Another sort of distancing parallel has been constructed in language, which thrives on the
abstraction of language structure (*langage*) from speech (*parole*), in which
residual 'pragmatic' aspects are lumped together. This sort of abstraction is foregone in Semiotic, and with it also all pretence to a special cognition distanced from concrete cognition.
   The burden is no less for film theory, because film perception is not
apperception. Viewing a film is not the cognitive processing of sensory
stimuli; rather, it is an action. When we organize sensory and other perceptive data by applying schemata to them, we are oversimplifying the
real process through which the mind relates to the real in film. We are
creating an artificial distance between concept and data, and in doing
so are giving the impression that concepts or schemata can be known

(and spoken of) separately. Both are abstractions; for neither can we claim 'naturalism' of any sort. Evidently, considerations of action or pragmatics would add nothing essential to this type of knowledge.

It is also less than adequate – as sometimes happens in semiological film theory – to theorize on 'cinema as such' and then to remember the social setting of its consumption in a 'film pragmatic.' This does not remedy the original abstraction, because there is no real situation of perception. As well, the 'social' setting ads nothing to cinema itself. Instead, such a 'film pragmatic' can remedy only the 'crystalline structure' of the 'language of cinema' (cf. Lévi-Strauss's critique of Eco's encyclopaedic liberty, v. *infra*) with a greater – if not arbitrary – freedom of interpretation of parallel 'readings.' Such 'wild' interpretations can only be imperfections (cf. Greimas's *De l'imperfection* and various *éthno-sémiotiques* q.v. Greimas 1979).

This sketched horizon of possibilities, and the location of Pragmatism therein, might raise questions about the validity of a behavioural approach. Can our theses claim to be a genuine representation of Peirce, since they contain little about that for which Peirce seems to be best known (e.g., the classification of signs, Speculative Grammar, and other subtleties)? Indeed, they mostly emphasize the naturalistic aspect (without foreclosing continuation into formal considerations). Foremost is the argument that signs have their natural place in the human behaviour of world appropriation and that they are not a self-contained reality.

However, there are three deeper reasons for a pragmatic interpretation of Peirce. First of all, as soon as one understands behaviour as the ultimate form of any experiential relation, a powerful basis of argumentation is gained. This is important especially on the wider horizon of contemporary non-pragmatic social theory, which is increasingly taking the place of former ontological and other totalistic theories (quite openly so in Luhmann). Yet its pretense is to be different. Thus, traditions of thought that Luhmann used to call 'old-european' are accused of clinging unreflectedly to teleological presuppositions: present cognition as aiming at a perfect, truer future knowledge. We need not decide here whether this is a pervasive figure of thought. If it is, it might apply to a number of 'Critical Theories,' but certainly not to Peirce's formal Pragmatism. Peirce is perfectly capable of justifying teleology and truth in cognition without presupposing any knowledge or grasp of the perfect state. For him, final causation does not determine efficient causes; that is, what causes the next behaviour is not derived in any way from the perfectly known reality, the perfectly adequate behaviour. Behaviour is just a form – although of generality – and not an instance of the Ideal, as I will emphasize later. It shows also that Peirce is more advanced and theoretically satisfactory than; for example, system theorists, who need the form of 'system re-entry' in order to justify themselves as theorists of a 'productive' infinite regress.[7] In Peirce there is no regress, no transcendentalism, and no foundationalism.

Second, deceptively simple as it may seem, the behavioural basis is treated immediately as a form. Thus it is not conceived of psychologically or psychological-rationally, as in most 'action theories.' We need not resort to psychological motives in order to explain the direction of acting. When we take our point of departure from behaviour, we are not simply extrapolating the directedness of acting. Peirce's Pragmatism is not Dewey's theory of means-ends rationality. Waks (1999) reconstructs Dewey's idea of the directedness of truth-seeking in science (to a large measure embraced by A. Schütz), which shows the limits of psychological accounts of teleology. Connecting means with ends cannot be a matter of psychological desire or uneasy doubt (the latter requiring a secondary experience of reflection about means). It follows that only a 'controlled conduct of behaviour' is considered relevant. Control and reflection are not the limit-cases of instinctive desire, and they are not modelled after that.[8] The feeling (desire, instinct, etc.) does not have to be suppressed; however, it can be treated as a degenerate form of a general relation. Not even instinctive acts are blind – they follow an immediate purpose. Thus we should not derive any false or unnecessarily limiting implications from the behavioural approach.

Third, the formal conception of Pragmatism allows a different grasp of continuity. It is constitutive for Luhmann's system theory, as well as for Dewey's pragmatic/Schütz's phenomenological action theory, that actions continue in other actions; a single action literally makes no sense. Peirce, however, makes his Pragmatism depend on a quite different continuity. No longer is it the permanence of the motivational or systemic trajectory of actions, where one decaying connects with another novel action toward an end. A radically Pragmatic view must comprehend the totality of all behaviour (however, not the collection of all behaviours) as resulting in the totality of all 'things.' It is not the ontological persistence of physical things that constitutes everything – rather, it is the persistence of habits of behaviour. However, it is not this totality which guarantees the possibility of the persistence of conduct. Rather, it is a form of continuity, which guarantees that the next behaviour will be a directed one. Peirce was emphatic that the form of continuity be anterior to any possible experience. In this way he made himself independent from on the one the ontological chain of causalities, and on the other hand, the motivational chain of action projects (in Schütz's and Dewey's sense). Continuity is more certain now because it is a mathematical (even topological) form.

The problem now will be to ascertain the applicability of a mathematical form to experience (this will also be the problem with the relational form: v. *infra*). Not every mathematical form applies to something experiential (e.g., certain types of numbers). So it falls to a different science, phenomenology, to investigate the real as it appears to experience. Hence phenomenology can only find as a universal 'general fact' that certain forms apply or not. If continuity applies to that which can be behaviourally experienced, this has some very interesting and important implications for action as a volitive reality. This relates to decisions in particular. In our context of cinema (which is much narrower than action theory), continuity implies an interesting facet for narration. It becomes the form of temporality, as we will investigate in the chapter on film narration (cf. §§4.1 and 6). Deciding on an end implies time, that is, creates time as meaning. So a behavioural conception of reality based on the form of continuity is a much more adequate framework of narration than, for instance, the referential existence of objects. With such a tool we will eventually be able to analyze narration as one particular form of decision (temporality) on the horizon of other forms of decision (with other temporalities).

These are some basic implications of the behavioural approach in the Peircean sense. When understood naturalistically in Pragmaticism as a habit of behaviour, cognition and experience leave no room for a second kind of cognition cognizing from a distanced, privileged vantage point the first. So much appears clearly from the preliminary sketch of the Pragmatic Semiotic characteristics (which at this stage leaves almost everything still to be determined). However, even this small determination does not imply that cognition is beyond control and critique. For film theory, another important implication from Semiotic is that cognition is a mediation. It does not 'connect' the mind directly with the real (*pace* Bazin and his advocacy of the 'realistic' essence of cinema); rather, it does so only through a third element, the sign. Also, this third element contains all the potential of communication between minds. The advantage for film theory is patent, in particular if this communication is controllable and if it can be criticized. No provisions need to be made for idiosyncratic 'readings' of films or for fuzzy applications of schemata 'against the grain' (cf. Staiger 1992 on the reception of Hollywood cinema). Allaying fears of orgies of arbitrary, 'postmodern' interpretations, in all its naturalism Semiotic is much stricter in determining the third element of mediation than some playful aesthetic minds would want. However, every communication – like every cognition – is an interpretation, which must add something new to the sign it is interpreting.

1.2 The Construction of Meaning

1.2.1 *The Novelty of Pragmaticism*

Cinema is meaning; but what is meaning? Nobody denies that explaining cinema is tantamount to explaining how it brings forth meaning. However, that does not imply that meaning itself is simple, of one kind only, nor does it imply that meaning can be expressed in all its kinds in one canonical form. Traditional logic has always treated the proposition as the ideal and normative expression of meaning. It has become increasingly clear, however, that this canonical form hinges unduly on certain classical European languages and their features; therefore, its claims to universality are unwarranted. As Peirce emphasized, there are languages that have no copula and there are others that have practically no nouns (not to mention no universal set of tenses and modes). So it is impossible to cast the thought process into an adequate universal logical form as long as the Graeco-Latin paradigm of proposition prevails.

For cinema and similar forms of meaning, this will certainly be a relief as soon as an adequate substitute is found. Evidently, it is awkward to express the meaning of a sequence of cinematic images in a proposition. To do so results at best in no more than an arbitrary abstraction, which is neither the comprehensive nor the univocal meaning of these moving images. Such (typically narrative) reductions of the rich meaning of cinema produce either some kind of précis or – for aesthetic effect – an even less controllable and more arguable description of subjective impressions. The fault is not with the meaning complexity in film as it exists; rather, it is with the conceptualization of meaning *in se*, where traditional limitations make it impossible to penetrate the inner workings of cinematic meaning.

The new promise of Pragmaticism is – in the last resort and interpreted thoroughly – provide a new logical form that is much more general and universal than the traditional canon. It also holds, therefore, a promising potential for the complex meaning of cinema. Its 'approach' seems simple enough and quasi-naturalistic: human behaviour. Much less can be brought into a propositional form than can be acted. We cannot not act – or, expressed positively (*pace* Watzlawick), we *always* act. This, then, is the broadest possible basis: something that is shared by all, over time, and is consequently the most naturalistic setting possible for any meaning reconstruction – including the film experience.

Through this reconstruction, 'action' becomes a heavily loaded concept; as the above sketched theses evolving one after another have already suggested, it expands the simple meaning of the concept to the point where it becomes comprehensive: there is nothing that is not action – or better, conduct of behaviour. The naturalistic framework remains the vital question. How do we act in a meaningful way? How do we need meaning to become capable of acting? How does this meaning precede our action in its own form? This is the basis of all argumentative constraint; at the same time, it is the everyday basis of Semiotic, which is intuitive and remains so at every level of analysis. However, we would be grossly underestimating Pragmaticism if we were to shrink it to a sort of anthropological approach. Such misappraisal reads Peirce through, for instance, the spectacles of existentialism, and this is not the wisdom of hindsight. Peirce does not depart from an anthropological fact, as Heidegger does from death. For the latter, death serves the function of providing the ultimate unity of all, on both a temporal and a world horizon. It thus assumes the function of a unique, most general category. However, its nature is that of a fact – not a 'general fact' in the Semiotic sense, but a universal fact – one that corresponds to Peirce's example of the unlimited gamble between a bank with unlimited richness and a group of players with an unlimited number of members (see 1903 Harvard Lecture I). Those who interpret Peirce's Pragmaticism along the lines of psychological pragmatisms (Mead, James) or a pragmatic anthropology (A. Gehlen, Heidegger) must lose its logical and normative content. That is its very marrow, however – albeit not exclusive of metaphysical, anthropological, socio-theoretical, political, and other implications (to which we will refer in their due place value and order).

Thus, Pragmaticism recommends itself for reasons of logic proper, (i.e., as a necessity of thought). Only in this regard does it lead directly to the postulation of Semiotic as a theoretical (Speculative) Grammar of all possible meaning. Pragmaticism is, therefore, not a psyche-centred, intuitionist phenomenology of action, one in which action becomes the 'action centre' of a will manipulating its universe, and, derived from this, the 'action correlate' of a world at the horizon of intentionality. As a strict necessity of thought, action as conduct is the correspondence of a hypothetical assertion. Hypotheses are conditional conduct. The conditions can be manifold, but the form is always the same: 'If y then you/I have to do x.' Here is the clearest difference from the propositional form, which casts modality into this form: 'If y then x.' Action is the foundation of meaning only in this sense of conditional conduct.

The first step in philosophical method, therefore, must be to formally analyze action-as-behaviour as such. The question 'what is action?' cannot be answered in a non-recursive way (i.e., without being itself an action). Thus, an analytic of our acting can only be mediate. It must presuppose itself and then find a way in which it observes itself acting. Clearly, this requires a highly complex method. If it were simply to beg the question, it could not recognize anything new; if it were to objectivize action, it would have to abstract from itself, not seeing itself as an action of thought. Also, our analysis cannot pretend to 'found' action on some postulated prerequisites. Such foundationalism cannot be successful, for the same reasons: there is never a first action, action is only continuous. An analytic of action must account for this methodological situation and reflect that situation in its results.

If we cannot start with a beginning (because there is no beginning in action that would justify a methodological approach based on an 'intentional' or other beginning), we can only start with the continuity of action from an arbitrary point. Our action, the next action, always relates to its preceding action, which is in turn related to other actions that precede both. As an ongoing action, it is also related to actions that follow. In the most general sense, this 'nextness' is formed only by meaning, but how exactly must for now remain an open question. It is not implied, though, that this nextness can only be a relation ruled by finality or by efficient causality.

This statement about action as such describes its first non-empty content, which is, however, only a formal content. At this point let us say simply that continuity of action shows that action can and must be described as form. We call this form meaning without any psychological connotation. Furthermore, acting with understanding establishes relations, not only as the form of action but also more generally as the form of all being. From a Pragmaticistic[9] perspective, being consists of meaning, which is relation. This is perhaps the intuitively most difficult novelty, since it runs counter to the almost 'natural' point of view that meaning is a true statement about a state of affairs, or language as mirror of the real. A relational view of meaning certainly does not deny this, but it must resituate this relatively as one of a number of types of relation. Later we will investigate the kinds of forms of relation in action that there are.

Regarding the specialty and novelty of Pragmaticism in this context, I offer two general remarks: First, meaning is not the result of an existential action (human behaviour or human condition); rather, it is the other way round: action as continuing is only expression of the nature of meaning as intrinsically not terminated or finite, and not terminable. Although this is easy to grasp in the infinite, continuous action, it is really meaning that is infinite. Many philosophers would grant this abstractly, perhaps, but in Pragmaticism and Semiotic every concrete meaning is infinite by nature. Second, from the perspective of meaning itself, difficulties arise with certain static conceptions and treatments of meaning. The sentence form, as proposition and assertion, cannot render the infinity of meaning. Because it is part of the nature of meaning to be infinite, we cannot abstract from it without an essential loss.

From these two general points about the specificity of Pragmaticism, we can in a short digression draw the line of demarcation separating his from other variants of pragmatism.

Every variant of pragmatism must find its own way of bringing 'meaning' or some equivalent into the concept of action, based on the action of a will on something material. This task is incumbent on intentionality, convention, historically contingent rationality, or language. With the latter, which is closest to Peirce, the difference could not be expressed in a neater way than in the validity claims of Habermas's *Fundamentalpragmatik*. As much as in Peirce's (still to be described) Semiotic form of meaning, the propositional form of validity claims is the focal point of the entire theory. Everything hinges on the possibility of a yes/no answer to a proposition vested in an adequate speech act. Habermas's argument must presuppose (or otherwise it does not work) that meaning – which has three worlds with corresponding universes of states of affairs, norms, and interiority expression – in its entire range can be reduced in lossless and complete form into the same propositions framed by different speech acts. So, more than by any of his anthropological and cultural assumptions (which are facts, and thus either true or false, but not necessary or not), his argument can be challenged by his linguistic-logical assumption.

Apparently, Habermas himself sees the constraints that propositional 'validity claims' would place on a theory with such a universal pretense as his *Fundamentalpragmatik*. The speech act philosophy wrapping the propositional claim is the closest he can get – on this basis – to a modal extension of linguistic logic. In film theory, a very analogous case is Bettetini – we shall return to this – who avails himself of Prior's modal logic to analyze what he calls temporal logic in cinema. Apparently, propositions would make it quite impossible to grasp the *post hoc ergo propter hoc* sort of logic in cinematic narration.

This core assumption is directly contradicted by the Semiotic form of meaning. All three forms of meaning in signs – which will be dealt with later in much greater detail – are counter to the three basic principles of traditional propositional logic: the principle of contradiction, the principle of identity, and the principle of excluded middle. Succinctly put, the meaning of Possibility (or mere quiddity or whatness) is not contradicted by anything – and yet it is meaning. The meaning of truth of existence, the closest to the yes/no alternative, is not when there is an identity between a state of affairs and a proposition; rather, it is a teridentity[10] between the two and a general. Lastly, the meaning of a general notion is always indefinite, and as long as it is not defined, a third (i.e., a middle) cannot be excluded. We will see later how these new principles of non-traditional logic are enshrined in the different sign classes. Taking the sign instead of the sentence as a (linguistic) standard case is, therefore, a way of overcoming the limitations of propositions.

The principle underlying this new conceptualization of the basics of logic involves extending the propositional relation (based on grammar and grammatical units) into the much broader field of cognitive relations. However, this presupposes – beyond a formal analytic of behaviour – that something other than language becomes the firm ground of meaning. The groundwork for an alternative involves everything that language can take for granted. What are the ultimate elements with which cognition deals? This is another way of asking: Do we have different kinds of thought, or is there just one type of thinking the opposite of thought, one uniform world such as it appears? The non-trivial, non-simple answer is a theory of Categories. Thereafter – if a careful examination of all possible thoughts reveals that there is no simple thought but rather multiple, n-tuple kinds of thought – the question arises, how do they relate? A theory of relations based on logical principles alone, and unsupported by grammatical conventions, deals with inclusions, the number of relates in a relation, their order. One of the simpler instances – for example, in traditional logic – is the inclusion of a term it can be more or less comprehensive, and only more comprehensive terms can stand in the major premise as general term, the more particular term, or proper name, in the dependent premise.

The relational nature of action – let alone its three elements, which will be discussed later – is not plausibly explained from action as the term is commonly used. The latter customarily concedes one relation – between a subject and an object. For Luhmann, theory of action is, again, an 'old-European' figure of thought (in his eyes to be overcome in general systems theory). Habermas calls it strategical action, while for Schütz it is the subjective meaning of a subject's action project. There are many other concepts of action in the same vein. So one might be inclined to assume that it is the 'natural attitude' (Husserl), which no one can seriously question. For Foucault, it is one of the traps of philosophical thought to construct the all-powerful subject behind everything, which through this becomes object. Film theory, too, has discovered and appropriated this relation (of existence). The two myths of cinematic specificity have been constructed from it – myths that can roughly be identified with two names: Bazin and Eisenstein.[11] The real problem is therefore not that acting is less than this simple relation, but that it must be shown to be more.

Formal theories in the realm of theories of action are an alternative to pragmatic theories; typically, however, they are also not based on logical problems of relations. The pure ideal form is certainly mathematical by nature. So it is not surprising that two major theories, comprehensive of but not limited to action, have availed themselves of the mathematical or even geometric form: R. Thom's 'chaos theory' and the postsemiological 'morphogenesis of meaning' (for a brief discussion, cf. *infra* 109, 175–8) and Luhmann's 'systems theory.' The Peircean approach, which is based on behaviour, precludes attempts to hypostasize purely mathematical forms. In its core argument, the general systems theory of Luhmann builds on Spencer-Brown's mathematical form of 'system re-entry,' which has nothing to do with experience. Here the form 'system' is applied to action, and the only justification for this is re-entry – that is, that 'system' is applied to systems theory itself. In the eyes of Luhmann, such an open regress is not hopelessly circular and infinite; however, it must reveal the blind spot – the latent tautology or manifest paradox –

at the root of every system. This is not the place to discuss problems with this circular reasoning. In contrast the non-circularity behind Peirce's 'formal' approach becomes evident. Peircean 'forms' are all rooted in experience as behaviour. It is from there that they obtain their compelling force. Mathematics as purely hypothetical thought can also admit (for instance) imaginary numbers which cannot be applied to something existent.

Formal theories, moreover, exist not only in explicit theories of action, but – in another vein – also in what Peirce might have called 'aesthetic conduct.' Such aesthetic theories owe nothing to Peirce's Pragmaticism, but have come up with a comparable claim that they extend the constraints of logic with formalism. By the same token, this has to cost them their universal logical relevance and make them 'logics' confined to the aesthetic domain. In the nineteenth century there were attempts to establish purely formal aesthetics, beginning with the work of Johann Friedrich Herbart and his pupil Robert Zimmermann. Images beyond representation, consisting of pure forms, are the domain of formal aesthetics, which has explicitly sacrificed all cognitive power (cf. Wiesing 1997). It is patent how this original aesthetic formalism was followed through into the aesthetic practice and theory of the twentieth century. Although Wiesing attempted to glean some inspiration from Peirce, Aesthetic Formalism is not of great relevance for a Semiotic aesthetic, because it is ultimately not cognate with the logic proper of relations.

Forms of behaviour must be justified, because behaviour is not 'formal' in the various formalist senses mentioned above. The formal justification stands, however, even if the comfortable way would be one that explains action through social, linguistic, or other conventions. Form alone is not enough whenever there are cognitive claims, and transcendental solutions have been excluded. Now there are chiefly two alternative possible justifications left: a psychological one based on the 'form of mind,' and a categorial one. Both have been raised in the broader realm of pragmatism. The psychological path was chosen by G.H. Mead and also by James. Peirce opted against psychology as a basis for cognition and cognitive behaviour. Yet, it must be admitted that even the first approach has succeeded in thoroughly overcoming the abstraction typically encountered in most psychologisms. Thus, there are no psychic contents in opposition to exterior stimuli, nor is there a solitary psyche connecting with an external matter; rather there is an intrinsic integration of cognition in a pragmatic, behavioural world relation. Therefore, with either justification there is no need to fight the battles of yesterday. Although the ideas from Wundt's psychological laboratory involved Peirce and Mead in some reflection, and even if there are still some remnants left in popular psychological epistemologies, in principle the philosophical state of the art has passed by psychologism.

Beyond pragmatic and formal theories of action, some might criticize the glaring absence of an important further alternative in justifying possible relations: Language and the 'linguistic turn,' the appreciation of language not only as the catalyst and transient in-between of mind and world, but also as a locus of the mediation itself. However, in both variants of pragmatism (Mead and Peirce), language plays a vital role. Whereas it is also true that pragmatism does not allow us to postulate language as the ultimate explanatory horizon. From this perspective would be another abstraction. Language and signs, instead, must be explained on a behavioural basis, and not the other way round (as happens in semiology, where the explanatory chain goes from language to system and to linguistic pragmatics). Therefore, the pragmatic consideration of language goes much deeper and is not restrained by the linguistic surface of natural languages.

The first viable explanation of universal forms of behaviour received its decisive impulse from Wundt. It was mainly Dewey who transmitted this impulse to pragmatism and to Mead. What sparked this figure of thought? The core of the problem was this question: What causes emotions in the psyche? Mead's answer did not involve considering psychic content, sensations, ideas, gestalts. Rather, he saw psychic content as being explained only through comparison with something else. In Mead's eyes this something else could only be reality. His psychologism was therefore actually a theory of the impressions of the real on the psyche, and not of intrapsychic dynamics. Yet the real itself is not a plain ontological factor; even less is it a sort of physical 'being'; rather, it is the context of the behaviour of an agent. Thus, emotions compare with action purposes.

1.3 Investigating Conduct as a Form

Peirce, from the beginning, justified possible relations in behaviour in a different way. Although he did not recuse psychological justification, he had good reasons to prefer another with a much broader scope – one that to him was much less prone to misunderstandings and psycholog-

ical limitations. At the same time, his alternative was much more difficult to follow. Toward the end of his life, almost desperate over the
difficulty he was having to make himself understood, he was prepared
to give the sop to Cerberus and to explain his theory in psychological
terms. Yet even then his explanation was categorial and not psychological, in spite of the impression his psychological illustrations might
have created. The categorial justification of possible relations in the
form of behaviour follows a different path, without being counter-intuitive. There is also an interesting upstream of a categorially founded
Pragmaticism in its 'metaphysical' consequences; however, this investigation is separate from, and above, the theory of forms, which concerns us here.

To conceive being as the form of behaviour might seem an offensive,
counterintuitive thought, admitted grudgingly as an heuristic tool to be
discarded after its useful life. Yet in a Pragmaticistic perspective, this
life span is perennial, as new interpretative relations of conduct of
behaviour toward the real are never terminated. Truth remains process
and seeking, and so does reality. So it is essential to truth itself that we
analyze the process of relating as the form of conduct. As relation and
sign, a theory of behaviour is the new Critique and substitute for epistemology. However, its object is not this or that action. Speaking of an
action in the singular can be two things: it can be a reductive abstraction, or it can be (comprehensive) form. There is never a concrete action
in the singular; that said, there is action as form in the singular. It can no
longer be the form of 'something' (i.e., among many other states of
affairs), of course, but it can be the ultimate form, of the most general,
universal origin of all phenomena. So the first question becomes this:
Which formal components (including continuity) are in the form of
action? A close observation of action (quantified as 'any action you
want') will show exactly three relations of different (formal) nature, not
less and not more. As a formal method, it must also claim that these
relations are operant in every action as soon as it has become a habit of
behaviour, which implies that it is based on meaning.[12] This form can
be spelled out as a practical relevance, thus ruling out any meaning that
is abstracted from meaningful behaviour where it is confirmed and
must be usable. In this consists the very difference between movement
and action. Movement – for instance, the moving images of cinema – is
also a relation of nextness. However, the type of relation is merely of
the nature of facts, which needs only a dyadic other for change;
whereas everything that is connected through meaning is no longer

mere movement. Meaning relates one to its other though a third, which is not of the nature of facts. An action brings forth its next, other action not as a (dyadic) movement, but solely as a meaningful continuation of a general idea that stands above all these single actions taken together.

However, the relation of meaning is not all that makes actions function as conduct. Although it is intuitively clear (but not yet proven at this stage) that action as such consists only in its being related through meaning, meaning alone does not yet produce an action. It depends equally on another relation – one that relates it to something existent. Later we shall see that in this consists the difference between a proposition and an assertion. A pure assertion, assertion – that is, without any propositional content at all – literally asserts nothing, even though it asserts perfectly. Peirce is poking fun at such assertive purity when he illustrates it with a perfect but empty notarial act that is perfectly unintelligible: 'We shall naturally take a case where the assertive element is magnified – a very formal assertion, such as an affidavit. Here a man goes before a notary or magistrate and takes such action that if what he says is not true, evil consequences will be visited upon him, and this he does with a view to thus causing other men to be affected just as they would be if the proposition sworn to had presented itself to them as a perceptual fact' (Peirce 1998: 140, cf. 5.546). This is pure existence without meaningful content. As a type of action, this creates an effective relation – but with nothing. Conversely, mere meaning is not confined by any constraint of fact – it need only be imaginable (something unimaginable is also not possible as an experience, only as a mathematical thought, i.e., 'imaginary numbers').

Another type of action, the third, is already conduct. Not only does it have meaning, not only is it based on factual constraints, but it is also controlled by an insight into laws of causal relations. In one of his lectures on Pragmatism, Peirce illustrated this with a fire accident, which his brother had rehearsed as a typical situation so that he would know exactly how to react in given circumstances. This meant he had the law of a conduct in his mind, even though he had never really experienced this situation before. In summary, a concrete, meaning-guided, self-controlled conduct of behaviour is exactly:

- one relation to a (possible, existent, or necessary) character,
- one relation to a character and its (verifiable, falsifiable) existence, *and*
- one relation to a character, its existence, and its must-be.

Each relation corresponds to a different ideal kind of action, which can be called an 'action' of feeling in the first, action proper in the second, and conduct or behaviour in the third case. The higher ordinal order contains the types of the lower ordinals, but not conversely. Thus, while an action (e.g., hitting a signpost) comprehends the feeling of something, it need not – yet – contain elements of causal knowledge.

At this stage of rudimentary pragmatism, such relations are realized in every action provided the action is under the deliberate control of meaning. Formal consideration of action, however, takes us farther than this. As final form, the complex of these relations translates into the sign process, passing through the logic of relations, which in turn have their ultimate base in what really is (i.e., the universal Categories of being and essence). The problem of justifying three relations in habits of behaviour can be treated in two separate questions. The first question concerns the invention of relations: What shows that there are not less than three relations, and are there more than three? The second concerns the question of justification: From where can we deduce such relations of conduct?

Clearly, a commonsense understanding of 'how we act' cannot suffice for a serious theory, which – in refuting apriorism – must necessarily substitute the latter with a proof that Pragmaticism constitutes a complete theory of reality *in se*. A deeper and already more formal understanding of behaviour is found in its relational conceptualization. Relations can be completely abstract if they remain in the realm of mathematical thought. As experience, however, relations combine the mathematical form with a *Weltanschauung* – they blend the purely mental with the hard resistance of real facts into logical laws of thought. Thus, relations as such are not sufficient. Reality must contribute in such a manner that not only is it open to relational treatment but also it does not exclude any possible experience. This seems an impossible feat if it postulates an experience upstream of experience (in which event infinite regress looms). This 'proto-experience' is the traditional topic of categories – a topic that in one way or another is focused on every philosophy that has not altogether dispensed with the reality factor. A pre-experience real – a sort of ontological cognition – is no longer feasible. Therefore, a new, non-transcendental method for finding categories of experiences as such must be established. Pragmaticism as a reality-aware philosophy must, then, prove that it is a comprehensive theory – one that is not limited to the downstream of first assumptions and that does not need to make an exception of its cognitive principles for the categories.

The basic idea of 'category' is as simple as the theories for grasping it are complex. Even in everyday conversation it can be discovered that to say 'is' can mean many things: the 'is' in 'this is red' is not the same 'is' as in 'this is new' or even in 'this is right.' Rightness exists in a different way than newness and redness. For instance, it cannot be indicated as such, and newness can be indicated only if something else is indicated in the same time. A question arises, then: What makes redness and freshness the same, and what distinguishes them from, say, fastness? In a convenient way they can be grouped under ultimate concepts, which interpreters must possess in order to process these ideas adequately in their difference. For red and fresh they need the ultimate concept of quality (i.e., that anything that 'is' has a quality, 'is' not without a characteristic). Fastness, however, already needs an ultimate concept, which is much more complex. It already involves comparing one subject for two different qualities distinguished by time. This combines the ultimate concepts of plurality and unity (cf. p. 569n31; we shall discuss Peirce's theory of categories and his struggle with the variety of ultimate concepts in the philosophical tradition in detail below, pp. 54–102).

In languages that use the 'is' copula as a tool to connect one thing – the subject – with another – the predicate – into a novel idea, such apparent sameness leads one astray. It has been discovered that such an ambiguity can be used profitably, for instance in a metaphorical abuse or other sophist device. Κατηγορεῖν simply means 'assert' (cf. *infra*). As soon as the business of asserting reveals itself as variegate and complex, the options are, in principle, only two: either exclude all assertions except the one of facts, or come up with a theory of assertion. The latter concerns itself with the actually possible differences in asserting. Exclusion is a solution that leads to an unrealistically purified language. Once purged it of all non-factual assertions, its ultimate ideal is the protocol sentence of direct observation of sensory data. This was thought to be the sole reliable basis of a strict logic, as it was programmatically proposed by the onto-semanticism of the Vienna Circle and early analytical philosophy (cf. Eley 1973). If the problem called 'categories' is admitted, however, a solution must be sought beyond language.

The ambiguity of 'is' is not a redeemable feature of Indo-European languages, to be overcome in an ideally clear formal language. Is it perhaps that being (nature or physis) itself 'is' in different ways? Such an intuition leads to ontology, which is meaningful only if there is more than one type of being. Peirce, however, addressed the multiplicity of meaning, being, and saying as a problem of behaviour: whatever is, must be the object of human behaviour, which can be grasped through the differences that this behaviour makes in behaving. Furthermore, behaving, in a non-contentual formal perspective, is relating. Thus, categorical differences must translate into differences of relating.

The category problem can easily be discovered in everyday language; however, it is not a linguistic problem and also applies to cinema. This may not be immediately evident. In conversation, we usually take note of the category problem, typically when by some blunder someone makes 'category mistakes.' When we respond to 'This book is interesting!' with 'You have a London accent!' we are creating a Babel of languages. Cinema, as much as meaning, is not exempt from this, because meaning always interprets some other meaning – that is, it can never start *ex ovo*. Cinema is not only internally organized as meaning upon meaning (montage, frame, etc.); not only that but it also has an interpretation interface with its viewers. Therefore, a category of meaning of one and only one determinate kind is always operant. When spectators 'misunderstand' such determination, they are committing a category mistake (i.e., they are mis-taking this category). A film, for instance, shows a knife. If the determinant category is final causality (which is the logic of narration), one sees a clue, a hint, or a 'smoking gun'–type conclusive proof of a (previously constructed) narrative. If the category is quiddity or whatness, such a sequence is 'documentary.' Nothing warrants the construction of a narrative logic, but one can see what something is (or – using other categories – where it is, or how old it is). The objectivity of documentary film presupposes that one does not commit the category mistake of constructing narrative causality; for narrative causality – presupposing a general reliability in the 'narrative contract' – aims exclusively at purposes and ends and not at anything answering the 'what' question. To prevent category mistakes like this, documentary film has put numerous devices in place, most prominently in montage. Another instance of categorical difference in cinema – and possible category mistake – is the playfully aesthetic contemplation, wherein any question of the type 'what is it?' and 'what is it for?' is inappropriate.

This is especially delicate in films in which the categorical determination is not standardized. Small wonder that the plethora of interpretations contradict one another. Later I will analyze in detail one such example of paramount categorical indeterminacy, Godard's *Je vous salue, Marie*. Some go so far as to state that any linguistic 'making meaning' from a film (basis) is falsifying, arbitrary, reductionist, and so on.

There is a point to this view: for example, Godard's smoke screen, while he was producing *Passion*, whereby he answered all questions on the 'about' of this film project with 'see' (the film dialogue starts with the question – ambivalent in French – 'Mais qu'est-ce que cette histoire?' which can be translated narcotized as 'What is going on here?' or in double-entendre as ' What is the (hi)story in this?' Then follows a series of 'categorical' theses on the 'about' of this film) images instead of scripts, is famous. This is precisely the category problem in his films.

In the richness of concrete meaning, 'category mistakes' have always been used profitably, notably for metaphors. Such mistakes, however, are really transitions from one category to another – in other words, interpretations of a different kind from the preceding one. The mastery of such transitions used to be the business of rhetoric. In this vein, the analysis of Godard's film will argue for a complex rhetorical reading, with or without preconfected figures of speech. The categorical toolbox of cinema measures up to this meaning-generating interpretation.

Categories can be deduced in a number of ways. As the ultimate difference of 'is,' they are universal by definition. In Aristotle, who first treated the subject who and contributed the terminology, it is not entirely clear whether categories are the ultimate forms of speech (for him this meant: about all being) or of being itself.[13] For Kant, categories concerned judgments and the mental faculties connected with them. Finally, regarding Peirce, the recusation of transcendentalism led him to deduce categories *a posteriori* from behaviour, most extensively in his late works. One might be tempted to interpret his deduction again in a transcendentalist or at least 'objective idealist' way. This would position the forms of behaviour outside (cognitive) behaviour itself in a precognitive realm of pure ideas (*a priori* to all behaviour).

As we have seen with the above phenomenological analysis of the continuum of behaviour, which evinced relation as its form, behaviour without form is literally not feasible. The form is operant in every single behaviour; however, the theoretical grasp of the form itself could become a problem. Solving this by comprehending form as transcendental idea or 'system re-entry' (cf. *infra*) is a temptation that can only be avoided when cognition is, without exception, anchored in experience. However, this is no impediment for Peirce, who goes beyond the immediate context of concrete behaviour. Having established the relational nature of behaviour, he investigates relations *in se*, undertaking an inquiry into the logic of relations. The precise comprehension of relations then bring him to his detailed analysis of one kind of relation

– the triadic relation – as the comprehensive classification of all possible signs. This order in Peirce's deduction is all-important. Otherwise – perhaps even in reverse order – one risks all shades of idealistic, transcendentalist, aprioristic temptations; Signs would perhaps become ideal types, and pragmatism and its derived metaphysic become superfluous superadditions without basis.

Given the importance of the discovery of all effective forms of behaviour – including cognitive behaviour – for all underlying structures of meaning as well, the burden of proof increases. Now all depends on obtaining an adequate grasp of habits of behaviour. This preliminary analysis or phenomenology of behaviour has evinced its continuous character. This continuity is totally different from the temporal totality in Husserl's phenomenology; which points to an immediate consciousness in the subjectivity of agents projecting their action plans into their future and onto their world horizon. It is also quite different from 'statistical' continuity, as Peirce in his 1903 lectures on Pragmatism illustrates with an amusing case of gambling (to which we will return in the context of narrative teleology when continuity becomes necessity). Continuity is not an unlimited number of single actions. It is not the famous case of an unlimited number of coins thrown, which customarily illustrates the normal distribution in chance events and thereby serves as the presupposition of any stochastic proposition.

The absurdity in attaining a completeness of all actions (i.e., without the capacity of forming a habit as a third) appears when we attempt to act with this kind of cognition. A statistical grasp of action is thus that it has no purchase on concrete behaviour; otherwise, one would not know what action to perform next. We know only which action has a certain probability for happening in a Gaussian-distributed set of actions. This makes for a deliberate abstraction of all motives and causes – which is, however, the essence of concrete action. By acting, every actor acknowledges through the effective action that he or she entertains a particular relation to other actions. One does not act one action, bring it to an end, and then act another, next action. If such acting were possible, it would be without meaning (i.e., without causes and motives). Now granting that all cognition is cognitive behaviour, there must be the same kind of continuity in cognition itself. We do not cognize by thinking one thought and then the next, and have a complete cognition when we have thought all thoughts on a subject. Any number of perceptions – or speaking metaphorically, 'bottom-up' concepts – do not make a cognition. This cognitivist approach requires a supervenience of 'top-down' schemata that can supply the unity of the one cognition of the many perceptions. The complementary metaphors suggest cooperation, yet there is no hint as to how to apply the correct top-down to the correct bottom-up. Does this entail the 'constructivism' of convention, of linguistic customs, of arbitrariness? Such an appearance of explanation only creates another meta-level of the problem, until a satisfactory explanation for the relationship of the two components is provided. The continuity of behaviour delivers this explanation, even though its basis is still to be clarified.

Behaviour-based cognition has a peculiar way of cognizing without reaching a unity based on completeness. Peirce does not reach this non-total unity by postulating one action standing in a relation to another action and again to another, and so forth. It must be admitted that this might be an easy and intuitive solution. It suffices to assume a successful relation between an agent and an object or fact. The further assumption of cohesion of facts among them, or of the physical world in itself, is the backdrop of the intuitive reasonableness in this solution. It creates or presupposes a one-dimensional world wherein cognizing involves no more than reaching that world successfully with the mind. However, the toll for this simplicity is too heavy. We forfeit the particular mode of reason to reach its cognitive unity – a unity that is not based on the factual unity of the physical world. In habits of behaviour, a unity is reached; in contrast, facts are unlimited and can never be complete. A habit has therefore integrated a time dimension in a particular way. Also, by the same token, it has immediately one qualitative character before it. This is when it gives its attention to something with no regard for all the rest.

In every action there are three quite different dimensions of the form, regardless of its content. Each formal dimension adds something else to acting. Abstracting of any one of them makes concrete action unreal and unfeasible. The consequence for film studies is that perception cannot be treated by itself. Furthermore, since there is no time in perception, because it belongs to a different dimension, one cannot 'add' time to cinema by grafting narration onto perception. One cannot perceive a narrative time construction. As we will discuss in the context of narrative enunciation, time consists in a comparison of the same in a state before and in an after.[14] That the comparison which makes narration can be treated analytically in a separate theory should not be denied. However, as a concrete cognition it is never separate; rather, it is different in the same cognition. It is customary practice in film theory that a theory of the image (perception, or perceptive codes) is elaborated, and then montage ('syntagmatically' or, making sense of the sequence of images directly, as narration). Then the elaboration is on 'documentary' uncaring production. When these elaborations come each as a different publication (see Aumont 1990; Chateau 1986; Bergala n.d.), it becomes even more difficult to see: every concrete film, as a form of cognitive action, contains all three jointly and cannot split them up lest it become incomprehensible. Images are not spatial, and narratives are temporal organizations – except as abstractions. Measured at their connection in real acting, every sign is always simultaneously spatial and temporal (space and time not, however, being on the same level of complexity).

1.3.1 Peculiarities of the Pragmatic Method

Before turning to the categorial forms of behaviour in the strict sense, we need to take a step back and negotiate some unfortunate common misunderstandings of the Pragmaticistic method. In the realm of ultimate forms, the result can only be as good as the method on which it is based. So if the pragmatic method itself is minimized, the professed claim to reach ultimate forms of every possible behaviour is greatly relativized and conditioned.

What is Pragmaticism in reality? Its extent and comprehension should not be contingent on the approach we chose earlier for its representation. Having chosen actual behaviour in the real world as an initial base – one has to start from somewhere, after all, and the late Peirce chose the same initial idea, enshrined in the Pragmatic Maxim itself – this is by no means to be taken as the last intuitive basis of all reasoning. This kind of intuitive basis prevails in some social theories, which in fact disallow or even discourage meaningful questions below the level of human action. Thus, to ask why we can act, or even act socially, is considered a non-pertinent question, because it involves a concept of society as society. Such a concept can no longer be meaningfully conceived of within society, and there is nothing outside of it, either. Therefore, the concept itself is dropped in favour of regional concepts such as 'national societies' or other units below the level of society (cf. Luhmann 1997: 16–43). In this problem context, intuitive foundation on the concept of human action appears as an anchor. Such limitation is not found in Pragmatism. The possibility of acting is neither presupposed nor intuitively accepted.

Pragmatism has a long history of being subject to inadequate critiques. Strangely enough, most of the older critiques go in the direction of doubting the reliability of normal behaviour as conceived by 'pragmatism,' reducing it to mere utilitarianism. Utilitarian pragmatism conceptualizes action as being governed by the irrationalistic subjective impression of utility, and its success is its proof (cf. Joas 1999: 66f). Such a caricature has its own function, however, and – not without nationalistic overtones ('erosion of french culture') – it served mainly as an easy whipping boy, for instance in Durkheim's lectures on 'pragmatism and sociology' from 1913–14 ('armed struggle against reason'). Other total failures to find an adequate purchase for pragmatism are those of Scheler, Horkheimer, and Lukács. Each of these failures had its own reasons.

All of these critiques focus on the question of truth. This is the typical reason for the demise of pragmatism as a theory advocating utility, and not the dictates of reason, as its truth criterion as 'true' philosophy would. Peirce, when his name was known at all, was perceived by his critics as a sort of American Nietzsche – as perhaps dangerous but not seriously so. In light of those criticisms, it is worth emphasizing that it is not the truth question that is truly new and unique in pragmatism. In our presentation we have deliberately neglected the following question: How, in the ultimate form of cognitive behaviour, is true cognition possible? Upstream to that question is how meaning is possible – that is, how can meaningful action in the physical world happen? This question translates practically into yet another question: How can action continue? Continuity is thus the fulcrum of pragmatic thought. On this basis, the question of true cognition is again posed in a novel way – one that bears not the remotest resemblance to 'utility.' Provided there is continuity, continuous action, or behaviour, meaning in certain circumstances will be true or false. In the broader horizon of meaning, at a given moment some meaning will be true, but the same meaning will be false at another moment. This does not suppress its being meaningful. Even something that is possible is meaningful, but it is neither true nor false. In Peirce's logical terminology, such meaning is vague. It is undetermined with respect to its truth characteristic, but it is liable to be determined in that regard at any moment ('I want'). There is also a third kind of meaning that is neither true nor false. All general meaning has a scope that is beyond truth determination, but at any moment ('you want') one can choose any instance and determine the truth or falseness of a general law for this instance. This kind can falsify a law, but that fal-

sification can never be verified in an inductive inference until that inference is complete, which is practically impossible.

In view of this concrete behavioural situation of cognition, the truth
question is certainly not excluded, but it becomes quite complex. Its
criterion is not utility; rather, it is the significant differences in its conclusiveness and determination. Truth becomes a particular case of
meaning, but it is not its presupposition. The primary question is
'What is this?' not 'Is this true?' The latter question is relevant only in
certain circumstances; in other circumstances it is not answerable; and
in yet other circumstances it is not desirable – it is an obstacle to the
exploration of the possible.

A second wave in the reception of pragmatism in the philosophical
debate was able to draw much more from the potential of pragmatism,
also with regard to the question of cognitive truth. For instance, in the
German philosophical debate Apel rediscovered pragmatism as a welcome extension of the limitations of the then prevailing speech act and
analytical language philosophy. Morris's earlier use of pragmatism (as
'pragmatics') in the framework of a basically onto-semantic research
agenda set by Carnap was no longer helpful at this stage. Thus, Apel's
was the philosophical recovery of a philosophical program much
richer than its early users had understood it to be (cf. Fisch 1986: 321–
55). In his interpretation, pragmatism was more than those famous
'practical consequences.' A number of Peirce's interpreters failed to see
more than a sort of Dewey-ish 'democratic truth' (cf. Oehler 1981a).

It is certainly true that the continuity of behaviour comprises the
social dimension in Peirce. In his later life, this gave rise to his 'social
metaphysic,' appropriately called Synechism ('having-part-in'). As in
physical nature, chance is different from mere factual tendencies and
from laws of nature, and the same holds for cognitive social behaviour.
Thus, the social mind is of a different nature than the individual mind,
which is merely actual and which in its findings is subject to chance. It
is the true and truly universal Thirdness, as will be explained below.
Only the social – as pure Thirdness – emphatically is in its full sense
(i.e., as it is intended to be in its perfect form). Yet no individual mind
ever 'is' the social mind at any given moment. Such a statement is by
no means natural and intuitive, even to a superficial, non-Pragmatic
present-day mind, which leans more toward all kinds of 'constructiv-
isms'.[15] At the other end of the spectrum there is still a Hegel-like philosophy of history, at times as a Marxist apotheosis of the hypostasized
social, at times as its postmodern negation as in Lyotard. In this regard,

Peirce's Pragmaticism is no more and no less than the result of his anti-aprioristic proof of metaphysical truths.

The father of 'practical consequences' is acknowledged to be Bain. He used this term to analyze the consequences of actions in contrast to inconsequential claims of inner states. Peirce must have been pleased with this doctrine's capacity to clarify concepts: what something truly is can no longer be determined of itself; rather, it must be gleaned from its practical consequences. Peirce merely dropped the forensic context. Later he was unhappy with some misleading expressions in his first published presentation of pragmatism in *Comment rendre nos idées claires*. The Pragmatist intuition is not new; rather, it is Bain's, and Peirce, considering his own 'scarce more than a corollary' (5.12), maintained the three-step procedure of belief, doubt, and inquiry. Thus far it is still Bain's psychology. In Peirce it becomes the scientific method, (i.e., that method's procedures of fixation of belief). Not psyche but rather economy of research in the context of Common-Sensism is the practical domain. Seen in a psychological key – and by his own admission, Peirce indulged in this perspective before his mature revision of Pragmatism – it is remotely comparable to 'cognitivism' in film theory and shares most of its inadequacies. The true import of Pragmaticism is already quite clear in Peirce's six early illustrations (see *Popular Science Monthly* 1877–8).

Pragmaticism does not even come as a theory of action; rather, it connects with the problem context of human understanding. 'Action,' at the time, was part of a surprisingly new answer (today, however, it has been adopted by a number of philosophical approaches). The typical way to pose Peirce's problem was in the form of an altogether practical question, for example, 'How does one find out what lithium is?'[16] This question is not exhaustively answered when we discover its salty taste or see its colour. For instance, the answer must include this element's psychopharmacological effects, which were not then known as well as future discoveries of effects not yet known to us. This open horizon of the unknown or the not-yet-known aspects is part of the phenomenon 'lithium' – that is, if we have a naturalistic, practical cognitive attitude. How can we account for this concrete openness, which is intrinsic to all cognition?

A more difficult but still practical question takes us one step farther: How does one cognize the hardness of a diamond in cotton (implied: first in an environment of only cotton)? The cognitive difficulty is in the conditions, which preclude direct experiential knowledge. How can we know this hardness, then? Clearly, the aim of this example is to expand the concept of experience so as to make its scope much wider than perception. This hardness is not perceptible and self-evident ('cotton'). It can be cognized only if we know what to do to discover it. Without question, this is a rather ordinary practical cognitive situation; that said, it is also eminently practical for cognition in/of cinema. The solution urged by this example is that the expansion of experience beyond perception must postulate a third element. We can apply this example directly to cinema, where cinema takes the place of the cotton. A film shows the diamond, and we can perceive its glitter, and so on, but we can never *perceive* its hardness. Nevertheless we 'see' a hard diamond. The third element consists of a Symbol, which enables us to possibly perform certain tests. Such a Symbol 'contains,' as a behavioural rule, all the tests that are possible at a given moment. In short, cognition involves, first, knowing what one has to do; second, cognition is not content with the rules it already contains. As a practical requirement, it must include a further element that enables the possibility of tests still to be imagined. Something perfectly known is therefore something known in all its practical consequences. Thus it is not enough, say, to correctly apply a concept to sensory perception data. We also 'know' the reason why this concept is applied correctly (when we know the rule).

Now the rule knows much more than its record of past applications. It may be true that one remembers all the instances when a diamond has been harder than anything else. The additional element in the rule is the knowledge of the reason for this behaviour – that is, why diamonds have to be harder than anything else. The necessity of a law is a logical value, (i.e., one that applies logic to factual experience). Yet logic is never experienced as a fact. We behave toward facts as if they were a necessary law (i.e., through our behaviour they become law). The element of logic introduces the dimension of time into experience. It first serializes facts, and then it closes ('con-cludes') the unfinished open series with an operation of necessity. This operation raises the question of whether it is more than a practical illusion. This is evidently the crucial point of Pragmaticism. How can it prove the reality of logic, or, the logical nature of reality?

In pragmatic (and thus actual) circumstances, is concrete question can be formulated: How can the hardness of a diamond in cotton be fully cognized? One might be tempted to use the 'diamond in cotton' (perhaps embellished, as a spacecraft *Mir* experiment in outer space) as an illustration for the (conventional) social construction of things, but this misses Peirce's point completely. Pragmaticism is all about a method of cognition that will ascertain true results if applied correctly. In the Pragmatic Maxim, the truth problem is hidden in the formula '(all) conceivable consequences.' In Space, one might be cognitively satisfied with a diamond not even touching the cotton, and there might be no practical use in 'knowing' better. Pragmaticism must therefore prove its worth by providing a method that advances cognition, for a 'fixation of belief' closer to truth, not just the successful application of a cognitive schema for data (which in the diamond example would be rather misleading). Peirce's life-long struggle was to overcome his early nominalistic temptation to settle for 'satisfaction,' for a 'construct.' He had to prove the epistemological method without a petition of principle (which he would incur when applying the method for the proof). Without proof, Pragmaticism would be the same kind of idle speculation as most of the pragmatism that followed (consider Peirce's criticism of James's position, cf. Gale 1996: esp. 580–4).

Peirce's full answer must be taken with due respect to all its parts. Cognition of a Symbol is achieved only when one knows every single and possible experiential context of it. 'Hard' can be known only if one knows all the circumstances in which hardness can or could be experienced. The counterfactual conditional is, therefore, very important to Peirce's definition of Pragmaticism. He does not reduce the meaning of a Symbol merely to past experience. His vision goes beyond 'Critical Common-Sensism' as the ultimum of cognition. This must be affirmed against all those followers who think they are able to shed metaphysical reflections and retain only pragmatism.[17] Pragmaticism can never be 'pure experience' (if that could exist). Instead, it retains the necessity that experience must somehow find its way through theoretical concepts or some generality beyond the experiential. Thus far it is only Peirce's claim, which must be taken as a Pragmaticistic creed. Yet he goes further, wanting to prove that the Pragmaticistic understanding of cognition must necessarily be like this. How can Pragmaticism be proved?

Premising that proof involves reconstructing of the cognitive process. This is done by utilizing extreme illustrations. As with all methods of expansive cognition, of course, these illustrations, too, are instances of 'diagrammatic thinking' (as it will be called). One such extreme case is the assumption of a real singularity, so-called 'Phaneron' (which excludes to imply more than that it appears before a mind).

Assuming[18] that one could experience something truly singular, it will necessarily be experienced as a mere feeling. This feeling cannot be represented, since through being represented it would inevitably lose its status of singularity. It would lose already by a compared feeling, as in '„' is like '„'. That would still be far from saying '„' is 'hard.' It follows that the singularity of a strict Phaneron would be strictly present, as long as it is present and not re-presented. A mere strictly present feeling is not 'hard.' Now, it cannot be denied that there are real Phanera even in normal mental activity. The human mind is indeed capable of taking something 'as itself' and also something 'as something else,' which is the difference between present(ing) and representing. In the former case the mind is only with itself and immediate. The latter, however, is an expression of the intrinsically dialogic nature of mind. Peirce affirmed on many occasions the importance of the inner dialogue. He understood that it is an operation of an individual mind that confronts itself with its other self.[19]

At any rate, as soon as *re*-presenting takes place, a feeling or Phaneron becomes a sign. Signi-fication, however, means referring to a generality, something beyond the singularity of a feeling. As we have seen, such referral – and this is precisely implied by the Pragmatic Maxim – is intrinsically directed toward 'all' circumstances – that is, to a totality. Only a totality is really general *and* contains all individual states; only then do we really know what something means. The connection of all concepts is the expression of 'all possible circumstances.'

Such an appeal to generality apparently contradicts our normal intuition and cannot pretend to be self-evident. The onus of proof lies with those who claim Pragmaticism.[20] Evidently, it is impossible to prove that one will indeed ever experience all circumstances. There is only one thing that can be proved. It is the form that produces the following thought of a thought – that is, that produces generalization. By taking the Pragmatic Maxim as something else, we would be reducing it to something lacking utterly in value. Ideologically, this makes it either a simple hope or a historical statement about futures (*futurabilia*). The cognitive value of either amounts to nought. Instead, there would be a cognitive value in Pragmaticism, if it is predictive. It would need to predict all future thought, however, in all actual and possible 'circumstances.' This is precisely Peirce's understanding of 'Reality' – strictly speaking, it is a *singulare tantum*.

Packing epistemological claims into concepts, however, would not solve any problem that appears to be unsolvable as it is posed. Where can a proof to that concept possibly be? Two key theorems become important in this context. The first, *conditional* conduct of behaviour, was illustrated earlier; the second – and a crucial one for the proof – is *Iconicity*. The proof proceeds by considering first that there is a form to this itinerary from one concept to the following one up to the final one. The form is in fact argumentation.[21]

The proof consists in the fact that arguments can be represented in a mathematical and thus in an Iconic-graphical form (cf. Fisch 1986: 370–2, with an important quote from MS649). Why need this form be an Icon? It is important to note that this is the only way out of circularity, which involves proving arguing through arguing and thus presupposing what is to be proved. It must not entail further interpretations. Therefore, this form must not be more than present while it is thought. It does not 'materially' contain all circumstances of an accepted Symbol. It merely represents the form-how-to-find a following concept of any preceding concept. Here one postulates a pure form of argumentation accessed in a non-argumentative, iconic way. Yet this form should nonetheless not be taken as the form we are thinking in argumentation. In arguing something, we simply respect this form obliquely when forming premises into a conclusion. Logic is not the content of argumentation, only its form. If it can be (re)presented in an iconic manner, it gives a foundation to arguing.[22]

At this point, we need not concern ourselves with the construction principles of such an Iconic logic with diagrams. In this instance these are lines, shapes for inclusion and exclusion, and also colours. With these aids and a set of rules, Peirce succeeded in reconstructing all logical operations, in principle. Some might criticize this, as it is often tacitly assumed that logic concerns propositions or assertions, which are almost impossible to think without their linguistic form. Such a presupposition would exclude any logic that is formal in a different, non-linguistic way. However, as unusual as a diagrammatic logic may be, it is distinct but not-different. There can be no question of logical arbitrariness, with a free choice among logics. It does not even change the 'epistemological' status of logic as a science. Logic can never become a positive science that can be verified (for instance, in hypotheses with the best fit of data, or similar procedures).

We still require proof of the link between logic and reality. Even if lines, shapes, colours, and so on are perfectly coherent in themselves, it is not yet clear that the real obeys these rules. If there were only a metaphysical speculation at this point, the upshot might be a postulate with

Reason absorbing into itself all the real, perhaps in something similar to the Hegelian State. This is certainly not the case with Peirce. Nor is he postulating an ontology of a 'logical physical world.' It should be understood that we do not fall back into a conception of the real as a phantasmagoric, precognized real. Peirce's procedure and proof is much simpler and more practical: the real, which is always a cognized real, follows logical rules when it is diagrammatically transformed into an assertion sheet. This is not the same as maintaining that the real becomes tangible and logical when it becomes a proposition. For a reflection of the actual cognitive behaviour, that would be too narrow and restrictive. The diagram allows also for the possibly real; in fact, it reflects the free play of imagination with possibilities, without any regard for any existent real.

The most important consequence, however, is that thought in diagrams can really be what Liszka (1996: 12) calls a 'bootstrap process.' It can prove itself as a logical form without a petition of principle.

Even though it is perfectly legitimate to speculate on the historical, social, and metaphysical consequences, without formal proof such an endeavour is idle hope, or even worse a social apriorism. If research as cognitive behaviour is never true, but rather is unending, for instance, the community of researchers and 'the long run' are important consequences, if the foundation of Pragmaticism is sound. For entirely different, political reasons, nowadays in some quarters doubts about the scientific process and progress itself have become a fad. Pragmaticism appeals to two – perhaps too remote, even though fundamentally concrete – finalities: the 'long run' of a process and the unlimited community of researchers spanning all times and cultures. Taken as a historical speculation (and a large part of the not so recent Peirce debate took it as such), there is much hope in these assumptions (or axioms).[23] Apel (1975: 350ff), instead, tries to frame Pragmaticism in a political, ethical communicational *a priori*; at the fringes of Peirce's system he sees the need for 'reaching an agreement (*Verständigung*)' (Apel 1981: 192). It is not just the agreement on the 'concepts and operations used in science,' but ultimately the purpose of science, that is the concern here.

Peirce's immediate answer might refer to his ethics of science. Ethics is, as much as logic, a science of the norms of conduct of behaviour. If it is not simply moralism; it must rest on the same formal proof. Kevelson (1993) emphasizes that the discovery of norms is an aesthetic process of cognition; this, however, is not yet the ultimate proof that conduct joins logic with reality. Now there are only two alternatives to this: formal or historical-social proof. For Apel, science concerns a community, which is a quasi-transcendental subject regarding which the cognitive finality cannot automatically be taken for granted. Its finality is not one of the 'movement of the Spirit'; rather, it is a historically contingent decision. The result of this 'proof' of pragmatism is a Critical version of Hegelianism, one that comprises societal agreements in a universal theory of truth. Yet Apel is not the only one who counts Peirce among the Critical Objective Idealists (cf. Esposito 1980 and Tiercelin 1997 on an anti-Apel note).

For Peirce himself, a volitive aspect of decision-making was more important as a condition for truth. As Pragmaticism, its essence is practical – conduct, not just action – and therefore it ethically requires that the fixation of belief be conducted under 'self-control' (5.533). The initial stage, belief, corresponds to Hegel's idea that 'we are in thought, not thoughts in us,' since we never start from zero in thought. A practical concern can only be how the *next* cognition is truer, not in which circumstances all cognitions in a final, ultimate opinion would be true. This requires the pragmatic cycle in three practical and ethical steps: belief–doubt–inquiry. Again, this norm is not a good will internal 'ethics committee' on research practice; rather, it is a condition *sine qua non* of cognition as such, once it has been conceptualized pragmatically. Insofar as far as it is cognition, every sign process enshrines such a norm – and not a hope – in following this pragmatic sequence. Pragmaticism is concerned here with cognizing as conduct, which as an ethical method of investigation *must* lead to truth. It cannot be more, or Peirce would be a Hegelian. Now Pragmaticism is easy to illustrate in any number of situations; however, illustrations are not enough to attain certainty. Peirce himself grew more and more aware of this as he tried for more than twenty years to rewrite that proof. A proof proper concerns all cases, and *de jure*. The first such proofs seemed to him illusionary, as Fisch (1986: 370–2) describes in historical detail. Only the mature Peirce discovered that Existential Graphs were crucial for his proof.

The proof of Pragmaticism is, avoiding a petition of principle, not more than a purely formal one. It could never be otherwise, unless Peirce's verdict on Hegel (probably) were not true: 'The Germans, whose tendency is to look at everything subjectively and to exaggerate the element of firstness, maintain that the object is simply to satisfy one's logical feeling and that the goodness of reasoning consists in that aesthetic satisfaction alone. This might do if we were gods and not subject to the force of experience' (5.160, 1903). Since the proof is a purely formal prescription, it can be followed mechanically without further concomitant insight into its reasons (another Interpretant). It resembles an experimental apparatus, or an electronic circuit, one that performs mechanically the logic built into it without having any insight. Experimentation is mental experimentation; it provides insight into the problem on which we are experimenting. We are cognizing not its logical structure, but rather its object – for instance, a chemical reaction or an unknown state of affairs. Existential Graphs constitute an experimental apparatus without further interpretation (which still has to be supplied for an experimental setup expressed in mathematical formulae). Peirce found in these graphs, which express logical relations, precisely that form which needs no Interpretants in order to lead to conduct. They fulfil the requirement of being the prescription of any conditional conduct of experimentation, without requiring a prescription for their own exercise: 'The system of Existential Graphs ... is the simplest possible system that is capable of expressing with exactitude every possible assertion' (MS654.5, 19 August 1910).

Existential Graphs represent Peirce's life-long intellectual struggle to find a non-regressive, non-transcendental proof for the Pragmaticistic theory of cognition. What do Existential Graphs actually prove? Merely that there is a method for describing completely the one necessary form of connecting concepts into a totality. This description is merely a prescription of a conditional conduct. The proof itself is established in such conduct alone. Yet the prescription must be iconic, since otherwise it would require a further Interpretant in order to be conclusive. Iconic conclusiveness is in doing – that is, in the present of doing alone. Therefore it is not transcendentalism in disguise.

1.4 The Categories of Behaviour

1.4.1 Required Characteristics of Ultimate Forms of Behaviour

The categorial approach to a theory of action has three important preliminary implications, which must be spelled out before they can be critiqued. So far we have concluded that any philosophy that is based on behaviour in a real world cannot avoid grasping realism; furthermore, this realist basis of experience cannot be itself an experience in need of further explanation. The exact nature of the forms of behaviour can only be explained on such a non-recursive basis – the Categories as ultimate origin of experiential meaning as such. From there it will be possible to draw some of the necessary consequences, in the two different directions of sign theory and the theory of reality. If we are to ascertain that it is a non-cursive and at the same time non-transcendental form, those forms must fulfil certain conditions, which alone can ascertain behaviour that accesses the real, through meaning, through identities of the object and the cognizing subject.

Categories as forms of behaviour need to be universal, complete, and necessary. Otherwise they will be bereft of any ultimate explanatory power[24] and will imply recursive, additional, or transcendental assumptions.

The first requirement is universality – that is, everything must be accessible through these forms. Every phenomenon of every kind must be a form of behaviour. In the beginning a universal category meant that everything which can be said must be concerned by it; in the pragmatic context, universality means that by the very moment something is 'doable' it already has certain characteristics. Everything that is, is accordingly 'doable' through one of the three types of action (cf. p. 34). This thesis is shocking only to those who want to retrocede before a phenomenal understanding of being. For such people there are domains which simply are, without being accessible to meaning or experience. The prerequisite to being 'doable' involves, then, the exclusion of all inaccessible being. This seems to be an undue, almost dogmatic limitation of what can be. A response to that critique is not the admission of simple incognizable being – for instance, explained as a 'safety zone' for future discoveries into which the human mind has still to penetrate. This is the case with the popular and fuzzy versions of film theory in which perception through schemata relies on an unlimited pool of stimuli to be processed by hypothetical schemata. Hypothesis is not so much a logical syllogistic figure in this context; rather, it is a stand-in for the inaccessibility shrouding the origin of stimuli in the 'raw' reality. Pragmatic universal categories, instead, do not identify the doable with the existent. This first response leaves open, within the range of the 'doable,' how the not yet done and not yet experienced is represented in the actual doing. A second response to those proponents of reality *in se* (i.e., reality as non-experienceable and inaccessible) is the critical counter-question: How is it possible to conceive of something that is by definition not knowable? It is meaningless to ask questions concerning the meaning-less, the unknowable, and to calculate with it even as a backdrop and guarantee for the actual experience of stimuli.

The postulate of universal categories must therefore find a different approach to evidencing that categories also apply to the not yet known, to the non actually known, to the possibly knowable.

A second requirement is that categories be complete. A list of categories can be useful – can guarantee that it grasps the principles of action as behaviour – only if it is complete. An heuristic device, misnamed category, cannot be ultimate form. It would still require further justification of its cognitive process. What is needed, then, is an explanation of action as behaviour that needs no further proof – that is, a proof which explains behaviour through still something else which lies before experience as behaviour. This would invalidate experiential cognition as the ultimate foundation and make it subject to something non-experienceable. If that were possible, 'action' would become a 'thing' among others, and the quest for a common form for all 'things' as they appear to us would continue. The claim that behaviour is precisely this form for all hinges on complete proof, not on infinite regress, which eventually is resolved in a decisionist manner. Some sign theories succumb to this danger by failing to arrive at some ultimate form in need of no further interpretation.

For instance, in Simon's (1989) sign theory, when he does not admit, in principle, any non-argumentative basis of interpretation, this leads him to an infinite regress. The result is that a sign can only be interpreted by another sign, and thus *ad infinitum*. A very similar situation arises in structural linguistics. When difference and positional values must be the only means of interpretation (or 'thought' in usual parlance), the definitional or determinational regress is at hand. An (involuntary) illustration of that danger, turned into something positive, is the playfulness of Eco's idea of 'encyclopaedia.' Here it is impossible to attain the concrete meaning of something, and one cannot but end up with circular, infinite, encyclopaedic referrals to other meanings. Peirce was perfectly aware of this risk of an infinite regress when he found his proof for forms of thought – for him cognitive behaviour – while remaining committed to empirical cognition alone. What distinguishes Peirce from Simon, Saussure, or Hjelmslev are the Categories and the logic of relations. Only on this basis – when Categories are the form (or *secunda intentio*) and not the object of a sign (*in prima intentione*) – is sign not equal to sign (i.e., there must be special classes of signs that make Categories cognizable not as objects). This excludes Categories as 'being' in the same way, as 'things' are through their cognitive representation in signs. Moreover, this implies that signs as they are used must be distinguished from signs as they are understood as forms. Categories, too, can only be cognized through a sign process (i.e., experientially), and not in a privileged, form-free cognition. In this cognition, then, there must be a way to somehow separate form from usage. On the practical basis of pragmatism, this special cognitive behaviour is expressed in the apparently paradoxical statement of the Pragmatic Maxim: the perfect understanding of an element must comprise '*all* practical consequences.' Such cognition of total knowledge cannot be concrete; nevertheless it is a necessary practical condition for cognition. This brings us back – with a vengeance – to the problem of the complete form of cognitive behaviour, which is a sort of cognition but one without presuppositions – a sort of finding the form of thought through thinking, cognitive behaviour (i.e., in signs).

The third requirement that an ultimate form must satisfy relates to the necessary number of Categories: they need not be more than are minimally necessary. But what is the criterion for this? Once it is recognized that behaviour of action is the naturalistic situation for cognition and not a faculty of mind or judgment, or a structure of a system, then acting as an ultimate, comprehensive form of world appropriation dictates formal requirements. At any rate, this excludes the possibility of falling back on 'being' – to be described in ontological archi-concepts – as the standard measure for cognition; for this, it would be necessary to know what it is 'to be' (such a godlike knowledge would be difficult for fallible cognizing beings to claim today). Structuralists, in turn, require at a minimum only one necessary category: difference, with which they organize a topological space.[25] This would certainly not suffice for the continuity of behaviour in the real world.

Some might challenge the minimum necessary number of categorial forms as too restrictive. We can see such a critique in the context of our assumed basis in habits of behaviour. This foundation could be required to justify itself for having sacrificed subjectivity as the ultimate ground – by the same token, for sacrificing time as a necessary dimension. Phenomenology and Existentialism have made time their mainstay, encapsulating all other determinations of being and cognition. From this perspective, any set of ultimate forms that does not comprise time must seem deficient. Such a critique – if pertinent – would be devastating for the professed claims of pragmatism, which would then be just another arbitrary 'approach' and certainly not a universal theory of being and cognition. Although semiology can dispense with time (and subjectivity and physical reality) on the basis of abstract language

– which makes it assailable from a hermeneutic/phenomenological perspective (as we see, for instance, in Ricoeur's taking exception to Greimas's theory of action, v. *infra*) – this critique cannot concern Semiotic. It is indeed the case that a comprehensively understood foundation in behaviour comprehends also these factors in its categorial determination. However, it is also true that the basis for this is not subjectivity. An acting subject encounters its opposite in an object; that is a relation of two correlates only. As soon as behaviour is seen in its continuity, it is no longer subjective but must transcend subjectivity into a larger, unlimited *totum*. Only when bound into such a connection is Semiotic able to introduce the time concept, but as a law that is itself the binding force. The contrast between Semiotic and the Phenomenological School can be case as follows: It is not time consciousness that produces the need to act (as 'Care of Dasein' or stretching from now to the end of death); rather, acting involves/evolves time. There is time because we act, and not action because we are temporal.

1.5 The Categorial Form of Behaviour

So far we have drawn some consequences from the 'Pragmaticistic turn,' regarding which the abstract problem of cognition is redefined in its realistic situation as cognitive behaviour: continuity, relation, form. The form of conduct of behaviour involves the form itself, and its analysis, but also the proof that it can measure up to its claim to amalgamate Real and logic: 'in intellectual life there is a tendency to value existence as the vehicle of forms' (Peirce 1998: 347; *Monist* 1905). Thus, proving that Pragmaticism is a sound method for attaining true cognition is a necessary preliminary. Once we have done this, the problem of the form in itself involves the task of constructing the entire architecture of a genuinely pragmatic theory of the Real (otherwise the proof would have failed). As outlined above, from the requirements of conduct (continuity, existence, qualitative character) arise the need for norms guiding this behaviour. This in turn consists in types of behaviour having their adequate (i.e., categorial) form. The idea of categories as the ultimate difference of meaning was sketched earlier (cf. 35). Only at the level of formal types of behaviour will we encounter the question of the signs involved in these processes. Signs, however, consist of Categories, which are those different types of relation that are contained in human action as such. Categories, ultimately, are a formal foundation of pragmatic world appropriation. Taking this approach,

Peirce can conceive more than a (content-empty) categorical imperative, as was the case with Kant's pragmatic.

Peirce discovered his Categories after a long and tortuous clarifying
process, long before he encountered pragmatism. Pragmatism, as it
were, was merely the ripe fruit of his solution for much more fundamental problems. This is important to bear in mind because it precludes Semiotic, as an appendix to pragmatism, from being reduced to
a version of social psychology in the manner of Mead, as still happens
unfortunately (as in Joas 1989: 41ff). However, it is legitimate to represent the Categories as the form of behaviour, following the Peirce of
the 1903 Harvard lectures on Pragmatism, even if we have to grant
that their scope is wider. Moreover, the Categorial perspective can
explain why he uses such key terms as Sign and Behaviour in a sense
that stretches common usage to the breaking point. Somehow the
scope of the Categories translates into a semantic inflation of these
terms. The Categories, then, and not a theory of human action called
pragmatism, are Peirce's true point of departure for a number of
important contributions to logic, mathematical theory, and metaphysics. However, even in his later years, by which time he had developed
a reputation as a pragmatist rather than as a Semiotician, he was able
(or forced) to explain the architecture of his system of thought in terms
of pragmatism.

Peirce considered his theory of Categories 'my one contribution to
philosophy' (8.213) even with the hindsight of advanced age. All other
concepts of Peirce's architectonic system are unified by the keystone,
the Categories. Thus the evolution in his treatment of the Categories
reflects the development of his entire thought. Tracing the development of the Categories in his thought will allow us to grasp how his
attempts to express the Categories in ever novel contexts evolved, and
enrich our understanding of the concept. In his earliest philosophical
inspirations there are already clear traces of what in his late philosophy would evolve – in a maximal formal reduction – into Firstness,
Secondness, and Thirdness. Although he concluded very early that the
definitive number of Categories is three, he repeatedly modified their
names and described their characteristics in terms of metaphysics, psychology, propositional logic, logic of relations, and mathematics. In
light of this genesis, some perceived Peirce as being forced to cast aside
his key theory time and again because of inconsistencies or contradictions. The prevailing view today is that there was an evolution, certainly, but no radical rectification. Peirce himself confessed, however,

that he began as a nominalist and ended as a realist; this certainly raises the need to explain and justify Categories in a different way.

Categories are having a profound impact on how we appropriate our world. Once the idea is there, a Categorial view amounts to admitting to a non-uniform world. It would be inappropriate, then, to refer to 'it' in the singular as if the Real were a single reality. In a naive way, this is often our natural attitude, as if 'facts' were the only corrective of our cognition. Yet if the world were accessible in just one Category, and if everything was of the same essence, there would be no need to consider the Categories. Only when there are differences in how the world appears to us are Categories meaningful. They no longer account for regrettable linguistic idiosyncrasies of speech-about-'the'-facts; rather, they account for a radical reconceptualization of the world as appearance. Only then does the 'how-it-appears' count emphatically, as there is no way to discount the mode in favour of the non-modal, direct possession of being. Having discovered three modes of world appearance, our only access to the Real is in three forms: 'is' is threefold, and any cognition that is not aware of the form it is in must 'see' a wrong world penalized with confusion in communication.[26] This is a category mistake.

The concept of categories, including their analysis and number, was a problem that Peirce inherited directly from Kant's *Critique*. As we will see, Peirce not only redefined and expanded the problem itself on the basis of Realist premises, but also transformed the concept of the Categories by abolishing both the Transcendental Subject and the Transcendental Object. In fact, in the wake of modernity – exemplified in the *Critique* – simple faith in cognition was thoroughly shaken, after a lengthy philosophical debate over how mental concepts relate to their Other, physical reality. The cognizing subject understood that it was its own operation, which synthesised what appeared to it as 'world.' The ingenious solution to this was to invent a figure of thought, transcendentalism, which stayed with us thereafter. The subject created its *Doppelgänger* Subject, called the Transcendental Subject. No longer was this the cognitive subject cognizing; instead, disconnected from its cognitive operation, it observed itself cognizing. The price for this was the loss of the immediacy of cognition; the gain was the self-assurance of posing the so-called Critical question. 'What can we know?' Kant's answer, transcendentalism, would infer the necessary forms of cognition. Cognition 'becomes' empirical only as synthesis of apperception and concept. Yet in itself it is a non-empirical, *a priori* deduction (i.e., through synthetic conclusion). This entailed a hypothetical assumption of all (cognizable and incognizable) objects as *Ding an sich* (thing-in-itself).[27] As a figure of thought, this is not so unlike the Structuralist transcendentalism, which is not Critical in the sense discussed – as Deleuze (1973) clearly points out.

Peirce in his early years[28] was puzzled by Kant's solution and did not agree with it. While the question remained the one emanating from the philosophical tradition, and not in disregard of it, Peirce found an ingenious new answer that retroactively also redefined the problem. This answer was based on his dissatisfaction with Kant. He began by arguing that if there were a *Ding an sich* – that is, an assumed incognizable world or an incognizable part of the world – we could not know of it. On the one hand, he initially accepted the necessity of *a priori* concepts, since there must be first premises to all cognition. On the other hand, the mode of knowing of these premises while speaking and theorizing about them could not but be absurd: those who propose them are forced to treat them as if they were objects of cognition. Before his 'New List of Categories' in 1867, Peirce's solution was a clear and avowed fideism[29]: if we do not know these premises, and yet they are necessary for all our cognition, then we must believe them.

It is fortunate that Peirce had already perused Schiller's *Ästhetische Briefe* by 1855, when he was only sixteen, and through them Kant, before reading the *Critique*. Schiller's idea was that Kant's rigour required correction through sensation. There are two impulses, the sensuous and the formal (cf. De Tienne 1996: 33–41). The first is meant for the finite, the latter for the infinite; similarly, singular against general, temporal against the eternal, *It* against *I*. Both lead to one-sidedness and prevent us from comprehending the complete reality. Ultimate harmony of the Good, True, and Beautiful can be achieved only in Aesthetics, when these impulses are moderated by each other. Sensation moderates Law through the Ideal of Beauty as the union of Law and Contingency: *Thou*. It, I, and Thou were Peirce's touchstones when he approached Kant's list of categories. It is interesting that Peirce retained this Schillerian inspiration until the end of his philosophical life, when he came back to aesthetics as a normative science (cf. Barnouw 1994: 161ff). The 'habit[s] of feeling' (Peirce 1998: 378; *Monist* 1905) have pragmatic consequences in that they control deliberate conduct and therefore are already the 'warp and woof of cognition' (1.381, 1890). Thus they are of especially fundamental importance. They measure our confidence in the validity of feeling – something very difficult to achieve in the wake of Baumgarten and Kant and their gashing of feeling as 'mere feeling.' In the context of film theory, the debate between the 'ontological film realists' and the 'imaginarians' could certainly profit from this Peircean insight.[30]

What were the consequences of this early inspiration for a novel understanding of the categories? It dawned on Peirce that the most general concepts regulating all thought could not only be constituted by laws of necessity. Thought can also be regulated by something that is not necessary. Although this sounds like an oxymoron, empirical cognition, experience, can be broader than that which the rules of necessity impose on thought.

Early on, Peirce began to remedy the arbitrary number and order of Kant's list of categories. Proving the exhaustiveness of the list of Categories is of prime importance (cf. *supra*). No thought can find its rule by trial and error, empirically, because in doing so it would already be applying it. Therefore, thought depends on ultimate premises that are necessary. Yet this necessity must be shown – it cannot be a matter of fact or an empirical list.[31] In the domain of *a priori* concepts there is no approximate truth as there is in all empirical knowledge: it is either truth or falsehood. Thus, it matters (to the early Peirce) how one deduces Categories as the ultimate necessity of cognitive operations, as analysis of *a priori* concepts. Categories cannot be observed as in science, nor can psychology yield reliable results. A science of thought-in-general is called for, one that investigates the elements of consciousness. There are two reasons why *a priori* concepts are needed. First, to understand propositions means to comprehend their terms. In Peirce's eyes, metaphysics cannot begin with propositions; rather, it can begin only with a sort of primal activity of the mind. Second, propositions must ultimately have recourse to primal truths. These truths must be either negative or universal: either is an *a priori* proposition, since every *a posteriori* experience is logically a particular and affirmative proposition. This early insight would accompany Peirce into his old age. For him it became a special science, which he first called Phenomenology and later, more distinctively, Phaneroscopy[32] (explicitly in 1.284, 1905). Also, the method of this science was bound to remain antitranscendentalist, insofar as the 'formal elements of the phaneron' 'that *I* have found in my mind are present at all times and to all minds' (1.284). The method would increasingly become purely experiential – albeit with an increasing burden of proof – but it started out as a psychologist nominalism.

A phenomenology of consciousness (in MS921, 'On the Definition of Metaphysics,' July 1859, W1,572; cf. Esposito 1980: 14ff) must deal with 'the elements of all that we are conscious of.' 'What can possibly be meaningful?' This question is striking, as it may presage generativism – in particular, that branch which investigates universals of language in a semiological way (cf. Greimas's *Sémio-narratologie*). Peirce's approach was quite different. First, he had to ensure that no meaning possibility was excluded. Therefore, he had to find an all-comprehensive 'state of mind' as the *a priori* disposition and activity of the mind. With typical ingenuity, he alluded to the comprehensiveness of all possible objects of the mind in this way: 'All unthought is thought of' (which is also the title of one of his essays). This enigmatic statement means that a (noematic) content of thought (the noetic act) can even be the 'unthought-of' inasmuch as it is reasonable to speak about it in a purely abstract and negative way (cf. Esposito 1980: 17). Far from restricting thought to 'real facts,' an idea is any mental content, including experience.

The counter-question is this: What is not an object of consciousness? Here the early Peirce perceives only one instance – when we do not use our faculties of mind properly. It follows conversely – if we use them properly – that all objects of consciousness are true. This can be tested against extreme cases such as the idea of 'infinite space.' Even when applying our mental faculties correctly, we never have a precise idea of such a thing. This is where the idea of Category begins to impose itself. Our cognition before it cognizes is also possibly under ultimate but unconscious ideas (e.g., infinity), 'incomprehensible truths,' which are there because they guide all our conscious conclusions (e.g., of spatiality).

Peirce found an empiricist answer to the problem of possible contents of consciousness,[33] compared to Kant's transcendentalist 'Ding an sich' solution. In 'Of Objects' (MS921, 25 October 1859), Peirce entirely and explicitly dismisses *noumena* (and therefore Kant's distinction between *noumena* and *phaenomena*). In 'That There Is No Need of Transcendentalism' (MS921), Peirce begins: 'There can be no need of Transcendental Philosophy if right reason does not lead to contradi[di]ctions of a priori principles.' Kant understands empirical cognition as the judgment-synthesis of *a priori* ideas of mind (*noumena*) and the manifold of sensations (*phaenomena*); Peirce must now clarify how objects of thought are explained without this transcendental distinction.

At this crucial juncture, the ultimate ideas guiding the production of meaning – categories – are redefined. First, in this most generally seen consciousness, we find as the first 'unconscious idea' that there are only objects in consciousness regarded as 'thought-of.' This – second – produces a chain from the ('outer') thing thought of, to – third – a thought itself dependent from it. The result is an unconscious idea of that dependency.

As a result we have an ultimate form for all meaning, which remains absolutely abstract before these three categories are used in one act. With a little stretching of a commonly used term – thought Peirce – the concreteness of meaning is enacted in 'representation.' For this form is evidently not just relating a thought ('theory') to an object ('data'). Rather, a mental content relates to an external object and 'knows' reflexively about this relation as one of dependency, and this is an interpretation. Such a tripartite process form becomes representation through usage, an act of representing, which calls upon an acting soul, which has a representation of itself as acting.

No further, higher and ultimate elements of meaning are needed.[34] The chain is thus complete. Notably, Peirce did not transcendentally deduce transcendental rules of experience as synthesis of a judgment (i.e., before any concrete cognition). However, the ultimate difference in meaning (and being) becomes not simply a formal one; even more, the Categories are welded into one process (of representation), which transforms those differences into an order. What used to be a differ-ence of ultimate ideas (causality, unicity, plurality, spatiality, etc.) is now an ordered chain of moments, which yield meaning only as a completed sequence. Of course, this does not imply that there can now be only a conception of uniform meaning, because those ultimate 'unconscious ideas' are formal. They provide the necessary form for how any meaning is formed, without prejudice to the content of mean-ing. The latter is formally determined by the thought-of Object (i.e., from outside).

This breakthrough constitutes a novel conception of the relationship between the mind and the real. The keyword is Representation. Kant's old watershed line – between contents of the mind (*noumena*) and appearances (*phaenomena*) from an otherwise ungraspable reality – has become redundant. In the young Peirce's seminal category theory, the consideration is formal, but it is also directly empirical as soon as the form is used. Therefore, the forms are real in their respective nature. One kind of real is represented before another kind of real. The mind is not unreal (i.e., the other of the real [data]); rather, it belongs to its own class of reality.

While Peirce retained the core, he elaborated, expanded, and clarified every single part of his new theory over the course of his life. The first decisive result was a clarification of the exact nature of his new categories, and an incipient relational comprehension of them. When this was presented to the public as the 'New List of Categories' of 14 May 1867, it is unlikely that anyone in the audience really understood him (cf. De Tienne 1996). As a result, one of the revolutionary consequences of categories conceived in this novel way went unnoticed: there 'can be no thought but in signs,' which follows from the foundation-idea representation. Conversely, the mind has no direct access to the real that is not mediated by a third. Thought is interpreting, and interpretation requires the precise order of the three categorial elements. This is the birth of Semiotic, the theory of all possible forms of representation. After his early breakthrough over transcendentalism, Peirce continued his struggle to better understand the highest unifying principles of cognition.

Peirce's early investigations can be summed up in six results: (1) His most important distinction from this stage is between 'thought' and 'thought-of,' which functionally substitutes the *a priori–a posteriori* distinction. (2) Kant's Transcendental Object, the *Ding an sich*, can therefore be dismissed. (3) The Transcendental Subject at this stage is still important, in a depsychologized form, as the perfection of cognition and Reality. Idealism and materialism ('naive realism') are therefore the only alternatives to realism, which is already foreshadowed here as a representational (Semiotic) understanding of reality and cognition. If matter and idea both exist, then neglecting one really means misunderstanding the form of cognition. The task is therefore to find a philosophical method for completely mediating between the two in order to truly reflect what cognition is. At the two extremities are matter and idea, or – in Peircean terms – pure Being and pure Substance. In between, there are three grades of their mediation, which is representation of the one before the other. Very soon Peirce abandoned Substance and Being, retaining merely the three representations, which are all that is accessible to human beings. It can be concluded only that the two extreme poles are the 'beyond' of representation without any content (and must therefore appear as idle speculation if not seen as the extremities beyond representation). (4) Peirce's opposition to foundationalisms of all shades is a consequence of mediation. This opens the path for metaphysic as consequences to be drawn from the mediational understanding of the nature of cognition. At this stage, however, his metaphysical[35] solution is still fideism – that is, God guarantees that cognition reaches reality. He replaces this only later, in his 'agapis-tic' metaphysic,[36] in which reality itself exerts a free force for being cognized. (5) Peirce stays within an attitude of Critique (in Kant's sense) by basing any possible metaphysic (theory of reality) on logic. (6) For reasons of logic, Peirce concludes that ultimate premises of thought cannot be deduced. Such a conclusion does not preclude the possibility and necessity of metaphysics; it merely determines that its method will always be one of a science of experience (later this position became fallibilism) and not of *a priori* ideas.

1.5.1 Method for Categories

A matter of such crucial importance as the Categories cannot be based on ephemeral insights; it demands a rigorous method. That said, the most general concepts governing thought are not illogical. Categories can be discovered, and they can be known in various ways that are not mutually exclusive. Furthermore, they can be known through a special kind of argumentative reasoning. Adequate argumentation involves the three different forms of abstraction (v. *infra* 63–4).[37] In all of these instances, it is not demanded – for the sake of not begging the question – that one place oneself in a precategorical space and observe from a neutral vantage point 'what' Categories are. Invention of Categories can only be an *in vivo* operation – that is, we must deduce them while using them in different actual forms of reasoning.

The deduction of Categories (whether we deduce them from con-sciousness or from phenomena) is argumentation that needs to con-vince in its domain of analysis. Consciousness, however, is not an object of thought but the *process* of thought. It follows that from the perspective of such deduction, one can never understand what Cate-gories are. Categories are about how we understand, but is there a way of making them an *object* of understanding? No ultimate, most general concept of thought can be further analyzed, otherwise it would not be ultimate. So we must find a way to treat Categories 'as if' they were normal concepts – that is, in the manner in which our normal under-standing takes place: in terms (i.e., in Symbols) – and nevertheless pre-serve their ultimate character. The procedure can also be expressed in the traditional difference between *prima* and *secunda intentio*.

The ideas of our mind are manifold: tree, house, sound, machine, bal-ance. Now, what matters here is not the number of different ideas but that they can be observed as unequal. Already at the level of sentences, every idea cannot be related to every other idea to form a new meaning. This is not explained by the lexical contingency of natural languages, because doing so merely begs the question of where this difference in ideas originates. Now it is obvious that it is this difference which is important for meaning, and not the material ideas themselves. Thus, the logical next question is this: What produces such difference among ideas? It is not enough to find different ideas. We must find the differences among ideas themselves, we must do so through (i.e., while using) these same ideas and terms. Then, from these 'oblique' observations, we will have to draw special logical conclusions in order to establish the differences.

Although actual reasoning is 'always-already' (in Heideggerese), the accomplished thought and its steps are never isolated even if they are manifest in that process as its logical necessities, in a special kind of reflection; however, we separate the elements involved. This 'open-heart surgery' of kind does not, indeed cannot, suspend thought; rather, it avails itself of three mental operations: uncontrolled awareness of every mental act ('of an artist'), an acute sense of observation of differences therein ('of a scientist'), and the power of abstraction ('of a mathematician'). As imperfect as it is, an observation of terms can also lead to comparable results. The young Peirce found this when he discovered his new Categories. The New List of Categories' logical procedure of thinking thought *in se* began with an abstractive operation called 'prescinding' (cf. Baltzer 1994: 41–57); Peirce further refined this logical operation in later years, and he never abandoned its use in logic.

The §5 of the New List (W2, 50f), 'One, Two, Three' (1.353, 1880), and §4 of 'Searching for the Categories' (W1, 518) describe how Categories can be found:

- Through discrimination, 'which is the mere recognition of the difference between the presence or absence of an element of cognition' (W1, 518);
- Through prescission [NL]/precision [S], which is a logical operation similar to abstraction. The New List (1.549) explained prescission as attention to one element of consciousness, neglecting another that is equally present. However, 'In general, prescission is always accomplished by imagining ourselves in situations in which certain elements of fact cannot be ascertained. This is a different and more complicated operation than merely attending to one element and neglecting the rest' (2.428);

- Through dissociation, 'which is the consciousness of one thing without the necessary simultaneous consciousness of the other' (ibid.)

Peirce's examples are indicative. It is not possible to discriminate, prescind, or dissociate red from colour, whereas each of these operations is possible with blue from red.[38]

	blue without red	space without colour	colour without space	red without colour
By discrimination	+	+	+	−
By precision	+	+	−	−
By dissociation	+	−	−	−	(W1, 519)

Here the behaviour of different Categories can be studied in words (or lexical units of natural languages). The logical quality differences among terms are an instance of categoriality, even though this seems much easier to conceptualize if we treat it as a question of extension and intension of terms (as Eco tries in vain to accomplish in Eco 1975). Peirce treated the latter topic extensively as a logical question of quantification. So, how is this connected with the Categories? That terms with an immense extension have a very low intension suggests a Cartesian space with the coordinates 'being' and 'substance.' ('Nature,' for example applies – extensionally – to almost every being, since only in its metaphorical root it does signify 'being born,' *natura*, equivalent to φύσις, and *nasci* to φύομαι or anything inherent to a thing from its origin. Otherwise, in its intension, it is simply the negative of 'art' and little more.) But what is the nature of those coordinate axes such that they can be differentiated? In the 'width' (i.e., information) of a term, two quite different modes coalesce without ever blending: whatness and thisness, quality–quiddity and haecceity.[39]

So far nothing is new in this; however, a third coalescing mode seems to be forgotten. This latter comes out in the logical operation of a discriminating abstraction (e.g., colour without space). Here is something (colour) that never exists without the other, its 'suppositum' (space), from which it cannot be separated. However, some logical operation provides the means to make it emerge as again a different mode. Here the decisive trait is merely cognitive in that something is cognized as a law. Thus, perceiving/imagining blue does not depend on a knowledge of its spectral wavelength; rather, spectral wavelengths as the 'idea' of colour contain the rule of how to produce blue (through subtraction or addition).

Thus three logical operations have the capacity to differentiate the space of all terms into modes. These modes are not deduced; rather, they are modes of experience (*a posteriori*). Their status is therefore not that of general truths; instead, they are entities that are proven *ad hoc* in any logical operation. This is the (negative) meaning of universality that is postulated for the Categories (cf. *supra* p. 59).

The logical operations of differentiation of terms date back to the New List and are of limited scope. What is the nature of these difference in modes of terms? They certainly cannot be taken as a universal linguistic feature (which, miraculously, inheres in all human languages). Such differentiation is better understood as the result of pre-linguistic operations; this is precisely the idea of Categories. Peirce repeatedly complained that logic seems to be inseparable from its linguistic supposition (cf. *supra*). If, as seems clear, the different modes as analyzed in terms are logical differences, they should also appear prior to their linguistic realization. They must be proven as necessities of thought and experience, not as linguistic features.

Conceptualizing 'necessities of thought' would be a pointless exercise if thought were a simple relation (adequation, association, or other 1:1 copy) between mind and reality. Thus, the initial goal of Peirce's endeavour here was to prove that the Simple Real (at least the one we think, experience, enunciate) does not exist at all; rather, differences alone produce meaning. Proving thought with thought is not an impossibility, provided the method is sound. It can only be a logical method, because humans appropriate reality through thought and thought alone.

At this stage, Peirce's (implicit) adversaries are all those who deny or abandon the possibility of thinking thought. There are those who think we can rely only on what we feel is logically sound (Sigwart with his ultimate reliance on 'Gefühl' was Peirce's 'preferred enemy' here). That scepticism – which is not confined to this one classical author in logic – would have still more advocates today. It really consists in all those ultimate tautologies, of which Peirce lists a few (v. Peirce 1998: 166ff).

For example, what 'desire' is can be defined in satisfaction alone, and 'consciousness' is what is immediately conscious. Peirce had a gift for logically illustrating such tautologies. Examples: a 'judgment judging itself to be true'; 'this proposition is not true'; 'A testifies that B's testimony is true. B testifies that A's testimony is false.' When projected into a court, this last one would involve a thought testifying to its own soundness. In a less obvious way, this is how conventionalism and constructivism explain the soundness of their own theory status.

In film theory we encounter plenty of logical tautology, as a later discussion of Bordwell's constructivism and of semiological film theories will show. The latter concern themselves with various extra- and intra-cinematic codes, but would not be able to justify the meaning thereby produced by any other standard than the fact that this meaning is thus.[40] Bordwell's 'science-theoretical' basis is not much different for its various 'schemata.' Production of meaning is taken as a fact, and this meaning is proven 'sound' on no other ground than the existence of such 'schema.' This is patently circular, and makes sense only on the basis of a strong nominalism: 'Res (i.e. schemata) sunt nomina' (the real reality of data is untouched by mere concepts). Unless one intends to discredit consciousness and proof of one's own theory status as 'grand theory' (i.e., worthless), efforts in the spirit of Peirce are necessary. There is no way to escape from this – even if we were to want to – since the only alternative is a naive belief in one's own foundation.

A sound method for proving the truth of one's own proposition is to logically defend the necessity of an outside element: without a relationship to external facts, there can be no truth. This is the result of the circularity of proposition proving its own truth. This means, however, that a proposition is not in itself true or false, as would follow from the received wisdom implied in the above circularity. Peirce guards himself against a very old but incorrect understanding of the proposition, on that goes back to Aristotle, De interpretatione: 17b26–28.[41] According to traditional wisdom every general proposition, enunciated generally, is either true or false. Yet general proposition is neither true nor false; it becomes so only if it is asserted. This means that it needs to be related to a universe of discourse that is shared by all participants in the assertion and by all proponents and all opponents of such assertion. Without this relation, a proposition still makes sense, but as mere possibility.

Clearly, this outside relationship of propositions is only a problem for general propositions, because singulars in a proposition – such as proper names and every kind of index – already relate it to a determined universe of discourse. That 'Kallias is white' (*de interpret.*) is true and meaningful only if the proponent and opponent know who Kallias is, goes without saying. However, 'all men are white' (*de interpret.*) can only be true or false in one given, factual universe of discourse. As a general proposition, it is undetermined and therefore neither true or false.

The defence of the differentiation of Categories – which has already appeared in the consideration of term differences – is more easily and effectively carried out in logic of relations. Even though this is also logic based on experience and not on purely hypothetical mathematical thinking, it is neither a contradiction nor a petition of principle that Categories are grasped in various ways. Although phenomenology perceives them clearly, it cannot prove or defend what it sees. At this point it would indeed be a temptation to assist with 'helpful' presuppositions of the type of psychologism, ontology, or philosophy of nature. However, these departments are not an influx but rather an outflow of logic. Phenomenology is upstream; in contrast, phenomena, the phaneron, is only the consideration of the experiential basis of thought as such, and therefore the presupposition of logic: the real as presupposed by logic.

These Categorial relationships have important implications for film theory. They will, for one, enable an answer to the problem of the specific nature of 'documentary film.' The relationship is necessarily between a content (propositions about some quality or characteristics of something) and a universe of discourse that is expressly specified as shared by those actually in communication. It cannot be, then, the universe of universes of discourse (i.e., what can be apostrophised as The Truth for all possible past, present, and future discoursants). Documentaries have no meaning as general truths unless with a strong indexical reference to 'our' known universe. It cannot be denied that such a basic 'documentary' relationship is also at work in another kind of cinematic meaning: narration. This is because narratives must be enunciated. So a 'narrative contract' must be established that is an indexical relationship in as much as it relates the narrator to the audience with a fiduciary bond. However, downstream of this contract, the meaning itself becomes quite different. As a matter of fact, it is based on a completely different relationship of more than indexical nature. I will argue later that narration *in se* is a meaning of temporality of a certain kind, one that is founded on a different Categorial basis. The enunciation of cinematic narratives thus also becomes an answerable question.

To illustrate the film-theoretical implications of Categories and their differentiation, let us look briefly at the cornfield sequence in Hitchcock's *North by Northwest* which Wulff (1999: 203–31, 256) subjects to a lengthy analysis, although he considers only the narrative meaning. There is no doubt that there are different things before the mind when we view this sequence. The first thing we discriminate (in Peirce's sense of the term) is the plot and, for instance, the psychological treatment of characters. This is on an identical Categorial level, which means that one comprehends either in the same manner. If someone used this sequence for agronomic cognition – of maize in particular – such cognition would use the same Category. However, one needs prescission (again in Peirce's sense of the term) to distance the (documentary) fact of a flat landscape from the scorching heat. In the case where there is a very 'contemplative' scene in a film such as a sunset, then the warmth of a colour can be perceived without simultaneously perceiving an ice desert. This reduces colour[42] to a non-relative quality that is not even a fact. Mere contemplation corresponds psychologically to this kind of meaning.

Thus a Categorial shift is an efficient manner in which to change meaning in cinema. It ruptures chains of narrative causality and interpretations or rhetorical-discursive representations of realities. Then it creates a place in the mind for ideas of a different kind. How is such a Categorial shift produced? It is one problem to conceptualize the Categorial nature of the Real, and another question as to how the Categories are actually managed in cognition. Propositions and language are certainly privileged but they are not the only vehicle of cognition and meaning. The nature of the Third Category is such that representation – which according to Peirce is 'germane to Thirdness' (1998: 171) is the most 'mental' Real. As such it always operates on signs or Representamina. This means that as soon as a (physical or imaginary) object becomes a Representamen, it changes its Categorical nature.

The mature Peirce always insisted that such a Categorial nature can be grasped very efficiently using logical relations. One of the collateral advantages in this procedure is that one is freed from the semantic and syntax of contingent natural languages. This makes an application to cinema much less awkward than using the metaphorical bridge 'cinematic language.' Thus the nature of any given cinematic image or sequence is more easily comprehensible when, for instance, a narrative logic is understood as a relation between three elements: a state before, a state after, and narrative teleology as the general idea of connection. This is certainly a complex relation, but it resembles Peirce's standard example of 'gift': the given object, the received object, and the idea of donation. Later, on the level of concrete cinematic enunciation, we will have to examine this in much greater detail. However, the reason why this is essentially different from a much less complex relation, such as cinematic colour perception, can best be grasped on this relational level.

Logic of Relations in the context of Categories is the bedrock of Peirce's original reframing of Kant's epistemology 'in transcendental respect.' The early Peirce's original problem was the reduction of 'the manifold of sensuous impressions to unity' (W2, 49) in the formation of a proposition. Now every proposition achieves union of being and substance. Yet substance always expresses a quality of something, which is therefore the first necessary element to be prescinded and is called Ground. Reference to a Ground cannot be prescinded from being.[43] The elements he prescinded in this manner are already relations and can be treated in that way.

What does the logic of relations add to the fundamental question of this novel Critique? After Murphey (1961), it seemed to have become received truth that Peirce's system changed fundamentally once he introduced relations. The first important study to prove the life-long coherence of Peirce's theory of Categories was Rosensohn (1974); but Esposito (1980), Pape (1986: 17–26), and Baltzer (1994: 15ff), can prove consistency through various stages of the development of Peirce's theory of Categories, as most others also contradict Murphey. Thus, there is no contradiction between the New List fundamental Categories of Ground, Correlate, and Correspondent and Firstness, Secondness, and Thirdness. To Lady Welby, the mature Peirce, from 1904 onwards, could therefore present his investigation of universal Categories in the New List in just these other terms.

1.6 Logic of Relations

One would not commonly think of words as devices for establishing logical relations. Yet such relations in the terms themselves become obvious as soon as they are analyzed. In Kant, terms are analytically 'dissolved' in a manner close to traditional procedures of climbing up and down the Porphyrian tree or scale. This means – for instance for a human – being analyzed as *animal rationale*, rational animated being, both terms being one generality level higher than the analyzed term. Thus the components of a term are analytically higher, depending on the hierarchy of meaning or being that is adopted. The terms of ultimate analyticity are those most simple terms which are known as categories. This traditional procedure has its typical shortcomings. Foremost, it presupposes an ultimate ontological order onto which the logical order is grafted; alternatively, such categories must be transcendentally cognized prior to cognition. A relational analysis is therefore indeed a novel approach. Relations are mathematical thinking and therefore are not subject to transcendental priority. Relations can be thought purely hypothetically. Then they merely have to be discovered in/as the forms of experience. This discovery is not new. Plato spoke of two sorts of being, one toward-itself and another toward-something (*Sophistes* 255c13–d1), and Aristotle listed this in many places as one of his categories πρὸς τι, which Peirce translated as 'to what?' (MS 477). However, neither of them recognized the central position of relation as inherent in all experience.

First, the forms of experience are phenomenologically discovered. This is called 'Ideoscopy' and 'consists in describing and classifying the ideas that belong to ordinary experience or that naturally arise in connection with ordinary life, without regard to their being valid or invalid or to their psychology' (SS24). Thereafter, they can be pre[s]cinded, and we find a system of logic (or necessary forms of thinking) by realizing what takes place in a proposition, in a concept – that is, by realizing the 'where' to which it relates. As a result we get the following: (1) from the relation to a property, the relation to Quality; (2) from the relation to a correlate, the relation to Relation (Ground – Correlate); (3) and from the relation to a correspondent, the relation to Representation (to a Correlate with properties). Relations being mathematical thinking and not transcendental, Peirce's method of differentiating[44] the necessary forms of thinking in a non-aprioristic way cannot avail itself of means other than the act of thinking itself.

'What' the 'cenopythagorean categories' (SS24) 'are' is not so much in function of the method of grasping and describing them; their nature comes out only as the differences expressed within one and the same descriptive discourse, not as the discourse itself. As universal Categories they apply equally, of course, to every phenomenon. Except that relations do not describe Categories, although the can define them in an abstract mathematical way. Before analyzing them relationally I will describe the different Categories as follows:

A. *Firstness* 'the mode of being of that which is such as it is, positively and without reference to anything else' (SS24). In the natural context of signs, the preponderance of this Category contributes the

Iconic part in the sign relation. Its Categorical function conveys Quality (Apel's *Sosein*, Hegel's *An-sich-Sein* or quite literally *qualitas*), but as the mere Possibility of existing,[45] (existence is competency of the next Category). As psychic process, it must contribute the 'unanalyzed total impression made by any manifold' – for instance of sensory data, of chance in general (and their functional equivalents at higher levels of semiosis)[46] – however, nothing that is perceived or remembered. At this stage one merely realizes.

B. *Secondness*, 'the mode of being of that which is such as it is, with respect to a second, but regardless of any third,' and which is 'experience of an effort' (SS24), factuality, the 'brute action' 'by virtue of its being opposed.' In volition, it is the Non-ego of the Subject. (In signs, the result of this Category is the Index correlate.) To illustrate psychologically the first two Categories to Lady Welby, Peirce used an example: There is, first, a pervasive stillness in a balloon basket; there is, second, a piercing, ear-torturing whistle. Both are instances of Firstness, yet the passage from one to the other is an event or effort, and thus Secondness. One might add: as soon as I must conclude that the reason for this passage is the deflating of my balloon, this becomes Thirdness. Secondness and Categories at large are not 'schemata applicable to data,' as mentioned earlier, because the presupposition of a dichotomic ontology is unacceptable. Constructivist schematism only works for a presupposed static and inert being ('data') and with intrinsically atemporal schemata. This must be said in the context of Secondness, the actual vis-à-vis of existence, because it is the most tangible mode of being, and dyadic relations seem to be natural (actually, Aristotelian). It is a (nominalistic) fallacy suggested by the subject/predicate form of the sentence, with its existential copula 'is.' Only the logic of relatives opened the possibility for the discovery of more than a two-place relation: 'One-place, two-place, and three-place predicates are basically different in logical form' (Oehler 1981b: 337f), which means that now there are three modes of 'is.' Yet the other two modes are of similar necessity, and their irreplaceable benefit (e.g., for what cinema is and does) will come to light when we reach an understanding of narration and aesthetic. If all being is not static but relational (not just cognitive relation, as follows from this theory of Categories and Semiotic, which indeed extends beyond the usual dyadic relation of existence), and if the 'cognitive schemata' have a life of their own (there is 'life among the legisigns,' cf. Short (1982: 285–310), this blocks certain simple accounts of cognition. Since Secondness necessarily comprises two related elements, it can be either genuine or degenerate. Genuine Secondness is anything acting on any other without law (e.g., reaction, existence); Degeneracy is when the two are merely similar to each other or identical. This is, then, quite close to Firstness, which is always identical only to itself.

The Welby letter mentions also a difference between an immediate and a dynamic object, which does not warrant antirealist misinterpretations. Any nominalist Peirce 'interpretation,' such as in Eco (1981), expects to find here a purchase for again introducing a separation between the 'real' and the 'rational'; Oehler (1981b: 341) considers such interpretations 'category mistakes.' This aspect will prove to be an important consideration in a theory of perception in signs, which are, however, triads.

In the Welby letter, Peirce also defines his Categories in terms of relations, and here we encounter Secondness as dyad. That is treated more extensively in the Syllabus (cf. Pape 1982: 99–120): 'The broadest division of dyadic relations is into those which can only subsist between two subjects of different categories of being (as between an existing individual and a quality) and those which can subsist between two subjects of the same category. A relation of the former kind may advantageously be termed a *reference*; a relation of the latter kind, a *dyadic relation proper.*' (3.572). In accordance with its composite nature, Secondness needs here to be classified with regard to the nature of the Second in itself, and with regard to its First. (1) The Second (relatum) is either a Referate (if it is a 'possibility such as a quality' [SS28]) or a Revelate, or in the Syllabus's terms a re-relation (if it is by nature an Existent, 'two objects of the same universe' of discourse [3.573]). (2) Its First can be either dynamic or immediate. If it is dynamic and an 'existential relation,' it can be determined either by its own essence, or by a real relation to the Second (e.g., an action). If immediate or a 'modal relation' (3.574), it can be either a Quality or Existent.

One must resist the temptation to interpret these diversified categorical relations directly as cognition. They play the decisive role only in certain cognitions (i.e., precisely when these are dyadically determined). A cognition is always a triadic sign. Even in those which are dyadically determined, we must always add the propositional conclusion: 'Then it is indeed thus ...' The whole point of especially dyadic relations is that there already are four different determinations here, which of course yield quite different cognitive results. For example, a Re-relate or Revelate can recognize the simultaneity of two existents (i.e., an event). A Referate, in contrast, contents itself with a sensation setting in. Film music is a case of the latter: it is simply there (as in all those virtual 'Hollywood orchestras setting in with lonely lovers on the beach'). In Jean-Jacques Beineix's *Diva*, however, the impeccable voice and tone of the diva is, as sign, completely different (only in the Secondness aspect of external meaning) – that is, it is of the former kind. The nature of the First in such relations is relevant because it determines whether a 'surprising' discovery, or 'only' an expectation or a possibility can be cognized (in the other, in the self). These are only some of the imaginable effects, which we can then build into triadic sign relations of the most variable kind. Moreover, they prove how enormously useful it is to examine cognitions in Categorical terms. It helps us discern whether we can recognize the differences in various cognitions – in Aristotle's sense, that 'where?' questions do not answer 'what?' questions. Of course, it is not as simple as this, and the relational conception of Categories provides us with a tool that is finer, more sophisticated, and closer to the real triadic manner of cognition.

Secondness is of considerable interest, because of two of its properties. (1) It is the most obvious of all relations, and if approached naively it can be taken as the only one. On this level it is quite common to treat all questions of 'reality' as 'does it exist or is it imagination?' In his letter to Lady Welby, Peirce tries to reduce the importance of dyadic relations; even so, he is quite aware that this is the most intuitive of the Categories. Secondness is the necessary form of thought containing the diversity of relations to an opposite; furthermore, it signals – because it is necessary – that without relation to an opposite there can be no cognition. (This alone answers the whole 'realism debate' in film theory and also the objections to it in Carroll [1988b].) (2) There are a great number of relations in dyads, as well as between a sign and its other or correlatum. In the chapter in the Syllabus on dyadic relations, Peirce differentiates a number of relation essences, naming them as follows (and finding accordingly convenient glyphs). re-x ('relation with a correlate standing to its relate in a relation to which the primitive name applies' – for example, 'A is loved by B'); extra-x ('any relation to which the primitive does not apply' – for example, 'A stands in some other relation whether loving besides or not'); contra-x (whose nature is 'the non-subsistence of corresponding relations to which the primitive name does apply' (3.575) – for example, 'A does not love B'); juxta-x (is contra-extra, – for example, 'stands in some other relation than that of not loving, whether loving or not'); com-x ('relation which consists in its relate and correlate alike standing in one relation of the primitive kind to one and the same individual correlate' – for example, 'A loves something loved by B'); trans-x ('there is an x-relation in which A stands to whatever individual there may be to which B stands in the same relation' – for example, 'loves whatever may be loved'); ultra-x ('relation which subsists between any given relate and correlate only in case the former stands in a relation of the primitive kind to some individual of which the latter does not stand in the same relation' – for example, 'A loves something not loved by B'); and super-x (trans plus ultra – for example, 'A loves whatever may be loved by B and something else'). Peirce deduces four divisions of existential relations only. This does not even consider modal relations such as 'being more intense than' (which really belongs to Thirdness).

C. *Thirdness*, 'the mode of being of that which is such as it is, in bringing a second and a third into relation to each other' (SS24), is the mediation of the former two in an Interpretant under the respect of necessity. It could be apostrophized as 'the cognition Category,' or ampliative reasoning. Its most prominent instances are the signs. Because of the Categorical constructiveness (and degeneration) of triadic relations, signs can become highly elaborate and differentiated. In this way they can reflect every imaginable kind of cognition. Thirdness is a concept, word, or argument, or – as a pure relation – it is like 'giving' (i.e., 'A gives B to C'). The third relation is the most replete, but it operates only through the former two – that is, it cannot be prescinded from the former two. The added value of the third Category shows in a small remark made by Peirce at the end of a long treatment of dyadic relations (Secondness) in the Syllabus. It is customary to treat terms as connotation and denotation. Terms are then seen merely with regard to existential relations. Yet this dichotomy is reductionist. It obscures precisely the third dimension, which is also a dimension of time. Terms also have a dimension of accumulated knowledge beyond their denotation and connotation. 'Concepts grow' (3.608). Yet in reading Eco (1975), one has the impression that his interpretation of Peirce suffers from a negligence regarding the precise nature of Thirdness. It is precisely through the logic of relatives that the unprescindability of Thirdness is established in signs. How can this single element be absolute? If Secondness is substituted with referential codes (which are instances of Thirdness), and Firstness by representational conventions, to what can Thirdness relate? Thus, even though Thirdness supposedly comes nearest to semiological options, it would be a serious error to suppress the other two correlates in their unique and unprescind-able function. In signs, this Category stands most prominently for the Symbolic relation.

This Category is not yet 'cognition in signs'; so far it is only the rela-tional base and ultimate presupposition. Signs relate as Thirds as their logical form. They are the only path to any concrete human cognition. Categories, on the other hand, are logical constructs with metaphysical consequences (albeit not synthetical *a prioris*). As necessary forms of cognition they are present in every cognitive act. The phaneroscopic mode in which they are cognized – and this is not without relevance – neither metaphysical nor transcendental. Such a mode of discovery is a consequence of the fact that they need to be necessary and at the same time of an empirical nature. We can know of such forms of experience only through direct observation or phaneroscopy; we cannot know of them through semiosic, triadic cognition. This is, however, the way we must reason about them once they are discovered phaneroscopically.

Categories have been understood as ultimate universal forms of thought or cognitive behaviour. In a literal sense, this is all they are, which is tantamount to saying that all there is (in between being and substance) is these Categories. Therefore Categories cannot be com-pared to anything else – put another way, they are not concepts which fit or do not fit sensuous data. It follows that Categories are also a com-prehensive theory of the Real as much as they are a theory of cognitive states. For a formal description, it does not matter whether states of consciousness or metaphysical modes of being can be associated with such elements. This would follow by itself from the claim that Cate-gories are universal. Thus we can indicate the first and immediate element as a *feeling*, which already produces a specific correlate in con-sciousness. It is not an indeterminate feeling – it already has a noe-matic content. This content, in a second element, is compared to other contents of the same sort. Such comparison results in a simple *relation to a correlate*. Feeling, then, is already related to something beyond itself (as a mental state). Furthermore, we return from the correlate to its Other, the *'thing' with properties*, which is related to the mind. Because there are 'properties,' there is the possibility of predication. This implies, before any predication, that there is 'Something,' 'pure being,' before any property. It is evident that this process goes from the immediate to the general. Later we will investigate such reflections on the metaphysical consequences. Before that – and that is the typically and uniquely Peircean consequence of sign theory imposing itself as necessary – we must address one of the most difficult questions at the root of Categories: relations.

From Peirce's philosophical architecture emerges a clear notion of the *onus probandi* with which the logic of relations is invested. He mentioned repeatedly that one would convince oneself of the Categories, as he described them, not so much on the basis of Phaneroscopy, as through an understanding of relations. Bertrand Russell was at odds with Peirce's philosophy, logic, and sign theory – and consequently everything built on it – because he could not concur with Peirce that there are no relations of higher adicity than three which could not be reduced to triadic relations. Obviously, sign theory in its entirety hinges on the triadic relation, into which it has no way of accommodating another relation. If there were an irreducibly tetradic way of conceiving of the Real, it could not be in signs, and therefore not cognitively. If, on the other hand, the Real could be reduced to dyads – to binary oppositions in the manner of structuralism and Semiology – one would have to abandon Generality as a Real.

There are – *nullo contradicente* – certainly relations of any power. Even relatively simple concepts can be analyzed as tetradic relations – for instance, 'sale': 'A sells C to B for the price of D.' This is contained in the general idea of sale. A search of higher-adic general concepts could certainly identify realities – and types of cognition – which require that more than three elements be brought into a relation. Evidently, this would increase the number of Categories to any power you want, because each relational adicity would constitute another ultimate concept of cognition of reality. This, however, defies the idea of Categories as ultimate concepts of experience. Consequently, it must destroy the very basis of Semiotic because the classification of signs rests on triadic relations as the highest form of cognition. It also destroys Category-based metaphysics, since the number of types of reality would increase beyond control.

It is still easy to show – for instance, in contrast to Greimas (whom Peirce did not of course know) and Kempe (whom Peirce knew and whom he repeatedly criticized) – that triadic relations cannot be reduced – *salva veritate* – to dyadic relations. However, this is not so easy for tetrads and above. Greimas's standard example was the 'gift' concept. This he analyzed as two dyads of one conjunction and one disjunction of two subjects with the same object (two 'faire avoir'). The passage from one to the other dyad is ascertained by another dyad of transformation ('faire être'). This can be repeated, *q.s.*, then. However, this does not preserve the concept of gift – *salva veritate*, which needs not only the transfer of objects but also the (legal, customary, etc.) idea of 'donating.' Greimas's attempt would qualify exactly for the challenge Peirce set up in order to defend his Categories. For Peirce, Representations are 'the best way of satisfying oneself whether Thirdness is elementary or not' (1998: 176) – that is, whether it is one of those irreducible and unanalyzable concepts that is necessary for thought and experience. To be able to render the idea of representation, then, without using in it the idea of Thirdness, would be to show that Thirdness is not elementary (i.e., can be analysed into simpler concepts). As the example suggests, this is not the case.

Peirce saw Kempe as a serious challenge, as evinced in Peirce (1998: 170–6). It would indeed have been a serious blow had Kempe (referring to problems of projective geometry) succeeded in demonstrating that in mathematical theorems of all sorts, all the relationships encountered can be represented with only two elements: coloured spots and lines. Spots can stand for any Quality, whereas lines stand for Reactions. Peirce shows in three counter-arguments that Kempe's theory applies only if restricted to (enumerable sets of) singulars and 'relations between single objects.' However, Kempe's exclusion of general concepts – Thirds for Peirce – is hidden. That his thought brings together a plurality, and not the unity of the many spots and dualities of lines, is embodied in 'the Surface upon which the graph is written as *one* whole which in its Unity represents the Category of Unity' (Peirce 1998: 175). Thus, this is the needed third element, without which Kempe's relationship theorem cannot assert any idea or general concept. Only then can spots and lines stand for a theoretical comprehension of relationships of that sort.

As far as the need for a third analyzable simple concept is concerned, this seems to have satisfied Peirce. However, the question remains. Must one reckon with more than three unanalyzable conceptions? There must be a proof for the completeness, and this is a *de jure* question rather than a *de facto* matter (i.e., a sort of phenomenological data gathering). Without the possibility of proving this, one would have to live with the lingering doubt that cognition could be more. A proof involves effectively reducing all other types of cognition. Now, relations possess the characteristic of formalizing any cognitive content. So a possible proof would be reflected in terms of relations.

As is so typical for Peirce, the approach he takes to this important question is based on mathematical theory. His logic of relations rests on a mathematical proof of the irreducibility of relations with adicity less than three and with reducibility greater than three. It is therefore not the reverse – that an ultimate ground of experience, or of most simple concepts, is the trunk onto which a mathematical confirmation is grafted. That there are no other forms of being and cognition besides the triadic ones, is not experience; rather, it is a formal mathematical proof. More complex forms of relations can all be decomposed into the three types of relation found in the Categories. This proof, known as 'reduction thesis,' far from being intuitive, is the object of the mathematical logic of relations (cf. its reconstruction in Burch 1991), and cannot be elaborated here. However, the thesis is relevant to more than the calculus of relations (to which it made a crucial contribution).

Given the Peircean system architecture, everything hinges on experience and on cognitive behaviour being relations. This can be compared with a chemical vision of the world. As soon as the periodic table was drawn, it became irreconcilable with seeing a world of chemical substances, possibly ordered along the hylomorphist lines of *accidentia* and *substantiae*. Peirce made extensive use of the chemical metaphor of atomic valency with saturated and unsaturated ions. Relations can be seen as unsaturated ions becoming compounds. This metaphor becomes tangible as soon as it is applied to logical calculus (cf. Burch 1991: 3ff). Reasoning proceeds, then, by relating thoughts, either as arguments or in the terms themselves. The logical aim is to establish which thoughts can be thought – that is, which behaviour is possible – because thought can correlate only what is relatable.

We are used to considering language as the principal determinant of what can be thought: which subjects can be related through which verbs to which objects. A logical perspective is broader and investigates subjects and predicates – that is, what can be said about a subject. Even though this is very conveniently brought into the form of a proposition it need not necessarily be so. Propositions can be 'hidden' in concepts; assertion cannot be. For instance, the concept of 'growth' encapsulates the idea that something changes its state while maintaining its identity; speaking of a 'son' encapsulates the idea of a parent having generated this child. The business of logic cannot be a lexical one, too narrowly tied to the expression capacities of a natural language.[47] Logical terms can only be formal positions in a process of reasoning; they cannot be lexical positions. Such a process of reasoning can be a syllogism or argument or its premises in the form of propositions or terms. It is only important that the nature of the connection being operated be well understood. It does not matter that we must use an English example – 'Caesar is owner of a horse' – but it does matter that in all cases of that type there be a relation between parts of a different nature. This logical nature can be grasped using the valency metaphor; Thus, 'Caesar' and 'horse' are correlates with only one unsaturated valency, whereas 'owner' has two (and 'giver' has three). It would not render the idea of ownership without referring to the owned (and the idea of giving needs the gift and the gifted). However, hearing 'Caesar' alone has no meaning at all. One asks immediately, 'and what?' That is, a second element of the same kind is needed: 'and a horse' – as well as an idea of relation: 'have the same size,' 'have an owner–owned relation,' 'have an affection relation,' and so on.

The importance of such a relational conception cannot be emphasized strongly enough. In the first place, it makes meaning independent of natural languages, and therefore applies also – *a fortiori*, one might even say, given the primordial importance of montage – to cinema. A logical conception of film does not have to deny the 'natural language' aspect of film inasmuch as it consists of iconography and montage conventions and styles, down to the characteristics of the photographic film. If this is perhaps comparable to a semantic and grammar, logic abstracts from such facts and considers only what thought operates on these elements; and thought relates. That meaning is created through relation applies also to cinema. For this context, it is important not only that propositions relate to other propositions, but more that any thought or meaning inasmuch as it continues in a next meaning does so. Therefore, images can easily be understood as a series of meanings that must be related. A relation of an image sequence that needs the support of narration is, as meaning, quite different from a much looser sequence of aesthetical impressions. Certainly, few have attempted to put forward a calculus of image sequences. Attempts such as Colin's (1985) are the exception, and Colin's is based on a peculiar version of semiological generativism. However, film narratologies are materially a highly restricted investigation of the relational calculus of the continuation of meaning. In fact, only a formal investigation can reveal how restricted this investigation is. It neglects all 'unsaturated' meaning of lesser adicity (as it must be formulated in triadic perspective of Semiotic and its degenerative adicities, monads, and dyads). Needless to say, meaning of the aesthetic type either falls through the grid, as we shall see, or is relegated to psychological treatment.

Thus – one might note in passing – the advantage of a logical concep-

tion of language and signs. Such a conception compares very favourably with theories that offer no more than a closed system with quasi-
logical binary codes. Sharing the same paradigm, Luhmann's Systems
Theory, Hjelmslev's language theory, and Semiology at large all treat
language at a level of abstraction that is above natural language. In
their generative versions at least, language is even seen as a formalized
quasi-calculus of meaning based on arbitrariness. *L'arbitraire du signe*
precludes semiological syntax from becoming a first-order logic of simple predicates. The reason for this is not so much that any truth values
are excluded; more to the point, the ordering principles of binary positional values are too simple. Thus, the whole weight of meaning production is placed on the practice of choice (manifestation of a virtual
position). Instead of a logical principle, this is a purely functional one
(choice for the purpose/function of social communication). Function
only has a purpose for another emerging closed system, where the
same question returns. Not that system theory – at least Luhmann's – is
unaware of the regress (every 'autopoietic' system is based on a tautology or paradox; or, with Deleuze, *l'objet X, mana, Phallus* in structuralist
theories). This exclusion of logic weakens all relational statements
within the two formalisms (expression, content) and with a universe.
The result is either a polemic with 'teleological,' 'old-European' philosophies of/incorporating language, or a 'weak' theory of the relational
forces of relations. Yes/no codes – so Luhmann thinks – cannot determine a closed 'autopoietic' system of linguistic communication.[48]

Peirce's formalism is logical and therefore goes much further in its
relational syntax and semantics. Modern logic needs not only a powerful syntax – which is the whole idea behind formalism – but also, explicitly, a semantic to which the syntax can be applied. The insistence on the
latter is warranted, because there is a conspicuous, dominant tradition
in logics that takes semantics for granted. The primitive version of this
is the one language–one world belief, which assumes that the horizon of
language is also the boundary of the actual universe (cf. Hintikka [1997]
on Russell and Quine). In such a theory there can be no doubt that syntax (logic or positional order) as it is applies to the world as it is; otherwise, the entire thinking process would be meaningless or an illusion.
'A universalist like Frege could never have developed a modal logic.
Why not? The answer is obvious. If language (our actual language or
any alternative that can do an appreciable part of the same job it does)
cannot be re-interpreted, it can be used only to speak of one and the
same world, what is to say, our actual world. No serious alternatives are

possible, and hence the notions of possibility and necessity lose their natural Leibnizian sense' (Hintikka 1997: 18). As we have seen already, with Peirce there can be no easy assumption that his logical syntax applies to at least one universe, and, if it does, to which one. The question of relational logic semantics must be addressed explicitly, comprehending also a semantic of the possible and necessary, including the interpretation of this semantic through this syntax. Here we meet the crucial function of the relational conception of the theory of Categories.

As interesting as it is *in se* that Peirce developed a notation for the calculus of algebraic logic of relations, that is not our concern here. His calculus provides a very practical approach to applying relations to relations in a number of algebraic operations (multiplication, negation, permutation, and joins). The behaviour of relations has been extended to topology (which Peirce knew as Listing's census theorem but which we now call the Euler-Poincaré formula); however, for Peirce this was a necessary part of his algebraic calculus of relations (cf. Burch 1991: 13–16), and not an application of the calculus of relations to the universe of experience. Furthermore, the use of natural language terms and their valencies in the calculus of relations does not constitute proof that experience itself is based on such relations or relational terms. The formalism of the logic of relations is merely a logical syntax that is not contradictory in itself; it is the result of logical deduction applied to itself, and it is comprehensive (cf. Hintikka 1997). This means that the logical calculus is perfectly feasible as an algebraic calculus regardless of an existent world; this, however, lends illustrative support to logical deductions. The syntax (Peirce called it 'notation') of algebraic logic needs not only a semantic but also an interpretation that applies that syntax to the semantic (cf. Burch 1997: 235). Now, the semantics of the logic of relations can be investigated as extensional or intensional semantics (cf. Burch 1991: 27–51). In the first case, it applies only to the sole domain of the actual, existing world; in the second case, it concerns 'the collection W of all possible worlds' (Burch 1991: 39, quoting Kripke). The significant feature of the first is that it alone contains two truth values, whereas the second cannot be described without the conditions which need to be satisfied that modal, intensional semantics can be applied to at least one of the possible domains W. This satisfaction must be provided by an interpretation.

The upshot of Peirce's (algebraic) 'calculus model of logic' (Hintikka) is that it applies to more than one universe (cf. also *infra* 304). Therefore, there is no straightforward application of that calculus and its formalism to experience (corresponding to Burch's 'Enterpretation' or extensional interpretation, where logical meaning is connected in certain ways with physical objects of a universe), which is of course the one of the existent universe. Yet this has been the tacit assumption of the 'universalist' tradition in language philosophy and logic, as is aptly recapitulated in Wittgenstein's aphorism that 'the boundaries of my language are the boundaries of my world.' Our experience is limited to the existent world; our thoughts are not. When a logic describes only this existent world, it can remain silent on possible worlds. For Russell, 'necessary' is therefore what is 'universally' existent (cf. Hintikka 1997: 18), and modal being, modal logic, has no meaningful use in one universe (for Quine). Peirce's calculus syntax, instead, calls for an interpretation, for a semantic that interprets its application to one of the possible worlds.

This multiplication of universes is required because of the triadicity of the relations, and is thus not an ontological but rather a logical requirement. Ontology, and most of the language-image-of-the-universe logic, thrives on the one universe that we know and in which we all live. Invoking other possible universes could be suspect as idle speculation if there were no perch for it in our way of thinking. If other possible universes be thought, and if in fact they are needed in order to think the present one, then we must apply a logic that can cope with this situation. This brings us to Hintikka's felicitously made point that the one universe of experience is the result of a logical frustration. Cognition, from such a perspective, can be viewed as a constant attempt to find counter-examples that prove it false. This effort is crowned with success in the case of other possible universes, but frustrated in the case of the present one. If logic consisted of only dyadic relations, what would be the point of going beyond the *terra firma* of the present universe and present language as its image? The mere fact that one can doubt what exists – which really implies looking for counter-examples – requires a logical relation to the possible.

Sign x = y, its object: such a dyadic relation could express the traditional (ancient, medieval, semiological) acceptation of signhood as a standing-for. It is understood that what the sign stands for is perhaps absent but even so is part of the existing universe (or as Eco defines his signs: they must function as lies and laughs). Clearly, this extensional relation does not allow us to account for possible objects. Peirce's analysis went further by recognizing that in every sign, in every cognitive behaviour, there is a place for the possible. While 'possible world' semantics is a meaningful result, it is rooted in a logical condition for thought in general. Thought can never be a simple identity x = y; it must state from a particular element that some other possible element is related to it under a rule. Thus, the real cognitive situation is never 'this chair is brown,' but rather 'this chair is brown (and all the other chairs are black, so it should be in the next room).' Brownhood, black-hood, and every other imaginable quality are in the domain of possibility (not ontologically, of course, but intensionally). A thought, then, which relates one of these possibilities with this instance does not really com-bine (two essentially identical); rather, it com-trines (*sit venia verbo*), because it can do so only because it sees a reason for it (the third element). Anything thought is therefore teridentical (x = y = z), not bi-identical: three elements must be thought together.

Given the predominance of extensional bi-identical logic, it is difficult to make a plausible argument for taking teridentity as the normal case, not as a peculiarity that is quickly reducible to a set of dyads. 'This chair is brown' and 'some brown chairs must be in the next room' and 'this chair is in this room' are all dyads, but even in their combination they cannot render the thought. Besides, the same applies emphatically to the often apostrophized 'presentic character' of film images, where an image of a chair shows this chair, but not the concept chair. In order to render the 'rule' of 'chairhood,' a director would have to show a series of dyads in images. The cookbook answer to this problem is usually 'montage,' which possesses the magical faculty of transforming dyads into a triadic rule. Where does this extra meaning come from? It cannot be accounted for by a montage of any ever-so-long series of chair images. It is certainly possible to shift the accounting outside of montage to some sort of 'extra-textual motivation,' tantamount to social convention. Yet this just passes on the problem to a further theory.

A closer look into the very cinematic perception, however, reveals that in the percept itself one already finds a teridentical operation. Common wisdom sees the percept as the simplest element in cinema and elsewhere. As soon as one looks at something, irresistibly a percept of that something appears in one's mind. Ostensibly, this is a paramount case of x = y, 'I see (here and now) a brown thing,' or 'this is brown.' In his 1903 Harvard lectures on Pragmatism, Peirce insisted on the share that generality has in perception itself. Seemingly, this was for no other reason than to fend off the usual nominalist Category mistake of placing the 'real reality' with sensuous impressions and a 'derived reality' with theoretical conceptualization. What Peirce's analyses showed in that context is how the immediate, irrefutable nature of a sensory percept to contain general elements is not contradicted. What is usually called perception is really perceptual judgment. As such it compares a series of irrefutable percepts, which *in se* cannot be erroneous but can only be followed by a second, third, and further percepts of the same nature. Thus, there is a clear affirmation (cf. Peirce 1998: 226) of the scholastic (in reality, Locke's) principle that 'nihil est in intellectu quin prius fuerit in sensu' (what is in the intellect has first to be in the senses). This said, however, there is no implication made that the sensory data are those absolutely certain – because absolutely simple – ideas on which all further reasoning can fall back when it wants to ascertain itself of its correctness. This is the worst kind of Cartesianism, which Peirce had already refuted in his youth (in his article series in the *Journal of Speculative Philosophy* (1868–9) concerning 'four incapacities'). For him, such an appeal to absolutely certain simple ideas was a form of authority argumentation on equal footing with the scholastic practice of settling arguments with 'auctoritates.' Actual thought, however, is never x = y, a binary relationship between a concept and data; even in perception it involves a third element of a general nature. Once such a foundationalist ideological fixation on ultimate first certainties or elements (which even in film theory is more pervasive than one might wish) is removed, the path is cleared for a comprehensive understanding of cinematic meaning. One thing is already clear – there is no meaningful way to address the problem through 'levels' of how filmic data are organized under different concepts. There are many variants of this simple figure of thought. In principle, they all misperceive the triadic nature of meaning.

What, then, is the point of a triadic logic, triadic experience and cognition, triadic reality? It is not a new metaphysical doctrine, a kind of dialectic idealism or materialism. It is not, in the framework of an old but narrow epistemological debate, a vindication of the 'coherence theory of truth' over 'correspondence theory.' Yet triadicity has profound consequences. These include the truth question, which acquires a more comprehensive frame once it moves beyond mere factual truth ('material truth'). As the analysis of perception evinced, a more comprehensive grasp of experience and, from there, of the possibility of behaviour under the control of reason is also included. The triad allows for a third dimension in the Real, continuity, or time in particular. It is not behaviour that brings triadic relations into being, but the triadic nature of being that makes controlled behaviour possible. Peirce's Pragmaticism is, therefore, not the usual 'pragmatic approach,' which declares axiomatically that the anthropological constant is the basis of thought. Anthropology is more a function of thought in general; it is not a truth condition. Peirce's 'triadomania' – as he called it – is ultimately a simple idea and a simple consequence of comprehending reality as cognized, presupposing only that it is cognizable. Cognition is part of the real itself, or, conversely, the real becomes relation as cognized real. There can be no surprise, then, that the study of logic – through algebra or graph semantics – becomes primordial for everything that follows from its results. 'Peirce often claimed that a thorough study of the algebras would convince one of the categories. So the algebras are related to the graphs by way of the categories' (Brunning 1997: 253). Such primordial logic would suffer most from limitations in the traditional logic of predicates, with its one world–one language premise. Peirce often apostrophized his logic of relations as the only adequate logical instrument for a really comprehensive cognitive grasp of all kinds of reality.

The logic of relations has one chief advantage to offer – it enables us to comprehend meaning as construction, reduction, and degeneration of relations. This benefit is not obvious as long as meaning is – in the wake of an unreflected 'linguistic turn' – equated with lexical units. However, a meaning is not what corresponds to a sign or a word or even a proposition. Meaning is not even what corresponds to/is bi-identical with a state of world or state of affairs. These are merely dyadic relations and therefore without adequate complexity. What the third relation – teridentity – adds to meaning is constructiveness. Only in this way does it acquire an essence of building relation on relation, interminability of interpretation and cognition, tantamount to an essential time dimension. This *time*, however – the inherent temporality – is not imported into meaning *in se* from its existential situation in the human subject as a mortal or temporal being. It comes from within, because it inheres to the triadic relation in itself.

The simple idea of construction is that relations of a higher adicity contain those of a lower adicity. Thus, a 'general fact' contains any number of material (existential) facts, but existent facts of any number will never become a general idea without being explicitly brought into that interpretative relation ('representation'). However, this is a general consideration and not a logical calculus. Without such calculus it is more difficult to comprehend the converse process of interpretation, degeneration, and reduction. This will also be a characteristic of signs and sign classes; it does not stand for a deficiency.

Degenerate signs are as meaningful as genuine ones – they just signify in a different manner. Understanding degeneration could remove
a lot of possible confusion from the many instances of degeneration in
sign classification. For instance, a sign whose main purpose is to designate a fact is still a triadic relation, which, however, emphasizes the
dyad of factual relationship it contains. If it were a genuine dyad, it
would not contain any cognitive value of even a minimal degree of generality. Such is the case, for example, with a pure monstration, (e.g., a
watch or a weathervane). A dyadically degenerate triad, however,
makes cognitive use only of the dyadic aspect in a sign. These, then, are
truth signs; for such signs the aspect that counts is a positive or negative truth value and not, for instance, a general idea. Even though this
appears to be an identity relation, bi-identity, between a sign and an
object, it is still under the teridentical control of a general idea. Degeneration also explains another kind of meaning. Triadic relations can
also degenerate into a collection of monads. The teridentical control
'contains' in this case only entities that are 'identical' with themselves
and with nothing else. The meaning is no longer 'roses are thorny'
(generally) or 'this is a rose' (true or false), but rather 'a rose (is a rose).'
Or in the same order, in the case of cinematic images: In the narrative
context of a sequence, 'roses are indicators of an amnesia,' as in Orson
Welles's *Citizen Kane*'s Rosebud (which can be grasped only as a general idea). In the documentary context of this film, 'there were roses at
this point in space and time.' Indulging in a moment of beauty: 'a rose!'

Again, what is so important for meaning must be grasped in a formal way, and not by way of examples. The formalized permissions of
how relations can be constructed can be represented in either graphic
or algebraic syntax. Peirce, who pioneered the former 'notation,' never
claimed that it was easy to use or elegant enough to become a manageable tool for representing valid logical argumentation. This is especially true when the syntax is written in a complete manner so that it
ends up as a convoluted grid of lines, inclusions, and spots and their
negations. However, a graph has one advantage over an algebraic
expression: it is intuitive with regard to the aspect it chooses to represent graphically. Burch preferred this method when stating his formal
proof of Peirce's thesis that all classes of higher relations can be
reduced to triads *salva veritate*, whereas triads cannot further be
reduced into dyads and monads. Graphs, being formalistic, are important for the reduction thesis itself because in this way the subjective act
of thinking is not used and analysed for the purpose of proving the

ways of thought *in se*. Such a petition of principle can be avoided – as is shown in the graph syntax of the logic of relations – without resorting to any form of transcendentalism. However, if the result of this is indeed that the triadic relation – which is the only cognitive relation – is the highest adicity needed for the construction of all further relations, the consequences for representation and experience cannot be overestimated.

Construction consists of logical operations on relations from the perspective of formal analysis of thought. For the purposes of operation, relations are represented as Cartesian products. Coordinate systems with 2 or n axes, for instance, define their space through 2 or n points such that any point is defined as $P(3,5, \ldots n)$ and a square or any n-dimensional object is defined by the corresponding function. Such objects can also be operated on, 2 points $P(2,2,4) \times Q(4,3)$ where $\times$ is one of the operators. A relation, first of all, can be negated. For instance, applied to a simple tetradic relative term, neg (sale) [sale is a term with four relates: object O, seller S, buyer B, and property transaction T. Thus, 'sale': __ gives __ to __ as __ {gift; ware; due} or 'medicine' __ gives __ to __ as __ {gift; ware; due} with the intention of __ {healing}]. A negation negates all. Permutation of a relation, second, means that the numbering of the adicity is changed. This presupposes that the order of relates is relevant – for instance, to meaning. Thus, applied to the same term, the same relate can become sale or theft. This might mean: BTOS, 'a thief brings into his property an object of someone.' Third, then, there is a join involving one relation, a selective deletion of one relate. Such an operation cancelling one of the relates transforms 'sale' into 'sale-without-object' as it were (e.g., lexically, as 'favour'). Fourth, a join involving two relations connects one relate of the first relation with one relate of the second relation. An example (taken from Peirce's 1903 Harvard lectures on Pragmatism) would involve two propositions: '__ is brown', '__ is a horse', into 'this is a brown horse' (both, however, are non-relative, that is, monadic terms). Fifth, an array as last operation gives a linear order to different relative terms.

With operations as the basis of every meaning the 'logical turn' supersedes any 'linguistic' or 'pragmatic turn,' which cannot really grasp the ever-changing nature of meaning. If the change is constructive, it is a growth of the generality of this meaning. In the contrary case of reduction, a given meaning loses generality down to the point where it ceases to be a relative term at all, or it becomes a monad. This is, for instance, a single percept. However, the operational capacity of constructions goes beyond simple relations, beyond relative terms such as 'father' and 'lover.' The logistic formalism suggests that constructiveness allows quite complex logical calculi. Here it is not mathematical hypothetical thought; rather, it amounts to a calculus of meaning. Conversely, this reveals meaning as calculation and not as an inert staple of lexical units *cum* syntactical order.

So far the construction and reduction of relations of any adicity seems unproblematic because it has been proved feasible. However, if this is transferred from a strictly mathematical calculus and applied to thought, it becomes apparent that thought as representation becomes impossible if it consists of relations higher than triadic. Tetrads may be a valid class of n-tuples for mathematical arguments; that said, it is impossible to find any cognitive behaviour or anything else in the domain of reality that is more complex than a thought. Thinking means establishing this typical relation among the three relates of a Quality, an Occurrence, and a Symbol. If it were an instance of tetrads or higher, this would involve a relate of still another nature, which can only be beyond generality. Phenomenology shows, however, that no such relate can be found. Thus, teridentity is in fact a quite special relation, special to thought. Thought is the triadic relation known as hypostatic abstraction. Here one brings under one general concept what is existentially quantified and identified as variable. The reduction thesis says no more than that through this procedure, any relation of any higher adicity can be replaced. Thus, the tetradic relation of 'sale' becomes 'sale-ness' or instance of the general idea of sale. Variables are *seller, buyer, merchandise*, which are quantified as singular terms: 'this (*buyer, seller, good*).' Teridentity and hypostatic abstraction, therefore, are basic to understanding thought as a relational process. They are also the decisive steps in a formal proof of the reducibility[49] of any relation into triads.

From construction – and reduction as its negative consequence – follows the idea of degeneration in such relations. As the examples above have illustrated, the impact on meaning is considerable. Evidently, such a conception of meaning is possible only on the basis that meaning is constructive (because it is triadic, etc.). Outside this assumption it makes no sense whatsoever to speak about degenerate relations and degenerate signs.

Burch gives this mathematical definition of degeneration: 'A relation of adicity $n > = 2$ is degenerate if and only if there is an integer $k > = 2$ and there are k integers $j_1, j_2,...j_k$; with $1 < = j_i < = 2$ for each j_i; and with

$j_1 + j_2 + ... + j_k = n$; such that for every $w \in W$ the value of the relation is a class of n-tuples X_w^n such that X_w^n is a Cartesian Product (Concatenation) of k classes of tuples $X_{w1}^j, X_{w2}^j, ..., X_{wk}^j$, with each X_{wi}^j being a class of j_i-tuples over D_w.' (Burch 1997: 242). This complex definition takes into account an interpretation for more than just one world – this would be the extensional interpretation or 'enterpretation' – in fact, for all possible worlds ('intensional interpretation'). Thus, D_w is a Kripke model of a set D, for domain, indexed by a member of W, a set of all possible worlds. This expresses the intensional understanding of Peircean logic, which applies to more than just the existing world, as would be the case for extensional interpretations. An n-tuples class [a subset of the Cartesian Product $(D_w)^n$, one domain of one of the possible worlds] constructed iteratively by the five operations, Peirce's 'relative products' – can also be reduced in the same manner. Degeneration of n-adic relations as mathematical operation consists in the lower relations being factored out from the Cartesian Product.

As usual, the best illustrations of degeneration are found in the realm of cognition, as cognition in signs, as we shall discuss in detail later. Within a cognitive relation, one can 'factor out' mere attentiveness to an event – for instance, in the form of expectation for something to happen or not to happen. The important point here is that this does not mean that such a relation is no longer a cognitive one of meaning; rather, meaning is reduced to interpreting with a simple yes or no (truth value), which is a relation between two elements. If it were not a degenerate triadic, but a genuine dyadic relation, such a thing would be no more than a weathervane or a watch. This is also the case for a television broadcast without a viewer or for a film screening without a spectator – a purely, genuine dyadic relation between the light beam's reflection and source (such genuine input/output dyads happen routinely in film-copying factories). However, this absolute deprivation of cognition is not taking place in a triad, degenerate as it might be. At least the constatation of a fact, or the perception of a quality, is a cognitive achievement that involves a higher class of relational complexity.

What the intensional interpretation of relations implies in relation to the (customary) extensional interpretation is not so immediately evident. Hintikka, as we saw earlier, has made the point in his critique of the one-language/one-world school of logic. From a cognitive point of view, one might harbour doubts about the relevance of theorizing on more than the one existing world. Its usefulness, though, is not a merely metaphysical subtlety, but a question of general cognition at large. As soon as it is admitted that the nature of cognition is to cognize necessity (i.e., that something is not factually so – *de facto* – but that a compelling reason makes it necessarily so – *de jure*), it is not enough to relate/appeal to facts, even if they were comprehensive. Such a procedure would amount to complete inductive inference, which is impossible, since induction has no means to prove its own completeness. Induction as a concept functions only in the belief that the number of cases is factually complete and therefore also logically completed because exhausted. Even for a contemporary philosophy of science, or science theory, this is an outmoded assumption. Apparently it has become a commonly accepted assumption that no scientific theory can ever be conclusively verified or falsified on the basis of data. One theory is preferred over another only on the basis of pragmatic considerations, and competing theories can concurrently explain the same set of data. One of the leading theorists of science, Mary Hesse, summarizes: 'Theories are logically constrained by facts, but are underdetermined by them: i.e., while, to be acceptable, theories should be more or less plausibly coherent with facts, they can be neither conclusively refuted nor uniquely derived from statements of fact alone, and hence no theory in a given domain is uniquely acceptable' (1978: 1). Contrary to certain naive assumptions in scientific practice – which Hesse describes as 'mopping up' strategies – Semiotic never assents to procedures that make 'objectivity' their hallmark or creed in the following manner: first, construct hypothetical models; second, verify or falsify them with data. As Peirce states 'The truth is that there are no data' (7.465, 1893). Clearly, this apodictic statement is only a metaphysical consequence of the Categories.

Abductive inference, therefore, is the quintessence of Pragmaticism and a requirement of scientific cognition. It presupposes no limitation to the existing world or other limited choices; to the contrary, it must transcend mere existence in two directions. In the first direction the realm of the possible acquires the same right to be real as the existent in the second; the general becomes the third reality. A general is clearly never real in the same way as something that merely/really exists, and it is impossible to think of a general as the sum total of all existents. If generality could indeed be expressed – *salva veritate* – as the sum of existent states of affairs, this would mean that it is not an irreducible relation, and thus a superfluous category. Now genuine necessity (i.e., not merely *de facto* quasi-necessity as exhaustion of all cases) is comprehensible only if it contrasts with what is not necessary. This implies the possibility of different worlds. In terms of logic in the ordinary sense (i.e., tied up with propositional structures of natural language), these non-necessities can be expressed in modal logic – usually with modal verbs of constructions.

The relational form of thought is the sign-form. Modal being can also be conceptualized very elegantly as classes of signs. This makes it patent that signs cannot be 'things' among other existing things in the one factual world. They extend intensionally, through meaning, beyond the factual world; not only that, but they only 'are' in relations and 'are not' factually mundane. If these forms of thought seem rather terse and abstract, and not as intuitively propositionally concrete as the Aristotelian list of categories (causality, quantity, etc.), this is only the consequence of their exhaustiveness and generality. The inadequacy of Aristotle's non-relative logic has long been recognized (cf. Bucher 1998: 198). Thus the introduction of relations would have disturbed the apparent concreteness of proposition-based, 'predicative' logic and its categorical presuppositions. Relation logic, however, does not exclude predicative propositional logic but rather combines perfectly with it (cf. Byrnes 1998). There have been successful attempts to prove that Peirce's first-intentional, propositional logic calculus is complete, even though he did not formally prove it himself. However, relations – as we have seen – also introduce elements (of what later was called 'undecidability') that go beyond strict requirements of what after Peirce (cf. 2.522 from 1883, a 1893 revision of the Grand Logic) became known as first-order logic.

With relations, Peirce introduced very important new elements into syllogistic logic (not just a rendering of syllogisms in a formal language and nothing more), and this had important consequences for the very definition of the 'epistemological' problem. Our way of conceptualizing how we cognize is profoundly affected if it is no longer self-evident that cognition is a matter of relating a fact to a concept. The third necessary element of cognition is a sign. It would be a profound misunderstanding if Peirce's idea of sign, or representation, were understood in the usual psychologizing sense as a shorthand or in-between placeholder for ideas developing in two solitary minds. This might be inevitable in the context of a phenomenological social theory such as Schütz's or Luckmann's, and even to a minor degree for Mead's pragmatism (v. *supra*, and *a fortiori* for Symbolic Interactionism). For Peirce and his Pragmaticism, however, it holds that its quintessence is 'the logic of abduction' (cf. Peirce 1998: 226), as the title of his seventh Harvard lecture on Pragmatism indicates. The ultimate form of human conduct of behaviour is triadic, and therefore has the form of representation. Acting (under self-control) means representing, which is the only cognitive form of world relation. The usual psychologism only sees the intentional will to act and its corresponding intentional object. Generalizing such a will, then, is an arduous but impossible enterprise, because the essentially dyadic will cannot be 'extended' into an essentially triadic generality.

1.6.1   Representation as Logic of Experience: Is There Truth in Signs?

Peirce thought that the best way to convince oneself of the appropriateness of the Categories was to investigate representation (cf. the sixth Harvard lecture, Peirce 1998: 208ff). This is not an attempt to beg the question (the elenchus being the ultimate forms of thought in general), nor is it a concession to foundationalism. Peirce's Categories are such that they need neither elementary simple forms nor a first 'Adamitic' thought-from-nowhere. The point of departure of even this fundamental reflection of meaning can safely be chosen even from terms, or (more precisely and comprehensively) Rhemata. It is only a question of method to avoid vicious circularity. For an anti-aprioristic method such as Peirce's, it was especially important to establish mathematical thought as thought-before-experiential-thought, as hypothetical thinking, as the place from which logic itself receives its formal proof (as in the logic of Relations and the reduction thesis). Logical graphs are a methodological addition in the sense that they show the practicality of logical relationships, which often are so well hidden in the terms of natural languages.

A novel relational idea of representation, however, becomes the well-founded upshot of all these logical conclusions. Representation, therefore, becomes the point that also condenses these underpinning logical reflections. Representation – that is, signs – makes (certain classes of) relations visible as meaning. Comprehending cognition as representation constitutes a veritable watershed, and is the demise of the very 'epistemological' question (as Peirce emphasizes repeatedly in his arguments against 'Erkenntnislehre'). The turn is more profound than the customary polemic against 'consciousness philosophy' hypothesises. Opposing to this a 'pragmatic turn' is only a small advance over a transcendental epistemology compared to the profoundly relational absorption of epistemology as achieved by Peirce.

This is most obvious in the nominalism debate with regard to the criteria for truth in cognitive behaviour. It is no longer enough to consider 'true' that idea which has a correspondence in real things – Thomas Aquinas's theory of *adaequatio intellectus et rei* (de verit 1, 2). If this were so, the third element in the representational relation would be redundant. The concept of truth had to measure up to the new insight of cognition as triadic relation, which to some degree is masked by the linguistic propositional form uniting subject and object with an existential copula. As form of behaviour, representation can never be the 'mere representation' of common parlance. As universal form, with representation as the only means to world possession for everything *quoad nos*, a new form of realism is possible. The real is accessible (exclusively) as representation in behaviour.

This understanding of representation cannot be shared by all those theories which remain fundamentally dyadic and therefore nominalistic epistemologies. Semiology, for one, is radically tied to nominalism and uses 'reference codes' that reduce representation to 'mere representation.' Being and substance (resp. 'meaning') are not mediated in this; rather, they are separated.[50] In this context it is inevitable that we understand signs as arbitrary relations. Arbitrariness is merely another way of stating that there is no logical relation, but only a factual relation of conventional connections, one that defies explanation and understanding.

Now, the mediation form 'representation' determines the realities of the real. The result of Peirce's early inquiries into mediation of substance and being is that Categories cannot be attributed (in a transcendental way) to the mind, nor can they be attributed (in an ontological way) to outside reality. They are both, because – as with the chemical elements of compounds – they are always bound to representations. Our appropriation of the Real becomes a question of the kind and the strength of the binding forces in the representational compound. It is not physical causation in the brain; nor is it the heuristic device of mental concepts to organize sensation; nor is it a psychological fact. The forces in the representational bind are living and varied, but they are located upstream of any concrete experience. It was Peirce's achievement that he comprehended that Logic determines Representation, which determines all possible behaviour; and this is the idea of the Sign. It relates a character (sensation, idea, feeling) to the brute fact of its real existence (in a precise moment and place, or not) through a force of generality (one among a choice of logical kinds of binding).

What is called logic here merits a closer relational analysis as it straddles the pre-experiential mathematical form and the reality of experience. This audacious (to most nominalist ontology, counter-intuitive) mixing of the logical and the factual cannot be assumed to be self-explanatory. It is certainly not the rule of forming meaningful propositions (in a given language). It is Speculative Grammar and not linguistic syntax. Peirce's architectonic assigned to it a much more crucial and central role. On the mathematical side is the abstract theory of relations; Experience comes into the picture as soon as a phenomeno-logical analysis reveals that the Phaneron has three essentially distinct parts, which then must enter into relations. Logic is more than the sole mathematics of relations because it is concerned with the elements of the experiential-as-relations. Its task is now to constitute the laws of experience inasmuch as they determine ideas (cf. W1,358f). This is indeed a rather crucial difference. While a mathematical theory of rela-tions can concern itself with any-adic relations, experiencing behav-iour is no more than a triadic relation, as the reduction thesis with its reliance on hypostatic abstraction proved. At any rate, as soon as it is a relation, representation can no longer be grasped in terms of mental states or psychological laws. The rule of certain types of relation gov-erns representation, and according to relation rules, various possible representations are conceivable. This will then be the concern of Semi-otic or Speculative Grammar.

Regarding the term 'representation,' it must be mentioned that Peirce was not happy with it for long. In his Cambridge conferences (1898, third lecture), he gives a historical account of the development of his logic of relatives (cf. Peirce 1992a: 146f), in which he concludes: 'It was also perhaps injudicious to stretch the meaning of the word Representation so far beyond all recognition as I did.' (147). He then deletes the following sentence: 'The word Mediation would have been better.' (282FN).

The concept of representation is central to the new concept of Reality – cognition of the Real – and cannot be restricted to the human mind (even though this remains the most important instance of representa-tion). In a metaphysical perspective, the interesting point is that some Reality is capable of representing another, which is different and not dependent on it. The representing Reality can be – and mostly is – a human mind, 'but so has a looking-glass' (W1,323), or something writ-ten, such as a capacity. Nothing that we could possibly know of is an essence interior to itself. Being means now that something represents itself to something else (e.g., some other mind).

However, there are further implications for the concept of representation. How far-reaching is it, and what does it mean that all is representation? Here is the point where epistemology gives way to Pragmaticism: if it is behaviour, it must be 'for some purpose' (which sounds anodyne enough, except that it then introduces final causality and teleology). This implies a Subject (volitive but not necessarily human), which takes it as being a representation of something. In the beginning, this was a statement of Anti-Cartesianism. Representation without a Subject, meaning a pure fact-ness without any generality, is incognizable. The same holds true for the complete lack of 'fact-ness,' an 'ultimate premise' without 'contamination' by empirical objects. In this manner one would obtain immediate cognition in intuition or pure undifferentiated Objectivity without a consideration for Subjects. Both effectively take dyads as norm and negate – or have no use for – triadic relations. The early Peirce called these two limits 'inner being.' Only outer being is conscious, because only representation as a triad comprehends a third kind of relation.

The full impact of representation as a theory of reality will only be seen in its metaphysical consequences, which however are contingent on the form of cognition (cf. W1,515; and not the other way round). After his early conception of representation, Peirce elaborated many further aspects of this idea, including the metaphysical implications, under various nomenclatures, until, after a lengthy pause, he took it up again in his late work. In between, he clarified further the Categorial-relational basis of representation, Phenomenology or Phaneroscopy, and he placed representation into the pragmatic framework. All of this maintained a remarkably constant core, which new elaborations in different keys could not substantially alter.

The idea of representation has many aspects, which should not surprise us if we take into account how closely it is related to the Categories as the necessary and sufficient form of cognition. Its prime and most formal expression is the relational one, where the different relational valencies each have a proper name: Ground, Correlate, and Correspondent. On this basis, other implications of each valency can be developed. Thus the sign process has a metaphysical basis, psychological states of subjectivity, logical expressions in predication.

First, in representation the mind sees that a thing is. The logical order is ordinally a first, but it is last in the order of experience (where we 'realize' that a thing is only after we have apprehended its characteristic and law). As a general presupposition the mind would necessarily merely have to acknowledge that something is being at all; without such a presupposition, it is impossible to think something. As such this thing is merely related to itself as being. This relational type is the First Category, as Peirce calls it in his mature works. As thing, at that stage its logical form is that of a connotation or term. In cognitive terms, a conclusion takes place, which relates properties (a Ground) to this thing. As a necessary form of being and of cognition, this stage of representation is also called Quality. To consciousness, this level is a 'feeling' and contributes comprehension (W1,491 or intension). Metaphysically, the object (noema) is pure Form or general essence (in a monadic relation), whereas it is subjectively (noesis) a Quality or internal mark.

Second, this thing with properties (or Ground) is related by the Second Category to a Correlate, which can be in the form of a proposition (or denotation). Psychologically, this relation can be 'attention.' To consciousness, this level is an 'effort' and contributes extension (W1,491). Metaphysically the object (noema) is matter (in a dyadic relation), whereas it is subjectively (noesis) an Object as the other of a subject.

Third, this represented thing is the necessity-form of a Correspondent, that is, the triadic relation to a correlate with properties (as described above). Its guiding Category is Thirdness. Logically, through comparison and in the form of an argument, 'something as this' is of type 'this' (e.g.; this, as orange, is an orange fruit-type; the same this, as orange, is an orange colour-type). To consciousness, this level is a 'notion' and contributes information (W1,491), psychologically as a thought. Metaphysically, the object (noema) is a concrete thing, whereas it is subjectively as noesis an actualized relation or Subject.

1.7 The Metaphysics of Pragmaticistic Semiotic

Before signs proper can be addressed, we need to consider a potentially nagging question: Is a monadic relation real? Is a triadic relation as real as a dyad (whose reality can hardly be doubted)? As mathematical ideas, relations of any adicity need not be real at all; it is enough that they can be hypothetically thought. However, we have already found that tetradic relations are mere composites of triads and not genuine. There is no reality of tetrads proper that is different from a triad of two triads – that is, two general thoughts in a third general thought.

As confirmation of his relational theory of Categories, then, Peirce had to attain a meta-factual (more than merely factual) proof of three distinct realities. In his later years, this was one of his strongest philosophical efforts, and he resorted to various formulations. The closest one to relational Categories is found in his Harvard lectures; elsewhere he develops many other aspects of his 'evolutionary metaphysic.'

Peirce's claim that there are ultimate, necessary, and exhaustive forms of cognition does not avail itself of a safety net such as transcendental thinking before (*a priori*) thought. It is the same cognition as any other. Therefore, these forms cannot be reduced to formalism; if they could be, they could stay on the other side of the material data. That would be a profoundly nominalistic ontology. So it is very important that these forms be real – not, however, in the sense that something real corresponds to them, but rather in the sense that everything real is these forms. Yet this is even more difficult to make plausible and intuitive as long as these forms are understood to be relations. If anything, relations could then be taken as 'mere mental forms,' perhaps relating real things; however, relating realities in themselves is not very intuitive.

Why is it so important that Categories, and therefore signs, be not mental forms or linguistic forms, but as real as (for instance) a signpost that I bump into while walking down the street? We do not find the answer in the later Peirce's peculiar foible for metaphysic. Metaphysical assumptions are inescapable for any theory, and the worst and most naive metaphysics turn out to be those which are not acknowledged. Peirce extensively analyzed one-sided metaphysical systems and their systemic defects (cf. *infra*). That said, one of the most insidious fallacies arises when certain theories postulate a total freedom from metaphysical assumptions (in the name of 'postmetaphysical thinking' or the like). Putting aside the very metaphysical question as meaningless and not answerable is no guarantee of freedom from such assumptions. In the worst cases such assumptions are commonsensical, generally taking the form of crude, Kant-icizing mental hypothetical schemata to be 'applied' data (which are really real). It is a facile exercise to have them, and their like, shot down with the customary accusation of ontology *more Cartesii*.

Categories are certainly already discovered in how we have to speak about the empirical; yet it does not follow that they are ways of speaking. Also, they are certainly discovered as mental laws; but it does not follow that they are psychological constants. Furthermore, they are certainly discovered as ultimate, not further analysable, and therefore simple ideas; but it does not follow that we must hypostatize the historically contingent mindset into logical universals. All of this can be used as a method of discovery; even so, we cannot jump to conclusions about the non-metaphysical nature of Categories. Only when phenomenality is considered in its completeness – by definition on a fallible, non-dogmatic basis – can we pretend to find those points where everything thinkable, doable, and possible converges. It is very wise and strongly advisable to assign highly formal names to these convergence points, in order to thwart premature conclusions. As we have seen, Peirce chose mathematical terms, and this makes it very hard to identify them with any one aspect. All aspects – those mentioned earlier and other possible methodical constructs – must be comprehended in such forms. However, except by negatively proving that something is not included, by definition there can be no conclusive, positive proof for Categories of experience that is more than mathematical proof and that has only a mathematical cogency (such as the reduction thesis). Whichever metaphysical system we are building on, the fallible results of a theory of Categories inherit this fallibility.

The reality as such of Categories cannot mean identifying not this or that existent thing. We must firmly keep in view the Phaneron in its comprehensiveness. Thus, metaphysic is contingent on what appears in the Phaneron. Had Phaneroscopy revealed that there is only one type of appearance – say, brute factual existence – the metaphysical problem would have found a simple solution: all there is is what exists, and that which does not exist, is not. The only theory that such a metaphysic has to develop is what existence is and how it relates to its being cognized (i.e., its 'cognitive existence' being epiphytic). All nominalisms *(res sunt nomina)* could be reduced to this point, with the *res* corresponding to singular facts and the *nomina* amounting to cognitive entities above those facts. Whenever the comprehensive (actual and possible) appearance before our eyes (minds, thoughts, acts) includes more than one type of element – without, however, resorting to some incognizable artefact – the metaphysical question is necessarily more complex. We cannot doubt that these appearances *are* appearances, otherwise nobody could know anything about nothing; however, whether or not such entities are mere heuristic devices, or historically contingent cultural products, or world appropriation, or something else, is a real question. An opinion in the first sense is indeed no bogeyman; it is actually held by Radical Constructivism (v. *supra*). Furthermore, sociological theories of knowledge offer profuse solutions in the second sense.

Peirce's metaphysic, then, is distinguished by the unusual count (>1) and nature of what it attributes to reality. By his own account, the count is unusual in that he sees an abundance of metaphysical systems or implied systems with only one reality, as well as some where two realities are admitted and, very occasionally, a metaphysic with three modes of being. To each mode of being there corresponds a different 'truth theory' – or better, a different normativity, as was outlined earlier in the context of Peirce's normative sciences. Trimodality is certainly neither trivial nor without consequences, nor does it make the business of metaphysic easier.

On the contrary, trimodal Reality is very rich in consequences. One of the most interesting challenges for film theory is to develop an adequate theory of time, because we can hardly think about cinema without considering time. What 'is' time, really? It would be enormously reductive to approach it simply as narration, because this would eliminate all the experiential and durative aspects of time. As we shall see, the quintessentially teleological nature of narration is a reality. In Categorical terms it is different from factual time (i.e., time as sequence of differentiating events of an identical object). Ricoeur's classical narratological treaty evinces the difficulties associated with thinking simultaneously about 'cosmological' and 'narrative time' (in other words, thinking in one metaphysical mode of being). We will have to investigate later how convincing it is to use Heidegger's levels of vulgar and existential temporality (v. *infra*); when we do, it may well appear as an attempt to accommodate hierarchically two modes of being in the one, 'genuine' being. As we shall see later, time comprehends – *must* comprehend – a third mode of being as well, otherwise it would not be. The facticity of temporal events must involve changes of an identical object. This identity is a Quality and therefore a mere possibility, illustrated by Plutarch's anecdote of 'Philip drunk and Philip sober' (3.93), as Peirce explains in 1896 in 'The Logic of Mathematics; An Attempt to Develop My Categories from Within': 'Phillip is drunk and Phillip is sober would be absurd, did not time make the Phillip of this morning another Phillip than the Phillip of last night. The law is that nothing dyadically exists as a subject without the diversification which permits it to receive contrary accidents. The instantaneous Phillip who can be drunk and sober at once has a potential being which does not quite amount to existence' (1.494). All of these constitutive elements of time – as a reality and as a cognitive experience – are lost if there is only one (kind of) real. Our discussion of semiological theories of narration in film theory (e.g., as encountered in Metz's and his school's Grand Syntagmatic), will point to their profound difficulties with time.

What are these modes of being? What is each single mode in reality? Universal Categories are cognizable, necessary, and comprehensive; it follows that Category-based cognition must also cognize three reality modes. It is no surprise, then, that one hundred years later, Popper brought up again a three-world model, one that somehow rediscovered three modes of being, albeit on a different basis.

(1) The Reality of Firstness is Quality without further considerations. In percepts ('Revelates'), it becomes tangible in the form of unappealable Whatness, before a series of percepts in one regard is transformed into a perceptual judgment (which is a Third). However, it is not limited to perception, as can equally be imagined. It is, to a certain degree, against common parlance to attribute being to (for instance) imagination. So it is only proper to qualify this kind of reality as being possible (which is not to say that it is potential, that is, a volitive object). A 'Real Possibility' is not an oxymoron. As monadic relationship only to itself, or as dyadic Immediate First of a Secondness (existence as defined relationally), or as double degenerate triadic relationship, its common reality is that it is Possibility or Quality. Because of its vagueness it is futile to determine this reality further, as one might try to conceive a perfect coherent construction of non-contradictory laws. There is no sum of qualities in their totality, even if there might be a limited number of semantic devices in all languages taken together. That there is real chance – 'tychism,' as Peirce called this metaphysical dimension – cannot be defined as the negation of necessity (this is seen from the perspective of the reality of Thirds). First Reality stands in itself; furthermore, nothing is constrained by past, actual, or future factual reality if one's metaphysic encompasses the much wider realm of the possible.

Clearly, comprehending or not comprehending the Possible has profound consequences for any understanding of fiction, or documentary, photography, all of which are stock problems in film theory. Often, but inadequately, this is the only question asked in the truth context. Questions such as 'Is it a true photograph?' and 'Is it fiction or documentary?' completely ignore the cognitive relevance and incidence of the possible. A photograph may not want to document anything; it may only want to play with qualities such as colour or shape. Later we will encounter striking examples of such cinematic pictures in Godard (*Passion* and *Je vous salue, Marie*) – that is, pictures which are incomprehensible as factual or narrative reality. There is even a 'truth' for First Realities, if one stretches the term to its breaking point. The unappealable truth of First Realities has only one chance of evincing – as a direct impression on the mind.

(2) Possibility does not concern itself with Existence questions; even so, this reality makes a difference. It is anything which is or which is not. Peirce is absolutely clear regarding the irreducibility of a reality outside the mind, which defines 'as that which holds its characters on such a tenure that it makes not the slightest difference what any man or men may have *thought* them to be, or ever will have *thought* them to be, here using thought to include, imagining, opining and willing (as long as forcible *means* are not used); but the real thing's characters will remain absolutely untouched' (6.495, 1906).[51]

Now, if there is one instance when a sophisticated theory of reality – not ontology but as based on Categories – is crucial in film theory debates, it is regarding the ostensible binarism of semiological film theory. Already at this stage we can see that such binarism cannot be reconciled with any theory that accounts for a true dyadic opposition between the dissimilar. The differential system of semiological meaning and signs is not the difference made by a fact or not-fact, as it would be if it were a true dyadic relation. As we shall see, the difference, there, is among the same – that is, among positional values organized in a homogeneous space. In other words, in a logical context of terms (or classes), the same can only be subjected to the abstraction of the discrimination type, not prescission and not dissociation (cf. *supra* 63). This suggests that the concept of sign in Semiology and Semiotic is completely univocal, because it is developed from completely different metaphysical bases. For our film theoretical debate, it will not be wise for us to confine ourselves to ramifications and deductions such as the two sign theories, or different pragmatics, or what Peirce called 'applied metaphysics' (cf. 6.555, 1887). In that debate, one would encounter no reasonable choices, only arbitrary options to 'use' one theory instead of another, or – what is even worse – a false friendship of similarity enabled by a profound misunderstanding. Such an eirenic hodgepodge is unwarranted in theory, even though there have been many attempts at a pan-semiotic merger. Semiotic and film theoretical statements must be justifiable on a firm foundation, *not* on univocality. Only then can such statements be compared to the ontological (Deleuze would say *transcendental*) assumptions of structuralist semiology.[52]

In semiological film theories, homological difference is assigned the primary position over dyadic identity. The rest – binarism, system, homology, conversion and substitution – necessarily follows. The peculiar reality theory of pure nominalist non-reality is mostly not reflected or otherwise justified, least of all as simple empirical, observable facts.[53]

(3) The third Reality appears also in a different truth claim, one that

is similar to the so-called coherence theory of truth. Its explicit description is the Pragmatic Maxim. The Reality of Thirds is specifically responsible for the potential of mediation understood as general truth. Therefore, it is also immediately related to the problem of the generality of truth. Peirce's non-aprioristic approach makes it necessary to draw the metaphysical conclusions from this necessary mode of human cognition. It is not superadditional or redundant – as Oehler (1981b) suggests – to spell out these truth conditions in a metaphysical theory, which in his later works Peirce called Synechism. In its best and most comprehensive understanding, Pragmatism is unthinkable without such a basis. However, Peirce's philosophical system – in particular and increasingly his late system – is so much a profusion of Thirdness that it comprehends the mathematical theory of Continuum as much as the Pragmatistic 'unlimited community of researchers.'

Realism – that is, trimodal realism – is not an elegant solution nor is it easier to accomplish than with fewer than three modes, since the burden of proof for modality, the proof for Pragmaticism, is immense. Before he felt compelled to abandon it, Peirce himself saw nominalism as the easier way. In a letter to James (13 March 1897), he wrote: 'This justifies giving nominalism a fair trial before you go on to realism; because it is a simple theory which if it don't [sic! doesn't (8.251)] work will have afforded indications of what kind of realism ought to be considered' (Peirce 1992a: 10). This explains his long struggle with the matter (which leads easily to discarding this with 'a skepticism about the clarity and precision of the positions taken by Peirce's writings' (Bordwell 1996: 106n6). As we have seen, however, it is the very concept of Representation or Sign – the only mode of cognition – that calls for a metaphysic of three modes of being.[54] The semiotic transformation meant also that at any moment we 'are' already in a very immediate sense of the word 'in thought' or 'a train of thought' (W1,494). There is no question that there follows as a consequence the radical temporalization of true cognition.

The mode of being of Thirds may be a little difficult to become accustomed to – except for inveterate Hegelians – because it cannot be grasped in a static way. Conversely, what does being-dynamically mean? The foremost among the cognitive consequences is that this being is no longer cognitively attainable, whereas a factual being is completely determined. The spiritual nature of Thirds allows cognitive behaviour to attain only sectors, never the complete being. It translates into a spiritual restlessness of perduring unlimited processes of interpretation. The cognitive grasp of Thirds is therefore intrinsically sectorial, but also cognizable in its totality. This is why we must be 'in thought' – in order to obtain new insights from a never totally determined general in a continuous chain of interpretations. What kind of Reality then, must correspond to such a mode of cognition? One does not cognize innumerable singular facts but something genuinely different. Facts are brought into one series and augmented with all possible facts of the same kind. Logically this is a case of hypostatic abstraction, as we have seen; that said, the other two kinds of abstraction are based on the same metaphysical Reality of Thirdness.

Perhaps the reality of a human being itself is the best illustration of the Reality of Thirdness. It is a locus of 'ongoing thought' not only in the psychological sense but also in the logical and metaphysical sense. This is the meaning of recognizing and treating 'man as a sign.' If thinking is an ongoing process, kept alive by thought itself, its Reality basis is particular and different from factual Reality. Thought is always a comparison between something past and general and something actual. It follows that it can only be one single interconnecting process of inferences. It is this requirement of logic or semiotic that necessitates an astonishing conclusion: Man himself is a sign ('a word' W1,495), because he participates in thought. He shares the symbolic nature of every other sign: 'A man denotes whatever is the object of his attention at the moment; he connotes whatever he knows or feels of this object, and is the incarnation of this form or intelligible species; his interpretant is the future of memory of this cognition, his future self, or the other person he addresses, or a sentence he writes, or a child he gets. In what does the identity of man consist ...?' This is a step away from all kinds of receptacle theories of a mind at the receiving end of its other, the world. Furthermore: 'But are we shut up in a box of flesh and blood? When I communicate my thoughts and my sentiments to a friend with whom I am in full sympathy, so that my feelings pass into him and I am conscious of what he feels, do I not live in his brain as well as in my own – most literally?' (W1,488). We are in symbols, literally and as rational social beings. As a consequence, everyone is a particularization of Us, a general soul.[55] Peirce did not arrive at this point through Idealist speculation, nor is there any vitalism involved in the argumentation. Compared to present-day philosophical problems of mind–body relationship, Peirce's is indeed an astonishing solution. For him, a separation of these two worlds would be utterly devoid of meaning: How could anyone *know*, if the other world were not connected? The 'semiotic turn' follows from thinking itself.

As early as the Lowell lectures, the New List, and the rest of a series of articles in the *Journal of Speculative Philosophy* (1868ff), it is apparent how Peirce thought the relationship between human mind and the necessary form of thinking in general (i.e., logic). The individual mind is merely a representation of the more general form. When there are two consecutive states of mind, the relation between them represents the abstract form. This allows us to substitute mental states with the form in each one of them, feelings with syllogism. However, in mental events the general form is the form of a sign relation. This explains the magic of the process of thought. In an expanding cognition, conclusions are not deductions (which would add nothing new to a thought). Abductional thinking is guessing; or, as Peirce would say later, there must be genuine chance in thought wherever it advances (cf. Richter 1995). Thoughts thus become fortuitous; nevertheless, they must reach their goal without knowing it *a priori*. The guarantee is not 'a higher form of chance'; rather, it is the presence of the form of 'certain relations' between mental events in the form of sign relations. Consequently, man must be given to himself as a sign: his thoughts as much as his feelings and his actual existence before objects.

The truth of cognition in signs is grounded in the Reality of Thirdness. Cognition in signs – even cinematic signs – is therefore not a *minus malum* when direct cognition is impossible. The Cartesian intuition of immediate 'Data' (cf. Ricoeur [1990] on the origin of Descartes's Doubt) is as much a phantasm of unadulterated, factual truth as the suggestion of arbitrary, 'hypothetical' models of data interpretation is a misconception of the nature of generality.

The infinity of the Reality of Thirdness can be expressed in various aspects. (1) The dynamism of being a Third is reflected in Peirce's evolutionism. (2) Furthermore, as development of truth it has a social implication; as 'logical socialism' it has been praised in this, the heyday of modern Pragmatism (cf. Wartenberg 1971). (3) Being and Society are ultimately held together by the very important mathematical theory of Continuity. However concrete and contingent it may be, cognition is ultimately true, not in its contingent historical subsistence but rather in a quasi-transcendental 'infinite community of investigators' (cf. W2, 271f), who form an 'ultimate opinion' (5.609, 1902) this is true 'in the long run' (Peirce 1998: 298, Syllabus 1903). Hope is an 'irrational' element in the context of a 'rationalization' process. Yet Peirce deemed it a necessary (i.e., logical), ethical, religious, and existential presupposition of all inquiry.[56] In particular, it is necessitated 'in the long run' by the assumption of a real inferential process as leading to truth. Hope is not simply the psychological underpinning of inquiry as a human act; it is an integral part of inquiry itself as a coming-to-cognition of the Real. Therefore, it needs a metaphysical foundation, since being observable directly as object is excluded.

How, then, can one prove that inductive inferences (including the inductive elements of abduction) will lead to truth? Peirce's doctrine of Synechism explicitly addresses this question. He first developed his answer in a systematic manner in the 1891–3 *Monist* articles, even though he discovered its central ideas much earlier. This doctrine is perfectly illustrated in the sign process itself, since any ordinal, iterative, triadic relation is as infinitesimally open at its lower end as at its upper end. Thus, a sign can be decomposed into all its antecedent Semioses (if such a need arises). This is why the first correlate of a sign ('knowing which I know something more,' cf. *infra*) can be called a sign again. In this way any knowledge participates in all other knowledge and can be traced back to experiences, be they direct or stored in language. At the upper, third position of Interpretant there is another infinitesimal process of progress (albeit not a direct one) in cognition. There are only adequate *opinions*, open to better understanding. The telos of 'better,' as a comparative word, is Synechistic awareness.

The Reality of Thirds is thus semiotically bound into the Reality of Firsts, as the lower end of semiosis. Cognition at that end cannot be grounded in the metaphysic of a final state. It must not be arguments but rather a kind of immediate insight, it must not be hope but rather aesthetic. Otherwise what it proves would be presupposed, a petition of principle. This insight constitutes a diagram: truth at this end involves us in thinking 'diagrammatically.' In real investigation we first expressly forgo Thirdness. In order to discover something new, we must introduce chaos into order (cf. Kevelson 1987; 1993). The material is manipulated 'preconceptually,' in thoughtful play and experimental thinking. As a 'method of discovery' in general, this new principle of investigative creativity is of vital importance. In cinema – especially in its aesthetic processes of discovery – diagrammatic thinking is the very foundation.

Such new disorder in intellectual play is essential at any stage of thinking. The human mind can somehow make out diagrammatic forms in the midst of disorder. If this is not a wild guess or an audacious factual claim, it must be explainable in both empirical and metaphysical terms. Peirce found the missing link between time and truth exactly in Continuity (cf. *infra*). For now it must be enough that we see in this play an indirect demonstration of the universality of Categories. Mental play indicates that cognition develops when it discovers hidden rationality through mental experimentation. It contains three elements: (1) the actually felt, (2) as much as the diagrammatical analysis of iconic and rhematic forms, (3) not just in the 'actually felt,' but from a general purview. Evidently, the danger of Platonism looms – pure ideas might be intuited. As an empiricist, Peirce would not admit that the deployment of Reason could simply be presupposed. Reason must still be mediated by a Subject that actually carries out the abstraction of the Form. The final Forms, Categories, are not pure forms, but they are still applied to representation.[57] Actual, lived representation produces formal representation as its own necessity. Only in this way can it become the object of metaphysical speculation. Without actual semiosis there can be no forms of Reason. Any deployment is that of representation and not that of pure Reason.

The *explanandum*, then, is the actual deployment of Reason in cognition along the sign relation. This is tantamount to asking, 'What brings truth into cognition?' Very aptly, this can be demonstrated by the various types of relations in the Categories (still as Phaneroscopy), when we apply them to cognition (Peirce's Critique) and draw the most general conclusions (Metaphysic).

(1) Initially, it is assumed that there is a complete 'unrelatedness' (i.e., to truth). No one can have knowledge of this stage, because we only know the related. Even so, this stage must be admitted as a limit stage of pure indeterminacy, pure chance. Being is in itself, or is the pure Potentiality of all being-possible and immediate and unrelated to other being? Peirce felt the need to defend real pure chance against all determinists. Possibility is real possibility. One can imagine this as a parallel universe (or, say, 'possible worlds') containing all that is possible[58] (but that is only a metaphor). Instead, a real possibility is by definition vague, not something (i.e., determinate). Therefore, it is unimaginable unless one takes the creative process of invention as precisely the imagination of the Possible. From there the reality of Firsts – a realm of the Possible, as a given (cf. Kevelson 1993) – follows. There is really an unexplained state.[59] Possibility is the possibility of becoming cognized. Pure chance still leads to pure Secondness, the existence of which cannot be denied.

(2) In order for Reason to progress, there must be a means of getting order out of disorder. From pure chance, tendencies appear under appropriate circumstances. This augmentation in order implies, in

relational terms, that something interacts with another or at least is related to another. At the stage of tendency, there is merely habit or an imbalance in disorder. It may be temporal, or it may be stabilizing itself. Something reacting to something else is pure Factuality, or Categorically a Second. There is no reason needed for that, as it were. Order, which is of an entirely different nature, will never result from chance and habits or tendencies. Statistics never produces laws.

(3) Order implies Reason. Only at this point must difficulties arise, for real order requires a plan or an orientation. Evolution can be claimed to 'evolve' only because there is an orientation toward an end. Some have tried to explain evolution as pure chance producing a stable state of affairs. Stochastic models then replace Reason to give a reason that explains why that evolutionary shape is as it is. Peirce, as a scientific evolution theorist, admitted this explanation only for what it is. In metaphysical terms, there is real chance (tychasm), and there are real tendencies (anankasm).

That there is something 'planful,' or that there is an orientation of something to react to something else, must be explained in its own right. Here is the leverage point of a Semiotic-diagrammatical ontology and epistemology. Orientation is principally a Third. As such it must be added to Secondness. One can also say that Reason, being essentially different, must be added beyond the mere brute haecceity of facts. The difficulty in joining mental and mere factual matter must not – as is often implied – be an excuse to reduce one to the other. Correspondingly, pure chance theorists must desist completely from explaining chance, because an explained chance is no longer chance, or it surreptitiously incorporates mental elements. Where is the difficulty? If one observes an unequal distribution of two properties in a population, it is not the fact that there are different properties that has to be explained, but that their distribution is not Gaussian, but selective beyond chance. Thus we have an unlimited number of particularities (pebbles can be yellow, grey, round, big, etc.), but only one generality catches the eye of an observer (e.g., that all grey ones are arranged in [an order of] stripes on a beach). The 'unusualness' of this order becomes an *explanandum* only before a background of chance (i.e., that every other state would be as probable as the one found there).

At this point synechism comes into play. The explanatory power on the basis of particularized elements reaches only as far as a chance state of world, or habit. Therefore, in the first place, a connection of all particular states is needed. This can only take place under a determinate respect. In order for Thirdness to result, the connection must be a real one and objective. Let us assume a time series – that is, particular elements arranged in a temporal sequence. The single, particular event needs no explanation, since this is apprehended easily. Yet seeing this or that as an event implies that it is already recognized as an event of that sort. What allows us to 'draw the line' between temporally distant elements? It cannot be completely past, for instance, but must be 'presently past.' In the case of a mental experiment, it must also be spatially contiguous, because experimenting implies the diagrammatic variation of one form.

Here, Continuity is the decisive point, joining the lower and upper ends of triadic Semiosis. Everything in this theory hinges on the Reality of that connection. Continuity must be real in order to result in something Third. One can understand how Peirce could declare his mathematical proof of continuity and then synechism as 'the keystone of the arch' (8.257, in a letter to W. James, 1897) holding together his entire system. His sharp criticism of James's pragmatism was ultimately that James refused to accept the importance of Continuity. Continuity is indeed the metaphysical proof of the anti-aprioristic yet nonetheless non-arbitrary nature of Pragmaticism, Semiotic, and so on. James' anti-apriorism, however, was unfounded and led him straight into arbitrariness.

Peirce developed his theory of Continuity in four stages.[60] There are two ways to comprehend Continuity. One is based on but not identical to,[61] the infinite divisibility of rational numbers or compactness. Peirce termed this 'Kanticity.' The other, 'Aristotelicity,' is based on the concatenation of limits of distances. It is 'the fact that adjacent parts have their limits in common' (6.164, 1903, *Century Dictionary*, s.v. 'Continuous'). Peirce develops Continuity denying that there are any discrete points in it at all: 'In one sense, then, continuity is totally different from any collection of discrete elements, but in another sense the larger such a collection becomes the more it resembles a continuum.' (Potter 1977: 27). There is no way to describe Continuity in terms of multitude; however, Peirce found a solution in the mode of connection, which must be immediate. Time is not part of that definition, yet it is one of the most important instances of immediate connection: 'Peirce's post-Cantorian definition, then, will depend solely on describing the mode of connection between continuous parts, without reference to the size or 'roominess' of such a whole' (ibid.: 30).

This is the key question: What does Continuity really prove? If these immediate connections are real, it follows that those forms, on which mental experimentation in diagrammatic thought turns, can really be thought. In our example of time, only form lets us see events of the Same. Forms must *be*, then, in order to be thinkable. Mentally varying such forms introduces Thirdness into Secondness, Mind into Chance. Connectedness can be temporal or spatial, provided it is immediate. Through this thought's happening, an ontological change of modality takes place, from Secondness to Thirdness. Chance and Facticity (haecceity) are actually connected through the Mind. This tells us how Peirce could interpret Continuity in a metaphysical key. It is a grave error to interpret this vital concept as merely a model of arbitrary arrangement, wherein the proper cause for what is ordered is in the objects. Yet such a figure of thought is quite common today. For instance, one of the most thorough theorists of structuralism, Petitot-Cocorda (1985a), finds himself confronted with almost the same problem as Peirce. He requires an objective foundation to the pure form of structure.[62] By virtue of being Continuous, the ordering of unorder mediating orientation takes place. Continuity can assume different versions. If seen in terms of consciousness, Continuity is time consciousness. As soon as there is time, particularized events are connected into a logic. However, this logic is not contained in the particularities, which are just themselves. Logic enters them only through that connection. As a consequence, there is a continuity of Ideas, psychologically expressed as 'attention.' Peirce's 'Law of Mind' is precisely that – one idea seizes another, one idea begets another, one idea, already connecting Firstness and Secondness, leads to the next.

How, then, does this evolution take place? Pure chance and the formation of habits were dealt with earlier. Now the 'occult property' from mental experimentation emerges – it 'comes to light,' as it were. The mind has before its eyes resemblances, which it associates on the basis of the 'occult substratum of thought' (7.394, 1893). In the final account, it is the reality of Continuity that necessitates thinking about an isomorphism of Nature and Mind. Mind and Matter are merely two perspectives of the same; Continuity is also a continuity of matter and mind. A 'law of nature' is not a mental model applied to disparate data; in Peirce's mind, it is the Spiritual in Nature. Nature is itself an Argument, a law functioning according to its premises. Semiotic Iconicity is then the Icon of the logic of nature, the presupposition that both argumentations can eventually coincide ('in the long run'). 'These premisses of Nature, however, though they are not the *perceptual facts* that are premisses to us, nevertheless must resemble them in being premisses.' (5.119, 1903).

When we return to the crucial cinematic problem of time, what Continuity means for cinema becomes quite evident. The lack of a proper theory of time has led many to fill the gap with narrativity and its intrinsic second-order-time, temporality. As a consequence, film theory has been at a loss as soon as there is no narration in film or to the degree that the narration is loosely knit. Some have resorted to the temporality of enunciation as a substitute or replacement of true (i.e., narrative) temporality. As an instance of last resort, this can always pragmatically provide a (teleo-)logic of action. Yet it should be clear that this sort of temporality is derived exclusively from the teleology of human action, and that technically it is a practical syllogism. Certainly this argumentation is not wrong; it is merely not at the level where time is indeed born. Narration is a highly advanced and complex cultural product. It is also a reflection of empirical societies, which recognize certain causalities as their own and refute others as illogical.

A cinematic work of art that wants to play on the very time register will not make use of narrativity. Instead, it must search for the order of an un-order. As the concept of Continuity suggests, the question as to which parts are brought into continuity is still left open. It could very well be the case that time is born with an aesthetic sibling. However, it is extremely difficult to use concepts of language for this process, which can only reflect the result. Now, the result itself is aesthetically open, and there can be more than one. It could also be the case that the process never does end. Of the very greatest works of musical art, it has often been said that they are never really 'exhausted' or known. Why should cinema be less inspiring? If we take the example of the 1994 Olmi film *Genesi: dalla creazione al diluvio*, we are reminded of cinema's potential to manipulate time proper genetically. If this film had not achieved the creation of time, its other content would be quite shallow. Interestingly, it creates time *and* temporality, but each by different means.

Cinematic time is only a very instructive example of how a certain cognition in signs is rooted in a perfect interplay of trimodal Reality. It could not be fully understood if less than three modes of being were acknowledged. It does not strictly appeal to evolutionary metaphysic or to mathematical Continuity, and time is not even specific to cinema. In the end, metaphysic is not all, but only a basis for grounding the sign process. On such a basis only, signs become a rich and complex matter, not just those impoverished placeholders 'standing for' some-thing else, and not a playful yet irrelevant orgy of 'connotational' cross-references called 'interpretation.' It is now clear in which sense signs partake in an unending process. The thesis was that all of this is not an ideal vantage point (i.e., of a transcendental communication process); rather, it must be observable at any moment in thought, and indeed it is forced upon us in cinema as soon as we comprehend more than just narration.

2 Semiotic and Its Practical Use for Cinema

Now we are finally in a position to use the full richness of Peirce's concept of Sign. We started in the previous chapter with a somewhat cryptic and apodictic statement – warranted by common obvious misunderstandings – that a Sign 'is' not something; rather, whatever is something is a Sign. The reason for this lies in trimodal Reality with its logical form of the triadic relationship, as expounded earlier. Once it is attained, this level of comprehension indicates the inadequacy – or univocality – of sign 'definitions' that make it one thing among others. It is not unfair to these sign theories to emphasize that they are grounded in completely different ontologies. This explains, for instance, the subaltern placement of signs (sign, image, and symbol) in the hermeneutical–phenomenological–existential theory framework.[1] The 'first reality' is clearly the intentional act of the subject, and only on this intentional horizon do signs acquire certain bridging functions toward the alter ego. The ontological root of the differential system of signification in semiology has already been mentioned, and will be discussed in detail (cf. *infra*). However, semiology is not even a classification of signs; rather, it is a taxonomy that assigns differences and identities to 'units' called signifiers and signifieds. As pure difference, signs 'are' exactly what is left over from what they 'are not.' The only analogy to this sort of being is meaning as a Cartesian space of whatever dimension. The absurdity appears when this analogy is applied to semantic or lexical units. Here the model functions only by presupposing a hidden generalization. Sememes are decomposed into more general semes, and generality is contained in the compositional semic units. Where this (and not another) generality comes from remains mysterious, or a sort of *ad hoc* operation.

The Semiotic sign concept is totally different. Here, representation is a mode of being, and only because it is this triadic mode of being are signs classified. This is of crucial importance for cinema; as we shall see, many more specific problems in film theory can be addressed from this basis. In this regard, one might say hyperbolically that there 'are' no signs; there 'are' no iconic signs, because iconic sign is not a discriminating concept. It is really a non-differentiating concept (not in the sense of Peirce's 'discrimination'), which applies to nothing in the world. Everything is (contains being) also iconic, so we must apply various procedures of abstraction to the whole of being if we are to distinguish Categorial dimensions, which then become modes of being.

Leading up to a Semiotic sign theory were pragmatic, normative, categorial, logical, relational, and finally metaphysical considerations; all of these remain constituents for the sign concept. Without this, straightforward talk about signs (as if they were things) is easily misunderstood, including a supposed sign nature of cinema and the Eco-esque theme of signs begetting signs through endless interpretation. Yet in the full breadth of Peircean thought, 'chance begets order' (6.297, January 1893). If Short (1981: 372) – certainly correctly – writes about the Reality of an evolutionary telos in Peirce, this also has something to do with signs, which have no autonomous function. Their interpretation is subject to an extrinsic telos, which is both an evolutionary Reality and a Category. The contrast with the semiological, and its Hjelmslev-inspired neo-hylomorphist, metaphysic is rather stark.

The Peircean concept of Sign makes sense (quite literally) on the basis of three distinct modes of being that it brings into a relationship. This is a crucial element of a universe (and all possible worlds), which without it would disintegrate into three different worlds. This would lead toward Habermas's dilemma with the three worlds theory, which he adopted from Popper. The three worlds are recognized as idealizations generated by different locutionary forces. It is only the lifeworld context that brings them together, although in theory it remains unclear how they relate to one another. The corresponding three validities of three discourses or critiques (to which suddenly another two can be added) have no logical connection, but only factual coexistence in language (cf. Habermas 1981: 45). The fundamental insight into cognitive differences of nature thus remains obfuscated by a lack of depth in the logical analysis of those natures. It is – as we have seen – the logic of relations in Peirce's Semiotic that makes every single sign a mediation of three modes of being.

Unfortunately, for most film theorists Semiotic in its richest sense is a closed book. The lack of understanding of the very problem can be seen as the chief reason for misunderstanding and also ignoring the solution that Semiotic offers. Most underlying ontologies – which can never be avoided, only suppressed and presupposed as common sense – are too simple and do not offer the complexity that is necessary for comprehending the sophistication of cinematic meaning (I have already illustrated the sophisticated temporality of cinema). As long as there is only one reality, the cognitive mediation of three realities loses all its charm and looks like overkill or redundancy. Then come the 'schemata' and 'devices,' which must provide the unity of the manifold, from bottom up or top down, and it is impossible to comprehend why, when bottom up or when top down (except that – not why – it is once this and another time that). However, it is also true that the Peircean Sign concept has proved itself highly appealing to the most sophisticated film theory in contemporary debate – Deleuze's.

Being as being-Sign – Peirce's unique solution to a fundamental philosophical problem of cognition and being – becomes a tangible achievement when applied to a complex problem such as cinema. Semiotic concerns the very subject matter of film theory. In fact, the concerns of film theory should not be limited artificially to whatever one is convinced is the specificity of cinema. In fact, the scope of film theory suffers from such impositions. Cinema is thereby reduced to analogy, it is (seen as) analogous to syntax, prose, poetic, literary style, perception, language, psyche, or dreams. It would be a profound misunderstanding to include in this list, as a further analogon, cinema 'as' Sign. Like everything else, cinema is, of course, Sign, but this is not interesting. *How* it is Sign, however, is interesting, because this involves a dynamic process of mediation, rather than film as some static object. Being-cinema, therefore, is a particular way of becoming/being-meaning. Semiotic is merely a particular way of thinking theoretically, in various ways, the trirelational process of becoming meaning. It allows the address of the single elements – correlates – in their proper regard/function within the process as a whole. Thus, it is possible to investigate the sign form in itself, the more-than-just-itselfness of something when it transcends its own whatness to become a more-than-itself ('knowing which we know something more' as Peirce wrote to Lady Welby). One discovers the complexity of such a form-of-'moreness,' and this is especially fruitful when we set out to comprehend the genesis of cinematic meaning. Cinema is patently not a monotonous form; it spreads itself out over the entire gamut of signification. Also, one discovers – in the reach of cinema – a complex approach to relating to existent otherness, one that is not 'checked off' with canonical reference to the documentary potential of film. Given cinema's complex form, one can expect a similarly nuance-rich manner of making available the outwardly resistant real. At the conclusion of this relational process, one discovers all of this richness as meaning – complex, subtle, and diversified. This does not mean that cinema can become all possible kinds of meaning. Certain mediations are not feasible owing to the nature of the cinematic sign form, and this is also significant. Even a superficial glance at cinema tells us that no really theoretical meaning can be achieved, in spite of certain sequences in the filmography of Rohmer (the Kant 'lectures' in *Contes d'hiver*, for instance) and Godard.

This sketches some approaches to investigating cinema in a Semiotic theory perspective, through which novel insights into film are possible. There is one advantage to the very broad philosophical context of Peirce: the Semiotic of aspects of the cinematic sign process can be undertaken as logical (what follows from the sign nature of cognized being?) as well as pragmatic investigations. Sign theory or pragmatics, then, is not an exclusive alternative; rather, it shows two sides of the same phenomenon. However, this is precluded when we embrace impoverished versions of Semiotic – for instance, as a decontextualized set of sign classes: the notorious three sign classes of icon, index, and symbol. The 'infrastructure' leading up to Semiotic is from the start essential and non-rescindable. As early as 1865 (W1,303), Peirce saw ('Semiotic is the science of representations') three types of representations: analogues (Imitation), marks (Signification), and symbols (cf. W1,322). A mark is equated with a denotatum,[2] whereas connotates are analogues because of similarities between the representation and that for which it stands. Symbols 'denote with connotation' (W1,308) and thus are actually what would soon afterwards be named a sign. In the mature Peirce the horizon for the 'science of representations' ranges from normative sciences to Evolutionary Metaphysic, but the Semiotic core remains. Semiotic has never been a simple matter of codes. Any debate or comparison with alternative film theories on that basis would be a sterile exercise. Conversely, Semiotic in its fullest sense bespeaks many hidden 'metaphysical' assumptions of current film theories. Therefore, we can and will come back to the pragmatic context of cinema, having fully integrated it[3] with representation.

2.1 Cinema 'Is' a Class of Sign

Sign classification describes all cognition, both possible and actual. This sweeping statement is not a factual one – as if anyone could have cognizance of the entire collection of past and even future thoughts. It is based on an understanding of what cognition is *in se* – one might call it a form or blueprint. It is thus entirely different from a Toulmin-analogous description of all sorts of 'natural' argumentation (which corresponds to projects of action feasible in a certain culture). It differs also from thought, as it can be produced by the potential of a language, its lexicon and grammar, and of course also by a meta-physical (in the classical sense of the term) speculation. Semiotic claims cognition and thought in general and describes it formally. 'Speculative Grammar'[4] investigates the horizon of everything that it is possible to think and say, the result being a classification of signs. Since we have already investigated the underpinnings of the possibility of such an endeavour, let us now turn to the classification itself, its meaning and its import for cinema.

As we know from our previous discussion of Categories, the formal idea is simple and radical. Three elements make up each act of thought, cognition, or other content of consciousness: (3) It has a purely rational 'grasp' of something General (this is just an *ens rationis* and needs neither to exist nor to be a mark of quality). (2) It has an existential vis-à-vis of some kind. Thus it is impossible to think what is not, was not, will not be, will not be possible. (1) It has a 'content' – that is, we always think 'something.' As soon as a thought takes place, these three elements are related and are one, and this unity of triadic relation is called a Sign. Generally speaking, and when there is no category mistake, we can define a Sign formally, in Categorical terms: as a perfect instance of a Third, a Sign's function is to bring a First into relation with a Second. This possibly cryptic formal description constitutes our next topic.

Another topic: It is the essential function of a sign to 'render inefficient relations efficient' (SS31). This rather inconspicuous remark effectively signals the whole advantage of Semiotic over, for example, Onto-Semanticism and early analytical philosophy (cf. Eley 1973). Peirce does not deny that there is the relation of Secondness between a Relate and a Correlate; thus, 'this hammer is black' is either true, if there is a relation of existence, or false, if not. However, cognition is more. In fact, such a relation is inefficient as long as it is not 'known' by Thirdness, by/as a Law: 'A sign is something by knowing which we know something more.' (SS31f). Thus, not by making a dyadic relation effective, but rather by making it efficient through a rule, we are making it a habit of conduct, according to which it can be acted eventually. The anodyne formal definition of the Sign relation, above, brings us radically into opposition with onto-semantic, 'constructivist,' 'cognitivist' accounts of cinematic representation, and also with the differential systems of signification. 'Signification' is not an autarchic nor autarkical domain; quite the contrary, it depends on the relation to an Object (opposing semiology) and to an Interpretant (opposing 'constructivism').

Peirce defines a sign as an 'object which is in relation to its object on the one hand and to an interpretant on the other ...' (SS32). This is seen 'from below,' where something is taken to be the basis of a further semiosis. Usually this object is taken as 'feeling,' which need not be the psychological state normally referred to by this term. Any state that adds a grain of chance will do. Also, a former concept can augment its chance part and thus become more insecure or problematic. Quite appropriately one can speak of qualities of feeling, since chance in a concept makes that concept less an instance of a rule. Yet the definition continues: '... in such a way as to bring the interpretant into a relation to the object corresponding to its own relation to the object.' The meaning of this addition is that the object must be the same for Interpretant and sign. Changing 'subject' is forbidden. One might remark a different thing on a physically identical object (here is an application of that differentiation between Dynamic and Immediate Objects). However, in this case it would be a different Immediate Object and not an augmentation of cognition of the same one. For instance, a physician might listen to beautiful oratory, the artifice of a consummate speaker, yet come to the conclusion that the speaker suffers from a bad cold; here, these would be two separate Immediate Objects, two signs.

First presupposition: We can discern here the *external nature of meaning* in Semiotic. Without externality, signs cannot be classified, because only an interpretational reference to one object makes a triadic structure necessary. Moreover, because of the ordinal, iterative essence of triadicity, triadic sign relations cannot be simple, but only (classes of) different triadic relational complexities. The significance of this variation in relational complexities is that they are general forms of thought, and this is the Real. The external Object is not simply there as the Other of a semantic unit. Its triadic being-there is full of consequences, as we know; but if triadicity is in itself complex, the Semiotic structure of Reality itself means that 'modal ontology' really is but one fundamental division of signs. Yet Reality is indeed modal, not merely existential as in dyadic relations. Categories are necessary really in their totality, as we have seen, and their number is exhaustive. It follows that if signs are triadic relations they follow the ordinal, iterative essence of Categories. If Signs (Reality) are relational, we have a principle of specification in them – that is, in the different complexity of the Correlates. An extension of sign classes has been presented by Spinks (1991) – albeit to the limits of the reasonable and reasonably verifiable, given that the entire purpose of formal reasoning is to reduce the number of forms of unification of the manifold (cf. Sanders 1970; Marty 1990).

Second presupposition: What does classifying signs mean, if everything in Semiotic Reality follows the meandering paths of logic, which is a necessary form of thought?[5] If being is being-related,[6] then any meaning-creating change in the relatable is determined by relational, Categorical means only. The science of interpretational triadic relation, Logic, is part of unified Reality. Sign is the expression of this union as it 'contains' mentality in its relation (First) and its existent Other (Second) with the purpose of bringing it to truth, making it a habit or law (Third). The organizing principle of sign classification is itself an application of Categorical triadicity in its *ordinality and iterativity*.

Third presupposition: We are now in a position to measure the consequences of another presupposition of a classification of signs. Iterativity, as a Categorical specification principle, entails a new possibility: there are *also non-cognitive relations*, non-Thirds, which can and must become effective. Every sign/being is an Interpretational relation to the same Object, external meaning. It is not a purely internal triadic relation (this is the difference between the logic of relations and Semiotic, the 'Philosophy of representation' (1.539, 1903). If it were all knowledge, such a world of signs could remain entirely internal, close to Eco's 'encyclopaedia,' in which everything interprets everything else. This needs no real external Object, as it consists only of perfect Thirds (what might be called the 'canonical sign,' that is, it is 'genuine'). If symbols 'grow,' if signs 'degenerate,' this means that a kind of relational 'valency' other than Thirdness becomes effective (in a complex way, as we will examine in the classification). Thus the formally, Categorically reduced abstract world suddenly becomes highly complex and concrete. We have radically different objects of cognition resulting from different types of cognitive relations. This encompasses world-not-unified-in-knowledge, but accessed from its Categorical unification base as different worlds (more radically than in Popper's 'three worlds'). Peirce himself classified sciences (those known in his time) according to these relation differences; each one is a different world presupposing only worlds Categorically above it in the ordinal ('hierarchical') order of Categories.

Fourth presupposition: This leads to another element that makes sign classification necessary: *'worlds' are really grades of complexity*. Peirce's logic of relations also circumscribes the various complexities of each element in a triadic relation. Depending on how many levels of complexity one takes into account, the tally of sign classes differs. It should not be surprising that the number of classes varies in the two better elaborated classifications – the Syllabus and the letter to Lady Welby. This is even more striking in that Peirce adds in a postscript to the letter the other classification – that of the Syllabus. The latter is less detailed (ten classes in three dichotomies) than the one developed in the letter itself (sixty-six classes in ten trichotomies),[7] which is not even fully spelled out (the tally of Spinks [1991] arrives at astronomical numbers, *ad libitum*). Not only that, but it is also based on different specifications, which makes their reconciliation seem impossible, as the Welby letter takes other, additional aspects into account. Since any specification can only be through Categories, classification proceeds by trichotomies that follow an iterative order.

One has to get used to Signs as classes; however, this that does not mean that they are counter-intuitive constructs. Whatever stands before one's eyes is a sign; we see only signs. Seeing, cognizing, means that a Sign operation has come to a term. One can cognize not only states of affairs but also ranges of possibilities and – the death of all possibility – strict necessities. A reflection of this diversity of one's cognition has led to the Categories and so on. Such a diversity, however, can also be tied to the materiality of the Sign itself, in the sense that what one cognizes is first determined by what the Sign as material essence empowers cognition to achieve. Empowerment must be understood in the broadest possible sense, not as a scale. Certain Signs do not allow one to recognize a fact,[8] others do not allow necessary insights. One could also say – oblivious to the distinct Sign materiality – that different 'worlds' (stretching the word) appear before the eyes of our mind. Yet since it is the Sign that operates such appearances of something, it is certainly more appropriate to take the Sign's nature seriously.

The first and basic trichotomy is the triadic Sign Relation itself. The following trichotomies specify the first by applying the Categories at three levels (two, after the basic trichotomy). Because of the different complexity of the different correlates in the Sign triad, the yield is ten classes (one class from monadic Firstness, three classes from dyadic Secondness, six classes from triadic Thirdness). This is schematically speaking, as the principal is a rather formal one (this will be discussed in detail shortly). It is, however, not so mechanical that classes are simply calculated with the trinomial equation $(a + b + c)^3$. Signs are recursive applications of the Categorical Relations, which were obtained through precisional abstraction (v. *supra* 63). It is also important to keep Peirce's classificatory efforts before and after 1903 separate. For instance, following Lieb's annex (SS160) – which refers to the years after 1903 – the number of classes can increase when we take into account the relational complexity of each correlate. This yields 10 trichotomies with 28 classes of signs, which is the remainder of the theoretical 729 classes, eliminating impossibilities of determination (mentioned in SS84) – that is, only lower-order Categories can determine higher ones. When Lieb adds another four trichotomies, his yield is 59,049 classes, of which only sixty-six are possible. What explains this apparent confusion in such an important matter? Apart from Peirce's ('backwoodsman') groundbreaking but evolving attempts, his commentators are excused by the scant and lacunary availability of important manuscripts on the topic of Signs. Peirce's principles of classification remain consistent over time – that is, they always entail multiple recursive application of the Categories – but the labels he gives to each resulting type differ throughout his many tables. Increasingly intense reflection resulted in a shift from the pure formal description toward a stronger concern from the order of actual reasoning.[9]

Yet trichotomies are not equal; each is different in nature from the others. There are two basic approaches to describing those classifying trichotomies: one starting from relates, and an other starting with relations (cf. Pape 1990: 46–52). When we take the relates considered in themselves (as below), we arrive at the first classification. Taking the relation with regard to its logical, Categorical nature yields those aspects that entered into the Welby classification. Yet in Peirce's manuscripts and notebooks, we find a number of further attempts to bring these two classifications together in a way that makes each more complex. This is the price that must be paid for relations less simple than expression-content relations of binary systems – but for relations to 'the same object' with triadic complexity. However, the matter of Sign classes – the formal, necessary forms of thought – is far too important to be left in this state of indecision.

We can clarify the problem of Sign classification by situating it in its actual context, a Relational conception of our experience. The chief 'irritants' arise in experience, where the connection to Sign classification is not so patent. Not surprisingly, this link has been severed in most cases where 'sign classes' have been abused for 'foreign' purposes (not just by Eco's iconism and that of his source, Morris'). Indeed, claims that there are only three elements – no more and as less – in this structure are certainly irritating. 'Why not four or five?' was Bertrand Russell's objection (cf. SS43). Objections such as these have found a mathematical answer – the 'Reduction Thesis' in the context of the logic of relations (cf. *supra*); they can no longer be countered at the level of experience in the only actual world, even less at the level of contingent languages. Thus the reduced number of forms of experience cannot be in doubt. It would be absurd to propose seriously as many forms as there are experiences, because thinking is always reductive ('synthesis'). So the real points of contention can only relate to the number and proof of their exhaustiveness.

This becomes obvious when we look at alternatives (omitting Aristotle's ten and Kant's twelve categories). We already know that in structuralism and semiology, the ultimate form is fundamentally binary, not only between the expression and content planes, but also in the ultimate elements within the planes. This means that every sense (one would not want to speak of experience in a semiological context) is sense *because* it is in a binary form: 'this'/'non-this.' This form can, of course, build up complexity with other binarisms (e.g., paradigmatic/syntagmatic;[10] Greimas's Semiotic Square, which adds binarism of three oppositive relations; generativism). Yet the ultimate form is $p/\neg p$, a dual relation. Only implicitly is there a third element in the all-unifying Whole, the *case vide*, Mana, phallus, zero degree, and so on, which is always present as the basis of homology across binary systems: phonetic with semantic, for example. However, this ultimate element is unequal to the other two ultimate elements – it is 'more ultimate.' So semiology can stay a binary theory because the homology element is ineffective when it comes to producing sense itself. A striking illustration involves the difference between Peirce's and Greimas's analyses of 'giving' ('don'). For Peirce this is a perfect triadic Relation: A gives B to C (cf. *supra*). This is the analytic content of the concept of 'gift' itself. Now, Greimas thinks he can reduce this, *salva veritate*, to '*transfer d'objet*,' expressed in the double formula of disjunction plus conjunction $S_1 \cup O$ plus $O \cap S_2$ (i.e., S_1 loses O plus O is gained by S_2). A dyadic, binary reduction of sense, however, cannot render the triadic operation of giving, which is 'something more' (cf. Peirce's definition of Semiosis). Undoubtedly, 'giving' can 'degenerate' into a dyad, when *only* the exchange is considered. This illustration reminds us how important it is to be certain about the exhaustiveness of the number of ultimate forms of experience. In this regard, Peirce's endeavour in his logic of Relations and theory of Categories cannot be overestimated.

This brief illustration of a Categorial analysis applicable to Signs is warranted in the context of the debate over the nature of cinematic representation. Taking in isolation just 10, 66, or 59,049 sign classes would make the task of opponents too easy, and indeed would miss the point. Compared to such simple accounts for meaning as binary systems or schematism-based theories, the complexity of Peirce's account would seem to be at a disadvantage. But this is not so if the claim to formally describe all kinds of thought is upheld (and not abandoned in favour of merely a 'hypothetical model' explaining some phantasmagorical 'data' from nowhere). In keeping with Peirce's epistemological question, strictly speaking it is not even meaningful to ask, '"What" is a sign?' This question cannot be answered without resorting to signs. However, keeping in the back of one's mind what can be assumed with Phenomenology, Signs 'are' but forms, as triadic Relations they are therefore concretized through Categorical determinations in classes.

We must keep apart the final product from its producing principles, the sign class from trichotomies. Classes are concrete. Trichotomies are Hypothetical Abstractions, when Categories are applied to the base triad of the sign. We describe classes, however, through their constituting trichotomies. What are we doing when we apply Categories recursively? Although this is a purely formal operation – and it is important that it be so – it constitutes sign usage, viz., signs are used as a cognitive relation of external meaning in an object.

Classification has one origin: the fact that every sign is *taken as such*. Conceiving of it as a sort of inventory gives, then, quite the wrong idea. Two questions arise from this approach: (1) What does it mean that we can 'take' Signs? (2) What does it mean that we can 'take' Signs differently? The second question indicates, simply put, that whatever is in front of our eyes is not yet indicative enough to tell 'what' this is, since we can take it such that it 'is' something quite different. Thus, what it is, for which cognition it strives or by which it is constrained, must be determined by precisely that purpose. This 'taking' itself – to consider the first question – does not imply that one is free to take or not to take as Sign. Take-as-Sign means to make sense, and whatever 'is' – even down to the level of perception (cf. *supra*) – already is-meaning. Even though 'take' is an active verb, it should not suggest the power not to take. It merely means that as 'controlled behaviour,' an interpretation in one or the other direction must be willed. As much as the act, as such, is not wilful 'application of a scheme over some data,' neither is the interpretation as process arbitrary; it must follow necessary forms of relations laid down in the Categories, because every Phaneron/being is thus determined. Also, the nature of Categories is such that there can be no new principles, only triadic determinations. Signs must be such complex specifications. Since they are Representations or Interpretations, how they stand before their judge (Peirce's metaphor), whose office it is to interpret, is decisive. This judge makes differences, speaking anthropomorphically. He either has or has not a sheriff – for instance, if a sign has/wants or does not have/want Secondness and Firstness to marshal. Evidently, this changes a sign and its 'cognitive power' decisively. In the negative case, it can only achieve a general cognition (the most abstract knowledge); in the positive case it means for instance external objects as existent. Both cognitions happen, even though a Sign with almost no objective meaning adds very little to cognition. Here we see how crucial it is to understand why and where Categories are applied to the sign relation.

Because it must represent external meaning, every Sign must always be a Relation consisting of three elements. On this basic and decisive fact every trichotomy is built. Usually, what is related is given as 'Sign in itself,' 'Object,' 'Interpretant.' This says no more than that a sign is a triadic relation that has three relates, each with specific valencies (valency as chemical metaphor is the capacity to relate different numbers of arguments into one unity-of-the-manifold). Only in this sense is it meaningful to speak of signs of Firstness (as we say for short throughout this book). The decisive determination of any concrete sign is here; with regard to its cognitive substance, this does not go far beyond the relational Categories themselves (cf. Müller 1994: 137f). The practical value of this base trichotomy is that it shows the event of relating itself in Semiotic-cognitive world appropriation. Thus, in every meaning event we can ('precisionally') abstract three relates, which are integrated iteratively in their being a Sign.

Going back a little in the history of Peirce scholarship in a narrow sense, it cannot be stated that the Sign operation behind the classification has always been fully understood. For this myopia the editors of the Collected Papers (cf. Pape 1989) have been blamed for significantly 'smoothing' Peirce's text precisely on sign classification, contributing an influential, misleading footnote. It did not help that until recently, most of Peirce's important writings on Signs were not published. It is not surprising that one of the major advances in Peirce scholarship has involved the realm of classification, since older books tend to rely mainly on the pioneering (but limiting) investigation of sign classes (i.e., Weiss 1945). This is true even for some of the already mentioned studies of Peirce's Sign classification, which tend to provide heterogeneous and contradictory results. Yet increasingly, we are now cognizant of the relational character of sign triads.

(1) Peirce, as we know, defined Signs as relations by force of logical bounds. This means there is always one and *only one character* supporting this relation (which can also be indicated through Hypostatical Abstraction, for example, 'redness' is the character holding together all things red).

(2) Furthermore, as we know, we 'are in thought.' This thwarts attempts at foundationalism, because every thought is a following thought. *A Sign follows [logically from] a previous Sign*. To maintain this, it is not enough to rely on commonsensical empirical evidence and intuitive belief in its truth; we must also explain by relational logic why this is necessary and what follows from this necessity. In this regard, the triadic Sign relation itself must give evidence of this necessity.

(3) If one character is the logical 'attraction' force in the relation, a further Interpretation – that is, with the same external Object of meaning – has two options. Option I: It must strictly *explicate* what it contains already as a Law. Only then is it 'genuine Thirdness.' (This, however, does not comprise, for instance, a new case of that Law, since if it did, it would add something beyond pure Lawness.)

(4) Option II: There are characters that *accede* to the relation. This is what Peirce calls 'degeneration,' because the Sign must somehow deal with these superadditional character(s). Under either option, the Semiosis continues. What grows ('signs grow') in the case of (3) is a more general generality, and generality, as we know, is a real addition to a direct cognition. Thus, without the interference of the other correlates of existence and quality, mathematical insight 'grows' more and more general. In the case of (4), instead, growth is the new Interpretation of new characters in the relation (of the same object, of course). This latter is chiefly of interest for Sign classification.

Now, if three Categories are the ultimate forms of thought, this accession can only be dealt with through further application of those Categories. So, the next question is this: What does it mean to further apply Categories to the sign relation, and what does this do to that relation? Thus reason for this question is, again, a formal one: if all Phanera are determined by Categories, the nature of the three relates of the sign can only be subject to the same ordinality and iterativity. Taking the instance of an acceding character (4) regarding the same external object, a new Interpretational task arises. At this stage (of cognitive endeavour), all depends on the type of this character, the 'Sign in itself.' There are three possibilities, or grades of complexity, that determine the meaning-to-be ontologically. (Greenlee called these the 'hypostatic' Categories, as opposed to 'factorial' ones, which build on this base determination; however, we can also stay within Peirce's terminology, speaking of 'universal' and 'particular' Categories.) This 'character overhang' – as we might call it – is now in need of unification, which alone will transform it into meaning and 'make something' out of it. Yet what can possibly be made out of it is not *ad libitum*, since it is predetermined by the nature of what will become the first correlate of this new sign. A character that is a monad will prevent its other correlates from being more complex than that. This means that this character of Possibility will, as a sign, relate to a monadic Existence Correlate, possible Existence, and to a monadic Law Correlate, possible Law. In other words, if a sign has in its first correlate a Firstness element, it can only have one of equal complexity in the second and third correlates. It will, for instance, remain 'mental image' (III), pure possibility to exist (II), because it is only a 'tone' (I) in its first correlate, which is 'potentially a sign.' As a basic specification of meaning, only a character that is Possibility or Firstness has an immediate and direct influence on all other Correlates. Other types of character can and must be further determined owing to their internal complexity.

Peirce struggled with the ramifications of Sign determination for much of his life, especially in his mature philosophy. As already noted, 1903 was a threshold year for him on his endeavour of classification. Beginning in that year we see him expanding the original ten Sign classes through the introduction of an additional Categorical principle. The original principle, which led to ten classes of Signs, was based on the fact that the Correlates themselves in the Relation are complexities. The new additional principle takes into consideration the Relation itself. From the base principle, an acceding character becomes Sign ('is cognized') through a three-times application of the Categories. Three times, because of the Representation purpose of the Sign, which can target an external Object only in a triadic Relation. Thus, to achieve this Triad, three Relates must be brought into a Relation. First, the three complexities are applied at the level of the 'Sign in itself,' which is the one concretizing character at the root of the relational effort. Depending on this First complexity, a Semiosis must 'go on' to a Second level, the Object, again applying (three times differently) one, two, or three different complexities. The same is repeated at the level of Interpretant. The triadic Relation is thus made complete.

The significance of the new classifying principle – the Relation itself – appears only at the Second level, where the founding character can also bring into play elements independent of this relation. The second relate is itself a dyad and has therefore a complexity of two. The meaning of this Categorical application is therefore to ascertain, in whatever is in that sign relation, an oppositive aspect. This is one of the aspects that is most intuitive and closest to experience. We do not stay in a sign universe closed in itself; rather, we encounter an outward, brute reality. For this reason alone, it is important that this oppositive dyad have two 'sides'; how exactly these two sides relate is also important. This insight is the root of Peirce's distinction between 'immediate' and 'dynamic.' Similarly, the complexity of the third relate is such that we can see three related elements, whose relations are distinguished as 'immediate,' 'dynamic,' and 'logical.' That which, in a sign, binds with a logical force is certainly different from that which binds by dynamic opposition; however, iterativity means that the latter is comprehended in the former. Again, this insight is not counter-intuitive, since we can easily understand what happens when we know something. It involves more than being confronted with it (Second Correlate), or merely considering it in one's fancy (which is what we do in the First Correlate of the sign).

As already noted, the whole point of this trichotomy is derived from the relation as such. It is not so much a question of a weaker or stronger relational force, but of the kind of force. Here again we see the fundamental importance of Categories (above) and Metaphysic (below the relational achievements of signs). The kind of force is rooted there and permeates all reality. The practical consequences of this trichotomy are the forms of 'degeneracy.' If the relation of a triad is genuine, all three relates are 'effective.' This presupposes that the relation concept, including the valency metaphor, is taken seriously. Thus a Second, if it is effective, is a Dynamic Object ('dO'): a sign, taken in such a way, relates to an actual and independent outside reality as much as to an immediate 'intentional' Object. The question 'Is this stove black?' immediately draws attention to the blackness – not as a General one, however, but as this which I see now in this stove outside-there. As soon as this determination is not meaning-effective, a Second degenerates into that which it immediately is. In the contrary case, we gain additional meaning when the Dynamic Object is distinguished as the point of curiosity and the object of discoveries.

Degeneracy yields even more meaning relevance when Thirdness is in the sign relation. Here a genuine triad is effective when the Normal Interpretant is used. This will be a relationing such that a general (concept) cognizes, from the point of view of a lawful must-be ('necessity'), that here (Second) in this (First) 'mental image of all past experiences'[11] there is a necessity. This First, then, is a sign (in itself) that represents (semantically, etc.) these past experiences.

The basic triad for all sign classes is the triadic relation of the Sign in itself. We might limit ourselves to Peirce's first classification in the Syllabus, the only one he completed (to his temporary satisfaction). Its classificatory terminology, as it stands in the Syllabus, is a Hypostatic Abstraction of Relational events in the Sign. Perhaps it will be easier to understand the significance and additional cognitive value of those abstractions if we first consider their setting. What takes place in a Semiosis? What is the reason for a new Interpretation of a first Sign in a second Sign? Why do characters, regarding the same Object, accede to a previous Sign? It must be understood that Interpretation does not necessarily mean a temporal succession of Signs or, even more cumbersome, a succession of words. Rather, the one Sign itself changes and becomes 'fuller' in meaning.

As an illustration, we could take the Sign (idea) of 'movement.' A little child asks, 'What is movement?' Someone answering this (actually quite difficult) question must then interpret movement. Depending on the interpretation, 'movement' can be a number of 'things.' In itself, movement is clearly an idea based on the regularity of a rule, because no one sees the succession of different states of a thing, but rather its general direction of spatial change. (II) This Sign changes in nature when another character of different complexity accedes to it. Let there be a change of speed of the very same Object; clearly, this event is by nature a Second, because it is no longer a pure rule; rather, an opposite of this precise moment of change is constitutive of the Idea (Hypostatically Abstracted, this is an Index). If this has become a Sign, with an appropriate Interpretant (let it be, Hypostatically Abstracted, a Dicent), and if this is based on the Quality of attention in its First Correlate (Hypostat-ically Abstracted, this is a Sinsign), the result is the Sign 'acceleration'. (I) Our illustration would take an altogether different turn if the acced-ing character were of the nature of a First, a pure Quality, as the sensa-tion typical of merry-go-rounds or roller-coasters (Hypostatically Abstracted, this is a Qualisign). This, too, changes the Sign 'movement' into something that could have an appropriate (Hypostatically Abstracted: Rhematic) Third Correlate in 'frenzy' or 'thrill of speed' (Le Mans feeling). The Second Correlate could only be a degenerate dyad – that is, a character that exists outside and beyond this dyadic relation of Opposite. In specie, here it is not constitutive of the Idea that an event takes place there; it might be just somewhere, or merely a possible there (Hypostatically Abstracted, this is an Icon). Besides, this instance of our illustration is the only sign determination that could not take place in another way, on the basis of the nature of its First Correlate. All other instances admit further determinations, of which we choose one. (III) However, why not change the course of Interpretation into the direction of Law, taking a character into (a) the First Correlate, which is of the complexity of a Third: a Legisign (in Hypostatical Abstraction). Let the acceding character be 'mechanism,' not necessarily as a physical object, but as a concept (plan, mental idea). Now the possibilities are many (six possible classes), but we choose the most general one. This choice means for (b) the Second Correlate that it is a Symbol (in Hypostatical Abstrac-tion) – that is, this character is there by necessity. For a plan it does not matter that it is realized in this or in that place. It could be realized, or remain a 'necessary possibility,' in all Objects that fall into this relation. The Third Correlate (c) could be of any Categorical nature, but we let it be an Argument (always in Hypostatical Abstraction). It is, then, not simply a concept of some mechanism; it is a scientific understanding of an engineering problem in which movements have an important share.

As answers to our questions, these illustrations indicate the reasons behind the Sign process of Interpretation. Every next step is formally less abstract and more concrete, closer to the concreteness of an experi-ence in its triadic structure. Ultimately, of course, the *why* question can only be answered metaphysically as part of the temporal truth process of cognition, a process that ends in an ultimate, adequate opinion. How-ever, as this illustration also shows, this is not merely metaphysical rea-soning – it is the concrete triadic structure of every Sign relation. As such it is open and liable to communicative verification. Since we dealt with this aspect earlier, it needs only a mention here, to keep the relational Sign process in proper perspective. The foundation of all those further metaphysical considerations is, in any case, the cognitive gain due to the Hypostatic Abstraction of the Semiosis, in those famous Trichotomies (which have so often been the object of simplifications).

In this abstraction, the base triad is divided according to (i.e., varies with respect to) (I) the material nature of the sign in itself, (II) the relation to Objects, and (III) the relation to their Interpretants. It must be borne in mind that these trichotomies are Hypostatically Abstracted construction principles of what will become signs. These are the subdivisions of the basic trichotomies:

Triad (I): The level of *the Sign itself*. The material nature of the sign constitutes the first trichotomy, which is triadic relations of comparison. Logically, this trichotomy is Possibility (Peirce 1998: 289f), which is not the same as Rhema, where the Interpretant takes something as mere Possibility. Possibility here involves more the establishment that there is 'matter to experience,' Quality (which reminds one of Substance in Peirce's early philosophy). This trichotomy can be divided from three aspects:

(1) Qualisign: 'nature of an appearance' (SS32) (or tone [4.537], or Potisign [8.363] – example: voice of uttering 'i'). Film abounds with aesthetic tools of expression. For instance, when a framing brings a large surface into the upper half, that surface weighs heavily. Peirce's example is the glyph '&' as opposed to the utterance 'and' and the word /and/ (the linguistic idea of 'andness'). It will be seen later that the cinematic object is often without identity yet has great similarity between its appearances. Frame-compositional techniques cannot vary much, and their potential for further Interpretation is limited. Very few of them wax into true Types or Legisigns. Showing characters from an extremely low camera angle is often but not always the Type for 'dominance,' 'menace,' and the like. Colour schemes are only to a certain degree subject to taste; it is up to the cinéaste to combine colours in such a way as to coherently 'set a mood.' The shift from genuine artistry to taste is perceptible. Chantal Akerman's *The Golden Eighties* is a clear example of taste, Godard's *Passion* of the former.

(2) Sinsign: 'individual object or event' (or token, Actisign – example: this 'the' – or replica). This is always a singular – for example, uttering a given word on a given occasion. This should not be a problem for film, which usually must struggle to achieve a general meaning from individual instances. The adage in this context is the problem of how to

show one chair but in such a way as to mean chairs in general. Only when film strives to say 'true things' (i.e., things of general relevance) is this difficulty almost insurmountable. Some try to go in the opposite direction – that is, they produce film signs of such extraordinary individuality that (general) meaning suffers greatly. That said, pure chance in film pictures happens very seldom, even in experimental film.

(3) Legisign: 'nature of a general type' (or type or Famisign – example: 'the' in English grammar). This is never individual, and it has an identity. In film this is rather difficult to discern. If one takes away spoken and written language, there are very few signs in film of the Legisign kind. Small wonder there are very few 'pictures without words.' Yet some fixed orientation points remain in film – for example, the central perspective, the reference to a frame and, of course, the resemblances to normal viewing conditions, with spatial orientation, and in temporal sequence, and so on.

Triad (II): The level of the *Relation of the Sign to its Object*. Following Secondness, this trichotomy generally answers questions concerning the constatation that there is 'existent matter,' in common parlance, or Actuality (cf. SS83, and without existence as a basic assumption, cognition would not be able to work). Existence means more than actual existence; it can also mean possible or necessary existence. The relation of the first trichotomy is basically monadic; the sign relation to Objects is basically dyadic. The Welby letter develops a classification based on that dyadic nature of Seconds, whereas in the Syllabus, each correlate in the basic triad is merely simply considered. Each of the two elements can be divided according to three aspects. The first trichotomy is from the Syllabus, which the Welby letter describes as referring to the Dynamic Object. If an Object determines the sign, this object can be either Dynamic or Immediate (this is not mentioned in the Syllabus). The actual, 'outer being' object ('without ... the sign') is determining as Dynamic. The object, inasmuch as it stands in the sign relation ('within the sign,' SS83), is the Immediate Object. (Peirce's famous example of a black stove might be useful to illustrate the difference: There is one actual stove, which can be the occasion to see a black stove, a hot stove, an old stove, and so on. Many Immediate Objects can be determined by the same Dynamic Object, yet the reverse is not true.) With a neglect of the trichotomy for the Immediate Object, the determination of signs through Objects can be:

(1) Icon, defined as 'the sign has some character in itself' (Immediate

Object: 'Descriptive' [8.352]). An example in cinema would be something that shares as a sign a quality with what it represents, regardless of whether it actually exists. Existence is not the focus here, because that quality is the same in both.

(2) Index, defined as 'the sign has some existential relation to that object' (Immediate Object: 'Designative' [8.352]). In cinema, and more specifically in television, various elaborate methods are used to denote the actual existence of the real; this, to such a degree that it has brought about a genre on its own, documentary. The documentary style consists chiefly in the avoidance of determinate signifying possibilities. For instance, it is an absolute taboo to interfere in the demonstration process by drawing as enunciation instance the general conclusion, beyond the concrete object of showing. The camera must not signal its presence through noticeable angles or movement. Its presence must explain itself, and it cannot resort to narrative causality. All of these are Thirds, which would make the sign a Symbol by being necessitant. Positively, Indexicality is a link between the showing and the shown. Someone wants visibly to talk to the camera (etc., spectator ...). There is a historical indication of when the material was shot, which gives it a historical placing as 'trace.' There are so many reality effects in cinema and audiovisuals that a highly detailed semiotic investigation is called for. Audiovisuals are especially and naturally apt for Indexicality. If language were not used, audiovisuals would be like photographs without titles of unfamiliar persons or objects (i.e., Descriptive Sinsigns). As such, they could not aspire to a higher sign class than a Dicent Sinsign. This logically translates into a demonstrative proposition without generality. Yet conventions outside the linguistic realm come to their rescue. Temporal sequentiality has a natural tendency to imply narrative causality: *post hoc ergo propter hoc*. Once this logic is established, a viewer can rearrange sequences in the proper logical order. In contrast, cinema must strive to dissipate this tendency if it wants to free a sequence from being anchored temporally and causally. In cinema, index and Symbol are on a constant Semiotic pivot.[12]

(3) Symbol, defined as 'the sign has a relation to an interpretant' – that is, it 'refers to the Object that it denotes by virtue of a law' (Immediate Object: 'Copulant,' cf. SS83 and 8.352, Peirce [1998: 291, Syllabus]). Symbols show what is already known. In audiovisual practice, there are rather scant instances of true Symbols. Television news (especially when poorly produced) 'illustrates' its messages with images. Because of its temporal sign potential, television can easily state some-

thing linguistically and then show it. In practise, this procedure takes on the power of a proof, even when the linguistic proposition in itself is debatable and the images in themselves prove nothing. The temporal connection of the two functions Semiotically as a Symbol, because it is referred to an object by virtue of a law. Corresponding audiovisual genres are 'public affairs' programs, variants of 'advocacy journalism,' all of which make for a rhetorical product.[13]

Triad (III): *The Representation of the Sign*. The mode of being of Thirdness is Necessity. The Third of a Third, then, is absolutely necessary, or true. There are three Interpretants (not mentioned in the Syllabus), according to the triadicity of Thirdness: the Destinate Interpretant, the Effective Interpretant, and the Explicit Interpretant (cf. SS83, SS162). It is too complex a matter to enter all the trichotomies of Thirdness. The 1904 Welby letter (SS33ff) outlines three of them, the first of which ('Signified or Normal Interpretant') is identical with the basic Thirdness trichotomy of the Syllabus. This trichotomy's elements are:

(1) *Rhema* (or Term), a 'sign of qualitative possibility' to its Interpretant (Peirce 1998: 292, Syllabus). Rhemes stand most prominently for linguistic terms. Pronouncing a term (a word) does not say anything; however, it does indicate the possibility that this term can be related in a sentence to a property. In cinema this seems a quite unlikely semiotic state: for where are cinematic terms? Here, the formal description of qualitative possibility must be emphasized. Cinema has to operate in a 'subtractive' manner – that is, the constative nature of its pictures must be dissipated. These pictures always seem to already state that this is so. Existence seems to be the minimal operating condition of film, because only existents are shown in photography. However, a sign is what it is taken for. This means that one can also take pictures to be imprecisions about existence and truth. Colours, forms, vectors, visual weights, and other formal features advance the taking of a sign as mere possibility. The psychological effect can be observed, for instance, in 'meditative' passages, in which inquisitive attitudes proper to 'news' are blatantly inappropriate to the picture. Conversely, such 'lyrical' passages are not tolerated in the news. This proves the existence of rhematic signs in cinema. The real question is a technical one: How are we to induce this 'taking as rhema' in a sequence of images? Here again, temporality can play a major role by imposing a rhythm that functions as rhythm, and by imposing similar prosodic means in lyrics. Our later discussion of Dreyer's aesthetic will demonstrate this.

(2) *Dicent* (or Proposition), 'a Sign of actual existence' (Peirce 1998: 292, Syllabus). In cinema, stating that 'this here is what it shows' seems to approach truism. In normal circumstances, cinema and audiovisuals are Dicents. One must make deliberate efforts to convey generality or to belie the immediate proposition for the sake of mere qualitative possibility.

When we compare this sign, in its unprescindable significance, with a cognitivist description of cinematic representation, the sophistication of Peirce's Semiotic stands out more clearly: 'Cinematic images certainly are representations of the people and objects of which they are photographs; the photograph (or the sequence of photographs that makes up the film) of Orson Welles represents Orson Welles. It also pictorially represents him; the capacity to recognize that this is a film image of Welles is the capacity to recognize Welles when and if I see him' (Currie 1995: 10). A film is not a representation of Orson Welles; rather, it is like a painting without a label. In a further Semiosis it can become an identification tool, an unintended *Blow-Up* of a real-life Antonioni. For Orson Welles's mother it could be a Famisign (i.e., the First of her Semiosis is already a sign of her son), and as with *Blow-Up*, its First is a Sinsign used to attach an identification label. Seen as a narrative, its Welles representation is minimized ('degenerate sign'); thus, Orson Welles becomes a mere Quality and, if follows, a Rhema for another Semiosis. So Currie is mistaken when he writes: 'But if our concern is with movies like *The Third Man* that present narrative fictions ... we are surely concerned with the representing relations that hold between the cinematic images and the fiction itself, its characters and events ... But the problem is that ... there are no such things as those characters and events, and so there are no relations, representing or otherwise, between the movie and fictional things. And so our image is not ... a picture ... of Harry Lime' (ibid.). The Rhematic sign class comprises the entire arch of narratological questions – questions that contemporary theories try to solve using communicational or pragmatolinguistic tools. The mentioned degeneracy of (any) sign into a Rhematic semiosis is tantamount to 'enunciation,' 'histoire–discours,' and 'Besprechen–Erzählen' attitudes (cf. *infra* for a detailed discussion). That we can narrate presupposes an 'uncoupling' (cf. Greimas). In more than metaphoric terms, the Indexical and Dicent (or higher) of a Sign must become (degenerate) into Icon and Rhema. Otherwise this sign would still refer to a determinate world, to an Orson Welles on the shooting location for a film on a certain date. Even in documentary film, narration is always a mere *narratio probabilis* (cf. *infra*) – that is, its point is not existence but possibility (this does not contradict the planned surprises of the *Poetic's* περιπέτεια). Welles becomes a Possibility to the same degree that he loses his existence. In Semiotic terms, the object relation is Iconic and the sign itself is restricted to Qualities. The idea (Interpretant) of this Semiosis is a mere Rhema. Yet as the term suggests, a Rhema is longing for a Semiosis that will relate it to knowledge type of cognition, in an abductive inference. In our example, this screen figure assumes a personality within a known plot. (We can neglect the photographic perception Semioses, which are automatic as long as there are no ambiguous percepts; cf. Nesher [1997] in detail.) Since a plot is always known in a given society (see below, Aristotle on ἤθη), it merely needs a Possibility to become Interpretant, a Rhema to become Argument.

Film theory based on Semiotic can dispense with psychology, including newly defined mental faculties such as 'imagination.' The way Currie understands this, it is really a representation semiosis, or 'simulation' (cf. Currie 1995: 144–55). Whether or not this is a personal or 'impersonal imagining' (Currie's §6.4) is beside the point of narration. Anticipating Ricoeur's illuminating insights (cf. *infra*), mimesis of action as essence of narration is always the construct of a teleological pragmatic logic. This is the Interpretant of a cinematic rhematic sign as much as any, otherwise quite different, literary bracketing device (cf. 'enunciation'). 'Once upon a time' functions semiosically as an 'uncoupling' de-Dicent, 'de-Indexizer'; it quite literally disorients spatiotemporally and constructs a new universe with a Symbolic, Legisign Interpretant: the plot. In short, what Peirce's Pragmatic Maxim has to offer as a description of inferential cognitions (mostly abductions) will become apparent. Plots are exact instances of the abductive completion of the picture, with the help of knowledge (plot structures, or Bordwell's *syushets*, are Thirds) and rhematic material.

(3) *Argument*, 'a Sign of law' (Peirce 1998: 292, Syllabus). In linguistic terms, this sign is a judgment unifying a quality and an object, usually separated as semantic units. This latter is not as nicely the case in cinema. Without the use of language in cinema, it is very difficult to imagine how films can make a true judgment, which will always have a general bearing. A semiosic process that produces Arguments must have at least a Symbol in its triadic relation, since there can be nothing general in existence. Thus, cinema's difficulty in ridding itself of indexical and iconic object relations is also responsible for its cognitive limi-

tation. Logic processes in argumentative signs are deductions. Cinema because of its very nature is pointed toward abductions (which has consequences for its representational objects and its intrinsic aestheticality). Again, however, it is a question of 'taking as' and of further continuation of Semiosis. Cinema must certainly make use of complicated strategies above and beyond language if it is to induce taking a sequence of pictures as a statement of truth (i.e., not merely as propositions on existence). Yet cinema is also especially felicitous because of its intrinsic temporality. Since there is also necessarily a temporal dimension in truth, it is possible for cinema to be a sign of truth from that perspective. We will consider this aspect in more detail below as a specificity of cinematic narration.

The richness of trichotomies at this level of Thirdness must be forgone and left open to other investigations (cf. the list of *desiderata* for future scholarship in Fisch [1986: 351]). Peirce mentions a few such richnesses in the Welby letters, without developing them thoroughly. Each sheds light on one cognitive nuance, taking into particular account psychological states of cognition (Firstnesses) and states of assurance of truth (Thirdnesses).

2.2 The Iconism of Cinema: A First Semiotic Approach

How does the classification of Signs help us understand film? It is time to illustrate how Signs affect film theory. However, because this will constitute the basis of all of the ensuing discussions of film theory, there is no need to anticipate how Semiotic is applied to some concrete questions in film theory. Here the focus will be on the principle. This must involve taking up the old question: What is – in principle – the essential in the Sign Film? What is the specifically cinematic? According to our definition of signhood these questions can be recast in this way: Which kind of meaning is proper to cinema by its essence? For such an eminent object of meaning it is important to indicate the logical forces that operate in film. To this end, we must understand the nature of Signs.

2.2.1 Is There a Meaningful 'Semiotic of ...'?

The Semiotic of cinema proper cannot be misunderstood as a static proposition – one that is excluded by the very definition of signhood. Cognition (i.e., Interpretation) is confined only by the Real as a whole, and even then it relates to the possibly real (which, as we now know, is one part of the real). Such an unending chain of Interpretation seems to defy any effort to chain meaning to a medium. The Semiotic of cinema cannot be compared to, say, the 'reality construction' of an autopoietic system 'cinema,' where it is the medium of that system which ascertains the systemic auto-reproduction and its environment, the cinematic reality. Similarly, the suggestion of a 'cinematic language' with its proper set of rules and elements would imply the possibility of a self-contained description of cinema. Semiotic, however, admits no bounds. Therefore we must exclude any 'regionalization' of meaning.

Here, however, the genitive case in 'Semiotic of cinema' does not imply a confinement or limitation. It is not an objective genitive (intended as the Semiotic belonging to cinema); rather, it is a subjective genitive (the Semiotic performed by cinema). In a Peircean context, this is the only meaningful understanding of the term. In this regard, the language paradigm of semiology differs sharply from a universal, Category-based Semiotic. Yet our Semiotic effort still concerns itself with cinema and not with general, universal meaning. Although interpretation cannot be stopped, it still must start at one point, which is the Sign itself. We will consider this point the zero point of interpretation, the point that determines all further cognition. However, in the progress of interpretation, other sources of meaning come into play.[14] There are two possible directions for cognition from the basis of a given Sign. One is a subsequent interpretation that is more vague, and the other makes it a more general cognition. Both must be expected also from the cinematic Sign.

This makes it meaningful to speak of a cinematic specificity – with the clear understanding, however, that meaning never stays at this stage. In the following investigations, for instance, we will use this dynamism in both directions, the heading of which will then be 'enunciation' (of various kinds). Although the cinematic Sign is specific, it is at least as interesting to reconstruct the paths of Interpretation that depend dynamically on the original cinematic Sign. For example, narrative enunciation is still cinematic – and more than cinematic. Here enters a logic that comes from outside cinema and is not completely covered by the cinematic Sign *in se*. Moving images must go through various stages of growing meaning in order to become Signs of teleology. Yet even in that narrative, teleological stage, the meaning is related to the cinematic Sign through a special and direct temporal relation. With regard to the opposite direction, there is a similar chain of Interpretation that allows the cinematic Sign, in its specific way, to become aesthetic meaning. Both directions can go so far that the meaning, then, becomes only remotely connected to the cinematic Sign. Other logical relations, to the extent that they are efficient, are the natural limits of a Semiotic of cinema.

What, then, is specific in the cinematic Sign? Not even cognitivist philosophies of film can dispense with framing the 'essence of cinema' (cf. Currie 1995: 1–16). Sign classification, however, provides a new and different answer to this indispensable question, and does not rely on 'schemata' and so on that 'explain data.' For the constitutive relations of cinema, the relational and formal idea of Semiotic requires a critical rethinking. Some will start, then, with how cinema relates to its sign material constraints, how the relation to the real is typical in cinema, and how this becomes a relation to meaning or thought, which is specific to cinema. In short and in the same order, specific to cinema are a chiefly non-linguistic Sign materiality, an outward real that is inescapably temporal with a space that eventually becomes temporal through narrative action, and a meaning that is chiefly non-propositional and inescapably aesthetic-perceptual. All of this is connected in a particular way with the First Category: Time, representation of pragmatic loci, aesthetic processes of invention of value. We will take up all of these suggestions arising from a Semiotic basis, and elaborate on them creatively in revisiting traditional problems in film theory.

Cinematic specificity also has an obvious relation to the 'iconismo,' which in semiology was a hot topic in the 1970s, with many repercussions for film theory. However, differential systems of cinematic lexical and syntagmatic units, and so on, are a static form of 'meaning,' Cinema in particular, though, is a difficult bedfellow for any non-dynamic understanding of cognition. This is manifest in the difficulty of introducing a temporal dimension into the semiological definition of the sign itself.[15] When we rethink 'iconism' completely, we can claim that cinematic Representation is an Iconic specialty.

2.2.2 How, Then, Is Film Iconic in Its Representation?

It is more than a way of speaking when we state that cinema is iconic. Now we are in a position to pinpoint this iconicity through the principles leading to Sign classes. This is more precise and also more formal than the term as it is understood in the common parlance of film literature, where it implies no more than the cinematic base of (not even moving) images. Instead, the cinematic specificity is indicated clearly, and is capable of formal description, in the Semiosic process itself.

First of all, there is no reason to deny film *in se* the status of a genuine Representation. Film is not a mere substratum of narration; nor is it the more or less negligible substructure of the level that is supposedly the 'real' representation of a recognizable universe (namely, narration). Regrettably, short-circuiting can be observed too often in the literature. This is perhaps due to the understandable desire to deal theoretically with a solid base in meaning, one that can be brought to propositional forms. Semiotic knows no such limitations; Signs start *before* the propositional stage. Also, Representation starts with anything that attains the fully triadic Relation, regarding an external Object of meaning. Therefore, to say that film is a Sign is the same as saying it is Representation.[16] It is important to bear in mind that film is a Sign even before it narrates.

Cinematic specificity, or the genuine Sign nature of cinema, is seen when we examine the initiation of Semiosis. As a relational event, a Sign brings three essentially different relates into one relation. This can be constructive or degenerative, as we have seen. Meaning either grows in generality and decreases in vagueness, or it becomes increasingly vague and less general. If meaning is entirely general, its Third Correlate determines the Sign completely. A Relation is not genuine (i.e., degenerate) if it encompasses characters or Firsts that are in excess of the complete determination of the Third of this Relation. This 'overhang' or excess of quality of some character is typical of cinema.

How does such a formal description translate into an imaginable meaning? Let us assume a handsome object 'G.' If 'gift' is a genuine Thirdness Relation, it determines perfectly all three Correlates of 'G' as gift – for example, in the legal context of betrothal gifts. Now this same Object 'G' is further concretized through a character that is not constitutive of the above, original Relation. For instance, in Olmi's *Genesi: dalla creazione al diluvio* one finds a classical gift episode – Cain and Abel's sacrifices, which in their differences have a character in excess of the concept of 'gift.' It is up to a subsequent Semiosis to make a Sign from this character. Let us assume that the acceding character here is something of the sort of 'grace,' 'emphatic acceptance' (in excess of the Relation 'gift' itself), or – respectively – 'bitterness,' 'frustration.' This linguistic description can, however, never render what we see in the film, so it is not contradictory if the combination of these terms does not make sense or is unrelated. As long as moving pictures can establish the relation, it functions as a degenerate meaning of a (visible, perceptible) character.

Our claim concerning the cinematic Sign is that it always and permanently, without the possibility of elimination, contains excessive quality of some character, over and above the logic of Generality mediating the Sign Relation.

Since this character is always in the First Correlate of the Semiosis, cinema is unredeemably laden with Firstness. So we can say, in an imprecise way, that cinema is Iconic. In reality, the nature of this First Correlate, the Sign itself – which also determines all the other Correlates – can in principle be of any of three types as described in the first trichotomy. If it is a Third of this trichotomy – that is, a Legisign (Famisign) – it can determine the Relation to the effect that it could contain an Argument. However, this possibility in principal is difficult to imagine in cinema. There are only a handful of examples of images and sounds (except language) that are Legisigns. The classical canonicity of Iconography, as we encounter it in treatises on painting, comes close to image Legisigns. In film, there are plenty of examples of Sinsigns and even more of Qualisigns. Sinsigns are mostly bracketed, through the 'uncoupling' procedure of narrative enunciation (cf. *infra*, §6.2, in detail), but this is not a fundamental impediment to the cinematic Sign. Nevertheless, most often we will find Signs that remain Possibilities, and then they are truly Iconic in the strictest sense of the term. Then, in fact, they can have only an Icon in their Second Correlate and a Rhema in their Third. All of this, of course, by the determination of the First, the Sign itself.

It is easy to understand why giving examples of this cinematic Iconicity is rather problematic if not impossible. When Peirce illustrates this Sign class, he usually writes 'the feeling of red' or similar immediate feelings. It is perfectly clear that this does not mean a colour value as per Itten's treatise on colours (cf. Itten 1970), but rahter this immediate sensation I have when seeing a poppy field or a sunrise, or the pale Nordic luminosity of Tarkovskij's *Offret*. It is truly a Sign of Possibility, because 'red-seeing' alone is not dependent on firefighters or traffic lights as a Relation. In a similar vein, if cinema is dominated by Firsts, this means that most of that excess must remain independent (remains an 'inefficient relation' [SS31] in the sense of Peirce's remark to Lady Welby) of any ('efficient') Relation – or precisely, that as Qualisign it does not determine more than that it is a Possibility. A First-driven Relation such as 'red' determines all three Correlates to a much lesser degree (i.e., with less of a logical force) than a Relation of Law. In such cases the logical forces are so strict that the existence of this character must even be a necessity (thus – psychologically speaking – paying attention to it and to its singularity is not worthwhile), and its Possibility is a rule (i.e., a Type). Rhematic Iconic Qualisigns relate instead to the existence of that character, as Icons, so that it could exist, somewhere and sometime; and as the Interpretation of this they offer a vague idea of something. Yet this is not nothing. It is already the unification of a manifold in the guise of an inkling of something, a faint idea of some Generality. (Besides, if we abstract this faint idea hypostatically, by speaking about it, it is no longer such.)

A counter-example of this cinematic Iconicity arises when the First Correlate is channelled into the stricter containment of a Third. This is the case when an 'inefficient relation' of a colour percept or even of something so imperceptible as rhythm (from dance and music, where it is not not perceptible, applied onto the cadence of cinematic montage understood as movement) – is built efficiently into narrativity. It is not that this colour is not meaningful in the first case, but that 'it' is clearly meaningful in a quite different sense when that colour is in a story plot.

Perhaps this result gives rise to objections preoccupied with this question: What kind of spiritual content or insight can then be achieved by cinema? We should not imply – as such a question does – that the normal case of spiritual content is cognition. We should not even imply that the cognitive is the most important part of cognition. Instead, closer examination reveals how vagueness is constitutive of cognition. In fact, Vagueness extends our findings concerning Iconicity or Firstness in Representation into the realm of Logic and Ontology. Thus, claiming cinema's special affinity to Representational Firstness involves further claims concerning its logical status and its Being: it is Vague. In Sign classification, Rhema (or Term) is consistently the Possibility of Thirdness. Even as a concept, this is not easy to digest; and if cinema is foremost a Rhema, we may want to know more about the kind of cognition it constitutes.

There can be no doubt that cognition for Peirce is always cognition of the Real; philosophically speaking, he is a Critical Realist. However, for this exact reason, there must be a place somewhere for the possible cognized (i.e., the possibly cognized and the cognized possible). Arguments, the Law aspect of Thirdness, are the knowledge already cognized. Under the aspect of Existence, Propositions are the actually cognized. If cognition of the Real as true cognition is somehow depen-

dent on the totality of cognition (the Ultimate Interpretant), this totality must be vaguely present in all cognition. Truth is a Possibility, the
Possibility aspect of the Third Correlate in the Sign Relation, but no
one wants to deny that truth is necessary for cognition as such. This is
the metaphysical function of the logical Rhema or Term. The Real is
not identical with the Actual or the Existent, of course – contrary perhaps to the common usage of the word. It contains Generality if it is
cognized – that is, to the extent of its being Argument (as a sign class).
It contains Vagueness if it is possibly cognized – that is, to the extent of
its being Term (cf. Richter 1995: 167ff). Terms are – with increasing
purity as Terms – only empty *significationes* (information), even though
they are effective Thirdness. It is through Pragmaticism (in the way
described above) that Peirce can treat them as Reals. They stand for a
'conduct' or a 'habit of behaviour' as much as do propositional signs.
For Peirce 'connotations' therefore really constitute universals with
their various degrees of vagueness. Investigating the area of pure
terms carries with it the inconvenience that any full cognition is never
a pure Term, but to some extent always an Argument or a Dicent.

Concerning cinema, the vagueness of the Semiosic outcome of the
Iconic Sign would be a real problem were no cognitive function to be
found for it. It would certainly raise objections against the practical use
of such a film theory, since every piece of narrative evidence in its definite meaning would invalidate it. An account of cinematic Semiosis in
terms of a logic of relations is perhaps not explicit enough to prevent
misunderstandings: Domination of Firstness in cinema does not imply
that it is only an arbitrary hodgepodge of something vaguely 'meaning.' Again, Iconic Signs, in film and elsewhere, are not the equivalent
of *objets trouvés* in certain domains of abstract art. They are not the
result of chance combinations of Semiosic pieces, a kind of Eco-esque
travail 'lavoro sul materiale espressivo.' 'Vague' does not mean
unclear; rather, it is the logical result of a fully triadic Relation of Representation, of a precise kind that can also be clearly and formally
described. As with any Sign, it participates in Truth, but not by way of
cognitive necessity. Whatever is chance, chaos, in the First Correlate of
such a Sign, is nevertheless the unification of the manifold in the Relation. When a Sign falls apart – when it becomes incomprehensible or
meaningless – it is precisely this unification of the Relation that is no
longer operational.

Cinematic Iconicity taken in itself – without any addition of reference to an Object or of necessities such as narrative logic – does not

allow for any precise meaning. It is constantly pressing for an increase in precision, as it is unsustainable to hover over impression after impression. Even perceptions are already the general aspect of a number of percepts; it is at that point that one can say that one has seen this or that (but 'this' is already a general idea different from 'that,' even though the percepts may be exactly the same). So it is better to think of Cinematic Iconicity as an excess of Iconic elements, and not as pure Iconicity, which would be an abstraction except in extremely rare cases of purely Iconic cinema. However, the Iconic has consequences for meaning, even as excess. It ties meaning to the real(m) of Possibility, but it is still a tie and not arbitrariness. It is not the wilful effort of an Interpreter to combine whatever characters he wants into a Relation. Thus, Iconicity and its logical sibling, Vagueness, are effectively based on a metaphysical state or mode of being. Peirce clearly avows this in his *Monist* articles of 1905: '... the scholastic doctrine of realism. This is usually defined as the opinion that there are real objects that are general, among the number being the modes of determination of existent singulars, if, indeed, these be not the only such objects. But the belief in this can hardly escape being accompanied by the acknowledgment that there are, besides, real *vagues*, and especially real possibilities. For possibility being the denial of necessity, which is a kind of generality, is vague like any other contradiction of a general' (1998: 354).

The introduction of Vagues, of Possibility as a reality, is full of consequences. If this is not just a psychological way of speaking about something one happens to know not sufficiently or imprecisely (also considered in the *Monist* article), it is indeed a precise way of cognition. One might even go so far as to see it as the most pervasive cognitive mode, as one of Peirce's most controversial and misleading examples shows. The quaint 'diamond in cotton-wool' is the most normal cognitive object, even though now everybody knows from chemistry books that it is really one of the hardest substances. However, it is not just pure imagination that this hardness would not be (or had not been) cognized (and one still needs corundum to find out). One must assume that many characters of many things are not known – or, conversely, that everything one knows is only imperfectly known and will remain so. Vague cognition, and not perfect knowledge, is the normal case. If we had perfect cognition, there would be no need for Signs. It would suffice to have the necessity of something, and from the law all single cases would follow and all the whatness of this thing would be perfectly comprised in the law ('if we were Gods,' as Peirce remarked obliquely on Hegel). However, we are still cognitively surprised, and we still come to terms with vague concepts. Now Iconicity is exactly the placeholder of the imperfect in cognition, the non-determinate.

Cinema, inasmuch as Iconic, relates essentially to the 'diamond in cotton-wool.' It is a truism that cinema 'lies,' but such a demise bespeaks a simplicistic notion of truth. Cinema *in se*, without a superaddition of logic of Generality, could never be true by a logic of Necessity, and not even by virtue of an Actual Relation (the documentary appeal does not stem from the cinematic Sign, but rather from circumstantial knowledge of the material conditions of filming). The Iconic nature of the cinematic Sign, instead, essentially reveals the truth of the 'merely' Possible, as if it said, 'This is really possible, you see it.' The Possible is linked to the Term or Rhema, if one makes a proposition of it – which cinema does not need to do. A Term asserts nothing but is a possibility of determination; thus is the Iconicity of cinema. Following Peirce's rendition of Rhemata as '– is red,' the logical status of the Iconicity of the cinematic Sign, if it were a proposition, would be a rich collection of predicates such as '– is warm, reddish, tranquil ...' Assertion would require that the placeholder be filled with an element, from which cinema *in se* can dispense itself. However, it becomes clear immediately that such a logical status is not sustainable. Although there is no syntactical pressure to complete the sentence in cinema, asserting a quality character of nothing determinate and leaving all attribution open would correspond to an extremely pure aesthetic attitude.

Whereas, if Iconicity is just a new aspect in an ongoing chain of Interpretation – one that relies on previous Signs – it adds to the latter as aspect a 'non-total knowledge' of their Object. This negative formulation is, in a positive reformulation, the doubt aspect in a cognitive act. Now doubt is certainly obstructive of knowledge and its associated certainty, but it also inspires the creative search for new certainty. This search involves mental experimentation – imagining the possible. Thus, this possible Object can be assumed to be 'possibly true' and so does 'not include the Utterer's ... total knowledge' (Peirce 1998: 355). In this context Peirce brings an important reformulation of the 'diamond in cotton-wool' example (of 1878).[17] States Peirce (1998: 354): '.. said that if a diamond were to be formed in a bed of cotton-wool, and were to be consumed there without ever having been pressed upon by any hard edge or point, it would be merely a question of nomenclature whether that diamond should be said to have been hard or not. No doubt this is true, except for the abominable falsehood of *merely*, implying that symbols are unreal. Nomenclature involves classification; and classification is true or false, and the generals to which it refers are either reals in the one case, or figments in the other.'

What is the point of this extreme illustration? The consequences of admitting of non-total knowledge – or non-final states of cognition – is an open question of how the unknown becomes known. So, if everything else were cotton-wool, how could one ever know of the hardness of diamonds? This concerns 'the occult state of things' (Peirce 1998: 357) in general: How can it become manifest? Now it would be useless speculation to grasp in anticipation what is not yet known, for this would amount to making the black box the core of one's theory. Yet advance in cognition does not depend on peeks into the black box; rather, it is already there in the form of Possibility. In this illustration, this Possibility is a case of constructing pure Quality ('– is hardest,' that is, absolute hardness can easily be imagined), but this case cannot be predicated of diamonds (assuming it is not yet known). So the subject 'all diamonds' lacks this quality of being the hardest substance. However, in Peirce's aggravated example it must, in such an experimental arrangement, lack forever the provability and proof of an oppositive Relation. As a Sign it has no Index (i.e., the hypostatic abstraction 'Hardestness' remains an Icon and is not brought into relation with diamonds), and so can yield an Interpretant that is no more than a Rhema.

Why should the question 'How can the not-cognized be cognised?' be relevant? Because of the actual existence of Symbols, which pretend to know – that is, pretend to cognize by general insight into causal relationships. So the 'sparkling diamond' as a Symbol of knowledge must yield to the 'hardest-substance diamond' as a new Symbol (and thereafter perhaps to a Symbol that includes its electrical and subatomic, crystalline, photon-bending properties). Iconicity pries open hitherto established knowledge. This mental play is possible because there are no singular facts. So even in a cotton-wool world there would be enough characters already attached to diamonds to insinuate the possibility of a new character, that of being the hardest element. The connection of those characters – and the similarity with others – is the domain of Iconicity inasmuch as free play of imagination (i.e., abductive inference). Peirce's ingenious answer, which he arrived at without abandoning Realism, is the 'would-be-conditional,' or what he called 'general conditional proposition,' which describes the behaviour of an object in all foreseeable and imaginable circumstances yet is also open to future possible discovery of further circumstances. This is the real difference between a diamond as the possibly hardest stone and the philosopher's stone (which has no other attributed characters).

Thus every object, or state of things, is somewhere in between its Possibility and its being perfectly cognized. In the context of the Pragmatic Maxim, Vagues as Possibles are real signs – indeed, they are the only signs producing ampliative reasoning. Cognition, then, is not the historically actual (or necessary) experience: it might exist somewhere, it might be true or false until found. It follows that the Iconicity of cinema is the element of Possibility, which subsists in every cognition. This, however, is only theoretically the case. Concretely, everybody who knows holds fast to the opinion to know all – until, that is, the next doubt arises (cf. Critical Common-Sensism).

A Sign of Possibility such as cinema *in se* hinges on its Iconic Correlate and its material quality. A moving picture offers little to express a rule that would suggest how such a picture must be taken or interpreted. It is a curious look at many objects, which could be many things. The moon, the lamp, the light from above in *Je vous salue, Marie*, are these objects, and more – which, however, one never finds out with certainty. If a Sign signals an 'and more,' it does so by virtue of its Iconicity. What one does not know, or not yet, or never knows, is still present as a suggestion. It is a cognition in search of an end, which it might probe or which remains suspended. In the first case it would be a problem, in the second it would be felt perhaps as a sort of wonder. Furthermore, the aesthetic attitude is such a wonder, a suggestion of an 'and more' that never attains the status of a knowledge. A truly aesthetic attitude is perhaps the only (albeit difficult to entertain) manner in which we can sustain the (in itself unsustainable) indeterminacy of the Iconic Sign. We will discover later, however, that there is no single aesthetic level of a medium so that all the rest is a determinate Sign and a cognition through causality. It is patently not so that cinematic aesthetics is limited to the pictorial level; on the contrary, Sign degeneration explains why any Symbol can – in double degeneration – become an Iconic Symbol. Thus, even a consummate narration teleology can 'decay' into an Iconicly aesthetic way of considering it. Understanding the story as a whole could – in an aesthetic attitude – still make one wonder *why*. The tragic effect – in particular, the incommensurateness of the inflicted punishment with the transgression, which leaves one in awe and 'wonder'[18] – is a queasy and non-conclusive state of mind. Certainly it is not an incomplete comprehension of the plot that accounts for inconclusiveness; rather, it is something based on a perfect understanding. In short, this takes place when Symbolic Signs acquire again – and as such remain – an Iconic nature.

The narrative logic, however, is the suppression (*Aufhebung*) of cinema *in se*. Notwithstanding the aesthetic degeneration of narration, it is still the narrative Sign that degenerates. It is the relapse not into cinematic Iconicity but into narrative Iconicity. For instance, the tragic effect as a meaning is different from the perceptive curiosity of camera view. Once the 'and more' of the Iconic overhang of cinema has been resolved into a narrative universe, it becomes a Correlate of a teleological Interpretant. One might give this a more hyperbolic formulation: 'The happy ending is the death of its film.' The default of sustainability in the Iconic Sign of cinema *in se* has yielded to a permanent law – narrative knowledge. These are the films as they end up in books: conclusively interpreted, temporal structure transformed into a teleological goal. Only at this stage do films have messages or morals. Yet this is no longer the specificity of cinema *in se*.

At this point, some film theorists might be overcome by the *horror vacui*: How is it possible to theorize about such a fluid, intrinsically vanishing object? If cinema is indeed essentially Iconic, there is no meaning in it that can be generalized into theoretical insights of the kind one finds in books. Such an impression is basically correct. Here we touch on the most Peircean element of Peirce's philosophy, as it were.

As we have seen, Categories are relational achievements. Now, in such a Categorical relation there are two infinites involved, an upper and a lower. The upper infinite is the infinite progression of relations, with lower triadic relations becoming the ground for higher ones. Signs are instances of triadic Relations: here we find this upper relational infinite when Signs 'proceed' from one to another (this can be 'diachronical' as cognitional progress toward fuller Signs, always concerning the same external Object, of course; and also 'synchronical' as enlargement of a commonsensical knowledge of a given epoch of a determinate matter). However, there are lower infinites as well. In the context of Signs, we see them in Peirce's seemingly strange habit of calling the First Correlate of a Sign the 'sign itself' (which makes sense seen from the upper infinite as well). We have seen that this is the character that can constitute the Semiosic Relation. From this it follows quite naturally that every meaning in Signs can be exposed to analytical treatment. Every Sign Relation 'contains,' as its 'simpler' elements, its Ground.

Yet it would be improper to 'analyse' (in the proper sense of 'untying') a Sign into its analytical parts. This would dissolve altogether the relational achievement of the Sign; and that means nothing other than a return to the cognitional stage before the Semiosic Relation took place. Analysis of Signs does not lead to their 'components,' however, as Signs are not composed of sememic traits of which they are a temporary collection. Instead, analysis is truly infinite. As we have seen, for the young Peirce, Being and Substance marked the limits of cognition. Thus Peirce considered them the fourth and fifth Categories respectively. Later he abandoned this thought because neither was relevant to actual cognition. In fact, once he abandoned those pure, infinite limits he grew fully aware of the true achievement of the Categories: they create relations. Substance is the metaphysical limit of cognition, but as unmitigated manifold (of sensation or any other qualitative mark), to be unified through Being (which is correspondingly pure Oneness).

These are the preconditions of cognition in terms of a logic of Relations. Seen epistemologically, observable in any cognition (i.e. in signs, as sole relation), a Sign can be analyzed into its Quality; at the same time, however, it is directed toward its Generality (cf. Baltzer 1994: 90ff). Furthermore, there is betwixt the two the domain of Semiosis itself. The mode of being of the Sign lies precisely in its being actual and contingent: it is not merely potential (as Qualities are), nor is it merely eternally true (as Generalities necessarily are). Being sign, however, means being simultaneously actual and potential and general, in this sequence (of ordinality).

Peirce's balloon example[19] illustrates this point perfectly. Initially, there is an infinitesimal point where there is just the sensation of a bang. As soon as the passengers become aware of the explosion, the actuality of a sign is given. Whereas the physical principle of hydrogen balloons suspended in the air (of oxygen and so on) is eternal. Despite its eternal generality, this principle needs an actual occasion in order to be cognized; at that point, for a passenger, it becomes a sign. Of course, actuality can also be imaginary in nature. Imagination is as much an occasion as a blow. It must only be stated clearly that without the two infinite limits, a Sign could never work.

Infinities are, as dictated by the logic of Relations, prerequisites of cognition in signs.

In claiming a special affinity, through the nature of its First Correlate, of film to Firstness, we are also claiming a special place for film in the Semiosic chain of cognition. This is possible if Vagues are Real (also in the sense of the would-be-conditional of the Pragmatic Maxim) and

True as much as their competence as sign class allows. Possibility is an unconditional prerequisite of cognition itself. We could think of Possibility in too narrow a manner by playing it off against existence, as is customary. In this way it is feasible to make fiction the opposite of the factual or real. Possibility is Real as well, but not by this existent. For our subject matter of Sign Representation, the unsubstitutable role of the Possible for the Factual is indicated by the First Correlate as irreplaceable for any Representation. However, the 'measure' of this weight is different (as the first trichotomy shows). If Iconicity is high in cinema – and if this constitutes a cinematic specificity – this bodes well for its importance and for its special achievements.

On this basis – the Iconicity of cinema *in se* – we can now investigate the aesthetic and narrative meanings in their special cinematic forms.

2.3 (From Film Pragmatics to) The Pragmaticism of Cinema

From Peirce's perspective, to be practical is not a bad recommendation for cognition. No insight can recommend itself that cannot be translated into instructions regarding how one must act in order to obtain cognition. We set out from human action, started by an inquiry into the nature of meaning stemming from a conduct of behaviour. At the end of this chapter we return to this point. Now Pragmaticism brings cinematic meaning back to its natural – practical – context. As Speculative Grammar, Signs are the core of meaning; even so, they are only a part, and the cinematic Sign *pars pro toto* of the practical use of cinema. From a broader perspective, Signs are merely a general form of cognitive action. In Aristotle's metaphysic, this was the function of the hylemorphism behind the physic. In Peirce's metaphysic, there are only Signs behind practice (i.e., which is no longer physic). Signs then, are metapragmatic; that said, we must take 'meta' in a purely formal sense. Once we have grasped the specifically cinematic Sign, we can now determine the specifically cinematic practice or conduct of behaviour. Cinematic pragmatism, then, is more then the global and necessary context of meaning; as a perspective, it is also an intrinsic consequence of the Semiotic approach.

Cinema as cognitive conduct of behaviour, then, is the all-inclusive context of any cinematic meaning. But does Pragmaticism also provide an additional aspect that is useful for a stronger theoretical understanding of cinema?

As we have seen, Pragmaticism serves a clear purpose, which one might call intellectual midwifery or maieutic. It is an explicit and practical method of cognition rather than a cognitive theory. However, cognition as it really *is* is never what certain abstractions want it to be – a perfect match of idea and data. Real cognition copes with and thrives on uncertainty. Thus Pragmaticism is but a recognition that uncertainty is the driving motor of the ongoing and unending cognitive process. Pragmaticism would not be needed if cognition were always certain and clear. This constitutes Pragmaticism as problem and traces its solution. As this problem, we can distinguish it from the altogether different problem of (what is often referred to as) pragmatics, as it is proposed in the usual 'pragmatics of cinema/film' and in Morris's triptych of semantic–syntax–pragmatic. Those pragmatics generally construe as problem a text/reader or spectator relationship, with a peculiar transformation of pure meaning into meaning(s)-for. The text is crisp and clear, whereas the spectator meaning is generally murky and impossible to reconstruct. This, then, is the hour of 'discourse,' *discoursivisation, mise-en-discours,* and so on.

Clearness seems to be the phantasmic ideal behind the methodic Cartesian doubt, where certain and true cognition is disturbed only by a *genius malignus,* whose nefarious action can be defeated by the self-assurance of the thinking subject. That genius still has its contemporary antagonists with a similar ideal, even in film theory. One such instance is the crisp and 'crystalline' (Lévi-Strauss: cf. *infra*) meaning hypostasized in semiology. The drawback to this hypostasis is that concrete texts are 'read' by concrete subjects, who spoil the crystalline structure with their own idiosyncrasies. Then the question arises of variegate 'pragmatic' communicational links between text and spectator and the fading out of a common horizon to all these 'readings.' Such discursivity constitutes a hopeless theoretical task. Pragmaticism is, therefore, not about – as Odin (1994: 44) puts it – 'rendre compte des multiples interprétations données pour un même film.' The theoretical concern of Pragmaticism is not the same as with the variability of interpretations of the same (i.e., clear in its meaning) 'text' in film pragmatics. Other film theories have neglected the pragmatic perspective altogether; that, or they have appended it for extrinsic reasons as a concession to the plain evidence that one cannot sustain that 'il n'y a que le texte' (Greimas). This sort of 'pragmatics' still thrives in the grammar paradigm for the social realm. Discourse makes text diffuse; pragmatics – one might say hyperbolically – make thoughts unclear.

Pragmaticism, on the other hand, is about a method for making thoughts clear. Once a thought is clear, there is belief. If one cannot conceive of a clear idea, one is in doubt. This idea is not as simple as it sounds, though. Most notably, it does not make thoughts clearer, but clear. This suggests a completeness of a process. This, it follows, implies two questions: What is the *terminus a quo*? And what is the *terminus ad quem*? Put more plainly where do doubts come from, and to which state do they tend? If, and only if, Pragmaticism were about psychological states, these questions would be quite idle, but this discussion is really about thought, or about meaning as the only approach to world appropriation – in other words, about everything-*in-se*.

It is understood that belief is a state of relative stability – one that originates in doubt and terminates in doubt. This does not mean that doubt comes first – only that belief is intrinsically fallible. First there is belief and practical certainty, with its intrinsic potential uncertainty. Peirce notes very carefully that one needs a real doubt, not a methodical doubt in the manner of Descartes, in order to disrupt the normal state of belief. The really interesting question, however, is how what became doubtful becomes certain again. The formal answer to this question (along with its proof) is found throughout the Categories–(metaphysic)–Relation–Sign chain of argumentation. It is evident that for Peirce, the formal side of Pragmaticism became increasingly important as he developed his thought. This, however, did not eliminate the pragmatic answer, which is the practical (i.e., behavioural) concern with clearness as a presupposition of being able to act (meaningfully).

Therefore, Pragmaticism as a whole (in Peirce's rephrasing of his own famous concepts) is about the three 'grades of attainment toward clearness of thought that are rendered distinct from one another by qualitative differences; the first and lowest imparting what may be more specifically called "Clearness", i.e. readiness in employing and in interpretatively applying the notion, idea, or other Sign to which it relates; the second imparting Distinctness, or analytic understanding of just what (2) constitutes the essence of that meaning which the first grade has rendered Clear; and the third, or Pragmatistic, grade imparting what perhaps I might be allowed to call Pragmatistic "Adequacy", that is, not what has been, but what, ought to be the substance or Meaning of the concept or of other Symbol in question, in order that its true usefulness may be fulfilled' (MS649: 1f). This (mostly unpublished) semi-popular essay (various drafts between 1909 and 10^{20}) was apparently intended as an amplification of the seminal texts of Pragmatism that were written in 1873 and published in 1877 in *Popular Sci-*

ence Monthly ('Fixation of Belief,' 'How to Make Our Ideas Clear,' and so on). These manuscripts contain some strikingly illuminating examples for such grades. For instance, a line is an instance of Clearness and is in this regard extremely similar to cinematic perception. Nowhere in the world do lines exist; nevertheless, one sees lines even where there are none. For example, rays of light are never straight and are therefore not lines – not even in empty space. It follows that the straightness one sees cannot come from what one sees; it must come instead from a general idea. 'Now if the Reader understands that a clear apprehension implies the mental possession of a canonical, typical, or pattern image together with the power of comparing others with it, the example of the idea of straightness will afford him a clear apprehension of Typical Clearness, which, I repeat, for each idea consists in (not merely requires,) a power of immediately and truly affirming or denying its applicability to any image that may present itself' (MS649: 11f).

The question is, where does this clearness of thought come from? Peirce tried to shed – without reneging on it – the psychological criterion of the first formulation of Pragmatism in favour of a logical conception, which he expounded systematically in his Harvard lectures of 1903 (cf. *supra*). So it is not just a question of attaining belief over doubt in the psychological sense, as an inattentive reader might have deduced from the *Popular Science Monthly* articles. This point is especially important when it comes to the first grade of Clearness, which can be considered the crucial one for cinema. In the psychological sense, there is no doubt in this grade. Percepts cannot be appealed; instead, they are what they are. Only perceptual judgments can be corrected, once further percepts suggest that what was perceived previously is not complete and led to a wrong general conclusion in the judgment (cf. *supra*).

So the primordial grade of cognition is in perceptual certainty, and there no doubt is possible. However, it is immediately transformed into another kind of clearness, which is more of the Pragmatistic kind and which can indeed be appealed. Peirce indicates this as early as the 1877 articles, which juxtapose various fixations of belief. The 'lowest' method is 'tenacity,' leading by way of 'authority' to the 'scientific method'; each of these has a different grade of clearness of thought. Tenacity encompasses neither a habitual nor an authoritatively imposed certainty of how to act; it only knows what it wants to do with this singular object. This certainty applies only to my individual self, without any consideration for the broader social context of meaning (close to Greimas's «*imaginaire social*»). However, this by no means devaluates this grade of clearness; it does not even imply that it will eventually be superseded by a higher grade. Of course, the 1877 articles concern themselves mainly with extolling the scientific method; this, however, should not deceive us into considering this grade a purely practical dummy that lacks the pragmatic grade of clearness. As we can deduce from Peirce's later expositions of Pragmaticism (e.g., 1903) – in particular, his astonishing insistence on the percept in the cognitive process – this grade is really the *conditio sine qua non* of any cognitive certainty. That context (which Peirce calls the first 'cotary proposition'; cf. Peirce 1998: 226f) indicates, with its explicit assent to the Scholastic maxim *nihil est in intellectu quin prius fuerit in sensu*, that the purpose of the first grade is to provide whatness to any cognition, 'about' which it is. Because this process is 'not sufficiently conscious to be controlled' (227), tenacity would be the proper behaviour of acquiring it. As a matter of fact, to find out, for instance, whether or not something is straight (i.e., is a line), one should have the tenacity to correct percepts until they become clear perceptual judgment. The other two cotary propositions, however, indicate that it would be meaningless to isolate the first grade of clearness; standing alone, it would not be clear at all. In the Harvard lectures, Peirce went to great lengths to explain that Clearness at the end of the belief–doubt–inquiry sequence relies on Continuity, Synechism, and Categories and is not a psychological alternation of moods. Only the whole of this context can count as the proof (which some still see as vanishing) of Pragmaticism that stands as a guarantor of truer cognition, provided that cognitive conduct is guided by ethical effort and self-control. Isolated from this context, the Pragmatistic claim is scandalously close to relativism and constructivism.

How does Pragmaticism relate to cinema? Where in cinema is a grade of clearness of thought? And where is a method for attaining certainty, which is a condition for the practical use (i.e., for the meaning of a behaviour)? We must now investigate the three grades of clearness for cinema – in particular, we must ask which method is available in cinema, and what its various practices are.

For the pragmatic comprehension of cinema *in se*, the line example is highly useful as an illustration of seeing what is not perceived. As individuals, we are certain about what we perceive – that is, we do not doubt what we see in cinema. That said, what kind of final judgment is required can remain undetermined at this grade. Rarely is this judgment a purely perceptual one. Are we supposed to see a line, or a shape, or a face, or a smile, or something else? A multitude of perceptual judgments must be made, but which ones we actually make depends also on the higher grades of clearness of thought for which we strive. Thus the pragmatic doubt in cinema, which gives rise to a fixation of belief or to Clearness and then Distinctiveness and Comprehensiveness in thought, is and remains endemic. In other words, it is never finally settled as an opinion. It is even essential to cinema's nature and effect that its non-conclusiveness – down to the perceptual judgment – remain in effect over all grades of clearness.

What does all of this mean for meaning in cinema? The Pragmatic Maxim, and its proof, make meaning contingent on a behavioural condition. Especially with the Pragmatistic grade of clearness of thought, meaning corresponding to this grade must translate into a perfect knowledge of how to behave in all possible circumstances (v. *supra*) and is usually a habit of behaviour. Now the relative indeterminacy of cinematic perception, with its suspended perceptual judgments, must prevent such behavioural knowledge. This follows only, however, on the basis of the meaning of cinema *in se*, without the aid of meaning from a different source. In that latter case, the cinematic Sign would become the First correlate of an altogether different logic, which also has a clearness of thought of its own. The behavioural ground of narration, for instance, is not the same as for cinema taken in itself, without narration (and such films do exist). In its purest instance, one would see moving images with no order other than their contiguous temporal succession.

Suffice it to recall certain Godard sequences (mentioned repeatedly in this book): What clearness of thought does one gain from sunlit water lilies reflecting in dirty water (repeatedly in *Je vous salue, Marie*) or from clouds (opening sequence of *Passion*)? Godard made certain there was no way to obtain any help from whatever narrative context.

Examples such as these illustrate perfectly the limits to the Pragmatistic grade of clearness of thought in cinema *in se*. Looking for such a grade leaves spectators bewildered and confused. The obvious question – 'What does this mean?' – can never find an answer other than to content itself with this reply: 'Exactly what you see, and no more.' One cannot tell what it means, because one cannot find a habitual way to approach this object in all its practical consequences. It is enough to perceive one practical meaning. This perception is so immediate that it is quite difficult to even remember it: these images do not perdure, they cannot be known as something except what they are immediately. The situation is even worse, from a Pragmatistic perspective, when the perceptual judgment, which decides that these are water lilies, turns out to be irrelevant. So even the formation of perceptual judgments can be prevented in cinema *in se*. It is, as it were, the cinematic equivalent of abstract art. Such a procedure can achieve an effect of pure cinematic form, which is no more than this.

Thus, from a Pragmatistic point of view, the certainty and meaning of cinema *in se* is at the exact antipode of Scientific cognition in Peirce's sense. Godard's water lilies or nenuphars are totally unlike the cotton-wool diamond (or the lithium of Peirce's habitual illustration of scientific knowledge). Here it does not matter that one cannot come up with a plan of experimentation describing all the biological, chemical, and mechanical (and so on) qualities of water lilies (or that this plan is irrelevant). However, nenuphars can very well be subject to the scientific kind of cognitive behaviour, even in the audiovisual form – for instance, in instructional aids. Such a use does not invalidate the 'cinematic' cognitive behaviour, but it does make the essentially cinematic a rarity. After such evidence of genuinely cinematic meaning, which is Clear but not Comprehensive, one must take into account that cinema *in se*, as a pure form, is in fact the exception. There is almost no boundary to the ancillary uses to which cinema and the audiovisual form in general can be put. It therefore still holds true that film 'is' different at each grade of clearness of thought. Film, in other words, can be brought into every kind of cognition. It serves then as a typical constraint to that cognition, which might achieve results of higher generality if it were not bound to the audiovisual form. Thus, 'scientific film' is not necessarily an oxymoron. One could not, however, produce science, attain scientific cognition, with only film.

In the pragmatic consideration of cinema, the film-theoretical consequences of Peirce's Pragmaticism are substantial; they separate, at the levels of both problem and answer, film pragmatics from Pragmaticistic cinematic meaning control. Under both approaches, meaning is derived from the principle of action; however, only Pragmaticism goes beyond a purely intentional comprehension of action. Analogically, the divide is between a film 'pragmatic' comprehended as deriving from action as intentional act in the usual way, and a derivation from action as a method of attaining clearness of thought. The watershed is the cinematic meaning itself, where a Pragmaticistic understanding cannot even meaningfully make a distinction between a pragmatic multiple 'reading' and the clear meaning-as-such (determined by semantic and syntax). Meaning is all about becoming clear – not, however, uniformly so, but clear in different ways. This was never a change in psychological moods, a sort of short-circuiting of the extremely onerous ascertainment of the possibility of such clearness of meaning from its Categorical basis down to the classification of Signs. Clear meaning, then, has a formal warrant, but it also functions on the practical level. Without the formal grounding, however, the different grades of clearness on the practical level must appear as mere psychological chimeras.

Thus there are – provided the cognitive behaviour is effectively under (Categorically grounded) self-control – no wrong or 'multiple' interpretations. As far as the respective Sign goes, all signs partake in a clarification of meaning, but in specific ways. Semioses cannot be confined irreversibly to one correct reading. Conversely, although doubt or chaos is a necessary part of cognition[21] (cf. *supra*; we will come back to this point in the context of film aesthetic), this freedom is by no means a licence for capricious, inconsistent ('hedonistic' according to Peirce [1998: 189], Fourth Harvard Lecture, 1903) interpretation. Even aesthetic meaning is perfectly controlled. It is neither an inexplicable subject event of an aesthetic 'genius,' in the sense of a post-Kantian 'genialic' aestheticism; nor an arbitrary 'work of invention' in the sense of Eco's (reneged mostly, though, in Eco 1997) *iconismo* theory and its invention of new 'content' in combination with new 'expression' values. We will take up this discussion in detail below.

But a Pragmatistic investigation of cinema as a whole does not stop at the first grade of Clearness. If it had to stop here, it would imply a rather crippled cognitive tool for attaining clearness of thought. For purely aesthetic purposes, the Clearness of cinema *in se* is enough; in fact, it must be preserved.

Another grade, the second, is Distinctness, which can be attained by 'authority' as method. We may be a little astonished at how this grade of clearness relates to the method of authority, which – besides – the young Peirce quite happily described in vivid colours almost as a precursor to Orwell's *1984*. Apart from the popular formulations and divagations on dogma, propaganda, and truth politics, the matter as such is perfectly consistent with Peirce's logical theories (cf. *supra*). Distinctness of thought corresponds to dyadic Relations, which are relations of singular facts. As we know, facts have a corrective function, always have truth values, and correspond to a type of behaviour that Peirce calls ethical. Facts exercise authority, the truth value demands to be believed – upon a 'clash with its outward reality.' To fix a belief based on facts, therefore, entails a behaviour that strives to be as docile as possible. Its regularity is based not on a general insight, but rather on training. Peirce illustrated the practical consequences of this behaviour in two autobiographical stories. The first relates to how he trained himself to lift weights with a rather complex contraption,[22] the second to how one of his relatives trained himself mentally regarding what to do in case a fire broke out in a given location – an action he found himself able to take when, all of a sudden, one of his cousins caught fire. The point of these illustrations is that facts instruct, not by teaching rules but rather through automatism of efforts.

Can cinema produce Distinctness of thought? In light of the 'documentarism' prevailing in certain film schools, this seems a rhetorical question. However, if the determination of cinema *in se* as intrinsically Iconic (v. *supra*) is correct, the real question arises: Where does the patent reality appeal ('documentary') come from? Cinema *in se* does not provide such docility by facts. The perceptual judgments of cinema *in se* give rise to representations of certain characters or qualities. It does not matter in this context where such qualities exist, nor can it be deduced from cinematic perception how such quality should relate to an existing being. The quality is the same as a dreamed one, as fantasy or fiction, as 'reality TV' or a news item, as a piece of evidence in a science fiction narrative. In cinema, a supervenient condition is required for a Relation to existent reality. Here the support of a previous knowledge of the ordinary production conditions of film is necessary. If it is not known within which parameters a 1:1 relationship between an existent real and the film or video material is either necessary (which it no longer is, in the contemporary practice of computer-generated 'animation'), or possible if admitted, and if that relationship is also impossible within other parameters (everything else except sight and sound), no reality effect takes place. In such a case, not even the 'reality markers' (those apparently superfluous little details of token unwilled presences in the image or on the sound track: imperfect sound, on-location contingencies in the background, handheld camera, etc.) can function as indicators or as evidence of ordinary production conditions. This knowledge is a belief of the Pragmaticistic kind and is required if cinema is being used to represent existing reality. The fixation of this kind of belief – a distinct clearness of thought – is, however, somewhat relative. Nobody in their right mind would use audiovisual signs to find out the temperature at some place or time; and not even webcams are absolutely reliable sources of information about weather events.

On the basis of belief (scientific or technological knowledge), cinema functions as 'documentary.' It helps attain a distinct thought, whether this-quality is the case or not. There are limits and conditions to this new capacity. This-quality must be a clear thought produced by cinema *in se* and not by something outside cinema. Also, the technological knowledge governing the dyadic relationship between audiovisual material and this existent being must be available. This same basis also limits the relation and conditions it further when it comes to measuring the possibilities of manipulative interventions.

The third grade of clearness of thought, Comprehensiveness, is even more problematic than Distinctness. It is rather difficult to imagine how cinema could become a vehicle of scientific method for making ideas clear and certain. With regard to general ('scientific') meaning in particular, it is very important to consider its starting point. Pragmaticism assumes that the first and normal state is belief, or the absence of genuine doubt. This is a kind of naturalism *ante litteram*; it is also the opposite of any foundationalist approach. Thus, also in film, the initial state would be one correct interpretation in which belief is fixed. Film, like every other cognition, will first marshal all our knowledge as it is evident to us. Yet that knowledge comprehends more than a technological know-how as to the grade of Distinctness.

From this starting point, which is common to all types of clearness of thought, the scientific method must attain its new clear thought as a theoretical insight. In the context of cinema the question arises whether such insight can be reached in and through cinema, with its intrinsic Iconicity. It seems that cinema lacks exactly those features which are decisive for this grade and in this method: Symbols. Language, for Peirce, is the treasury of knowledge – with 'growing Symbols.' Scientific clearness of thought seems to presuppose Symbols, of which cinema *in se* apparently cannot avail itself. Film normally provides forms (two-dimensional shapes, colours, positions, etc.) that allow us to recognize what we know: 'A clear apprehension implies the mental possession of a canonical, typical, or pattern image together with the power of comparing others with it' (MS649: 11). Those who do not possess, do not recognize. The intrinsic Iconicity of cinema *in se* seems to prevent any definitive apprehension, because the applicable type is not determined. So the effective meaning of a cinematic image depends on the belief antecedent to the image-as-idea. If, for instance, the belief system is a narrative universe, the 'doubt' presented by the next image can be successfully integrated into the antecedent narrative belief. That the Legisign character of audiovisual forms comes 'naturally' can be excluded, although it is also true that it can be achieved. To recognize rule-based elements in cinema would be to imply some specific learning, which is quite different from more formal signs such as phonetic sounds and scriptural graphs.

To address this problem, one can also look at the complementary side: Is there a real doubt in cinema? It is more interesting to consider how film signs can become doubtful. It is easy to observe that belief in film can be impeded, in the same manner as words can be distorted, or pronunciation can be slurred: images may not be distorted, but their representational character can be suspended through extreme devices (photography, angle, movement, etc.). Such a cinema is doubtful – or better, it has produced of a chaos in order to instigate the discovery of order in it. This destruction proves, conversely, that a cinema contained some constructed knowledge that it no longer represents the clearness of thought of which it has destroyed. In principle, this constitutes the Semiotic operation of degeneration, but how does it take place as fixation of belief in films? In this respect, we can observe that a film can only very rarely, if at all, shatter our world knowledge as such. Even ethnographical films of totally unknown cultures merely show what is known. In a film, doubt does not usually cognitively undermine entire universes; more typically, it contents itself with a planned destruction of selected assumptions. For instance, neither science fiction films nor the plethora of animated cartoon films could function without the selected suspension of belief in certain laws of physics, which are generally known.

What, then, is the belief of the third grade that cinema is capable of fixing, using its own methods? If the Semiotic analysis is correct, cinema as a Sign cannot defy its constraints, which have been described as Iconicity (cf. *supra* §2.2). However, since meaning is constructive (cf. *supra* §1.6, esp. 85–9), Signs always interpret other Signs – and be it a thought-sign. There is no difficulty in principle in admitting cinema as scientific knowledge, most obviously in the case of film theory; that said, this Sign relation has cinema in its second (and first) Correlate only as an instance of a much broader General thought (for instance concerning cognition as such, the nature of narration, or the nature of pictorial representation). This sort of cognition of cinema, although undeniable, is not relevant here. Cinema in itself would hardly generate such a real doubt from, and through, itself alone. Such scientific doubts are contingent on theories taken in themselves – and in their own dynamic. So the only relevant questions are those which arise from cinema directly, as doubts concerning a clearness of thought of Comprehensiveness. In order to delimit the range of such doubt, here we can limit meaning to comprehend only *this* film. Now, the classical range of meaning that comprehends a given film as a whole, and not beyond, is called either text or narrative. This is a specific kind of meaning, because aesthetic contents itself with a clearness of 'what stares one in the face,' and the logic of documentarism involves collecting truth values on the basis of whatever clues can be discerned. Such kinds of clearness do not need to comprehend the film as a whole. Therefore, one might *per exclusionem* define as Comprehensiveness that which is congenial to cinema and also to its highest grade of clearness of thought, narrative generality. Narration shares the same logic as the scientific method, teleology, but, contrary to science, it limits its purview to the boundaries of a given text: it provides clews instead of clues.

Comprehending the whole from its aim, then, is in cinema the third grade of clearness of thought, and this amounts to a meaning of a single action. Action is not yet a habit of conduct of behaviour; it is attached to the immediate, ongoing closure of one teleological initiation. The Pragmaticistic method makes visible how something is part of an action, down to perception itself (cf. the contribution of 'volition' in perception in Peirce's understanding of it – Nesher 1997). Meaning is inherent in action because it is subject to values as a necessary part of its directionality (cf. *supra*), which is determined by elements beyond itself. From the classification of sciences, we know these elements as Normative Sciences – here, in particular, Logic.

What film must do, then, as a first step beyond pure physical movement, is focus on values. Only value makes an action out of movement. What weaknesses film has in representing generalities, it turns into strengths by making those values accessible which determine the one action in focus. Values, however, are inherently Iconic (cf. *supra*) and therefore in principle well within the range of cinema. Values are Firsts of action; therefore, as Signs they will always be immediate experience and never truly general. They are percepts of a very fundamental kind, grounded in the very possibility of acting. So it is not feasible to show values as if they were objects, as if they existed. Conversely, without values it is not only impossible to act, but also impossible to narrate. Since narration does not consist in protocol sentences of physical movements, it will only be instituted through a perception of 'one action' (known since Aristotle's *Poetic*: 59a22f). Action consists of its constitutive value, the invisible goal it intends to achieve, even if action is seen as an achieved goal or result. Besides, Pragmaticism, is simply the systematic explication of this fundamental assumption. Thus, the true *incipit* of a narrative is not the magic formula 'once upon a time' (or the equivalent in many other languages), but an intuition of a goal of one action. Granted, cinema through its Iconicity is not open to scientific cognition in the full sense of the term; that said, through its Iconicity teleology is not only within its reach, but is effectively applied to – or subsists in – one action. Being fictional action implies that this narrative is merely possible (and probable in the sense of the *Poetic* 51b31f, εἰκός, the probable, and δυνατόν) and does not have to live up to the constraints of an 'outward reality.' This latter aspect, however, falls under the previous kind of clearness of thought. Nothing prevents cinema from combining both, or all three, in one enunciation. There is only a residuum of ethic in all narration, and also in its logical *incipit*, which is related to the credibility of the narrator or narrating instance. It forms, as it were, the protasis 'I tell you now a story of my own imagination, which is ...' of the narrative apodosis 'an old magician once upon a time ...'.

If cinema intends to make values visible and conscious, it has only the usual Pragmaticistic way to do so, to make previous values doubtful. For instance, ethical and teleological values become doubts through an avoidance of presenting understandable narrative 'points of view' (in Branigan's sense, cf. *infra*). Once teleology has become a belief, cinema is instrumental in 'knowing which we know something more' (8.332), or a re-'fixation of belief.' Typically, it is here that a 'small scale' generality constitutes itself in the form of narrative typos, again in the sense of Aristotelian (and even more so in Brechtian) *Poetic*. This enables us to understand teleology as a 'contingent logical' constraint, which is merely based on custom.

If the third method of fixation of belief were lacking in cinema, it would be precluded from any new and lasting cognition. Conversely, one could recognize the cognitive limitation of cinema if one could not conceive of a rememberable idea. Remembrance is a matter of generality, to such a degree that if 'Symbols grow,' memory is the growth including the grown.[23] A purely aesthetic experience must vanish with the moment, unless it is interpreted as an instance of some general character (in the perceptual judgment). The same is true for truth. One can imagine a series of experiments that are all either true or false at a certain point, but only as part of an inductive process do they become part of a cognition. A single 'experiment' is without any meaning – it would be a mere event. Therefore, memory and cognition is a crucial test of the capacity of cinema, for this 'grade of clearness.' Instead of diagnosing an irremediable iconic limitation in film, we must consider the process of new cognition in its entirety. In fact, the 'lower' grades of clearness are by no means suppressed; they must instead be contained as relation (cf. MS649) in the 'higher' grades.

Because of the non-psychological character of belief in Pragmaticism, an issue arises, which must find an resolution, without which Pragmaticism ultimately cannot convince. Cognition is always a mere fixation of belief. Even if this is neither an individual belief (as for Clearness), nor one that is socially imposed (Distinctness), even the third grade is still belief (or common sense). At this point Peirce must assume an unlimited community of researchers.[24] But this is not a factual assumption; rather, it is just another expression for the impossibility of concluding interpretation. This astonishing but necessary conclusion was emphasized earlier in the context of an apparently counter-current base assumption of the comprehensiveness of reality appropriation (this was the meaning of the diamond example, cf. *supra* 43–4). Thought is an unending process-in-progress based on truth. Truth, however, is merely the finality of the progress toward truth, the perfect mediation, or full Reality. 'If we were gods' (5.160), we might anticipate this Ultimate Interpretant, and it could very well look like a system or – as Peirce felt – like a perfect mathematical Symbol. Before that, however, there is merely an orientation toward it, which needs at any given moment elements of chance in order to proceed. Those elements must be reintroduced into the stable system of 'settled opinions' or knowledge. They represent the chaos side of cognition seen from a perspective of knowledge. Novelty, if it is true novelty, always emerges from chaos.

Here, then, we are confronted with two infinities, which are completed with Possibility as third infinity. Cinema must partake ultimately in these infinities, and this is the real import of Pragmaticism of film. Otherwise cinema would lack a cognitive potential. If this method of cognition had only 'hypothetical models of data explanation,' there would be no laurels for film to gain. Indeed, it would exclude cinema from any serious cognition and limit it to the area of 'making believe,' of constructing the 'veri-similar' of narrative universes.

2.3.1 Cinematically Being

The more famous it became, the more Pragmaticism had to struggle not to be underestimated as psychologism. The dangerous misunderstanding of a simple doubt–belief alternation receded once it became clear that Pragmaticism concerns itself with types of clearness of thought. Yet another way of arguing against a psychologist reduction involves emphasizing the Realism embodied in the Pragmaticistic method. Its proof is a chain of arguments passing through logic, the logic of relations, and metaphysic as result of this logic – and not as usual as presupposition – so that the clear repercussion of Peirce's philosophy in its entirety ensues: that our reality or world – encapsulated in Signs – is modal being. In other words, when we grasp something cognitively and we say 'is,' then 'is' is one of three modes to be.

Cinema, too, 'is' something in some way. This may sound truistic – or worse a *bêtise* – in particular, to those who believe simplistically in a uniform material reality that is opposite to immaterial ideas and somehow related to the former. How cinema 'is,' instead, is a substantive question. It is a quite remarkable achievement that there are different modes of being in cinema. As always with Signs, one does not cognize the Sign, and one is not conscious of 'meaning.' Something 'is,' however, which means 'is meaningful,' 'is through meaning.' Also, in talking about film the purpose is to talk about that which film makes meaningful, the being which film discloses.

Thus, one has to inquire about cinematic Signs in a Realist sense, as corollary evidence of Pragmaticism, by posing an explicit question: 'How do they say "is"?' A trimodal cognitive appropriation of being recommends itself strongly also by common and known practices. In cinema, too, one encounters quite established practices of saying 'is' that have a very high cultural recognition rate. Cinema as art is one of the foremost cultural frameworks, in which case cinema 'is' Possibility. So if cinema 'is' art, it is not – as is usually said – a sign that relates to the existing reality as a merely hypothetical possibility (namely, as fiction). As aesthetic reality, 'is' means 'is possible as one of innumerable possibilities that are not considered now.' Aesthetic cinema is the possible world, but without the limitation of the copula as in propositions and language (v. *supra* §1.2.1, esp. 24–6). As such, it does not have to negate partially existential propositions through qualifying additions. Cinema shows quite non-grammatically: the round shape is_possible romantic (a sun, warm colour, perfusion of light, overwhelming ...).

Now, if a film commences to present itself as (i.e., is taken as) 'moving photography,' then suddenly all of this becomes true or false. This relation can be tested, as we have seen, on the basis of technological knowledge. Only here does film become visible as film-sign, in its material Sign character, as that no-thing opposite to something, toward which it relates as true or false. Every thing which is is_true (is_false). The round shape, which I see, is the sun.

The reality that is object of a film which narrates is totally different. Here the world is filled only with elements that lead up to something. So here, cinema is 'is leading towards.' Every thing that is is_for (is_necessary_for, is_superfluous_for ...). The round shape, which I see at this plot juncture at high noon, is, must be, certainly the sun of justice.

At the issue of this Pragmaticistic conceptualization of cinema, cinematic meaning flows back into its natural bed of a world appropriation through human action or conduct. It has been argued that this is the most comprehensive context of every possible kind of meaning. It is, however, not the apparently plausible argument of the 'naturally transcendental' notion of action, which cannot be criticized in a meaningful way. From that assumption can be derived all the conditions of its possibility – for instance, as 'basic actions,' or in a *sémantique de l'action* in the manner of Ricoeur; however, all theorems still hinge on the 'natural given-ness' of a human acting something in time. Pragmaticism has chosen another, much more fundamental phenomenology, upstream of acting subjects and their constitution of meaning. Here meaning is first, and then comes the possibility of action. Other (pragmatic, 'fundamental-pragmatic,' 'intentional-pragmatic') theories place acting or action first and then endow it with the requisite meaning.

Pragmaticism is a theory of cognition, or a very comprehensive 'cognitivism.' Cognition not only can but should be practical. For film theory, this was an obstinate request made by one of the most formal theories in the field, cognitive constructivism. One can try to pension off 'Grand Theory' in favour of many little regional theories ('middle-level,' see Bordwell [1996: 26]), if one feels uncomfortable with the 'big picture' theories, which are so barren when it comes to practical problems. This desire to explain actual, practical problems is legitimate; however, it is also clear that this worthy desire must find means of fulfilment. These means are not always available. Constructivism in film theory basically saw two avenues to making theories practical: psychology and action. Cognition seems more practical if it is explained by means of apparently familiar psychological states. If these states are abnormal, a quite complex psychoanalytic theory is called for (the epistemological basis of which is still far from clear). Carroll (1996a) declares it incompetent for normal psychic states, which are supposedly better explained by cognitivism. This, however, is also its limitation, since cinema is thereby confined to rationality in the broadest sense. For example, cognitivist attempts to come to terms with film aesthetic have – not by chance – a tendency to be Formalist and nothing more (cf. *infra* §6.4.9.1, 414–20).

Practical theory – living up to it as ideal, or giving it up as oxymoron: this is the alternative for film theory, as the oscillations of contemporary debates make clear.

3 What 'Is' Cinema?

How can we compare film theories? We could formulate a practical problem and then compare what theory X and theory Y have to offer as solutions. In the best of all circumstances, this would yield a panorama of views, but it would not enable a decision on the theories. All theories could address the problem, but what would tell us which treatment is better?

Some film theorists claim for their (mostly 'middle level') theories a 'best fit' to data. This is certainly no solution. What is 'best' in a theory fit? Albeit suggestive, this functions only metaphorically (clothes fit bodies). 'Fit' misconceives theory and data as different, as if there were data outside theory. Comparing the constructed data with the constructor theory is, thus, the question, not the solution. Theories don't fit; they are good. For a theory is always more than any collection of any amount of 'fitting' data. Can we know what makes such a theory a good (or better) one, then? The only way is to understand the theoretical construction of its object; data add nothing to this construct. For this we need to comprehend why this problem is treated in exactly this manner – that is, this theory's construction principles of the object, through which we see the problem. What we then see through theory is its data, which can be constructed in such a way that surprises are either possible or excluded; but no theoretical generality can ever be falsified or verified by the existence or not of its data. Some theories can learn, others can not.

For any problem treatment, the convergence point is the comprehension of the object itself. All treatments, and all problem solutions, in their totality and in their silences, enunciate in the first place what cinema is *in se*.

It is much more promising to conceptualize cinema as such – that is, the epistemic 'cinematic object' – than to approach problems of cinema in different theories. When we take this approach, theories become comparable and can be criticized. We will also likely be placing Semiotic film theory in the context of the most explicit and reflected contemporary film theories. Without question, there are real differences between film theories at a deep level. There is no theory-free way in which to understand film; all claims otherwise should be rejected as ideological – as simply a refusal to acknowledge what is assumed on a deeper level to be the 'nature' of cinema.

The nature of cinema as a Sign relation was laid out in earlier chapters. In this chapter, we will draw the consequences, relating the representational achievements of cinema to perception, time, reality, language, and system. This is how other theories reconstruct cinema. In a nutshell, cinema 'is' either a special sign relation, or a special kind of time, of a qualified textual entity.

Many theories have tried to explain the nature of cinema – see the panorama in Aristarco (1963) and Casetti (1993). Discarding the zero stage of 'savage' film aesthetics, in its early incarnations film theory – then a budding academic discipline – adopted a phenomenalistic attitude and became descriptive and psychological. Soon after the language paradigm took over. Was this merely a change in meta-language – as Mitry (1987) strongly suggests – or were we gaining radically new insights thanks to the new paradigm? There is no doubt that semiology constitutes a new and relatively rigorous meta-language. But is semiology actually a new way of understanding of cinema, or is it just a faulty application of an inadequate paradigm? In §3.1 we will discuss what semiology sees, and what it obfuscates; then, in §3.2, we will consider Eco's seminal theory of iconism. That there is a radical alternative to semiology will be seen in our concluding topic, Deleuze's new ontology of cinema as moving matter (§3.4). In between (§3.3) we will touch on cognitivism (or constructivism), an emerging current in film theory that gives us occasion to probe, in a Semiotic way, the question of perception.

Without further implications, let us call these assumptions the 'being of cinema' – what 'is' cinema. In the contemporary debate there are five principal, alternative, implicit or explicit concepts of the 'being' of cinema (although not all are sophisticated enough to recognize and state this as ontology, and probably one could find further budding conceptualizations, which are of very minor interest). The five are as follows: (1) the broad strand of semiology,' (2) some remnants of a prescriptive 'production aesthetic', (3) Deleuze's ontology of movement, (4) cognitivist constructivism, (5) and 'film pragmatics.' These basic approaches do not always coincide with – or subsist within – one strand of film theory, rather, they are reconstructions of various bases of a number of contemporary theory approaches. Here, a caveat is necessary: some strands are hardly unified theories (and some admit as much); furthermore, older approaches – phenomenological, hermeneutical – still survive in a modernized form. Some strands are eclecticist and merely emphasize one approach among the many they incorporate; they return to the others when it is convenient despite their deep theoretical incompatibilities.

(1) *Semiology:* The first important ontology of cinema, semiology, shelters its entire hidden metaphysic within its core, Homology. This fundamentally structuralist belief is a universal constitutional principle of 'what is.' For instance, it 'manifests' itself as (but does not restrict itself to) belief in the homology of expression and content planes (for a detailed discussion, cf. also *infra* 177–80). How the dual planes of the *arbitraire du signe* are indeed modes of 'being' something is a question to be addressed later. At that time, attention will be paid especially to the difficulties these modes of being encounter with pictorial and cinematic representation and cinematic temporality. Semiology and cognitivism share certain basic assumptions (with due regard to their not being unified theories). For example, constructivist film perception theories and their supposedly opposed immanentist semiological theories of cinematic codes *sub specie semioticae* are equal, because both have a dualistic ontological basis, even though they utilize different elements. Semiology is known for its hylomorphistic dualism; Schemata-guided constructivist perception is too similar to the theoretical intuition in Kant's schematism to be a fundamentally novel theory.

To ask, 'What is cinema?' is not a rhetorical question because, as a construct, the answer is far from evident. No doubt, what we see in cinema is meaning, and not pictures, just as one sings a song and not musical notes. Now, meaning is not 'data.' Only through the 'trick of familiarization' ('anti-*ostranenje*') by way of Homology can meaning as 'content' be taxonomically arranged in the same manner as, say, phonemes. Is it reasonable to overlook the difficulties in semiology in equating ('serializing') expression and content in their givenness? Deleuze (1973) argues cogently that this homology of two structural series is part and parcel of structural metaphysics. This on reflection, implies a new form of transcendentalism. In structural transcendents there are two modes of being: the pure form of structure and its 'incarnation' (as Deleuze calls it) in whatever amorphous matter there is (incest taboos into reproduction, purity into food, language into world). As Deleuze lucidly puts it, 'L'ambition scientifique du structuralisme n'est pas quantitative, mais topologique et relationelle' (1973: 305).[1] This ontological presupposition – including the structuralist equivalent of Kant's Transcendental Object ('l'objet = X') – can be negated (cf. supra 121).

(2) *Production aesthetics:* Even this class of approaches is contingent on a clear answer to 'what cinema is' (its 'essence'); the answer then becomes the meta-language of theory. There must be something that can be described. This typically translates into, 'What are the constitutive rules of cinema? Structure was the one rule of semiology – even *de rigueur*; soft rules of 'Film Grammars' amount to an enticement of essentialisms. (Not even Currie (1995) escapes this rule, by way of 'description' of essential traits of cinema, which happen to fit his theory.) Most often, unreflected language analogies as suggested by the term 'Grammar' postulate rules. Such rules, however, are derived from production ('montage,' photography whether black and white or colour, and so forth) and then construed as the phenomenon itself. Sometimes this is done in a sophisticated and quite interesting way, as in Mitry, but he uses it in an entirely different theory of cinematic 'being,' one that is reduced to sheer phenomenality. This does not hinder him, though, from using the second Peircean trichotomy as substitution for his phenomenological rules (Mitry 1987, cf. 575n53).

Earlier attempts (starting with Sprottiswood) to construct film grammars or rule systems allow us to use film as a tool, like language. However, the grammar metaphor is based on the analogy of the sentence. The difference between well made and poorly made films is supposed to arise from rules by which the well made abide. Now, there are rules for well-formed picture compositions (let us say) such that deviation from these rule is considered ungrammatical. That said, we do not produce well-formed films the way we produce well-formed sentences. Metz denied even the possibility of such grammatical correctness, and rightly so. Syntax becomes a weak analogy as soon as the unit under consideration is a chain of sentences or text. 'Text grammars' are as grammatical as film grammars; the *tertium comparationis* is merely formational and compositional rules on a diachronic axis and the idea of a whole being more than its parts (sentence ≈text).

At the base of endeavours like this stand the following axioms:

meaning means rules; rules hinge on a game to which they can be applied; and cinema is such a game with a closed set of rules. Generally, this does not go so far as to investigate the logic of such rules, as long as they are followed in a given game. But this theory choice already amounts to making cinema a convention. If it 'is' convention in essence, its rules need no further justification than that they are a fact. Cognitive achievements, which could be criticized, cannot really be claimed for conventional rules; but neither would they normally be excluded on the commonsense basis of 'photographic truth.' Mitry, for example, is not strongly concerned with cinematic cognition as long as 'rules' can be described as if they were mundane objects.

(3) *Deleuze:* The question 'What "is" cinema?' receives a highly ontological answer from Deleuze as well as from the Bergsonism in which his film theory is grounded. However, Bergson and Deleuze are far too subtle to allow a meaningful brief characterization. The ontological status of *'le Tout'* is complicated; it also has a time dimension. Because it hinges ultimately on a concept of the Whole – which is quite different from Synechism – and on how we can know of it, its repercussions for cinema are profound. How do changes happen in film? If they do not happen in signs, but rather in the time of physical movement, they cannot constitute primarily a movement of cognition and its force. Thus even the progress toward the *totum* is a singularity of Semiotic. Its sign base and its pragmatic, social setting as singular, however.

(4) *Cognitivism:* The discrepancies between Semiotic and cognitivist constructivism are almost as interesting and profound as Deleuze's divergence and require an explicit discussion. It is not easy to discern how constructivism defines the being of cinema, given that it has no unified theoretical basis. Seen from the perspective of the history of philosophy, it amounts to a basic Kantianism, which then compares to Peirce's Realism. This must be taken very cautiously, however, as cognitivism shows little concern for explicitly unifying all objects of cognition into a sort of Transcendental Object. Here we will try to supply such a focal concept for the foundations of constructivism (which is clearly more explicit and less piecemeal than the intellectual gesture of regional, middle-level theory often encountered in cognitivism). This concept is the system idea.

Cognitivism is rarely vested in epistemology; for its claims it relies mainly on the (environment) psychology context. Thus in film theory it 'defines' film as a set of 'cues.' Despite the theatrical connotation of the term, the Subject (or quasi-Subject 'author,' text, or some physical reality) is not the 'director' giving cues. Cues really come from nowhere. We would not be doing justice to constructivism and cognitivism by burdening these with the problems of subject or consciousness philosophy. They have more in common with the system environment relation assumptions of general systems theory and radical constructivism. From this perspective about being and existence, the only reasonable statement can be, 'There are systems.' Functions, elements, relations, order, and other systemic achievements are regulated by the concrete system (be it psychic, social, or even narrative), which defines what 'is' (i.e., what it can 'see' but also what it selectively excludes). On these grounds, cinema 'is' not; rather, it is/functions as narrative system. (Highly instructive on this point are Schumm [1990] and Wuss [1993].) The elements of narrative systems are representations (cf. especially Wulff, in Schumm [1990: 26–8]), which thus constitute the smallest entity this system can 'see' – and through which it can see its reality – on the basis of its own selectivity. Yet the systemic achievement of narration is not representation itself; rather, it is a typical orderly relation of narrative elements as teleological selectivity. How much this theory is worth as a narratology will be discussed in another context. The point of interest for now is a critical understanding of the 'reality construction' achieved by cinema as a whole, before any further determination. This, then, is what cinema 'is,' according to constructivism.

(5) *Pragmatics:* An understanding of what cinema 'is' in the form of an implicit ontology plays a major role in film pragmatics (cf. the representative lot in Müller [1994a]). The gist of this specific debate (there is a broader one relating to reception theory and hermeneutic at large) involves introducing communicational aspects into the object/being cinema. This debate's interest arises from two things: the supposed abstraction of pure text as opposed to its reception or communication; the double 'ontology' it reflects with regard to the being of cinema and the receiving subject. To some degree this still reflects a Kantian transcendentalism inasmuch as it cannot unite cognition with pragmatic. Regarding this central point, as we have already seen, Pragmaticism is more successful. Therefore, the communicational, 'pragmatic' aspects of film are not a necessary topic for Semiotic and will not be raised here. In fact, raising them would unravel the Pragmaticistic approach in all its comprehensiveness. The full Pragmatic concept of signs already answers the presupposition of film pragmatics. Besides, the pragmatic aspect of 'cueing' the spectator and 'viewer activity' in cognitivism is only an apparent one (in Morris's prevailing communica-

tional definition of 'pragmatics'). The set of communicational events is sharply reduced through this 'activity,' with corresponding 'cues' on the other side. How both sides avail themselves of a common meaning horizon is hardly imaginable. Basically, this is still methodological solipsism, whereas it is typical that all shades of pragmatism presuppose shared horizons (Peirce's, Dewey's 'democratic truth,' Mead's 'generalized other,' as much as Habermas's 'life-worldly' discursivity). The obvious and extensive admixture of reception aesthetic elements (which is in the hermeneutic domain) in the film pragmatics debate (in particular Bettetini and Casetti) is possible on the basis of this common horizon. Clearly, a third strand of influence (and the list in Müller [1994a]: 8f) has not omitted a single eligible cognate pragmatic is here the 'pragmatic' of Narrative Grammar, the 'communication axis' of its enunciation theory.

Yet pragmatics is not Pragmaticism, not even its 'stripped down' variant. It should be evident that the horizon of meaning is not a matter of the text itself, but of communication, which is Morris's heritage. A lucid account of the types of questions and possible answers is provided by Odin (1994: 42–5), who epitomizes the object as 'LE spectateur' (45). The latter is the same sort of abstraction as LE texte – this, despite Greimas's 'il n'y a que le texte.'

Of these five divergent comprehensions of what cinema is, certainly the two most interesting and challenging are Deleuze's and semiology. The broad school of semiology and semionarratology in film theory will be discussed below in two phases. The first focuses on the core of semiological film theory, the problem of order. However, the notion of order presupposes a special, 'film-adequate' answer to the problem of units. This has made iconism especially attractive; yet instead of remedying the problematic core, it has added to the burden carried by semiological explanations of cinema.

3.1 Cinema 'Is' Syntagma

Under the common umbrella of the sign, semiology is among the most conspicuous rivals of Semiotic. Semiology 'sees' something other than Semiotic. As soon as we examine the details, we encounter a rift between very fundamental assumptions. Notwithstanding a number of attempted syncretisms, it will be shown that Semiotic and semiology are still truly unreconciled today and probably always will be if the basic insights of both are to remain intact. Thus, one must choose. In the theory of signs there is no middle ground. Furthermore, the choice must not be arbitrary; rather, it must be based on the better arguments, and uncovering them will be our first and foremost purpose here. From our perusal of Semiotic – including its modal understanding of being – it will become obvious that in semiology, signs are never modes of being.

The very sign theory in semiology has evolved, however. Hjelmslev's glossematic is one of the logical continuations of de Saussure's Cours de linguistique générale[2] and might be seen as its theoretical perfection; yet at the opposite pole there is a functionalist offspring of Saussure with Trubetzkoy, in which semiology evolves in the direction of communication. All of this has repercussions for an understanding of the sign itself. A systematic and historical description of semiology is beyond the scope of this book (for this, see among many others, Eco [1975] and Albrecht [1988]). There is also abundant critique of semiology. This is the big picture of semiology. The small picture is just the view of a detail, unthinkable without the big picture. Even so, this discussion will be limited to what has become relevant to the reception of semiology in film theory. In this regard there are two dominant sources, often quoted quasi-ritually. One is the 'grande syntagmatique' of Metz and his school. The other is Eco whose impact on film theory is not due to mere chance. We will see how Eco's definition of the iconic sign underpins Metz's theory of syntagmatic. If cinema were normal language with a proper 'articulation,' its syntax would not be a problem. Since it is not a language, the iconic sign has become the other source of film semiology. Apparently it was felt that 'iconismo'[3] precisely describes the constitution of the pictorial potential of film. Among those resorting to iconism are Beilenhoff (1978: 30FN34), Siegrist (1986: 33ff), and Opl (1990). As well, Metz acknowledges Eco's iconist contribution: Eco has become Crown witness and guarantor of the semiological basis at large of cinematic syntagmata. As a consequence of such layers of presupposition, we must deal with two separate theoretical problems: (1) syntagmata as the typical semiological manner of dealing with narrative time, and (2) iconism as a threat to the differential basis of semiology. As a side effect we can examine Eco's supposedly Peircean basis, which he pretends to bring to bear exactly on his conception of iconism.

Beginning with the first theoretical problem, we have to see how the problem is defined immanently in the system. Metz distinguishes between film and cinema. Generally speaking, the latter is narrative; the *differentiae specificae* of film are not so clear. There is a long discussion in Odin (1990: 29-57) about the necessary distinctive marks needed for codification and articulation (compare this with Currie's [1995: 1–16] similar attempt, which is apparently independent of Odin's more detailed effort). In its Metzian form, film semiology hinges on a subtlety that is decisive for its object of study. The question is, 'Can cinema be counted as 'langue' or 'langage?' Depending on how we answer this question, film semiology is or is not possible. Yet the question itself is sensible only against the wider background of Saussurean differential systems with their characteristic levels. De Saussure carved out a language study domain and identified it with that middle ground between the spoken word of a concrete utterance (*parole*) and the upper-limit assumption of a human nature in a society communicating through language (*langue* translatable as 'language faculty' or linguistic competence, provided that one does not read it in a mentalist key). At a different level, language itself is articulation (i.e., it should render *Gliederung*). Articulation requires discrete units with typical distinctive markers at the same level. The problem for film semiology is that cinema evidently has no articulation of distinct units (those bearing any meaning). This makes it a means of communication governed by language faculty or linguistic competence, and *not* by rules of language.

The Metz School, before its psychoanalytic turn and after its return from psychoanalysis (cf. Odin [1990]) – presents itself as a fairly compact and internally coherent research tradition. It has already found its historiographer in Colin (1989). In a summary, Chateau (1986: 14) limits its concerns to 'les difficultés suscitées directement par l'élaboration d'un modèle de représentation de la structure du film.' Semiology of cinema is thus confined strictly to whatever can be 'formalized,' which is a 'petit nombre de classes de "faits filmiques" auxquelles peut être attribuée une propriété essentielle du point de vue de l'étude des systèmes de signification' 24.

This limitation is not entirely a self-imposed one, but also stems from the inherent intractability of film with linguistic methods. Given such methodological dependence from alien presuppositions, the main concern becomes, how much of those can be grafted upon film? The most 'transcendental' presupposition is de Saussure's level differentiation of faculty, language, and utterance, as described above. How is this, however, 'analysed-into' cinema? Not even utterance partakes in a communicational, speech act, difference, but is the discursive, production part of three code systems. A supposititious parallelization with cinema loses all intuitive appeal, starting with the problem of levels of cinematic code, which have to prove comprehensive in order to comprehend all meaning found in film. However, film semiology comes up with an inventory at best, and what becomes inventorized takes on the name 'cinema.' The strength of the inventory list is merely commonsense, obvious observations. All its explanatory power (i.e., differentiation, articulation, levels) it draws from de Saussure's linguistic methodology, which can function only when factors of human communication other than meaning are excluded methodologically.

Semiological doxa must account for meaning also in cinema; but the method here is fraught with unexpected difficulties. This imposes to split the meaning problem into two different semiological enquiries, contingent on the peculiar nature of cinematic 'expression material.' The first inquiry, syntagmatic, concerns itself only with narrativity, postulating in its formalization a specific difference to other (likewise not-discrete, unarticulated) cinematic expression. The challenge of semiological doxa through cinema is that because of the lack of discrete units and double articulation it is not a language (*langue*); However, at least as language-faculty (*langage*) it should be suitable for formalization, not as syntax, but merely as narrative syntagma. The resulting *grande syntagmatique* appeals to common sense and is not counterintuitive, despite its weak methodological, doxastic grounding. Somehow, this is the way we understand parts of a tale and how they relate to one another. Thus, the major stake is in the second semiological inquiry, which is actually foundation to the first and concerns itself with the image-sound substratum, subjecting it to Eco's iconismo.

A theory with rigorous claims, at any rate, should not be established on common sense. All its rigour and formality film semiology derives from its homological doxa in articulation and difference, in spite of its commonsense result. If it is judged not by its results, but by the underpinnings, complex assumptions about the nature of language, then the 'original sin' of film semiology is inherited. There are unquestioned philosophical assumptions in the very definition of semiology. The level difference between language and language-faculty, for one, is based on linguistic facts of articulation of units (which do not apply to film), and this alone explains a crucial difference: between (pure) language and language-faculty, an imprecise tool of social interaction (all the while carefully avoiding mentalist implications). Such a theory hinges on (linguistic) facts. But its first principles, the primacy of difference and the consequence of systematicity, cannot pretend to be facts. This is not reflected in semiology. As repeatedly stated, by Petitot-Cocorda (1985b) for one, phonology has assumed the status of a model. Only here this principle yields a perfect explanation, and thus becomes the champion of system, difference, and articulation. Petitot-Cocorda has also shown, however, that this homological operation scarcely fits phonetic reality. For even here meaning (content) provides the real distinctive features, and not the units and articulation of expression material.

In this spirit of semiology, Chateau (1986: 33) first draws up 'une liste non redondante et structurée des propriétés du langage ciné-matographique qui se prêtent à une formulation sémiologique.' Highly descriptive, but of a non-coherent nature, this property list contains only current film practice observations hinting a possible linguistic rel-evance. The first such property is 'discontinuous communication' (i.e., the severance and unidirectionality of communicational situation). The first position in this list of to-be-syntagmatized cinematic features has only one purpose: creating a pure linguistic tool. Only independent from situation and empirical users can film qualify as an independent domain of meaning. For this it must not dependent on communicating subjects or minds. But can it simply be observed? Since we see only what we know, communication has to be reduced to transmission of messages in order to leave the construction of meaning in its entirety to the downstream of discontinuity. As second property, (acoustic and visual) sensory groups are reduced to typologies. The only purpose in this remains the same, for the constitution of linguistic systematicity, by a twist of homology, needs to turn sensory material into expression (not even cinema specific). How is it done? The trick is the arbitrary sign relation with its belief that articulation of expression entails seg-mentation of meaning as its counterpart. This is far from self-evident. Meaning segmentation for being used must be an intelligence of some sort. Petitot-Cocorda (1985b) compellingly argued that segmenting expression independently from content is philosophically naive. We cannot short-circuit non-trivial problems such as cognition with what appears to be simple observation of two simultaneously changing orders. Up to this point, Chateau follows faithfully the homological doxa with articulation (P2) following on discontinuity (P1), but he offers no further theoretical justification, let alone for the context of cinema. Crucial questions remain open or doxa, even those close to cinematic codification. If we follow Petitot's suggestion to put the horse back before the cart: How can there be cognitions to be encoded? Or how do they decode mechanistically, without intervening cogniz-ing agent (*vulgo*: subject)?

A third property solves the following problem: What classifies sensory material of visual ordering into either planned or real, *tournage* or *filmage, mise-en-scène* – based cinema, (i.e., drama), or documentary sort of real objects before the camera lens (Chateau 1986: 34)? A complex system of referential coding is needed; Or is it merely an empirical statement about production practices? This stage allows film semiology to branch ontologically into meaning-the-real (analogous to the referential potential of language to say 'this' or 'today') ordering-the-order (analogous to syntax). Now the door is open for the fourth property of cinema, its comprehensive codification. Both classes of the ontological divide of cinema can exploit (i.e., codify) five communication channels (three auditive: noise, music, and verbal language; two visual: written language and visual images). Both classes need not use identical codes on each channel. All of this seems to be pure observation, but it has a very tangible usefulness: the number of code systems can be multiplied *ad libitum,* building on lower-order codes. There can be theatrical codes based on codes of social interaction, on linguistic codes, on conversational codes, on kinetic codes, on proxemic codes. Within this pluricodicity – but what are the criteria used for distinguishing these codes, if not cognitive ones? – film semiology claims merely to represent a subset of film structure. Cinematography itself is a broader language.

Language in semiological contexts always translates into rules, and rules must be matched by a competence in their users. There is no cinematic competence (Chateau concurring with Sol Worth) corresponding to language competence in cinema and a corresponding grammaticality; there is only performance. However, Chateau seconds van Dijk (speaking about literary texts) when he perceives larger structures based on supplementary rules. These 'superstructures' are often found in poetics (e.g., prosodic rules and narrative syntax). This is certainly a boon for film semiology, which must rid itself of too restricted a model of linguistic grammaticality. Cinematic competence, therefore, comprises the rules for inventing new rules (by the producer as much as the viewer). 'La privation de langage cinématographique standard, soit l'inadéquation du film à une supposée communication ordinaire, signifie qu'il est vain de rechercher d'emblée une grammaire standard pour le film, d'autant que l'absence de critère de grammaticalité ne permettrait pas, en tout état de cause, de distinguer un sous-ensemble de segments filmiques bien formés' (Chateau 1986: 59). Understanding/ competence is equated with the grasp of virtualities. This is a common feature in all semiology, one that follows directly from a differential system of place values. A (positional, topological) value is defined by what it is not. Thus cinematic language (*vidèmes*, *cadèmes*, *édèmes*, etc) is defined as performance, which in standard language is only one side. Supposedly regulated on a grammarlike basis, performance means no more than a grasp of cinematic acceptability: 'On se trouve ... d'emblée déporté vers des jugements correspondant à des acceptabilités (modèle de performance) qui mettent en jeu, à la réception, des classes socio-culturelles d'usagers et, à l'émission, des genres cinématographiques.'[4] Suddenly the communicational aspect of film comes back, but now it is relegated to the concept of text. Thin syntagmatic theory gives it a slant toward textuality. After syntax proved to be irretrievable in films now of interest is the role of enunciation, enunciators, and enunciatees, which is already a narratological problem (cf. *infra*).

Fundamental objections that are not from a Peircean perspective[5] have been levelled against the semiological treatments of film. In particular, Deleuze (1985)[6] criticizes those special cinematic 'codes.' His struggle against linguistics and structuralism is directed against the very Saussurean, structuralist roots of semiology, of which he is very much aware (cf. Deleuze 1973). Treating cinema as a language involves a perspective of sign arbitrariness and the difference of planes: *signifiant* and *signifié*. As a consequence, film theory becomes an inquiry into the 'pluricodicity' that governs cinematic signification. At whom is Deleuze[7] targeting his critique? Semiology 'dissolves the very sign itself.' Deleuze (1985: 342f) juxtaposes the two domains: 'La langue en [scil. de l'énonçable, qui possède sa logique propre] tire des énoncés de langage avec des unités et opérations signifiantes, mais l'énonçable lui-même, ses images et ses signes, sont d'une autre nature ... La sémiologie ... tend à fermer sur soi le "signifiant," et à couper le langage des images et des signes qui en constituent la matière première.' Among other implications of the multiplication of codes that are 'closed within themselves' is that the sign, being arbitrary, can be replaced without loss by convention. The failure of semiology in cinema analysis is complete,[8] measured against semiological claims to establish a *de rigueur* knowledge. Only lawlike syntagmatic codes can be the objects of scientific rigour. Codes are the 'linguisticity' of language and make language operational. The object of his critique (Deleuze 1985: 41) are the two distinct, closed 'moules' (moulds), analogical and digital, into which semiology casts everything: a differential system of two arbitrarily connected continua, 'digitalization' and 'codes.'[9] Indeed, Metz (1968) explicitly accepts Eco's[10] idea of the codification of images (cf. *infra* §3.2). Syntagmatic – that is, Metz's 'passer d'une image à deux images, c'est passer de l'image au langage' (Deleuze [1985: 53] quotes disapprovingly) – betrays a thorough misunderstanding of the image. Deleuze's verdict: no film theory can be made on the basis of semiology.

Apparently, it is Order against Image – two mutually exclusive definitions of the cinematic object. Yet Deleuze's counter-concept is not itself free from ontological presuppositions. The Order (of differences) is as much a transcendental object as Deleuze's Movement (which comprises the mind). Their respective (onto)logic goes this way: either 'deux images' with their differences must force the question of how they relate (paradigmatically and syntagmatically); or one sees image as *singulare tantum*, containing in itself movement (i.e., its own changes). Deleuze answers the ordering problem of images in film (syntagmata) in an ontological way: the 'image' itself, and not what it represents,[11] is either chained or a whole. As we will discover shortly, such a radical counter-proposal is not self-explanatory.

With regard to cinematicity, the explanatory power of the grand syntagmatic standing on its own is relatively weak. It orders units of narrative content, yet it leaves open the fundamental question as to which differential principles are responsible for generating these units themselves – which, as is known, is done in moving images. Thus the meaning-generating principles of the syntagmatic basis must become the focus of our attention. If its representational power does not present time or action space to syntagmas, they are literally order of nothing. The narrative 'real' may be of lesser importance in film than this image 'reality,' which never completely disappears into narrative meaning. What sort of articulation and differences in moving images create meaning? That the 'natural way' to analyze an image is to section it into its parts seems self-evident. But what *are* parts of an image, in particular a moving image? Phonology is the primary paradigm also for visuals (compare to the 'miracle' of sound transformation from noise into phonemes). It has been described but has not been theoretically explained, except in Petitot-Cocorda's topological theories which give a mathematical explanation of pure form (or Gestalt) and of form *in se*. Visual semiology has been quite prolific with description (although it taps Gestaltist wisdom), but it cannot sustain a theory proper (which explains the strategic weight of Eco's iconism theory).

Following the analogy with phonetics closely, in keeping with structuralist axioms, one would begin by differentiating distinctive features within the matter of expression (the first 'mould'). Homology would then allow for an arbitrary but structurally analogous difference in the second 'mould' of meaning ('matter of content'). Distinctive features are themselves not observations. One would not be doing justice to structuralism to think of it in an epistemological way. Through distinctive features an 'episteme' of an observable becomes possible, not the other way round. Thus there is no infinite regress looming here. The structural mode of thinking prevents circular arguments. Let us assume the following structural scenario: (1) Distinctive colour marks in an image differentiate a topos as a line. (2) Paradigmatically there is a differential value to other forms such as circle, square, and so on. (3) On the content side, homology provides a way of differentiating notional marks of 'line-ness,' 'square-ness,' and so on. (4) Within this structural field of topological forms, certain notional combinations yield the identity of one form. Epistemological thinking is tempted to object that one must already know the notion of a line in order to recognize its shape; thus the above sequence would seem inconclusive, or circular, or a regress. This means being oblivious to the 'magic word' in structuralism: homology (or the law of a series, in Saussure's axiom of 'l'arbitraire du signe'). When, for instance, Aumont (1990) describes extensively geometric and other forms, this is not intended as a psychology of perception. We could, however, fail to notice that this is conducive to cinematic meaning. The leap into *meaning* of geometric forms is, however, no problem for structural thinking, because there is homology between a geometrical form (becoming expression) and a notional content (very basic, to be true). It is no answer to go into the descriptive details of visual semiology. In the axiomatic assumptions, the core question itself must be addressed: 'Is homology "true"?' Only then can we ask, 'Is it true that the idea of a line is structurally identical to the topology of certain colour differences in an image? Does the phonetic archetype work in a strong sense for images?'

Clearly, the nature of the expression material imposes strong constraints on how sophisticated meanings are possible. What results from forms and shapes is scanty and does not measure up to the patent richness of representational meaning in images. The structuralist legacy is responsible for the limitations in semiological film theory with regard to both Order and Image. From this perspective, Eco's iconism is an enormous extension (or weakening?) of the structural dogma itself. Sign arbitrariness perhaps has some plausibility for language, yet if it comes to resemble 'motivation' it challenges the very structural explanation. Moving images are so obviously 'motivated signs' that it becomes highly counter-intuitive to maintain an arbitrary relation between the expression and the notional content.

However, the syntagmatic attempt to grasp time as Order is not a fatally flawed intuition (as is evidenced by the earlier discussion in §1.7 and in the discussion of narrative enunciation §6). Time is indeed a series linking two different states of the same in a third respect, change. Here semiology is handicapped greatly by its language paradigm, which contains only two solution principles: either the tense model or the syntax model. In film theory, Bettetini and the Milan School have chosen the first path, Metz and the French School the second. However, both models rely on distinct units, which must relate to one another according to an established logic. Instead of relating the 'identical' 'in different states' to itself, and in doing so originating time, semiology relates previously abstracted units. At this point the interest in and hope with regard to Eco's iconism surfaces, and this has had a considerable (albeit not always obvious) influence on film semiology. The relation, both temporal and representational, is no longer ruled grammatically but rather 'iconically.' Unfortunately, this concept in the Morris Eco tradition lost none of its problematic character once Eco vested it with his 'encyclopaedic' semanticism.

Our crystallization point still involves signs producing the 'real' of cinema. Can the 'real' still be constructed if 'motivation' forces its way into homology and arbitrary sign relation? If cinema is a sign, how is it a sign? The lack of articulation (this is what motivation means, not just a lack of double articulation, as Metz suggests) in cinema entails a negation of signification. Eco is not a major film theorist; even so, his inquiry into the nature of the sign, with a *faux*- perspective on Peirce, has become highly meaningful for the semiology of cinema. Most visual semiology has concentrated on the expression material side, which has yielded scarce content segmentation; Eco, in contrast, focuses on the content side and its segmentation.

3.2 Cinema 'Is' Sign Function

It is iconism, and not the differential system of geometric and other forms, that delivers the 'real' to syntagmatic order: the representational object hinges on iconism. The constitution of cinematic meaning occurs on the basis of a particular kind of sign, which is not just a 'moule' (Deleuze) such as phonetics, discrete and capable of (double or triple) articulation. This kind of basic sign is iconic and is thought to be constituted of particular problems of segmentation. In connection with this particular sign, three topics hold interest for us: (1) its representational achievement (i.e., whether, how, and how far); (2) its representational provisioning for syntagmatics (i.e., how it delivers time) and (3) whether we are justified in bringing iconism into a 'sibling' relationship (perhaps as 'creative rewriting') with Peirce's Iconic Sign. In this context, Eco's and others' reconciliation of Saussurean and Peircean sign theories gives us occasion to (a) review the nature of signs in a Peircean framework, and (b) question Saussurean assumptions about the nature of signs from a Peircean perspective.

Would Peirce pass the entrance examination to the semiological universe of discourse as his 'coaches' Jakobson, Morris, and Eco apparently thought he might? What makes an answer to this question more difficult is that de Saussure's school had various ramifications, if not heterogeneity. For instance, Hjelmslev's Glossematics became influential for Jakobson, who established Peirce as the father of semiology. An altogether different tradition is Morris' – chiefly semantics and meant as a extension of Carnap's philosophical program. Its other parts, syntax and pragmatics, must be understood as part of this extension (cf. Apel [1975: 20 *passim*]). Through genealogy or syncretism, Eco's iconism has inherited Peirce, but not necessarily a genuine Peirce. 'Has Eco understood Peirce?' is the rhetorical question of Tejera (1989). His answer comes close to a flat no. Especially, if such important concepts as Categories and Index and Icon are sacrificed, Peirce's admission fee to the semiological universe of discourse may be too high. The impulse to merge the two sign theories goes back to Jakobson at a time when it was still possible to exploit Peircean Categories liberally and 'creatively' (cf. Portis-Winner ([1994: 126–9]). He accomplished the astonishing feat of raising the number of Categories to four, thereby defeating the triadic architecture of Peircean thought. Eco (1976) must be credited with an accommodation more faithful to Peirce (while still using him as a quarry for a different construction).

Iconicity, both the common term and the radically disparate theories behind it, is indeed not a bad choice for focusing a debate between likewise radically different sign theories. This dispute involves theories of Reality and cognition at large. This clearly has profound consequences for the cinematic object. Eco's project idea is to transform Iconicity (Morris's and, by extension, Peirce's) into representational analogy. Analogy implies a sign, a signified other, and the rule of comparison. For Eco it is enough that this latter is a distinct feature in both 'reality' and representation, not a logical operation. For example, particularities in a landscape would be represented in the particularities of a map (e.g., same height in same line). In keeping with the arbitrary sign function, this construes two different juxtaposed planes. This dyadicity prevents the triadic understanding of Semiosis comprehending a logical Interpretation. Juxtaposition suggests (to a mind in Peirce, and to a differential system in semiology) a comparison of parts. Only this enables the segmentation of a landscape. If anything can be first decomposed into semantic markers or sememes, any concrete thing is a multitude of 'cultural units' to be recomposed and assembled (we should be aware that this is not Peirce's Semiotic unity of the manifold). Thus it will always be possible to find one of these markers in common with another thing. A landscape is a cultural unit that can be decomposed into a multitude of single features. If there are no markers shared directly with a two-dimensional thing such as a map, we can establish a transformation rule to provide it. On the presupposition that altitude can always be measured in the same, constant way, it can then be transformed into colour coding, and so on.

Iconism then, faces two different problems: (1) What governs the transformation from one code system into another? (2) Which process ascertains the decomposition into the right sememic marks? After all, we are still in a sign universe, whose units are units of meaning (at least in one articulation), and not beans or atoms to be broken down 'naturally.' The answer to (1) brought Eco to Morris and to a communicational reconceptualization of the sign as function; this will be our next topic. Problem (2) later led him to Peirce's sign theory, which he presented in a notable reinterpretation. He must have attached considerable importance to this idea, since he divulged it, as a Peirce interpretation, in roughly the same form on at least six occasions, as evidenced in Eco (1979: n1) and in *Langage* 58 (June 1980). Indeed, this sort of Peirce interpretation is important for his argumentation strategy as a whole, as we will examine briefly.

If Eco's iconism seemed so promising for the syntagmatic order of film semiology as an escape from the quagmire of differential systems, the hope lay in sign 'motivation.' Notwithstanding Peircean reminiscences, the territory remained fundamentally a collection of segmented sememic units and their arbitrary combination with an object. Transcription (of object properties, which are in themselves a differential system) involves organizing a translation rule into graphical artefacts, which Eco calls 'code' ('Rappresentare iconicamente l'oggetto significa allora trascrivere per mezzo di artifici grafici (o di altro genere) le proprietà culturali che gli vengono attribuite' (Eco [1975: 272]) – for example, (Morris's) verbal onomatopoeic expressions. Similarly, indexicals (or any other 'deictic' elements) are 'operationalized' as toposensitive sign. That an 'expressive artefact' 'functions' as sign for 'something else' is often not capable of being governed by a rule; rather, it must be instituted through communication as a code. Motivation here means that 'standing for' uses a similarity between the opposites to facilitate that 'for.' Tirelessly, Eco (1975: 261ff) demonstrates that all of these similarities are also based on conventions. Iconic motivation is needed when the expression artefacts cannot easily be reduced to differential 'marks.'

The ultimate borderline is a semiological theory of perception, which is evidently difficult to describe in terms of code. 'Motivation' is no more than a special sort of attribution (of sememic content units to a token-without-type expression artefact), one that is more constrained than in pure arbitrariness. The problem at the root of motivation is not the mechanism for connecting binary planes to a sign function when one of the planes is systemically deficient. This shakes the foundations for the whole explanatory power of semiology, if the relation of an abstract system to concrete units in this system can exhibit various *rationes*. This really introduces an alien element into differentiality, since *ratio* strikes us semantically as another term for 'mind.' (Besides, it is in this context that Eco misinterprets the Peircean type token distinction as standing for this system unit relationship. The third element in this triad, tone, is dropped silently.) There can be an easy (*ratio facilis*) type token relation, in which the system clearly defines the position of the unit, and there can be a difficult (*ratio difficilis*) relation when the unit is underdefined and has no clear position (Eco [1975: 246–8]). This is when a code, which of course is always between types (expression and content), needs considerable 'work' (*lavoro*) in order to establish it. Iconism is located on the difficult *ratio* side of expression artefacts, which relate to no precise rules establishing the system.

Eco's whole point is that the *ratio* of a token to a system must be established, even in the most difficult cases he discusses. One of the really hard cases is perception (1975: 312–15), which avails itself of a perceptive model in order to become a unit in that system. Does this solve the problem? No. It merely pushes the question one concept further, so that we can ask the same with regard to the modelling of the perceptive model. Are the innate ideas *a priori* or acquired forms? Eco is tight lipped where there would be a real philosophical interest. The very idea of systems suggests that they are in place, in function, because without some sort of inner organization there would be no elements. The notion that there are elements without a system, semes without a lexicon, amounts to a contradiction in terms. 'Motivation' must at least involve a motivator and a motivated, and this opens the opportunity for us to discern at least some system features on the motivator's side ('model' is an architectonic need for 'perception'). In Eco's semiology, strictly speaking, this never goes beyond the status of a postulate. The conditions of its possibility are never proven, never reflected on. The biplanar point of reference, including arbitrariness, remains in force. Without abandoning his reference, Eco could have expanded his semiology within the framework of systems theory. Instead of a simple multiplication of code systems, they could be ordered in subsystems. Thus the sign function could be better understood as specifications of a system of communication (cf. Merten [1977]).

However, the fundamental question of signs is not solved through postulates. We need to have clear ideas regarding whether signs are dyadic relations of expression and content, or triadic relations.[12] This changes the whole picture, and is not a question of details in sign typology (or 'sign functions'). Regarding these two completely heterogeneous conceptions of signs, the hinge is a man whose merit it was to have kept alive an interest in Peircean Semiotic even in the meagre years, when his works were largely unpublished. Originally, the admission of less-than-arbitrary signs was motivated by Morris (quoted on iconicity in Eco [1975: 257]). Iconicity, as understood by Morris (1946),[13] has one element in common with semiology: cultural arbitrariness. Its main point consists in social pragmatics. Eco's own verdict in the iconism field ('useless') despite its clarity, perhaps does not fully measure up to the philosophical reflection in his source: 'la categoria di iconismo non serve a nulla, confonde le idee perché non definisce un solo fenomeno e non definisce solo fenomeni semiotici. L'iconismo rappresenta una collezione di fenomeni messi insieme, se non a caso, almeno con grande larghezza di idee'; yet he goes even further to question the idea of the sign itself as inapplicable: 'È la nozione stessa di 'segno' che risulta inadoperabile' (1975: 282f).

The substitute is sign function, which emphasizes the functive of joining expression with content (which is not exactly the idea of signhood in Morris and is completely alien to Peirce). Eco's significance for a film theory conceived as syntagmatic order is based on the dissolution of sign into sign function. The compactness of code system thought was considered in this way to be preserved. Outside these semiological constraints, iconism had a life of its own, before it became a source. We will take a brief look at Morris's concept of this, because as a source it promises to be richer than its recipient.

Also, iconicity plays a certain role as a Peircean heritage. The task Morris assigns to sign theory is not to solve Peirce's original question of true cognition of the real. There is no cognition in signs, here. Cognition having taken place, there can only be a more or less coordinated use of communication artefacts. Not all of these artefacts are up to the highest standards of regularity. "Iconicity is thus a matter of degree" (Morris [1946: 7.2]). But degree of what? Morris's answer is 'of what it denotes,' which is precisely the Object. A sign that shares physical 'properties' of its object is but a less real of a (sensory) real, as it were. A sign will always be a mental thing to Peirce, but not to Morris. If he does not want to fall back into a *receptaculum* concept of mind, where exterior sensory data (or percepts) provoke associations (constant not by the intervention of God – as in Berkeley – but by conventional use), he must postulate behavioural conventions as absolutes.[14] In the case of iconicity, sensory data becoming a sign is very difficult to explain, unless we resort to what Morris calls 'idealistic metaphysics' (Morris 1946: App. 2]). 'For if "sign" is defined in terms of mind or thought, then we cannot furnish an empirical criterion for determining whether a certain thing is or is not a sign' (ibid.). Explicitly he understands his philosophy as behavioural completion of Carnap's logical Onto-Semanticism. Thus his sign theory wants to be measured for how it provides this support. There are objects and subjects of behaviour. Objects are only the vis-à-vis, the *other* of a behaviour, whose behaving is *ipso facto* signifying.

This dyadic relation eliminates 'mentalism'; furthermore it leaves no place for Quality and 'outward clash' upon sign processes. Even iconicity is defined from behaviour, because only in a behavioural relationship is the (physically) other important. With icons it is the sensory qualities of that (physical) object which become the object of the sign. They are the invitation through which 'the interpreter highly activates in himself his dispositions to respond, and can by the study of the icon acquaint himself with certain properties of what is signified.'[15] Eco explicitly accepts Morris's definition of sign ('si accetta la definizione di Morris [1938] per cui "qualcosa è un segno solo perché è interpretato come segno di qualcosa da qualche interprete"'). Eco's antimentalism calls for a concrete interpretant, for physical persons who can be observed (1975: 27). As behaviour, in any case, it needs a rule, and this quasi-normativity is statistical for a 'normal' Subject; it is substituted in Eco with a given concrete Culture as quasi-Subject of a convention. The problem with behavioural rules is alleviated when perception is treated as iconic but merely initial sign: Behaviour selects response to certain stimuli. These become sign, whereas the refuted ones do not.[16] When we treat iconicity as sensory data taken over as 'preparatory stimuli' (i.e. for the rule-governed behaviour) from the object itself, we run into the same epistemological problems as we do with Eco's 'raw percepts' (cf. *supra*). The elimination of true Thirds can yield only as reductive a metaphysic (as Peirce described it in 5.79, 1903). They differ only in what the triad is reduced to. Morris's signs, as preparatory stimuli, cannot validly be determined by behaviour: they are merely actual, and determination on the grounds of actuality is not general. Meaning – more than the statistically verified use of actual signs – requires a Law or Thirdness. A truly universal, valid, and true concept can never be 'sensory stimulus'. In the wake of Carnap's similar *Protokollsätzen*, both can be defined no further than as having 'prognostic relevance of theoretical concepts.' Peirce had answered this with his triadic relations. He foresaw *avant la lettre* what Apel (1975: 20ff, referring to [5.77–81, 1903]) termed 'reductive fallacies.' Eco's reduction to codification stipulates Laws without Reality (Quality and Facticity). Thirdness would inevitably become an empty concept, deprived precisely of its mediation function.

Another type of reduction (behaviourist) of the triad to a dyadic relationship of observation is realized in Morris; his declared intention was to fight Peirce's 'unmodern' mentalism. Through his programmatic support of Carnap, he effectively inherits a metaphysical foundation. Although emphatically sharing Peirce's pragmatic premise (as he understood it), he rejects as 'mentalist' a normative logic that would form the sign as rule. His would be a *post factum* logic (if this were not a contradiction in terms) established by conventions of behaviour. These conventions can be observed and analyzed statistically, resulting in quite stable sign-behaviour relations. (Not so surprisingly, this idea in the guise of the 'generalized other' found its way into Mead's *opus magnum*, edited and compiled by the same Morris.) If it was intended as a Peirce interpretation, Morris had to suppress the distinction that was so important for the late Peirce between the 'dynamical interpretant' of a sign (the individual psychophysical effect of a com-

munication) and the 'logical interpretant' (normatively correct conceptual interpretation). Thus, he had to admit that rule-based behaviour
itself must simply 'be presupposed by semiotic and [can] not be
defined within it' (Morris [1946: Glossary, s.v. 'Behavior']). With this
presupposition he frees himself from having to make explicit the metaphysical assumption that is buried in it.

Morris's second epistemological premise is 'science.' But how is science possible as true cognition of the real, in an antimentalist framework? How can anybody observe *ab extra* one's statistically average
pragmatic interpretation of a sign? Evidently, investigators themselves
must first have understood that a sign vehicle is mediated with a fact,
and how. However, only by self-interpretation can they do so, because
it is precisely that which they are doing when observing. Furthermore,
it is not only whether someone mediates some fact with some sign
vehicle, that is in question; it is how a habit (of such mediation) should,
or will be, formed *properly* ('adequate opinion') in the long run. In principle, that will be decided by all communicants, or, vicariously in one's
own logical justification of one's habit. The first case will never happen
concretely, the second is only a theoretical possibility. Nevertheless,
the logical normative Interpretant needs always to be part of the observation, which by that very fact ceases to be merely observation. It
becomes Interpretation instead.

So far, we have been looking at reductionist attempts to explain
iconism. The term also plays an important role in Lotman's film aesthetic, but there it has more of a function as a *Kunstwollen*-type of artistic
usage. We will return to it in that other context. Furthermore, I should
mention that Mitry picks up the term 'iconic,' even in a triadic constel-
lation, but in a completely independent reflection on the genesis of a
new language, which supposedly is especially close to the process of
thought. These, and some minor uses, are no longer the 'fodder' of syntagmatic film theory along the lines of Morris and Eco. The purpose was
to keep the integrity of differential meaning systems. This meant that
Eco had to reject some of Morris's basic ideas about behaviour in connection with iconic signs. Merely the communicational-turned-cultural
conjunction between sign and object remained; however, Eco transformed this into sign function and type token cases. Whether or not this
is a satisfactory solution, for film semiology and as the concept of a sign
theory at large, must (to be just) also be considered in the context of
Eco's use of Peirce. This is the second source of iconismo, as was mentioned earlier.

The entire promise of iconism relates to the novel means for reseg-menting content when there is no type of the token-of-expression arte-fact. Even though Eco's early efforts focused on iconism on the expression side, it was still difficult to understand the need for this difficult type token relationship. Was there too little codification or too much? We should approach his later 'creative' reinterpretation of Peircean sign theory concepts as a contribution to the original problem of iconism. It is only worth arriving at new codes of expression if doing so will result in new content. Certainly, we should not treat Eco's (1976) work as an authentic interpretation of Peircean sign theory – for that matter, he does not claim that it is. That said, it is through this reinterpretation that we can comprehend iconism's sememic potential to expand content.

Eco's argumentation[17] starts from his concept of 'signification,' without any relation to Categories or equivalent groundwork. It defines the problem of sign functions as one of 'disambiguation'. This is obvious only if signs must produce clear positions in the system of meaning (i.e., not true cognition). 'Clouds of content' or expression are a problem. One attraction of Peircean interpretational signs is that they are used to solve this problem, which, let us remember, is altogether alien to Semiotic. The triad as the intrinsic relation of a semiosis opens a path to semantic decomposition, provided we understand it in Eco's sense. For him, briefly, signs are momentary aggregations of sememic marks, which are conveniently projected onto an object. (This is how the distinction between dynamical and immediate objects is exploited.)

It is obvious, as a first point of critique, that this misses the very idea of Generality and its non-substitutable function in Signs.[18] 'A sign becomes a clown, who takes off one mask only to reveal another' is Esposito's (1980: 362) colourful précis of Eco (1976); he gives him the predicate 'pragmatic' (at best), but not 'Pragmaticistic.' Fumagalli (1995: 311n) believes that Eco has abandoned this position (although he does not provide supporting evidence as to how this could happen to such a central tenet without threatening the architectonic structure). There are, however, two other fundamental objections from a Peircean perspective that we must deal with. One is in connection with the 'derealization' of the Object. As soon as the Object becomes a convenient container of sememic marks, this is the end of Haecceity, that is, the very idea of Secondness. Another subtle stumbling block is this: How can it be possible that in the Sign relation, Ground should be different from Interpretant? Eco uses 'interpretation' as a kind of procedure for assembling sememic marks (in the 'ground') into a new sign. Peirce's Quality becomes 'qualities.' His witty juggling with terms from very different stages of Peirce's sign theory development, for instance, Ground and Sign change places in the terminology of sign theory, obfuscates the fundamental difference in functions between a First and a Third. As we know, Categories must be ordinal and iterative in order to be ultimate forms, and a Third is (knowing) 'more' than a First (see letter to Welby). Eco offers no answers to the problems Peirce was trying to solve with the Categories. The reason why there are irreducibly three Categories is that Peirce sees in them the bedrock requirements of cognitive forms or being. Sememic containers are, of course, no substitute for the 'outward clash' or the externality of meaning. All of this defies the early Pragmaticistic belief that any cognition needs real problems, an impulse from outside. Otherwise, attention to chaos would not be paid.

How does this relate to the iconic foundation of cinematic syntagms? Evidently, nothing can be placed in a syntaxlike order if there is no representational object. Since the crucial part of cinematic representation is not linguistic, an ordered presemiotic real is embarrassing. Thus, iconism constitutes an ingenious attempt to order the unordered, the primordial stage of ordering, which coincides with the primordial stage of 'being something' (i.e., different). The problem lies at the beginning of order: How does the discrete enter the continuous? Unlike Peirce, Eco has room for 'presemiotic' reality, which is non-differential by definition; thus order for him involves inventing a process (called 'perception') by which difference can be introduced. Syntagmatic film theory depends on such percepts, iconic signs, for cinematic representation as a whole. As we have seen, iconism is an extension of the differential order of semiology into the realm of 'difficult codes.' Needless to say, this entails an enormous complexification of arbitrary sign functions and of the expression side. In terms of type token codes, the content side is not as easy to grasp if we are prohibited from referring to mental categories. As a result, the sememic marks, and the encyclopaedic organization of marks in their entirety, have had to supplant 'facile and difficult codes' for content organization.

Even after such a notable expansion and complexification, we cannot properly criticize the semiological idea of differential meaning organization except at a fundamental level. Eco's 'transformation' has pointed us precisely to the place where the hinges of this sign theory can be criticized and compared with others. The question is this: Sign function or Sign Relation? This encompasses the entire debate. Let us assume for now that three mechanisms are satisfactorily explained: one, disambig-uating the positional determination of content tokens; two, a reliable functive com-Bination with an expression token; three, that Eco finds a mechanism for this decomposition of sememic marks (= interpretation[E] [in Eco's sense]). Now the question is still, 'What is the purpose of inter-pretation[E]?' The question is not, 'How can this content token be com-municated?' because there surely would be communication codes for this. Instead, if truth (Peirce's 'knowing more') as the purpose of inter-pretation must be eliminated, why would one interpret[E]? We notice the different theory design in the questions, which then become meaning-less in the respective other context. Although it becomes in semiology meaningless to ask truth questions it is meaningless in Semiotic to ask questions of truthless communication. For Peirce, there are no lies; there are only deceptions, because at least the liar knows truth. For Eco, the ultimate achievement of sign theory is that it explains how to lie and how to joke. How such a communication could function is unimag-inable. This results from a conclusion from objections to Morris's 'sta-tistical rule' of usage, which Eco uses as an argument for his communic-ability theory.

Are signs functions or Relations? It seems evident that the difference between a convention-based and a Category-based sign theory must appear also in capacities, which a theory has or has not. For cinema in particular, the change from iconism to Icons is fundamental. Semiotic makes obsolete the semiological problem of how signs are ordered: no longer do they simply 'stand for something else' and combine with it in a codified way. If this 'something else' already stands in an ordered relation to the sign (as in a Triad), syntagmata (or syntax) must consti-tute a redundant secondary order (i.e., not the real meaning determi-nation). Conversely, for temporal order, Semiotic offers an entirely new approach to making a Sign (i.e., meaning). We must not let our-selves be deceived by pictorial representation, which is the *princeps analogatum* of Eco's iconism. The relationship between painting and reality is also applied to the representational achievement of time, which is implicitly comprehended as narrative time. This, however, is exactly *not* the cognitive achievement of the relational triad Time.

For Time it is not at all important how the facticity of two events is experienced. It may well be that there are Iconic facts, a simple succes-sion of percepts. This corresponds to a purely interior experience of passing time. Facts can equally be indexical and then relate to outside events in their truth values. This corresponds to movement in the physical world and also to normalized movement in a clockwork. Symbols can also be Facts, yet they are related to the outside world through generality. Thus they are not suitable for stating singularities – they are always 'general facts.' Iconicity, as in every other Sign process, also contributes to the cognition of time. However, this contribution occurs at a point that is totally different from the way in which it is conceptualized by syntagmatic film theory (cf. *supra*). There are two reasons why syntagmatics lacks the capacity to grasp time. (1) The units on which syntagms are based in themselves marginally different or differentiable, either as units of representation or as continuous temporality. In either case, this entails an incapacity for double articulation, which is a fatal flaw in the semiological generation of meaning. (2) The result is a merely analogical use of the concept of syntax. Non-discrete units cannot form a syntax as second articulation. Yet only from a syntax can tenses arise, and without tenses there is no 'time' in semiology. It is literally unthinkable to establish an arbitrary sign function – even weakened 'iconically' or as 'motivated' – between an expression and content if the expression cannot be differentially articulated. Semiotic takes a quite different approach. In a triadic sign process it relates two (indexical or iconic) facts under one general respect. This general respect can be syntax, of course, but it can also come from another Symbol such as narrative enunciation. Later we will see how Semiotic enables us to account for time as experience (something that is not possible in semiology), just as it enables us to account for time as temporality (of a pragmatic causality). At this point we must get a clearer view of the cinematic problem, which iconism has not solved. The question of what cinema represents – or better, what its representational object is before it becomes (and in order for it to become – narrativity as pragmatic logic – is still open.

3.3 Cinema 'Is' Percept

Recuperation of the Real for film is, ultimately, the issue raised through cognitivism. A basic intuition of cognitivist film psychology is that the cinematic meaning must be related to the real – a glaring absence in semiology.

How does cognitivism translate this intuition into method? The decisive questions are two: What is taken as *explanans*? (That is, which meta-language is adopted to explain the object?) And what is the *explanandum*? (That is, what can be covered by cognitivist theory?)

In order to take account of cognitivism's strength as theory *per se*, we deliberately decontextualize it from its customary place. Often, for poetics or aesthetics of cinema, it figures as initial 'connection in series.' Its supposed function, its utility, is to deliver the *explanans* – or logic of theorizing narratives – to narratology and stylistic, which then turn 'automagically' into a special type of psychology. A short-circuited cognitivism as narrative spatiotemporal action space is quite different and obscures the logical diversity of constituting narrative and experiential spatiotemporality. Cognitivism must convince as cognition theory at large, and as theory of cinematic experience *in se*, which can comprise but must not be confined to cinematic narration.

3.3.1 What Are the Common Traits of All Variants of Cognitivism?

'Cognitivism' is not a unified theory. At best, it is an approach with certain fairly typical traits. Those who call themselves cognitivists customarily emphasize that cognitivism is 'piecemeal' and not a unified theory (still less a 'grand' one; cf. Carroll in Bordwell 1996: 39). It can even be seen as an 'attitude,' at least. A really nice way to put this is Carroll's 'dialogical theories' or 'dialectic conception of film theory' (ibid.: 63). Yet even 'competitive theories' compete in the same game. The 'rule set' is truth claims about an object, which in the case of cinema is an object of meaning. A minimum requirement for a common denomination theory is that we 'see' the same object in a common coherent metalanguage. The versions of cognitivism are many and diverse, but any critical reflection will enable us to stay within the limits of the similarities among methodologies. We should regret that constructivist/cognitivist film theory has been assigned the role of a rallying cry in the polemic against psychoanalytic and other 'fads' in film theory: this reverberates on the pages of the collective volume *Post-Theory*, assembled by Bordwell and Carroll. Some Berlin scholars (e.g., Schumm and Wulff 1990 pursue this approach in film theory as well, although without the polemical overtones.

First, the common object converges most generally on a certain notion of perception, which signals the shift towards a psychological methodology. As one key to the cinematic object, perception becomes a necessity when we approach cinematic meaning not through linguistic meaning but rather through description of psychological functions. This all-important, fundamental, methodological option of cognitivism differs from two alternative approaches: epistemology (as the cognized reality) and phenomenology (as immediate consciousness). This is clear from the respective perspectives: whereas cognitivism sees interiority (psychic functions) as objective entity, epistemology relates interiority (thought) to external reality, and phenomenology sees interiority (immediate consciousness) as subjective entity, not described as object and not a function of its noematic content, its protensional acts.

Thus the cognitivist mundane exterior hinges on psychological interiority described non-introspectively as cognitive object. Notwithstanding the objectification of subjectivity, the methodological point is that the psychic object can still produce the fundamental difference 'in' versus 'out' (this comes in the guise of oppositions such as concept vs data and Currie's 'models matching input'). Once we have established this founding difference, it does not matter which perspective we see it from: outside or inside. Whatever can be said is intelligible only from its dialectic other. This difference, however, is a psychic difference and is not an option for realism. This is why constructivism can come close to Radical Constructivism, an instance of Systems theory. How would systems theory enter Constructivism[19]? Despite its silence, and despite its lack of reflexive concern about its principles of construction, the system paradigm enters by way of environmental psychology. Much of its argumentative power is drawn from this idea, which allows for anti-mentalism and non-subjective functionalism. However, few cognitivist film theorists investigate their grounding in explicit theories of science. In all justice, it must be admitted that for most film theorists, constructivist and cognitivist theories assume a merely ancillary role. Investigating the basic constructions of any downstream meaning is thus relegated to positive sciences (e.g., experimental psychology), without any further concern about their conceptualizations of meaning construction. For example, Bordwell is not in the first place constructivist; he is neoformalist and therefore constructivist. We need not concern ourselves with the success or failure of the amalgamation of two heterogeneous strands of theory, as long as the junction between the two is clear. That practical end is relevant upstream, as it limits the depth and purview of the theoretical development of constructivism. Also, such practical ends are a concession so that constructivism and cognitivism can become very broad churches. Constructivist constructs provide 'cinematic specificity' within the framework of Formalism. 'Normal' contrasts with 'literary' perception (the Formalist Литерарност). As a necessity of theory design, it colours Bordwell's constructivist account of cinematic perception. In Bordwell (1981), the 'normality' of familiarized (or 'automatic') perception is taken for granted and remains unaccounted for. So there is as yet no concern about perception and psychology. As problems only of unity and disunity, artistic strategies of defamiliarization are disunifying. This is the aesthetic preoccupation of Formalism.

Thus not every psychologism leads to introspection of solitary psychic subjects. In contrast to all these forms of *verstehende* psychology, the interior could also be treated as an unknown variable that is described perfectly by its reactions. It is enough that the fundamental difference is maintained. This is to some degree common to various other psychological frameworks for film: Hugo Münsterberg's film perception psychology (close to consciousness philosophy), the phenomenological French film psychology of Mitry and Cohen-Séat, and even Arnheim's Gestaltism.

Second, there is another foundational difference, one that is grafted onto the first but of greater practical use – two hierarchical levels: 'automatic' versus 'poetic' processes, and 'automatism' versus 'judgment.' Formalism operates solely on the basis of such changes in levels, from which it gleans all aesthetic relevance. For Bordwell's (1985) non-linguistic, cinematic poetics, defamiliarization is the aesthetic layer above normal constructivist perception; the same is replicated in cognitivism (Bordwell 1989b, 1990, 1992), with Formalism as a background. A similar difference is found in Currie (1995). The difference between inductive and deductive processes – which are not even the gist of constructivism[20] – has been overemphasized. Automatic perception involves the 'inductive' application of models to data ('cues'), whereas deductive reasoning selects consciously matching models. Every perception terminates in automatic conclusions, or higher judgments, although not necessarily in linguistic propositions,[21] for which the appropriate terms are 'templates,' 'bottom-up' and 'top-down' processes and so on. They explain the application of schemata to all sorts of cognitive operations. Especially important for Formalism is the construction of a narrative. The supposed advantage of schemata is that there is no longer a need to construct narrative grammars (as Semionarratology attempts to do) that would explain the sequence of action logic and the generation of their total as more than its parts (which Ricoeur's hermeneutic narratology attempts to do).

As a Constructivist Bordwell assumes that certain basic processes are common to all perception. A spectator not only 'perceives' sensory stimuli but also 'constructs a perceptual judgment on the basis of nonconscious inferences' (1985: 31). These inferences are non-conscious, because they are not subject to effort and because they happen automatically whenever we do not make an effort to prevent them. We will always see colours.[22] The virtually automatic processes are the so-called 'bottom-up' processes, whereas the 'top-down' ones are 'more overtly based on assumptions, expectations, hypotheses' (loc. cit.). These are the 'schemata' that guide hypothesis making; they are epistemologically close to 'scripts' or 'frames' in the context of narration and world cognition, according to Nieding and Ohler (cf. Schumm 1990: 44–7). Bordwell writes that 'constructivist theory permits no easy separation between perception and cognition'; even so, his Formalism required that this distinction be made.

Having 'cues,' 'environment data,' 'stimuli' on the one hand and 'hypothesis-testing,' 'expectations,' 'assumptions,' 'prior knowledge,' and so on the other, replicates the pattern of Kant's amalgam of rationalism and empiricism. At a higher level of reflection this has produced the transcendental entities of synthetic construct and apperception. Constructivism, however, considers the explanatory power of psychological *a prioris* sufficient, and shows no concern for the intrinsic differences among types of 'prior knowledge,' 'hypotheses,' and the like. Not even Kant's typification of schemata, which results in essentially different kinds of cognition, has been instructive when it comes to diversifying constructivist schemata. The 'dynamic nature of the Constructivist account' (Bordwell 1985: 31) is a virtually eternal process of hypothesis testing ('schemata'). It can be thought of as coming to a halt only through psychic satisfaction or arbitrary decision. 'Incoming data' would continuously destabilize the percept as an identical Some-Thing until 'satisfaction,' 'confirmation and disconfirmation' put an end to it. This is the major difference between the successful 'unification of the manifold of senses' in a judgment – as Kant understood empirical cognition – and the satisfaction of a psyche. Bordwell's cognitivism is in no way a genuine temporalization of cognition, as seen in Peirce's Pragmaticism. This, if we discount satisfaction – it is no less arbitrary than the semiological or glossematic content expression combination. Notwithstanding the inflow of data, this is never the determining cognitive factor. It seems that it is solely the hypothesis itself, or the schemata (whose task it is to organize sensory data into 'things'), that 'is' in a strong sense. This is why Bordwell's cognitivism is not truly realist. It must always start from the assumption of primary schemata, and it cannot really deal with the real impact of an outward reality, of real chaos (in spite of 'data'). In light of the complex Peircean theory of any type of experience (i.e., sign classes), not enough aspects of the actual cognitive process have been considered here – for example, we have not considered the complexity of the real before the mind. However, the metaphoric licence or suggestive richness of these operational concepts prevents one from precisely reconstructing all the epistemological implications.

Bordwell's constructivism and later cognitivism seem concerned mainly with a psychological theory of cognition; in contrast, Currie's concern is re-cognition. By turning now to Currie's cognate but more philosophical account, we will encounter the meaning producing/conceptual skeleton (which must be stripped of antisemiological, antipsychoanalytic polemic). We will find that Currie's topic is more revelatory regarding the research-guiding foundational problem. Various contexts show that there is a consciousness of the problem of how cognition relates to the real. Polemically, it is the standpoint against the 'artifice, conventionality, codedness' (cf. Currie 1995: 79) sort of theorizing that concerns itself with a contrasting 'realist' account of (film) perception. This task of establishing some 'Likeness' between percept and the perceived object is clearly more arduous than explanations that rely on convention, and is, in fact, in its understanding of the problem much closer to Peirce (but by the same token, cognitivism is more remote from constructivism).

The reality question enters through traditionally understood concepts. Clearly, 'schema' (in Bordwell more a metaphor than a concept) somewhat resembles Kant's schemata, Table of Judgements, and list of categories. In passing, Bordwell refutes such implied kinship as unnecessary for Constructivism[23]; that said, he has inherited, in another form, the epistemological problems. A rudimentary description of the principal process of cognition (i.e., as spatiality) segregates two processes. The first of these involves 'automatism' (also a metaphor), the second a (propositional?) judgment. Yet in terms of logic, there is no criterion of separation so far, as both apply concepts to data (which are supposed to be neatly separated entities). In any case, the real question, which led to Kant's laborious efforts to individuate categorical forms of such an application, is deeper than this. Cognition does not function with just one form, 'concepts.' The whole point of separating categories (traditionally ten or more) is the insight that irreducible ultimate concepts can never be abstracted to this extent. 'Applying concepts to data' says no more than [whatever] ' – is.' This is an empty enunciation, one that does not even contain the possibility for negation, that ' – is not.' 'Is' – as Aristotle knew – is inevitably said in diverse ways (cf. *infra*, 567n26).

The most basic critique of the commonplace 'data versus concept' is discussed elsewhere (*supra* 90, *infra* 205). In light of the second common characteristic of cognitivism, it might be more appropriate to ask, 'What is the reason for it?' 'Concept' and 'data' are not equal. In short, cognitivism/constructivism is in need of a level drop or disparity. The handwriting of 'synthesis,' or the reduction of 'the manifold of senses,' is on the wall. As Currie reveals, the innocuous 'bottom-up' and 'top-down' inferences suddenly become wide-open problems of logic. What are the laws that allow this reduction? What is the (relatively more) synthetical nature of the 'concept' compared with the (relatively) non-synthetic 'data'? To make the situation more complex, 'data' in themselves are most often concepts at a different level. The pure data at the bottom are either abstractions or very rare cases of complete invention. They must be so startling and novel, without the admixture of general elements 'under' which they are meaningful. Not even cognitivism goes so far, because pure data do not 'fall under' concepts 'automatically.' (Or would it be better to say that concepts search 'their' data, that is, general facts contain all their conceivable instances?).

In Currie's philosophically more explicit and reflected description, an automatically 'triggered' recognition mechanism, something 'sub-personal,' 'happens within me' (1995: 83). From a Semiotic, logical point of view, Currie's (crime fiction? metaphor) 'trigger' cannot conceal that this is still a procedure in which a generality brings a character into relation with a (possible) object. It is only through the insinuation of the chosen metaphor that the agent of this process is 'features' (e.g., certain spatial features of 'horsehood' in the triggered recognition of a horse), which unify in the concept ('horse') 'above it.' Currie (1995: 81) describes this as a 'capacity to associate some visual feature of what I see with the concept horse, thereby enabling me to *bring* what I see *under* that *concept*' (emphasis added). This associative capacity suggests a non-mental replica of mental operations of thought. It can only consist of a planned selection of features that fit. This raises a problem: what are the laws of this capacity for selection? Currie seems to halt the looming infinite regress by expressing his belief in the self-organization of the organism. We might conclude, then, that there are two horses, one self-organized and one judgmental, because on the other side of automatism is something 'personal,' which 'I do' (83), and which is no longer the domain of recognition but rather that of 'judgment.'

Stripped of their cumbersome sophistication, 'trigger' (feature association) and 'judgment,' in quintessence, remind us respectively of Kant's apperception or transcendental aesthetic, and synthetic judgements (v. *supra*). This simplicity makes critical appreciation difficult, since it leaves so many essential questions unanswered. However, cognitivism recognizes a valid distinction: not everything that becomes a concept is the same type of cognitive act or conduct; concept is not equal to concept. This observation is not nearly as precise as is necessary; even so, it agrees with the basic intuition of Peirce's earliest Phenomenology. 'What is' (in its totality, as it appears to us in a non-uniform way) can be differentiated (v. 63) into types of concepts. So far the agreement, expressed in psychological and logical terms, respectively. 'I perceive white' is different from 'I see white froth from the mouth of this horse as symptom of its exhaustion.' Peirce logically distinguished three kinds of concepts. Some allow one differentiation, while others include all three. 'Trigger' concepts – which are really concepts of qualities – can be logically dissociated only from other concepts. The idea of red can be dissociated from blue, but not more. It cannot be discriminated from the idea of colour; however, colour can be precised from space. That said, Currie's 'horsehood' is not precisely a concept of the lowest kind and thus cannot be 'automatic.' All three distinction types can be applied to this concept. Thus, 'horse' can be discriminated from 'dog' but not from 'animal' (there is no horse without animal, there is but animal without horse); 'horse' can be precised from 'body,' 'strength' (there is no body that does not belong to some animated being such as horse, but horse can be thought without thinking of its bodily existence], and 'massive' can be dissociated from 'racy'). Or for the other illustration above: exhaustion can be discriminated from nervousness (or any other theoretical insight into bodily states), but it can be thought without this horse or other animal. Whitish froth can be precised from non-froth (colourless saliva), brown nostrils, or whatever is seen at this moment on this horse, but whitish is just whitish and not not-colourless (as it must be perceived when it is in this horse's mouth). Currie's 'trigger' can be merely this one percept of a white; but as soon as it is compared with something else, it is a perceptual judgment of a series of percepts and/or possible percepts. It involves a capacity to think generally of all the other possibilities or factual percepts.

However, Peirce's distinctions of concepts into (what he later understood as relational) 'valencies' contain much more than cognitivist drops in level. They also show the 'containment' of lower within higher relations, and this logical analysis constitutes the real constructivism of meaning. Stripped of its psychological clothing, automatism adds nothing to the explanation of difference among concepts except a perspective of subjectivity (i.e., 'personal' or 'impersonal'). Only here does it make some sense to change the perspective side, when 'personal' means that something is conscious and volitive (i.e., really self-controlled conduct). Logic does not require this perspective, nor does it need a change in perspective.

Furthermore, the nominalist undercurrent of Currie's conception of what he calls 'features' raises questions. Of course, any cognition and recognition concerns features. In fact, 'feature' is a logical predicate, and a 'concept' is the subject of which the predicate becomes an attribute in a proposition. So again, the distinction is logically meaningful only if we can distinguish *kinds* of features.

Features are different in the way they constitute relations. We know now that 'features' of mere quality (psychological feeling, metaphysical Possibility) are monadic relations (i.e., as representations they are monadically degenerate triads). Their nature is constituted only by their position in the cognitive relation and has no bearing on the physical nature of outward, Dynamic Objects. Thus we must abandon the misleading plurals in 'features,' 'data,' and similar concepts, which suggest that a mass of incongruent bits of something can be unified by the one 'schema,' and so on, into what it is thereafter. A horse is never the mass of spatial features, colours, and other bits of information. What can be brought into unity is only what is (cognized, interpreted as) similar. A horse, then, is never a percept; it is indeed a recognition of a relatively abstract concept, which can be precisionally distinguished from a sheep or a cow but not from yellow (colour feature of a parrot) or from deep (spatial feature of a well). That we recognize horses – the 're' in recognition – means that we have concepts of animals (or of speculation objects, or of transportation means, whatever 'horse' means as a sign), not that we store spatial patterns of horses and dogs. These patterns are qualities, which become predicates, or better Rhemata, of different semioses, one of which might eventually be 'a strong horse.' Obviously, many generalities take part in this 'recognition.' Therefore, a horse is never the result of a 'triggered recognition.' It is a plain judgment, one that compares similar things to constitute a relation.

However, if indeed the 'content' of thought is only qualities of feeling (everything that can be distinguished by dissociation: red is not green, but whether it is a red circle or a rectangle is irrelevant), then the similar character constituting the relation, the 'concept,' is in fact almost 'automatic.' (Again, we should not be misled into thinking of semantic units here.) This is because all thought contents of this sort are only possibilities. No consideration is given to existence (Currie's problem with illusion) or to necessity (it does not matter whether what one thinks of must be so). A quite different kind of 'feature' is a character that 'features' existential relations of any kind. Anything that is or is not constitutes an existential relation, which can, in a proposition, be either true or false. Currie's 'horse' example (op. cit. 81) might fit into this slot. Usually it is not a sign of 'horsehood' (except in the context of veterinary medicine, for instance) but rather of 'horse or not horse.' However, as we see in those dreaming, slow- motion, long-angle stock-shot horse races – seen in a number of Western films and television trailers of sporting events – there is indeed a way to reduce horses to qualities of feeling. Now, which of the three alternative horses do we recognize? In terms of relational Semioses, the difference is crucial. Thus there is no simple automatic 'horse recognition' capacity in our organism, as Currie (cf. op. cit. 80f) assumes.

Currie's depiction example points out also the resulting difficulties inherent in differentiating between relations of quality and those of existence (First and Second Categories). On the one land, there are triggering features (of a horse picture); on the other there is the horse itself and the picture horse sharing those features ('likeness'). This difficulty is typical of data and concept separation and their synthesis. Only according to these premises is a picture different from the real thing (cf. op. cit.: 82). Only when we begin to understand semiosis as types of relation is the real thing accessible as real representations (of different modes of being). The existential mode of being is just one possible mode, but it is not representation-free, non-'depiction.'

Other examples of 'bottom-up'-ness are colour perception (Bordwell) and the recognition of the letter 'F' (Currie op. cit.: 81). For Peirce, as we know, this is a much more complicated cognitive process than its name suggests. It does not get up from the bottom by itself. As we have seen, 'F' recognition is a problem solved in the first trichotomy of the sign classification. Even the simple red is no less a triadic representation. Only because there is a concept of 'redness' (colour is even more abstract) is some thing red. 'Bottom-up' and 'top-down' are neither; they are always more than this dyadic vector, in a triadic relation (some represent it as a pyramid).

The notion of 'automatism' is an artefact of the psychological perspective in experimental psychology. From accessing a phenomenon in a given methodological way, it does not follow that the cognized object behaves identically. The extraordinary advance of Gibson and Hochberg was that they introduced 'meaning' into the discipline of experimental psychology. At least, this was the point where sole physiological automatism could no longer yield a reasonable account. Up to this point the claims of sensory auto-organization, which looks already quite 'meaning'-ful, are questionable. But, if the driver's seat is taken by 'meaning,' fully 'bottom-up' processes (genuine inductions, including the abstractive statement of a general rule on the basis of a perfect common character of all its cases) could never be concluded. Abductions, therefore, are the nearest to bottom-up; however, this presupposes that we already have a reflected idea of the nature of the generality contained in Representation as much as in abduction.

Cognitivism and constructivism borrow the basics of meaning from 'science.' Scientific discourse reconstructs from facts, but only from those facts it succeeds in seeing methodologically. Those methods, however, take into account diverse factors, even in experimental psychology; indeed, some include the fact of meaningful interaction with one's environment (some do not). Building an epistemological superstructure on factual findings of science must therefore beg the question.[24] At the very least, a presupposition-less 'method of methods' such as Peirce's phenomenology must not place itself outside the range of critique. If the scientific doxa of an epoch must vouch for truth (assuming we find this idea still useful), it will overstretch its epistemological status. There are indeed good reasons to avoid the argumentative circularity of state of cognition and form of cognition through an analysis of the epistemic process itself without presupposing it. Against Currie's argumentation, must be critically remarked that this 'as science knows' is the problem of 'automatism' as *explanans*. It can never explain why the result of 'the organism's background knowledge' (cf. Fodor in Currie (1995: 85) is meaning.[25] Meaning, however, and not perception, is what cinema is about. It is even a matter of meaning with (the cognition of, or better, thought content of) colours. Currie's automatic trigger example is inappropriate because 'horse' is already the replica of 'horsehood.' However, the latter, with all automatism, will not be innate in the brain. Before becoming memory content it must be – at least the first time – grasped as meaning (i.e., in a triadic sign relation) (much more in the case of 'F's, cf. op. cit.: 86). If 'automatic' does not mean more than not being arbitrary, it should not be used in connection with horse recognition. Indeed, it is not automatic whether this–here is understood as horse, or danger, or force, or Jungian archetype. Furthermore, the difference between 'recognition' and judgments is not of an inside/outside perspective, but rather of logic. Propositional judgments simply add one more type of being to the understanding: Facticity. Logically, this is different from the first impression of 'recognition' (which is Semiotically a rhematic Icon), as it is the relation of existence (propositional Dicent sign).

The problem with cognitivism as a method is not so much its psychologism and the two main characteristics connected to it. The double level of cognition can be criticized and reduced to a single cognitive process, even though this obliterates its usefulness for Formalist aesthetics. If recognition is not a variant of Plato's anamnesis, it is also an act of interpretation, 'knowing which we know something more'. The failure to grasp ampliative reasoning *in se*, either triggered or as judgment, merely bespeaks the deeper problem of its use as an epistemological method. (1) It is precisely the theoretical deficiency of cognition without signs. *Ab ovo* cognition looks for generality in the organism or in innate bottom-up schemata (both of which must be established previously by psychological science). Such a theoretical account merely relocates the problem itself to its first premise. Explaining the premise, then, starts begging the question, explains a *quaestio juris* with a statement *de facto*.

Not so with signs, when every cognition is an interpretation of signs. (2) As has been critically remarked against Bordwell, the real real is the schema itself. Data – or better, reality – have no corrective function in cognitivist cognition. Schemata can be exchanged but not changed (at least, where this change would come from is not visible). Although 'hypothesis testing' can go on forever, perhaps never coming to a truly satisfactory end, the hypothesis itself does not grow in determination. It will be exchanged with another hypothesis affording greater satisfaction. The pressure of reality – in Pragmaticism, as presence of 'real doubt' – is the corrective function of further triadic sign relations. Thus cognition is always recognition and in the long run 'something more.' Re-cognition is constituted as the First Correlate in every interpretative Relation, while the Real becomes a more determinate Generality. (3) True generality is also atrophied in cognitivism, either as knowledge of the organism (or F-recognitional capacity) or as schema; it never arises as a genuine law, which is experienced as necessity in the cognitive act.

However, the 'recognitional primacy' of 'really seeing' (v. *infra*) might receive a strongly sympathetic interpretation in the context of Pragmaticism. Properly reinterpreted, it resembles in some aspects the cotton-wool-and-diamond example (v. *supra* 140–5). It is indeed the reality context that allows for ampliative cognition, and for additions of further attributes, or growth of knowledge. From a positive perspective (1) cognitivism recognizes, at least implicitly, two modes of being or realities (albeit they cannot be treated logically separately). (2) Advocating 'realism,' cognitivism surpasses the arbitrariness of semiological sign theory. (3) Also, there is a rudimentary sign theory in Currie (which can be gleaned from his 'F' example, op. cit. 86ff). There he assumes a 'capacity identity' in the recognition of this image of 'F' and in the recognition of 'F's: 'For every F, it is possible that the F-recognitional capacity is acquired pictorially, but it is not possible for every F-recognitional capacity to be acquired pictorially' (1995: 87). Here he addresses, in fact, the central problem of the relation between cognition and reality (understood as existence).

This very same problem is also the ignition spark for a Semiotic theory of reality. In dismissing Kant's *Ding an sich*, was Peirce not attempting to render aprioristic assumptions obsolete? Similarly, was it not justified to give up Being and Substance as Categories, since they are but the limits of cognition? In a literal sense there is use neither for pure objectivity nor for pure forms of mind, because there is no way to know of them or to deduce them free of contradiction. What, then, is exactly the cognitivist thesis (as far as it can be gleaned from Currie) regarding this central problem? And how is it solved in a Semiotic way? We will see the key to that in Peirce's Immediate Object as 'internal' (SS32), 'Idea,' 'mental representation' (he certainly did not mean to reintroduce a rationalist *res cogitans* or what resembles it so closely). That 'some outward being' determines Semiosis is what cognition is all about. His Dynamical Object in a sign relation is indeed a token of Realism, but of a more radical kind than the cognitivist version.

For both, the real problem is: 'How does what is not mind come before the mind.' In other words, 'How does the real get into the sign without ceasing to be real and independent of the mind?'

Currie has three arguments for his cognitivist solution. First, Cartesianism – including the 'methodological doubt – is killed off as a result of its faulty problematic, as a sort of bogeyman (which is not of interest here, since for Peirce post-1867 this is really kicking at an open door). Second, the question is put more precisely as a Cartesian *homunculus* whose office is 'matching the visual input with a series of stored models of known objects' (Currie 1995: 86). This sounds anodyne enough, provided we do not consider the real complexity of 'matching.' This is not even the synthesis of apperception and intellectual forms in the manner of Kant. Instead it presupposes a modelizing of any cognitive object. What a model is, in connection with knowledge, remains obscure, as much as the meaning of 'match' (with something other) is enigmatic. It is perplexing that Currie relates this match to the existential problem of illusion (as Descartes's methodological doubt). It shows that he does indeed see something important – Quality, Quiddity, or 'Whatness' – but also that its interpretation is logically wrong: Quiddity *in se* – the 'cognitive content' of some character – can never be true or false; it is only possible (not even impossible, because such an insight can conceive of what [is impossible]). However, questions of 'matching' and modelizing are of basic importance for any sign theory, whether it goes by that name or not. Constructing models is the chief business of signs, but the intrinsic logic of this operation is decisive and of sole import to the result of meaning. However, for truth values of existential relations, illusion or 'reality' suffices much less, and two oppositive elements other than model and input are needed. As we have seen, existential vagueness combined with imagination of possible characteristics is of great consequence and potential for film.

Third, the match making is underpinned by two postulates, which are also based on this logical confusion: capacity identity and the 'weak thesis' of recognitional primacy. The gist of the former is that the recognition of concrete depictions of 'F' is the same capacity as the one which recognizes (the 'F'-hood in) 'F's. In Semiotic terms, to recognize the replica, or token, would be the same as recognizing the type. Evidently, these capacities are not identical, because they are different signs if we cognize them *as* type or *as* token. However, the iterative and ordinal nature of Categories – and *per extensionem* of trichotomies – comprehends the lower (-adic) in the relation with higher adicity. In this context, this means that the recognition of types also comprehends all possible and existent tokens, but not the other way round. In the case of 'F's, though, the mere token of a graphical shape F is not the letter 'F,' but merely the instance of a design. Unless 'capacity' means no more than a general ability to think, the logic nature of that mental act creates two different realities. Currie's intuition is right: every cognition involves a generality. Cognition is indeed the comparing relation of a generality ('F-ness') with a (distinct) Quality ('F' 'f' '**F**' '*F*,' etc.) in an instance of it, here or there. Unfortunately, he does not develop his intuition into a comprehensive theory of signhood. The first sign tri-chotomy merely states that at the (logical) start – because the sign itself determines the cognitive relation (as we have seen) – we have F only as 'F-ness' (type), *or* this 'F' (token), *or* 'F' '*f*' 'f' 'f' (tone). According to these different bases, we cognize completely different realities with the shape and the letter 'F'. In the absence of this, the capacity-identity is crucially important for a theory that has no possibility of reflecting the Law-ness of thought as a logical operation (v. *supra*). Postulating iden-tity merely contours the quagmire of finding a basis for relating logical necessity in cognition with actual mental contents (the knowledge-matched input, which might even be an illusion).

How are these capacities (either) acquired? This question is addres-sed in the postulate of the 'weak thesis': 'really seeing things has ... "rec-ognitional primacy" over seeing depictions of them' (op.cit: 87). In Pragmaticism, this means that generality is primordial, and through this knowledge of generality we can recognize depictions or replicas. This argument could apply to schemata as well (also in Bordwell), which are primary (or the sole reality), and whose primacy is explained with 'previous knowledge.' Although schema (which strictly speaking explains nothing, except in postulating a regularity) has (as an innate, 'hard wired' form or as knowledge) its exact logical status and genesis shrouded with indeterminacy.[26]

The realist endowment of the 'weak thesis' is, however, compro-mised by schema–data difference (also 'cues,' etc.). It remains unclear which side of this watershed reality is found. As epistemological the-ory, constructivism still shares with the empiricist strand in philoso-phy the separation of 'synthetic constructs' from data. Percepts are thereby reduced to sensory stimuli plus (more or less 'automatic') judgment, the function of judgments being a disambiguation of the sensory data. Sensory data (or experimental data) and judgment (or the synthetic construct that exists as linguistic description) evoke the same *aporia* that was responsible for the demise of empiricism (cf. Eley 1973). There are no data. This is not just a Peircean postulate; it is also a consequence of scientific method. If data are always languaged and therefore inextricably amalgamated with concepts, what sense does it make to separate them? They do not exist as separate entities. The smallest unit attainable, then, becomes the percept as an inseparable fusion of both.

For film perception the stakes in genuine realism are considerable. Not only is it needed for the corrective function of reality in cognition, which defies any schema. What is the spectator supposed to con-struct when, in language or 'structure,' the 'con-' is achieved beforehand? What remains is the task of applying-correctly-to-'states of world' (which pre-exists in an encyclopaedia, as Eco might say). Moreover, realism provides an opening for the non-factual in perception. Before they become perceptual judgments, percepts are possibly existent, not yet controlled for existential relations with truth values. Cognitivism made an effort to save the real percept from the prerogatives of semiological arbitrariness. In view of the plural modality of the real, however, it would be instructive to shed light on the question of reality, reality cognition, and cognition in signs.

3.3.2 Cognized Reality and Cognition in Signs

This is exactly the subject matter of Peirce's distinction of three 'respects' (Normal or Final, Dynamic, Immediate) in Interpretants, Objects, and the Sign itself. In every experience, or more generally in any mind content or Phaneron, we find necessarily that a triadic relation takes place (Categories). The force of attraction in such representing triads is a logical one, but whatever is (experienced) is already attracted – that is, we always have the final result and never analytical bits and pieces. We must keep this in mind also when discuss this last development of Peirce's classification, which as a method is analytical. From the 1903 classification we know (v. *supra* 127–32) that the second trichotomy (Icon, Index, Symbol) determines the sign by the Categorical nature of the Object, which can be Possibility, Existence, and Necessity. The entire classification of 1903 considered only the internal Categorical structure of each of the Correlates; it left unconsidered the Relation itself. Thus it was always clear that provided the triad stands, it has three Correlates, and these must be certainly less abstract than the absolutely most general idea of cognition *in se* (as 'triadic Relation'). The Sign as such – that is, as Representation of an external Object of meaning – is too abstract to be analytically helpful, but it is there (i.e., it can be prescinded) in every thought act (more than that cannot be said). Any other Sign must therefore be more concrete, and only through the recursive application of Categories can there be concreteness. Being a triad, Categories are applied similarly three times for three Correlates, which, thus determined (i.e. 'degenerated' from 'genuineness'), are a Relation of a concrete Sign. This concreteness can be as spurious as a vague feeling (Rhematic Iconic Qualisign), or as abstract as a 'vast Argument,' the complete law-nature of the Object. As Sign, however, it will always be a Relation of any three of three determinants (trichotomies).

After 1903 Peirce started to consider not only the Correlates, but also the nature or the kind of Relation (to one external object of meaning). This not only adds complexity (ten instead of three trichotomies), but also brings signs closer to their actual usage. Signs (of whatever abstractness) always 'are' already in Relation, and through this Relation we 'have world,' experience whatever we experience. When we consider the manner in which something stands before our mind through this Relation, we discover very differentiated Realities. This constitutes a swan-song for a unified 'data' collection universe, which usually differentiates 'the [stream of] Data' according to input channels (visual, etc.). If data means 'given,' then we observe quite distinct forms of givenness for the entirety of things. In Semiotic – more specifically, in the three respects (logical or normal, dynamic, immediate) of Signs – we have a theory of experience that grasps reality *in* different modes, *as* different modes.

A 'something' standing before the mind can (as a first-level division after the Correlates Sign itself, Object, Interpretant) be threefold.

(1) In the Immediate respect, there is the least 'mentality' or rule. All that relates to an Immediate Interpretant is the object of my feelings; all that relates to an Immediate Object[27] is 'just there'; all that relates to an Immediate Sign itself is the most inconspicuous of Signs, one that does not involve more than taking anything spontaneously as a sign of meaning (which is then interpreted by another Sign).

(2) The Dynamic respect concerns anything that stands before the mind (has meaning) because of an existential Relation. When this happens, the meaning receives its character from outside, in the existential vis-à-vis of an Object. Thus there can be no 'dynamic sign itself,' since a First Correlate alone is monadic. It brings nothing before the mind, which receives meaning from its actual (or necessary and thus also actual) existence. A Relation in a Dynamic respect brings before the mind something that is interpreted such that it is made merely an object of mental reactions (passion or surprise, which are the lower limit of mentality). Such things are true of false.

(3) The Normal respect is meaning, because it is an experience of an Object that is logically necessary. Therefore, only Interpretants as triads can bear a Normal respect. External Objects, which they interpret in this respect, are necessary beings; this cannot be said of anything before the mind that only exists. Of course, necessary things must also be exis-

tent and possible and are necessarily true. Only a Normal (and therefore Final) Interpretant has an Object that stands up to General valid cognition. A certain indication to that interpretation is found in Peirce's 'Ground arms!' example (Peirce 1998: 430; 1907 Letter to the editor of the *Nation*, Variant 2;) cf. also 4.572, 'Prolegomena to an Apology for Pragmaticism,' October 1906–January 1907), consistent with 'mentality." One might object that there is really no Final Object, which would be an absolutely necessary Object. It might appear as just an outlandish upshot of Sign classificatory speculation, a token of idealism, once it is realized what this really means. However, one cannot forget that Semiotic is also part and parcel of Peirce's metaphysical investigations. How would such an Object be, anyway? It must be that aspect of the second correlate of the sign function which is Law-like (i.e., a Symbol in the 1903 classification), and which stands before the mind as Normal. That kind of necessary Object will only be at the end of all cognition. From a Pragmaticistic perspective, in an Ultimate adequate opinion the Object of cognition must be truly necessary. Yet even in Critical Common-Sensism, Finals are truly anticipations of the 'ultimate, adequate opinion.' This involves Peirce's metaphysic, which therefore has a diachronic dimension and is evolutionary. Seen this way, the necessary Object becomes the rationality of Nature itself. Except that we can never know of it in our necessarily hypothetical (sublunary) cognition. Here, then, is another implication of the final state of cognition, of the adequate opinion about the Real.

It is not just the final but necessary limit of Semiosis that is of interest in this new attempt after 1903; it is the classification itself. 'Something' becomes (represented) through a Triad only. The force that binds this Triad is the degree of necessity of this 'something' as it stands before the mind. There is no contradiction to a less epistemological and instead more Semiotic consideration, since the (more than the individual and psychological) mind is in fact the Triad. It is a consequence of this if we can say that the Correlates of this Relation are accessible to the mind in a different way. The Sign itself will always be Immediately accessible. The Interpretant can also be accessible Logically. In the first case, the mind would see merely something-as-sign, spontaneously cognizing something as potentially meaningful. In the latter case, the mind has the complete, necessary, and true knowledge, both of something (Dynamical Object) and as Sign (i.e., also Immediately present).

Whether, and that, we interpret something somehow, that we make something a sign, is not Peirce's concern in this classification. In the last resort, the question behind any sign usage is this: is there a necessity, a compulsion to interpret in this and not in another way? This constitutive question must be reflected also in the classification. For practical purposes, we can understand this as the question of rule, which determines sign usage. Rule – and this is the proviso – must not be understood as constraint by conventions. For a Pragmaticist it is clear that such a constraint must always be a habit of behaviour or conduct. As we know, such habit is the result, at the third grade, of true chance (Tychasm), as much as of statistical predictability (Anankasm). How far this, then, has become a linguistic, semantic convention is not crucially important. What counts is that it is a practice. In cinema, this practice, this presence of rules, is in force only conditionally, as a Norm of the practice, as we have seen. Thus it is even more important that practice, as third grade of Sign usage after rules, be reflected in Sign classes.

Therefore it is evident for Peirce that the regularity of the world is what causes the regularity of Signs, and not the other way round. This, then, is real realism, and it is much more radical than that professed by Currie and cognitivism. Realism – and this is important for film – is not physicalist (materialist) such that the brain as part of matter is determined causally. In Peirce Realism is always conduct (practice). Habit is of thought, of sign usage, since thought is eminently conduct. It is just that Peirce does not postulate that all thought is lawlike; only one of his ten Sign classes is the perfect triadic Relation of the Normal Interpretant. This, then, enables film to assign a crucial, frequent, and customary role to less-than-necessary cognitions and even to sheer possibilities.

The question of cinematic illusionism, as raised by Currie, finds an answer here. First, if only a Sign itself stands before the mind, pure Qualities make no propositional claim at all, as they are Possibility. Second, however, the relation to a Real can be of two natures (in addition to the Real Possibility). He makes a distinction between 'dynamical, or dyadic, action; and intelligent' or triadic action." (MS318.25; 5.472, 1907). Each has a different Object, experiences a different Real. 'Semeiosy, or action of a sign' (MS318.28) also concerns the less 'intelligent' variant, which makes it a viable, direct operation of the will, for example. A good illustration is provided by Peirce's own examples – for instance, of the 'Ground arms!' command of an officer. Even if he must suppose that his soldiers speak English according to the rules – of grammar, of being, and of circumstantial sign usage – 'it is not essential to the action of the sign.'[28] (Peirce 1998 430). The mental representation (or Immediate Object) in the officer's mind is simply, 'The butts of the muskets be brought down'; of this, it is inappropriate to ask truth questions, as it is just there, immediately accessible to the subjective mind. Whereas the butts themselves, as an identity, are the Dynamical Object, which the mind accesses through existential, circumstantial constraints, as it is there or not there. The hypothesized 'Final Object' is a liminal monstrosity of the cognition process 'in the long run', when Being is perfectly known in Laws. Referring to a different but comparable example of responding to his wife's inquiry about the weather, Peirce states: 'The *Dynamical Object* is the *identity* of the actual or Real meteorological conditions of the moment. The *Immediate Interpretant* is the *schema* in her imagination, i.e. the vague Image of what there is in common to the different Images of a stormy day. The *Dynamical Interpretant* is the disappointment or whatever actual effect it at once has upon her. The *Final Interpretant* is the sum of the reply, Moral, Scientific, etc.' (8.314, 1909). If the officer had to reflect on his action, he could form a sign with a Final Interpretant.[29] Its corresponding (Final?) Object could perhaps be a certain consistent image of the world, organized as will.

The cinematic object, then, need not be restricted to propositional universes, automatic or judgmental, as the 'real' it represents. This is just one kind of objective vis-à-vis of film (as of many other signs). However, it is vital to know the exact nature of objectivity, if only to offer a faithful account of what we really experience in all its richness. No Sign can ever be meaningless – that is, be without an object of some kind. Yet in cinema we notice 'slippages' – even ambivalences – between the ways in which some objects must stand before the mind. One way is the Reality of Possibility (which is only a metaphysical Reality, but which is highly relevant for the experience of time). Most people may find this difficult to maintain, and they are justified by common language usage, which opposes 'possible' to 'real' (Peirce, instead, opposes possible to existent and necessary). Film often does not insist that we know what we are seeing; it employs instead a number of specific techniques to display a 'vague Image' (8.314). Thus, we must account for this possibly Real as much as the existentially Real of the documentary way of Objectivity. As we shall see, every narration tends to become monument and document (Ricoeur's Mimesis III). For this season, most cognitivist accounts would fit well into an important function of narrativity; however, they also neglect the necessary Real, the Objectivity of the Law (besides the Possible). Necessary Reality stands before the mind in a Normal, or Final, Interpretant of the Sign. A complete picture of cinematic modes of experience of objects of meaning should not exclude this necessary cognition. As abstract and as general as it must be as a Sign, there is truth in cinema where the main consideration is not the existence of the object but rather that it 'must be.' Of course, film is not usually a treatise of science; that said, it can prove more than the 'evidence' of facts can – for instance, as the visual simulation of a Law.

All these objectivities are the operation of the Sign relation (which might even refer to the same physical body, as three Objects in three Interpretations). The dyadic action of a sign is different from its 'intelligent' Semiosis; moreover, the absence of a truly monadic action of a sign (which is an absolute inferior limit of signhood, as we have seen) does not mean that Firsts – even at this aspect level of classification – are not part of any of those semioses. It is evident that as an Immediate Sign itself, such Firsts can only be felt immediately and would not subsist as more than 'just being taken as' sign. Even Peirce's own Phaneroscopy is a case in point, a philosophical method for reflecting such an absolute First, the Phaneron. As foundational science, Phaneroscopy must indeed treat pure Firstness. Yet it can and must be Critically surpassed in genuine Reflection or Thirdness. However, Peirce acknowledges that as Intuition or 'vague Image,' it is absolutely irreplaceable: a necessary source of insight and discovery and the basis of (subsequent) cognition. In this light, the strict discourse part of phaneroscopy is Thirdness, but the intuition (which is always already a Sign) is pure Firstness (v. 75). Firstness as Category, however, is a prescinding abstraction of concrete Semioses, which are Relational 'valencies.' 'Indecomposeable' and Immediate as they are, each of these valencies also has its 'hypostatical abstract' necessity, which must be understood through generalization. Yet, in spite of this prominent instance of a merely Immediate Object, higher representational Objects are the basic operation of experience. It can be experience of the Real in the form of a judgment and expressed or expressible in a proposition or argument.

So it is of considerable importance to cinematic representation that there be various objective realities. The distinction between Immediate and Dynamical concerns cinema directly, but this has nothing to do with the so-called 'profilmic' reality and the semiological, veridictional 'reality effect' in cinema, or the 'illusionism' topic. Instead, all reality being mediated through signs, this mediation in cinema produces kinds of reality. Olmi's *Genesi: dalla creazione al diluvio* allows us to observe this distinction in kind directly, with regard to time. Even though the physical time is identical (so to speak), one experiences one kind immediately. 'Time begins' and there is a world that simply is, without direction and without change. Once there is an irruption there, time begins. 'Time began' is the second kind of time, which is naturally narrative. Its experience is in the 'now' of narration. One might even imagine a third kind of time, which is not an object in this film. The Final Object 'time' is its true Symbol, when time is perfectly cognized. One can find this in Godard's *Je vous salue, Marie*, in which the Pascal-ish professor makes it an argument intended as true (shots 27-35). Time as Immediate Object can only relate to a Quality. It will therefore be experienced directly and in no other mode. Thus, this time cannot be spoken of, although one sees it in Olmi's film. Time as Dynamical Object is among the most common of cinematic objects. In this film, however, one observes the onset of narration as the genesis of a new reality. This is the birth of history, and history is crucial for the human mode of being. Furthermore, time is really an 'angelical' object of knowledge – a Final Object of truth as it were – as soon as this truth becomes unbearable for humanity. The fall of Man is connected with the knowledge of time, which immediately turns into manipulative knowledge. (Consider Godard's 'exploitative ant instruction' scene in shots 65 to 68 of *Je vous salue, Marie*, in which Eve at the same time brings time to an end in quoting Hölderlin's last words before his death.) As pure signs, the difference could not be more obvious. Godard's sign of time is Rubik's cube and stochastic formulas; in contrast, in *Genesi: dalla creazione al diluvio*, narrative time is the imagination of a narrating father and his son. Direct time instead is a sign of the now of an irruption into the eternity of non-time. Three 'times' stand before the mind as different Objects, but in a triadic Sign Relation of meaning. They comprehend three kinds of temporal Qualities, which must be of different weight and of a wildly different nature. Its three kinds of Objects are proof that Quality in Signs determines the objective world as result of sign relations. Only through the mediation of an Interpretant as a third Correlate can a judgment be made that time is identical in all three cases. As Objects they are different; they constitute distinct kinds of Relation. Also, of course, for the spectator, who relates subjectively to three realities.

These examples make it clear that the differentiation of objectivity is crucial to an understanding of cinema. There is no reasonable way to accomplish this with schematic judgments of a propositional nature, or with semantic marks and encyclopaedias. In such cases, film would be limited to 'arty' variants. One can make a semantic (extensional and intensional) walk through the witty aphoristic allusionist cinema of Godard. Here it is absolutely crucial to activate an encyclopaedia of connotations. Otherwise his work would be impossible to understand (cf. *infra*). Furthermore, how would schematic judgments allow us to grasp the sheer feeling of open possibility in the immediate time experience?

Cinema needs all three kinds of Objectivity, standing before the mind in their specific difference. First of all, cognition needs an occasion. Second, its pragmatic setting calls not only for a startling starting point but also, just as necessarily, for new 'material.' What advances it is Firstness or *'mentality.'*[30] This realm of the real possible, even as it is constituted as sign, is different in nature from necessary things. Only when we assume the reality of Possibility is it not cryptic to say, 'Remember it is by icons only that we really reason, and abstract statements are valueless in reasoning except so far as they aid us to construct diagrams' (4.127, 'Grand Logic,' 1893). It is only through an outward world (cf. 4.157, c1897), both as Quality and Opposition, in the form of an 'idea of feeling' (4.157, c1897), that true cognition literally works. However, in order to become cognition,[31] in order to become signification,[32] that world must have an Interpretant. As much as factual 'Outwardness,' Qualitative cannot be suppressed in a realist sign theory. Outside this context, it is impossible to assume that the outer world is itself 'logical'; or that evolution, as it were, is a process of logic-ization to which the unlimited progress of truth in cognition corresponds.

We can conclude now by summarizing the richness of Sign theory and its advantages over cognitivism.

1 Semiotic is fine-tuned to respect *all* possible experiences (but this descriptive power is based on very simple forms, recursively applied).
2 There are many more kinds of meaning, or empirical operations, than just automatism and judgment. On a *uniform*, logical foundation, we have at hand all the principles for diversification.
3 There is both more and less in meaning than cognitivism makes provisions for. More, because there is more than propositional truth – there is also real necessity. Less, because the lower level of automatism is too high for mere signs of Quality.
4 For cinema, the upper level of Semiosis (i.e., the Final Interpretant) is in common practice beyond reach. Only when we examine carefully

the givenness of accomplished necessity in concrete signs do we notice also a potential for cinema as aesthetic sign. If it contributes to the discovery of norms, it is the first stage of Necessity. Regarding the lower limit, there is much more for cinema than colour recognition and the like. This potential is often overlooked because of our excessive concern for narrative universes. Spatiotemporal action space is not the lower limit of the Sign potential of cinema.

3.4 Cinema 'Is' Moving Matter or Time

The real *articulum stantis et cadentis* for any film theory is how it can cope with time. The experience of time as such is already a formidable object of inquiry, regarding which quite a number of the major philosophers were left puzzled (v. *infra*). This fact certainly does not simplify the task of film theory. Narration is one means by which most film theory has mastered this. Yet time is more than that which narration succeeds in configuring.[33] So, it is not the temporality of time but the very experience of it[34] that is the crucial hurdle to be taken by theory. Only then can we gauge the extent of time as a meaningful dimension that is left untouched by narrative temporality. It is intriguingly meaningful to transform time as experience into time as meaning. Yet at what enormous cost comes the (admitted) artificiality of meaningful narrative time. The vestiges of time before its textual configuration remain important for cinema.

Cognitivism is surprisingly silent about time proper. It had no difficulties in admitting tense-based schemata of narrative causalities. Time proper 'comes' before any causality. Thus it is very much worth investigating attempts to reflect on the coexistence of cinema and time, which (much more deeply than narrativity) touches on the nature of film, (i.e., the cinematic sign itself). (1) In a first round we recall those harbingers of semiological film theory, who conceptualized time other than as syntax. (2) It was (Bergson via) Deleuze, however, who introduced the thematic of time, with *éclat*, in film theory. (3) A Peircean film theory, aware of cinematic time, must therefore come to terms with (this variant of) Bergsonist time theory. (4) We might expect its 'natural' opponent to be the time theory of the phenomenological tradition after Husserl. This debate will arise in the context of cinematic narratology, because phenomenological film theory proper has not developed (as Deleuze did) a theory of cinematic time. Instead, Ricoeur relies heavily on this philosophical tradition for his outstanding narratology.

3.4.1 Cinematic Time as Enunciation

Morris's theory of iconism had to serve as an extension of semiological sign arbitrariness in cinematic object representation; Bettetini makes a similar attempt with regard to time representation. Notwithstanding its otherwise firm semiological affiliation, Bettetini's theory of cinematic time offers some interesting innovations. This is owed to a surreptitious introduction of a hermeneutic approach in the form of Weinrich's reception aesthetic. Interest for cinematic temporality is thus embedded in a broader narratological problem (which will concern us later). Bettetini's construction, following Weinrich, requires two sorts of time, *Besprechen* and *Erzählen* (roughly equivalent to *énonciation* and *énoncé*, *discours* and *histoire*). Cinema itself, by enunciation, produces time before it produces narrative temporality. How is time taken in charge of cinema in a direct but not yet narrative way? In agreement with Morris and Eco, by 'reproducing' or motivated 'iconic' signs (cf. Bettetini 1979: 27) we can establish a strict bi-univocal relationship between the two times of sign and object: one passively mirrors the other (Bettetini's *specularità*). Bi-univocal cinematic time is considered the 'iconic' representation of the time of experience.

The interesting point in Bettetini's theory of cinematic time is where it creates continuity. His solution is based on taking 'syntax' literally as composition. If elements must be composed into a unity, the question is, 'What unifies?' Here Bettetini proposes logic as the binding force of what used to be mere syntax or juxtaposition. Enunciation – which has its own time – intervenes textually in the time of the enunciated. Now, time cannot be grasped by propositions – that is, by dyads enunciating a state as true or false. It requires a logic of composition proper, in the framework of rhetorical figuration. For logical theories base on propositional dyads – taking into account existential relations – there can be only one escape: modal logic. In propositions, time is emphatically only in a (mathematical, measurable) system of onto-semantic logic; in a system of natural language, it is much less precise. For von Wright[35] and Russell, time lacks bi-univocity (a 1:1 relationship) in a natural language's representation of time. This form of time is multivalent: what 'long' means is established by the context in (and for) unique or singular circumstances. In a natural language communication act, enunciation can ignore a signification that can be related exactly to objective time. This 'imprecision' is attributable to the symbolic (i.e., connotational) nature of natural languages.

Cinematic time differs from tense because cinematic enunciation produces a direct time. An older differentiation is found in Mitry, who counts temporal bi-univocal relations of represented and representation[36] among the 'logic of facts'. This contrasts with another way of representing time in a 'logic of implications' (Mitry 1965). How are implications attained? It is through the limitless interrelation of objects and facts[37] within the temporally fixed frame of cinematic enunciation. A complex interaction of these two logics, following Weinrich, cannot be suppressed, and this produces an 'always other meaning.' What are in themselves strictly bi-univocal temporal pieces change their interrelations constantly. Taken in themselves, however, pieces constantly produce complete perceptive units in a 'logic of facts'; together with the other logic, this constitutes a process of 'assimilation' and 'distinction.'[38]

Which of the two logics, at a given time, represents time in cinema[39]? First the temporal 'signifier' (a tense equivalent) relates logically to its 'signified.' The concrete mode of how that logic relates influences the resulting 'time,' creating a particular 'time.' Enunciation uncouples the two universes of representation/enunciation and the represented/enunciated[40]; whereas the 'logic of implications' governs the represented, representation can signify temporal change and shifting of sense. The enunciated object of temporal organization (the represented 'real') has a logic different from the temporality of the organizing itself. Bettetini, concurring with Laffay, assumes a specifically cinematic, trans-semantic 'logic of things.' Images contain 'things' as a cultural form, whereas concepts rely on semantic. The probability of their occurrence being reduced, images require rhetorical logic in order to make their 'things' veri-similar (*vraisemblable* in Greimas, 'doxastic' in Bettetini).

Thus, three logics signify time in cinema: (1) On top there is a narrative or 'deterministico-doxastica' logic (Bettetini 1979: 68). As linguistic standard its causality is detemporalized, thus determining the sequence of events, which events *can* happen, and in which order they must happen. (2) The 'temporalizzatrice-doxastica' (ibid.) 'logic of things,' specific for cinema, dissolves the former by making the strict logic of the narrative less constraining. Cinematic narratives only connect the veri-similar, not 'hard factual and present truth.' These two logics are capable of a number of unusual interrelations. Their cooperation determines cinematic 'style,' 'genre,' and so on. (3) 'Temporalizzatrice' (ibid.) – 'implication' logic – creates temporal order through cinema techniques such as 'editing styles. It is the most difficult to formalize. The propositional copula 'is' relates 'what is' in a detemporalized way. Cinema shows things 'now.' What they 'are' is therefore difficult to determine. As a mere temporal articulation cinema 'is' a re-cord[41] or memory. These pieces of record are joined into a whole by modal logic. The logical necessity of this join on an instance of modalization, which adds meaning to anything downstream (i.e., the temporal dimension).

Bettetini shares with colleagues from the Milan School a predilection for enunciational hierarchization – with a twist, however. He combines this familiar linguistic concept with logic and with cinematic specificity in representation. Modalization[42] (cf. Greimas 1979, s.v. 'Énonciation') is already part of enunciation as a concept, but here an attempt is made to expound it in a more strictly logical direction. The simple idea that enunciation subjects its enunciated to its conditions as if it – the dictum – were bracketed by modes (of truth, necessity, volition, and obligation) is applied to time. This is not precisely a linguistic element (tense); even so, Bettetini connects it to the existential situation, and dependencies, of human existence. This is a hermeneutic, existence-philosophical idea, grafted onto cinematic time as experience (as we will encounter it in Ricoeur's narratology, cf. *infra*). Here exactly is the novelty vis-à-vis the Eco/iconism strand of film theory (v. *supra*). However, this hermeneutic figure of thought is semiologically fractured; thus, the 'originary'–'vulgar' (Heidegger)/*Urbild–Abbild* (Gadamer) level hierarchy becomes a simple textual dependency chain. This dependency, then, is configured logically. Becoming subject to modes is rightly seen as a logical operation, and thus does not fit into the truth values of propositional logic. Propositions can only negate[43]; that said, in time something that is not, is not yet, perhaps, but is never not at all (there are no all-quantifiable negations in time, except at the end of all time).

Bettetini's amalgam of heterogeneous ideas cannot completely efface the traces of its origins. The logic of temporal implications is definitely a Husserlian topic. 'Immediate time consciousness' constitutes a classical attempt to think of the temporal relations. Yet its point is that it is not logic, but rather immediately conscious. This is the originary mode of time. Is it possible to fit this intuition into the Procrustean bed of semiology? Modal logic promises to be a valid substitute for iconism-based, tense-substituting time theories. Now the enunciator and enunciatee have the choice and obligation of picking one among different logics. To pick the right one, they must know the enunciational level on which they are.

The contrast between logics as cinematic specificity presupposes that the 'other' logic has made itself available. Modal logic is a difficult logic, because it defies common usage logic. It is never false and cannot be negated. Bettetini opted for Prior's AN ('and next') logic,[44] which explains what is true now and false in the next moment – for example, temporal, doxastic, and deontic (cf. Prior 1967) predicates and the like.In this way he found the missing link to semiological figures of thought. Cinema – after the model of the logic of grammatical tenses[45] – would not remain an exception to the need for formalization. This project of formalization remains a sketch, however. A fundamental problem is whether logic can be applied to the arbitrary relation between signifier and signified. The object of logic is predicates, and modal logic concerns the modality of predicates. Even though it is not impossible, it seems that outside of well-formed sentences this hardly makes sense. A signifier has none of the qualities of a premise.

The 'logic of implications,' comprehended as modal logic, achieves a more thorough grasp of time than iconism film theories. Yet, modality has not really reached the core of time; it has only reached 'saying time.' If cinema does not tell, stacked in layers of the telling and the told, there can be no trace of time at all. That film is an object of duration is a banality if it is not understood as meaning. Everything has a duration, including laws of nature, which have an eternal duration. However, here the meaning itself encompasses the all and always – it must be so, otherwise it would not be understood as law. Cinema as meaning evidently encompasses a quite different time. It cannot be taken as 'simply there' – not even in Husserl's 'immediate time consciousness' – because this would be a meaningless (literally) time. This durational time *simpliciter* does not become meaning by being told in a narrative. It is time only by being meaning. As cognitive object, it exists only as meaning and not physically. This time-honoured classical insight responsible for the aporia of reflection, led to the classical contraposition of Augustinian psyche-logical time theory of mental unification of three times and the Aristotelian physical-logical one of countability (of movement). Time 'is' thinking of past and future; it is not the infinitesimal point of passage of future into past, which we call present. This applies also to cinema *in se*, not as a textual medium of narration. Perhaps Bettetini wanted to grasp original temporality as implication (i.e., the 'now' implying everything past and future). The whole difficulty, which is not solved by this film theory, is how implication operates in order to become time. It cannot be the eternal implication of 'all' instants united into one necessary law.

The kernel of Peirce's Continuity, as a mathematical theory of necessary forms of thought, is precisely that the thought process is describable as an unlimited process of relations. However, non-limitation can be there only as a real Possibility, which will always be limited by any actual thought. It does, however, remain a necessary part of any thought as thought (i.e., triadic relation). Rather than being one of the liabilities of natural languages, this Peircean conception of thought has an important consequence: relations in terms are never entirely 1:1 relations. Logical terms are always to some extent Vague terms (cf. Chauviré 1995: 120–35 regarding Russell's dependence on Peirce; see also 169ff). In spite of this indeterminacy of any thought, the nature of time experience is different. Vagueness is a Continuity of Thirds, whereas time is at the opposite end of the Semiosic relation. It is Continuity of Firstness, at the lower root of a triadic relation.

By stacking levels of enunciation, Bettetini freed himself from the confines of semiological syntax. Yet the grasp of cinematic time proper is still lacunose. Levels therefore are levels not of time but of enunciational hypotaxis – which, however, stands. If it were possible to comprehend these levels as different types of time, as meaning, the result would be a highly time-conscious film theory, one that exploits the layers of time for very specific cinematic meaning constructs. A comparison with Metz's cinematic enunciation theory, written many years after Bettetini's, shows the result of an incapacity to make use of enunciation for time generation.

3.4.2 Cinematic Time as Intuition and as Division

Deleuze's choice to opt for Bergson allowed him to pursue the enigma of time experience in an absolutely different way. He also uses two different times (or time and temporality), albeit the two are distant from the Husserlian phenomenological–hermeneutical approach. The 'specificity of cinema' must comprehend time. With Deleuze, time resolutely enters film theory. Temporality as movement is at the core of his philosophical film theory. His reflections on fundamental cinematic concepts[46] are unique in the contemporary debate. By assigning such a central role to time, he covers the cinematic phenomenon in its entirety. This is not a 'film-as-film' sort of theory, nor is it a veiled narratology posing as film theory. Quite the contrary – cinema ceases to be supplementary to other theories. The way in which Deleuze theorizes on the cinematic image is intriguing indeed: 'Image'[47] is a function of 'action' or 'mouvement.' Image is commonly treated as representation of 'something' (to some mind or to intermediate organizations such as narratives). In Deleuze, it is the pivot of an entirely new understanding of temporal 'being.' His is the first cinematic theory to centre radically on the 'moving image' or, in common terms, the changing being. What gives Deleuze a particular purchase on the image, even as an original mode of being? It is with Bergson (mostly) that Deleuze cut the Gordian knot of the linguistic paradigm. If language has a purchase on the real (which cannot be questioned outside language), the image's onto-scopy makes it clear that the real cannot be taken for granted. It is not imprisoned in language, but can it be accessed directly in an ontology?

What is the problem to which Deleuze provides a solution? What does 'image' address? In her review, Ropars-Wuilleumier (1994) suggests that Deleuze resorted to the (easiness of) image as a sort of self-evidence, as the place where language in its differentiating nature fails. Yet this does not take into account the altogether different basis of Deleuze's argument. For him, being is not a-temporally differential at all; rather, it is movement and time. Thus it makes no sense to ask for the 'meaning' of images, if meaning really means difference.[48]

Deleuze proposes – contained in this concept of 'image' – a theory of thoroughly temporal being. The real 'is' not, it is in movement. For this, would have to circumvent the 'idealist' trap, tearing apart Subject and Reality. This is from a Bergson/Deleuzean perspective, or rather Bergson in Deleuze's interpretation (henceforth called B/D), which is different from Bergson's philosophy (this difference will not be investigated here). Supposedly, this trap is also found in phenomenological film theories. Deleuze outlines a metaphysics of cinema most clearly in his 'Second Commentary on Bergson' (1983: 83–103; Bergson himself wanted a metaphysics of science[49]). This project enables Deleuze to argue for a counterintuitive equation of cinema to what was formerly the 'subjective' mind. When this argument is taken to its end, it no longer makes sense to oppose an understanding subject with a factual object, since the two are forms of the same thing. Reducing the subjectobject dichotomy answered the epistemological question of science; this had to entail what we might call a 'materialist ontology.'

If we are to understand Deleuze's unusual theory of cinematic being as movement, the most useful vantage point is the 'Whole.' This is not simply a consequence of his systematic theory design. Ultimately, it has fundamental philosophical reasons, as will become clearer later. Strangely, the extremely systemic nature of his film theory has mostly not been taken into account. For instance, Leutrat (1988: 143–61) comes to see a hodgepodge (*rhizomes*) of impressionist insights into film. Instead of a 'livre vivant, qui bouge' (161) with unwarranted claims, it might be of more help to see its thorough organization. In fact, everything in it is part of a whole and is only justified by the whole. Misrecognizing such a dependency – treating Deleuze's statements as theorems instead of parts also of an intellect movement – robs them of all plausibility. The system – that is, the Whole[50] – changes all: every element falls in place.

3.4.2.1 The Structure of Deleuze's Film Theory

Deleuze's theory of cinematic being also contains some 'Peirceish'[51] material, it is true, but this remains rather inconsequential (cf. *infra*). Cinematic images as metaphysical *images* of movement: That is comprehensible only if being itself is movement. In its original Bergsonian version, *image* is an impulse for a centre to act; but then every-thing that reaches a living matter and launches a re-action is *image*. In Bergson's ontology, *images* are not yet mental/'spiritual' entities; they are only the universe as it presents itself at the (inter-)*face* of living, reacting matter. Deleuze chose not to exploit Bergson's theory and to make full use of its mental parts. The systemic approach made Deleuze unfold his film theory as a suite of *images*. It is not a typology, nor is it strictly a classification.[52]

What cinema could possibly be, and look like, was basically prescribed by the ontology of movement. Even the place that was left for Peirce to fill was imposed by the mental stage of the reaction action chain. Once this disposition is in place, description of the systemic singularities is an exercise of deduction and application. Cinematic images are stages of movement within the Whole, yet they do not really take the place of a cognition centre (*vulgo*: 'mind').[53] If cinema is really the imitation of the centre of ordering, then that mechanism has various stages: from the first contact, to the executed action, when the centre has passed on to the Whole the action exerted on it.

Deleuze has a longstanding interest in cinema, which can be traced throughout. After a long preparation in antecedent works, theatre and especially cinema organized the systemic parts of his thought. So it might be said that the systemic organization had long been in his mind and was only catalyzed by cinema.

It is highly significant that Deleuze's outline is designed as a double symmetry: (symmetric) *image-mouvement* mirrors (symmetric) *image-*

temps. Every logically possible part has its correspondence in cinematic practice. It is very instructive to study the structural plan – how B/D is outlined and cinema delivers its concepts in a mutually congenial way. At the same time, the structural plan is incomprehensible except as a B/D one. Deleuze's organization has two crucial design principles: Symmetry[54] and triadicity. These complementary, contrasting principles shape his thought and are absolutely not fortuitous; the vibrant, indeed, oscillating, ambivalent fascination of Deleuze's film theory stems from there. In fact, this organization constitutes the '*taxonomie*' and '*classification*' (Deleuze 1983: 7), which only reflects – as symmetry – onto-logical, Bergsonian necessity, and – as triads – Peircean sign relations.

Volet 1 ('action' plus 'zéroïté' in book 0, chs I, II, III) & *volet* 2 ('spirit' plus the 'Tout' in book Ω, ch. X) stand for the symmetric organization of thought, wrapped by 0 and Ω. Each *volet* contains 3 books, with 3 chapters each, with 3 §§ each; this organizes thought relationally, as triadic sign-categories) *Volet* 1: tries to project Peirce's 3 Categories (books A, B, C) on the being of movement. Book 0 wrapping volet 1 lays the veritable foundation of the Whole at the same time in Peirce's Categories (where *zéroïté* translates Medad) and in Bergson's (*Matière et memoir*) Movement. This results in (book A) the Image, (book B) Action, and (book C) Crisis. *Volet* 2 moves on to the next level, the Whole, based on (book D) temporalizing signs, (book E) time, and (book F) thought itself.

This is an organization of thought, in the first place. Only then it is a text organized in two volumes and XII resp. X chapters. We tried to reconstruct Deleuze's thought by grouping each three chapters (Deleuze's roman numerals) into a – what we call – 'book,' and each three books into a *volet*, which make – together with the two wrappers – together the two volumes. Movement dictates the path: First, around the very important concept of the action-image-reaction chain (*volet* 1); second, around the spiritual, and therefore temporal, intervening in that chain.

This explains why equating B/D types of *images* with Peircean Categories is limited to the first volet. It becomes clear also why the linguistic option is diametrically opposed to B/D. Semiologically, action – even communicative action – is reduced or abstracted into pre-established societal conventions. This is a sin against Bergson's verdict on 'Idealist' contemplation; even more, it is a further abstraction from material reality.

Deleuze's film ontology works only as a whole and as a description of the Whole. Cinema is not part of Being; rather, it squats on the whole of it. *From Perception to Action*: we cannot of course take this first-step term in its common sense; rather, we must take it as structured and planned in terms of Bergsonian metaphysics. The symmetric layout requires some explanation. After introducing B/D and assigning cinematic pieces to each concept (book 0), the logical First in B/D film theory is not surprisingly the *image-perception*,[55] quite literally *per-* and *capere*, or catching the ever moving; nothing can be set in motion without receiving an im-pulse. There is objective (Whole) and subjective (*Face*) perception: 'sera subjective une perception où les images varient par rapport à une image centrale et privilégiée; sera objective une perception, telle qu'elle est dans les choses, où toutes les images varient les unes par rapport aux autres, sur toutes leurs faces et dans toutes leurs parties.'[56] (Deleuze 1983: 111). The next stage is *image-affection*.[57]. This is the first part of the body's reaction – its arousal, filtering, and so on. Already acting on the interface itself, it is almost cogent that Deleuze identifies the central human interface-with-the-world as 'image-affect': 'L'image-affectation, c'est le gros plan, et le gros plan, c'est le visage' (ibid.: 125). Yet the face is only the beginning of the affect, which continues in quality, power, and space (*qualités, puissances, espaces*): 'nous distinguons donc deux états des qualités-puissances, c'est-à-dire des affects: en tant qu'ils sont actualisés dans un état de choses individué et dans les *connexions réelles* correspondantes (avec tel espace-temps, *hic et nunc*, tels caractères, tels rôles, tels objets); en tant qu'ils sont exprimés pour eux-mêmes, en dehors des coordonnées spatio-temporelles, avec leurs singularités propres idéales et leurs *conjonctions virtuelles'* [ibid.: 146]. Necessarily thereafter comes that which first induces action: *image-pulsion*, which consists of the nature of the pull (ibid.: 179) and the object of the pull (ibid.: 180). Then comes the centre itself: image-action,[58] whose description calls to mind certain narratologies (cf. ibid.: 197f). Deleuze detects two forms of image-action: *la grande forme* follows the scheme S-A-S' (meaning from a situation to a transformed situation through an intermediate action). *La petite forme* follows A-S-A' (from action to a situation to a new action). The latter leads to the dissolution of the merely movement-based image through a dissolution of sensomotoric causality. Up until this point it was merely matter in movement without intervening factors, which in B/D could only be *souvenir pur* and mind.

How Peirce is drawn into this structure is interesting. His Categories are equated with parts/polarities of matter–movement. Firstness appears when a movement has been perceived by a body and leaves an impression (and is therefore equated with the *Face*). Secondness or Opposition is the Action–Reaction logic, exemplified in the 'Duel.' Thirdness is already at the fringes of action before its dissolve into Mind. Deleuze admits that Peircean signs have defeated him; this is not difficult to believe after such a reinterpretation of the Categories, which after all are necessary forms of thought and being.

There are two Wholes in B/D: the Whole of Movement and the Whole of the *souvenir pur*.[59] Both are found at the actual moment of reaction (Second?). These Wholes are identified with, respectively, the whole of the Iconic Real and the whole of Interpretants (the known). As for the first Whole, Iconicity is Quality – but amorphous as it were, not an opaque screen within movement proper. The role of Categories comes to an end when Thirdness establishes the relationship between the parts of movement (= action, i.e., this much is retained from the logic of relations). *Images*, typified through unfolding movement, find a natural cohesion in their interrelation, after which a division into parts is destructive: parts only make sense as parts of the whole of action. Deleuze managed the astounding feat of projecting irreducibly distinct ultimate forms of Reality onto the one being in movement. Now it is not disputed that Categories have metaphysical consequences and that Bergson's philosophy is also clearly metaphysical. This, although the fundamental difference between Peirce's Critical and Bergson's ontological derivation is so overwhelming that not much space for conciliation seems available. Bergson's Real, however, shares with Peirce's irreducible modal Realities that it is also not unimodal. Being-in-movement is not grasped by way of propositions – after all, also trimodal being is beyond dyadic truth relations. With some interpretative effort, one might also project the iterative sequence of the ordinal Categories onto the parts of movement, which then becomes a sequence of (medatic) monadic, dyadic and, in its final stage, triadic relations. So far all of this compares well with Peirce's relational analysis of the relative term 'movement' (v. *supra*). However, there is Really Quality that is not Struggle and not Law, real Opposition, distinct modes of being, just as there is Really Law. There is no higher or more constructively complex being than Law. In just the same way, there is no Reality beyond thought, Categories being expressions of this inasmuch as they are Relations.

Clearly, the 'motor' of unity in Peirce is thought in its most comprehensive sense. There is thought not only in the human mind but also in the Reality of all possible worlds. In Bergson, movement as such, and not thought, relates. Moreover, movement does not relate in the manner of thought. Deleuze seems quite aware of the difference in pattern, both as a theory of being and as theory of thought. This has clear implications for the possibility and procedure of thought, which must be derived from conceptualizing the real as movement. This was also Bergson's intention in formulating his anti-idealist position. His solution – the two kinds of time – allows Deleuze, at this delicate stage of his film theory, to shift gears into another mode of Bergsonist being, virtuality. Only the Whole as such is virtually intuited. The realm of *souvenir pur*[60] or memory is pure virtuality. It will be clearer shortly that Bergsonism needs a 'non-empirical,' ontological mode of access to this virtual whole: intuition. Within a Peircean frame of thought this is as questionable as Kant's *Ding an sich* and other incognizable entities. Had Deleuze fully acknowledged that Pragmatic Maxim with its counterfactual conditional as the strongest bulwark of Realism, he would not have been able to think in virtuality. So the organization of these different virtualities or pure relationships is crafted around the notion of time and memory, in this form that is not of Peircean descent.[61]

Since time can never be a concrete entity or a remembering without the moment of reaction, pure time is a pure abstraction. This is why Deleuze speaks of 'temps direct.' How can this be imagined? In B/D, memory intervenes for the mind into movement. This would now be reversed, in that it is no longer the movement that dictates what is to happen, but the until now only virtually (and not directly) present time. One must remark, however, that even now time is never solely present. It is still *mouvement*, pieces, 'nappes de passé,' false representations (but representations nevertheless); it is still a believing and problematizing visualization of the yet invisible, in which time has intervened. How is this done in concrete terms? To find an answer we must again move to the details of Deleuze's structure: *Le Tout*. Beyond the parts of the movement – of which he analysed all imaginable parts one after another – a new entity arises: the Whole. This is the whole of an entire movement. As such it is always – contrary to the thoughts of Zenon – perceived as one whole. In a Bergsonian meta-physis one can, moreover, also imagine a Whole of all synchronically and diachronically interacting movements. The question is, of course, how a mortal human can know this. Originally, for Bergson the answer must be sought in scientific attitude, based fundamentally on a *sens commun* (cf.

Bergson 1959: 219/76). While in natural perception we perceive only the one image at hand – as a whole one – scientific cognition and philosophy fill the gaps between the not perceived, or the perceivable. Thus it extends toward the Whole, which is never perceived.

Cinema would (exceptionally) be the first case in which the 'natural attitude' could directly attain the Whole. It was not difficult to think of cinematic practices exemplifying all of the different parts of movement. The other part of Bergson's ontology is a bigger challenge. Indeed, cinema seems so intimately tied to natural perception that the notion of (Bergsonian) *image* seems also intranscendible (image being that filtering process toward a possible action, which is proper to organisms). Deleuze's film theory is based in the first place on the equation of Bergsonian and cinematic image, both being the expression and articulation of movement. Somehow, then, he must overcome *image* as the basic principle or theorem in order to find a cinematic equivalent to Bergson's scientific cognition. Practically, he accomplishes this by a historic perspective. After the rise of Hollywood, the *image-action* definitively entered a lethal crisis. An aesthetic avant-garde found different means of cinematic signification. Here, however, the problem is one of theory, which goes beyond historic reconstruction: namely, 'what would allow us to construct theory within that ontology?' A merely historic rendering of developments that cannot be further understood by theory is useless as well against Deleuze's intentions.

What could possibly be beyond action, then? The reaction of a mind (memory, *affectation*) is coming to its natural end, the Whole is envisaged. A first step in transcending the action reaction cycle is seen in what Deleuze calls purely optical and sonorous situations. No action is exerted by these, no reaction elicited, namely, beyond sensory-motor situations, which are inevitably prolonged into action. Neorealism was a protagonist in transforming the *image*. The action-freed space became 'espace quelconque': disconnected and empty, not turned toward and centred on a developing action. In Deleuze's classification of signs, this becomes 'opsigne' and 'sonsigne,' which are objectivizing 'constatations' (Antonioni) or subjectivizing 'instatations' (Fellini). The question of the cinematic image 'après l'image-mouvement,' passing through the 'dissolves' of *opsigne* and *sonsigne*, becomes more and more one of 'image-temps.' In his fight against materialism, Bergson insisted on the otherness of (pure, that is, not actually remembered) memory or *souvenir pur*.[62] Without the intervention of the mind, cerebral reactions are nothing but reflexes or 'matière.' Mind, however, intervenes in the form of memory, and this is precisely where temporality is introduced. In Bergson, no other mental intervention is thinkable. Time and 'esprit' are materially the same, because single memories are retrieved from a purely virtual deposit and then related to an actual present of perception. That deposit in its pure virtuality is time in a crystal – 'temps-cristal'[63] in Deleuze's parlance – because it is tied to an actual present moment as its virtual mirror or to its immediate past.[64] For our present purposes what counts is that (1) time becomes a factor of the image, (2) the constitution of time in the present moment is like a crystal that 'dédouble à chaque instant en présent et passé' (ibid.: 109), and (3) its function is the materialization of the mind.[65]

The Sides of the Time Crystal Based on that *dédoublement* at the very core or crystal of time, Deleuze can now construe film theory around the different parts of the crystal, much like he did when constructing it around movement and its parts. Deleuze's classification at the *pensée* stage – also far beyond the Bergsonian ontology – goes in several directions. The first are various forms of falsehood, a cinema-technical destruction of normality in the *image-mouvement*. Then comes what Deleuze calls 'noochoc,' where thinking takes over the constitution of world. Various forms of mutual or reciprocal influence between image and thought are possible. One of these is nothing other than the mythical, mental automaton of Eisenstein (one of Deleuze's preferred authors on cinema). Yet there are also other montage-related concepts. While in classic paintings the *historia* is certainly an element of *image-mouvement*, it is the mind that must provide for it entirely. Only in cinema does movement act directly on the human brain, making the mind work from outside.

Once confidence in the reasonableness of the world is lost – which could be proved by intellectual processes – except perhaps for suicide, there are only two other possibilities: Belief and Theorema. If one cannot show the world as full of sense, one must change it into this sense by believing, or by making the world a pro-blema ($\pi\rho o$ = before, $\beta\lambda\acute{\epsilon}\pi\omega$ = to look) through a Theorema, such as Pasolini's famous one or Bresson's world of freedom of choice, or by making irrational cuts. Following this line of thought and transcending it, there is a confidence in the body, the corporality of dance, ceremonies, everyday being-there. The consequences are similar: 'l'espace de corps' is not one of choice; rather, it is the obliteration of choice. Much as death, blank screens, or simply irrational cuts and 're-enchaînements.' Or in the genuine politics of people with its power of fabulation, constructing its own (hi)story. Such a cinema is waiting for the masses to follow. Moreover, we can avail ourselves of the power of the word (not of language in the linguistic sense). As when cinema experiments with juxtaposing sound and image, as layers, consecutively, without unifying them in the movement's normality.

Here the symmetrical theory structure of Deleuze's system comes to its close. Certainly, it is a new and quite original way of reflecting cinema in an ontological manner. Yet it is much less so with regard to Peircean Semiotic, which, we trust, can effectively overcome Deleuze's ambiguities. To a run-of-the-mill film semiologist, the most counterintuitive could be that Deleuze's cinema is not 'something,' a well-confined object, a well-known social practice perhaps. We are used to seeing cinema as an object of meaning in the neighbourhood of linguistic artefacts or theatrical means of representation that has no use for the Whole – other than the homological whole of the Structure. Cinema is the Whole. The Whole is cinema to the extent that it creates a whole. Such a thought is less provocative if compared to the wholeness of temporality in Heidegger's existential analysis. Or, in comparison to Nietzsche's wholeness of Life, life context (*Lebenszusammenhang*) in a new way.

What is cinema? Deleuze gave this question a new and explicit answer. If being is movement, then cinema is also movement, but unlike every other being it is emphatically temporal, on both sides of the 'crystal.' However, the tribute for Bergson's 'anti-idealism,' of abandoning the mind matter distinction, is a high price exacted for being-movement. A critical examination of Deleuze's film theory as cinematic theory of being is possible only as a step backward before – or at the root of – Bergson's philosophy. It concerns centrally the question of time, of cognition of time, and of cognition *in* time.

3.4.2.2 Bergson's Philosophy of Time

Image as Time is Bergson's new solution to an old philosophical problem. The core insight regards time, comprehending movement above all as the Whole, and not as the sum of different states of an object (as in Zenon's paradox of the never-arriving shaft, or Achilles and the tortoise). Only when we break down the whole into momentary cuts, 'coupes mobiles,' can the object be seen as a state of movement, or as a mobile. The Real is Movement, not the mobile. Against the Eleatic's paradox, it is the shaft flying from here to there that is real, not the shaft at a particular intermediate state.

Every answer presupposes its own problem. We have seen that Peirce's theory of the Continuum tackled Zenon's paradox as well – its repercussion was a solution we are tempted to compare with Bergson's Whole. What kind of problem did Peirce see, and was it the same as what Bergson saw? During that epoch, the philosophical problem of time was being reconsidered by many thinkers. Kant's solution to it, in a Transcendental Aesthetics, was no longer satisfying. Yet a return to (pre-Kantian) pre-critical rationalism or associationism was out of question. Among all recent attempts to reach beyond Kant, the most outstanding have been Peirce's Evolutionary Metaphysics, Husserl's Phenomenology, and Bergson's Vitalism. All three share the problem they inherited from Kant. They recuse Kant's apriorism. Yet without apriorism, how can time be thought? How can it be thought that all experience is in time? Without any previous experience of time, without an *a priori* form of time, what is time?

Let us first turn to Bergson, from whom Deleuze received his inspiration for his treatment of time in and beyond movement. Foremost, time is radically disconnected from a transcendental aesthetic; 'image' always stands in the context of Matter, *in specie* that of bodily action or of a corporeally acting *face* or person. 'Image' was developed in a debate with the experimental physiological psychology of that epoch (cf. Deleuze 1983: 83), in particular that of Wundt and the Leipzig laboratory. There is an important difference between Wundt's 'materialist' physiological psychology and the explanation of memory in Bergson (1959: 272/143fn). Memory even more than instantaneous perception poses a problem for all non-mentalist thought. For Bergson there are two movements involved in memory that together yield distinct 'perception.' One movement is centripetal, coming from an outside real object into the brain; the other is centrifugal, going out from 'pure memory' or 'virtual objects' (v. *infra*). Centripetal movements on their own yield only automatic reactions based on passive perception (S-R type), whereas a more and more actualized memory would result from the second movement on its own. Bergson is now denying Wundt's notion that both memory and attention are fixed to cerebral substances such that the brain is a sort of memory deposit. On the contrary, there is a virtual perception influenced by the intention of memory.

It is perhaps worth noting that de Saussure was a pupil of Wundt and that his general linguistics was inspired by Wundt. De Saussure's linguistics are concerned about the common laws of signification *langue* rather than in the individual subject *parole*; in the same vein,

Wundt's physiological interest is in the empirical nature of a *Gattungs*-subject. De Saussure strived to establish a systematic as-sociation of *signifiant* and *signifié*; similarly, Wundt established the (four-step) *Reflexbogen* ('arch of reflexes') from sensory physiological stimuli to the exercise of psychological will through muscles. Wundt knew drive (*Trieb*) only as the most general concept, both as explanatory and as physical driving force; in contrasts, Bergson's departure point was from a more philosophical concept of action (i.e., of an object-manipulating body). Bergson in his metaphysic recognized and criticized the limitations of psychophysiology, and he did this masterfully, but at least in the beginning, he did not think of cinema. In fact, Bergson is much less contradictory as psychophysiology (as it was then), and his work constituted a step toward modern scientific epistemology.

From a psychophysiological perspective, the collection of sensory data under the concept of 'image' amounts to epistemological progress and defeats materialism. The concept of representation is deemed an Idealist aberration. Thus *Image* corresponds to nothing artificial or conventional; rather, it is strictly matter at the entrance (or *face*) of an acting centre, which is equipped with some selection mechanisms supported by the faculty of virtual action (in the cortex). Everything coming before that centre of action ('centre d'image,' that is, human being or living matter) is not in itself raw matter. Rather, it is image; however, it has to be thought of as being image in the natural perception sense of the term. Bergson postulates a mode of knowledge that transcends the contingent, natural 'image' perception, that infers not-yet-perceived (namely, science). We can deduce scientifically even if we cannot perceive naturally. We must reckon with the broader universe of perceived and unperceived ('acentré' in Deleuze), or with matter as such (Deleuze's *image-mouvement*). Grouped around this centre – from which reaction comes – are the filtered outward blows or impulses (*image-perception*) that activate the reaction (*image-action*) through the intromission of affects (*image-affection*).

Bergson's latter notion is especially interesting because it is the direct expression of bodily existence. Action is not thought of immaterially or abstractly, but rather in terms of a corporeal freedom, or will. The body is the guarantor of reality (against Realism). Through affects, the centre of action perceives its corporality without being able to act on it. Everything receives impulses from everything else; that said, it is the nearest images which produce perception and elicit re-action. When the perception is too near, however, it disempowers action (as in the case of pain), because there is no distance.[66] Affects, being interior, have a mediating effect on action: 'C'est donc la perception pure, c'est-à-dire l'image, qu'on doit se donner d'abord. Et les sensations, bien loin d'être les matériaux avec lesquels l'image se fabrique, apparaîtront au contraire alors comme l'impureté qui s'y mêle, étant ce que nous projetons de notre corps dans tous les autres' (ibid. 365/264). From there it is not far to consciousness and mind. To avoid falling into Idealism however, the site of mind is always action–reaction and not Hegelian pure spirit.

The entire material universe is comprehended as consciousness, viz. virtually acting upon each other. The effect of all actions is to neutralize one another. In an individual mind, however, that eternal *consecutio temporum* comes to a halt. Here, the past is not constantly produced by the passing present; rather, it is enriching a present in the form of a freely recalling memory (cf. ibid. 365f/264f), which is also virtual action. As a theoretical concept, *image* is oblivious to language. Bergson criticized philosophical theories that treat cognition inappropriately – as a problem of representation (of an object to a mind or vice versa (cf., e.g., ibid. 356/253). There are an unlimited variety of 'beings' within the Whole. Since every matter acts on every other so as to constantly change the whole and the relationship of all parts in it, living matter introduces a certain *stasis* in the movement. Here the reaction is not immediate; rather, it is mediated by selection and retardation. Such a state is called *une coupe mobile* – or, more plainly, 'thing,' or, in Bergsonian terminology, *image*. Things are defined by the action on them of a centre of action, sometimes equipped with mental consciousness, and memory.[67] Clearly, there are not an infinite number of things, although there are an infinite number of states of movement. Selection and retardation – the characteristics of the interface as much as the choices of the acting centre – determine a concrete thing or image.

3.4.2.3 Deleuze's 'Bergsonization' of Cinema

Matter being temporalized in 'images' is an unusual conception and one that is (more than metaphorically) close to cinema. Through the nature of time itself, it is also close to the spiritual – already so in Bergson's early work. Furthermore, Deleuze attempts to combine Bergson's and Peirce's approaches to this question of time, which is now open again. This philosophical problem finds an original response, within the history of thought (cf. Deleuze 1983: 8) and art, in cinema. There are junctions in the history of thought where thought alone leads no further – where it requires insights from outside, from music, art, and cinema. Here, Deleuze sees his contribution. The cinematic object enters a new dimension by entering the context of a history of thought. Anything less would not do justice to Deleuze's film theory, which is theory in the fullest sense of the term. Semiology, the prevailing approach to cinema, in his eyes is not up to this task. It fails exactly where cinema can contribute most to the history of thought – by helping redefine time as a fundamental dimension of being. Ropars-Wuilleumier (1994) has unearthed the fundamental discrepancy between these two approaches. However, she does not fully appreciate Deleuze's philosophically audacious proposal, because she measures it in terms of its disagreement with semiology.

Seen in the context of a history of thought, Peirce's theory of the Continuum (as discussed earlier) stands out as strikingly similar – and fundamentally different as well. For Peirce, also post-Kantian, this is not the Continuum of the synthesizing mind as opposed to the manifold of sensations. Rather, this theory is based on a Continuum of (modal) being. Furthermore, in Peirce there is no dichotomy between an immaterial Spirit and a mindless material being. From a Bergsonian perspective it is important not to take Peirce for what his work is not: a philosophy in which the synthesis, the Whole, is entirely the work of the mind. The Real itself is continuous.

Obviously, an ontology centred so clearly on movement is quite suited for film. The reason is of course not the banality that film has moving images. For Deleuze the profound reason lies in an ontological assumption concerning every being and being as such. It is not intuitively clear that being is time and duration. Yet alternative intuitions such as Constructivism are only apparently less ontological.[68] Deleuze – who must be credited with a quite interesting interpretation of Bergson – in his film theory merely makes use of some central Bergsonian concepts. These concepts play a structural role in his theory's design and deliver their explanatory power to the core of his explanations of cinema. One could even say that his theory amounts to a creative continuation of Bergsonism. At any rate, it is incomprehensible without Bergsonism.

Thus the question: What *is* Bergsonism? There is undoubtedly a development, from *Matière et mémoire* to *Évolution créatrice*, as outlined in Deleuze (1966). Its latest gestalt prevails in the work on film theory. Generally speaking, Bergsonism is a Platonist ontology, from the philosophical method (intuition) to the archi-platonist ἕν καί πᾶν, the One and Whole. This is discussed as the question of Bergson's monism, which does not contradict an intermediary dualism. Evidently, the Whole of Deleuze's film theory builds on the platonism of its infrastructure, both methodologically and formally. If being were not memory and time, it would be difficult to conceive of cinema 'as object' as image (which only as such is movement and time). The basic question, and a much less mystifying one in light of platonism) – is this: How can one know? Intuition is the answer, which happens to be close enough to the immediate apperception of essence of platonist θεωρία. It follows that an attitude of Kantian Critique is by no means possible. Intuitively, the philosopher discerns as natural 'articulations of the real' (cf. Bergson 1959: 1292) two different beings that are different in their pure essence ('différence de nature'): matter and memory, or duration and actuality, accessed by remembering or perception, respectively. Note well that Deleuze follows Bergson: his film theory is theory in the original, platonist sense of the term; it is genuine ontology. Anyone who forgets this must feel terribly bewildered when cinematic images become matter and also become mind. In sum, it is quite difficult to understand this theory without reference to Deleuze's earlier work on Bergsonism (Deleuze 1966), which establishes its ontological foundations.

Deleuze knows ontologically through 'Intuition,' which eliminates a number of otherwise excruciating problems. The very discernment of essences makes temporal duration a separate entity from spatially divisible extension. Ontological intuition does not suppress the fact that both essences are usually (*de facto*) not pure, but rather *mixta*. Yet they can be seen in their pure state (which they are *de jure*; cf. Deleuze 1966: 35) 'beyond the bend of experience' ('tournant de l'expérience'; Bergson 1959: 321) – that is, tracing out the lines that lead beyond experience. Some problems become 'inexistent problems,' some 'badly posed questions' (in Bergson's 'Introduction, second part'; Bergson 1959: 1271ff). If we do not regard differences of essence, when the problem is posed, we are led to suppose merely differences of degree, of more and less. In a way that reflects Kant's demise of 'metaphysischer Schein,' Bergson debits intelligence itself with a tendency to this sort of error. So this error cannot be suppressed; it can only be fought against. Ontology as 'intuitive counter-intelligence' is thus explained, as it is in Deleuze's film theory.

All of this is merely presupposed by Deleuze. In his '1st Commentary on Bergson' he seems to pretend that there 'are' simply two different natures (essences). 'L'espace parcouru est divisible ... tandis que le mouvement est indivisible' (Deleuze 1983: 9) describes, without warning, ontological differences, space and time. Far from treating this as self-evident, he presupposes an ontological method for differentiating between the two natures. Moreover, a certain anti-Kantianism runs through this commentary (without being named as such). With the help of ontology, he attempts an outright reversion of the Transcendental Aesthetic. The first page of this commentary contains so many capital presuppositions that it is anything but self-explanatory. The model of Kant's Transcendental Aesthetic is indeed the pure form of a geometrical space, which Kant transposes on time. Kant's sole arguments assert themselves as reductions *ad absurdum*; he cannot argue empirically in the Transcendental Aesthetic without contradicting himself. On the other hand, Kant affirms that time is never *experienced as such*; rather, everything is *in* time. Deleuze's entire film theory hinges on this unnamed (and even less discussed) ontological basis. He follows Bergson in *Matière et mémoire*: the 'purity' of forms, of the curves, is behind the bend of experience and can never be the object of an empirical experience. Purity is exactly what Deleuze sees in cinema – intuition therefore, and not empirical, and not even a matter of intellection.

So if indeed the (possibly badly posed) problem is how time becomes thinkable, there are at least two strong alternative answers that do not have an ontological basis. One is phenomenology and the analysis of *Dasein*; the other is Peirce's evolutionary metaphysics. Yet it is preposterous to surmise principally the same sorts of 'pensées' that Deleuze attributes to his 'grands auteurs de cinéma' (cf. Deleuze 1983: 7f). Beyond (and instead of) concepts, these authors can think (!) in movement-images and time-images. However, one can think this only if one possesses the ontological intuition that matter is thought. Strictly speaking, it is meaningless to discuss details of Deleuze's film theory on a non-ontological basis. Like every ontology, it stands and falls only *in toto*.

This could be the place were Peirce enters the debate. His theory of Continuity is also capable of solving the problem of Achilles and the tortoise (cf. *supra*, albeit in an entirely different manner). Deleuze did not notice this, though, when he fitted Peirce into his ontological film theory by identifying some states of the movement with sign classes (albeit 'en changeant le sens'). Deleuze is certainly right in placing the entire film problem in the context of time. Time, however, as all philosophers agree, is not 'some thing.' Therefore, cinema cannot be just like any other object in the physical universe. Why? Because it is so intimately connected with the ever-evanescent and difficult-to-grasp time. Furthermore, we must expect the discourse on cinema to share the fate of time discourses. Every film theoretician who is really aware of the time dimension must concur with Deleuze that time imposes a difficult choice on the then-cognate film discourse. There is no escape from invoking the 'realist' nature of cinema and its unique truth relation to the unaltered real. Time is never – *pace* Bettetini – 'just there.' So difficult is it to speak about time that every meaning of the verb 'is' changes in this context. Perhaps the only alternative is to opt for safety, by situating one's film theory downriver of the time cataracts. But this could never result in an honest film theory, because it avoids the core of film.

Deleuze's thesis stands: cinema is movement. Bergson himself had a quite different opinion – which Deleuze notes in passing – in particular with regard to film. Of course, Bergson never proposes an explicit film theory. What he repeatedly refers to as 'cinematographic illusion' in *Évolution créatrice* is merely an important example – one which, by the way, exemplifies exactly the opposite of Deleuze's opinion on cinema. For Bergson, cinema remains exterior to movement itself; it is like natural cognition, perception, language, intellection. 'Sur la continuité d'un certain devenir j'ai pris une série de vues que j'ai reliées entre elles par "le devenir" en général' (Bergson 1959: 754). Language proceeds in this way – by taking an infinite number of instances, cuts and views and then connecting them from without with tenses. Thus, language, like cinema, possesses only a general idea of becoming. Yet it has no grasp on this becoming, or on becoming itself. For Bergson, then, film is natural cognition, which is essentially different from that other form, continuity, which lies in action itself. 'Pour avancer avec la réalité mouvante, c'est en elle qu'il faudrait se replacer' (ibid.: 755). Bergson uses a neat metaphor for this procedure: to install oneself inside. What does that mean, in light of Deleuze's understanding of cinema?

At least in Bergson's eyes, cinema is not on the side of the whole, but on the side of Zenon's paradox: the unlimited divisibleness of instants, without ever reaching oneness. In the context of the aporia of thinking time, Bergson's originality lies in more than the fact that he resists the temptation of overcoming that impossibility of reaching one wholeness with psychology. After Kant's Transcendental Aesthetic and after psychology in the Augustinian-phenomenological vein, this effectively constitutes a third alternative. Yet never before has ontology been placed so emphatically in the service of temporality. This is not the place to estimate Bergson's achievement, however. The problem is cinema. Immediately, we would like to know how Deleuze can contradict Bergson regarding cinema. Could it be that by investing cinema with attributes of an ontological nature, Deleuze is changing the architectonic principles of Bergson? Unquestionably, cinema stands in the philosophical problem context of time. Time (duration, memory), however, is not cognized through natural perception. One way or another, all philosophical theories agree on this. Thus, by contradicting Bergson, (i.e., by stating that film is not natural perception), Deleuze is maintaining indirectly that it opens the way to genuine time (movement). This genuine time is reserved not for natural perception, but only for ontological knowing. Cinema for Deleuze, is therefore onto-'logy' (where image takes the place of logos), truly *capax temporis*. Furthermore, ontology means intuition, which is beyond intellection. So cinema in its truest essence, time, is intuition rather than perception. Certainly we must take into account that things, including cinema, are *mixta*. That said, cinema in its truest form would attain the pure essence of time. Stated in such unambiguous terms, Deleuze's claim is extraordinary and philosophically revolutionary.

Deleuze does everything he can to conceal the ontological nature of his concepts. While arguing ontologically, it is still possible to see a point in distinguishing two natures. Clearly, the constraints of this kind of argumentation are left behind if the meanings of its concepts assume increasingly concrete features. Speaking of the Whole as if it 'were' (even as an open one in permanent becoming) undoes the work of intuition. Deleuze does not neglect to remind us of the 'spiritual' or 'mental' nature of duration; however, this is not mental in the usual meaning of the term. 'Mental' here is best understood as a remnant of platonism, where 'is' still makes sense. Conversely, it is not visible or experimental as such, not even in principle (if the human mind could also grasp the whole cognitively in its still-to-becoming side).

All of this gives Deleuze's theory an ambivalent character, in the sense that ontological and empirical entities thrive on the same planet. Moreover, we cannot undo Kant's *Critique* so completely. Yet this mixture of the ontological and the cognizable is the ultimate reason why we feel so bewildered by cinema. In Deleuze's mixture, cinema illustrates step by step an ontological theory, even by expanding it with relational aspects (which are not present in Bergson). No surprise, then, that it cannot be followed 'naturally.' Ontological reasoning is different. This knowledge is still present as methodological awareness in Deleuze's Bergsonism book (1966: esp. ch. 1). In his film theory, Deleuze assumes a type of reasoning that is essentially ontological, although intuitive (in the common sense of the term) in its descriptions. Only those who accept an ontological conceptual universe can see what he is describing; those who do not will find it difficult to digest the reasons why certain films are 'mobile cuts' or 'pure remembrance.' Not even the schema of his film theory divisions are sensible: some works of cinema are on the side of the whole, others are on the side of movement and its parts.

To show its ontological foundations, I offer next the basic tenets – stripped of their cinematic content and motors of development of Deleuze's film theory:

A first nature, 'line of objectivity' is divisible and therefore spatial and accessible through perception as opposed to memory. (a) All things in themselves are light. This means that it is not the mind that sheds light on matter, thereby making it cognizable matter. Instead, matter itself provides its own illumination. This is clearly against a Critical attitude. (b) Being light, things (matter) are hyper-mobile. They are under the impact of all other things, in as much as they impel them (i.e., give them im-pulse). The consequence of this is that things are eternally changeable momentary states or images (= a particular state of *matière*).[69] (c) Only in particular images does movement come to a halt. The condition is that these images have particular receptors, which act, as it were, as filters. Upon such *faces*, then, perception acts. (d) This reduction of mobility, or filtering, constitutes a reduction of the many disordered movements into one directed movement. This happens only with regard to an intended action and in living matter. (e) In these circumstances, between Perception and Action an Interval opens, one that can be filled by/with 'affection' if the acting ends or if *faces* are momentarily immobilized.

Memory is of a different nature than this. It contains the whole. All things being *mixta*, memory creates relation in everything (insofar as it is changing) to the whole. It creates in the changing an opening to the open, because the whole is always open (cf. Deleuze's first Bergson commentary). (1) Remembering means, first, assuming an attitude of attaining the past as such. Time is not the fourth dimension of space (cf. Bergson's fight against Einstein's thorough misunderstanding of relativity). Different by nature, time is principally the whole. Duration is thus only a virtual multiple, not an actual multiple like space. Time is in various stages of contraction. In its most decontracted mode it is matter; in its most contracted mode, it is an immediately remembered moment. (2) In remembering, we necessarily choose a level. Every level contains the whole of duration, but in different forms of contraction. We can remember long durations and short durations (which 'materially' comprise the same event, but each time are 'part' of a different whole). (3) Thus, remembering also means choosing a contraction level. The difference between time and space must be kept in mind; time is not the 'abnumerable,' the number of parts. Longer durations do not contain a greater number of parts (instants) than shorter durations; both are more or less contracted wholes.

These two (very sketchy) lines of theses, corresponding to perception and remembrance, amount to a bird's-eye view of Bergsonist ontology. Its platonist nature stands out much more clearly once we exclude 'erroneous opinions' from the philosophical tradition (e.g., Zenon's privileged moments such as finality, and the implicit ontology of modern science with its *instants quelconques*). The entirety of this ontology describes cinema. However, this did not show itself clearly in its infancy as a new technology (cf. Deleuze 1983: 11). Cinema became a crucial cultural phenomenon once it began to unfold its ontological diversity. Thus Deleuze can claim: 'Le cinéma ne nous donne pas une image à laquelle il ajouterait du mouvement, il nous donne immédiatement une image-mouvement. Il nous donne bien une coupe, mais une coupe mobile' (ibid.). The history of cinema would go from the imitation of natural perception to its truer essence as whole. Deleuze has no hesitations: 'Le cinéma retrouvera exactement l'image-mouvement du premier chapitre de "Matière et mémoire"' (ibid.: 12) It ends, therefore, in the domain of the spiritual, even though it starts off in the 'numerable' of perceptible parts. In this sense, cinema 'utilizes the concepts of Bergsonist ontology' perfectly, and signals the commencement of a spiritual culture.

3.4.2.4 *In Defence of Bergsonist Cinematic Being*
A first real challenge arises from Husserl's phenomenology, which is contemporary with Bergsonism as well as analogous as a philosophical revolution. Deleuze argues at one point with the phenomenology, of Husserl and Merleau-Ponty. An interesting argument, coming from Merleau-Ponty, irritates Deleuze: that cinema is – a kind of *epoché?* – unlike the normal intentional being in a world horizon, normal 'natural' cognition being always 'consciousness of something' and therefore

not Idealistically a form of judgment ('concept') combined with empirical apperception. Cinema is suspect in that it makes an unreal out of the real, an image out of the real world. This can only lead to a falsification of intentionality or the intentional being-within-a-world-horizon.

Even imagination, a temporal mode so clearly central to cinema, is – through intentionality – in the phenomenological world horizon. In spite of its being either unreal, or past, or both, it effectively generates $εἴδη$. It is the concrete object or $εἶδος$ one intends, in the now of phenomenological time, that guarantees world and a world horizon, and not the other way around (cf. Eley 1973: 438). Phenomenology is, if nothing else, a novel way to approach the image problem. It is not yet another attempt to reject that cumbersome subjectobject dichotomy by sacrificing one or the other. There is no Subject in Saussurean semiology (in fact there are only combinations of units); nor is there a sense-constituting Subject à la Kant in *Gestalt* theory since innate or at least ever-present *Gestalten* are responsible for the constitution of sense. As a philosophical program, phenomenology also sets out to bridge the abyss between Subject and Object. It achieves this through a new approach to intentionality. The intentional-being-with-a-world is not objectivist; rather, it is intrinsically relational, an originary cross-reference of expectation and fulfilment. An object is what fulfils an intentionality. Peirce's 'there are no data' also applies to phenomenology. The image serves as a placeholder of the world in the mind, and philosophical analysis can reduce its purview to this $εἶδος$ of intentionality. This indicates clearly why Gadamer's *Wahrheit und Methode* dedicates so much effort to describing the mode of the presence of images, in particular religious images. Thus it would certainly be interesting to have phenomenological film theories, in continuation of a recent effort by Casebier (1991), who unfortunately fails to consider time.

Deleuze criticizes the phenomenological understanding of the perceiving subject from a Bergsonian perspective. According to this, the physical world or movement still relates to 'poses,' with the only difference being that these poses are existential instead of essential (Deleuze 1983: 85). The perceiving subject is still thought of as a vis-à-vis to an object, which remains, as it were, in the outside world. Although evidently not as fully as in Bergson, the perceiving Subject for Husserl is immersed into, and confounded with – even a part of – the physical world. It remains intentionality and does not become part of the relation of subject to world (as thought of by Husserl and the tradition following him). Deleuze calls it 'pose' or posture.

What does this criticism of intentionality intend? Since antiquity, the problem has always been how to think of movement; this is another way of expressing the problem of how to think of time. The paradox of Achilles and the tortoise, and that of the arrow and the shaft, are well known. What the paradox makes utterly clear is that the source of the dilemma lies in the posing of the problem itself. In antiquity, one of the best answers to this dilemma was hylomorphism. Here every move-ment is tied into an ontological change of being, which is thought of as being 'composed' by form μορφή and matter ΰλη, *actus* and *potentia, accidens* and *substantia, existentia* and *essentia*. Movement can thus be thought as 'act'-ualization of a potential; every concrete (<*con-crescere*, meaning grow together!) being, then. is what Deleuze calls a 'pose,' – that is, a privileged moment on the way to a telos. It falls short of thinking of the whole of a movement, because it thinks of movement as being in privileged moments. Modern science is different only in that it eliminates privileged moments such as teleology.

For Bergson every movement can only be comprehended as other than a closed system. Here the ontological theory of 'pure remem-brance,' of duration, arises as an alternative. It is *translation*, in the atti-tude of remembering, that produces the open and whole: 'coupes immobiles + temps abstrait' renvoie aux ensembles clos, dont les par-ties sont en effet des coupes immobiles, et les états successifs, calculés sur un temps abstrait; tandis que "mouvement réel – > durée concrète" renvoie à l'ouverture d'un tout qui dure, et dont les mouvements sont autant de coupes mobiles traversant les systèmes clos.' (Deleuze 1983: 22). Thus according to Deleuze, phenomenology also thinks of move-ment in poses (cf. Deleuze 1983: 85). This constitutes a converse deduc-tion from the non-ontological theory status of phenomenology. When an intuitive grasp of the whole is lacking there remains an idea of only parts of the movement (namely, the ones we are intentionally being with). Undeniably, Bergson thinks of movement as other than the retention and protention of the phenomenological now. Husserl contin-ued a psychological tradition of thought that began with St Augustine's three presents; from there, the psychological side of the time phenome-non continued to subsist (cf. *infra* 348). Husserl's phenomenological time, however, is also a whole in duration; it goes from the *eben noch* ('recently yet') to the presently present and the immediately coming.

There is an interesting parallel: both Husserl and Bergson pay a very high price for their solutions to creating a whole. In Husserl, this price is in the fundamental division between the whole of immediate time consciousness and that which is alienated in the flow of oblivion ('versunken im Fluß des Vergessens'). The result is another, secondary or derived intentionality, imagination. Bergson pays the price in the 'difference of nature,' in perception and intuition, in the difference of ontology. If actions result from perception and affects, which in turn can remain virtual actions ('rêve') or become real reactions, there is an alien element in that chain. Virtuality is a second order of real.

The second challenge, Peirce, merits a final remark. What can be said about Deleuze's effort to decorate his Bergsonist film theory with Peircean sign classification? After all, it has no incisive consequences. It leads, however, straight to the core of the central question: What is a cinematic image? Is image (that interface of a centre of re-action called) *image*, or is it a triadic sign? Or is there no difference between the two, as Deleuze's pastiche theory suggests? Or is the surreptitious spiriting in of signs without their Pragmaticistic, Categorical, and Metaphysical underpinnings actually a new attempt to bring about *coincidentia oppositorum*?

For Bergson Peirce would probably be an Idealist. Peirce still allows for two independent orders: one of raw Facticity and Quality the other its representation in the system of Interpretants. He believes only that in the long run they will coincide as the ultimate adequate opinion on the Real. Bergson takes his (vitalist?) distance from Kant's Idealism[70] explicitly and radically, which is relevant in this context. Peirce instead might raise the same critical objection against Bergson as against Kant's *Ding an sich*; in fact, something in Bergson makes it impossible for him to reflect critically on his own theorizing. Bergson must write about *images, mouvement,* and so on as if he had knowledge of them previous to his reflection. He does so on the basis of *sens commun* and 'science' (in its trans-historical entirety). Yet his common sense is not reflected Critically as a non-transcendible *a priori* of every cognition, including his own, as is Peirce's Common-sensism as the historicity of cognition.

It is astonishing how Deleuze manages to save the potential of Peircean sign classification. How does he circumvent the evident importance of the very idea of representation as definition of sign in Peircean Semiotic[71] without sacrificing its potential? By his own admission, he is eclectic regarding what he adopts from Peirce, and he destroys the coherence of Semiotic argumentation. With it dies both the purpose and the idea itself of Category, so that when speaking of signs Deleuze calls them Firstness and so on. Deleuze employs ontological terms[72] that defy the principle of Semiotic. He uses signs in a Peirceish way, but without strictly intending them as Peircean: 'Nous prenons donc le terme "signe" en un tout autre sens que Peirce: c'est une image particulière qui renvoie à un type d'image, soit du point de vue de sa composition bipolaire, soit du point de vue de sa genèse … nous empruntions à Peirce un certain nombre de termes en changeant le sens' (1985: 48). Semiotic is 'wrapped' by B/D, linked by mere classification. Categories are transformed into B/D as follows: 'image-affection' (for Firstness), 'image-action' (for Secondness), 'image-relation' (for Thirdness). It is unclear, and does not really matter, why Deleuze decorates his various stages of ontological argumentation with Peirceish labels (see Deleuze 1983: 291f). He borrows the following terms: *Dicisigne, Icône, Qualisigne, Synsigne* = sinsign (from singular, in Peirce), *Empreinte, Indice, Marque, Symbole, Opsigne, Sonsigne*. Not surprisingly, some of Peirce's sign classes are lacking. Because he did not acknowledge the Categorical pivot of Peirce's classification, his translation of the triadic sign relation into a Bergsonism had to fail. 'Categories' are actually images; however, where cognition becomes an interstice between action and re-action, the Critical purpose of Category is lost.

Taking exception to Peirce's supposed abandonment of his original approach to signs (as threefold images) in favour of logic[73] makes no sense except for an ontology of duration. It is the originality of Peirce's sign relation – its unique relating of Quality, Facticity, and the supra-individual interpretation – that Deleuze does not acknowledge. For Peirce, a sign is never the relation of an acting centre ('image-action') to a universe in movement ('image-mouvement'). For him, sign is still thought of from the unifying point of view of a subject (this is the idea behind Secondness or Opposition). The Pragmatic Maxim as critique of Kant's *Ding an sich* categorically vetoes all attempts to assume cognitive positions that cannot be accounted for Critically. Bergsonist ontology is in such a position where it can never be falsified, and cognizing being as movement becomes platonist intuition as an exceptional kind of cognition beyond Critique. It is intended as an ontology of science, upstream of science itself, but appealing to the evidence of 'sens commun.' The method of methods justifying these ontological concepts, however, is not in itself scientific.

Ontological thinking leads to criticism of Peirce for mistaking categories, the three images, as simple facts. Instead, Deleuze (1985: 47): '… que la priméité, la secondéité et la tiercéité correspondaient à l'image-affection, à l'image-action et à l'image-relation.' Peirce's mistake was that he lacked the intuition that before everything there is Movement; thus, we must amend his list of Categories by preposing a 'zéroïté' (cf. Deleuze 1985: 47) as the true basis for subsequent Categories (which, however, stop before Fourthness, for ontological reasons). An interesting parallel between this basic 'zéroïté' outside cognition and the *Ding an sich* (also incognizable) cannot be further investigated. There is in any case no non-cognitive vantage point on the incognizable, which is thus sheltered from any Critical argument. There is only one alternative against all sorts of ontology: not arguing, but not practising it. 'There is no cognition without signs' (5.265; W2.212, 1868) might never convince an ontologist, but at least it is a clear option for making one's own theory accountable. In B/D terms, the absolute point of reference is time, not cognition. Time is the place from which all being flows. All being is only diversification and modification of the movement.

3.5 What Cinema Becomes: Theory Objects Compared, Reconciled, Rejected

Not even an excessively irenic temperament could reconcile all of these theoretical approaches to cinema. Are they still about the same object, film? What cinema is – and even more, what can be derived from its essence – has found no straightforward answer. Cinema defies all plain definitions. What makes it so difficult to arrive at an adequate grasp of cinematic meaning in all its comprehensiveness, complexity, and subtlety? Cinema is more than narration. It is not just a kind of language, and its capacity to construct meaning goes far beyond perception. Anything short of a theoretical grasp of the poetical, aesthetic, cognitive, and documentary potential will not be adequate for cinema. All of this depends on the answer we can provide to the question, 'What is cinema?' Cinema's potential is formidable. It captures the visible real in images; not only that, but it is uniquely capable of manipulating time. So far we have encountered a number of more or less ingenuous ways to tackle such a potential theoretically.

(1) In the semiological model, meaning as topology – including its film-theoretical extension *iconismo* – could ultimately not explain Generality, which is essential for meaning. Those who think in 'codes' can think only from the vantage point of a system assigning a place to every singularity of the codified. It is difficult for semiological film theories to overcome this constraint, which confines the meaning admissible in cinema to the differentiated. Like iconic representation, semiology also

has notorious difficulties with time, even as film theory. The methodological restraint against considering *parole/discours* as capable of theory blocks any approach to the psychological philosophies of time. The
principal limitation resulting from this method is a fixation on the two
remaining marks of time: syntax and tense. In film, then, not much is to
be gained. For one thing, there are no cinematic equivalents of tense
codification. Furthermore, any narrative substitute does not result from
a syntax in the strict sense of the term. Syntagmatics build on the successful achievement of representation: only if, temporal universes can
be represented can they be ordered in a quasi-syntactic manner. Strictly
speaking, this is the task of a poetic of imitating action (μίμησις
πράξεως) as an arrangement of acts (σύστασις τῶν πραγματῶν).

The code-based representational achievement of cinema itself is
profoundly insufficient. For this reason, an amendment has been
attempted that applies 'motivated signs,' Morris's 'icons.' These contribute the dissolution of arbitrariness in the semiological sign relation,
which must directly concern the explanatory power of systematicity.
What is left from arbitrariness in motivation? Eco's iconism tries to
save as much of 'system' as is feasible in a procedure of communicational disambiguation. This introduces a system behind the system of
signs (here, an infinite regress looms).

But does this help with the representation of time? 'Is' time at all as a
motivated sign, and not as syntax or tense? Bettetini draws a coura-
geous consequence by reanchoring time in enunciation. Mediated
through Weinrich, he returns effectively to a hermeneutical and thus
psychological time concept. Cinematic enunciation becomes, first, an
institution of levels of time (not so much hypotaxis and its textual
marks, and not principally a matter of logical modalization – despite
AN logic), where by the base level is by its nature an existential experience of time, and not temporality as meaning. What is left of semiology, then, if we again anchor time in the subject? Semiology as such
becomes a regional film theory. This still allows us to deduce tense
effects and equivalents in a semiological manner. Ricoeur, in the
hermeneutical tradition, makes this point in his critique of Greimas,
the semiologist. Cinema as object remains in an ambivalent state when
treated from a theory, which is essentially atemporal.

(2) In Deleuze, time becomes thinkable, but not as an external fact
and not as syntagmatic effect. The failure in integrating Peirce into this
film theory highlights the central problem of an ontological vision.
Whole and Parts, 'tout' and 'dividuel,' remain contraries and cannot be

thought of together. Even though this dichotomy is not conceptualized as level (or as drop in level, as in phenomenology), this makes time as it is experienced and cognized almost unthinkable. Bergson thinks about having direct access to time by means of intuition; Deleuze configures this ontological intuition for cinema but without changing it in its essence. So we must accept that as a result, we have two different regimes at the watershed of that 'différence de nature.' One is perception, the other is intuition, which mixes in the concrete matter of things, the *mixta*. Perhaps it is the penalty for all ontological thought generally that it is impossible with this theory for us to account for the nature of the 'difference of nature'. Neither is it possible to argue without presuppositions why a wrongly posed or inexistent problem is wrong or inexistent (this is not a *quaestio facti*, but a *quaestio juris*).

In Peirce's scheme of things, we can never have direct access to time. Time 'is' in the sign itself, as the novelty of a cognition, whereas time as entirety is to be grasped only through Continuity. We must not think of this as a transcendental presupposition. Through its being in signs, time is empirical throughout. It is never whole but always 'wholer,' as it were, more entire. Now, what of the two Bergsonist natures? Bergsonism stands for 'wholes.' From a Peircean perspective we must ask whether we need wholes, and if we do, why we do. This question becomes highly relevant in the context of time or temporality. As an experience, time is a vector to a whole. Therefore, it is not only change, which could also be circular (i.e., not vectorial). Totality, and not just the 'now' of cinema, is also presupposed in Bettetini's concept of enunciation time (and through his implicit latching on to the hermeneutic tradition, from which he inherits a *Dasein*-analytical temporal wholeness).

Thus the only serious point of contention between Bergsonism and a Peircean perspective relates to the type of presence of the whole. Is the ontological presence feasible at all, as Deleuze postulates? Is intuition not that sort of non-cognitive, non-criticizable attitude change which is untypical of cinema, but at best is typical of some traditions of philosophical thinking? Is it true, as Deleuze contends, that cinema 'utilizes the concepts' of Bergsonism because it is temporal? Both Deleuze and Bergsonism tend to obscure the principal difference between the ontological attitude and the empirical, between intuition and perception. No doubt, the need to change attitude is accounted for. We can doubt, though, that time needs the ontological attitude and that it would otherwise be inaccessible. This doubt cannot be argued, however, because it is based on ontology. Again, like all ontologies, it is either true or false in its entirety. It is impossible to falsify parts of it, because that would require a confrontation with empirical facts, which is inadmissible and inadequate for ontology. So the reasonable thing to do is keep it or to dismiss it *in toto*. Even more so, if it is a non-Critical ontology and therefore not even to be measured with the operation of the cognizing mind.

Thus, when cinema is claimed to be 'movement' in the context of Bergsonism, this amounts to a contention that cinema as an attitude is intuition and not perception. By no means, however, is 'movement' to be taken here in the common sense of the term. In this common sense, it was understood in Aristotle's *Physic* as the numerable and therefore not as a whole. 'Movement' is invisible, and so is movement; both are mental acts of intuiting a nature or numbering. The platonist ontology behind the 'movement' is justified by other means than perceptive experience. Movement as numbering instead incurs into an aporia of thought the Achilles–tortoise paradox. Bergsonism must oppose all formal, anti-ontological theories. If time becomes a form of the perceiving mind, it is a mere formal whole. In Kant's Transcendental Aesthetic the schema of time is a whole only because it cannot otherwise be thought of without contradiction. One would incur into an antinomy if a period of time could not be thought of as necessarily being part of a whole. As a consequence, sequentiality and simultaneity would no longer be thinkable and *a fortiori* perceptible.

Semiology is a similar sort of formalism. By defaulting on anything comparable to the Transcendental Aesthetic, however, it remains blind to the apperception side. Its synthesis does not require schematisms of time and space. There is, however, a deeper rift between an ontological and a formal approach, one that separates Deleuze from semiological theories of all stripes. Semiological film theories with their fundamental atemporality are at a disadvantage when they come up against the thorough temporality of Bergsonism. Deleuze constructs his theory of cinema as the whole or parts of Bergsonism. The concept of a more than formal whole must necessarily escape to theories based on differential systems. One can only deny the whole as superfluous, but this denial comes at a high price: it must banish temporality from the realms of its theory.

It seems evident that for cinema, theories with a grasp of time are superior. Time is without doubt a special object (i.e., non-object). Therefore any theory that fails to recognize this special mode of being of time will not be adequate. Yet there are a number of theories that meet this requirement, and on the basis of some of them, respectable film theories have been developed. Until we have considered film theories in the phenomenological tradition, we can make no final judgment between Deleuze's Bergsonism and Semiotic. Furthermore, we can make that final judgment only if a determinate presence of the whole is required. Peirce would have denied the possibility of knowing the whole – the evolutionary whole as much as any other. For him it would have sufficed that any concrete cognition is part of the whole. It is not necessary that the whole as such be present, as long as the vectors point toward it.

Peirce's self-restraint enjoys a practical advantage. He does not need to change attitudes, there is no intuition for the 'other nature.' Everything is on one register of being, everything is cognized, but there are modes of cognition. Firstness, the prevailing of Icons in sign relations, enables a perfect and sufficient mode of cognition of time. Furthermore, there is no difficulty changing from one mode of cognition to the other on the same 'object' of time. Therefore, choosing Semiotic is more than warranted. In particular for film, the different modes of cognition, all of them simultaneously possible, are an obvious boon. Witnessing *Je vous salue, Marie*, Godard's film about the permanent becoming of All, is complex enough to defy any reductionism of the cinematic object.

(3) Constructivism could at best be Kantianism (but diminished by the labours of a table of categories and of a Transcendental Aesthetic). It treats time, if at all, in the manner of schematism. Yet its schematisms appear from nowhere. Picturesque metaphors suggest a natural growth of forms that inform perception. Also, the central theorems of cognitivism (constructivism) cannot achieve the explanatory power of relational Semiotic. Some important concepts lack sufficient explanation. To begin with fundamentals: 'Why (caused by which power) are schemata applied to ('cues,' 'data,' 'stimuli'?)?' Thus, 'What produces a synthesis?' Is it produced from outside (i.e., the cognitivist equivalent of Peirce's 'we are in thought')? Or from inside (i.e., from the distinctly different strengths of cohesion forces between these two elements, which, lacking a third General one, are subject to the same criticisms on this point as semiology)? Furthermore, the activity of a psychological subject must always be postulated, from whose volitive teleology (and not true cognition!) the purpose of cognition must be deduced.

Semiotic, the triadic Relation of the Sign (including Generality), lacks the peculiar deficiencies of the film theories discussed earlier. As the above discussion has shown, the real advantage of a Semiotic film theory is that it has such Signs at its core: cinema *in se* is comprehended as an Iconic Sign. Its triadic Relation encompasses the broad realm of logical possibility. Such a fundamental determination of the being and cognitive status of cinema *in se* leaves open a certain number of cognitive paths while closing others.[74] All further sign determination, all concretized meaning, builds on this. It follows that if cinema is a Relation of Performance (which in Classical film theory was hypostasized as the 'photographic' in film), it is so only under Iconic conditions. Cinema *in se* is essentially a playful reasoning that is independent of existence and logical necessity. As such it is neither false nor true. In contrast, a Relation of Performance is epitomized in propositions, which are either false or true. A documentary 'photographic' film becomes, as textual genre, reportage; this indicates a change in the Sign nature of what could even be of the same material as Relations of Comparison. The latter could also yield to Relations of Thought. This is usually at a later stage in film; and as we have seen, its production – except for the teleology of narration – is highly precarious.

A relational Semiotic does more than provide us with a stronger grip on the Real. Especially relevant to cinema, it constitutively includes time; thus cinema becomes a peculiar object, quite resistant to objectivizing. Except for Bergsonism, no other theory really provides the means for reflecting on different modes of being, which are so crucially important for the time nature of cinema (and of course for its aesthetic nature). We have observed the limitations of cognitivist rationality, which can grasp merely one of three types of Relations (i.e., the Existential propositional type). Thus it must fail at least in that Relation which is the experience of time. Also, in the intricate complexities of aesthetic and rhetorical meaning, the entire Relational arsenal is involved.

As a conclusion and result of our inquiry into the 'what-ness,' nature, essence, or objectivity of cinema, we can now test the core of this theory in a very difficult work of cinematic art. In Godard's *chef d'oeuvre* we can observe its analytical capability for a very concrete but almost elusive meaning (one that is not so tremendously avant-garde when compared to classical rhetorical figuration).

Intermezzo: Cinematic Imagination of Godard's *Je vous salue, Marie*

If there is a film whose analysis can profit from a Semiotic approach, it is certainly *Je vous salue, Marie* (*Hail Mary*). This film is complex enough to challenge any theoretical concept of cinema. Among its layers are straightforward (and 'straightbackward'?) narrative parts. There are sheer images that are non-subservient to narrative meaning. There are comments and parallelisms. There is heavy irony. So problems arise: What will enable us to comprehend all these variegate parts? And what makes these parts function as parts of a whole?

Any partial concept of cinema will see preferentially that with which it can deal and leave for the rubbish heap that which does not fit. For this film 'is' many things at once. Moreover, those many things do not supplement one another in an easy configuration; rather, they seem to tear apart any contingent joining. Starting with the puzzling introductory film by another hand (who happens to be Godard's wife), we easily eliminate unhelpful subplots, symbolic universes, and music as bearers of significant signification. Thus, if film (from a cognitivist perspective) 'is' spatiotemporal representation, there is much redundant material. If film 'is' perception, there is too much to think about and to be argued, alluded to, theorized, rhetorical, spiritual. If film 'is' stratified codes, it is very easy to distinguish those strata, but then there is the problem of 'unlocking' their internal organization and their 'commenting' interrelationships. All of this greatly disturbs the independent arbitrary sign relation of any one stratum. Lest it be taken in charge by an overarching code: usually this is the opportunity to take advantage of enunciation. We have already noted how this 'solves' the arbitrariness of signification, especially in connection with time.

Before we begin considering this work of art in its entirety, let us test the Semiotic analytical method against a tiny portion of the film: a short, recurring sequence of nenuphars or water lilies. Without a doubt this is one of the most enigmatic sequences, one that stubbornly resists all sorts of interpretations; yet it has a strange aesthetic charm. At the same time, it must play an important function for the meaning of the film *in toto*, since it is emphasized through its recursiveness. Here we can exemplify changes in the Sign Relation as meaning constitution. From the perspective of the logic of relations, these Relational changes are changes in Relation types of Thought, Performance, and Comparison, until they constitute one and the same material in Godard's *Je vous salue, Marie*: the water lilies.[75] This constitutes a 'natural sign,' which as a Sign in Godard's film is maximally open to diverse meanings. This sign could tentatively be circumscribed in its final but not immediate meaning as follows: 'The algae water in fermenting agitation, with magnificent water lilies and a mirroring sun, wants to imply that somebody has/is created/creating Life, here.' This is a quite daring interpretation. It certainly does not recommend itself strictly on the basis of this percept, but it can of course be supported by multiple Grounds of Interpretation, which are unique and specific to this film in its entirety, but which are not listed here (cf. *infra*).

This is a perfect example of a triadic Representation or Semiosis. Now, depending on the relational degeneration (respectively constructiveness) of the Sign triad, it is more or less than a dyadic (degenerate triadic) Relation, which is the usual conception of 'sign.' Clearly, this nenuphar sequence does not pretend to indicate anything. Thus the meaning can only be a general or a possible cognition. The proof is *per exclusionem* of its alternative: it would be a dyadic Relation, which is either true or false, if this Sign could be rendered *salva veritate* in two propositions: (1) 'this water is warmed by the sun' (A > B: sun > warm water), and (2) 'this warm water contains life/algae' (B > C: warm water > life). These and many similar propositions of facts could be the dyadic rendering of our sequence of images. (An additional external condition must be met, that these images are interpreted 'photographically,' that is, with the technological knowledge of the 1:1 relationship of certain attributes on celluloid and an outside reality [rendered linguistically with 'this']).

One should perceive, then, two – or any number of – distinct facts in this sequence (facticity supported by the knowledge of photography). However, at this cognitive junction one can choose openly among three alternatives. First, true statements of these events ('someone has perceived all these qualities [warm, algae-green, stone-splash, air-bubbles coming from the dirty watery solution of organisms, and so on] at a given time and for a given duration'). As a cognition this is probably not at all interesting. Yet one is forced to perceive the same facts repeatedly during the course of the film; this is either to enforce boredom or to hint that the series is justified by a cognitive process that demands to surmount facticity. Second, with the mind and knowledge of a biologist, one 'sees' fermentation, developing life, evolution. This means that all instances of the same kind are cognized cumulatively as one general insight into Nature. Only in this case are the two propositions united in a general law. Perhaps this is as outlined above. Alternatively, in the film itself this interpretation might be supported by and identical to the careful exposition of the Professor's understanding. Third, however, we can disregard biological and photographic knowledge and simply perceive what stares us in the face. Thus, bubbling algae can stand for everything possible, and its cognitive value is imagination. That interpretation is supported by the aesthetic regard with which these sequences are shown and repeated. Since the cognitive status of imagination does not allow for conclusive reasoning, the circumscription of the comprehensive meaning of these sequences is merely one possibility. But it must be imagined – it is not enough that it is imaginable. When it is imagined it 'is,' otherwise 'it' never comes to light. Invention is therefore the cognitive function of aesthetic.

Yet that aesthetic synthesis (in the sense of unification of the manifold) is Godard's whole point – and anti-Pascalist counterpoint – in these images, which are repeated like an organ point in an organ concerto whenever the symbolic meaning requires. It is God, for whom the sun stands in these images, who creates Life (and who also created Life in Marie). If we understand this meaning in this Sign, we have grasped that the sun creates life, and therefore that the warming of the water is done to this purpose in order to induce in me the impression that from this warming originates Life. In the film's artistic strategy, the organ point becomes the really plausible support of the narrative, which never attains the status of a *narratio probablis*. This observation calls for a deeper investigation into Godard's rhetorical artistry, which seems to accomplish an impossible feat. By generalizing the improbable aesthetically, he transforms it into the only plausible interpretation. Godard has even purposefully removed (or ridiculed and discredited, as with the Pascal Professor stochastic proof) all other evidence that could lend credible support to the central plot. The inconspicuous aesthetic sequences become the pillars of the plot without ever being part of it. Without a proper understanding of their meaning process, the key to the entire film would be irretrievable. It would be lost as a whimsical, high-brow, 'artsy,' meaninglessly playful, and unintelligible art film.

Regarding the cognitive types in general: A dyad is expressed in a proposition, which is true if the fact exists and false if it does not. Yet there is no 'intelligence' in true/false proposition, which would require a 'smart' inference to a General, a purpose that is beyond the purely factual. That the sun shines in order to bring life is a Relation, between three elements, of a specific kind. Triadicity (i.e., Sign) is essential for understanding; as we have seen, meaning is always an external object in Relation to which are two elements. In our example, one relation is between sun and water, the other relation is between life and the same water. This is clearly more than in the first relation alone, which means that something else was added in this new wholeness: understanding – for example, that here (in this same external Object) life is originating. The linguistic rendering of our example may not be the best, or it may be too simple for the complexity of the imagery; but (seeing) it is really striking because if we are incapable of synthesizing such a triadic Relation, what we see is really meaningless. Dyadic Relations yield only insignificant results, a photographic rendering of an existential, quasi-propositional fact of a water lily in dirty water; but they do not yield the purpose of that rendering. We are navigating with this example in the realm of Sign Relations of thought, which are the easiest to talk about. In spite of their difficult (i.e., rhetorical; cf. *infra*) achievement, as consciousness content they can be rendered in sentences as far as their logical necessity goes. The same material can also be an Iconic Sign Relation of comparison, when it is not used rhetorically, as Godard evidently wants it to be used. In principle, we cannot render this linguistically without destroying its nature. A playful comparison of what I see with something else is, however, the initial stage in the invention of meaning. In a later, detailed description I will argue that Sign processes of this sort are at the root of cinematic rhetoric. Once the rhetoric link of meaning 'stands,' the Relation of thought becomes efficient and is the meaning of that image.

Admittedly,this is a difficult cinematic example, but what would be an alternative theory to account for this? We can try the schematism of (Bordwell's rendering of) constructivism: 'top-down' and 'bottom-up processes.' The most charitable interpretation of these metaphors would equate them with the logical operations of deduction and induction. But this would leave a significant gap that again fully justifies the wisdom of limiting this to metaphoric usage: it gives an idea of the sequence of premises, *a maiore ad minorem* in top-down, *a minore ad maiorem* in bottom-up processes. Yet there is no conclusion, and this is really the whole point of logical inference. What was criticized earlier arises again in this example: as a bottom-up process, we should get 'sun [plus bubbles, etc.] > warm water' (taking all lower-order recognition of visual forms and so on for granted). Strictly speaking, this already contains an admixture of top-down processes, which are neglected here for simplicity's sake. It is not derived from the *same* cognition that a top-down process (life originates from warm water) relates to the same object; it requires a new dyad for it to be thinkable. We can theorize that ever new, more general schemata are applied until we come to the macro-proposition, 'life originates from warm water.' How then, do we explain that it comes to this and not to an entirely different 'direction' in the application of more general schemata A > B, B > C, C > D ... ? This cannot be answered with sequences of dyads. The water lily image points to that impasse because there is no natural way to impose one most general schema; rather, there are many somewhat vague ones. 'Interpretation' thus becomes unpredictable, because *narration* as highest schema is prohibited by the textual strategy of the film. The only alternative left is to apply style schemata. Yet even these must relate (triadically) to defamiliarizing general schemata,[76] which do not exist here. Therefore, even 'style' (let alone rational cognitive perception processes in the manner of Peterson's description of avant-garde) does not reach this image: 'What does it mean?' cannot be answered (not even with 'trouvailles' [cf. *infra*], which before 'ending up' or not must first be found).

A difficult image, which this one is, reveals hidden presuppositions and point to the explanatory power of the Triadicity of Sign Relations. Even for 'simple' cinematic images, we have to include Generality in the triadic Relation if there to be is understanding. Dyads such as those envisaged by schema theories may yield truth ('schema application fits data'), but they are not Signs. Once this principal step into Triadicity is made, and the nature of the being of the Sign is determined as one of the basic trichotomy, the interesting points for a subsequent meaning determination involve the narrower determination of sign classes. This is concretely, then, the direction of Interpretation, of its predictability, of 'what does that image, etc., mean?'

The advantage and value of Semiotic for understanding cinema lies precisely in a Sign that is triadic and not something else. Being Sign comprehends more than dyadic facts (i.e., [this sign signifies that] 'X has done Y'). It also comprehends the possibility of interpreting 'Y is an indication for me that X has done it,' or 'X the agent makes me believe that it has done Y.' What do we gain from this? We gain the awareness that all meanings are placed on a Continuum of Interpretations. There are no pure facts (except as Ground of a Sign), there are no unrelated Dyads, that stay juxtaposed to one another. A and B and C does not permit us to conclude 'ergo D.' 'And' is merely a pseudo-conjunction, one that has been recognized as such since Boetius (cf. Brunning 1994: 124). All true Relations are Triads or higher *n*-ads. In this way, Triadicity makes possible an enormous multiplicity of meaning, one that is far beyond facts and that does not need to be left to the arbitration of the psyche (perhaps constrained by 'motivation'). The unexplained remainder of volitive forces, as was criticized earlier in the theory design of constructivism, is in principle superfluous in Semiotic.

The impact of the classification of Signs becomes fully apparent in the context of the Continuum of meaning. Making classes means that we are making meaning more concrete in Relations. It is not difficult to conceive of 'grand' meaning unities resulting from 'small' ones; meaning is always the unification of the manifold. Godard's water lily images are a perfect albeit difficult example of this. 'Narrative schemata' that would be required in order to integrate those water lilies do not exist, or they are obliterated by Godard. From this we come to the importance of the Relations in the Continuity of Interpretations. Not even this Continuity is simple, but it can be determined, as any Interpretation (i.e., it can never have the rigidity of a schema). How we ever arrive at narrative Interpretation strategies (i.e., Semioses) at all will be thematized in chapter 5. In this context we are seeking a more general understanding of only rhetorical strategies of Interpretational guidance. The 'argumentative' (or pseudo-argumentative) view of enthymemas, besides, fits well into the much more complex Semioses of cinema. Here, too, reference to 'tropes' is no explanation, except that they are habits, as is every true Thirdness.

In this complicated reconstruction of meaning, we cannot avoid referring to semiosic Sign determination in the Continuum of Interpretation. Furthermore, another avenue for film Interpretation, one that is important for a truly full understanding of cinema, becomes possible at this point: there is a further Continuity that becomes interpretable 'into life' (or history, or society, or Transcendence in the sense of what Peirce refers to as 'Neglected Argument'). This is possible only Semiotically or in a psychological-hermeneutic key. It will also be discussed in the next chapter as the problem of time experience, which connects me Iconically with my present point, as well as with a telos beyond narrative teleology (as Truth).

In Godard's film, this short, recurring sequence has method. It is centrally placed, as a series of contemplative halting points in the overall film discourse; moreover, it is an example of how he creates meaning as a whole, including in those passages which are narratively viable. Our Semiotic interpretation is therefore also a model. Godard has a filmographic history of theorizing about cinema through cinematic means. This has the advantage that whatever his theoretical concept of cinema is, it has an immediate proof. The film we are discussing constitutes an important turning point in Godard's theory of cinema. Very probably it cannot be considered one of his 'easier' ones; quite probably most spectators are struck first by how difficult it is to understand. Predictably, his theory on the nature of cinema is as complex as the film. Although his reflections are important, this film was not made for the purpose of theory, nor would it be adequate to treat it as an exemplification of that theory. Notwithstanding this proviso, theoretical discourses in a meta-language convey their understanding of cinema, which turns out to be more or less adequate when confronted with this film. Semiotic can unearth why this film is difficult to understand; it can also suggest alternative means of perception.

Godard is one of those directors who have an extremely reflected awareness of the nature of cinema – in particular, of the cinematic image – and who put that awareness into practice. Moreover, almost every Godard film contains remarks about its own cinematic status. He is well aware that even in cinema, image entails iconography. Small wonder that filmmakers become iconoclasts – in a reflective and effective way – before they 'deconstruct' narrative genres. Even though it is rather untypically narrative, *Je vous salue, Marie* is nevertheless a good example of Godard's grappling with the iconic potential of cinema. This is even more interesting because he explores here the explicitly transcendental theme of religion, which must forcibly transcend the 'image-able' and the imaginable. We can observe Goddard's struggle with the resilient image, which he strives to fill with a representational content *contra naturam*, as it were. To this end, Miéville and Godard destroy and use iconography malleably, making it manageable again for genuine meaning. Images used to stand for their objects in an unproblematic manner; here they stand for what they are *not* re-presenting (they stand for what they are not; *prae* – before our eyes – is the wrong object; and not *ens* – 'being' is 'directed toward our inner senses – which is counterfactual to our outer senses).

The images in *Je vous salue, Marie* display pure meaning, not illustrations of theory. Yet this meaning is far from simple. We ought to be astonished by the procedures Godard uses to achieve this complexity. The first observation relates to the obvious inconclusiveness of his narrative strategies. Either they are too dense to allow a proper deciphering, or they are heavily loaded with non-narrative elements. These elements, by not contributing to the construction of a narrative universe, actually represent a level of meta-narrative signification. Through sheer complementarity every beyond-of-narrative is defined as commentary. In this case it is merely a useful construct, albeit one that does not explain much of the meaning those images convey. Although the narrative is clearly there, it is not self-contained; rather, it is strongly determined and influenced by meta-narrative, discursive elements – not primarily discursive as in a direct allocution, but discursive through narration. In this sense *Je vous salue, Marie* differs fundamentally from earlier Godard films such as *A letter to Jane* and even *Tout va bien*; this allows us to look at it from a narratological point of view and makes it reasonable to do so. This does not necessarily reduce the film ('juste une image' in Godard's well-known expression) to a 'text' – a notion loathsome to Godard – nor does it imply a disregard for the image (the 'passer des image' cf. #105). It simply takes the narrative as the modulated and the rest as the modulation.

Metaphorically speaking, Godard makes images speak metaphorically; he does not 'silence' them to mere images, as Cavalier does in *Thérèse*. The quality of these images is immensely different. Godard's images are decidedly images of something, albeit not representations of their objects. Opposed to this are images as the composition of pictorial elements or of entirely isolated, rarefied objects becoming tableaux. How, then, do images speak that which they do not or cannot show? It would be facile to answer this by resorting to verbal language. Godard strives in every sense to tear apart what in an image could become closed in any way. Language plays an important role in this, but so do music and rhetorical transformation, such as symbolization of images and of montage. If there is a cinematic iconography in the sense of a usual depiction of objects, Godard is systematic in destroying it or finding substitutes for it. Moreover, in the same vein, the absence of a frame in Godard's image has often been noted. This constitutes his difference from 'fauxtographies,' the enshrined icons of the real. The consequence, however, has been a differently, non-iconographic or iconoclastic, cinematographic construction, one that pieces together and pulls apart what amounts to a rhetorical construct of dissonant elements. In this regard, a careful analysis of *Je vous salue, Marie* is highly instructive. The extreme fragmentation does not allow us to constitute a separate signification of image or narrative or sound or music. Rather, all of these elements must be comprehended on an equal footing – often simultaneously. There is no illustrating one with the others (e.g., music of narrative mood), and there is no mere allegorization. Thus, a non-comprehension of the music makes the image utterly incomprehensible. In hindsight, we find that identifying the piece of music comments on the narrative.

In *Je vous salue, Marie*[77] – in this sense the opposite of the closed narrative interior world construction in Dreyer's *Ordet* – the plot does not easily allow the construction of a *fabula* universe. Instead, there are residua of narrative logic belonging to two universes, as well as a number of non-narrative or half-narrative universes. Moreover, the ever-present rhetoric does not invite the spectator to identify with the character, as it does in *Ordet*. Rhetoric argues, comments, and draws conclusions and is often on the verge of extradiegesis. Though at the other extreme from *Ordet*, *Je vous salue, Marie* nevertheless achieves a profound aesthetic effect.

First, we can examine the narrative skeleton. Having identified that it is principally a narrative film, the spectator must interpret various signifying elements with respect to their belonging to possible universes. Innocuous as this may sound, it poses a serious Semiotic dilemma. Any object presented with a quality will give way to a semiosis as soon as it has found its Interpretant; the Symbolic context of those Interpretants constitutes a pragmatic universe. Now Godard 'subtilizes away' the natural Interpretant from the Object it naturally belongs to. If an Object is no longer the actual occasion of its Interpretant, it must search for, or allow a search for, a new Interpretant. An iconography usually facilitates such a path of Interpretation. In *Je vous salue, Marie*, however, these paths lead us astray into interpretational *cul-de-sacs*. Iconography stops being a device of recognition (in the sense of Currie 1995, cf. *supra*) and becomes an Icon, or a process of discovery. Furthermore, we must take into account that images are the most immediate means of conveying clearly exactly one idea (catalogues, encyclopaedias, etc.); this gives rise to the received wisdom that images never lie. Thus, an image of a horse can never mean a dog, whereas butchers and language allow some 'dogs' to become 'hot dogs.' However, images have not yet reckoned with Godard's *hérisson, âne*, red lipsticks (v. *infra*). The undoing of such a firm connection is for this reason even more difficult to achieve: an image is what it is, but here it is something else. In Godard's work it must become a sign of the invisible: '*l'image aura sa plénitude*' as Ishaghpour (1986: 297) quotes him, but in the present tense it first consists of an emptiness. The Semiotic problem with this film is that not even Godard can dismiss completely the débris of iconographic representation.

It is possible, though, to recognize the shape of a construction in its entirety as narrative worlds. Eco calls this the possible 'extensional disambiguations' of narrative texts. These constructions remain visible throughout. One construction, however, shines brightly through, and is founded on the frustrating holes, contrasts, and inconsistencies of the base constructions. Sorting through images, sounds, and speech must lead to a compacting and also to groupings: every group has its intention, a kind of 'topic' or the coherence of a semantic disclosure (or semantic isotopy). Sometimes this leads to an extensional inference, or to narrative universes with or without causal connections among them or their parts. These parts can then be indicated in the form of a macro-proposition: 'this is xy.'

In *Je vous salue, Marie* it is possible to identify five extensional universes.[78] (U I) a triangular love affair, Juliette – (without a Romeo)– Joseph – Marie, with episodes of jealousy due to the appearance of a putative rival, Gabriel, and the extra-marital pregnancy of Marie. This is the main thread, which most people will recognize as what the film is 'about.' (U II) A linear, logical romantic relationship and love affair between a professor and a girl named Eve until their bitter separation. This thread is also easily understood, although there is no apparent reason why it figures in this film. The following are among the merely narrated or book universes: (U III) The canine Feuerbach: the dogs' liberation from the enslaving faith-projection in man (Marx for dogs) in the novel read aloud by Joseph in his taxi and elsewhere. The appearance of dogs and barks at various places always belong to this universe as well. (U IV) The cover story of a book Marie brings to Joseph about St Francis, who confronted God unarmed and poor. (U V) two stories, one told by a mother to her child, the other told by one of the two male patients in the doctor's waiting room. The mother's story is about the stars, the patient's is about his problems with pictures, painting, and writing. The (considerable) remainder of this film either fits nowhere or fits into more than one universe, depending on our interpretation. It is not possible to identify whether these bits and pieces are meant to constitute a separate universe or not. With some difficulty, we can understand them diegetically of the universe in which they are embedded. Narratively speaking, here they are pure retardations that do nothing to advance the narrative but do not disrupt it either. Yet how should we take it when Marie is reading from a book or speaking in voice-over? If it is part of the narrative, it is only barely so. If this is a purely discursive element – and we could interpret it as such it sheds light on the narrative.

In these narrations there are many foreign bodies such as those mentioned. The various narrative strings do not advance one another; and simply keep the rest in suspense. Moreover, with regard to pieces of narrative logic, alien elements such as these compel us to ask how they are related. In the same vein, the juxtaposition of different narrative universes within the same work requires a rationale. In *Je vous salue, Marie*, universes do link, but only quite loosely. There is no reason – beyond pure coincidence – why the protagonists of universe II use Joseph's taxi (of universe I), nor does it strictly belong to the narrative U I that the dog novel is read aloud, or that Marie reads (or perhaps speaks) as monologuist in voice-over. There is a clear sense that we should not simply be accepting all of these narratively meaningless elements as 'dead moments.'

In this film, Godard's narrative universe is actually a precise form of causality. The narrative texture (if not entanglement) in this film does not reflect the usual form of pragmatic causality that constitutes narrativity. (We will consider this more closely in the following chapter.) Clearly, the connectors chosen by Godard go beyond this sort of causality, which, furthermore, is frustrated to a certain degree. If this film does not fall to pieces (i.e., if it is not an anecdotal sort of film), it is because we can discern some other glue under the narratives. Behind every representation stands causality, which opens passages from element one to the next. This is also the case with images (both Deleuzean action images and thought images) as long as they represent. Only when images glue naturally together in the pragmatic sense, does the question of a nexus among them become superfluous. In this film, however, they often become isolated elements. They threaten to become meaningless juxtapositions of unrelated material. For instance, if seen narratively: Toward the end of the film what do all those train and rape field images have to tell? And what meaning can a spectator invest in the following hedgehog shot?[79] (the riddle will be resolved shortly):

239	11	with hedgehog	*Il faut prendre le cul dans sa tête, et puis avec le cul dans sa tête*
240	11	50 cm	*se rendre au niveau du cul et s'en aller à gauche,*
241	11	as #239	*ou à droite*

Traditionally, all non-necessary argumentation has been assigned to 'rhetorical' figures. This being so, what can rhetoric achieve, and how? This leads us quickly to ask what causes causality. This question has been considered since antiquity in rhetoric – in particular for the (logically) not so compelling reasons. In the present context, it is certainly safer to avoid posing the problem as one of the 'truth of images.' In common parlance, the notion of truth conveys the idea of unfailing causal relation. This is conceivable only in an ontological philosophy such as Aristotelian metaphysics. However, if images such as Godard's (of the 'evidence' sort) are precisely not compelling, their connection cannot be one of truth, since such a relation would have to be necessary. In Aristotle's, *Analytica Prior* (II.23 68b9–13) there are two sorts of conclusions: deduction (syllogism proper or συλλογισμός ἀποδεικτικός, [not διαλεκτικός, ῥητορικός]) with a strict (ἐξ ἀνάγκης) necessary causal relationship, and induction (ἐπαγωγή). An apodeictic syllogism is the only scientific cognition of causes; in contrast, rhetoric, syllogisms argue through enthymeme (ἐνθύμημα) or paradigm (παράδειγμα). This distinction relates to the type of causality involved. With the former, all of the premisses can be made explicit and deduction necessarily produces a conclusion from a general to a particular. With the latter, there are no true generals among the premises. Here only the verisimilar (τό εἰκός) is available, which can be counted as being or having been recognized (ἔνδοξος) by a group of people, or at least by an expert's doxa. In practical social matters, in which there are so many possibilities for action beyond self-control, there are no generals leading to necessary conduct (as Peirce stipulated for cognitive conduct). Thus any causal link from an antecedent to a consequent is 'in force' only on the basis of a common pragmatic foundation. Living together must have bases in unquestioned and unquestionable premises; this corresponds to Husserl's and Schütz's 'Lebenswelt,' the horizon of life. Any narration is at best probable, if it construes its links on that verisimilitude, which is a term common to Aristotle's *Poetic* and *Rhetoric*.

Now, a narration can certainly pretend to derive its necessity from facts. Yet there are Facts and there are facts. Facts can be eternally true or they can be particular. If something is considered particular, it is comprehended only on the basis of an imputed practical generality. It must be recognized as a standard behaviour, as it were, or as a usual state of affairs. For Ricoeur, this imputation can only be derived by conceptualizing human acting as such (v. *infra*). What is of interest here is merely the type of connectives. The deceptively anodyne narrative connectives 'then' and 'thereafter' do not signal temporal ranks; rather, they are logical in the manner of dialectic syllogism. This presupposes the understanding of the whole, which therefore (or consequently) must lead to this next element. The normal, relative compactness of narrative universes, a result of narrative causality, is logically identical to the permitted reasons (αἱ αἰτίαι) in rhetoric, the premises of which are mere 'signs' (σημεῖα or τεκμήρια), hints at best, and because of their unreliable deducibility they are prone to (or at least usable for) fallacies. So while Aristotle [*Rhetorica* I.2 1357b 1-14] considers it necessary to conclude that 'a woman who has milk must have given birth,' a typical example of the second kind is also typically narrative: 'Lovers are useful to the state, because love between Harmodios and Aristogeiton overthrew Hipparchos the tyrant' (cf. *Rhetorica* II.24 1401b 9–12).

Our discussion of Pragmaticism could help expand Aristotle's narrow understanding of rhetorical logic. We do not need to follow Aristotle's strategy in order to distance rhetorical from ontical, 'true' logic. After all, Semiotic, as Speculative Grammar is only the first, formal aspect of Speculative Rhetoric; it is an inquiry into all possible discursive arguments. Furthermore, it is not by chance that signs achieve meaning only through being embedded in pragmatism (i.e., through being used). This is a fundamental departure from the ontological presuppositions of Aristotle. Rhetoric – especially in the understanding and practice of Gorgias, the renowned sophist – could become a problem and a temptress only for an ontology. Perhaps it is be better to say that philosophy became what it became because it comprehended the gloss of the logos as not being in the efficacious speech of the sophists (σοφιστεύειν is clearly intended as derogatory). Its true gloss is in the truth, a value in itself, in the consciousness of a spiritual order of values and in the corresponding dignified lifestyle of those who professed the truth (the προαίρεσις τοῦ βιοῦ, but a φιλόσοφος βίος): philosophers. Socrates became a role model against Gorgias. The true being became an anchor against the sophists' partisan bending of truths for their own convenience.

However, there was no time in this ontology. It was abused, and as a result of that abuse, the time-bound form of truth, sophism and rhetoric, were discovered. Peirce admits no plain being as point of comparison for Grounds. For this would indeed mean necessity, which corresponds to authority arguments. His idea of Anankism has already been mentioned: if everything were as it is, this would be totally ἐξ ἀνάγκης (Aristotle, *Topica* I.1 100a 25–7, *Analytica Prior* I.1 24b 18–20, II.23 68b 15–37). His counter-position was his belief in the universe of absolute chance (τυχή; and Tychism). Certainly, if everything – the logical structure of the (cognized) world – is thoroughly based in sign relations, there must be a corresponding theory of being. Peirce reached this conclusion through his tripartite theory of modal being. Although he would also admit and postulate the reality of there being absolute chance (Tychism), the most common representation of being in propositional form makes a different presupposition. It would be nonsensical to form propositions (and to use them in assertions) if there were no (anankistic) constraints in being, if things could be arbitrarily thus or not thus.[80] Making a proposition is an act of faith in truth, and truth relies on existent or imaginable (being) Objects.

Cognition, however, goes further than the constraints of existence. The ethos of science is guided in its generalizations by the Reality of laws. Thus, a third mode of being is agapistic, since the act of cognition is freely consenting and not constrained; it is cognitively 'lovingly taken by the hand' of a general truth that wants to be discovered. This is the metaphysical backdrop of a general rhetoric, Speculative (i.e., theoretical) Rhetoric, or Methodeutic. It looks into the 'formal conditions of the force of symbols," which is 'their power of appealing to a mind,' or, more generally, 'their reference in general to interpretants' (1.559, New List): the 'laws by which in every scientific intelligence one sign gives birth to another' (2.229). For Semiotic, it is important that there be a corresponding sign for every mode of being. Moreover, if being is like this, there are only signs (the Real is signs because every sign must have an Object), and signs are also the points of comparison for subsequent signs and not being. Also, every sign must contain its ground ($\alpha i \tau i \alpha$), the reason for its semiosic connectedness; this is part of its definition. Aristotle treats signs as of minor value (if they are no $\tau \epsilon \kappa \mu \dot{\eta} \rho \iota \alpha$). In a less anankastic metaphysics, no sign is certain and necessary – at best, it is common sense for its time. One would conclude therefore that there are no true apodeictic syllogisms or deductions; there are only dialectic syllogisms. The verisimilar is the best one can attain at a given moment; truth herself is only a telos of discovery. What we find in Godard – the transitory meaning of elements – is in fact the normal situation for any discovery, only at a higher intensity.

Speculative Rhetoric shows us how to constitute something novel from elements. This is always accomplished through 'the force of symbols' appealing to a mind (1.559). In this sense, Rhetoric is employed for a meaning that grows. Godard make use of it to explore 'incarnation' and 'femininity' and to reach a deeper understanding of them. What are the argumentation procedures, what is the 'force,' for advancing new formations of meaning? Undoubtedly, some apodeictic forms of argument efficiently impede their being broken up into new formations. In Godard, as the following descriptions will clearly demonstrate, the opposite tendency gains room. All of a sudden, certain images or syllogistic placeholders no longer conclude. An image can be a sign of such a kind that it represents an apodeictic argument, one that allows no doubt that things are as they are (represented here). Godard instead 'elementizes,' decontextualizes, isolates. He asks for a meaning. Erratic enigmatic elements, Iconic signs in Indexical occurrences, need new Interpretants. Invention of interpretations passes through the meaning of a pragmatic context. This is where rhetoric takes its place. Rhetoric suggests novel pragmatic contexts. Godard packages at least three such contexts into this film, in effect offering three different paths of conviction ($\pi\iota\sigma\tau\iota\varsigma$, the point of convincing). In point of fact, these paths of conviction can be reconstructed as three argumentation theoretical types that correspond to three different 'forces' of referring to Interpretants. With regard to Speculative Rhetoric, the matter-of-fact argumentation type of the Professor–Pascal–Eve narrative is different from the utter confusion of Joseph, from the underdog suspicion of Feuerbach-for-dogs, and also from Marie's supreme understanding. From within the narration, the archangel duo is the rhetorical postulation instance, one that demands a cognitive choice to be made from among the clearly stated alternatives.

Not necessity, but discursive interrelation of parts, is what one finds in Godard's film; it follows that 'dialectical' reasoning is of another force than (appealing to a mind with) the power of laws. Connectives here are not of the necessary kind; moreover, not even the narrative universes are left untouched. Normally their illusory quality is a function of their compactness – linguistically speaking, of the perfect 'uncoupling' from the communicative situation. In this film, however, these illusionary narrative universes are broken up through the introduction of rhetoric reasoning. Although rhetoric is intrinsically of the same logical nature as narratives, in the enunciation situation it is hither of the uncoupled narrative universe. Weinrich's *Erzählen/Besprechen* (or Benveniste's *discours/histoire*) dialectic relies on this fact. The logic is the same but it applies – or can apply – to different objects. Images thus become connected narratively, and at the same time rhetorical connectors make images an element in their own line of argumentation. This is quite intriguing to observe. Suddenly, single parts of the narrative – single phrases of the dialogues, pieces of music, images, parts of images – become elements in isolation. One expects enthymemic logic to make them meaningful.

For instance, in shot #309 there is an almost meaningless image of an open mouth in close-up; at the same time we hear clearly (an exception in this film!) the final chorale from J.S. Bach's *St. Matthew Passion*: 'Wir setzen uns mit Tränen nieder: und rufen Dir im Grabe zu: Ruhe sanfte, sanfte ruh'!'. Certainly there is also a weak narrative link to shot #306 (Marie's putting on lipstick), but there is no good reason to dwell on a close-up of painted lips with a wide-open black cavity, and this in the very last shot. Rhetorically, however, this makes sense. Through the text of the chorale, we are induced to see the empty tomb. Yet we see it through a double metaphor only: this adorned, black, open mouth is like the three Marys weeping at Christ's tomb. Once the parallel between Mary's and Marie's life (first metaphor) has been established, this last action of theirs is given a theological meaning through the chorale (second metaphor). There are other examples in film history of music providing the key of meaning to an otherwise outlandish narrative. For instance, the title of Vilsmaier's *Schlafes Bruder* is a direct quote from a chorale in Bach's cantata *Ich will den Kreuzstab gerne tragen*. We learn what this film is all about only when the 'Brother of Sleep,' (i.e., Death) is welcomed while the chorus sings, 'Come oh death ye sleep's brother.' Once we know this, we can see the film's meaning when it is shown to us in the final sequences of the film. Unless and until we know this (and there is no other place to glean it from except the chorale), we cannot interpret the film as anything but another of those 'unhappy love stories.' Moreover, in both *auteurs* there is a deep sense of non-thematic, non-narrative meaning that only music as a non-representative art can convey. The mood the music strikes is not attributable as expression of a character's subjectivity (as it is in most classical Hollywood cinema); rather, it has an outright significance for the meaning of the film itself. In Aristotelian terms, those σημεῖα must lead to a (shaky, unnecessary) general: Mary is the mother of a new mankind, and she finds a certain kind of peace at Christ's tomb (as sung in the chorale). Only this imputed general makes arguments of the non-necessary kind convincing. In the case at hand, an open, empty mouth alone does not prove anything or argue for anything. Only once the sign answers (ὅτι because) a 'W'-question does it have the power of a proof. The supposed general premise, put as a question, might be this: 'Where can the Soul ('der Seelen Ruhstatt sein') find peace?' The second premise might be, 'The Saviour himself found his peace at this tomb.' Rhetorical conclusion: 'Then the Souls will find theirs as well.'

Of course, it is usually rather too much to ask the sole narrative to provide its general premise. The narrative tells particulars, which become comprehensible if they are referred to generals (of action). This must be clearly presupposed by narration as such (accepted as εἰκός since Aristotle's *Poetic*). Yet in Godard's case the general is supplied rhetorically, in addition to and in contrast to what the narrative suggests as its pragmatic general. Thus it asserts itself again that the broader context of narrative logic is the discursive logic of rhetoric (which is true as well for Genette's discursive concept 'récit'). In forensic rhetoric in particular, this logic is a source of meaning about the narrative, not in the narrative about the events. It is certainly responsible for the principal mischief that rhetoric is customarily accused of making by philosophers: amplification (αὔξησις) of facts. The reason why something is amplified can only be in the argumentation logic of the orator.

Godard's rhetorical strategy is relatively clear. First, he provides elements through isolation, following which he establishes discursive links between them. The way this can be done is named (though not at all explained) by traditional rhetorical figures (irony, metaphor, etc.). Also, it can consist in providing premises to be imputed by the enthymemic meaning. The image can easily become like any other argumentative element, even while keeping (more or less loosely) its position in the narrative connection. Images as premises are not unheard of, because of their linguistic (imaginatory) usage in figures of speech. Yet they are only premises in the context of an argumentation. Godard argues parallel to the narration, and does so without giving up the narrative contract (i.e., without uncoupling from the communication situation from the spectator). The strategic context of argumentation exists in the manner of an identifiable register of meaning, which can coexist with the narrative register because it comments the latter. Thus an image can be commentary and narration at the same time. As a result of the interplay of the two registers, narrative and discourse,[81] that Godard is using, various analytical consequences arise. The foremost would be the most evident – that the narration must be interpreted from the perspective of an equally coherent discursive system.

Godard can extend these discursive parts to the point of 'information overload.' The narration is accompanied by a bizarrely high amount of useless but somehow meaningful information; even more, all of this is sometimes packaged into the extremely crowded sound track. Extradiegetic music (extradiegetic to such a degree that it does not even relate to moods), voice-overs from unknown universes – and all of this mixed with another strange thing: the diegetic dialogue seems to be divided into some key sentences of clearly comprehensible narrative parts (excluding even environmental sound) and less audible (almost inaudible) parts that nevertheless are sometimes an intradiegetic commentary of the diegesis. Overabundance of information can only mean that these must be new signs. In other words, they determine an Interpretant to refer to the same Object. Signs grow in this way, and acquire new meaning, and this is exactly what must happen with the already meaningful parts of Godard's film.

This juxtaposition of information calls for an explanation of how it affects meaning. If juxtaposition is not a choice forced upon the spectators (i.e., which of the lines to follow and which to drop from their attention), then the meaning through combination might be called rhetoric and dialectic. Here, however, there is not just one rhetoric comment on the basic narrative line. Instead a multitude of elements can comment on one another: extradiegetic elements commenting on one another or on the diegesis, and the various diegeses commenting on one another. Which part of the global text a given other part is commenting on, we cannot determine in advance and almost never with certainty.

Consequently, Godard's direct theoretical statements of 'generality' gain their comprehensibility only on the premisses of that commentary, and beyond them. The broadly discursive parts – on body (soul, virginity, corporal beauty, sex, image, etc.) and on writing, politics, and so on – are not foreign to the film. They are really the *argumentatio* after the *enarratio* in a rhetoric discourse.

The main narrative event in *Je vous salue, Marie* even has its own authentic interpreter, in double appearance: the two angels Gabriel (the revolutionary) and his double, the angel girl. The two have slightly different roles. Perhaps Godard, the interpreter, was uncomfortable with merely one side of that role in this divine play. They comment on the behaviour and attitude of Joseph; more importantly, with their at first glance, cryptic theoretical propositions they also explain the mystery of incarnation, Marie's virginity, and the proper path to comprehension: faith ('Il faut avoir confiance!' shot #143). Such innerdiegetic exegesis of diegesis is far from direct, however. It is introduced into the narrative as a conflict with Joseph and as a rhetorical conflict with the canine Feuerbach novel that Joseph[82] is reading with his dog. The classical trope *prosopopoieia* is thus very directly used. Angels and dog novel are mutually exclusive exegetes of the central theme, fighting for Joseph's attitude (#73 'Il n'y a pas d'miracles!' versus #193 'C'est ça "je t'aime"').

Besides intradiegetic commentary, Godard uses a certain number of symbols from nature (one has been used above as an example of Semiotic Interpretation of the same Object) and consistently two types of music: Dvořák and J.S. Bach. Furthermore, a number of extradiegetic sound events such as wind, barking dogs, strokes of a tower clock, and so on gain meaning only through being contextualized intradiscursively. Neither nature nor music symbols are related diegetically or psychologically to the narratives. Thus they can be considered as symbolic commentary, general premises to other elements that by this means gain in a higher sort of meaning. The immediate interpretative task is to identify those other elements whose meaning should be changed rhetorically. Those symbolic elements can be of two sorts: one is of the common sort of cultural heritage – for instance when the wind can stand for the Holy Spirit; the other can refer to elements of a different narrative universe – for instance, barking dogs refer to Joseph's novelistic Feuerbachian creatures. As clearly established symbols, they relate from an abstract symbolic universe to narrative contexts. This provides the narrative with another level of meaning that is independent from its literal diegetic meaning. At certain points, when music or nature influences the narrative meaning, the symbolic level is broken. In these instances there is no independent narrative meaning. Instead, the narrative becomes allegorized. In #305–9, only Bach's 'Ruhet sanft' (St Matthew Passion) indicates the narrative meaning of lipstick and the tightening close-up of Marie's 'embalmed' open mouth. It is in fact the empty tomb, its universal salvific power (#300f), sung by the choir after the Deposition from the Cross.

302^{cars}	GABRIEL: *Ma Dame!* [klaxonne] *He, Ma Dame!*	M: Bach's *St Matthew Passion*,
	MARIE: *Oui, quoi?*	Final chorale ('Wir setzen uns
303 $^{2m\ Gabriel}$	GABRIEL: *Rien. Je vous salue, Marie!*	mit Tränen nieder') ('und rufen Dir im Grabe zu:')
304$^{2m\ Marie}$	[BELLS]	('ruhe sanfte')
305$^{Marie\ in\ car}$	[lights cigarette]	
306^{1m}	[close-up, putting on lipstick]	('sanfte ruh'!')
307^{50cm}	MARIE: [voice over][near][good audib.] *Moi, je suis de la Vierge; et je n'ai pas voulu de cet être.*	[repetitur]
308^{mouth}	*J'ai marqué l'âme, qui m'a été. C'est tout!*	
309$^{open\ mouth}$		('sanfte ruh'!')

Another example is *Quia respexit*, #294. When not in allegoric relation, these symbols provide narrative counterpoints.

When we sift through extradiegetic events on the sound track and in images, the picture of signification strategy becomes much clearer. As alien bodies, they are symbolic inserts with all the cryptic meaning of symbols: Moon, Sun, Cornfields, *Ur*-soup broths and sounds, flowers and blossoms, landing aircraft. Or they appear within the narrative: – for example, in #32 in the allusion to Blaise Pascal, who is blinded by Eve (yet there is another noteworthy symbolism in the music: 'Behold! whom? the bridegroom!' which continues, 'Behold him, like a lamb'):

32IIC^{head 50cm}	*Nous sommes pris des extraterrestres. On n'est pas nés d'une soupe d'aminoacides, brusquement, par hasard.* [Music ends] *Rien à faire, les chiffres sont bons!* MALE VOICE: [off] *Et s'il n'y avait pas de hasard?* PROFESSOR: *Exactement, cette invraisemblable vérité: La vie a été voulue, désirée, prévue, ordonnée, programmée par une intelligence présumée. Éve, mettez Vous derrière Pascal!* EVA: [off] *Eva, Monsieur, Eva!* PROFESSOR: *Oui, mettez Vous derrière Pascal, et rendez-le aveugle.*	JS Bach: *St Matthew Passion* Nr.1 'Sehet, wen?, den Bräutigam'
		'Bräutigam'

Or the quotation from Heidegger in #128. These can be quite hidden allusions and symbolic comments – for example, the *locus* in Heidegger, which can only be clear to someone who knows the exact reference.[83]

128^{Villa Paradis} window	EVA: *À quoi Vous pensez?* PROFESSOR: *Le soir, il change sa figure et son propre sens.* EVA: *Heidegger, Trois conférences à la* PROFESSOR: *Bayerische Akademie.* EVA: *En 59 Savez Vous pourquoi il n'a pas été publié*	D: Table bell

Evidently, there are degrees of how clear interpretation can make itself, as the last example indicates. Some of the rhetorical commentaries packaged into *Je vous salue, Marie* could seem too obscure to be noticeable. This would make them virtually anodyne. Yet can they therefore be discounted as of no importance to interpretation? There is quite a variation in how, and how far, Godard makes certain things understandable (and this starts in Godard with sheer audibility). For example, in foreign-language dubbings the entire 'Feuerbach for dogs' narrative is much more audible than in the original.[84] Thus certain parts of this film are almost like some sculptures in Gothic cathedrals, as it were. They are in such remote and hidden places that they can never be seen by anyone (except the stonecutter who carved them centuries ago, and who in carving them was in effect carving a memorial to himself and certainly to the honour of God). However, there is clearly a *hierarchia veritatum* in *Je vous salue, Marie*. The important messages are made entirely clear, even at the cost of eliminating environmental sound on the otherwise overloaded sound track. Thus, even partial sentences are isolated, and that in both directions. The 'speeches' of Marie's that are most inaudible are the ones in which she is answering God ('C'est un grand secret'). Whereas everything that has to do with her virginal body is as clear as a public speech. In these latter speeches it is up to the images to become contrapuntal (i.e., where the force of that which is seen is fully achieved through the voice-over dialogue, which is itself credentialed by the images). Instead of becoming a treatise on virginity, or something similar, *Je vous salue, Marie* flaunts nothing as evidence; instead, it hammers its message home through repeated non-contrasted demonstration. It keeps the open fluidity of a mysterious beauty – but a fluidity that is not in the service of seduction or of another common narrative topos. It can only be seen, through all means: vision happens through music and narrative alike, but ultimately it remains Iconic vision. However, in all of these rhetorical interpretations, Godard does not abandon the viewer. Instead, he literally offers tracks to interpretation.

The overall effect of these procedures in *Je vous salue, Marie* is to display the various possible attitudes toward the principal theme. As a narrative this is plain enough, although it offends one of the principal rhetorical virtues of a narrative – namely to be *narratio probabilis*. The narrative here is so highly improbable that everyone except Marie refuses to believe in it. One possible way to overcome narratively this stumbling block of improbability would have been to encourage the spectator to identify closely with the main character Marie. Godard instead chose rhetorical distancing. If we take Dreyer's *Ordet* as the antipode in this respect, the identification with Inger can become almost incantation. In the narrative of *Ordet* there is almost nothing tortuous or distracting (in the sense of the rhetorical strategy of *disgressio*). In contrast, in Godard's *Je vous salue, Marie*, close-ups of Marie are broken by voice-overs, which distance us from her interiority. We do not comprehend from inside, as it were, through some psychological sharing of interiorities. In these intimate instances, Godard bombards us with discourses, which (and we never find out which) could be read from a book or be Marie's own reflections. Rhetorically speaking, the stasis or *status questionis* of this narrative is one of *status qualitatis*,[85] meaning that the determination of the essence of an event is in question, not its factuality. When Marie sees her physician, this becomes equal to a *prolepsis* of the kind of *praeparatio* (one prepares the audience for the stunning aspect of what is later narrated). The entire film must thus be understood as a circling of the question, 'What does Marie's virginity mean?' Access to that meaning is mediated rhetorically, at a rhetorical distance from the narrative, as different attitudes toward that meaning. These attitudes are in detail doubt, (s/d)eduction, and faith.

Doubt, the first alternative of interpretation, is mainly centred on Joseph. Note the simplicity of Joseph,[86] who – wearing sunglasses – requires evidence (e.g. #112): '"Voyez, voyez, je vais avoir un enfant et je ne connais aucun homme. Joseph me croit pas. Dites-lui, c'est vrai." DOCTOR: "Non, dis pas ça sans arrêt, petite."' He is finally allowed to touch Marie's virginity (#158: 'Voilà touche!'), but only after a fight with Gabriel does he give up understanding and accept loving Marie without ever possessing her. What comes into play here is a repertoire of various possible interpretations of the standard story of betrayed love (#96: 'Pourquoi tu ne dis pas que tu as rencontré d'autres hommes, ça simplifierait!'). From there, the question becomes, 'Does soul act upon body or vice versa?' This question arises against the alternative interpretation patterns of two books, one of a refusal to believe (even in the possibility: dog novel), another of acceptance (Marie's book on St Francis, another pauper). Joseph's path to understanding is a progression; even so, Marie will always understand better.

The theme (and game of interpretation of (d/s)education revolves mainly around the Professor/Pascal plot line. Although this strand of narrative is, with one exception, never in diegetic relatedness to the Marie narrative, it enters a rhetorical relationship. It is interwoven by means of direct contrasts; it is also, at the joining of shots, voiced over so that it is directly commented on. Shot #132 shows the naked Eva (about to seduce the Professor) and voices Marie[87] – 'Je crois que l'esprit agit sur le corps, le transfigure, le couvre d'une voile qui le fait apparaître plus beau qu'il en est' – on the two kinds of beauty, two nudities, and body/soul. These together make this narrative comprehensible as a counterpoint to the Marie narrative, toward which it represents a contrary attitude. Thus the Professor/Eve relationship is in almost every detail the opposite to the Marie/Joseph relationship. Starting with the Professor's proof of God, which he reaches through calculation (Eve is first seen holding a Rubik's cube!), this compares to Joseph's quandaries and his Feuerbach for dogs world. The Professor's faith is as strong and as straightforward as his numbers, which lead him also into Eve's 'Paradis' (*sur la route d'Annemasse*) (#115) (and not, as with Joseph, into the fight with Gabriel and Marie's 'je t'aime'). Only if we catch the hints about Pascal does this comment become fully understandable as an attitude. Pascal is the inventor of probability calculus; not only that, but his well-known 'pari' or betting on God plays a role, as does his mystical fire experience on the night of 23 November 1654. The blinded Pascal calculates the probability of evolution and concludes that only an extraterrestrial will accomplish this. However, shortly after this, 'Le moment est venu ... et l'endroit aussi' for his temptation and fall. Although we see on paper, 'Coder la vie jusqu'à DIEU' (which explains the idea that intelligent beings would accumulate an enormous knowledge in the course of evolution but would have to transmit their knowing of their intelligent origin), we hear, '"est-ce que vous tenteriez pas de transmettre le secret de l'origine?" EVA: [off?] "Mais peut-être nous avons eu le message depuis toujours?"' In this dialogue Eve suddenly whispers, in acoustic close-up and very audibly, which cuts her from the diegetic context and places her in an 'eternal,' transcendental enunciation. In the fatality of that 'secret de l'origine' there is no decision to make; there is only the logic of following as precisely as clockwork, which at the moment of temptation – Eve is eating her apple – is ticking loudly. Embedded again in this narrative string are implicit exegeses: very directly, the quotation from Heidegger, which is narratively unwarranted. Trakl's line 'Abend wechselt Bild und Sinn' in Heidegger provides the occasion for speaking about 'Geschlecht' (gender, sex, sexuality, generation) precisely, but as a curse.

Faith is the final choice of interpretation. Marie's attitude of faith is perfect and unshakable from the beginning. Her first line in the film is, 'Je me demande si quelque événement survenait dans ma vie.' It is especially because she must discover what this means for her corporeality, sexuality, and femininity that Godard outlines a discourse about soul/body. She becomes the model for a female sexuality transformed by God, for virginity as open: 'Être vierge, ça devrait être, être disponible ou libre' (#112), as opposed to Juliette (nomen est omen!), who says, 'Moi aussi, je suis une vrai femme.' (#137). Marie, although she harbours no doubts, must suffer many pains, and not simply in terms of the classical seven sorrows of Mary: Stabat Mater Dolorosa enumerates them all. Furthermore, the fight of humanity, for humanity (#228), between the Devil and herself, is a motif taken from St John's Apocalypse, which Godard has worked into Marie's discourses.

The rhetorical arrangement of elements of image, music, dialogue, and sound can escape total confusion only if the textual rhetorical strategy lends a helping hand. Because Godard offers three principal interpretation attitudes, many figures or symbols beyond the narrative universes make sense. Furthermore, since they are available simultaneously, they enable us to interpret each track from the perspective of the others. Eve's dire destiny is indeed interpreted (sometimes in voice-over) by Marie's words and history. These three attitude models are left whole and are not narratively interwoven; the course of events proves which one is correct. In order that things not become too simple, Godard has built into this main theme its double. Just as with the listing of alternative attitudes toward the Almighty (illusion, calculable, Lord of life), there are at the same time and with the same distribution three alternative attitudes toward Woman. Joseph risks being turned into a Romeo by Juliette; similarly, the Professor is like Adam dragged down by Eve's passing him the apple. Juliette has a female body, as does Eve, but they are of very distinct kinds. Juliette tries to settle (albeit rather cheaply) various deals with her prospective lover; however, the illusion does not work as it should. Her female body is never exposed – there is no male relation to it. Eve's body is the only truly naked one; it is naked and laid bare in the biblical sense of the term. To the male gaze it is seductive, reducing both Eve and Man to objects of possession. The traffic between them is commerce, the *merces* being the bodies. (There is a clear hint of this Enlightenmental attitude in the dialogue exchange about the exploitation of ants in shot #66f: Eve, too, has read this in *Scientific American!*). However, this value is exchangeable with every other value (e.g., money). In the departure scene, Godard allows the Professor to pay back in kind: in Swiss francs.

209 II AB $^{180°\ 2m}$ EVA: *Ta femme et ton fils ils comptent jusqu'à combien?*
PROFESSOR: *Je comprends pas.*
EVA: *Salaud! Je m'excuse!*
PROFESSOR: *Ça va, ça va.*
EVA: *Tu me racontes que ta femme est en prison et pendant ce*
210 II AB ^{1m} *temps tu couches avec moi?*
PROFESSOR: *Éve, je t'en prie!*   D: Train
EVA: *Eva! Éve, c'est fini! Fiche le camp si c'est ce que tu veux.*
D'abord, rend-moi les trente deux mille francs!   D: Blows horn
PROFESSOR: *Oui, je te les enverrai!*
EVA: *Tu est vraiment un pauvre type!*

In this second computational, probabilistic attitude of disbelief, the appreciation of the female body is to be taken quite literally. Certainly it is in the key shot #132 (v. *supra*), where the transformation of the female body takes place, from Eve to Mary. A new attitude transforms the gaze into contemplation, 'transfigures' the object of desire into beauty: 'when the spirit acts upon the body.' 'The spirit covers the body with a veil and makes it more beautiful than it is.' 'Veil,' of course, has only a meaning inasmuch as it is barrier to the (possessive, appropriating) gaze. Joseph sees the beauty of Marie, his bride, only when he does not touch her humble body: 'C'est ça: je t'aime?' (#193; likewise, 'JOSEPH: "Il faut arrêter [de] te montrer toute nue avec lui maintenant!" MARIE: "Quia respexit, Joseph!"' which quotes directly the 'quia respexit humilitatem' from the *Magnificat* [#294]). Also, Godard takes a strongly practical approach to outlining for each attitude the consequences for sex. Taken together, these are types of carnal knowledge: Juliette to Eve to Mary. Men are bound to become knowledgeable: Romeo Joseph (Doctor) to Professor to Joseph. This cannot be said of *Prénom Carmen*, in which men remain unenlightened and are everywhere confronted with enigmatic women. Since the theological discourse coincides with the sexual, the two become mutually supportive. In fact, from the perspective of a relator, the male relation to a woman and the human relation to God are identical. For interpretation, however, this helps a lot. The various strands of narrative and symbolic information are unified as soon as the spectator understands the unidirectional orientation. This still leaves plenty of room for unattributable parts, which have no pragmatic connection with any strand.

Once we have grouped the secondary elements (i.e., the non-narrative ones, and those not taken as narrative) in a rhetorical relationship around the three principal interpretational attitudes, we are left with the problem of the free-floating symbols. How are they attached to the rest? Only after we have clearly set out the global theme can the symbols display their signifying potential. For example, we quickly ascertain that the narrative is not really about a triangular love affair. The first appearance of Marie begins with her voice-over (#21): 'le grand événement pour moi est là.' It is noteworthy that Godard here introduces one of the symbols: the moon. From Marie's voice-over we comprehend that it is 'De l'amour, je n'ai vu que l'ombre.' Having been introduced in this way, the symbol is used consistently throughout the film, as the earthly shadow of the shadow of the sun. Godard even folds his own theory of symbols into this context ('Comme on s'aperçoit dans l'étang des reflets d'un nénuphar. Non pas tranquille, mais invité par les rides de l'eau. Si bien que ce reflet tout déforme, vous échappe en partie.') – that reflections invite through their interspersion, which also partly conceals. By the same token, we understand how symbols work, as Godard pronounces his theory as a symbol itself. The 'comme' commences so abruptly that no element of comparison is immediately visible. It is a temporalized image working entirely by itself, and only the context forces us to look for its application, which is quite remote. What it signifies can only be understood poetically (*ornate*, in rhetorical terms) –that is, in the sense of speaking about one thing while meaning another (*in verbis translatis*). Thus in Marie's speech the reference point of 'comme' is her having seen the shadow of a shadow of love, not the original. In this way it refers to something that is already a metaphor ('ombre') – and metaphor, however, that is charged with meaning from another repertoire ('et la puissance du Très Haut te prendra sous son ombre' [Lc 1,35])[88] and from Plato's cave. This need not be clear from the outset, since it will be developed throughout the film. The functioning of symbols as clear second meanings once the 'comme' has been fully understood is not only shown here but also (metaphorically) explained. If such symbols must function beyond diegetic contexts they must be neutral enough that we will not mistake them as diegetic elements. Godard uses only a handful of images from nature. In order of appearance (1) Tree with meadow, perhaps identical with #10. (2) Water, apparently at a lakeshore or in a puddle, sometimes associated with a corresponding sound, sometimes with the junglelike sounds of birds, frogs, and the like. This sound and/or image is consistently associated with ideas of evolution and the creation of the world. (3) Moon, which is always associated with an epiphanic event of God in the life of Marie only (4) Aircraft approaching an airport, seen through trees. Initially this can be associated with what turns out to be two angels arriving in Geneva by plane. Generally, however, it stands for the concrete coming of God – for example, much later, at the birth of Marie's child. (5) Sun, in different stages of daylight and clouding. It is introduced in shot #42, with a wind sound. It is 'the Moon one shadow removed,' or 'l'amour' itself (cf. #24–7):

24	3 moon		
25 I B	Marie 1m	MARIE: [over] [N[89]][G] *De l'amour, je n'ai vu que*	M: ends
26 I B	as #24	*l'ombre, oui, et même l'ombre d'une ombre. Comme on*	
		s'aperçoit dans l'étang des reflets d'un nénuphar. Non	
		pas tranquille, mais invité par les rides de l'eau. Si bien	
		que ce reflet tout déformé, vous échappe en partie.	
27 IIIC	Eva with a	*Cependant, le grand événement pour moi est là.*	M: Bach,
	Rubik's cube	FILM-VOICE: [off and over]: *Et le soleil, enfin visible,*	St. John Passion,
		se met à appliquer sur les océans primitifs. Alors, la vie	CHOEUR: 'Herr
		est apparue, dit-on, [music starts] *tout-à-fait par*	unser Herrscher'
		hasard. Il y avait de l'hydrogène, de l'azote.	D: [Laughter]

(6) Traffic lights, changing from yellow to red. These appear only once,

in conjunction with Marie's acceptance of God's will. (7a) A pair of eagles high overhead, and (7b) woods from below. These are associated with the Professor's lecture on the manipulation of nature's equilibrium, 'survival of the fittest,' decodification of the secret of the beginning. They end with the sound of bombers. (8) Blossoms of yellow flowers. These are introduced rather late (#191), when Joseph must find a relationship to Marie's body according to the Law. They are used identically and with similar shots as #10, going from single flowers, to a flower garden, to a field of flowers, to a meadow with isolated flowers (a red poppy, incidentally), to a train in far perspective. Even the 'hérisson' shots evolve from this pictorial complex. The ideational complex therefore seems to turn around the topic of Marie's virginal body – in particular its beauty, with the veil covering her flesh making it appear more beautiful than it is (cf. #132). (9) Tree by running water. (10a) Train, seen both after the Professor's departure and as the background of the poppy field. This seems to be connected with the consequences of sin in both of its appearances (#197 and #211) as something that separates mankind. (10b) Garden with flowers; meadow flowered with yellow flowers (cf. *supra*). (11) Hedgehog (v. *supra*). (12) People's legs crossing the street. This represents the going out into the entire world, after Trinity (#300f). (13) (Semi-diegetic) snowplough. This stands for Christmas. A newborn baby's voice is heard. (14) Magnolia tree in blossom. This is clearly associated with Marie through intercutting – a praise of Marie in #285 ('Tu es bénie parmi toutes les femmes') to be compared with #1, the two decisive trees (of the destiny of mankind, perhaps). Shot #81 shows the joint use of two symbols: on the sound track, a stone drops into the water, as we heard and saw in the opening shots. Simultaneously in the image we have a clouded sun.

Clearly, these symbols are used consistently in *Je vous salue, Marie*; furthermore, they are obviously associated with theological themes, which cannot be expressed directly in images. They prove to be reliable interpretational guides to the transcendent meaning of narrative parts, through which they are interspersed, as are music and extradiegetic sound.

Is it correct to say, as *Ishaghpour* (1986) does, that Godard rediscovers nature to such an extent that he is in danger of approaching travel advertisement photography? Only by giving nature back its aura, by making it myth again, does he create a beauty besides that.[90] Perhaps this film does not fit as nicely as Ishaghpour would like into Walter Benjamin's theory. As pertinent as it may be to speak of the figuration of ancient paintings, of the film's epiphanic structure of the holy in the mimetically rendered world, it is not in this way that nature gains its aura – if it does so at all – in *Je vous salue, Marie*. The world of Marie remains almost entirely profane (as Ishaghpour also admits), yet the symbols stand out in that they are never part of the world in the suburbs of Geneva. They are an outright irruption of the transcendental meaning, the idea itself of the shadow of the shadow.

Separate from symbols of nature, there are allegoric, innerworldly placekeepers of the invisible: the voices, the angels, the landing aircraft, Gabriel taking off his shoes on touching ground, and the ending with the red-painted lips of Marie. These intradiegetic references, however, are treated entirely differently from the symbols of nature, which only tangentially touch the world and make irruptions like the Word into Marie's life. There is only one parallel to their pure, extra-mundane essence: J.S. Bach. Like the symbols, his music is chopped up and irrupts in fragments into the mundane from nowhere. Like the symbols of nature, music is treated consistently by Godard. Bach's music is always used to signify the presence of the sacred and the holy Passion, whereas Antonin Dvořák's cello concerto and his symphony always mark the presence of passionate love. Regarding sound, we find a consistent use of wind sounds when the Holy Spirit irrupts,[91] and we hear barking dogs when there is the temptation of incredulity. Both are easily understandable, besides, from the repertoire of the two texts that are central to this film: the Feuerbach for dogs novel and the Annunciation pericope. In addition, the sound track of symbolic images sometimes replaces the symbolic image itself.

Apart from pure symbolisms, there are some interspersed extradiegetic images that must be read as metaphors of the dialogue text. The donkey figures in the traditional iconography of the birth of Christ, who was born 'entre l'âne et le boeuf'; in *Je vous salue, Marie* the donkey also represents Joseph. Similarly, when Marie is speaking of her sex, Godard shows us a 'hérisson' (hedgehog, the argot word for the female pubic parts in #234). This passage is also a clear demonstration of Godard's consistent use of fixed symbols and allegories: Sun – 'hérisson' (cf. #294), when Marie explains her anatomy to her son. These images are allegories, not symbols. They require the context of the text to become clear, yet even then they remain isolated, since there is nothing that builds the pragmatic bridge to understanding.

These symbols (i.e., this non-narrative rest) exacerbate the theory problem. How are we to take *Je vous salue, Marie* if the standard approaches fail? Narration – either familiar or defamiliarized – is not good enough as schema to cope with this film. That which would allow direct arguing rhetorically for one's case – a sort of documentary attitude – is impossible without communicative linkage (decoupling, which would jeopardize the narrative closure). Here it helps to take a different approach.

A Semiotic approach will make it possible for us to arrive at a more global view. There is no denying that all of these transdiegetic parts are meaningful and serve a purpose. But what does Godard's purpose accomplish through this tripartite textual strategy? On first glance, we find a narrative that is permanently fissured by foreign narratives, images, sounds, and monologues that are not directly pertinent being outright philosophical statements. On the other side of the narrative we find a parallel and coherent symbolic enunciation, which is transcendent meaning, layered over the narratives. Moreover, between these we find narrative elements that can be comprehended only when we take the symbolic elements fully into account and when we read them from their own perspective.

Let us return to the Semiotic of the aesthetic and rhetorical meaning. In this film particularly, the sign procedure at the junctions of these parts is quite interesting. (1) Because of their narrative causal context, the transdiegetic parts require an Interpretation where a linkage to the narrative chain of Interpretants is barred. The Pragmaticistic effect, after such a destruction of belief, must become real doubt. (2) Therefore, excluding Indexical meaning (cf. *supra* 162, §2.3.1), they can only be Icons. It requires a special care in cinema that these signs have the 'same Object' (as they must have in the sense of Peirce's definition of the sign in 2.274, as described earlier) without remaining narrative. This cannot be achieved in a simple and straightforward way, because the connection between sequences – or between images and extradiegetic sound, and so on – is never automatic. There is always the danger that the work's texture will be unravelled. Later on we will have to investigate the intricacies of Godard's cinematic rhetoric in detail. In languaged texts (i.e., where the First of the sign is of the nature of a Legisign, and the Second of the nature of a Symbol), especially in Classical, preromantic novels, auctorial digressions are most likely to be encountered as philosophical comments. Cervantes's deliberations, which he scatters throughout the *Don Quixote* narrative, are among the most famous examples of this. In cinema – in this film, at least – the attribution of Interpretants can remain entirely open.

(3) Each one of the part-linking Interpretants of this film has the same Object, whereas in other forms of sign relation, symbolism can directly impregnate the narrative universe without becoming narrative itself. Unquestionably, this is restricted to point interventions. The principal purpose of narrative Interpretants is always the orderly temporal construction of a probable universe. However, since the Representamen of this universe is a Thirdness, a Firstness can and does intrude cannibalistically into the chain of Interpretation. For the resulting sign, this means that it is a degenerate Interpretant (i.e., it will be specified by a Firstness). (4) What happens when from within a narrative purpose (and every Interpretant is a purpose) a new purpose appears? If this does not lead to an interruption of the Interpretant chain – to a new 'topic' – but stays related to the same Object, this can only result in a new meaning dimension for an already narrative sign, and thus the meaning of a narration that is invisible and cannot be narrated. As we have seen, in this film even that purpose of Interpretation is coherently constructed in the various symbolisms. This is important if the meaning is to be more than a local accent and is to be given the chance to provide a transdiegetic meaning to the whole narration.

The meaning of a narration cannot be attained under different conditions while staying within the immanence of the text. Otherwise, and under normal conditions, interpretation would follow the narration. Thus it is left to the spectator, under normal circumstances, to view the narrative as a whole and to provide it with a comprehensive meaning, often in hindsight. After this, Thompson's 'trouvailles' (cf. *infra*) must be 'added up' by someone, otherwise they will simply be lost. In this film, Godard has already started the interpretation process. However, this interpretation cannot pretend to postulate a necessity other than, and parallel to, the narrative interpretation. The excess figurative meaning must be grafted onto the interpretation of the narration as narrative necessity. And this must happen in such a manner that neither meaning cannibalizes the other, but on the contrary enhances it with a new vector of interpretation.

Narration is one kind of logical relation. Rhetorical, figurative meaning establishes a different logical relation, notwithstanding Aristotle's enthymematic commonality (v. *supra*). Without denying such a difference in nature, we can resolve the contrast Semiotically as Interpretation in the correct order. Provided that the narrative meaning has been successfully established through a teleological relation (cf. *infra*), an Interpretant of the narration in its entirety, or as such, relates it to a logical necessity beyond the narrative universe. The credibility of this particular pragmatic and narrative universe – which it remains as Replica of a Type of probable world – in this existential or imaginary dyadic relation remains in place. However, by nourishing doubts about its purpose – or, in our case, about the purposes of parallel narratives – it calls up questions of normativity (in the Peircean sense of the term). The reason why a narrative is worth narration need not be conveyed in a 'pre-text' or a detached discourse; it can also be woven into the narrative warp. 'Weaving,' however, is metaphoric parlance for a complex Interpretative relationship that must be established either case by case or with the support of the customary tropes or other figuration.

Argumentation beyond narration (i.e. not directed toward the construction of a probable narration) asserts itself as a general cognition of values. These values might instantiate themselves in narratively concrete existential relations (propositions of two-value logical truth). However, figuration and narration are related only if the figurative discourse is about pragmatic values and not about random theoretical objects. From our discussion of Peirce's Normative Sciences we know that such values are peculiar: inescapable but never existent. This cognitive state makes such values rather evanescent – we can perceive only instances. To illustrate using our film example: A narrative in which a biology professor disproves the calculus of chances for evolution is more or less plausible. Furthermore, it can be theoretically more or less convincing that God created the universe. Thus, theory can stand in a more or less evident discursive relation to narrative. However, it is only when we understand the existence and act of God as a normative value that the aesthetic effect becomes meaningful as such. This is not to deny that the biology professor with his theoretical conclusions cannot be understood as the Interpretation of the narrative, bringing more light into the strictly narrative logic. For instance, this very same episode heightens the narrative probability of the political intellectual victimization of the exiled Czech political refugee: as choice between entertaining a theistic belief in creationism and paying the price for it, instead of professing a materialist philosophy. However, in spite of the artistry of this dexterous interweaving of comment and narrative, there is not yet an aesthetic meaning. This is not a meaningful insight into the purpose of this exact narration and the aesthetic feeling of its worth in being narrated by someone for someone else. Only when the normativity itself can be discovered in the figuration can it enter into a logical relation of aesthetic meaning to the narrative. Otherwise, the figurative form indeed does not 'add up.'

Thus in order to 'add up' aesthetic and figurative meaning, it is not absolutely necessary to resort to Gadamer's *Urbild* of humanity in its plenitude. Although this is certainly not wrong, it hinges emphatically on psychological insights. Not 'adding up,' however, is not an option, because an aesthetic that cannot become meaning is pointless and without effect.

From a purely formalist point of view, if we decides to look at this film from the perspective of narrative fissures, we could try to subsume it under the known forms and rationales for keeping narrative illusion at bay. Much ink had to flow to demonstrate the influence of Berthold Brecht's theatre theory on Godard,[92] – in particular, the former's 'V-Effekt' (short for 'Verfremdungseffekt') and his notion of 'episches Theater.' It is, however, noteworthy that *Je vous salue, Marie* goes beyond Brecht's practical finality. Yet even then is 'epos' – as traditional and Brechtian idea – an Interpretant intervention into the narrative universe itself. This also answers the claim that 'trouvailles' (of a Neoformalist account of artistic style in Thompson [1988]) never add up in aesthetics. There are certainly features interspersed through the narrative or enunciationally bracketed out of it. In Godard's films we find instances of both: the strangeness of symbols in this film, but also the strangeness of a scene where Godard in person comments on the friendliness of the French State Radio personnel. These strange elements demand Interpretation which they are denied from within the narrative. Thus 'trouvailles' are actually signs that must necessarily include a generality. Except in the narrative framework they appear as erratic blocks of singularities, as patches of meaning. However, if we notice them as such, and nevertheless are able to interpret them, this means that another sign process has been completed. We have succeeded in determining another general Third. If this new generality derives no centrifugal force from the narration, this is the result of a transnarrative meaning bestowed on the narrative itself.

From the above illustration, it would follow that the aesthetic effect, as pragmatic value of narrative purpose, transcends the narrative. This conclusion is not incorrect, yet it must also be noted that this meaning retroactively becomes part and parcel of the narration itself. Seen from inside the narrative, the aesthetic meaning becomes an Iconic Sign and the figurative meaning can become Indexical. Thus it has to become an element that is narratively not determined. The first prevalent kind,

Iconically degenerated Thirds, cognizes a generality in the manner of a feeling or subjective intuition. In *Je vous salue, Marie* this happens very frequently and has two principal fields of application. First, everything relating to God is Iconic sign – for example, the moon, the sun, and the big, round lamp in front of the gymnasium. Also, there is the open, adorned mouth together with the final chorus of Bach's *St Matthew Passion*. Second, all matters of femininity are signs of the first type. Certain images of the naked body of a woman bespeak (either) the male gaze / (or) a contemplative view of a woman in its diversity as look. It can only be deceptive when concepts such as 'beauty' and 'desire' are used for this sign relation, because these concepts suggest more clarity and evidence than is offered by the frail image reality. In both cases, to maintain that these images of the first kind are 'about' this or 'about' that requires some temerity; but any 'about' is not warranted narratively. If they were 'about,' they were not narratively degenerated as the first type. Yet they could certainly *lead to* such an 'about.' In this film they do only with the help of clear theoretical enunciations. It is through Marie's reflective thoughts about water lilies, reflections in the water, shadows of shadows of the light, that we understand explicitly the 'about' of such images. Likewise, we learn from dialogue parts (the Doctor, Marie's, Eve's, Juliette's) what women are 'about.'

Nor is the second sign degeneration a relation bonded by a force of (narrative) necessity (appealing to a mind). Rather, it functions differently in a fundamental way. One has the Interpretant, as it were, but it is not immediately clear what it interprets. Instances are generally witty remarks; they could be irony if only we could see or know what they are referring to. As they stand, they are witty subscriptions to non-existent images. Perhaps the most brutal instance is Godard's (already mentioned) surreptitious introduction of Heidegger and Trakl into the secret of sexuality. Pascal, name of a punk boy and owner of a Rubik cube, is only apparently a more ironic reference to Blaise, the probability calculus genius. Marie's lines toward the end of the film, about her son's coming back at Easter or Trinity, and also her 'quia respexit,' are enigmatic emblems. The audience must reason 'about what' they are witty remarks, given that they do not fit absolutely into the narrative context. Such lacunae never constitute a hint to the solution of a riddle; there are no police film allusions in this film. If we understand, then they are about the true context of the narrative, the glue of meaning that holds symbols and narrative together and gives the latter a transcendent meaning.

However, for this sign class meaning is not the feeling of an idea, but the search for an Object. More explicitly, the sign relation is specified by a Secondness. In signs of the second type, knowledge of Heidegger, Trakl, and their theories about sexuality is presupposed; yet it is far from evident which cognitive Object they are alluding to. It is strictly not seen on the screen, but understanding it, we are offered a better understanding of the narrative. In the first case, however, all we need to do is abandon ourselves lyrically to suns, moons, and water lilies. This abandonment leads us to be carried away from the visible to the other, invisible. If we understand, then it becomes intended by the artistic strategy, built into the very purpose of the film. Both types of Degenerate Sign relations explain the difficulties of understanding this film. Even their simultaneous presence might be felt as bewildering, especially because they produce such a contradictory impression. If sign relations of the first kind would prevail, the overall impression could easily be that of a 'poetic' film. Cavalier's Thérèse might be such an example, where the consistency of one type of Iconic sign relations sets the unified mood of a poetically argumentative type of connectors. Godard's interspersed wittiness, instead, calls for a quite different sort of spectatorship, one that is constantly alert and looking out for unusual connections to an invisible Object.

As we come to the close of this Intermezzo with *Je vous salue, Marie*, the practical importance of a proper understanding of the object, cinema (which is intentionally more vague than a 'theory of the film image'), should be apparent. The complexities of meaning can certainly not be countless, because otherwise there could be no understanding. However, they are more complex than some film theories like to admit. The pride of a theory should be that it is capable of *not* reducing meaning – for instance, to narration. Speculative Grammar (i.e., Semiotic), as a theory of meaning has a nonpareil grasp of meaning subtleties. So much so that it might seem 'suspect' to some because it is not 'consistent, rigorously argued, and (above all) clear.' (Bordwell 1996: 106). Peirce's intent was to 'make our ideas clear; making meanings as complex as those in this film clearer would be no small benefit.

4 Narration in Film and
   Film Theory

de Te narratur Fabula

To paraphrase Garfinkel 'If narration is the answer, what is the question?' With this question, and in a typical Pragmaticistic frame of mind, we are now ready to approach a peculiar form of meaning. In the beginning, it was important to allow plenty of room for the representational achievements of cinema as a whole.[1] This meant paying special attention to meaning other (and more) than narration. The challenge of grasping the meaning of Godard's *Je vous salue, Marie* highlighted the need for such a free space. Nevertheless, narration is still the most conspicuous form of meaning in cinema. To understand it well – in particular, to understand how to locate the source of its meaning – remains crucial to film theory. As we might expect, especially after encountering Bergson in Deleuze's film theory, the different accounts for this source are wildly and fundamentally at variance. In the debate at hand, Semiotic argumentation must prove its basic reasonableness, and not merely in its narratological ramifications. Semiotic is rooted in Pragmaticism, which offers an excellent natural frame for narrative meaning.

To this end, the chapter at hand will first (§4.1) show that time experience is a foundational sign that can give rise to – and that is a nonprescindable precondition for – narration. Furthermore, a sufficient cause for narrative meaning presupposes, as a further Categorical specification of the sign, an Occurrence in a special Now – enunciation, as it is called in most of the present literature. (This will be the focus of §6). Only from there as the third necessary ingredient, can a teleology of narrated action be meaningfully established). This roughly outlines narrative meaning as it can be derived from Peirce. Only a thorough debate (in §5) with two of the more important narratologies will enable us to see the Semiotic advance. One of these is epitomized by Ricoeur's phenomenological existence-analytical narratology. As a theory of time transformation, it is very different from Deleuze's ontology of movement (v. *supra*). The other, in sharp contrast, explains not time but rather the idea of narrative action; this is Greimas's Semio-narratology. As by-product, at the end of our investigation (§6.3) we will see the possibility of a film rhetoric that is cognate with and close to the form of meaning in narration. For the moment we will leave aside the aesthetic treatment of narration, a topic reserved for this book's final chapter.

4.1 The Narratological Question, Peirce, and Cinema

First let us consider the question of narrative meaning itself. How does it function as a sign? And what is its unique relationship to cinema? In general terms, narrativity is a human concern, not simply a special problem of Semiotic or literary theory. The Hopi people of the American Southwest considered the narrated to be the real and of the merely experienced to be the unreal (cf. Weinrich 1964: 308, referring to Whorf). There is indeed philosophical wisdom in this view: a rehabilitation of narration is appropriate (recall our earlier discussion of representation) if the real is concretely cognized not so much in propositions ('the world is round') as in conduct (perhaps as in Columbus's way of thinking). If it is true that our world cognition is neither a mental act of judgment, nor a matter of forming propositions, but instead a habit of behaviour in the universe of real objects, then we cannot leave narration to literary theory. Rather than being a discipline and a special domain of inquiry, it is an epiphyte of our only tool for 'having world': action and conduct. Pragmaticism must be credited for the revolutionary conduct of behaviour leaving behind epistemology. It contains in a nutshell a theory of narration – narration, however, with considerable philosophical relevance. Thus, Pragmaticism finds itself competing with philosophies that also assign some pivotal role to narrative meaning (these accounts will be debated in §5).

Philosophy has long concerned itself with narration, and the questions have not always related to aesthetic. Narration was bequeathed to us by Aristotle as *Poetic* (which already distances itself from Plato's distrust of narratives); that said, a pivotal role cannot be assigned to poetic within the architectonic structure of his philosophy. However, and against Plato, no longer should narration be seen as copy of a copy of the Real Idea (which only the Philosopher is capable of contemplating, and whose form only he can surmise). Rather, in narrating one imitates actions. Aristotle's insight is still entirely valid. Not even film narratology can disregard narration's intimate dependence on real, actual human action. By the same token, narration is fundamentally different from action. It is merely, or much more, its representation, imitation. Narration is when action becomes warped or 'textus.' (There is no need to deny this transformation – not even in the name of 'anti-diegetic' cinematic specificity.) Thus as soon as film represents actions it must create a whole, a texture of parts of action. Cinema complies with this rule, since the teleological approach to representing human action[2] falls almost inevitably into a narrative form.

So if narration is an answer, what is the question? Perhaps it needs to be emphasized that there is indeed a question, and not just a classification problem relating to a cultural form. Narration is a special meaning that is not already comprehended as a sequence of propositions. 'Text grammar' (and the like) states the problem (typically as order beyond sentence rules), but does it give an answer? Is there hope that such an approach will lead to an answer (cf. *infra* 372–3)? The narration phenomenon itself raises intriguing questions. How can there be propositions that are not assertions (even though they are used), but that depend on a single, primordial true assertion (v. *infra* 402–3)? If everything is treated as a statement, then most narratives are lies or 'fictions.' However, if there are perfectly comprehensible linguistic phenomena that state nothing, 'extensional disambiguations' (in Eco's narratology, cf. *infra* 392–4) are in peril of missing the particularity of such a meaning.

We can formulate the problem at various levels, starting from the most anodyne narrative. The basic miracle – the compelling force – of narration becomes discernible when we ask this simple question: Why does a narrative continue? Questions like this are no longer simple if we remain aware of the fragile nature of the 'double contingent' (Parsons) human acting, communicative acting, representing action. Action can and must stop the moment there is no sequel, no next action 'docking' at the previous action; thus narration as the representation of action must inevitably break down once the compulsion of an inner necessity is lacking. Some narratologies take this necessity for granted, though they shouldn't. Does this compulsion stem from action, or should we locate it (less naively) merely in the power of the narrative form? Questions like these place an enormous burden of proof on 'generative' theories (as we shall see in the debate between Ricoeur and Greimas). Yet even then it is hard to deny that the form's momentum lies in something exterior. Pragmatic logic relies on human action for its constraints. Narration therefore can never be a self-contained problem (of text linguistics); it must blend into broader philosophical questions.

Starting from a formal perspective, we can regard films as works of text. The term 'content' tells us not so much that film relates to a world, but that it is organized as a whole. The whole can be either a rhetorical organization or a narrative structure. The coherence of the whole of meaning cannot be observed. Only apparently is it reified as causality; in fact, it is result of a textual form. Narration treats temporal sequence as a logical consequence (i.e., as causality), and thus defies a logical verdict against the *post hoc ergo propter hoc* sort of argument. In all of this, form is of clear theoretical importance. Its investigation is therefore vital to underlying philosophical problems. Some, like Foucault, would maintain that the Form is the cause of problems because it suggests false answers. In any case, the mere existence of a narrative Form has consequences. Understanding it in certain ways will inevitably have repercussions when we set out to define and solve philosophical, epistemological, historiographical, and social problems[3] that depend on narrativity. The enigma is that narration, as a result of its formal nature, produces its own unity, which then comes to a natural end. This is not explained by a supposed analogy of the narrative form to propositional structure (as postulated in Fundamental Syntax; cf. Greimas 1979). Instead, it is based on the idea of action. This has profound implications for the act of narrating (and even for textual organization).[4]

The narrative form is rooted in action because it can never produce its own temporality by itself. Action, common action, social praxis, and therefore narratives produce time. Now the decisive question becomes, 'What gives origin to human time, narrated as well as acted[5]?' Without an answer to this, there is no possibility of explaining the meaning of texts or films. There is no narratology that does not have at least a hidden (sometimes merely implied) root in the time-generation potential of action. However, action need not be the ultimate key, if time itself is conceivable in a theory. Thus time will become our focus. There are various reasons for this line of thought. Narration is ('exists as') always a representation of time. Temporality is not subordinate here. The creation of time is the very foundation of meaning in narratives; that foundation is not the semantic representation of a universe, as is so often suggested.[6]

Yet it is as difficult to cognize time as it is to give it a textual form. This is not so clear in everyday life. Time is as easily taken for granted as it is difficult to comprehend. And it is even more difficult to comprehend the transformation of time through representation. This is when time must become a sign – when it must exist in a sign relation.

4.2 The Semiotic of Narrative Time

We should avoid taking an ingenuous, reductive approach to time. Time can never be addressed as if it were an object, as long as it remains time (and not a weak replacement such as order). Now time is even more than just action, as Peirce's struggle against a reductive understanding of pragmatism has so clearly indicated. Although time is in action, comprehending this 'in' is really a question of understanding the peculiarity of a particular Relation. In certain various ways, we gain an understanding of time, this Relation must therefore eventually become a triadic relation of a Sign. Peirce would not be Peirce, however, if he were to offer only a simple conception of time. Before time becomes 'time' as an object of understanding, it must build on certain preconditions, which like everything else can only be in the Categorical order – that is, iterative and ordinal. By its very nature, the Sign of Time can only be a triadic relation whose Thirdness thus forcibly comprehends a First and a Second. Because of its Categorical structure, a sign of time is able to fall back on its basic constituents. As sign, however, it will do this only by way of sign degeneration (which is really through a Categorical specification of the triad, as we have seen). What is time as a genuine Triad? An example would be the concept of evolution. If this sign is specified by a Second, it could become, for instance, the idea of acceleration. In contrast, a case of a raw intuition of change is a double degenerate sign (v. *supra* 124–6). So far, there is nothing special in the Relational Sign process with regard to time; however, as we shall see, the various modes of being of time, comprehensible in a theory of being (metaphysic) as the law of time, offer some particular constraints also to the Sign of time.

It is reasonable to examine the time of the First and the Second of this triadic relation of time, because it amounts to this question: Is time also non-mental? We can escape this question only if we can exclude the idea that time is either less or more than 'a Cognizable that ... determines some actual or potential Mind' (8.177, undated letter to Lady Welby; cf. also 7.356). Ordinarily, this question is automatically precluded if we approach time from a psychological standpoint. Then, of course, the 'physical' (Ricoeur's 'cosmological') reality of time either remains unnoticed or is tacitly presupposed (Husserl) or is flatly denied. Yet in Peirce, time need not be excluded. However, if time 'is,' there are no 'provisions' that it is in a mode essentially different from all other being (comparable to Kant's *Anschauungsformen*). Generally speaking, everything between pure being and pure essence is determined by Categories. If time 'is' at all, it has a Categorical nature. This question is not trivial, especially for Semiotic, which is not nominalist, since Signs must Interpret the same Object that they have in their First and Second Correlate. Thus the Sign of time must have something of time in its First and in its Second as well. What is it, then, that constitutes time as a mere Quality? We must approach this question separately from the fact that we do indeed cognize time only in Signs. Furthermore, as basis for our cognition there must be something 'conducive to' time. Purely Firstness time is a monadic Relation, just as a dyadic Relation is in time as pure Occurrence.

As a metaphysical theory this is not so difficult to find in the late Peirce, where it is conceivable within the framework of Tychasm and Anankasm. As we shall see, it is also conceivable from a strictly logical perspective. Our question is only this: From which theoretical perspective should we observe the underpinnings of the Sign of time? In between the mathematical Continuity approach and the metaphysical, *Naturphilosophie*-like approach is the site of Semiotic comprehended as Logic. What time is as a monadic logical Relation is the problem of a temporal First, which is required as a basis for its cognition. Feeling might be a psychological instance of this, but not every Monad is a feeling, nor does time need to be a Quality of Feeling. From the metaphysical law of time (cf. *infra*), we will understand that the monadic element *in the being* of Time, its oneness, calls for a specially degenerative Relation *in the cognition* or Sign of it. Less problematic is the almost normal dyad of the Sign relation of time, which is connected with its being as different states of the same subject (i.e., events). Often overlooked is the logically different nature of the triad of the Sign relation of time, which is, however, the quintessence of narration.

Semiotic assigns a pivotal role to signs even in epistemology and metaphysic. We have already discussed what this means for a conception of the Real and for cognition. Cinema 'is' really (i.e., is a sign), and as sign it comprises modes of being (logical). As one mode of its being, it is in a peculiar way time. As we will see in the context of the metaphysical law of time, being time is a prerequisite to signs, which are non-necessary (i.e., contingent) Relations. Although some Signs certainly have a temporal Object – that is, although there are some explicit signs of time – in all other signs time can be either be 'subdued' or 'emphatic.' In a given sign, time might play no significant role (even though it is still present). However, when it does play a significant role, it mostly assumes the appearance of narration. A maximally a-temporal sign of something 'eternally' valid, such as a chemical compound in a book of chemistry, can become temporalized again. For example, when the compound is discovered (in its history of invention), or when in the history of the cosmos certain conditions had to be present in order to produce the compound, or when the compound's mere possibility is inferred, we can see the temporal mode of that compound. Signs with fixed meanings are rather the exception to the process of discovery (i.e., semiosis).

The investigation of cinema reveals the semiotic incidence of time in two ways: narrative[7] and aesthetic. (In television and documentary film there is a third way of being a Sign of time [a dyadic Second], in which the focus is on the difference between two states or events [of the same subject].) Narration and aesthetic constitute two poles on a semiotic spectrum. As narration, time is cognition; as aesthetic, time is discovery. Thus a narrative is understood from its ending, whereas it is a matter of aesthetic experience that a narrative begins with startling wonder (and may never lead to a conclusive understanding). In both instances the triadic sign relation relies heavily on Firsts; but in aesthetic experience it must live with a hypothetical choice of perhaps a multitude of Thirds. Instead of a reduction of the multiple (of senses), this sign produces a multiple of meanings. In this regard the aesthetic sign is pure temporality. This opens an avenue for a particular 'aesthetic of time,' as will become evident when we analyze some films in detail.

Cinematic narration 'is' (has being) as a Semiotic object of a particular kind. This means, it 'is' not simply as if there were only one mode of being, which would follow if meaningful sentences were restricted to propositions. Evidently, narrations are 'problematic' propositions. In most cases of fiction, even those 'based on the true events,' narrations are openly false. Furthermore, truth values are something no proposition can avoid, and this is the case even with unasserted propositions. What makes narratives even more problematic is the constitutive fact of their teleology. Now facticity, which finds its adequate expression in propositions, is completely devoid of finality (teleology, purpose). In stating mere facts, we are not speculating on their supposed aims, purposes, or ends; rather we are restricting ourselves to anything that can be named with 'is' or 'was.' This rule is flagrantly violated in narrating. Without at least an inkling of finality, of the ends of an episode, its elements must remain purposeless. The text can never come to its end. This end is at a different level from any of the elements or episodes, since it is the one general idea that unifies elements falling under it. The particular nature of narrative meaning is linked to the reason driving its operation; as we will see later, two types of causality differentiate propositions from narrations. Moreover, this reason is also the reason why narration is inherently unable to make (true or false) assertions.

To demonstrate that cinema is capable of this special meaning, narrativity, we must show the pivotal nature of teleology. As the absolute minimum requirement for narration, teleology is final causality (i.e., purpose). However, the mode of being of a purpose is not visible, as it were; rather, it must be inferred as real (but not existent) in the visible (or existent). For any proposition-based theory, this would be an awkward position, since there is no way to state finality (except as reified in this concept). 'These are the ends' is an inadequate, 'inconclusive' proposition. Such a peculiarity of the purpose is therefore also a problem of adopting an adequate theory.

A preliminary remark needs to be made here. In explaining teleology, is it not enough to resort to such a theory as we find in Aristotle's *Poetic*? Here the generation of this kind of meaning is explained as 'imitation of action' ($\mu\iota\mu\eta\sigma\iota\varsigma$ $\pi\alpha\xi\epsilon\omega\varsigma$). However, if we look closer and see how the possibility of imitation is explained, we will find in the end that praxis and imitation have their common denominator in the $\eta\theta o\varsigma$ (customs, contingent of a culture). Thus we get no further than the everyday evidence of a life-world (much in the Schützean sense of an 'unquestionable horizon of the lifeworld'). This becomes then a *quaestio facti*, in its last resort, and can no longer claim to answer a *quaestio juris*. This leaves us at a loss precisely where we need to explain the possibility of teleology. Purpose is never explained by facts, and this is not as far as Aristotle goes in his *Poetic*.

Conceptions of purpose can be given many names. Peirce in his later work called it sympathy, love, Agapasm (cf. 101–8, 262, 571n36). We now find ourselves in the realm of metaphysical, *naturphilosophical* speculation. Concepts closer to the narrative phenomenon would take into account primarily action as an idea. Action is first of all desire (seen from a psychological perspective 'from within'), and desire strives toward a General, exactly one case of which one expects to occur. Up to this point a number of alternative philosophical accounts of action finality are available. Fortunately, this is also the exact point of departure of Pragmaticism. Explanations of (narrative) purpose are feasible (and need not be tucked away into 'schematisms' of some sort). This kind of problem is very close to the foundational intuition of pragmatism. Thus, Peirce's Harvard lectures of 1903 serve as an excellent guide for the problem of teleology. Inexorably, this will lead us encounter all the major knots of the narrative problem, such as finality, values, action, and time.

For a Pragmaticistic approach to 'purpose,' we must choose our starting point carefully. Peirce is far from anchoring pragmatic cognition on the contingent foundation of an $\tilde{\eta}\theta o\varsigma$, as in the *Poetic*. The opposite, however, is no option either. He admits no outside purchase on the cognition of the real, and neither a crude realism nor apriorism is a choice.[8] Thus, even cognizing cognition, pursuing 'purpose' it is already done from within a purpose – that is, from a cognitive conduct or project. Just as every cognition is but a next cognition, every purpose is but a continuation of an ongoing conduct of behaviour. In the present context, the keystone of this antifoundationalism is the 'dynamic principle' in the presupposition itself. Although this reflects a naturalistic attitude (which Peirce called the scientific method), it still can be justified (v. §1). However, in practical terms justification is an empty exercise, because by living and thinking we are already proving that it is possible to live and think: *ex esse sequitur posse*. However, this kind of proof is not *a posteriori* foundationalism for human action, as might be the case in other theories. For instance, the 'imaginaire social' in Semionarratology is simply a formal deduction of meaning structures in the propositional form; it needs to be proven by a postulate of 'thymie,' which is an assumption of an anthropological constant. As we know from our earlier discussion, this is not the case with the dynamic principle in Peirce's Pragmaticism.

An understanding of narration, then, cannot be achieved by starting from abstract thinking as a form, in the Kantian manner. Nor can we understand narration through abstract language in the manner of Greimas's generativism. Only when mental acts are *in situ* of a conduct of behaviour, in a world of an outside reality and as a continuation of thought, can purpose of action be explained. The Pragmatic Maxim expresses nothing less than this. Human acting, as conduct of behaviour and not as single acts, thus can become the veritable (empirical, a posteriori) basis of philosophical reflection (as was outlined in §1.1.1). As its Interpretation, narration of behaviour cannot differ fundamentally from behaviour itself. When we consider sign theory as the quintessential result of the Pragmatic Maxim, but only as Form and as Speculative Grammar, narration as the concrete train of thought is an expression of the continuation of sign Interpretation.

The idea of 'purpose' as central to pragmatic meaning – and *a fortiori* to narrative meaning – has an important consequence for theories of narration. Those which limit themselves to extensional treatments of narrative universes (including certain psychologized variants that treat 'point of view' knowledge of such universes in the minds of characters) miss the point. This cannot account for purpose, barring the path to time.

Further steps besides these are necessary for narrative meaning. Peirce's first 1903 Harvard lecture (1998: 136f) provides an interesting example of the basic insurance problem of risk assessment. Insurers know only 'what' it is they are insuring when they venture beyond the stage of statistical analysis. Statistics calculates the incidence of a certain species of events among a genus of events, on the basis of a normal distribution of probability.[9] However, this ratio of two infinite multitudes will never be able to result in a cognition of a conduct. If storytellers, instead, recount a firestorm as an 'accident' (the 'ad' contained in the term suggests already a vector which, for instance, might come to its fullness in a biographical teleology) they must already use a different logic than one which cognizes statistical ratios. For insurers, 'really knowing' means following the logical path of a storyteller inventing a generality. This makes their risk a true or false case (i.e., token of a general type).

The link of probability to narrativity is even closer than mere logic: both are conduct. What the illustration in the lecture makes also clear is that we already have two conducts which are different by nature.[10] Cognizing the nature of something is a characteristic proper only of the purposive conduct (compared above to storytelling). Statisticians' conduct is necessarily different. How the different nature of conducts is grasped in their different values – or, as Peirce calls it, 'goodness' – was discussed earlier. Thus we recognize the conduct of behaviour of statisticians when in their acts they follow the value of truth. They can form propositions that are completely understood if the relation to existent objects can be either true or false. Another type of behaviour is exemplified in artists, who merely need to open their eyes, without either making truth judgments or cognizing laws.

All of these values are relevant for narration, because teleological purpose comprehends the lower-adic values in a specific way. Thus, the value of 'aesthetic' behaviour – related to the *summum bonum* that is nondescript (i.e., does not make differences) – gives to narration motivation (from a psychological perspective), a drive to act. Even truth is important for fiction, which must be anchored in the reality of a narrator (regarding narrative enunciation; v. *infra*). Any conduct that is cognitive follows a third kind of value or goodness, the regularity of general laws. As purpose this goodness is of particular relevance to narration.

In contrast to real action in situations of pragmatic consequence, narratives as representations of action 'are' pure teleology of acting. Although both are Sign, narration is a Sign of behaviour, one that in Thirdness is categorically further specified (v. *supra*) as teleology. That latter cognitive conduct is guided by a different Value. In narration as conduct, there is patently no 'reality constraint,' as there is with pragmatic behaviour. Anything is feasibly narratable provided that a narrator can convince me of its credibility (Aristotle's εἰκός). The only constraint regarding 'outward reality' is the truth of the narrator's enunciational intention that now wants to tell me something of proper invention. However, cognitive behaviour as such is under a constant reality constraint, and this difference (in the Second Correlate) constitutes narrative meaning ('narrative contract').

We have identified three prerequisites of narrativity as such – purpose as narrative teleological causality, the existential reality of enunciation, and normative values. These share one peculiarity: all three conditions are a determinate transformation of time as sign processes. Time, then, is both the pivot and the condition of the possibility of purpose: narrative and behavioural. If follows that we cannot comprehend narration without an implicit idea of time.

How can time be comprehended within a Peircean framework? As a basic principle, if time has any Reality, it must be determined Categorically, as noted earlier. Time as an object of philosophical reflection is reputedly almost impossible to speak about in the way we speak of any other object. Yet in a non-objective way, time can be – and has been – discussed in a number of indirect modes. The Augustine Husserl line of thought chose the psychological mode (as immediate time consciousness). Peirce, instead, adopted a formal mode. The consequence of this choice certainly does not lie in the fact that time can never be an object. It is treated as one in simplicistic accounts (and also in a number of narratologies), in which cases it is actually reified as an experiential (or grammatical) aspect. This corresponds roughly to Bergson's *dividuel* temporality; 'Le Tout' is time as non-object. In a similar way, time 'is' Continuity for Peirce – that is, pure mathematical form, before any phenomenon. Hence we can say that everything is Continuous; this is instantiated in that everything is time. These two terms would have the same 'extension' if it were not a contradiction in terms to speak of abnumerable sets as 'extended' when they are beyond any extension proper. Consequently, time is never 'full' (and in the 'fullness of time,' there is no more time), and the same is true of Continuity.

Being formal does not contradict being empirical; this form is the condition of the possibility of experience. Time is the precondition of change (which is then experienced). The metaphysic of time, however, is not enough. If every experience and every cognition is in signs, it follows that unless it somehow enters the sign process, it 'is' not (now a question of cognitive objects). As such (i.e., no longer as pure form), time must logically become a triad and thus trimodal. As a Third, it 'comprehends' a Second, which comprehends a First. Time as mere pure Third can only result in a sort of Hegelian philosophy of history. This is similar to poetic, because it can be thought only as pure Thirdness. Poetic is a figure, a figuration (Aristotle's $\mu\bar{v}\theta o\varsigma$) of every possible action that can be conceived. As Revolution, Utopia, Cockaigne, or Lubberland, it is imagined as a reification of Hegel's 'being in and for itself' regarded as a totality of time. However, from a Peircean perspective, this is a deficient conception of time.

For time, there must, as part of the sign, also be concrete occurrence. As Secondness, time is event. No sooner do we bring events into propositional form than they acquire truth capability. Occurrence is in the first place a matter of lived conduct of behaviour (at least as narrative enunciation). Yet it cannot be lacking in narration. Under the aegis of the teleological Thirdness of poetic figuration, the brute facticity of events subsists inside narratives as a degenerated, weakened Thirdness. Perhaps it is enough that it becomes the 'otherness of the next' (event) in narrativity: something must come next. This is certainly not the same intensity of surprise, but it must suffice as Second in a narrative Sign of time. It is not predetermined, then, how this otherness will be realized in the various kinds of narratives. For the time experience, an actor's surprise, or frustrated expectation would be enough.

The least intuitive part of the time sign process is its First Correlate. Perhaps this is a problem of reflection more than one of experience, for it is difficult to restrain ourselves from thinking of movement or change (which is already change into another). Firstness in the sign relation and as Categorical specification is defined in practical terms as Now, and therefore Immediacy. This must at once invoke the 'immediate consciousness' of Husserl's psychological analysis of the time experience. However, even from a logical perspective it is possible to conceive of this immediate now, as a kind of 'infra-temporality' of the Moment. To achieve this idea we need only restrain ourselves from abstracting (i.e., Firstness from a Second). Beholding, as it were, momentarily stops the course of time into a moment. A moment without a next is the basis for every other next moment, or chance.

When we change the level of reflection from sign theory to *Naturphilosophie*, this experience of time corresponds to absolute chance. It would be inadequate to approach chance negatively as absence of order. Instead, it is a necessary moment of order (in its diversity, though). This reality must also have a Poetical correspondence – narrative chance, as it were; otherwise, since it is a necessary Correlate, there would be no time in narration. Now this is rather difficult to imagine if we approach narration – in the Aristotelian manner – from the teleological idea of $\mu\tilde{\upsilon}\theta\text{os}$. However, once we remind ourselves of the implications of the Semiotic concept of Sign (as a consequence of Pragmaticism), 'plot' as teleology is not all: the abstraction of teleology is not the real Sign. Rather, every Sign signifies only through its use or enunciation. For narrative time this has important implications. Thus, the Moment originates in the act of telling, narrating. The same is true for change, even in its weak form of surprise caused by the otherness of a next element (or in its stronger form, as narrative $\pi\varepsilon\rho\iota\pi\acute{\varepsilon}\tau\varepsilon\iota\alpha$). Only in the Sign's use is otherness real. The Moment, as part of the time experience, is the closest that time experience can get to chance. It is not ordered, and it is not referring to a second as the idea of change does. Both, however, are necessary as conditions for the possibility of teleology, and thus also of narrativity. Narrative-time-as-moment is still genuinely time, since moments remain moments of something, some quality or character. Quality 'presence' is momentaneous, not the moment itself. For poetical practice, the implication is that in narrating, images appear and are beholden as just here, whether they are concrete or not and whether they are instances of a law or purpose or not. Time, including narrative time, will never be complete if we understand it merely as purpose or teleology. It would be impossible to narrate if there were not something that – during the narration – gives rise to Moments and also to the experience of Change. Although this truth – without the theoretical consequences – can be found in the *Poetic* (what else is κάθαρσις?), it has been given a psychological twist in modern poetics (as we shall discuss later).

However, we do not need to resort to psychology in order to be granted access to those foundations of time in the immediacy of the flow and the brute facticity of this change. Time has a being not only in a psyche but also in any Sign process – for instance, quite typically, in the narrative Sign. In such a manner time becomes conduct. Only in this way can it be conceived Pragmaticisticly with all the advantages. This comprises a perspective from the end, as 'all conceivable consequences' (in the Pragmatic Maxim), which could then be only the perfectly adequate conduct of behaviour. All-quantifiers are a very peculiar operation of thought, however. They are necessary, and we have seen concretely with regard to narration that it is not feasible without teleology. Yet they need the basis of the chain of 'next behaviours.' There are (i.e., are existent) only next Interpretations of the same external Object. Final Interpretations ('all') are only there as Tokens of a general Law. The 'sense of an ending' in narration thrives on narrating and its Sign generation of Moments and Change.

Yet, neither moments nor change make sense if they are not complemented by the relative closure of a narration. For this reason we can comprehend narration as a Sign process that comes to a relative conclusion as long as it Interprets the same Object. Conversely, a narration has reached its end when Interpretation changes over to another Object. In the texture of living conduct, this is to be expected quite often. Cognition processes are interrupted by distractions or surprises. Narration, in contrast, is much better protected against premature object changes through the 'narrative contract.' The same effect can be achieved through certain audiovisual means that prevent the diegetic universe from being disturbed. The strongest logical coercion for narrative closure and unity comes from teleology. By representing the purpose of conduct narratively, teleology constitutes a final Interpretant in such a way that indeed it contains 'all conceivable consequences.' As cognitive act it is therefore closed; it is no longer cognition but knowledge (enclosing even surprises of narrative περιπέτεια).

Teleology is as non-substitutable as the Moment, and this brings us to the third necessary element of the time-Sign as it is represented pragmatically in narration. The planned surprises in narrative vicissitudes come as close as possible to the function of the Opposition in the triadic sign relation. Concrete cognitive Objects never amount to the 'complete meaning of a concept' but merely to *this-new* meaning which I cognize now. Cognitively, this corresponds to the crucial difference between understanding a law and understanding a fact. In much the same way, it shows up narratively as the difference between the end of a plot and a surprising suspense, a new turn, a *coup de théâtre*. In some theories, meaning as pure novelty is difficult to grasp (e.g., as a positional value in a system of semiological meaning). For Semiotic Information, an event is one of the simplest elements, present in everything that is. In other words: Signs become Signs only when they are being used, *now* and for *this*. This is exactly the general condition that is represented in narrative περιπέτεια as planned surprise. We always already know something. Thus, every Interpretation is concretely a mere continuation of something that is treasured. For instance, in language: 'symbols grow' ([Peirce 1998: 10, in 'What Is a Sign,' [1894]). No behaviour would be possible without the event-nature of being; even less would narration be possible.

In the 1905 *Monist* articles, Peirce explicitly addresses this question 'for the purpose of illustrating the nature of Pragmaticism.' For example, in 'What is Time' (1998: 357f): 'What is the intellectual purport of the Past, Present, and Future?' (357). Typically, his concern in these articles is conduct or behaviour rather than psychological accounts of time. Behaviour need not be solely actual – as is inevitably the case with the psyche – and its 'depth dimension' as knowledge and habit stands out immediately. In behaving, therefore, 'the Past is the storehouse of all our knowledge' (358). On the forefront of behavioural depth, 'future facts are the only facts that we can ... control; and whatever there may be in Future that is not amenable to control are the things that we *shall* be able to infer, or *should* be able to infer under favourable circumstances" (358). The question is not one of behaviourism or behavioural learning. Rather, it is, 'How is new cognition possible without the availability of *a priori* forms?' This is the domain of the future and of behaviour directed toward the future. For the Present, that means: 'There is no time in the Present for any inference at all, least of all for inference concerning that very instant. Consequently the present object must be an external object, if there be any objective reference in it. The attitude of the Present is either conative or perceptive ... The consciousness of the present is then that of a struggle over what shall be; ... the Nascent State of the Actual' (359). This account is quite different from the ones we encounter in traditional (say, constructivist) epistemologies, in which present constructs are what 'is.' However, it demonstrates clearly the central place of the time dimension in cognition. We cannot cognize just what is; we must also implicate future influences on our behaviour. The problem of Time in the context of Pragmaticism is exactly this. 'What is real?' – that is, 'What can be experienced?' – is not a question bound to the present tense. Nowhere else is this clearer than in a narrative, which answers problems of 'what is' by developing a determinate future for 'what is.'

4.2.1 Continuity

In a Pragmaticistic perspective, time *in se* is presupposed by time as a Sign. Signs are time, and metaphysic is the basis for cognition. However, time is-in-Signs in a very particular way; it is not just Signs' presupposed metaphysic. Therefore, the temporal dimension of cognition must certainly be a first and immediate concern; that said, it can be treated separately from the metaphysical problem. Already in the 'Four Incapacities,' Peirce wrote: 'no present actual thought (which is a mere feeling) has any meaning, any intellectual value; for this lies not in what is actually thought, but in what this thought may be connected with in representation by subsequent thoughts; so that the meaning of a thought is altogether something virtual ... At no one instant in my state of mind is there cognition or representation, but in the relation of my states of mind at different instants there is' (1992b: 42). The metaphysical reality of time is not denied, but neither is it reduced to a present (or even triple present) state of mind in its reality. The temporal dimension of cognition must rely metaphysically on the Reality of a First, pure Possibility, mathematical Time. This makes for a rather peculiar experience if we are asked, 'How does one know of a pure Possibility?' This pure Possibility can only be a genuine (i.e., not discrete) Continuum, which must be of an entirely hypothetical nature. Its mode of cognition is diagrammatic thought (v. *supra*). Thus it is impossible to conceive an exact idea of a Continuum, which never comes to an end. No one has ever seen a line (v. *supra*) as a result of perceptions and cognitive conclusions. In the same way, we cannot cognize the continuation of time (or its regularity, directedness, and irreversibility). Furthermore, what exactly is 'pure possibility,' positively cognized and not as a complete negation of necessity? We need not recapitulate Peirce's 'The Categories Defended' lecture in order to demonstrate the irreducibility of Categories (in particular the First). Cognition as a Third, and thus cognition of time as also a narrative, iteratively comprehends 'its' First. Yet continuous time as in the First Correlate of a Sign can only be understood hypothetically (as a never finally conclusive abduction).[11] In the complexity of the narrating act, this position is taken by the Moment; it is hardly noticeable, nor is it meaningful in itself, yet it is crucial. In a Symbolic Sign, just as in a narration meaning, there must be general law of a teleological purpose, but that law must still be grounded in Possibility: 'Hence to assert that a law positively exists is to assert that it will operate, and therefore to refer to the future, even though only conditionally' (cf.'Reason's Rules,' 1902, 5.545).

We can conclude now that narrative, poetical practice is the work of time as Sign processes. Even though the Thirdness of teleology 'contains' the Moment and the Event, narration evidences and produces them on their own. We have already noted the intimate connection between narrative temporality and the process character of the Sign. However, we will understand the full signification of being-temporal only if we are able to distance it from 'existing-temporally.' Time can also be anchored to human existence, as opposed to either cognition or being as such (in its Categorical nature). Narratologies that are based on the time of subjective existence (such as Ricoeur's) diverge from theories of temporal being. Only the latter can involve pragmatic conduct as the sole means of cognizing and appropriating world as temporal. Narration here is merely a special representation of such a world constitution.

Such a change in the 'theory design' compels also a relocation of the 'strategical position' of Time in the architectonic structure. As Continuity – a mathematical concept not of cognition but of hypothetical value – Time is not yet a phenomenon. Instead, and without being a concept, it formally grounds all phenomenality and provides the conditions for its possibility. This makes its 'proof' a highly delicate matter and one that is similar to – or part of – the proof of Pragmaticism. For this reason we should expect it to be quite unlike normal cognitive objects. Consequently: (1) Time cannot (yet) be the object of a Normative Science (in the architectonic structure of the classification of sciences).[12] (2) *A fortiori* it is no object of a science of Idioscopy, nor is it any sort of empirical object. This points to where a Peircean understanding of time principally differs from traditional conceptions of time. Consequent to (1), there is no meaningful Peircean equivalent to a Kantian Transcendental Aesthetic, nor is there even any need for *a priori* forms. If time were an *a priori* form of apperception, for Peirce there would be no time. In which place, then, do we 'know' of time? Peirce's alternative is not (2): time is not an abnumerable thing that can be grasped by observing its increase or 'running out.' It is not an abnumerable set of discrete moments.[13]

The Peircean approach is altogether different. It has a number of 'manifestations' in his thought, at all levels. For instance, the need to transcend Normative sciences to explicit metaphysical questions becomes evident when Peirce discusses the central concept of community. The 'unlimited community of investigators' is Continuity (cf. *supra*),[14] which takes the place of Kant's transcendental concepts. Another instance of the true Continuity is encountered in the iterativity of Categorical relations. These are immediately realized in the Sign triads, which as we have seen (cf. *supra*) have three dimensions of Continuity. One of them is that signs are interpretations and are therefore unlimited by nature: any given sign is whatever it is interpreted to be by a new sign. The temporal aspect in this is not that interpretation must come to an end when everything is interpreted (cognized). Rather, interpretation is never abnumerably complete; it is open and ideally final.[15] The Pragmatic Maxim is therefore a perfect expression of the Continuity of being. Evidently, all of these mentioned contexts indicate how altogether different this perspective is from, say, a conception of a time totality seen as a Heideggerian Being-a-whole ('Ganzsein'). Even here, time is of a different nature from events in time, which receive their 'coordinates' only from the system's zero point (cf. Ricoeur 1985). The totality is deduced from Care ('Sorge') as existential analysis. Sorge causes action, historiality, history (cf. p. 361). The enormous difference between this Wholeness of a 'Being-toward-death' and the ideality of a Peircean Continuous ultimate could not be more evident.

Time is reflected explicitly in a number of Peirce's works – for example, in 'Some Amazing Mazes, Fourth Curiosity' (*c*.1909, 6.325f) – mainly in connection with the keystone to his entire thinking, Continuity (cf. Potter 1977). Its mathematical theorem character makes Continuity 'supra-concrete' since it 'is' before any phenomena. It is the formal–mental precondition for any reality cognition as such (which is much more than 'mere mathematics' in the sense of mental play). Yet being purely formal, is not the same as being a pure mental form. Provided it can be proven that being in its entirety is Continuous, then Form is united with Objectivity. This proof is the Sign, as reflected in Sign theory.

There are four phases of Peirce's understanding of Continuity, which centre around his debate with Kant and Cantor. Time is a central instance of Continuity. In his definitive comprehension of it, he distinguishes between mathematical time and experiential time. The former cannot interact with existent things. It 'is imagined to be a mere *possible-*

ness' (6.325); the idea behind this is that infinitesimal point of passage between the past and the future called 'now.' This is a key example used against Georg Cantor and in support of true Continuity. Its point is that true Continuity cannot be discrete, abnumerable or supernumerable. Peirce uses Heraclitus' river example[16] to emphasize that time proper does not exist – that it is of possible rather than existential nature, even though all things happen in time. Mathematical time is without beginning and without end, because it is only possibleness and what is possible is without limits, truly infinite. Peirce demonstrates that this ideal Time, like its 'parent' principle Continuity, has no absolute instant, or is of 'absolute definite before-and-afterness relatively to all other instants' (6.326), because lapses that are after a point B and before point Y can be multiplied *ad libitum*. As a consequence, an instant has to come from outside – from an existential, 'brute fact,' which is assumed to be the point of before and after. Similarly: 'While we must *adopt* a standard of first and last, there is nothing in its own nature the prototype of first and last.' ('The Logic of Mathematics; An Attempt to Develop My Categories from Within.' [1896], 1.498).

Thus when *human* time is experienced, its birth is owed to a Symbol and not to the virtuality of true Continuity as in the ideality of time. On its own, however, the adoption of a point is not enough to make it an initial point from which experiential time starts. So far this point is merely a fact. Much more is needed in order for that point to become a temporal fact (i.e., an event). The problem of how time becomes sign is rather complex, as shall be seen below; in principle, however, it depends on a First Correlate, which is 'possibility.' Consequently, in a semiosis time can only be an Icon, but mathematical Time alone is not a semiosis. Experiential time plays the central role in the process of discovery, the continuous novelty of cognition. Again, it is never the direct object of a thought,[17] but instead the 'hidden engine' in the process of thought. The arbitrary setting of a zero point for time, which is inscribed as Index in that semiosis, is also not so simple as event, because no event can be a singular fact. The complexity of the time Sign continues in the Third Correlate, which must relate to the same Object as the other Correlates, thus inheriting their peculiar nature. Is there a sign of time in se? Even if time determines signs, the question is how much a temporal Sign or a Sign of temporality can preserve of the mathematical nature of Continuous time. Mere continuation could only determine Iconically a temporal Sign. Yet as full semiosis, time as we experience it is first constituted by the Dicentic Interpretant: 'This is set

as point zero.' Time, then, public, experiential, and referential, is constituted directly by determining that Indexical point of reference from
which every moment is Indexically determined. These are the absolute
conditions in which Time comes into 'existence.' Through that process,
time becomes *ipso facto* communicable and public.[18]

Since Continuity is the cornerstone of Peirce's entire system – the
basis of its novelty and of a new conception of Time – we must not be
astonished that Peirce did not produce a theory of time as we have
seen it in Bergson and as we shall see in Husserl and the rest of the
Phenomenological tradition. He did not have to. Nor did his assumptions compel him into a Transcendental Aesthetic. Nor did he need to
ground his firm phenomenalism in an analysis of consciousness. For
Peirce, Time is not an apperception form of sensory synthesis, nor is it
one of the fundamental psychic acts of reality constituting consciousness. Time need not be the prime concern of a philosophy that gives
rise to Semiotic. The primary position is taken by Continuity, which
stands for the most Peircean of all insights, the total connection of
everything in various fundamental respects.[19]

The necessary consequence of Continuity is modal ontology. And
one of the strangest and most astonishing results of modes of being is
that Vagues are real (cf. Peirce 1998: 354). How can it be that (someone
claims that) there are elements which are not well defined? Is it not
counterintuitive to assume that at times, using deictic words as 'this!'
cannot even approximately indicate what is meant? Furthermore,
where it is – in principle – inappropriate to ask 'Are they X or not?'
because the principle of contradiction does not apply? Such are Vagues,
and since all is in Signs, Vagueness is also a property of some terms.
Because Vagueness is not a diminution of some complete state, but as
much a Categorical necessity as existential determination, Reality[20]
must be claimed also for Possibility, and also for Generality. As (metaphysical) instantiations of Continuity Time and Vagues they are related
to (if not being the immediate consequence of, or leading directly to)
the (logical form) abduction and the Pragmatic Maxim in its would-be
conditional: 'A state of things has the Modality of the possible – that is,
of the merely possible – only in case the contradictory state of things is
likewise possible, which proves possibility to be the vague modality"
(Peirce 1998: 355).

Evidently, Continuity completely changes the conceptualization of
traditional time theories as either physical or psychological, including
the aporetic either or alternative. This unacceptable choice is avoided

by means of a Triadic Continuous understanding of the Real. Also, many theoreticians rely on implicit time theories reflecting this sort of separation of physical and psychic universes. This has acquired the status of truism, as we can see in a random albeit representative example of psychological arguing: 'It has been argued ... that time per se is not experienced; rather the experience of time passing results from the simultaneous perception of change and stability' (Werner 1985: 87; in an entirely pragmatic context of pace and rhythm in interpersonal relationships). In this extract, the 'data' of the physical world are change and stability, and time is the perception's synthesis. As we have seen, this cannot even remotely explain narration, which is one of the most common human acts. Without the Reality of a Third, Time-law, teleology would never become part of the phenomenon of time. All of the various modes of being are needed – namely, Actuality, Necessity and Possibility.[21] Universals and Vagues (as much as Propositions) are not merely modes of cognition – they are real Modes of being, including being cognized (5.547, 1908). Clearly, this must have immediate fundamental consequences for the problem of Time. Thus, as past, time influences our Actuality and so is 'a particular variety of objective Modality' (Peirce 1998: 357, *Monist* series, 1905). Real, cognized Time, in its three dimensions, is not a mere *Anschauungsweise*[22] or 'something' in and through which all that exists is apperceived (as Werner's source, Gibson seems to believe). Time *is* then exactly three Modalities of being.

Time is real (1.489), although in some special mode; it is not (as is customary) reduced to pure existence or to pure change. For us, the immediate need to understand time arises from narration, where it is enshrined ineluctably. Yet narratives obviously transform only one part of the time experience. Owing to their Sign class, they can omit otherwise essential parts of time. Now this does not destroy the temporality of narrative time, which relies instead, somehow, on a peculiar kind of integration, which can only be grasped through the Relational and Categorical nature of triadic Signs.

4.2.2 Semiosis of Time

How does Time become experience and cognition of temporality? This problem is dealt with explicitly in 'The Logic of Mathematics; an Attempt to develop my Categories from Within' (1.488ff 1896[?]; cf. also Peirce 1998: 357, *Monist* 1905). Here is more than just the familiar Categorial territory. Among his various attempts to provide a metaphysical underpinning to the Categories – which are still concepts relating to cognition – this is one that considers especially time and space. The unique vantage point in this paper is not so much a mathematical theory of Continuity, as its extension into the cognitive domain.

This paper constitutes Peirce's effort to show from the basis of necessary principles of reasoning (*logica utens*), but with no further assumptions, that 'this necessity must spring from some truth so broad as to hold not only for the universe we know but for every world that poet could create" (1.417). Such a broad and universal truth, even before mathematical reasoning, is nothing less than the 'most universal categories of elements of all experience, natural or poetical' (1.417; taken up by Hintikka's 'possible world logic' cf. *supra*). Where is such a truth necessity for Time? Evidently, it is not yet at the level of the most universal Categories, because Time is not as universal as they are. Therefore, Categories must also apply for Time. Now, 'the third category of elements of phenomena consists of what we call laws when we contemplate them from the outside only, but which when we see both sides of the shield we call thoughts' (1.420). Furthermore, we have seen (in §1.6) that the completeness of these necessary truths can be demonstrated through mathematical reasoning ... 'why there should be these three categories and no others. This reason ... will be found to coincide with the most fundamental characteristic of the most universal of the mathematical hypotheses, I mean that of number' (1.421; i.e., Continuity).

As soon as we draw the necessary conclusions from this trimodal general 'broad truth,' it follows that Being itself must also be trimodal. As triadic being, all must be general in some way; it is not enough that it exists. Here Peirce makes a vital distinction between necessary and contingent. Some thoughts are so universally true that they are 'eternal' and 'above time.' Only these thoughts – in signs – are instances of the perfect mathematical form of genuine triad. Genuineness 'involves the idea of a third not resoluble into a formless aggregation. In other words, it involves the idea of something more than all that can result from the successive addition of one to one. This "all that can" involves the idea of every possible something, and therefore of generality' (1.477). Every triad is a law, but some triads are less than 'thoroughly genuine' (1.480) and can thus be mere laws of quality or the regularity of facts (which are obviously more and other than the quality or the fact itself). The third class of genuine triads are laws of logic, and here we come to what is basically Peirce's version of what today is called argumentation theory. If a triad governs Quality (Firstness), we can speak of a 'law of quality'; if Fact, it is a 'law of fact.' All genuine triads must involve a Representamen 'of some kind, outward or inward' (1.480), whose function it is to mediate between an object and a thought. For the time problem this is of interest, because this understanding precludes sign-free immediate consciousness of time. Even time experience is ineluctably a mediation.

As we have seen, there are various sorts of mediation in thought (i.e., by laws). Laws of qualities (later important for Peirce's theory of perception (v. *supra*) are of lesser interest here, since time belongs to the realm of laws of fact. This means, in principle, that Time is not a law of thought. Semiotic, then, is never philosophy of history (in the Hegelian sense) and cannot be obtained from this Categorically conceived time theory. It is not the Spirit itself that gives itself a temporal manifestation. Time is still pegged to the dyadic form of event. There is a fundamental difference between generality (in genuine triads) and the world of fact: the latter 'contains only what is, and not everything that is possible of any description. Hence, the world of fact cannot contain a genuine triad. But ... it may be governed by genuine triads.' (1.478). This is why there are still laws governing facts, as opposed to bare facticity. Thus, laws of fact can be divided (in the manner of degeneration, that is, further Categorical specification, of triads) into the logically necessary and the logically contingent. Logically necessary facts are extremely difficult to comprehend, since they mean that something must exist *and* does exist. They can only be eternal facts – still capable of being true or false. Yet of the laws of fact, 'the most universal are of such a kind that they must be true provided every form which by logical necessity must be thought of a given subject is also a form of its real being. Calling this kind of necessity, metaphysical necessity, we may divide laws logically contingent into laws metaphysically necessary and laws metaphysically contingent' (1.483).

This is the decisive and consequential step from logical reasoning to the broader area of metaphysic[23] (Peirce's variant has been compared to Schelling's *Naturphilosophie*). Only here Time can be treated properly, because time is not essential to thought (even though, must be admitted, thoughts take place in time and follow one another). Time inheres to factual events; by introducing a dyadic character into the triad, this also introduces worldliness. The question then arises: is it a necessary being (i.e., is it also necessarily true) or is it a contingent being without sacrificing its essence of law? If the latter, it can be true or not, while still being as general as a law. Obviously, this Peircean answer is not a simple one. It is certainly much more complex than all those naive time theories which imply that time simply exists. At this point we can put paid to the notion that Time is a metaphysically necessary law of fact (i.e., in Peirce's understanding a 'law that whatever exists, although its existence is a matter of brute fact, irrespective of any qualities, must definitely possess or be without each monadic quality' [1.489]), because it is precisely not 'eternal' as a thought (here Peirce distances himself sharply from Hegel, as we have seen).

The contingency – in the sense of 'not necessarily involved in the literal extension to being of the necessary laws of logical truth' (1.488) – in metaphysical laws has itself a triadic constitution. Not every (non-necessary) being is assumed to be under the same sort of lawful grip. Being can be quasi-necessarily contingent or it can be so contingent that it is not tied to any generality that is beyond the subject itself. At the upper, more generality-containing end, there is the law-nature of Time, which imposes 'upon the subjects of dyadic existence forms of reaction analogous to those of logic' (1.488). Why is Time not such a compelling law as logic? We have already seen that the laws of the excluded middle and of non-contradiction do not apply to time. Such a subject can have contrary attribute inherences, and this must defy the strict logical laws that apply to thought.

Yet we can still apply laws of time, by taking the contrary attributes in sequence. The sober Philip and the drunk Philip cannot be thought in one thought, but they can be thought together. In such cases like these it is not impossible to think in one thought, because the generality of thought requires us to comprehend all possibilities. Thought is not the sum of all occurrences (facts) of a subject, which would be as many thoughts as there are occurrences; rather, it is a unity (of occurrences and all possible occurrences) in a general concept. We cannot achieve this oneness if the maximum we can think is two states of one subject. We can only realize this oneness as sequence, logically as consequence. The same thought, as metaphysic, results in modes of being, which even though lawlike are dyadically specified. The lawlike lies in the conclusion (i.e., these are not facts 'Philip is sober' and 'Philip is drunk,' but rather laws of facts), when we say that the sober and the drunk Philip are one and the same, although we cannot think him without a non-contrary attribute. As consequence, laws of time imitate logic in the closest possible way for facts. The necessity is less than with metaphysically necessary laws, because it consists merely in the force of the 'junctions, between the possessions by a subject of contrary attributes, to be related to one another like premises and conclusions, as before and after' (1.489).

As every law, being a triad, Time inasmuch as a contingent metaphysical law of fact has three 'clauses' (which are Correlates in Relations and not so much propositional predications). This postulates from being, inasmuch as it is of the general mode of law, that it comprehends three 'elements' that are comparable to the three distinct elements of logical reasoning in generals. So the first clause of the law of time is its monadic requirement. For temporal being this means that a fact exists in *this* time and *during* this much time. Formulated as law, as soon as something is temporal, it is one subject as different states, expressed as different statements of the same subject. 'Time is that diversity of existence whereby that which is existentially a subject is enabled to receive contrary determinations in existence.' (1.494).

If a law of time should be formulated, this must be its First clause, on which everything else is based. At the same time, it indicates what this law applies to, which is clearly not being-as-such (this would no longer be a contingent metaphysical law). This is, then, not a sweeping metaphysical statement implying that all being (not being as such) is temporal. At the upper limit, Peirce admits to some true (i.e., existential) beings that are so pervasive and universal that they almost approach the generality of a logical law.

At the lower limit of being-in-time is being-in-space. The determination such a being receives is different from the temporal determination, which has the force of a consequence of conclusion. Indeed, we can imagine spatial determination in very much the same manner as with the semiological sort of positional system (once semiology is applied to being, as an ontology, which would contradict its nominalist nature). What counts here is that this is determined solely on the principle that something has not the same positional value as another thing in an imaginary space of meaning and of expression. Semiology can be seen as a subset[24] of Semiotic, one that is restricted to one kind of determination and that lacks the grasp of temporal determination. This has implications for logic and for thought that reach far beyond what semiology is prepared to admit.

Being-temporal, then, is being existentially capable of receiving contrary attributes while being existentially one subject. Therefore the dyadic requirement of the time law is that one of the contrary states of an event is first, and that of two events one is first (1.495). This under-

standing is certainly not counterintuitive, however, its wider significance is less clear in its consequences. First, there is an absolute
inherence of thisness in the time experience. Second, there must be a
standard against which the comparison contained in a sequence can be
made. Third, this dyadic is so obviously different from the triadic
requirement of the continuity of time without a limit (including a
beginning), that there seems to be a contradiction in the time experience itself. Thisness means comparison, in the experience of time. Time
clearly cannot function as a monadic quality alone, nor can it ever consist of a general knowledge of, say, finality. In principle, it follows
from this that narration inasmuch as sheer teleology is different from
the experience of time, both metaphysically and Semiotically; it needs
to 'imitate' existential contrary determinations (as 'metabole'). Time
depends on the experience of dyadic nature of this first being different
from this second. Yet from where do we receive the first point of comparison for our experience? We must set this point whenever we start
experiencing something as temporal, because nothing in itself is first.

Time experience thus depends also on knowledge, which then
serves as the standard point from which we start comparing. Therefore
'we must adopt a standard of first and last, there is nothing in its own
nature the prototype of first and last' (1.498). The alternative would be
that contained in our time experience we should find an absolute reference point for any form of thisness – for instance the experiential presence of an absolute beginning or of an absolute end. Heidegger's
being-toward-death would be such an alternative, which gives time its
determination. Peirce, in contrast, has his reasons for holding on to
Continuity, in the triadic requirement of time experience as in essence
having no limit. The logical expression of the dyadic requirement lies
in a sequence of propositions that follow one another. If two propositions on the same subject are both true, events are unconnected or
simultaneous. If one of the two propositions cannot be true if the other
is true, we must conclude that one follows the other in a temporal succession. This gives form to knowledge; in other words when cognizing
we say one follows from the other.

The third clause of the law of time is the triadic requirement "that
time has no limit, and every portion of time is bounded by two instants
which are of it, and between any two instants either way round,
instants may be interposed such that taking any possible multitude of
objects there is at least one interposed event for every unit of that multitude' (1.498). How can this be thought together (as we have seen, the

unity of thought is the very nature of law) with the second clause? The answer is that time in itself has no limit (expressed topographically, 'since every portion of time is bounded by two instants, there must be a connection of time ring-wise' [1.498]). Yet this does not preclude events from being limited to portions of this ring. The dyadic requirement of time-as-experience interrupts the closure of the ring of time-in-itself and applies a standard to its operation of comparing. Time-in-itself must be different from events for the following reason: 'For since the instants, or possible events, are as many as any collection whatever, and there is no maximum collection, it follows that they are more than any collections whatever. They must, therefore, be individually indistinguishable in their very existence – that is, are distinguishable and the parts distinguishable indefinitely, but yet not composed of individuals absolutely self-identical and distinct from one another – that is, they form a continuum' 1.499).

Why is it crucial for the being of Time that it be Continuous? First, otherwise it could not be a law. Continuity is the only triadic requirement in the logical and metaphysical determination of Time. Indeed, Continuity is a potent unifier of the multiple, which in the case of time is not the multiple of senses but the multiple of the abnumerable events or the abnumerable contrary states. Just as thoughts can unify in a logical form, Continuity unifies being metaphysically. That continuity is also the ultimate guarantee of the process of Interpretation in the Sign is related to the interpretability of Reality, in keeping with a realist sign theory. Opting for Reality instead of a system of positional values (as in the semiological sign theory) must have these metaphysical consequences. Without these consequences, Semiotic would dangle in the thin air of idealism. Second (connected with the first), there would be no unification, only moments. Therefore, there could be no narration either, but only events and changes. An episode refers already to a portion of a whole, where it subsists only under an already established narrative teleology. In this way the triadic requirement of the law of temporal being connects perfectly with the requirement of teleological time for narration.

All three clauses together form the law of time – that is, they describe the logical nature of that part of being which is subject to time. As mentioned earlier, beneath the lower limit of the law of time there are contingent metaphysical laws 'which have no relation to logic. And with this division another is closely connected, namely, the division of the latter class of laws into those which are imposed upon objects as reacting upon one another existentially, as merely coexistent, which are the laws of space' (1.488). The most contingent laws are those 'which are only imposed upon objects in so far as their mode of existence is in its own metaphysical nature that of a subject, that is, laws of substantial things' (1.488). Being not being simple, there is no single, uniform being, and even less is there a material, raw physical being that in the form of data can then be subject to the cognizing mind.

Here is also the ultimate reason why Constructivism would have difficulties grasping the cognition of time. For it is evident that the signs ('top-down schemata') used for experiencing time must be capable of experiencing precisely this, which is so different from colours (monadic Quality) and from spatial parameters. We explored earlier how the Sign form adapts to this special cognitive object Time. We have also already explored the conditions for the possibility of representing Time in Symbolic Signs (which is, as with teleological Signs, again somewhat different from experiencing time). In those earlier discussions, we had to take it for granted that Time is not narration; we now have analyzed why this is so. Time is represented in narration, but the unifying force of time is narrative finality, which is not contingent on a dyadic structure of events. The temporal element of event diversity is not anchored to the same subject, but rather to the narrative enunciation as *origo* of narrating *this* universe. Thus, the subject identity through diverse states is strictly the same narrator subject, first as living and second as narrating, in a pragmatic or fictional state. This provides the necessary foundation for the narrative time effect of teleology. It also suffices for the setting of a secondary, derived zero standard for the before and after of events. These, then, become events of now-I-tell-you-that after now-I-tell-you-this. The temporality of narration imitates time not only in teleology but also in the sense that it spreads out the idea as before and after. Now it becomes purposeful, through the order in which an 'aiming element' is narrated. Through this purpose, we automatically make a comparison with the temporally next element as the logically second element of the same subject. Such automatism is only reliable under the premise that this teleology is enunciated. This is (Pragmaticistic) belief; whereas confusion in the order of narration – that is, presentation of plot information outside a strict logical order – is not a real doubt. Its clarification can be suspended, as long as the belief in the foundational narrative end can be maintained. Thus it is a real *post hoc ergo propter hoc* logic that needs only to follow final causality and that is not contingent on efficient causes. In the experience of time, however, the order of first and second is determinant for a causality that becomes efficient only in this logical order. However, the teleological imitation of events in narration does not transform the final into an efficient causality.

Peirce himself mentions in passing this difference: 'Imaginary events, the course of a romance, are represented as having relations like those of time among one another, but they have no real places in time. A historical romance connects itself, more or less definitely, with real time; but that is because it "makes believe" they [the imaginary events] are real events. It is, then, only existentially real events which the law of time represents really to have places in real time' (1.492). All of this is fully understood only in the context of Signs of Time, which will have their experience in their Second Correlate, but which will relate to the Continuity of Interpretation in a way different from the Continuity of Time-in-itself.[25]

To conclude, let us now draw consequences for two of the most distinctively Peircean aspects of an understanding of time: (1) One 'adopts a standard of first and last." (2) Time is a Continuum (1.499).

Regarding (1): Other than with Heidegger (cf. *infra*), the Peircean philosophy of time has no absolute *terminus ad quem* (death) as zero reference – nor a *terminus ab quo*, for that matter. True Continua are infinite and supra-abnumerable. Thus, there is always a next instant. Assuming some experience as standard makes time practical and experiential; however, that standard is not the origin. Time as thought-like being has its origin in any two contrary states of an event, provided they can be related. By necessity this results in the demise of psychological approaches to time (as triple present). Instead of thought and triadic law, in the psychological Now time becomes whole and one through the psyche. Thought is more than existence. Law of time is more than a feeling of passing (which is, however, its monadic requirement).

Regarding (2): Now there is no doubt that thought is lawlike in nature. It is less obvious that law can comprise time. The usual way of approaching events logically is that causal links, as mental form, are added to data. Schematism as we encountered it in Constructivism works in this manner, but it is founded merely on *a priori* forms, not on Real generalities. True Continua are real, however; their reality is the presupposition that time can be a law of being. It follows from a Pragmaticistic argumentation that Time is capable of becoming a sign relation and therefore cognizable experience. This Thirdness of the law of time is inherent in subjects as form. Albeit in a similar way to the forms of thought, with time these forms are 'analogous' (1.500).

Of fundamental importance are the consequences of all this for cinematic narratology: (1) There is no further need to construct another Being-a-whole outside of time (cosmological, physical, movement) in a humanized variant as psychic temporality. The wholeness of time from a Semiotic perspective is that of being a Real Possibility. (2) Time is real, but it does not exist. Its being is that of a metaphysical law and not that of truth states. So in a certain way it is similar to a logical sign relation. It Represents a dyadic difference of contrary existential states in one subject, as a logical law analogous to thinking as a process.

Regarding point (1): Although time requires a differentiating relation between two contrary 'thisnesses' in an event, it would still be impossible without the unity being one pure Continuity of all possible events. So it becomes law, because it cannot be limited to dyadic facts. Time without a monadic Quality could not be experienced: *this* subject with *this* duration is needed. If everything was as eternal as a mathematic formula, there could be no time, nor could there be any possibility of action. There is no proof that such monadic Qualities must be (this is why it is only a contingent metaphysical law); but if there are such Qualities, they appear phenomenologically as monads. This mode of being of time (i.e., law) is the condition also for its cognition – that is, for corresponding Semiotic processes. From statements (for the monadic requirement) to propositions and general arguments (for the triadic requirement of Continuity), we have all the corresponding logical forms of the experience of time.

As always, the more complex forms comprehend the relationally simpler ones. Having arrived at a general understanding of time – for instance as history, evolution, cosmic durations – we must have the thisness of changes and the statements of actual states. We can imagine how time as triadic cognition can degenerate, but it will always be a degenerate triad and therefore a degenerate Sign. Depending on the nature of the First in the Sign relation, such a degeneration can be forced. If there is narration, the First must be a (Rhematic Symbolic) Legisign; possible degenerations of narration were discussed earlier as Moment and event imitation. Even though Time is a metaphysical law, it is – through its triadic logical nature – also cognition and Sign. At a later stage time, already as meaning, is linked to conduct of behaviour. As was illustrated earlier, self-controlled action as cognitive conduct fulfils all the requirements of a law of time, including the part of Continuous generality. Action can go on forever, as Interpretational conduct. Without this presence of limitless continuation, it is not human action.

As a later discussion of Ricoeur's poetics will reveal (cf. *infra*), such a theory amounts to a clear solution to a foundational problem of narratology. Ricoeur's approach finds an entirely different (Existential-Phenomenological) solution to the time unity problem; that said, Continuity results in no less coherent temporal unity. If time could not be thought, in the sense of 'states thought together,' narration and narrative configuration would be arbitrary acts of conventional schematization. A logical default of this sort is owed to a failure to comprehend the being and sign relation of time.[26]

If we succeed, however in making time constitutive of the sign relation, then there is more than a syntagmatic, and more than even a psychic unity – there is a Real temporal order. Semiotic wholeness in its entirety is based on the metaphysical unity of the world as a cognizable. As we have seen in Peirce's understanding of time, this is not the result of a fallacious 'metaphysical appearance,' which is a false belief. In this metaphysic, however, there is a very special sort of generality, Continuity, which is pre-phenomenal. Its ultimate ramification for the social and temporal concreteness of cognition is Pragmaticistic conduct of behaviour. This narration as its representation can blend into Pragmaticism as a whole, as one form of it. This Pragmaticistic logic is not 'outside' an 'authentic' (in a Heideggerian sense) temporality, it *is intrinsically* time.

Regarding point (2): Oneness of time in a conception based on Continuity easily finds its way into the manner in which time is a sign. But at the same time, the dyadic difference must also be represented. Continuous Oneness does more than provide the conditions for the possibility of understanding the necessarily different semioses of Time. It also enables a sign process that presents Time merely as Quality, including in otherwise more complex semioses such as narration. Time used to be conceived of as incognizable, as an *a priori* form of apperception. If it were that, it could never become a sign process. From a Peircean perspective, we can so far agree with Heidegger (1927: 432 n30), who criticized idealism for its countability concept of time movement (i.e., for being intrinsically identical with Aristotle's concept [cf. *infra*]). The numerable alone – different states or the discrete as such – is not time; it is merely its dyadic requirement, the basis of its experience. Although it is not discrete, the 'now,' the present moment, is also not time. If time is triadic in its being such that it can also be understood as triadic sign relation, then all of this is in the sign. Two 'nows' are thus contained in the dyadic requirement of the time law. Although one 'now' cannot yet attain the status of being cognized as timelike, a comparison of different states must presuppose at least two signs of 'now.' The time sign can thus shift its 'attention' to any of its constituent correlates. It can be awareness of passing, but at the same time it can never become entirely oblivious to Continuity, which gives it unity. Also, it could be awareness of evolutionary law, without forgetting the dyadic difference of change.

4.3 Cinematic Time

For cinema, the particular importance of a modal understanding of time and time semiosis stands out as soon as we attempt to analyse the unusual time relations in certain films. There is no point in investigating – *nemine contradicente* – cinematic narration as such. A Semiotic theory of literature could consist only in its comprehensive understanding of the entire range of possible meaning, where the major part is already covered by language-based theories. Beyond those theories, the 'literary' upshot of Semiotic is quite interesting. This can be demonstrated only with unusual works – particular, works of cinematic art. Although narrative manipulation of temporality is normal practice in cinema, some films achieve a particular presence of time that effectively transcends narrativity. Such a borderline position where time is no longer a consecution of moments, but only Wholeness – without, however, destroying narration – thrives only on the cinematic Sign. Olmi's Genesi (v. *supra*) provides a general idea of this. It would probably be preposterous to assume that there is a pattern of transcending narration common to all films. Thus, our later analysis of Dreyer's *Ordet* will provide only another, diverse example, not the formula. Olmi's Sign Represents the before-of-time; Dreyer transcends narration into after-time.

These examples of exceptional cinematic quality are a challenge to any theory that claims to grasp time. According to the usual concepts of time, what we perceive in these films can never be visible. It is more than beyond explanation – it is not there at all (which perhaps reflects the adage that 'we see only what we know'). These films, with their deeper, transnarrative quality, could not have been made with a mere teleological idea of time. They narrate in a different temporality, as it were, one in which pragmatic purpose is invalidated. At best, this sort of time can become finality ('closure,' as Bordwell suggests for Dreyer), or a strong beginning; it cannot become a whole. As a first principle, we must reject the notion that transnarrative time is incognizable and without meaning. Such incognizable entities can be expunged without difficulty in the antitranscendentalist context of Semiotic. If the 'whole' of time were such an entity, it would not be worth defending and we would not even be aware of it. Thus, finding evidence of it in a work of cinematic art amounts to cognizing it as meaning and to relying on this particular mode of Reality of Time – that is, it amounts to presupposing a theory that is neither nominalistic nor psychologizing. The crucial point involves not the simple claim to such a particular temporal meaning, but rather the demonstration and Semiotic reconstruction of its functioning. We must shift our attention to those Signs in which dyadic aspects of consecutivity become irrelevant. This is so for both *Ordet* and *Genesi*, but in different ways.

Before we approach one outstanding example of this particular meaning, it might be interesting to review the conceptual arsenals of various theories of time and cinematic narrativity. Any understanding (or misunderstanding) of time cannot help but have an immediate impact on our understanding of narration, of ways of narrating, especially in cinema. So let us take three well-known alternative concepts of time and put them to the test.

(1) Deleuze's Bergson-inspired film theory is perhaps the only film theory capable of intuiting the Whole of time as a meaning *sui generis*. This, however, has a price. As we have seen, it permits an organic evolution of narration as particular instance of movement. Cinema must be narrative as long as we understand it as movement. As soon as movement comes to an end, and thought sets in, time begins to 'crystallize' – a nice metaphor for saying that something else has taken over the entire stage. However, cinema is by then already beyond narration, because in this theory context it is no longer thinkable that the same Time is also a Continuous Whole. For its theory of time, Bergsonism needs the difference between the Dividual and the Individual, between Space and Duration. Space is thus thought of as dividability and time as Wholeness. The mediation between the division and the whole, however, becomes a matter of ontological attitude. Time is there as intuition only, as an ontological object. Therefore, time must remain by nature outside the sphere of judgment, and consequently outside of Critique. Evidently, a Peircean film theory does not involve a dichotomy of time-movement (which is the dyadic requirement) and time-time (which is Continuity beyond parts). One can think it all together, in the very sign process itself.

(2) Seemingly, there is no direct impact on film theory from a Kan-

tian understanding of time. Despite appearances, though, the quasi-transcendental schematism of time as 'concept' of order is widespread. Casebier (1991: 3f) is certainly right in taking nominalism as the overarching approach in film theory (and he provides many extracts in support of this). From his vantage point of phenomenological immediate consciousness he must see this reductionism also in Cognitivist film theory. This is especially virulent in conceptions of the temporal essence of cinema. Time is understood in a merely formal way. Thus it becomes the Other of experience (v. *supra*, Werner 1985). It plays a unificatory role precisely because it is not experience. Bergson overcame this dichotomy; in doing so, however, he lost the Critical potential inherent in Kant's transcendentalism. Instances of this time concept in film theory abound, so it is merely for the sake of providing examples to mention the formalism of Neoformalism. Bordwell, as a Formalist and even less as a Constructivist, can integrate time only as temporal ordering.

(3) Of greater interest, although certainly different from Peirce, is a phenomenological-existential understanding of time. It was noted earlier that Husserlian phenomenology could have provided an interesting and non-nominalistic theory of cinematic time. Although it seems that this thread has never been taken up, Ricoeur proves its general value for narratology. Surprisingly, Casebier (1991) neglects Husserl's and Heidegger's investigations of time consciousness. Yet Heidegger has had a much broader (albeit somewhat latent) influence on thinking about time. Foucault and Derrida are avowedly Heideggerian when it comes to understanding an authentic being-whole, which is so dependent on temporality and Care. The philosophical problem named 'time' as inherited from Kant was a problem of unification. In taking up St Augustine's psychologism, Husserl located the wholeness in the immediacy of the psyche (Caring Being-toward-death, in Heidegger). The disadvantage in both is the loss of generality, which can be thought of in Peirce. Just as death is *'je-meinig'* (Heidegger 1927: 240: 'in each case one's own'), the psyche's wholeness of time is limited to one's immediate consciousness (in St Augustine, in front of the eternal God). Evidently, that is a solitary way of thinking of time. Not surprisingly, Ricoeur felt the need to correct this limitation by applying an external pragmatic logic (cf. *infra*).

A 'natural' advantage in film theory for the phenomenological-hermeneutical tradition its inherent psychologism. This has been demonstrated with great success by Reception Aesthetics and the Reader

Response theory. Over Metz's loud protests, this tradition has formed alliances with enunciation theory (v. §3.4.1), which was originally a purely linguistic theory. Metz's objection has a strong basis: *énonciation* has no original and genuine relation to questions of identity and subjectivity. We shall see later that enunciation can be understood perfectly as a dyadic determination in the sign process. Thus it is not the 'natural' setting for an intuitively correct intersubject communication that could offer an advantage to hermeneutical literary theories. This is not even a unique purchase on narration. Unique, instead, is how the temporality of narrative configuration is deduced from the originary time in an immediate consciousness. Critical questions must be raised at this level, in light of the derived capacity to explain the real qualities of narration. Anticipating our more extensive debate, it is clear that narrative unity remains dependent on the unificatory achievement of the immediate consciousness of time. This comprises the public nature of what can be communicated, but also of what is socially shared in narration. These ramifications, however, are to be compared not with the alternatives, but rather with the core. A debate with Kantian time concepts has taken place from within the phenomenological approach. Deleuze, for his part, has distanced his philosophy of time quite pointedly from phenomenology. Thus we are left with the task of critically discussing the problem from a Peircean viewpoint.

Peirce is in contrast to all three alternatives. Like those other conceptions, his must affect our understanding of cinematic narration. In this Semiotic has two main advantages. The first is that it offers a more adequate understanding of cinematic narration (see §5). The second will reveal itself later when we explore how aesthetic objects are created (e.g., through a narration).

In any case, Deleuze and Ricoeur share the merit of articulating the ineluctably temporal essence of narration. In/through the end, a narrative evolves out of time and not from objects. Thus the semantic core of a narrative is not a concept but an action (i.e., as conduct a desire toward a future state).

Transnarrative Time and aesthetic (in Peirce's original sense of the term) are related. This meaning can originate only in the First Correlate of narration, by aestheticizing narration (which is not a contradiction in terms). The reason for this kind of Interpretation relates to the nature of narration itself, which does not allow for a supra-narrative Interpretation with a meaning beyond the narrative. At any rate, the 'moral' of the story does not count as such a meaning, because 'moral' contains only teleology and is just another way of stating the narrative purpose. That narration cannot be extended into a narratively modelled life (in spite of the usage of narrative and film models in politics, terror attacks, etc.) is due to enunciation. At some point the enunciation of a narrative will terminate its narrative contract as fulfilled, at which point narrative time will also end. Only when life is no longer lived but represented – that is, as taking place under an obligation or as a destination – does it become a narrative, but at the price of having-been-live. Only then can one narrative amalgamate with its other and coincide a hypostasized enunciation with the I-now-here enunciation of a concrete narrative text.

Degeneration of the narrative Sign, of its teleological meaning, can take place in two ways, according to its constructive elements. Teleology degenerates into dyads – for example, when it is reduced to waiting for the next right event – and is then experienced as 'suspense.' Narrative relationality, however, is also capable of monadic degeneration, which was apostrophized earlier as Moment. This is more a metaphoric term and is intended in a sense almost contrary to its literal meaning of 'movement.' It is a meaning of time before movement, before it becomes change. Its logical form of production is interesting. A Moment is not a physical unit yet it is still a monadic degeneration of narrative logic. As such, it is close to perception – aesthetical in Peirce's sense. Now the question is, what is percept in narrative temporality? This seems self-contradictory. Is it not intrinsically knowledge? We need to know (i.e., to possess cognitively) the narrative end, the purpose of narrative action, which is never visible as such, in order to understand even a single element. It cannot be denied that teleology is indeed constitutive for narration. So the next question is, what can we perceive in a teleology?

Purpose is certainly the initial cognition required for narrative teleology. Folded into this cognition, however, is a pragmatic value, which in narration gives value to the desired outcome. As a normative value this is quite particular, because narration is not behaviour in the full sense. It is not itself guided by a direct truth value; rather, it is anchored solely to an act of narrating, which is truthful in the sense that it vouches for the creation of an artificial universe with no further reality constraints. Narration, as final value of purpose, is a logical value that differentiates narrative elements as leading more or less cogently toward the desired end. Next to these two normative values, narration also enshrines a monadic normativity that does not differentiate. It is simply admirable and not the choice between admirable and not admirable. As we saw in our analysis of the Normative Sciences of all types of self-controlled conduct, presupposing a basic desire is necessary for action as such, even before we decern what should and what should not be done.

This normative value is also fundamental to narration. It can no longer be cognized; only perceived aesthetically. Thus the Moment is only a temporal expression of a basic, non-discriminating pragmatic value before any choice is made between objects of desire. This can only be a stage before action, a moment before the *incipit* itself. The not yet present vector is the stasis of time but not the absence of time. A vectorless time is a whole, not yet unfolded or unfolding. As a double degenerate Sign of teleology, it is however still time as meaning, not as a meaningless physical entity.

This wholeness is quite different from totality. Even as a meaning it can never transcend narrativity to become a philosophy of history (as in Hegel). It is a whole that does not know everything. The monadic degeneration of narrativity produces only a whole that can be admired *in toto*, not as a total or the totally grasped. Furthermore, this is still a determinate kind of narrativity and is not reduced to an atemporal, pure image (image without historia, only pure aesthetic qualities, comparable to Kant's *Naturschönem*). Evidently, this time without vectors is also a time without a standard zero point as point of reference. It is, as meaning, the oneness of time before time unfolds.

The decisive practical question is now this: How does this kind of narrativity prevail as Sign against the pressure of teleology? There is no answer to this question. It is evident that the logical character of such a Sign is not constraining and has no necessity. Consequently it can only be shown and experienced. Logical constraints function only in teleology. All that showing the Moment can do, therefore, is evidence the Interpretational irrelevance of teleology, the confinement of its determinant role for Interpretation. *Genesi* and *Ordet* confine in a rather different manner, though. Before all time there is no purpose (yet). Thus, *Genesi* makes the camera meander over waters, aimless also in terms of meaning. In *Ordet* all purpose ends with and in death, and does so in such a way that it does not nurture any hope of amending (Propp's narrative function 'K' *Réparation du méfait ou du manque*) and thus of strengthening hopes of meaningfulness.

The representational effect of time is strongest when a standard of reference is established. Thus, giving up such an anchorage in a zero point for the time of action has its effects. Action itself is 'freed.' This alone makes for a considerable strangeness in narratives. Furthermore, that 'freedom' can be taken as such, and when it is, the result is pure aesthetics. In *Ordet* we will encounter one of the most extraordinary examples of a liberation of time, from within time.

Yet cinema disposes time quite freely. Time can always be 'taken as' a point (end, summit, beginning, disappointment, etc.) for pragmatic intervention if a semiosis requires it. Furthermore, time in cinema can be a Continuity or a flowing present, if there is no need for pragmatic reference. In *Thérèse* there are moments of pure contemplation, in which Time has no aim, goal, or telos and nothing is to be reached. In one sequence, an old nun is being washed, and in her dying (#122–38 and 143–50 in the published *scénario*; Cavalier [1987]), time is timeless, as it were. Remarkably, this takes place in a narrative film. It would surprise us less in a music feature; consider, for example, some sequences in François Girard's *Thirty-two Short Films about Glenn Gould* and in Jean-Marie Straub's *Die Chronik der Anna Magdalena Bach* (inspired by her *Notenbüchlein*). Thérèse can be taken as Cavalier's consummate aesthetic achievement, because it unties language from reality with regard to time so that the pragmatic grip on temporal organization becomes looser if not completely lost. One might say that the only remainder is presence, time passing.

We can now test this Peircean Semiotic insight against one of the most impressive of all cinematic narrations: Carl-Theodor Dreyer's *Ordet* (which appears on almost all '100 best films in film history' lists).

Intermezzo: Two Kinds of Narrative Time in Dreyer's *Ordet*

Ordet is without question an intense and remarkable narration. However, we can do no greater harm to this film than by constraining it to narration. In fact it is a paradigm for how the narration-constitutive 'purpose' can be transcended by narrative means – how 'purposiveness' itself can give way to a transcendent instantiation of time.

Ordet exhausts narration as 'order through time.' This is clearly already felt to be the exhaustion of narrative credibility, yet astonishingly, the credibility gap is not critical to the cinematic impression. What would be destructive for any other closely knit narrative has – and we will see how – been assisted by Dreyer's cinematic form. We are now in a position to grasp the intricacies of different productions of time, which would be impossible without an understanding of the modes of Time. Without this subtlety, we would merely perceive teleology: all time (schemata) in narratives as ordered by a purpose. For the temporality of resurrection, as shown in *Ordet*, this would be a catastrophe. Such reduced temporality would miss the subtlety of Dreyer's narration. Furthermore, we would also miss the enormous difference between this and Godard's narration of the same subject (v. *supra* Intermezzo, 248).

Perhaps this sketch makes astonishing claims. Is it perhaps easy to discover any representational ambiguities, which would allow for the appearance of representational questions about the quiddity of objects? Certainly not, as all is plainly clear. In this regard, *Ordet* is quite unlike Godard's *Je vous salue, Marie*, which plays aesthetically with doubtful meanings of represented objects. Rhetorical figuration is Godard's way out of meaningless, rigid discourse; Dreyer stays within the narrative configuration. He does not achieve what he does by stepping out of the screen toward the audience, which is what rhetorical cinema does. From safely behind or on the screen, Dreyer leaves its temporal universe through the door of eternity. Although the topic is very similar in both films, Dreyer's is quite dissimilar from either Godard's or *a fortiori* from televangelist shows.[27] The point to prove with *Ordet*, aided by a Peircean time theory, is that it involves a different form of temporal reiconization of a normally completely Symbolic semiosis: narration.

Rarely is *Ordet* interpreted from the perspective of temporality. Time does not seem to be the subject (or the *syuzhet*). The debate over its interpretation most often focuses on its religious or feminist or formal significance. However, the fact that resurrection is not only the narrative pivot but even the title itself should tell us something. As a narrative project this is certainly extremely difficult and in need of great mastery. Lacking this mastery, the film maker would be in constant danger of lapsing into a banal Disney fairytale, a miracle of the crisis-reversal type, or just an imagery of wishful thinking. Dreyer succeeded in avoiding these traps, so he must have found a way to deal with time: the end of time, time at a total standstill in death; and beginning with emphasis. Time in *Ordet* is not the subject itself; rather, it is the condition of the possibility of the subject 'resurrection.' All of our written accounts here will be bound by the sentence structure, or narrative précis – under the rule of a purpose (a clearly defined class of Signs) and are therefore caught in its teleology. That said, cinema is not bound to this mode of temporal being.

Every film has its own fate in film critique. This has been especially so with most of Dreyer's films. Indeed, there has been an ongoing fight over the interpretation of what at first sight does not even seem to be an overly cryptic work. Dreyer has been praised and loathed for his spiritual cinema, his aesthetic, his humanism. In his book about Dreyer, Bordwell criticizes these approaches for taking as a given that Dreyer is making sense without difficulty, clearly and comprehensibly. He insists instead that there are incoherences and even strangeness to be found: 'If we read the films as "about" some slippery religious or psychological states, we ought to realize that this infinitely elastic principle of interpretation pays the price of insipidity. I shall try to show that the films' primary importance is not thematic but *formal* and *perceptual*' (1981: 3). It is true that the temptation of falling into 'genre overcoding,' as Eco (1979: 19–23) calls it, is always present in film discourse. Dreyer's narratives clearly show their colours. Also he uses in his narratives strong (innuendos of) novelistic conventions. Indeed, not everything needs to be said once the genre of the course of narrative events is set. Dreyer's films lend themselves to being seen as *variazioni con tema*, so to speak; not one of them is cryptic or is an entirely novel type of narrative. Dreyer himself declared repeatedly in interviews that up to a certain point he always tried to respect his audience by adhering to their viewing expectations. Yet such use of narrative patrimony, this strategic choice to stay within the bounds of tradition with regard to narratives, does not preclude originality on Dreyer's part. He cannot be interpreted adequately by 'intertextual competence' alone, and film discourse should respect his claim that beyond a certain point he feels solely responsible to his artistic conscience and not to the audience's approval.

Femininity: *Ordet* According to Drouzy

What is the 'authentic Dreyer interpretation' war all about, then? Certainly, one of the most deviant arguments involves basing interpretation on biographical facts, or even on Dreyer's autobiographical statements. When we do this we are retreating into a crude auteurism. Clearly, it is not Dreyer, the human being, who is communicating through his films. On the contrary, the films are referring not to their physical author, but rather, at most, to an auctorial instance within them. Films are and must be perfectly understandable without the least knowledge of biographical facts. Most interpreters generally would subscribe to this; nevertheless, there is a tradition in interpretation that attempts to read texts in a bad sense 'against the grain.' The text thus immediately becomes a symptom to be deciphered psychoanalytically. In this way – it is believed – we can uncover either ideologies or the author's psyche. In the latter case, this leads inevitably to a therapeutic narrative, where persona defines herself as/is her own (hi-)story.[28]

This tends to be the discourse in Drouzy (1982), who identifies (rather convincingly) Dreyer's natural mother and who also conjectures (less convincingly) on the identity of his natural father. Dreyer himself, when he was eighteen, undertook this sort of research into his origins. Having learned what Drouzy (probably) later discovered, he kept it secret (except from his wife). Dreyer's 'official' autobiographical notes indicate that his childhood was very painful – a fact highlighted by some critics of his films. Given these 'objective' coordinates, we need little imagination to guess how Dreyer's personality became what it was. Accordingly, Drouzy discusses which symptoms Dreyer's traumatized psyche could have chosen but did not choose, except one: his eternal preoccupation with the figure of a victimized woman and her struggle to free herself from her bonds. This symptom appears only in his films, not in his private life or elsewhere. Drouzy's point is that the narrative of Dreyer's films must be read as a sort of psychoanalytical reappraisal of the past. But part of what? Of precisely those facts Drouzy succeeded in uncovering. His therapeutic reconstruction narrative is supposed to be privy to the psychological state of Dreyer's mother, Josefine Nilsson; furthermore, he writes as if he had privileged access to Dreyer's own interiority. He deduces Dreyer's traumatic experiences with a 'sharp analytical insight and depth view.' This sort of knowledge is the domain and prerogative of novelists. In a historiographic narrative, this sort of conjecture is inadmissible. The time of a film in this sort of interpretation is of course emphatically past (which is *also* a teleology, though in the other direction).

The main problem with Drouzy's work, aside from these methodological questions, is reflected in his stated reasons for writing this type of biography. He defends himself against requests for privacy from Dreyer's family by claiming that the information he has succeeded in gathering will help us understand what Dreyer was trying o say in his films. If this were really so, Dreyer's work would be merely a highly idiosyncratic 'labour,' psychic travail, bereft of all universality, mirroring only his personal trauma. Hermeneutically, such an approach can only be qualified as therapeutic.[29] We would immediately have to bracket out all of Dreyer's truth claims and interpret them as distorted veracity claims.[30] Drouzy's interpretations of Dreyer's works are consistently therapeutic. With a discoverer's complacency, he notes throughout that Dreyer was concerned only with showing women who become victims of their trust in unworthy men. These 'symptoms' of Dreyer's trauma constitute, as it were, Dreyer's wounded psyche longing for redemption from unbearably destructive suffering: from *Präsidenten*'s daughter Victorine Lippert, to *Jeanne d'Arc*, to Anne Pedersdotter in *Vredens Dag*, and to *Gertrud*. Only this makes possible such unheard of things as miracles and resurrection from the dead such as Inger's in *Ordet*. Even if this could identify one of Dreyer's subjects as comparable to other authors' preoccupations in their films,[31] it is dangerously narcotizing as an explanation.

Film theorists should not be psychotherapists. They should not be trying to explain Dreyer through his films, but to explain his films *tout court*. To this end, they should take these films literally and not as symptoms. Until 1982, this would surely have been the typical viewing experience of any spectator who had not read Drouzy's revelations. Drouzy's interpretation of *Ordet* is no less objectionable. His argument for an 'authentic' interpretation of Dreyer's work is directed against 'spiritualist' appropriations that would make his an antireligious exegesis of a feminine mystique. Dreyer, he argues, had for more than two decades an especially dear project, which was finally aborted: a film about Jesus. He meant both *Ordet* and *Gertrud* to be preparations for it (cf. Bordwell (1981: 221)).

To look for intertextual cues in that aborted film, there is no other place than its published script. To demonstrate the non-religious meaning of this film, Drouzy argues as follows: (1) *Jesus* is an 'oeuvre prosémite,' Jesus is but a 'juif parmi les Juifs.' In this, Dreyer shows 'un sens quasi infaillible de l'incarnation.'[32] (2) Jesus happened to become caught up in the political struggle against the Romans. He is merely 'une victime exemplaire, un idéaliste, compromis sans s'en douter dans un imbroglio politique ... Son Jésus est un homme authentique et exceptionnel mais n'est que cela' (ibid.: 330). 'Pour expliquer sa conduite et sa prédication il n'est nullement nécessaire, selon le cinéaste, de faire appel à une Parole révélée ou à une transcendance,' according to Drouzy, with regard to a project that was prepared for a film like *Ordet*. (3) Miracles in Dreyer's script are easily explained. Drouzy is careful, however, not to declare that it is Dreyer who explains them thus: 'par une communication télépathique ... clairvoyance ... la salive [et] la boue

[qui] possèdent des vertus thérapeutiques.' This means exactly cheapening Dreyer into a fairytale. (4) Regarding Jesus' declarations of his divine origins: 'il faut les comprendre dans un sens figuré' (ibid.: 331). (5) The reason behind all this is that 'La foi en Dieu implique une trahison de l'homme' (ibid.: 332) – a pop-Nietzschean argument. (6) Jesus is a partisan for the poor, in particular for poor women ('Jésus féministe avant la lettre'). Drouzy supports this claim by noting that Dreyer brought into his script three neotestamentary scenes with women (without saying that there are many more). 'Si durant trente années de sa vie ou plus Dreyer a été fasciné par la figure du Nazaréen, ce n'est donc pas dans le contexte d'une problématique religieuse, parce que Jésus était Dieu ou prétendait l'être. Au contraire! C'est plutôt, selon la logique d'une pensée humaniste, parce que ne l'étant pas il pouvait d'autant plus facilement prêcher la fraternité universelle, prendre la défense des faibles et en particulier rétablir la femme dans sa dignité ... l'idée-force qui a inspiré ... la réhabilitation de la femme et des valeurs féminines comme condition, à la fois nécessaire et suffisante, pour que la terre des hommes devienne humaine et habitable' (ibid. 333).

Is this an interpretation of Dreyer's script, or is it Drouzy's theological treatise à l'envers? Drouzy does not even render Dreyer's narrative nearly exactly. Certainly it is pertinent to Ordet that Dreyer was planning this film and did not want to jettison his ideas completely. Here, Johannes follows closely the incarnational aspect of Jesus, in Jutland as much as when portraying Jesus[33] not as a Thorvaldsen Christ with nordic traits but as the Aramaic Jew that he was. Not so for Drouzy, for whom Jesus was some sort of revolutionary malgré lui. He suppresses indications to the contrary, which in fact figure prominently in Dreyer's rendering as miracles and as Jesus' own declarations about his identity. Drouzy's constructs fail completely, however, once we notice that there are no 'normal' explanations of miracles in Jesus. It speaks for Dreyer's historical fidelity that he did not show Jesus as God. Nowhere in the gospels is 'God' applied to someone other than his Father. In Israel, Jesus saw himself only in apocalyptic, prophetic, and general theological terms such as messiah (= the anointed one), Servant of Jahwe (Jesaiah), son of God, son of man (Daniel), and so forth. And his contemporaries saw him the same way.

Drouzy is short-circuiting an acceptable historical argumentation by making an argument e silentio of the absence in the New Testament of theological (hellenistic) concepts from the third century. Dreyer did not suppress what would have supported Drouzy's argument. So we

find all the scenes that indicate the divinity of Christ during his existence on earth interpreted gradually and progressively by his disciples
after his resurrection. Examples: the entire Lazarus scene (Dreyer 1971:
182f); the scene in which the Samaritan woman learns from Jesus that
He is the Messiah (149); Peter's confession of Jesus' Messianity; and
even the Transfiguration scene, in which Moses says, 'Verily you are
the only Son of God and chosen to establish His Kingdom on Earth.'[34]
If there is a single argument that invalidates Drouzy's interpretation, it
is that Dreyer not only retains, but alters that scene.

The quality of Drouzy's theological treatise is dubious, his interpretation of *Ordet* is lamentable. It is not based on formal observations;
rather, it is an exercise in applying faulty theological theses to a recalci-
trant filmic content. In this regard, the thaumaturgical aspect of Jesus
is at the core of *Ordet's* narrative, in which Jesus is represented by
Johannes. It is quite clear that any stylization of Jesus as a revolutionary, a preacher, or similar did not interest Dreyer to the same degree as
his healing power and redeeming presence. In *Jesus*, the resurrection
narrative is lacking (just as it is in the gospel of Mark, by the way); its
important place in *Ordet* is proof enough that it was of key importance
to Dreyer. So it really is surprising that Drouzy tries to explain 'le
mécanisme de la résurrection' (340). The mechanical parts are the mystical fool, the child, and 'la femme' (343). This latter 'a été la victime
immolée pour la réconciliation des hommes.' Perhaps it would be
more precise to say that Inger has become the victim of Drouzy's prejudgmental interpretation, since in *Ordet* there is nothing at all that
allows us to maintain that anyone is responsible for Inger's death. Conflicts with men did not bring about her death, yet her resurrection
brings men to reconciliation (Peter and Morten), healing (Johannes),
faith (Mikkel), and love (Anders, but also Anne), and brings to her two
daughters a mother. In a word: the fullness of what theology and Pastor Kaj Munk, the author of the homonymous play (which is Dreyer's
script) would call salvation, and what the New Testament and Inger
call 'Life' in the strong sense of the word (i.e., *Ordet*).

There is no point in discussing Drouzy's faith in psychism and '*télé-
pathie*,' since the film itself offers no hints in this direction.[35] His reconstruction of the narrative is focused sharply[36] on his biographical
trouvaille of the redemptive force of the woman.[37] Sometimes he is even
quite wrong – for example, when he states that Dreyer visually composed a universe that is only horizontal. As proof of his figurative
meaning of the term, he states that there is 'aucune échappée sur le

ciel' that Dreyer has created a prison atmosphere with his low, beamed ceilings, which represent all those who are 'écrasés par leur cadre de vie – lui-même symbole de l'esclavage intérieur auquel dogmes et sectarisme les avaient réduits' (ibid.: 342f). On the contrary, the tightly closed universe of Borgensgård[38] is broken up by the vastness of the heavens. Consider here one of the mood-setting opening shots, in which Johannes is shown, high angle from below, preaching his Sermon on the Mount in the dunes of Jutland. This is matched by the amazing flood of light that enters the room where Inger's casket has been placed. At this moment there is again no ceiling enclosing a narrow universe, but instead a true visual 'échappée sur le ciel.'

Drouzy's theological premises are wrong; furthermore, his interpretation demonstrably runs counter to Dreyer's intent. Any cognitive effort that is lawlike must restrict itself to narrative 'purpose,' which is but one (albeit comprehensive) mode of time. Yet Interpretation, especially of this film, should not be limited to that type of meaning. There is also cognition of Time (in narrative form) in other modes, including abductive modes of cognition (cf. *supra*). This avoids sterile debates on the religious meaning of *Ordet*, which is typically understood (cf. Drouzy) as if it were a lawlike cognition. However, this film shows that religious cognition is not the operation of the application of a General law. This is epitomized precisely in the transfiguration of Time. The failure to make a distinction has especially nefarious effects on *Ordet*. Is this film to be interpreted as 'religious'? (A debate usually rages about this.) We cannot decide this question in the same way we can clearly decide on the interpretation of the narrative universe. (This is dissimilar to Godard's film, in which exactly *this* is left unclear, and in which the abductive, rhetorical meaning decides over the narrative universe, cf. *supra*.) *Ordet*'s narrative is exceptionally clear and closed. On this representational basis, through a strict temporal, chronometric order (we are not allowed to skip time, the clock dictates its pace until it is stopped), Dreyer creates a time dimension out of time – a different time.

Ordet's Narrative

Having restricted our purview to narration, we can best clarify the spatiotemporal representation side by following a hierarchical approach. *Ordet* contains precisely three representational universes: besides the principal one, there is Borgen's tale of Johannes's studies and psychiatric anamnesis. Furthermore – and this is highly significant – coexisting with the principal plot is the ambiguous but coherent symbolic universe of Johannes's madness. The relation between these three is far from a simple juxtaposition in the manner of 'parallel montage' cinema. Without ever blending together, they comment on one another. Yet they never coincide. For a classical narration, this is rather unusual in that it violates a basic principle of Aristotelian *Poetic*. The first poetic definition is that tragedy (drama, narration) is an imitation not of men but of action and life and happy and unhappy fate.[39] In 50b23–5 of the *Poetic* we find listed exactly three prerequisites: (1) completeness of the action ($\tau\epsilon\lambda\epsilon\acute{\iota}\alpha$); (2) whole ($\ddot{o}\lambda\eta$) action, that is, in all its parts; and (3) action of a certain length ($\grave{\epsilon}\chi o\acute{\nu}\sigma\eta$ $\tau\iota$ $\mu\acute{\epsilon}\gamma\epsilon\theta os$). Dreyer and Munk place logical parts of the dramatic action in the other strands. Logical wholeness is achieved by having a beginning, a middle, and an end (50b26f: $\tau\grave{o}$ $\ddot{\epsilon}\chi o\nu$ $\grave{\alpha}\rho\chi\grave{\eta}\nu$ $\kappa\alpha\grave{\iota}$ $\mu\acute{\epsilon}\sigma o\nu$ $\kappa\alpha\grave{\iota}$ $\tau\epsilon\lambda\epsilon\upsilon\tau\acute{\eta}\nu$). This prevents one action from ending or from continuing in/as a second action (as is the case here). If there is any doubt, we must establish the respective 'middles,' which are defined as the point where the change of fortune, the $\mu\epsilon\tau\alpha\beta o\lambda\grave{\eta}$, takes place, and there are two in *Ordet*.

Dreyer's narrative artistry lies in the fact that we cannot decide which universe takes over. Johannes, being part of all of them, is, of course, the pivotal character. Because narration is imitation not of men but of action, localization is not a problem here. The two dramas share contiguous spaces: Borgensgård and Peter Petersen's house; as well as three not clearly defined locations: the dunes (during the search for Johannes), the marsh where Mikkel is cutting reeds, and various stretches of the road between Borgensgård and Petersen's. Dreyer is especially carefulto establish visually a temporal unity. He avoids flashbacks and flashforwards. The one exception to this is therefore all the more remarkable. The narrative contains a decisive temporal ellipsis: after Inger's death, Johannes disappears for three days.[40] All of this gives a non-problematic structure of spatiotemporal contiguity to *Ordet* – obviously in keeping with its origins as a dramatic play.

Praxis imitation, plot structure, is no less straightforward in *Ordet*. Except for the very end, there are few surprises. The actions and reactions of the individual characters, once they have been introduced, are both normal and foreseeable. The narrative *Locus* is established in the very opening shot and music, after which we are introduced to each character in succession. Very skilfully, Dreyer associates one person (Johannes) with one initiating narrative *disequilibrium*. Thus the viewer receives all necessary pragmatic clues; this allows the ordering of all events into meaningful temporal successions of single tasks. These tasks bind the cooperating and antagonist characters into a single universe of a single narrative action. Once the principal task is identified, the principal actor is also evident. Once this task is completed, the tale is over, and all other tasks must have fulfilled their ancillary function. This is the principal strand.

Yet Dreyer's film is quite deceptive in its simplicity. To make real sense of *Ordet* (as if it were a whole), we must read it both backwards and forwards. When we do, another universe appears from each direction. In each universe, the same event has a second meaning. If we consider them in an ordered and separate way, the question of universes is settled with the protagonist, the task, and the action. Taking the first scene, this question is open but only minimally so. The first alternative reading requires Borgen to be the protagonist (the entire Borgen clan being the 'actant' subject in semionarratological terms). His task relates to a family saga–type of patriarchal care for the tribe and its black sheep. The second alternative places Johannes at the centre. The universe is now the coming of the Kingdom of God. All events become signs of its hidden presence, and this instils, in the spectator a foreboding of the final event. All of this produces distinct qualities of time. Family sagas have roots in the past, and the past casts its shadows. The Kingdom is here, is now, but it is not visible, not in a now-moment-among-others – there are no historical events in this hidden Jesus/Johannes universe. It has all happened (the Jesus narrative juxtaposed as transparency onto the mad universe of Johannes). It must all still appear. This latent strand is especially strong, and it is responsible for a 'non-clausing narrative closure' in the timeless openness.

In terms of Poetics, this is an impossible narration. Even though it displays features of a kind of $\mu\varepsilon\tau\alpha\beta o\lambda\grave{\eta}$ (Inger's resurrection), there is no real end in time. What could count as an end? Narration being the imitation of praxis action and not of people, pragmatic logic ends actions through completions of tasks. This resurrection is not the solution to a problem. In this sequence the focus is by no means on 'order restored' – that is, it is not on the restoration of an initial disequilibrium. We witness instead how all the people of that universe step out of their 'worries of this time' and how they enter into the universe 'eternal and the same' (twice emphatically in sequence #68; Dreyer 1970: 298). For Dreyer this transformation of time is so important that he mentions it even in the dialogues. However, in reality it is his direct formation of time, which is achieved through cinematic means alone. It is present as a Sign process and strictly speaking has no need of an ancillary Sign process in language (in biblical usage these explicit confirmations of miracles by bystanders are called ἀποφθέγματα). This imagery is of such a type that Inger's life, and Johannes' existence within his new identity, cannot simply be imagined as continuing along the same trajectory. Teleology is suspended. In spite of this, there is no threat to the compactness of the Borgensgård universe. This is because of the peculiar way in which both imitations are interwoven. We cannot decide which one dominates, since the main events make sense in both universes. They differ merely in their temporal approach to the same representational universe. How, then, does Dreyer achieve this peculiar temporality effect? How does he succeed in creating two kinds of time simultaneously? The deceptive simplicity of the 'preferred' reading as saga is slightly threatened from the start. The revelation of the Kingdom is hidden in the camera treatment of Johannes. The overwhelming evidence of the saga indicates that Johannes is enormously odd, a made prophet, yet the camera shows him as indeed a prophet. The low camera angle, the reverent distance, the framing with clouds – all of this reveals him as the promised One (#10 ibid., 241). Seen from the end (i.e., the resurrection of Inger), this was the beginning.

What this means in terms of enunciation instances and narrative sanction (cf. *infra*) can be mentioned here only with respect to its temporal implications. The enunciational point of narrative enunciation is a test of closure, very literally the telling of an end (i.e., teleology). As each enunciation passes a judgment over the protagonist and his task, the viewer is called as judge. With this film, the thrilling experience – and narrative aesthetic – lies in the gradual revision of that judgment. Enunciation (anticipating any critique of undue personification) is a theoretical construct that is the quintessence of narrative probability and possibility. The poetic general concept is (in 51b31f) εἰκός, the probable, and δυνατόν, the possible, which is convincing (51b16). Only the probable and the possible can be the object of poetics, even when the poet represents actual occurrences. Thus the facticity of an event does not make it representable. In consequence, it is only the probable and possible in an event that can ascertain the narrability and credibility of the enunciator. Poetry is about universals (καθόλου 51b7). Dreyer's film, seen as poiesis, presents a choice between the two universes and as such is a struggle among disparate universals. It does not, however, proceed according to the knock-out principle: it is not a police story in which one of two alternatives must turn out to be extensionally deceitful.

This film is also a clear example of how unavoidable enunciation instances are. Their true and unique function is to enable us to understand the task itself. As soon as spectators have understood what the film is about, they share with the enunciation instance the knowledge about the object of value of the narrative action – that is, the task – and they are capable of judging how well it is being or has been completed. *Ordet*, however, is the odd instance of a narrative that has no clear 'aboutness.' What holds the text together, its unification principle, is to be changed on the fly. Near the end, toward the death of Inger, the 'task' of the family patriarch is no longer meaningful and he cannot accomplish it. If the second unifying principle has not taken over by then, the saga can only become a sad deadlock by the time of Inger's wake. It has not even the strength of the decadent decline of a family (as in Visconti's *Gattopardo*). Everything is loose-ended, including the disappearance of Johannes and his eventual but pointless return. Borgen's task cannot be completed, but this is unnoticed –that is, there is no growing uneasiness with the protagonist, as soon as the alternative universe with its own enunciation is firmly believed in as the prevailing *narratio probabilis*. This is probable only in the Kingdom.

These worlds are held together by merely cinematic means. There are no auctorial comments or other interventions of meaning manipulation; these are more typical of Godard's figuration tropes in *Je vous salue, Marie*. The achievement of one narration with two different universes is even more remarkable because there is not even the support of a *narratio probabilis* for the second universe. That improbability results from the narrative logic of the principal saga universe and not from auctorial outside intervention. From within, there had to develop a separate probability in conjunction with the growing credibility of Johannes. On his trajectory from madman to principal enunciation instance, Johannes changes also his *auctoritas*, his 'right to tell,' the very 'narrative contract.' People once commented on him (explaining his madness to the pastor and to the spectator); now he is commenting (seeing, understanding truly) on that other dead-ended universe.

Taking into account that enunciation logically establishes a purpose and that in order to do so it establishes a certain mode of time for realizing this purpose (narrative teleology), we can observe contrasting enunciations in differing temporalities as much as in extensional universes. It is quite unusual, though, for one work to contain more than one enunciation. Even the strictest parallel montage–type cinema is not a simultaneous 'double feature.' Its very existence as one film is a customary guarantee that everything in it is somehow connected. Thus even the authorship of Miéville of the part *'vie de Marie'* in *Je vous salue, Marie* does not stop us from seeing all of the parts as one film; the temporal logic that allows this is to interpret the second part as a continuation of the first part, which implies one narrative purpose. Only through this temporal device is it possible to suppose one narrative universe in spite of the unconnectedness of the plot universes. The narrative unification principle, enunciation, is so strong that it conquers even such gaps. In the case of Dreyer's film, however, one unification presents no doubtful lacunae, or jumps, or audacious inferences. It cannot be connected with a further thread, because all of the elements fit perfectly. The second enunciation is therefore an alternative unification, under a new temporality with less than a narrative purpose. It is not even Godard's hidden rhetorical agenda, which has no need of a different time and universe. The two enunciations unify in two different ways, and the alternative way in Dreyer is imposed through time, which in retrospect becomes purpose, replacing the previous purpose. It is almost as when someone learns to read: after that achievement, a letter will always be a letter and not a graphical shape.

The Danes practically specialize in alternative enunciation narratives. One enunciation makes perfect sense, but then there is a not so obvious key to a different unification, which we usually notice only in hindsight. This pattern is found in Gabriel Axel's *Babettes gaestebud* and in Lars von Trier's *Breaking the Waves*. In both, the alternative vision becomes compelling in hindsight even though it is not achieved by the same temporal means as in *Ordet*. Dreyer's mastery of this is unparalleled. It is subtle enough to subsist in universes and mimetic-pragmatic logics that are not revealed as false, in hindsight, but make perfect sense even in a second logic. For universes (and the corresponding enunciation instances) are unifications under the *Poetic*'s principle of imitation of action. This means that as semantic extensions, they must make sense not as spatiotemporal connectedness, but rather as credible action spaces (namely, extensions of a pragmatic task). The one action of the entire film, however, is usually built up as a supra-ordinate pragmatic task from single, coherent actional tasks, with synergetic or weakening correlation. How these correlations function proves the inferential walks not only of coherent mimetic (not extensional) universes, but also of reading patterns. In *Ordet*, for both alternative universes there are exactly seven mimetic mythos units consisting of characters (Poetic, ἤθη, 50a9) and tasks (50a10, διάνοια, which sets off actional trajectories). It is known that the character, ethos, introduces ethical categories into dramatic genres. Aristotle (48a2f) aims at the 'typical representation of men in general' as better (σπουδαίους, βελτίους, in tragedy) or worse (φαύλους, χείρους, in comedy) 'than we,' the ordinary.

(1) The *escape of* Johannes initiates the narrative treatment of his insanity (##2-13[41]). His main problem is the unbelieving world,[42] but this is in the other narrative universe. The bridge between the two is the 'holy fool' figure, who fits in both universes.

(2) Borgen sees all his dreams as the patriarch and superego of the Borgen family shattered as a result of Johannes's ministry (#11), Mikkel's faithlessness (#11), Anders's marriage plans, and the death of a male heir. Johannes's universe makes him appear as a Job-like figure.

(3) Anders (#14) wants to marry Anne but encounters resistance from his father and later from Peter Petersen. Together with his brother Mikkel, he will be the unexpected and unmerited beneficiary of the Kingdom, in the other universe.

(4) Inger's narrative *disequilibrium* begins with her becoming involved in others' difficulties – specifically, with Mikkel's (#12) and Anders's (#14). She becomes the vicarious agent in the climactic struggle with Borgen (##20f). Thereafter, unexpectedly, she goes into labour, which leads to a stillbirth and to her death in childbed. Her position becomes a privileged one in the Johannes universe, because she is the chosen site of the revelation. The Kingdom is in her, hidden in her womb as Life, and thereafter as new Life.

(5) Peter Petersen is first seen confronting the problem of how to keep his daughter Anne within his congregation (#23). His goal becomes to win over Anders and Borgen himself; an 'anti-program' to (2) is thereby created. When seen in retrospect as part of the Johannes universe, he is the matching part to the pastor and doctor (6), with the complementary program of a repentant.

(6) The pastor and the doctor do not experience narrative *disequilibria* and so have no goals in the saga universe. Their role is limited to reacting, to doing their job. Dreyer does not let them evolve. They remain the same until the end. In the Johannes universe they become the most formidable opponents to the revelation of the Kingdom.

(7) Maren and Lille Inger face their mother's death with great equanimity, so there is no narrative struggle for them to undergo. However, in the Johannes universe they are the first and only ones who see the

hidden, from the beginning and unwaveringly. They are a very literal illustration of Johannes's biblical macarism over the little ones, to whom the mysteries of the Kingdom are revealed: 'At that season Jesus answered and said, I thank thee, O Father, Lord of heaven and earth, that thou didst hide these things from the wise and understanding, and didst reveal them unto babes' (Matthew 11:25 [ASV]).

Given this multitude of narrative threads, and this in two initially exclusive inferential walks, it is not so clear what the film is actually about. In terms of Propp's narrative functions, there is no single protagonist with his '*quête*,' antagonist, fight, and marriage. Dreyer's great achievement was that he succeeded in threading the same characters into different plots. Moreover, the *dénouement* of each plot focuses on a different character. Speaking in Proppian terms, in the Johannes trajectory of the family saga universe there is no 'villain.' Everyone is aware of the 'damage caused to a family member.' This makes Johannes one of the chief objects of the narrative action, whose irreparable state hurts the clan, tarnishes its reputation, and damages its high hopes of fame. Yet from all this, no 'mission to help' arises, because fundamentally there is no hero with a competence for 'Reparation.' Thus the danger looms that a sensible narrative action will not be able to develop; this would bring the narrative to an end at its very start (assuming there is not a spark of hope left that this could change). The whole poetic effort would thus be in vain, since there is no possibility of achieving any pity or catharsis. When a narrative is completely foreseeable, this kills the inner dynamics. Thus narrative schemes (of predictability) must be broken by the astounding ($\tau\grave{o}$ $\theta\alpha\upsilon\mu\alpha\sigma\tau\acute{o}\nu$ 52a2), the plot line must be broken by the unforeseeable ($\pi\varepsilon\rho\iota\pi\acute{\varepsilon}\tau\varepsilon\iota\alpha$). Unless Johannes is put to a test, he will never be able to reveal his character and greater-than-normality. Every narrative plan needs its built-in surprise, then, for it is this which creates the pitiful and merciful identification with the hero. Being 'hopelessly mad' is not a narrative program; this madness must lead to insight ($\grave{\alpha}\nu\alpha\gamma\nu\acute{\omega}\rho\iota\sigma\iota\varsigma$) and pathos.

This thread coming to a halt, there is, luckily, the Anders strand. The old Borgen refuses to allow any alliances with the lowly Petersen clan. This problem causes damage that must be repaired, Inger, it seems, has competence and tries to make those repairs. But she fails, and when she dies, there is no hope for a solution. Again we have come to a narrative dead end, with no peripeteia in sight. Luckily again, reparation is in sight through the rise of a still greater conflict: Petersen's refusal to let his daughter marry a Borgen. In the Mikkel subplot the villain in some way is old Borgen, but this is clearly a subordinate structure. In Greimas's terms of actantiality, Mikkel becomes a mere 'opponent' to the actant Borgen clan. The damage cannot be repaired, it can only subside. Still, the clearest scheme is the Borgens' struggle with Peter. (Here Anders wins over Borgen as his 'helper.') Gradually this becomes a sort of showdown (in which we encounter Propp's classical fairytale functions of 'departure,' 'transfer of one kingdom into the other,' 'struggle,' and 'marking of the hero'). Yet no victory or reparation is imaginable.

As a result of all this all the subplots come to a halt, stagnate or are hopelessly stalled, just at the point where Inger's drama sets in. The dramatic lines are sufficiently developed that all sorts of 'transgressions' or abnormal states can be felt, for example, insanity (Johannes), unhappiness (Anders), desperation (Borgen), and cynicism (Mikkel). These are all suspended and add to the dramatic cataract of Inger's struggle with death. In a certain sense then, this is becoming the central subplot, but with a curious twist: the only hero with any competence for reparation finds herself drawn into an abyss. This is not her '*épreuve qualifiante*' (in Greimas's sense). Nor can she obtain an 'Accomplishment' of a 'difficult Task.' The narrative is posed to end in a tragedy without catharsis, not even in the sense of a glorious family decadence (as in 'The Rise and the Fall of the House of Borgen'). Is this finally the completion of the Aristotelian schema? The turn-around is astonishing, but no one has the faintest insight (i.e. 'into the *fatum* of the gods'). Pathos, a precondition of any catharsis, risks being empty. In rhetoric, it is pathos which facilitates the argumentative, enthymemic jump. Convincing in narration is therefore a very similar quasi-logical process. We follow by identifying, not by reason. Yet with whom, with whose trespassing (ἀμαρτία), are we supposed to identify? The entire judgmental process is endangered: only through a trespassing can binding or solving (δῆσις, λῦσις) be credible. It is highly unsatisfactory when the end of a narration becomes meaningless, a meaningless death. In narrative terms, even worse is the fact that all the run-up conflicts in the family saga line become meaningless so that there is no point in repairing them. Up to this point, the clear actant consists of various actors, all of them together being the 'Borgen clan,' against the 'Petersen people' in a conflict over a liaison between the two clans.

It is now that Johannes comes into play. Only with regard to narration (later we will consider the aesthetic dimension in Dreyer), is the juncture with the main plot of interest. It is a matter of both credibility and temporality. If we believe his claims, we also accept his transtemporality. Johannes is first auto-mandated (in Greimas's sense). From the normal universe, he is sent by Maren alone. Both are extremely incredible. This changes when the saga universe is in complete disarray, but very gently. It is here that we learn that Johannes's universe has always been taken seriously by the two girls.[43] For them, the two universes have always been unified. They alone anticipate the final narrative state. They alone are therefore guarantors of the 'one action' imperative. For the rest Johannes has been a mere narrative retardation. Understanding that, we must make a choice, somehow solve the problem that is Johannes. His problem can be conceived of as his madness, as Mikkel explains. Will the solution be death, with Kierkegaard being the culprit (as Borgen wishes), or an asylum (as the pastor suggests), or (as the doctor gives hope) a sudden breakthrough into sanity? If none of these, then we must opt for taking Johannes seriously and see *with* him a problem in the unbelieving world that must be repaired. *Tertium non datur*. The choice between refusal and acceptance of belief culminates in the climax of the film – the highly dramatic scene at the catafalque – a climax that has been prepared from the opening sequence.

Form: Bordwell's *Ordet*

The narrative construction of *Ordet* hinges on a parallelism: Johannes's madness, and his representation as the Messiah. He is present as an absence from the universe of normality, but completely present in the alternative universe of his mission. This parallel universe is entirely coherent and makes sense as a faithful enactment of a venerated narrative: the life of Jesus. The interesting fact – and proof of artistic skill – is that these two universes relate to each other also as mutual commentary. The 'world' is commenting on his insanity and making sense of it. At the same time, Johannes is commenting very precisely on the role he ('My name is Jesus of Nazareth,' #27) is/plays for almost everything that he observes round him. He does this to such a degree that it sometimes becomes embarrassing. So he draws from his milieu various ways of dealing with this uneasy communicational situation. His effect on everyone is quite strong, ranging from shame (Borgen) to shock (Pastor) to negligent indifference (Mikkel #7) to pity (Inger #7). Only with the children does he find what he is seeking: faith. Through his camera work, Dreyer makes certain that Johannes poses a reaction problem to everyone, including the spectator. As already noted, the very first sequence testifies to the 'faithful' vision of the camera, in contrast with the eyes of all of the narrative characters. In later sequences the camera maintains its respectful attitude (distance, angle). In one of the culminating scenes, during which the girls for the first time express their faith in him after their mother's death, the camera follows him like a disciple, in a famous 180 degree panorama. For the spectator, then, Johannes's universe is far from inaccessible or hermetic. It's just that it is only completely incompatible with the other universe. This forces us to choose: Which one fits into which and is explained from its perspective?

If it is generally true that narration is a manipulation of time, this analysis demonstrates that it is the artistic weaving of overt and latent threads, and not the usual parallel montage, that necessarily produces effects on the time dimension. A superficial survey of the narrative texture forces critics to make an awkward choice between 'lay' and 'religious' interpretation. This choice cannot be avoided by sticking to formal devices, because forms are discovered only through their function. 'What purpose does this formal device fulfil?' is asked only in hindsight – that is, after the purpose has been fulfilled. Furthermore, threads are clearly distinguishable not by their spatial universe (which is precisely *not* separate), but by their different *time essences.* Semiotic allows us to better understand the nature of time as a whole; here we see the narrative consequences of that transtemporality mentioned earlier. Unfortunately, there is not the usual material proof of this, as stills (the usual ones displayed in almost all publications on *Ordet*) are incapable of capturing time. Even if an entire sequence could be enclosed, it would have to show two times at the same time (which is just a difference in semiosis). Dreyer himself, in 'Thoughts on My Craft' (cf. Skoller 1973), called this procedure 'abstraction,' defined as 'abstracting himself from reality in order to strengthen the spiritual content of his work.' In Dreyer's own words, this is an aesthetic achievement. Yet it is an achievement in the narrative continuity itself; it is not limited to frame composition and similar devices. In the present context the point to be made is merely with regard to narrativity – that is, the classical poetic problem (aesthetic considerations on *Ordet* will be dealt with later). Form does indeed affect 'content' – more precisely, temporal content. Conversely, unless we account for the formal difference in the time semiosis, we cannot discover the distinct threading, let alone the difference between 'normal' and 'transcendent' meanings.

The key to understanding time is the narrative position of Johannes. If we fail to account for the parallelism of the two universes, we will inevitably misinterpret the very 'macroproposition' of the narration as a whole. We will misinterpret *Ordet* as the drama of a dogmatic squabble between Grundtvigism and Inner Mission, or as the narrative closure provided by different understandings of Christianity (cf. Bordwell 1981: 144) or, as Drouzy (1982: 335f) suggests, as the story of a domestic tyrant redeemed (as always in Dreyer) by the feminine genius of a woman-victim. Bordwell finds *Ordet's* narrative closure especially problematic and difficult to achieve. It seems to him narratively improbable, in that he feels that Dreyer was compelled to circumvent various narrative traps (and he quotes Milne as an example of criticism misinterpreting the difficult Christian closure [cf. ibid.: 147]).[44] The problem boils down to a sort of macroproposition, with all its ideological, transtextual, and semantic overcoding. The one Bordwell is proposing (and he cannot see two of them) does not allow for miracles in the usual sense (in his view, such a closure would be problematic). Thus Dreyer is, as it were, forced to resort to various countermeasures, both narrative and representational. From here it becomes apparent how Bordwell's further analysis of *Ordet* is based on a determinant macroproposition, and a problematic one at that. Theatralization and Sparseness, as he calls it, is a formal strategy intended to make 'Christian closure' (a formal[!] device) – itself an *enarratio incredibilis* – credible: 'The resolution of this religious narrative requires a miracle. It is not that Dreyer is 'a religious director' and had found in *Ordet* the perfect narrative. Just the opposite: Dreyer's typical narrative unity finds in *Ordet* its most thoroughgoing justification – religion. Christianity becomes Dreyer's most overpowering formal device. If the narrative draws on such potent forces, what could trouble it?' (ibid.). This is true if we take into account only the family saga universe. Bordwell fails to recognize the hidden parallel universe of Johannes's 'madness': 'I shall suggest how the film's mode of representation pulls it away from any simple or direct transmission of this Christian tale. Yet *Ordet's* narrative itself, for all its unity, is not free of inner difficulties' (ibid.).

Without a doubt this is well observed. Yet those inner difficulties are not an accident. They are placed before the spectator as a choice to be made, one that involves an interpretational choice of alternative enunciation instances, alternative sanctions, alternative macropropositions. Through Dreyer's formal treatment alone, should the 'tale' become

Christian? There is ample evidence that the 'tale' is already not so simple. 'The' tale is effectively a non-ending, open-threaded, non-conclusive narration – that is, if the universe of it is the Borgen saga. It is hard to see how this saga's closure can be called a miracle. After all, which noticeable, previously announced task is accomplished by a miracle? An absolute requirement for the genesis of a purpose as temporal unification? Dreyer had no need to bend the saga with formal devices, since it already contained its parallel interpretation or alternative reading. 'Christianity' is not a practical device for overcoming the rarefying effects of formal strategies. Furthermore, the narrative logics (closures) of both universes are quite apparent, in their unmitigated and unreconcilable contrast. One must lead to its 'natural' stalemate in order for the other to take over and finally become dominant. Certainly, in Dreyer formal devices do serve the narrative. They are not independent bearers of signification, as in the rhetoric of Godard's *Je vous salue, Marie*. Dreyer need never step out from behind the narrative surface. All signification comes from his actors.

Is narration the only means of generating meaning in *Ordet*?[45] Can all meaning be described pragmatically? This is suggested by Bordwell's analysis. Faithful to his Formalist theory, both his formal devices concern the representation of a pragmatic *Locus*. Time, the problem of its representation, seems to be taken for granted. It has variously been observed (cf. Petric 1975: 109f) that in *Ordet* the rhythm, established by the very opening shot and music, is important. So what has Dreyer added – for instance, with his steady quasi-musical rhythm – that runs through the whole film the way a theme runs through a fugue? Whatever he has added, is it an addition to the narrative?[46] Beyond pragmatics, the rendering of human action, Dreyer opens another, aesthetic dimension of signification, one that is based on another temporal dimension. The aesthetic, as a transitory First (cf. *infra*), can only be described in its effects on an Interpretation – for example, on narration.[47] Instead of describing the most obvious formal devices and making sense of them in order to achieve a particular narrative closure,[48] we could try to interpret them as a particular aesthetic openness. Dreyer did not choose to achieve this openness through the dissolution of narrative closure.

Bordwell's main category, 'theatralization,' considers pragmatic representation alone.[49] Why should 'cinematic means' attain – in their functional definition – a 'separation of the text and its representation'? Such a separation is in principle nonsensical, because every Sign or text must have an external Object (cf. *supra*). Representation is therefore a *conditio sine qua non* for non-empty Signs (cf. Peirce's sarcastic example: 'I remember ... a prayer as follows: "O Thou, All-Sufficient, Self-Sufficient, Insufficient God." Now pure Self-consciousness is Self-sufficient, and if it is also regarded as All-sufficient, it would seem to follow that it must be Insufficient' (1998: 161, 3rd Harvard lecture). Bordwell, however, considers it something in contrast to plain speech. So far it is in keeping with ancient rhetoric, which treated various levels of *ornatus* over the *oratio simplex* as an object of separate study (cf. *infra*). Perhaps some late treatises on rhetoric obfuscated the original communicational and representational context of varieties of *ornatus*, thereby bequeathing a dangerous misunderstanding to posteriority. Separation as an object of study might be feasible, but not, however, in the reality of sign usage, which is what Formalism calls for. Even presupposing that aesthetic effects could be produced by a pragmatic representation and an 'estranged' or 'unusual' pragmatic representation of the same, this is just a further Interpretation (semantization) of the same represented external Object. Formalists might not admit as much, but any meaning is semantic and need not be described in terms of psychological effects. It bears more resemblance to a very weak version of the *'V-effekt'* in Brecht's theatre theory (cf. *supra*, itself a reflex from Formalism).

Clearly, from their function, neither formal device has a bearing on time and the narrativity proper of representation. Here spatial metaphors, including 'distancing,' have no meaning, because the anchor of Time in the Secondness of different states is already a particular kind of 'distance.' In other words, there is no 'estrangement' in time, only a comparison of a difference (of at least a First with a Second). What remains of Time in the narrative purpose is already itself, in its pure state, an abstraction from the dyadic experiential element of time, but never to such a degree that it could do without the difference of states and the monadic quality of duration.

Neoformalism seems to apply merely to representation, and where it has no purchase, it overlooked completely the temporal essence of narration. However, even in the represented there is almost no trace of that particular spectator distancing (and interaction – so central to Brecht's epic theatre). Estranged distance presupposes a comparison with some normative Generality ('familiar'). In *Ordet* the Generality would be non-'theatrical' behaviour and non-'sparse,' abundant use of available film techniques (for obvious example, 180° camera movement!). Compared with a very noticeable difference from that which we see, this might give rise to an ulterior Interpretation. If at all, it would be only a very transitory device, yielding – even in Bordwell's analysis – to something entirely different in the final scene, in which no distancing whatsoever can be discovered. What is worse, that very climax would certainly bc in total contradiction to theatralization (and *a fortiori* to the epic theatre concept). There is no point in separating 'usual'-ness and 'unusual'-ness in *Ordet*. Dreyer accomplished his effects through rather ordinary narrative and cinematic means.[50] He used the cinematographic arsenal very 'restrictively' because he did not need more. Form in *Ordet* is largely subservient to the narrative, and is not its own coherent track of meaning.

Time in *Ordet*

What makes Dreyer's film an outstanding work of art (in particular, art of narration) is not that he achieved the representation of a universe. Rather, his signification of time makes this work unique. It is an outstanding narration, a creation of times. Therefore, it is more worthwhile to uncover the secret of this temporal art. We know from the modal being of Time that temporal art allows for more than one cinematic mode by which to represent temporality. One is based on the Continuous element of the law of time, which as a Sign makes it determined by Iconicity. Another is based on a Generality, a Sign of pragmatic sequential logic. Pragmatic logic is clearly prominent in *Ordet*, such is the dominant nature of the narrative closure; there are hardly any noticeable foreign elements from outside the narrative universe. Even the emergence of a parallel universe does not lead to the disruption of the main family saga universe. This is not *nouvelle vague* cinema with two parallel narrative universes. The emergence of the alternative universe is hidden and is not 'motivated' in subjective visions either (*Rashomon*-izing, as it were). Our analysis of enunciation and universes indicates narratively a Kierkegaardian *aut aut*.

In the narrative structure of this film, the visitation and resurrection sequences are pivotal, so there is no better place to analyze Dreyer's mastery of time. *Ordet* is in a narrative form but at the same time it is beyond narration. When and how do we notice the emergence of this other time? Here the cinematic nature of Dreyer's narrating comes strongly into play. Only cinema can bring to the fore temporal qualities (without tenses) through direct switches of logic, through a change in the nature of the sign process. The pragmatic logic is based on action, the beginning of an end, but there is another sort of temporal logic – that of Continuous presentness.

Continuity is, of course, not merely a matter of memory, a continuity into the past. The particular Continuity of *Ordet* is the continuous presence of a monadic Oneness, Whole, an ultimate Entirety. This effect can be noticed immediately; it is not a philosophical speculation we are applying to cinema. We need not be in possession of time theories in order to perceive the change in time nature. The sequence of the visitation and Inger's resurrection is of such a Quality of time having no further vector in it. This is so strong that from this point on, in hindsight, we notice this same time nature earlier in the film and even in one scene of the opening sequence. These scenes are not difficult to spot, since they are all connected with the Johannes universe. So the eerie impression that time stands still is not narrative information (a sort of ritual figuration from Mikkel's stopping the clock at the hour of Inger's death, which is clearly a custom with metaphoric significance); instead it is produced directly by cinematic means.

A comparison with other famous scenes in the film history point to the peculiar nature of the eternity of *Ordet*. It is not time standing still, as in the anxiously endless moment of fright during the gunfight in Zinnemann's *High Noon*, or in the eternity of Clouzot's *Le salaire de la peur*. Eternities like these are produced only through a narrative purpose that culminates in a climactic *épreuve décisive*. In Inger's environs, time (of any sort of purpose) is at its end. Therefore it is still. The stopped clock corresponds perfectly to a way of narrating that in this moment brings time to a halt.

Two technical questions arise: What kind of Sign process is this? Which First and Second Correlate can produce it? We are looking for cinematic means, not elements of Speculative Grammar. The second question in the order of analysis will be answered first.

We must have an impression of stasis only when there is no longer a comparison between different states. This means, for the Second Correlate of the Sign that constitutes our sequence, that the strongest emphasis is placed on the everlastingness of the same state. Time stands still because the main character is only dead and nothing more. The clock stands still. All other actors do not go anywhere but merely back and forth and back again. The camera performs the same slow, endless, lateral movements back and forth without purpose. Even the mourners' song is monotonous. When there is nothing left to do, no purpose left in anything, we do the accidental, in a perfunctory way. As a matter of custom, some of the minor functions of funerals are performed, with a clear and outspoken aimlessness. Such aimlessness reminds us strongly, albeit without formal references, of a Beckett-like *Waiting* that is not waiting because it does not know what it is waiting for.

These and other elements can be unified as temporal Sign diverse from temporal advances in the logic of narrative purpose. Of course there is not only a lack of contradiction but also the clear implication that this duration also represents Objects. Yet this representation is everlasting and not advancing – that is, it does not invite comparison of the different states of the represented. For instance, there is no suspense with Inger's waking up, nor is there any suspense (only challenge). Johannes will live up to his promises. This is the distinctive mark of this sequence, not representation or the represented Object.

Once we realize the peculiar nature of the First and Second Correlate of this Sign process, we can answer the first question with more precision. Having the Quality of duration ('leaden,' as it were) as First, there being no emphasis on the Second (i.e., degenerate) as Struggle or difference, the Third of this Sign can only be a Generalization of the Quality of duration. This corresponds perfectly to the feeling of 'numbness' in connection with dying. Such a degeneration prevents Interpretations as 'evolution,' 'purpose,' or other 'fulfilled' temporalities. We are instead left with the oneness of all temporality – with an empty oneness or sameness of time without purpose.

As soon as we observe the advent of Johannes there appears another sort of eternity, one that is no longer empty. Now time is 'eternal and the same.' However, the pivotal sequence does not terminate by falling back into a 'happy ending' purposive time. Even after Inger's resurrection no task is accomplished, there is no new beginning. It is not, as might be imagined, the return of the mother to her girls and the family and the Borgen clan (whose continuation as a saga could be imagined). It is just life: 'Now life is beginning for us' (#68, 298).

So even in the decisive transformation of this narrative, Dreyer remains uncompromisingly in the new temporality, which can be thought of as a whole. Furthermore, from then on the representational Object must change its nature. If the focus is no longer on the difference of states of an existentially identical subject (or better, their narrative imitation, as mentioned earlier), the Object world, the narrative universe, must likewise become timeless. Objects freed from time can stand isolated in themselves under a different kind of Generality. Flooded by light, Inger's visitation parlour is from a different universe with scant connection to Borgensgård. Inger's life does not quite continue, but it begins emphatically.

If narration is the orientation of time, Dreyer orients it toward an eternal present. In this semiosic context it would be highly inappropriate to imagine how Inger resumes her daily chores and how she will die eventually as a grandmother. The narrative cannot go beyond her resurrection; it has reached the new age of eternity, with no further vector in it. Thus it can also transform through its temporality the normal pragmatic logic of things, expressed in the teleology of the Pragmatic Maxim as 'all conceivable consequences.' Instrumental in all this is the way in which Dreyer succeeds in reducing the dyadic element of state differences so that that element remains a General Object.[51]

Dreyer achieves this extraordinary aesthetic effect by producing different modes of time. Failure to comprehend this would lead to a narrative (purpose-guided) comprehension of the pivotal sequence, which through its non-closure must appear unsatisfactory. This, however, is not the point. It is not at all a miraculous Proppian 'reparation of a damage.' Only if time as essence of narration is not given a monopoly over meaning, and only if the differences in the modal being of time are taken into account, will an artistic achievement of the magnitude of *Ordet* be fully recognized.

5 Narration, Time, and Narratologies

Apoc 10,6s: Tempus non erit amplius

Not every theory of narration conceives narration proper as a production of time. 'What is a narration?' finds very different answers. Aristotle's *Poetic* defined it as imitation of praxis. Ricoeur locates this imitation in the imitation of existence. Hermeneutic narratologies see narration as reflecting the immediacy of consciousness in a derived temporal extension. Semionarratology comprehends narration as a linguistic meta-universal. For Deleuze, narrating reflects an approach to time that divides movement into parts.

All of these theories are time-aware, and contain time as a more or less central aspect, but 'time' is never the same 'thing.' Then there are theories which see the main achievement of narration as being the production of a universe, either as Russian doll of layers of alienation or as the opposite direction of strategies of extensional and intensional disambiguation (as in our past discussion of Olmi's *Genesi*). As part of the unidirectional nature of this universe, there is certainly an irreversible time vector, but it is not the result of narrative arrangement as such.

The diversity among these approaches has not always produced an interesting debate but has often produced a theoretic syncretism. We will develop a Semiotic approach to narration as enunciation in a later chapter. The investigation of Signs has already touched on a number of questions arising from the practice of storytelling and the writing of history. Together with our analysis of *Ordet*, this earlier investigation will form the basis for a discussion of the reasons why these theories of narration are so diverse.

5.1 Ricoeur's Mimesis

Peirce, Bergson, and Husserl were contemporaries who shared the same intellectual climate and who were somewhat aware of one another. The phenomenological-hermeneutical perspective, then, is the ineluctable intellectual environment of Semiotic (as much as Bergson was for Husserl). Hermeneutics was prolific as a literary theory of narration, whereas Pragmaticism has no prominent narratological offshoot.[1]

It is easy to forget that even as an aesthetic narratology hermeneutic remains solidly anchored to its roots in the analysis of immediate consciousness. At that level it compares with the Sign process, so we will debate it at that level. Few hermeneutic narratologies are as comprehensive and deep as Ricoeur's investigation of 'time and narration.' For all its originality, it comprehensively blends the many strands of hermeneutical and existentialist theories of literature, poetics, and aesthetics. For all practical purposes, Ricoeur's work constitutes the state of the art in hermeneutic poetic. Film theory is still very much in need of a comprehensive understanding of narration *per se*. The prevailing commonsensical idea of narration still has an exclusive and unreflected penchant for teleology (cf. *supra*). This is often hidden behind terms as commonsensical as syntagma. In this field Ricoeur, who is especially attentive to the origin of narrating in time, can be instructive.

Roles (extra- and intra-diegetic), subjectivity, motivation – important narratological problems like these enter hermeneutic through its philosophical foundation in consciousness. These are certainly central topics for literary theory of all sorts, where they are most often disguised as psychological common sense. Some film theories rely heavily on this sort of psychology – in fact, too heavily. The problem is that psychological personifying identifications with 'visions of camera,' 'characters,' and other 'foci of mind' never explain a camera perspective as meaning. Even some cinematic enunciation theories are in danger of psychologizing (in this case, even on linguistic facts). The whole truth of such statements is a metaphoric equation of eye with lens, suggesting an equation of consciousness with film-as-quasi-subject. Overstretching a metaphor taken literally is no explanation for narration *per se*. This points to the critical and clarifying potential of Ricoeur's theory design, which sharply differentiates the level of immediacy (of consciousness or existence) from the strictly narrative level. This allows him to remain true to Aristotle's definition of narration as the imitation not of persons but of actions. This will help us reframe the role problematic into the coordinates of action, including its intrinsic dimension of time.

Many of these insights hinge on their philosophical foundations. A debate from a perspective of Peircean time theory will reveal whether such insights can also be understood as Sign process in lieu of consciousness. If this undertaking remains mere paraphrasing, it is pointless. It is important in this debate to separate the three principal stands of Ricoeur's narratology, because each strand has its own response and is not as tightly integrated with the other strands as one might think. These three strands are: (1) Husserl's, in particular his reception of St Augustine (based on their common psychologism). (2) The concept of human action developed in basic accordance with Aristotelian *Poetic*. (3) Existential analysis and hermeneutics, which provide the missing link between time and action in the form of Heideggerian 'Care.' We gain a clearer picture of Ricoeur's theory design when we strip it down to its bare argumentation plan. What is the pivotal role assigned to time that in this particular understanding of it, can answer this question: How does *all* become a whole?

It is not intuitively clearly why time can fulfil such a central function (which is not unlike Bergson's *tout*). With a simpler theory, such as Constructivism, everything is cognitively and causally linked because above all there is the idea of one reality of data. So, apparently, the problem does not even exist. Yet at the same time, Cognitivists do not go so far as to admit any kind of truth, because there is an ultimate arbitrariness in cognitive schemata (cf. *supra*). In functional terms, this amounts to phenomenalism, but its consequences are not as radical. There are still data as ontic ground of cognitions, whereas phenomena constitute a radical departure from ontic foundations.

In this way, and this way only, the problem arises as to how phenomena become one whole. They can do so only by appearing before a consciousness. Kant's phenomenalism was unified by categorical forms of judgment, and Peirce argued for a thorough categorical-relational constitution of all phenomena. Phenomenology chose a different option: the mode of experiencing – itself and in its immediacy – which became the measure. Now there is nothing comparable to time which as an experience constitutes oneness. If we have nothing except by being experienced, there can be only one question with regard to time: Is it one because of itself, or is it one because it must be experienced in order to be for us? Having opened this hiatus between mental form and objective existence, we must meet Kant's option for the apperceptional form with a counter-question about the objective grounds in movement. The Aristotelian physical concept of time then becomes interesting as a counter-position. Ricoeur's 'rival' time concept, then, is always physical time (cosmological, calendar, movement, *a priori* formal). It is confined to measuring movement or the 'something in movement' (number), which is the ontological definition of (physical) 'time.' Having to do with movement, it is intimately tied into hylomorphism (in particular what the Scholastics later on would call the distinction between *actus* and *potentia*).

Once ontological reasoning is no longer viable, 'change' becomes a difficult thought. If being as such no longer fulfils the role of totality, it must be 'reconstructed' in Subjectivity. In Foucault, this reconstruction has the disadvantage that it exists merely as duplification, in a parallel Subject. As double it is no longer part of the Subject of experience. Time as such cannot be perceived, but everything is *in* time (Kant's thesis: *KrV* A183, B226). From that point on the only relevant question becomes the *a priori* temporal form of perception in the Transcendental Aesthetic. Its derivates from the mind ('im Gemüt,' *KrV* A20, B34) go down to the Schemata (i.e., of categories), where they yield (in three analogies of experience) three properties of time: permanence, succession, and simultaneity. These properties are still formal; even so, they describe the actual time experience rather well. There seems to be no such preoccupation with totality in Aristotle, who understood Time as numerable according to before and after in movement (τοῦτο γάρ ἐστιν ὁ χρόνος, ἀριθμὸς κινήσεως κατὰ τὸ πρότερον καὶ ὕστερον *Physica* Δ 11 219b1ff).

The numerability of physical movement, however, suggests a mind able to number. As long as the mind is not seen as the opposite of being, the problem of a psychological constitution of time does not arise. St Augustine, however, saw a mind as the foundation of the time phenomenon, excluding physical determinants. 'What "is" time?' Ricoeur asks with St Augustine; and as an answer he finds 'intentio' and 'distentio animi' (psychological notions whose rediscovery would become important for Husserl): I, as a subject of consciousness, can only conceive of time in the two directions past and future. This is how Ricoeur (1983: 19–53) reads St Augustine's *locus classicus* on time (*Confessiones*, Book XI). St. Augustine finds in these concepts an answer to the Sceptics' argument that time is a nothing between past and future. Actually, when we try to measure time, the past is no longer and the future is not yet; this leaves only the present, which, however, is an infinitesimally small point between the future and the past. Therefore, according to this fallacy, time does not exist. St Augustine, then, from this aporia, resorts to ordinary language, which allows us to speak (but how so "sed quo pacto?' Conf. XI: 15,18) and think reasonably about time.

What makes St Augustine so interesting is that he makes it possible for us to solve the problem of the unity of time. This is why Husserl (1966) took him up again. He even recycled the song example, which indeed illustrates well how time becomes a psychic totality in the triple present. A tone and the duration of it: in the interior time consciousness (i.e., as long as I hear it) it is one tone that is 'still yet' ('immer noch') and 'just now flown by' ('soeben verflossen'). I 'retain' it, as it were. Simultaneously I expect immediately a perception from the non-perceived. At the other end, it 'relapses' into the 'flow of oblivion' ('zurücksinkend in den Fluß des Vergessens'). The distance ('Strecke') between the two is 'held,' gives duration; the Now-point ('Jetztpunkt') and the retentions are one, a temporal totality.

Especially important is the fundamental dichotomy in the nature of time: there is the Same ('Gleiche') and there is the Other ('Andere'). In both Heidegger and Foucault, all future development of temporality is informed by this pair. The basic insight is an understanding of the duration, the one tone, as being a Same in its one intentionality, which Husserl called 'longitudinal intentionality.' Thus it is not a series of intentional objects, which change and can then be serialized. The Other must be distinguished sharply, as it flows back into the flux of oblivion. It can be recovered from this flux in any arbitrary order, through remembrance. As imagination it merely imitates the model of the original consciousness. Thus what had originally been the source point, now in remembering can be taken by any set-in point. This lacks exactly a time halo ('Zeithof'), the duration belonging to it. The primary memory instead is a passing till the point where it descends ('versinken') into the flux. The secondary remembering brings back images from the really gone. It reproduces a time object in a representation ('Vergegenwärtigung').

Husserl's point emphasizes the nature of the time object as being already 'one after another' and as therefore not the result of a serializing act of imagination. The Other, instead, is accessible only through Re-Petition (the very important term 'Wiederholung,' bringing back, which is so central to Heidegger and Foucault). History, Stories are 're-petitioned' because their object is the Other, merged into the flux of oblivion. A story happens imagined 'as if' it had duration. This strict difference in nature is the heavy price we must pay for temporal totality. The Other is left outside as the discontinuous, which is quite at odds with a Peircean Continuity of time, being, and thought. This precludes everything outside duration from being thought of as being one. When we fetch it back, through remembrance, into the 'halo of time,' it becomes a re-given ('Wiedergegebenes') at best, but there is no guarantee that this can be done. The past 'is congruent' ('deckt sich') with the immediate past at the point where it merges into the flux. By remembering, I relive it. It is therefore a second intentionality by setting an arbitrary point of 'initiation,' which integrates it into time consciousness. Through these settings, which assign to every initial point a different place, we construct a time series. The opportunity of a second intentionality is that it 'repeats' the first, and thereby creates in a similar way a protentional content as preremembrance ('Vorerinnerung'). There is expectation also in the repeated, which is fulfilled in the present. The present therefore 'colours' also repetition. The totality of immediate consciousness having been attained, we are left with three problems: (1) How can we achieve the unity of the different fluxes of remembrance? In Husserl, the unity as a wholeness is based on the unity of consciousness. (2) If the two intentionalities share one now, we must still constitute this formally. Otherwise it will not be possible to determine two events as simultaneous. (3) Husserl must refer back to objective (physical) time in order to ascertain from the manner of 'flowing by' that the seriality really is a continuous one. The flow itself is actually discontinuous – a sequence of arbitrary jumps. Thus continuity is indeed the primordial totality, and the discontinuous is the derivate of a reappropriation.

5.2 Heidegger's *Ekstasis*

With Heidegger a radical reorientation takes place. Retention loses its primate, which is taken by protention, when time is no longer one with regard to flowing into the past of oblivion. The new totality is attained by stretching out from the present into being 'ahead of oneself'[2] ('sich vorweg') by caring. This means being incomplete, having potentiality-for-Being ('Seinkönnen'). The present, instead, is present-at-hand ('vorhanden') because ready-to-hand ('zuhanden'), without a dimension for what is not yet or is no longer. Care ('Sorge'[3]) has the advantage of stretching along by having its secret in a Being-toward-the-end ('zum Ende sein'), which belongs to the incomplete, the imperfect, that which still can be. The end of Being-in-the-world, however, is death.

This concept of totality has decisively shaped Ricoeur's rewriting of Aristotelian *Poetic*. It is the kernel of narrative configuration ('mimesis II') as teleological logic. It will be necessary to describe in detail how the structure of Heideggerian temporality has since been transformed into narrative logic. At any rate, the 'sense of an ending' has its origins here, even when it is applied to a sphere quite different from Being-toward-death. Ricoeur's justification for this transformation must be highly problematic, then. For Heidegger, death is never social, but 'in each case mine' ('der je meine'). But this is so for all existents; if we were not mortals we could not understand novels, even though there have been some narratives about immortality (in cinema, Sally Potter's *Orlando*). With temporality having its origin in the end, death is lonely and is not transferable as experience. It is therefore important that in our fixation on the present, the everydayness, we not overlook the authentic, the primordial ('das Ursprüngliche'). Outside 'Bezeugung' (attesting, testimony) from the existential, which is in 'conscience' ('Gewissen'), it cannot be analysed. Attesting, I am responsible before my own existence. Testimony and responsibility in the context of temporality is certainly new. Furthermore, it has important consequences in both Foucault and Ricoeur. In Foucault it becomes (in a Nietzschean key) responsibility before life itself (cf. *supra*). For Ricoeur this is the ultimate reason for 'refiguration' ('mimesis III'), which does not end time with its end (cf. *infra*). Testimony, however, has a disadvantage: the 'existentiales' ('Existenziale') depend on authentically lived existence, the 'existenziell' ('das Existenzielle'), which by its very nature is highly personal. As well, in Heidegger existence has very stoical traits.

Such is the originary mode of Dasein of 'Sorge.' Yet there is a hierarchy of time ('Zeit'). Temporality ('Zeitlichkeit') is the originary tension between the now and death. Only here, in temporality, is time a whole, but as solitary experience. The 'anticipating resolution' ('vorlaufende Entschlossenheit') transforms Care into Being-toward-the-end ('Sein zum Ende'). When I anticipate, future ('Zu-kunft' or 'ad-vent') 'comes toward' my now. As such it is the origin of unity and of temporal duration. Having-been ('Gewesen-Sein') of what 'came toward' yields the past. It is accepted as 'thrownness' ('Geworfenheit'), in which one accepts also guilt or 'response-ability.' The present can no longer be the infinitesimal point of passing from the future into the past. It becomes the time of worry, concern ('Besorgen') with the things at hand, of everydayness. Existence toward death is a whole, but its temporality of Care is already ek-static (standing out) in these three, co-originary ecstases of time. Historicality ('Geschichtlichkeit') repeats (in 'Wiederholung') 'radical temporality'. Consisting of the 'stretch' of the Dasein between being born and dying, it produces the 'connectedness of life.' It adds movement and Self-constancy ('Selbst-Ständigkeit') to the *Dasein*. Only now can something 'happen' (by 'temporalizing' 'zeitigen' itself) in an original sense. That which happens is history temporalizing itself in the stretching duration of Dasein. The Self is therefore Movement, Self-constancy, and Connectedness, both as responsibility (guilt) and as promise.

Given our usual understanding of history, it is a surprise that in Heidegger history is not found the realm of 'our common past.' History is still in the solitary existential *Dasein* and does not refer to a public thing concerning all of us. If it is a given, it is only to one person in her thrownness before her own death. Yet, in this way history can become a concept of true unity. If it were portrayed as a construction of an abstraction effort (G. Simmel) – as a sort of Kantian concept applied to a manifold of (disparate) data – Heidegger's history concept would be genuinely one. As one's existence itself, it can hardly be placed in doubt. Not surprisingly, the givenness of the one temporality in *Ekstasen der Zeit* has been understood as an Iconic sign process, as Apel (1975: 202) remarked. Now Firstness is the mode of being of metaphysical truth. In this point some see a kinship between existential-hermeneutic and semiotic approaches (In Apel's transcendentalist interpretation [1973: 178–219], they converge in principle in the ultimately historic and communicational comprehension of truth.) Furthermore, like existence, this oneness is connected more with my ad-vent or (the) future than with my having-been or (the) past. Clearly, in narrating this temporal being we must remain aware of the solitary origin of time-as-one. It can never misconceive itself as objective relation of past facts. Even when it tells the present, it is not objective; rather, it is rooted in the fate of an existence, a subject-toward-the-end. Should it surprise us, then, that Heidegger took the present and its tales as the greatest danger to inauthenticity, to oblivion of Being in time?

History as thrownness must first of all take over one's heritage in resolution. 'Taking over' what is 'handed down' is not an automatism; it could also be refused. Thus, the authentically historical is not only the ad-vent or potentiality-of-being, but also the fate of the 'having-been-there Being-there' ('dagewesenes Dasein') in its three forms. This limitation is factual and is inherited as fate ('Schicksal') of being (free) for death, but it is also taken over as heritage. It is also my destiny ('Geschick'), which is common from my primordial being-with others. In destiny my solitary fate breaks up. Primordial Dasein is being-with and happen-with. Thus the destiny of a community is more than the co-occurrence of many subjects. It must as much be taken over as the 'heritage.' Only then is it history ('Geschichte') in the sense of pastness of things within-the-world. Heidegger's historicality concludes in the 'repetition,' which is the explicit handing down, a return to the potentialities of the 'having-been-there' *Dasein*. Thus it enables us to disavow, to refuse the influence of the having-been on the future. The three ekstases are reunited in the resolution of the taking over of historizing, happening. Repetition is therefore the futural aspect of historicality, and the ad-vent, future produces being-a-whole.

Equiprimordial with historicality is intratemporality ('Innerzeitigkeit'). This attempts to think that the historical takes place 'within time.' One must 'reckon with one's time.' Yet by reckoning, one has already pulled temporality into the present-at-hand, levelling it off. Even if *Dasein* owes everything to its pro-venience ('Her-kunft'), it is not just thrown into the world. In this way it is also with the things ('equipment'), as much as it is with others. Care thus becomes concern, provision ('Besorgen'). The third ekstasis, the present, is calculating and manipulating with the 'equipment.' As a result, temporality becomes time and acquires three characteristics: (1) it can be dated, (2) it has extension, and (3) it is public, compared to the solitariness of death. Regarding (1), only now is it possible to date events. Whereas in the original connectedness of life, elements have their places assigned by existential care, now they are on a scale. Existentially, it is not difficult to weigh the importance of events. On a scale, however, events can only be counted, beginning from an arbitrary zero point. Yet the real point of reference is the now point. All events that are not yet (and how long they will not yet be), relate to now; the same is true for what is gone and for how long it is gone. To be able to localize these moments, I must go down to things, the 'equipment.' Then I am (e.g., with Romans and all the equipment of their past world). However, one can forget the provenience of those now points from the Care. Regarding (2), the interval joins datability by creating sectors of 'stretchedness' (ex-tension), which have been 'since that' 'to that.' (This is not to be confused with the duration of life, originating from the Care.) From this arises the thought that each event itself has an extension. Moreover, it gains self-constancy because it can be isolated as no longer being within the unity of a Being-toward-the-end. Regarding (3), time can be called 'vulgar time' proper. It is *vulgaris* in the literal sense of *vulgus* – it is a public and common time of the concern with 'equipment.' Certainly it is not the case that all share their being-toward-death. Instead, thrown, we experience our being-with. By becoming oblivious to its original derivation from Care, Being-with very soon becomes everyday being together. Once ek-static temporality is levelled off into a concerned, countable world-time, it becomes vulgar time.

Is the hierarchization of time too high a price to pay for the unity of time? The 'natural' perception of time as a continuum, or even as unlimited but countable, is from such a perspective almost a misunderstanding of the authentic nature of time. Authenticity can only be reached through the radical closure of existential finitude.[4] As a seminal foundation of time experience, it is radically opposed to St Augustine's Otherness of time: Eternity. Here the soul enjoys its truth, stable and grounded in God, with no need to move. Care is radically different from Hope. If caring *Dasein* is the other of concerned being-in-time (and also 'in time'), eternity – and its vector in the present, hope – offers a unity traversal to time. As a unifying principle, eternity is diametrically opposed to infinity, including the formal infinities of Kant and Aristotle's countability. However, it is prone to being no longer thinkable in its complete otherness. We can only negate time specifically (cf. Rev. 10:6s: 'time will no longer be'), or speak of 'the end of times.' Heidegger makes eternity as negation even more specific by referring to the 'end of my time.' The advantage of such a miniature eternity, compared to Kant's abstract unity, is that it can be experienced without the need to duplicate the Subject into a Transcendental Subject. If – from a Semiotic perspective – time can be thought of as a Real Continuous Possibility, however, we need no longer define eternity in terms of an end. Possibility is not thinkable either, because 'is' is more than the actual.

Ricoeur's narratological theory design hinges on time as existential analysis. Yet for two crucial reasons he was not totally satisfied with the outcome. He needed to break up the nefarious effects of the finitude approach; furthermore, he could not agree completely with the hierarchical understanding of cosmological time as inauthentic obliviousness of the originary temporality. Without going into a critique of the fundamental design decision at this point, it is not difficult for us to imagine a theory of narration on the basis of this existential analysis alone. As long as unification is tied to the authentic but solitary experience of time, narrative unity must forever remain a derivate of lesser dignity. Is there an escape beyond the boundaries of the very approach of existential analysis, possibly without giving up what has been obtained in time analysis? The strong point undoubtedly is a new way of thinking temporal unity as totality. In terms of a positivist (transformation of Kant's formal apriorism into a) world of directionless, unlimited change, Being-toward-the-end is more easily thinkable. At least it does not lend itself so easily to substitute totalities such as 'progress' and 'historical advancement.' The emptiness of pure chance cannot be held for long without some surreptitious reintroduction of ordering principles.[5] Time postulates a reason for its 'one after another,' even if this is taken for granted in its sublunary version of the realm of human action. There is no such granting for nature (albeit for sciences of nature there is such a reason). Stochastic descriptions of chemical 'reactions' are 'temporary' equilibria of completely reversible non-events. By merely introducing any kind of 'truth' into this area, we factually create a direction, as we have seen in Peirce's analysis of the triadic and dyadic requirements of the law of time.

Deleuze and Ricoeur (through Husserl and Heidegger, who admittedly had Bergson in mind when they arrived at their alternative time theory) intended a more profound comprehension of time; to this purpose they drove their understanding of time into concrete forms — that is, in the sense of how this time is taken in charge or 'owned.' Cinema just as much as narration is an 'owner' of temporality. These forms have inherited from the principal time-before-forms that they are not sequence but totality. In Peirce, this nature of time is contained in Continuity. In Deleuze, cinema's capacity to intuit the whole is constitutive (at least in its more spiritual 'incarnations'). Existential analysis leaves Ricoeur's conception of the whole with the problem of solitariness; whereas by definition the vulgar time is no longer whole, but a flow of nows. Thus Heidegger (1962): 'Nevertheless, the "they," which never dies and which misunderstands Being-towards-the-end, gives a characteristic interpretation to fleeing in the face of death. To the very end "it always has more time"' (477). 'Dasein knows fugitive time in terms of its "fugitive" knowledge about its death' (478). As we have seen also in Peirce, time is not time as collection of events unless a law aspect becomes part of it. The difference with Heidegger is only that every Sign of time must contain this part; otherwise it will not succeed in completing this temporal Sign process. With hierarchies, this problem is more complicated. Casting temporality into narration, which is certainly not solitary, Ricoeur must provide means for remembering its primordial provenience (if he does not want to lose the whole). He avails himself of the important Heideggerian concept of Repetition. In fact, his understanding of poetics as imitation of action is not by chance tripartite. It repeats exactly Heidegger's ekstases of temporality. Speaking of the objective, cosmological time, he proclaims narration as the source of human time ('que le temps devient temps humain dans la mesure où il est articulé sur un mode narratif, et que le récit atteint sa signification plénière quand il devient une condition de l'existence temporelle' [Ricoeur 1983: 85]). A task so arduous must push the requirements on the essence of narration to their limit. For the ascension of narratives to their truer and fuller meaning is achieved only when they remember their Caring provenience, which is the ultimate function of refiguration.

5.2.1 Ricoeur's Rereading of Heidegger with Aristotle

Conversely, this kind of conceiving narration is also a windfall solution to the solitariness, the hierarchization problem in Heidegger and the corresponding irreconcilability with the cosmological concept of time (Ricoeur [1985–133]: 'Être quelque chose du mouvement et être quelque chose du Souci me paraissent constituer deux déterminations inconciliables dans leur principe.' How this conciliation is operated will become clearer after we elaborate of the three quasi-ekstases of narration. Two further instantiations of narration (usually not considered as essentially different from narrative teleological configuration) are instrumental for this reconciliation: the *vox narrativa* and the historical 'trace.' The former is the textual trace of a human temporal being as true foundation of the possibility of narrating; the latter is the unavoidable reference of the real of the past, which forces its way into a narrative (including 'fictional' narratives) by way of responsibility (also as a Heideggerian concept) and the fiduciary narrative contract.

Ricoeur's narratology starts as a rereading of Aristotle's *Poetic* of mimesis of action. However, a clear interest is evinced in this rereading, which amounts to an impregnation of Heideggerian analysis with pragmatic logic and is not an exegesis of the *Poetic*. In this reinterpretation the pivot of pragmatic logic is teleological configuration (mimesis II), while the framing (re- and pre-) figurations have the task of anchoring narration in existence. This explains the tripartition of Aristotle's one mimesis. In this way Ricoeur is drawing a classical philosopher in two modern directions. To start, the one *Poetic* mimesis of action is instilled with acto-rial temporality (and truth) – that is, through three parts of true temporal existence. The drawback to this extension relates to how it retro-acts with the idea of action itself. If acting can go on forever, as Heidegger's understanding of it as being merely 'instrumental' suggests, then its authentic unity lies outside. The intended pragmatization of existence, which is the second extension into existential analysis, remains external. With this extension, narration inherits the two consequences of authen-tic unity – the solitary state before death, and a hierarchy of time as authentic and vulgar. Mimesis of human praxis, however, means much more and much less, and perhaps even something else. It is greater through its inclusion of actorial, auctorial, and reader existence. It is less, however, in the core of the concept of action itself. This loss has two sides. One is that we find unity only at the authentic level, which a log-ical unity of pragmatic logic can merely imitate. The corresponding opposite is that action itself becomes nominalistic. Praxis is not, as in Peirce, pragmatic conduct, a conduct of cognitive effort and purpose, which finds its unity in truth and – fallibilistically – in each triadic Sign process. Time is merely – as law of time – the re-enactment of logical principles in being, as we have seen, but it 'exists' through logic. Thus there is no need for a hierarchy of being, which is taken care of in the unlimited Categorical specifying determination of all Relations (cf. *supra*). Care instead, as unifier, has no logical 'finious' wholeness, as in Peirce's evolutionary metaphysic. Only as *Dasein* is it one; as instrumen-tal, public praxis it is open and without end.

Now, outside *Dasein*, any concrete practical action can – in principle – assume an arbitrary finality. With regard to cognitive acts, the result is nominalistic. On this point Ricoeur accepts the technique of configu-ration (his mimesis II integrates certain aspects of Greimas's generation of narrative meaning) as an arbitrary imposition of a narrative teleol-ogy – within the bounds of the probable of mores of a culture (as in the *Poetic*), of course. A reparation takes place only in a further mimesis, which 'remembers' its provenance from authentic being-before-death. It puts an end to the endless, but the force to do so is only borrowed and must remain imaginative or normative. As ethical value it must – as *monumentum* or *documentum* – 'admonish' the reader to postulate jus-tice, the realization of what is concretely not realizable.

This is a reparation, but it is not a correction of the original approach; human praxis is still the improper, and is in itself not unified. Even the hierarchy of time cannot be abandoned lest there be not even narrative unity. This postulates that an appeal for some form of justice can be called for from every narration – an ethic derived from authentic human being. In light of the consequences of Ricoeur's theory design, we will finally have to consider two questions: Is it more an extension of the *Poetic* or is it a welcome, necessary correction of the intrinsic psychologism of existential analysis? Then, is the alliance between pragmatic logic and existential analysis successful (provided it is not a *mésalliance*) or does it remain an emulsion of heterogeneous elements?

In Ricoeur's theory design, temporal unity is irreplaceable. It can only be matched by an artificial unity, imitating the authentic one, in the Otherness, the non-Self (Heidegger recognizes two Self-constancies; as we know, the other is the Other, non-Self in the datable world-time). With the artificial unity of narrative temporality in the mimetic pragmatic logic, we risk losing the link with existential temporality. Consequently, narrative unity must not be self-contained; instead it must receive its unity as temporal unity. It operates, however, as the logical unifier, with a borrowed force making finality thinkable as logic.

The linking of narration to existential temporality is ascertained in two places: in the reader or author (downstream), and in the concept of historical 'trace' (upstream). 'Trace' is an especially interesting notion (reader theory will be examined in the context of enunciation and *vox narrativa*). In principle, every 'entirely past' (in Husserl's sense) is the Other, strange. By definition it is outside the temporal unity. In material terms, traces are found in historical documents, or better, sometimes in monuments, or in any sort of remains of people who are gone forever. A trace is definitively past; it is all that is left of something that no longer is. As such it has a double nature: it is objectively past, and it is something that can be reattached to its 'provenience.' How can this be achieved? Traces must be configured. Narrative configuration can be taken quite literally – it involves giving a figure to the strange, Other. This artificial act is analogous to the ekstases of temporality (in Heidegger's analysis of originary time). Ricoeur attempts, hyperbolically, the ekstasis of the Other. Now, the ἐκ of a στάσις means that this something steps out of the ground of a Oneness. The Other, which became trace, stepped out of a no longer available Oneness in a different way. To call it 'equipment' of a past, as past world of a Being-in-the-world, still suggests the ability to bring it back into unity. To call it trace, however, is to take its definitive pastness seriously. Traces are marks of an infinite continuation of time; they are things that can only be grasped as marks of a pastness.

Understanding such marks is infinitely more difficult, since there seems to be no bridge to temporality and its ekstases. Ricoeur therefore needs a substitute Oneness, which can no longer reasonably be a Being-toward-death. Traces are erratic blocks. Only through a detour via another kind of 'provenience' can unity be achieved. This works in a manner of 'attesting' that is entirely homological to the ethical principle which constitutes authentic temporality in 'testimony' (cf. *supra*), the 'responsibility before the dead.' Just as I 'take over' the 'responsibility' of my 'Being-toward-the-end,' I take over that before the dead. The dead are functionally a 'collective Subject,' as it were, one that has no death of its own except in me. Thus another unity – a purely formal one – must be constructed for the dead, which is literary, narrative configuration. This is experienced only in the act of reading. Thus it must be followed by a refiguration, mimesis III, otherwise narration would have to remain purely formal. Configuration, which is embedded in this way, ascertains the applicability of the logic of human action to history. Action is the same experience as the 'act of reading' (which is the title of W. Iser's seminal book on 'reader response'). Although applied to history, pragmatic logic must suggest – through the act of teleological configuration – a collective subject, 'as if' it existed. Now, we know that the substitute for a collective subject is the dead. Their subjectivity, however, hinges on the subject of the reader. The impression of a certain circularity is certainly not unwarranted, but in this case it is the hermeneutic circle.

How can literature, stories, accomplish such a task with 'traces,' since figuration is an artificial unity of the alien Other in a pragmatic logic? There is no question that narrative or historical causal connections are factual, as the decisive fact in this unification is the time of *Dasein*. The point is that narrative configuration of traces can remain composition of the alien, provided it is 'composition of actions.' For Ricoeur, objectivity in history lies in the facticity of the traces, which are essentially appeals that 'teach' (as *documenta*) or 'admonish' (as *monumenta*). Narration limits itself to providing the logic, the teleology, for something that by its nature does not have one. As long as the true topic of stories, not only history, is 'trace' – in all their derivation and 'provenience' – the narrative technique finds a frame of comprehensibility and unity (it resembles 'concern,' but only in teleology). Even when they are 'fictional,' narratives remain true if they refer to that 'responsibility.' They become the fantasy product of the unrealized possibilities of the dead. Testimony implies that this must be done by concretely existing and acting subjects. The reader/author, as much as the 'repeated' action (on the basis of the 'traces'), share a common essence as temporal beings. Only through this common ground does narration bring traces into a secondary present, in (the time of) the reader.

5.3 Aristotle's Poesis

In Ricoeur's theory, pragmatic narrative logic is less important. It is also much less decisive than existential analysis. It need only ensure that it can *represent* action. His theory can do without a theory of human action proper. This is probably covered by Heidegger's manipulation theory of the equipment, which is ready at hand. Added to this, he needs only the logic of human praxis, which has its form in narrative, textual representation. Then it is not even a strict logical claim, because he does not deduce (from which other premises?) but rather describes some (and not necessarily a comprehensive list) of the 'symbolic resources' of pragmatic logic (cf. Ricoeur 1983: 87), an ancillary 'logic' without first principles. This is indicated in the structure of how the logic of the mimesis of human praxis is divided into three necessary steps.

Prefiguration, Mimesis I, constitutes the initial steps of the conceptual network of a logic of action. Its function is to deliver the logical scaffolding of a pragmatic logic, primitives of action 'as an idea' (a *'pré-compréhension du monde de l'action: de ses structures intelligibles, de ses ressources symboliques et de son caractère temporel'*; Ricoeur [1983: 87]). The general structure of action (*'réseau conceptuel'*), which is logically different from the structure of physical movement, is taken from Danto's theory of basic actions. It consists of a complex of six concepts: every action has (1) finality ('but') (2) agents, who do their work and who therefore have (3) their motives ('motifs'). They act in (4) circumstances, determining what is possible, and in (5) interaction with others, for the purpose of a (6) bringing about change in the physical world.

This 'conceptual network' must rely on some presuppositions. Since it has no foundation of its own, we assume that what concrete acting is is something that is generally known. This is problematic when we adopt Danto's 'basic actions' as 'symbolic resources' for a concept of pragmatic logic. For one thing, it does not really blend into existence analysis. If the idea of action is indeed derived from the (manipulating) 'equipment-at-hand,' it is still dependent on the solitary Care. Once it becomes social, Care loses its link with authenticity, including the originary, existential 'being-with' sociality ('*Mitsein*'). How can it be that such a symbolic resource is truly a coordination of meaning, which is required for action and which is more than just manipulative? Ricoeur's existential phenomenology argues that action is unthinkable and unsayable without an implicit notion of time experience.[6] Every concrete human action takes place not in time *sensu stricto*, but in temporality. It takes place in a 'now' that is directed toward a future of action in the form of Care and is marked by antecedents. The derivation from Care still cannot be transcended: 'Saying "now," however, is the discursive Articulation of a making-present which temporalizes itself in a unity with a retentive awaiting' (Heidegger 1962: 469; also Ricoeur's quote). Existential temporality is only repeated in the intratemporality of concrete action. The drawback to this anchoring to Care is that action, if authentic, must share in solitariness. If it is reduced to the ready-at-hand, it is public, measurable-with-a-clock, and inauthentic. Acting in public, 'vulgar time' means acting inauthentically and in a manipulative way, which must influence meaning itself.

Ricoeur hints at how we must conceptualize the symbolic resource for action. Only on the surface is it a mere linguistic presupposition, because an action that is told is not an action that is performed but rather a syn-tactical entity.[7] The verbal or similar interlacement (in short: discourse) produces a 'deed' or '*intrigue*.' Ricoeur's idea is that the representation of action depends on the symbolic resources and not on action as such. However, even though symbolic resources alone can illuminate which aspect of the deed becomes thematic, it can create this logical effect only on the basis of a cultural fact or contingency. As a temporal logic (i.e., narrative causality), cultural mores are no more than plausible. Certainly they are logically less compelling, let alone authentic, than the originary time of Care. The linguistic stock of symbolic resources used for representing action is very small because it is not based on real acting, real pragmatic conduct of behaviour.

Is there at least a bridge between the two logical constraints of such different origins? If it is not the strong 'being-with,' the link of similarity must be provided by a lesser element. The role of Schütz's 'life world' phenomenology of intersubjectivity is such a bridge with 'being-with.' Seen from a temporal point of view, social validity of interaction becomes the chain ('*Zusammenhang*') of a generation (ibid.: 164ff). Coordination of action is a phenomenological given of valid action over time, where there is no need to make a topic of the unproblematic horizon of meaning over generational gaps. In order to be valid, however, this meaning must become contemporaneity, which in terms of existential analysis is still a relation of private and public time.

The logical strength of Ricoeur's symbolic resources is probably deliberately weak, because he reserves the unifying strength for time. In other theory designs symbol has – and needs – a role that is much more substantial. Action as such is not the link – contrary to Peirce's Pragmatic Maxim, for instance – so there is no need to explore the logical requirements of action. Here the universality of human acting is the guarantee both of reality and of understanding/communicating. Neither are narrative prefigurations and their symbolic resources hypothetical reconstructions of social coordination à la Mead and Habermas. Not even in Greimas is there a need to provide a logical equivalent to a 'social imaginary,' a deduction of linguistic universals from the basic features of propositional processes. It is enough that there is a fundamental description of the pragmatic logic of represented action.

Ricoeur's analysis lacks a mimesis 0 – a pre-mimesis as it were, a true pragmatic or analysis of the possibility of human action – of the sort that is achieved in Pragmaticism (cf. *supra* §1.1.1). If there were more than just symbolic resources at this stage, if there were a true coordination of meaning as a logical constraint, this would require that those resources be understood as Replicas of a Generality. In Ricoeur the procedure is reversed. Although the resources of tenses or equivalents vary greatly among linguistic universes, the existential equivalent of their Generality is the temporal existence of the reader.

Con-Figuration, Mimesis II, is the technique of the imitation of action, or action in the form 'as-if,' resulting in a '*mise-en-intrigue*' (a sympathetic translation of μῦθος in the *Poetic*). Additionally, for Ricoeur it is a composition of time, but not in its originary mode. Vulgar time is already in the public domain of action, which through this technique receives its substitutive temporal unification. Notwithstanding this temporal effect, time is not the source of unification in the narrative technique of imitation. Here a clear, logical schematism is in operation without any foundation in the authentic time of *Dasein*. This does not go so far as to derive the schematic order from the proposition structure (as we will see in Greimas) or from other linguistic features. However, once he has shifted all the weight of synthesis to existence, Ricoeur can content himself with a quite nominalistic secondary, order-creating synthesis. Merely conceptual 'schematisms' must result from this design decision because the true synthesis (Thirdness for Peirce) is in the reader's existence. The mimetic synthesis interlocks with the authentic whole only at a later stage (mimesis III). Only here can the ties to the reader's existence produce being-a-whole as the idea of justice (for the characters of the story). Thus imitation stands for the non-authentic order. It involves neither the fabrication of lies nor an analogy to the 'really real reality.' Indeed, if there is a conflict between what actually happened and what is credible, Aristotle says the choice must be the (typical and therefore) credible. Configuration is, then, a concrete application of pragmatic logic to what is in itself not configured because it is not logical. This is as much the case in social reality as in texts. So for both myth and action, mimesis functions as literal com-position (i.e., positing into one whole that which is disparate and heterogeneous).

The mimesis of action has three aspects.

1 Whole: *Mythos* transforms the flow of events into stories. The transformation of 'doing' into 'acting' is the difference of mere successions of changes and discrete units. Only acts of doing something determinate can have units or steps towards it. Steps are logical units, not physical ones. 'Becoming-a-story' only connects actions into a meaningful whole, one that is more than the sum of its parts. The sum of episodes is not yet a narration, in spite of television serials (which are not a sum of episodes; rather, episodes tend to be repetitions of the same whole).

2 Unification: Configuration as a necessary function accomplishes the concordance of the discordant ('concordance-discordance') (cf. Ricocur 1983: 65–75, 103). For the purpose of imitating actions, a unity of such disparate elements such as intrigue, characters, surprising turns, and ideas is composed (cf. *supra*, Aristotle's six parts of mimesis in 1450 a7–10: ἀνάγκη οὖν πάσης τραγῳδίας μέρη εἶναι ἕξ, καθ' ἅ ποιά τις ἐστὶν ἡ τραγῳδία· ταῦτα δ'ἐστί [1] μῦθος καί [2] ἤθη καί [3] λέξις καί [4] διάνοια καί [5] ὄψις καί [6] μελοποιία). Here the semantic of action passes from paradigmatic to syntagmatic, from an isolated act meaningful to a minute human task to a perceived finality of a broader action context (which can even be as broad as historiography). Added to this unity is chronological unity, which unites with an achronic concept that which is chronologically apart. A story must be of one time and duration (cf. *supra*). The manifold of events is united in one conceptual con-clusion. Thus, the dianoietic concept becomes the unifying substitute for time. Assuming the concept is (a

Peircean) purpose, that teleology is an artificial and arbitrary whole. This purpose or teleology is founded in the narrative contract alone and thus presents the reader with a '*Quête*,' including inherent 'methods of (pseudo)-discovery.' That whole, as quest that has a chance to be concluded, must be carefully established as a probable one. Already in the *Poetic*, the length or μέγεθος (i.e., the 'natural' end of a narration) is determined not by a temporal measure but by a purpose – that is, of inspiring fear and pity (φόβος καί ἐλεός).

3 Schematism: The temporal synthesis of heterogeneous actions is performed chronologically. Events become episodes. In comparison to Kant's Schematism (cf. *supra*), narrative logic is similarly automatic in creating the Whole. Like the application of categories, historical schematism produces the effect that a narration can be followed, in the double sense of the term: there is a synthetical force both intellectually and in the sense of a *post hoc ergo propter hoc* causality. The result is a temporal extension.

These three aspects have a threefold result:

1 Linear representation of a 'then ... and then.' This presupposes an act of insight (dianoietic) that direction to the sequence of 'thens,' episodes of a whole.

2 The sequence is principally open. There is always another 'and then.' For Kant, the only 'seizable' in time is not that it is infinite; rather, it is a partial extension of the infinite. Time cannot be thought of as limited, just as causality cannot be terminated (not even by a big bang or black hole). History, however, has the precise effect of setting a final point. It is the theme, narrative figuration, position, that in truth is a com- or ad-position. Narrative closure is not time but thema (literally thetic, setting of a final point).

3 Stories, finally, peremptorily impose time as irreversible. Through dianoia, the thematic insight, narration means that it is read from the end. Everything that is between the configured beginning and the final point has an irreversibility in its own right. By this stage we can construe Kermode's 'Sense of an Ending.' Knowing the whole (in the sense of *totum*, not *omnis*), we read in the beginning (but with hindsight from the end) the conditions and the manner of its ending.

Narrative intelligibility is not constructed *ab ovo* every time it is used; instead it avails itself of narrative schemes.[8] Calling them 'schematism' grants them a quasi-intuitive status; in the manner of Kantian schematism, they become 'eine Eigenschaft unseres Gemüts' (*KrV* B37, 'a property of our mind'). This will become important for Ricoeur's debate with narrative formalisms. However, since this is not an apperceptional schematism, it is culturally established as a work of rules. It is only as a cultural form (i.e., in a tradition of narratives) that this schema of a *totum* becomes configured. Speaking of narrative 'schematism' is almost metaphoric usage, since there can be no trace of true necessity in it. Schema gives no more than a pattern that admits infinite variations. Historical developments occur at all three levels – of the schematic form, of the genre, and of the type – and certainly they differ between any two cultures.[9] This alone should dispel any analogy with schematism proper, since there is no such thing as a narrative category that would determine a schematism. Aristotle had 'stable variants' from the general pattern, with tragedy as its purest incarnation. Comedy 'suffers' from foregrounding (for the pattern rules) the character of actors too much, whereas historical tales are the furthest from the scheme because they require diegesis. Only literary theory can explain the substance of what became, historically, a schematic pattern in various epochs through the dialectic of innovation and sedimentation. Thus the Occidental tradition developed eventually into one of genres (Frye's mythoi) such as tragedy, comedy, and so on, each of these permitting only certain forms of narrative causality. At any stage of formal advancement, Classics (i.e., exemplary single works) retain their model nature. Paradigmata, then, are always subject to innovation, especially through poetic efforts that constitute deviations when compared to the classical paradigm. Furthermore, these deviations can occur in each of the three dimensions of a paradigm.

Mimesis II, despite its technically literary aspect, becomes in Ricoeur a temporal configuration. It must contribute to the task of unifying the Other, the strange. Therefore, as an Ecstatical imitation, configuration is in the present, in the ready-at-hand (being 'zuhanden,' which is in the etymological neighbourhood of 'Handlung,' action). Concern creates its own world-time, an extension as far as concern reaches. Configuration thus presupposes the idea of an acting, striving being, who may or may not have forgotten its provenience from the Potentiality-for-Being.

Refiguration, 'Mimèsis III,' is materially the final stage. In Ricoeur, however, it is the origin of the possibility of narration. Contrary to Mallarmé's adage 'toute chose au monde existe pour aboutir dans un livre,' everything terminates really in a reader (or spectator). In a certain sense, this is contained in Aristotle's idea of the κάθαρσις of the spectator. It is not enough that narration is based on the fact of acting being human (mimesis I).

The idea that 'mise-en-intrigue' is capable of (trans)forming the source from which it sprang is the quintessence of hermeneutics. It stands for a dynamic transformation of fixed meaning, and does so in hindsight, *a posteriori*. All efforts of interpretation thus become highly contingent and necessarily idiosyncratic. Such a 'joker in the pack' seems suspicious and difficult to treat and is rarely fully accepted in literary and film theory. Here enters the debate between Ricoeur and formalist approaches to narration, in particular that of Greimas. Ricoeur's central assumption is that in the last resort, narrative closure is achieved not by textual means but rather by the telos of life, of the finite existence of the reader. Narrative closure is by no means the end of a narrative. In order to understand it, we must have understood the entire potential, of which the story is one of its realizations. The surprising turn of the story, περιπέτεια, 'coup du théâtre,' can be understood because it was a possibility. This already goes beyond pure formal schematism – it is actually a threat to it. Refiguring the concretely configured is the task of mimesis III. Thus, it is a necessary text function to direct beyond the text.

A question arises: Where does the potential for potentiality come from? In terms of narrative literature, where does the potentiality of apocalyptic (in its variegate forms, even the most banalized ones) come from? Furthermore – the example dear to Ricoeur – there is the case of the psychotherapeutic discourse. Its power lies not in its well-formed configuration as a story, but in that it serves as a springboard for a personal transformation. If it could not open possibilities, new alleys of imagination, its narrative essence would change. Instead of therapy it would become a verdict. In the double sense of Schapp's 'Entangled in stories' [*In Geschichten verstrickt*; cf. Ricoeur 1983: 114f), one's personality is one's prehistory, which has the strangling effect of verdicts and at the same time can possibly open its own way out of its own entanglement. Jauss's literary theory of the *vis comica* (cf. *supra*) is another case in point. Comedies inexorably pass their sentence on the ridiculed subjects and thereby have a liberating effect for the judges spectators. To achieve this, they must transform the life of the spectator.

Ricoeur's theory of the narrative potentiality blends with, and repeats, temporal ecstases. Refiguration is the narrative equivalent of the openness of the ad-vent, future in the Caring Dasein. However, in this approach all openness depends on the textual anchors in existence. It is not the texts, the peculiar sign relations of some texts, that are open. Openness is existential openness. A text can only be as open as the open potential of an existence of the reader, which, however, ends in death. Conceptualizing the reader/spectator involves considerable risks – in particular, the Reader might be misunderstood psychologically or empirically. In fact, it is a purely textual instance (a very old insight, which, again understood, inspired Metz's diatribe against personalized enunciation). Ricoeur does not confuse the role of the author or reader in the text (not necessarily within the textual universe) with that of the human being who actually reads. He merely maintains that the former cannot be without the latter. The intersection of the text universe with that of its receiver is 'temps de l'agir et du pâtir' (ibid.: 109), which is what Gadamer meant with *applicatio*. In the Text, the refigurational potential is derived from the Receiver or Author, as their Potentiality-for-Being ('Sein-Können').

In view of his theory design, we must not impute Hegelianism to Ricoeur. The refigurational potential is not 'philosophy of history' in the evil sense of the term (all kinds of determinism). Ignoring the 'Hegelian temptation' makes sense with *Dasein*-analytical premises. Narrative potentiality is rooted in Potentiality-for-Being but in a special, derived way. The anchor in existence is 'traces' (cf. *infra*); the temptation to cognize a historical totality is principally thwarted when the potentiality is pegged to the traces of the dead, the having-been-there (who had *Dasein*: *die Dagewesenen*). What could not be realized in their life causes in responsibility the need to narrate their story, and by narrating it to make it whole. Therefore, refiguration is not an absolute teleology of history, but the open telos of closed lives (having-been-toward-the-end). The potential in refiguration is to be seen in the context of taking over the destiny, the being-with of those who have-been. That responsibility is no longer a general teleology, consciousness of the course of history. Instead, it is the expression of a general desire for Being-whole. Even history, fictional or real, wants to be whole. It is not enough that a story comes to its end. The whole created by narrative technique is a borrowed teleological logic. Endings are transcended existentially into their wholeness.

In mimesis theory, Ricoeur has delivered an imitation of action (as in the *Poetic*); he has also provided a mimesis of Heidegger's analysis in the outside, the Otherness of temporal existence. He has done through narration what existential analysis alone cannot achieve. The result is not so much a hermeneutics of action as an extension to solitariness. An analysis of public existence as temporal is, however, always dependent on the analysis of Dasein. The tripartition of mimesis is an indication that it is a borrowed pragmatic logic. It cannot function outside itself, which is precisely the bone of contention with formalist narratologies. The narrative schematism of configuration is not really one in the strict Kantian sense; rather, building on existential temporality, it is a kind of cultural *a priori*.

Ricoeur's repetition-in-narration makes it possible to repeat history as the taking over of guilt, which seemed to be restricted to the authenticity of Caring *Dasein*. Because narrative logic is conceived as repetition, it no longer precludes (axiomatically, as it were) a reopening of sombre chapters of history, which are 'sorrow'-ful, 'care'-ful, precisely because potentialities of human action could not be realized. A transcendent authenticity of human existence translates narratively into a transcendental fulfilment of human action beyond its intratemporal constraints. What justifies a return to the past is not the past for the past's sake, but instead the past for the 'not yet,' the potentialities' sake. This unique achievement of narrativity as repetition of potentiality-of-Being is possible only according to the premises of *Dasein* analysis. Ricoeur does not accomplish this as a philosophy of history. The difference is that although a potential refers to a whole, it cannot even name it as the philosophy of history does (and as this century has had occasion to observe as ideologies becoming reality).

The reason for such wordlessness lies in the inauthentic mode of vulgar narrative time. Authentically, the whole is death; but there is no equivalent to the unifying force of death in history and in its unrealized potential and in historical guilt. It is still evidenced by the hierarchy of levels of authenticity on what totality and finality depend. In Peirce the wholeness of the cognitive potential is neither (ideologically) realized, as we have seen, nor is it derived from another, authentic and experiential whole. Instead, it is Real in every Sign process as General Third. It is reflected metaphysically as ultimate opinion, which is, however, not an existent object. The driving force here is cognition (taken in its full Pragmaticistic breadth, of course), in which time has a role that is crucial but not isolated.

Narration theory has no 'natural' object that urges itself into our minds. Only in one given philosophical context 'is' narration something. In the *Poetic's* understanding of narration as mimesis of human praxis and not of human beings, narration was a pragmatic device for producing cathartic effects in spectators. For representation, this meant it had to be typical rather than realistic. Another such purpose (pathos) is found only in the Rhetoric, where it is sharply distinguished from cognitive truth as purpose. At any rate, the purpose of narration was not to render a world faithfully. Narrating as such already meant the 'defamiliarization' of a universe into a typos. In the hermeneutic tradition we have in principle a vexing and radically different alternative understanding of narration proper. It makes the unifying purpose more topical than any other theory. Even at the derived, vulgar level as a mimetic theory of social configuration, it sees a unifying potential by overcoming solitariness for interaction.[10] The Order of time constitutes everything human. In this way, Ricoeur's approach differs principally from other attempts to define the order of narration through a whole that is constitutive of an order.

In view of this origin of narration as theoretical object it is at least as interesting to see the reasons why it became an object of problematization, as to see what kind of object[11] it is. Unification as purpose creates 'narrativity' in hermeneutics. Other ways of questioning, however – Foucault's nominalist narratology, for one – defined human Order as the discursive order of things, held together by relations of power. Deleuze's Bergsonism is a third way to grasp narration. A different principle constituting the typical order of narration has been identified in linguistic quasi-universals. There can be no doubt that grammatical order is a universal needed for functioning speech; even so, there is no easy step from sentence to text order. Since narration exists, explaining this fact only by linguistics calls for an order-constituting principle below the sentence surface. What Greimas called 'deep structure'[12] is a point in case. The difference between unavowedly transcendentalist universals such as Greimas's and a 'responsibility before the dead' cannot be greater (insofar as I am based on the ground of what their tradition passed on to me).

The first implication is methodological. *Daseinsanalyse* can only be comprehended in reenaction or in testimony, and Ricoeur's insistence on the re-entrance point into the existence of the reader's time in the act of reading is very necessary to a hermeneutical theory. Understanding is 'divinatory' (as Schleiermacher called it; cf. Gadamer 1990). The usual metaphor is 'melting horizons' (i.e., with another subjectivity). What the case in understanding as such is, is even more so in matters of *Dasein*. Ultimate existential conditions such as temporality cannot be communicated; they can only be shared, in testimony. Now, there can be no proof that this identification (i.e., *idem*-fication, same-making) happens – that is, that the result will be felicitous (usually referred to as 'glücken'). To prove it, we must presuppose it already, which is to say that understanding (which is not a purely phenomenological eidetic reduction[13]) is circular albeit not a vicious circle. Thus the extreme solitariness of *Dasein*, also identification as the understanding of the other solitary being, is in the sharpest possible contrast to the linguistic universals of Greimas's Narrative Grammar.

The opposition between the narratologies of Greimas and Ricoeur reaches deep into the comprehension of language itself. If there is a meaningful way to speak of universals in Ricoeur, these are by no means universals of meaning. His recusancy of semiological nominalism is his due from a hermeneutical position. His principal dispute with semiology is directed against its abstract immateriality. If narrative schemes are but the universals of the 'social imaginary,' no transformation of time in subjects is possible. In his longstanding discussion with Greimas, the prerogatives of materiality and existence were reclaimed. His universals are not transcendental; rather, they are contingent on a given culture as its semantic resources. Thus 'configurational' universes created by narratives are not, in his eyes, nominalist intrusions into narration. For his terminology distinguishes between semantics and semiology. The latter deals with signs that are defined only by other signs. Narrative universals here can therefore only stem from the essence of signs themselves and not from a world or action outside of signs. The former, instead, is concerned with larger units of signification such as sentences and beyond, but it is assumed that a sentence and *a fortiori* a text always refer to a world. Their meaning, though, can be established through their internal position in a system.

For Ricoeur this conception of language in general would put an end to tendencies that exclude the world of experience from the textual world. Yet severing the linkage between the two is the methodological *a priori* of linguistics. For Ricoeur sentences are always *about* something; they never merely *mean* signifieds (by differences). There is no arbitraire du signe here. However, that language as Same ('le Même') has its match in its Other ('son Autre') of the world cannot be deduced from language alone. Ricoeur's antinominalism is not yet a realism. His comprehension of language still depends on hermeneutic presuppositions, which are functional. That is, there must at least be communication, and therefore the being-in-the-world-and-time of communicators. This is a consequence of existential hermeneutics. As much as narration is unified through its descent from the authentic time of *Dasein*, language is ineluctably referring to a world because it comes from communicating subjects, and not because it is self-contained in producing meaning (through its own means, however).

The nominalistic problem arises only with language taken strictly in itself. Since the languaged nature of reality does not imply, conversely, the realistic nature of language, the exact determination of the relationship between the two is an open question. There is the immanent (Ricoeur says 'semiotic,' Frege says 'Sinn') system of mutually defined signs; there is also the referential (Ricoeur says 'semantic,' Frege says 'Bedeutung') system. Nevertheless, the 'world' universe and the 'signs' universe cannot be reduced to either. Once we have separated these systems, we must determine their relation. De Saussure opted for the arbitrary of signs, and nominalism. Ricoeur, instead, while admitting that the two systems are separate, chooses experience as the common ground of both language and the real. Experience, however is not accessed again in the dichotomy of apperception and concept, or sign system and reference, but rather phenomenologically as immediately given.[14] Instead of being a (methodological) autonomous object with its own laws and rules, language remains subject to its representational function. However, even with these premises, Ricoeur must admit a (relatively) autonomous operation of the 'symbolic resources,' following their own 'symbolic mechanics.' In spite of all the emphasis on temporality and the temporal nature of narrative configuration, there is a lawful operation (to which the entire volume Ricoeur [1984] is dedicated). Again, in this strictly narratological context, his argumentation strategy emphasizes the enunciation aspect (as existential anchor of narration). Nevertheless, even in this narrow, 'maximally minimal' interval there reigns a logic proper (ibid.: 63–71). For other narratologies this is the very core. Ricoeur cannot avoid it, and as a consequence, he cannot avoid debating the foundations of non-hermeneutic literary theories.

5.4 Greimas's Semiosis

The thesis that Ricoeur argues is nicely formulated (quoting Bremond 1973: 133): 'les 'nécessités conceptuelles immanentes au développement des rôles' relèvent davantage d'une sémantique et d'une logique de l'action que d'une logique véritablement narrative' (ibid.: 70, i.e., refutation of a narratological logic proper, its subordination under a pragmatic logic and semantic). This is all Ricoeur needs to prove against Greimas; because if it were possible to deduce such an autonomous narrative logic, the temporal nature of the compositional constraints would be disavowed. Certainly, this diametrical opposition is not just between Ricoeur and Greimas; it is also between hermeneutics and semiology, between phenomenological and nominalist approaches to reality and language in arbitrary sign convention.

Semionarratology is a respectably thorough attempt to describe principles of order that make the parts of speech a totality of meaning. It is much more than a literary theory. Its approach to questioning the object narration – or texts and all major linguistic organizations generally – is intrinsically different from other approaches to narrations. Without naming it as deduction, the deduction of linguistic universals of processes around the production of meaning was called generativism. This terminology reflects the fact that language does not exist as the sum of all possible combinations of its elements; rather, it is a set of rules that produce these possibilities. Ricoeur apparently is not unimpressed by this idea. In fact, after renaming it (a little metaphorically) 'schematism,' he finds the constrictive force of its automatism quite useful. This does not follow from his own semantic structure alone. His repeated and strenuous debate with the Semionarratological force of generation (or constriction of order) cannot be avoided. So much in his narration theory depends on the 'configurational' potential itself as it is produced by the linguistic medium. Yet Ricoeur is not alone. Doubts have arisen in other quarters besides about the strictly logical claim of Semionarratology. Budniakiewicz (1992) suspects that simple pragmatic syllogisms are the base of Semionarratology. Petitot-Cocorda (1985a) pushes the drive to found the logic of narrative grammar onto topological forms. Outside these extensions or critiques, what exactly is being claimed by the narrative logic of the Paris School of Semionarratology?

Although still considered a work in progress, the fundamental positions are clear and have been described often. Its quintessential instantiation is the 'Semiotic Square.'[15] What task is it supposed to accomplish? The product of language, in the semiological understanding, is a meaning effect (*effet de sens*), no less (i.e., it is autarkic in this respect) and no more (i.e., it has no relation to the physical world or to the mind). Further, the fundamental linguistic act is a proposition. The objective is to deduce all meaning effects from a small handful of primitives. Now, if a proposition is 'to make be,' and its primitives therefore are 'make' and 'be,' a first genesis of meaning is a disposition of 'to make' (an enunciated of making) and 'to be' (an enunciated of being). The 'be' of 'to make be' can be any of the following possible states, described in the 'Square of Veridiction' (cf. Greimas 1986: 34ff): (1) A being (*être*) is shown (*paraître*) (and then its primitive semantic effect is to be *true*). (2) A non-being (*non être*) is shown (then it is a *lie* or *illusion*). (3) A non-being (*non être*) is not shown (which is *false*). (4) A being (*être*) is not shown (i.e., it is concealed) (which is *secret*). Being is in contradictory relation to non-being and in contrary relation to appearing, being to non-appearing is in a relation of presupposition. This close resemblance to Aristotelian logical oppositions is not fortuitous, but because it is the 'natural logic' in Greimas's eyes.

These four positions are in the first place formal positions (cf. Greimas 1970: 138). If invested with semantic content, they control at a very fundamental level the impression of reality by the sign system. Moreover, in a more superficial level of a given semantic field, they can control the static and dynamic relations of the elements. The question is now, on what can this hope of a deduction of all meaning effects be founded? This claim is somewhat reduced when we postulate only a 'generativism' of meaning and not an elaborated structure. It is evident that a primary role is given to the opposition relations in the Square. Another assumption – much less explicit but of equal importance – is the factual pre-existence of language. That it functions as a tool of communication in given discourses is presupposed. However, everything hinges on the fact that meaning effects are brought into existence by 'enunciating' subjects. If there is an enunciation at all, then it must be 'about' something. This is the implicit premiss. What semionarratology must avoid at all costs is the deduction that there 'is' indeed something or that a existent reality 'informs' language. From the perspective of Narrative Grammar, meaning shows merely how language operates in a self-contained and self-explicated manner: it creates the 'reality' it needs, but only as effect. All further assumptions are not covered by its method. Nevertheless, this *illusion référentielle* is necessarily established by an act of enunciation.

As our earlier debate with binary logic showed, the main weakness in Greimas's deductions concerns his unquestioned binarism. This corresponds logically to a two-valued logic (one that is subject to the principle of excluded middle, etc.); it is also an ontological option. Two values can treat existential relations adequately. All truly General statements, Laws, Arguments in the strict logical sense are out of reach.

Insofar as he needs them, Greimas has shifted truly General terms into his general assumptions on language and about anthropological constants. This enables him to avoid accounting for truly General processes in language, such as cognition. Ricoeur has made this the subject of the Other of language (cf. *supra*), which is much more than the existence of worldly objects – it also includes a lawful universe.[16] The triadic principle in Peirce is essential and can never be reconciled with a dyadic binarism, as much as binary opposition is essential for Greimas.

If we are to attack Semionarratology, except on its fundamental binary option, we can do so at two soft spots: (A) the exact logical nature of the Square, and (B) the suppressed traces of its existential setting in enunciation. Ricoeur is doing exactly this. For Ricoeur, narration is not a mere meaning effect; rather, it is inexorably linked to human experience. It is the world of the reader, who must serve as link between the textual world and the object world. What a text really achieves in terms of world relationship cannot be understood from linguistics. If a narrative has 'refigurational' consequences, sign arbitrariness cannot but cut off the purpose of narration.

Ricoeur concurs with Greimas regarding the functional understanding of narrative forms in Propp's sense. The relative stringency, the minimum conditions, and the non-arbitrary order of narration were first described by Propp, albeit without a far-reaching theory. Yet this propelled Greimas toward 'homologization.' The result was the idea of a Narrative Grammar, a comprehensive text syntax with rules for generating meaning. Because it is beyond the level of sentences, it can no longer follow linguistic features. The strength (cf. Greimas 1989: 555) of such a layered model is that unlike Chomsky's generativism, its surface level is not overloaded with an all-explanatory logic of both syntactic and semantic unfolding. Even when expanded into a generativism, everything hinges on the power of logic. The manifestation relation of depths and surfaces – the entire 'generative process or *parcours*' – is based on strict logical premises. This is the point that Ricoeur (1984: 85–91) criticizes as not really explicative of the narration.[17]

Regarding point A: Greimas's Square (cf. *supra*) claims, as taxonomy, strict logical relations. As a necessary unfolding of meaning, it must be automatic and universal and carry the force of a logical law. Only on such strict premises can Greimas (1970: 166) claim that both as taxonomic operations and as 'oriented' syntactic operations (cf. *infra*) they are 'prévisibles et calculables.' Ricoeur counters that this must ruin the narrative unpredictability; even so, it can logically be imagined that indeed everything is predictable with the same necessity as logical oppositions. This would not be new, nor would it be an innovative insight. It is simply one of the most basic laws of the most classical logic. The positions of both Ricoeur and Greimas follow perfectly in their mutual opposition the respective narratological assumptions. Ricoeur must hold – and not simply as respectful concession to poetical περιπέτεια – the principal openness of narratives. Narration is temporal and temporality is Potentiality-for-being; it follows that narratives's central achievement is that it creates open horizons. Greimas understands narration's form as linguistic operations. Because language is system and rules, anything less than closed totality would cease to function systemically. It must become completely inexplicable. His predictability and conjecture claims are typical not of narratology but of language as a whole. In defence of systemic narratology, the following can be objected:

(1) Not every position in a Square must be filled, although logically, all four positions must exist. These four position can then be implied or completed as necessary. To minimize narrative surprise, these vacancies might be good enough. At the same time, no narration can be really open as long as it remains a probable one. Perhaps it is alluring to speak of refiguration, but even then there are limits to the imaginable as long as the logic of figuration is still a narrative one.

(2) The formal aspect of meaning generation is not necessarily something to be held against Greimas. Ricoeur postulates that the real logic of narration is merely pragmatic, based on the real actions of human beings. Even then it has been described 'in analytical philosophy.' This description is not based only on 'ordinary language,' or on its repertory of verbs, which are different in any concrete culture. It also describes a logical content. 'Basic actions' (in mimesis I) are a logical scaffolding of the 'verb-ness' of verbs. They are the basis of true judgments, although their pragmatic nature makes it unreasonable to reduce them to simple 'adequation with existent reality' sorts of judgments. Clearly, they presuppose a more sophisticated metaphysic of reality than mere existence (however, Pragmaticism is not the topic here). The point is only that 'ordinary language' is reasonable. To the extent that it is reasonable, it is formal, and presupposes rules. Not because they are pragmatic, they are less strict rules (and even abductive reasoning is rule-based). What we can object to in Greimas's Square, though, is its exclusively deductive formalism. When we ascertain predictability on deductive premises only, meaning generation as

a deductive exercise is indeed imperilled by chance. Semiology does not seem capable of handling true chance.

(3) Ricoeur's objection that nothing surprising or new can happen in this narratology can be confirmed from another perspective besides. One of the basic operations in the Square is the contrary relation of semic elements. A standard example is 'black' as contrary to 'white.' Indeed, this hides a deeper problem behind the commonsensical appearance of the examples. How can we determine sememes (not negations) as relatable? They must be the same category and must be treated only in this particular regard. When we take 'black' and 'white' as same, we are presupposing the general idea of which they are the same. In other words, we are presupposing the triad of a sign relation with a Generality as its mediating correlate. According to a previous decision, blackness and whiteness can be taken either as (cases of) 'colour' *or* (cases of) extreme poles on a spectrum of 'darkness.' If this ontic hierarchy is not reflected, we must end up with an ontological concept of being. Taking Deleuze's word, a convergence point might be found in an 'empty square one' ('case vide' Deleuze [1973: 321–30], which can be taken by virtually anything: Object X, the transcendental object, mana, phallus, zero phoneme, or material value). Or it might be an abstract difference of being and nothing, from which we deduce all further determinations. The logical construction of the world as a taxonomy of meaning in the École de Paris[18] is at any rate based on deduction as a strict logical operation. There can be no chance. We can speculate on how a narratology would be if there are sign relations that can deal with chance. Those sign relations must be open ones and genuinely aesthetic processes of discovery. An amalgamation of Ricoeur and Greimas, then.

Regarding point B: Ricoeur's second principal objection to the narratology of the École de Paris concerns this question: By what's power is temporality introduced? In his view, 'oriented operations' – tokens of syntagmatic ordering – do not follow from the taxonomy of the Square. Instead, they introduce a full-fledged chronologization. It must have been symptomatic that Ricoeur found the inconspicuous remark in Greimas (1970: 164) 'production de sens par le sujet.' Indeed, this is not a *lapsus calami*; rather, since Greimas (1976), it has been taken up explicitly as 'enunciation.' Although there is an augmentation in meaning from deep structure to surface structure to discursive production, the latter cannot be a scientific object, because on the discourse level there are too many imponderables. Its sole objective is restricted to the analysis, the 'parcours de la méthode' (Bertrand 1984: 32)] of narrative programs as such. The concrete production of narrative programs is a matter of 'mise en discours' (op. cit. 30), whose procedure may differ greatly from analysis. This explicitly limits the interest of semiology to 'l'objectivation du texte.'[19] Hence, an axis of meaning, which is not easy to conceive of.

Especially criticizable in Ricoeur's view is the source from which meaning gains in meaning. As narration, this meaning must be gaining at that point along a temporal axis where the narrative discourse is most meaningful. It is not derived from deeper structures, but there is no source of time. In his debate with Ricoeur Greimas used a variety of metaphors to describe the relation along the axis. For instance, 'the figurative clothed narrative structures,' which is then 'abstractly' clarified: 'the mode of existence of narrative structures is a virtual mode of existence. Narrative structures do not exist per se but are a mere moment in the generation of signification.' Figures 'bear the traces of narrative universals' (all Greimas 1989: 557). Ricoeur, however, denies this relation of virtuality when he claims that 'because of ... the freedom of enunciation, and also the constraints of the last level ... figurativization has its own rules' [ibid.].

What does 'virtual-(actualized)-manifest' mean, anyway? Greimas's answer is that 'the problematics of levels is [sic] a strategy because the number of levels can be increased or diminished in order to facilitate the analysis and the construction of the model" (1989: 560). As the debate unfailingly showed, however, the connection between levels[20] remains problematic – an ultimately arbitrary choice of discourse into which another discourse is 'transcoded' (cf. Greimas 1989: 562). It proved to be difficult to transcode the very complex discursive level, which has depth structures of its own. Significantly, there is no agreement between Ricoeur and Greimas regarding how the relationship between levels can be understood. It is all but impossible to reconcile an ontologically understood generative narrative grammar with hermeneutic circularity. For the latter, the problem with the former is that it has limited power to explain predictably how narrative meaning is generated on the basis of a few polemical (cf. Greimas 1989: 595) principles of contrariety. Greimas happily admits that a number of meaning effects are dependent on enunciation – for example, actorialization, aspectualization (modality), and temporalization. For Ricoeur, in contrast, the very syntagmatic force of the Square is chronological. It introduces genuine temporal duration and extension into oppositional logic.

Taxonomy and orientation cannot by any means be identical if orientation introduces irreversibility. Transformation – as the 'make be' operation is called – is not a change in the form; it is really a passage of time. In narrative terms, the direction of an operation shows in the subsequent operation, as Ricoeur remarks, and finally in the global aim of the narrative itself.

So it is not counterintuitive when Ricoeur surmises that the novelty of the syntagmatic addition does not arise from the logical force of the taxonomic model. He argues that a semantic of action must be admitted when temporal sequence is introduced as logical force (cf. *supra*). However, his doubt that 'doing,' *'faire'* (cf. Ricoeur 1984: 87Fn), can be described in pragmatic categories without reference to acting humans plays too much on his own hermeneutic premises. It has been shown that there are other philosophical options for finding finality in action. In a metaphysic based on Continuity, this is no problem at all. Moreover, Pragmaticism is the best proof that an alternative comprehension of action is feasible. It even includes cognition in signs in its temporal dimension.

Enunciation – the ultimate locus where virtual and actualized narrative meaning is realized – the generative discourse level, then, served Ricoeur as Dasein anchor of a semantic of action. It is somewhat surprising, therefore, that the very generative principle – if not directly criticized as by Ricoeur – was implicitly recognized as insufficient. 'Virtuality' cannot avail itself of psychological states or of only logical constraints. Nor does it have the force of explicit transcendental arguments. Some fermentation around the foundational principles within the Paris School gave birth to a number of 'extensions,' which head in basically two directions. Some, like Petitot-Cocorda (1985a), move deliberately in a Platonistic direction. Others, like Zilberberg, move into a decidedly Hjelmslevian, nominalistic direction (both also in their respective articles in Greimas [1986]). A very interesting extension of the founding logic, and the very base of its syntagmatic force, is a theory of *'thymie.'* We might see in this a placeholder of corporality, which (after Schopenhauer) is the origin of the will. At a level of fundamental syntax (as 'dys-' or 'euphory'), it is a sort of libidinal general driving principle. At the narrative level, it operates meaning generating as 'thymic' forces. For narrative generativism, this means that it seems to draw its explanatory power from anthropological analogy, if not anthropomorphism.

Undeniably, Greimas is at his best and most convincing at the surface level of narrative Grammar. Away from the 'mal des profondeurs' (about which he is mocking his pupils?), he is dealing with text-organizing principles, which are agents (roles, actors, actantial functions united in different roles or in one, their competences, modalities of acting will, etc.) defined and educed by an initial problematic situation and necessary for its 'dénouement.'[21] Actantial schemes and functions apply to any narrative, whatever medium of discourse is used, and are conceived of as dynamic principles and agents between an initial disturbance of order and its final restitution.

Others, for example Budniakiewicz (1992), are pessimistic about the explanatory power of oppositional logical relations. It is true that Greimas deduces the explication of narrative meaning from the basis of a proposition (as its logical unfolding), yet this is still a step away from maintaining that this should really be the logical unfolding of a practical syllogism. Budniakiewicz is certainly right to opt for a less necessary logic (which this sort of syllogism is considered to be). She is still a step away from supposing explicitly human acting according to its mere idea. Ricoeur did not even attempt this thoroughly (cf. *supra*). Indeed, it must be a formidable task to deduce narration from the idea of human action, if a semantic of action assumes this task already as fulfilled in the representational achievement of language.

We need not repeat here the basic objections against the binarism in Semionarratology. In particular against the binary, dyadic pairs of oppositions in the genesis of narrative meaning it can be said that the 'weak logical' force in this consists of the intrinsic lack of generalization. As we saw in Peirce's analysis of the contingent law of time, there can be no strict metaphysical necessity in temporal sequences of events. However, binary oppositions provide even less than a law, which requires Thirdness. Conduct (i.e., any action that is more than just aimless doing) requires purpose, which is logically a Third. Greimas supplies all the purposiveness from the enunciation situation, which creates destination. The purpose of an act of narrating guarantees the dynamic of the basic Semiotic Square of a narrative (expressed in its destination roles), thus providing purpose to the pairs of oppositions. Therefore, Ricoeur's critique of the true source of narrative dynamic of purpose in Semionarratology does not hinge on hermeneutic premises; it can be verified in strict logic.

5.5 Bordwell's Formalism

Formalism is another contending theory of narration or poetic. However, this approach is much less formal as well as less demanding in its theoretical claim than Greimas's 'normalization' of it. First in historical terms was Propp's analysis of a limited set of narrative functions, which cover the entire field of possible fairy tales. We need not decide here whether it is permissible to count Propp among the Russian Formalists. According to Bordwell (1981: XII), Formalists are 'the most significant theorists of narrative since Aristotle.'

The question put to Formalism in this context of narration theory must be a limited one: What new discovery with regard to narrativity proper does it contain? It is of course its prerogative to define anew the object narration through a new way of questioning. Now Formalism[22] in a narrower sense saw itself as an (aesthetic) theory of 'literature-ness.' We can interpret this as being close to Aristotle's *Poetic* in one point – that narration is defined from a purpose point of view: a novel vision of things. Although the spectators' κάθαρσις was the *Poetic's* purpose, we could identify in the πάθος type of argumentation (v. *supra*) a familiarity with the 'trick of defamiliarization' in the Formalist approach. Principally, however, we find here a concern with the outside world rather than with spectators and subjects. Still, in the *Poetic* a universe in a probable and possible form was subordinate to the basic purpose. Now, instead, narrativity does not produce this εἰκός, but its significant opposite, the representational equivalent of περιπέτεια, the planned surprise turn-around. The problem is that this is the turn-around not of an action but of a universe. This seems to eliminate the mimesis of praxis from the definition of narration. Although the whole idea of action, teleology, and so on has not evaporated from Formalism, which still talks of 'events' – without, however, reflecting further on how events turn into a unity (of a plot).

Relabelling Formalism (for film theory) as Neoformalism has not yet changed these fundamentals; a 'normal,' 'automatic' constitution of textual, narrative meaning continues to be implied. Neo-Formalism argued that this constitution problem is addressed by a Constructivist foundation. There is no easy way to bridge the enormous gap between perception and a text, which is constituted by events and their unifying purpose. Evidently the *world* cannot be 'estranged'; it is a text that represents world, through its purpose (not necessarily in language, but at least in 'forming' concepts or διάνοια). Bordwell attempts to supply or presuppose the 'automatic' representation of textual meaning and a narrative universe without resorting to the pragmatic logic of action. Greimas instead attributes the generation of narrative meaning strictly to a logical concept – one that creates the idea of action as a deduction of the propositional act. 'Normal' and 'unusual' worlds have no relevance for a poetic proper. *Poetic* catharsis (as the gist of a drama) is not estrangement but rather the idealization – which is also 'unusual,' but in a different way – of the righteousness (δικαιοσύνη or ἁμαρτία; 1453a.8/10.) of human acting. This was the purpose of the *Poetic* in explaining in its rules and variations. Aristotle's Poetic chose pragmatic logic, the imitation of praxis, and Ricoeur wanted to follow him in this theoretical choice. The idea of human action, in all its societal conditioning, reigns to such a degree that even the desirable tragical transformation becomes an ideal of human action.

Without pragmatic logic and purpose, there is a clear need of another 'agency of change' in the drama (doing) of a poetic product. Now Formalism insists on the one pivotal transformation of 'making strange.' This is tantamount to asking two questions in a more technical key: (1) How does the production of text occur? (2) How does the production of 'strange text' occur as a transformation? All without a Ricoeur-like basis in *Dasein* as the sole guarantor of narrative totality through temporal unity. If (2) is thought to be responsible for the aesthetic effect, it is nevertheless clear that there are no two texts. The 'normal' text of representation is merely presupposed if someone deems 'strange' the text at hand. 'Estrangement' being merely a nice metaphoric field of homeliness, its oppositional character is clearly intended.[23] Thus the other, familiar and automatic pole of the ob-posited is in question. Even if 'auto-matic,' it is still 'matic' – literally 'moving in a hurry' – an act of changing that does not proceed by itself. Greimas saw the (logical or other) necessity in producing change or transformation. The theory of the 'social imaginary' has it that all of us possess that necessity. Then automaticity ensues and makes narrative functions reproduce themselves by necessity. Although Narrative Grammar abstracted all temporality, its theory of transformation can claim to resemble action. In Neoformalist narratology, instead neither rudimentary temporal nor pragmatic logic explains transformation or change. Even such basic Poetical elements as 'oneness' and 'boundary' must rely on the concept of action teleology.

Repeatedly, Bordwell declares redundant such narratological instances as the spectatorial and auctorial ones (not roles or humans!), which he pins to 'mimetic' and 'perspectivist' theories of narration.[24] Metz labelled this a redundant exercise in name changing, yet it can be understood strategically from the very theory design. Russian Formalism (which evolved into structuralism and was itself 'born out of wedlock' from de Saussure) was in its foundational difference not constructivist but at least rudimentarily linguistic. Only when we duly take into account this foundational shift can we comprehend Bordwell's claim to be doing away with diegetic instances. Once he does this, he finds that perception, as a vehicle, is more driverless than instance-driven. This is again an epistemological choice, and we need not discuss again whether schemata are epistemologically convincing. His antilinguist alternative claims to enhance the spectator's activity. Bordwell polemicizes with 'semiological' theories against their strong tendency to confine spectators to cognitive passivity[25]: 'A film, I shall suggest, does not "position" anybody. A film cues the spectator to execute a definable variety of *operations*' (1985: 29). What he is really criticizing is the tendency of some semiological sign theories to confine all temporal elements to discourse (i.e., to the outside of the linguistic object proper: *langue*). However, is his substitute really better able to explain the highly temporal sign process of narration? In this respect, doubts quickly rise when we consider the cognitive product of spectator activities he has in mind. That product is a constructed universe, which is called 'fabula' when it is a narrative construction. Bordwell does not explain how a universe becomes a course of events (*infra* 385). These events are thought to be pre-existing, inferred, placed there by their own means. 'A film cues ...' is supposed to be different from an entity that exists only because someone ('énonciation') constructed it into existence.

The linguistic differentiation of 'énonciation–énoncé' is, however, not so toothless. In its extension through Genette, it even allows for a further ('realist') level between discourse and a universe. Every plot (Genette's 'récit'), with all the techniques for ordering and arranging the parts of the whole, does not only 'mean' an 'histoire' (this would roughly correspond to the *fabula*). More importantly, there is also always an intended state of the world (imaginary or empirical). In terms of narrative, this distinction is not empty. It is precisely relevant to the positioning of the characters and even of the narrative instance (*vox narrativa*) toward that outward world (positioning them toward the text is part of the definition of enunciation). Everyone's individual horizon is not coextensive with everyone else's – even the author's is often not the most general one – but all refer to a single point of reference: the actual world. However, this narratological differentiation explains nothing – it classifies dependently of a communication act. Enunciation means no less than that the interwoven aspectuality of this world is in the plot. Yet this necessarily presupposes an instance through which we are granted access – precisely the *vox* or 'the cueing film.' That *vox* (enunciational, auctorial instance) is indeed part of the plot, not of the world. It stands for the narrative configuration as such; it produces the unification of a narrative time and through this the unification of a narrative universe.

Narration is a truly transforming operation. The *fabula* – the object of the plot's representation – differs essentially from the intentional object of an eventful, real, one world. Conversely, without the teleological transformation in the narrative attitude the narrative universe would be as open as the world universe. Logical closure is important for narration, but for cognition it amounts to an incapacitation. If the viewer's (re-)construction of all the aspectualities onto the imaginable world were always and infallibly a faithful one and complete beyond the limits of narrative teleology, the two would coincide. The world becomes imaginable, and on this becoming reposes the ability to narrate. Narration therefore means becoming 'probable and possible' (Aristotle's εἰκὸς γένεσθαι καὶ δυνατὰ γένεσθαι; 51b31f). This production does not depend on the perception of the physical world; rather, it is constructed from a pragmatic logic and is utterly social.

Radical Constructivism takes this constructed character of the aspectual narrative probabilities to the extreme. Not surprisingly, it has become very attractive to theories of literature, such as that of Schmidt (1988). Yet here, in the *fabula*, 'perspectives of the real' are through narrative perspectivism, which achieves in viewers the existential illusion of a real world of the narrative (except for intentional 'realist' effects, which are especially extreme in the literary *verismo* style of G. Verga). Bordwell describes 'the plot,' or 'the film,' as releasing its information to the spectator successively and piecemeal. Is this factually different from enunciational, narrative perspectivism? *Fabula* is merely the ideal convergence of all perspectives, the historical (*histoire*) of a story and the reality (effect). Every signifying intervention and manipulation thus takes place in this interval between plot and *fabula*. It would be a mistake, however, to attribute any non-artificial 'naturality' or 'objective reality' to the *fabula*. It is still a construct, an ideal convergence of configuring acts. The interstice between the artefact and its signified cannot be closed with a simplistic equation. In reality, the *fabula* requires a logical instance that unifies all narrative perspectives into one 'What-ness.' *Fabula* is not the automatic result of perceptive schemata but an explicit and voluntary act of configuration. Without this work, there is literally nothing to tell. Enunciation, *vox narrativa*, is only a handy metaphor and should be judged solely on its analytical merits.

Terminologically, it unites useful and undeniable features that can be separated from the *fabula* and the plot. There is no need to discuss the dangers arising from its personification, but it is indeed a useful reminder of the artificiality of acts of configuration. As it unifies textual interventions, it constitutes a clear rupture from 'perceptionist' naturalisms. Enunciation does not simply exist linguistically, through 'shifters,' 'deixis,' and the like, as Bordwell contends. Furthermore, it cannot be counterposed to the differentiation of a pure state of the world. What it *is* is a narrative logic (*fabula* or events oblivious of their configuration), from a *sujet*/сюжет (and in addition, media-dependent devices, 'style,' which, however, is the subject of aesthetics).

A use of enunciational instances – even beyond the narrative- transforming unification – is that which construes only the δυνατὰ, that which becomes possible. In Bordwell's understanding, narration is also a defamiliarizing transformation. In spite of the polemical gesture of formalism, even the 'device of defamiliarization' construes no more than what is probable – εἰκὸς. There is no point in emphasizing the unusual through comparisons with the physical world. Narration has already closed its own world from the outside. However, as it is the device of temporality which operates that closure, it is necessarily built on a 'comparison of two events in their difference' (Peirce). Thus, defamiliarization reveals itself to be a transformation into a narrative oneness. The *fabula* is not the world. As a transforming construction, it is narration and as such is that sort of episteme where in any text, any part can be related to a unifying perspective.

Narrative texts owe their cognitive force to the whole resulting from relating perspectives. Hamburger (1968), Iser (1976), and later still Ricoeur (1985) all highlighted one basic and constitutive feature of narration. It can be described thus: in epistemological terms, regardless of the temporal means of construing, there is a difference between perception and narration. The latter is an instance of reflexive judgments (cf. Wagner 1973), whereas the former is an apperceptional judgment: the very act of construing teleological links into world-states goes beyond perceiving reactions. Understanding causality adds reflexiveness to the causes. By narrating, subjects express their awareness that it is their thought which lends purpose to object-actions. Causal comprehension follows a single route through the maze of all possible chains of realized consequences to a single initial action. Therefore, the seminal point of a story may very well be its 'moral.' It is the reflectivity of the thought that originated the tale. No reality tells itself, because in reality it is a narrative which, owing its existence to a mind, lacks the reality of reality. This is far from being merely a truism: the origin of narration in the 'configuring' act engraves traces that eventually become cultural forms of causality or genre. Without configuration, no listener, reader, or spectator would understand narration as narration. There is a mental proviso contained in 'once upon a time,' which starts off narration by bracketing it from mundane reality. Reflectivity, then, is the one mental operation where both author and reader create that transforming bracket and thus narration.

How this translates into textual features is another question. In linguistic terms, however, this is exactly what is behind the *énoncé– énonciation* difference. Metaphorically speaking, only the latter is the bracket (because in reality it will always be present, and must be so for grammatical reasons in language). We are not expressing this idea when we differentiate *fabula* from *sujet*. It is already situated beyond the configuration act.[26] Here is exactly that narration-constituting gap which is lacking in Bordwell's theory – a gap he deliberately accepted in exchange for 'cinematic specificity.' Notwithstanding this, cinema must not neglect reflectivity; after all, it can achieve it by its own means; otherwise, there could be no 'récit en images' (cf. Bergala s.a.).

Having eliminated the auctorial instance in film, Bordwell[27] must introduce functional equivalents through the back door. The 'cueing film' (cf. *supra*) substitutes auctorial instances. Narrative construction is not done with perception schemata. Leapfrogging directly from perceptive schemata into *fabula* is unduly economical and does not account for the exclusively pragmatic logic of which the narrative universe consists.

Owing to this logic alone, there is a chain of (apparent, i.e., narrative) causality. Thus the presence of causal impressions indicates the presence of temporal unification. Peirce demonstrates this as that law which connects two events in their difference. In the narrative purpose, therefore, time subsists as law, as a Third. Aristotle's poetical maxims of turn-around and certain length ($\mu\varepsilon\tau\alpha\beta o\lambda\dot{\eta}$, $\mu\acute{\varepsilon}\gamma\varepsilon\theta o\varsigma$) denote this narrative logic of time producing a whole (including a probable and possible universe). Neither perception nor defamiliarized (narrative) universes explain a turn-around within a whole-in-becoming.

Generally it must be doubted that spectator activity can remain so primitive as to be capable of applying schemata only. The real requirements for narrating were already indicated in Aristotle's terminology and suggest that there must be more. As we discussed in the context of

Cognitivism, only the endemic doxa of an unreflected nominalism can explain such an oversight. Real cognition is different. It cannot function through the application of schemata, but only in truly ampliative signs. Thus it is not the schema 'causality' that constitutes an order of events. Here lies the entire secret of the Pragmatic Maxim. Its essence is not the belief regained after a doubt; rather this new belief is more than the one that was destroyed by doubt. The insurance problem illustration (v. *supra*) in the first 1903 Harvard lecture (very appropriately titled 'Pragmatism as a Principle and Method of Right Thinking') also illustrates the cognitive gain through narrativity. The ratio of chance is not the cognition of the risk – for instance of climbing. Rather, mountaineers have cognition of the risk of climbing, which is not only more (their data are certainly fewer than those of an insurer) but also of a different nature. Here we have one chain of causality forming one Generality that is an ampliative Symbol of the many actual and possible instances. *'Symbols grow'* and 'omne symbolum de symbolo' (Ockham) says 'What is a Sign?' (Peirce 1998: 10). Empirical social sciences are in the same epistemological situation as the insurer; even so, it is not so customary to stay within the bounds of existential propositions. Drawing general conclusions from data is not the same as applying schemata to data. A hypothetical inference (in the logical sense of Peirce) is more: a genuine amplification. It is the insight of Semiotic that such an amplification depends on a sign.

Narration is very similar. It is made not of events but of episodes. When two different events are compared in relation to a third General idea, they become an episode of one purpose. The institution of narration would already be the result of the fundamental difference between the two events of narrating-as-act (now) and of the narrated. The *causa finalis* causality of the narrative universe is produced as a law of time that relates two events in a quasi-logical manner (cf. *supra*). Therefore, enunciation is crucial in order to institute a different causality. *Énonciation/énoncé* is a customary linguistic dichotomy used for expressing a logical transformation. In fact, in language (i.e., in Legisigns), we must constitute causality quite unlike in actual experience. Here the causal effect depends on the possibility that a *difference* in the sign usage (as prior event) can be established. Traces of the causality effect can be verified in languages through the Legisigns made available – for instance, through the differential use of verb tenses or through adverbial groups. Certainly, enunciation has a broader meaning than this logical one – through personal and modal deictic elements, enunciation achieves all sorts of dependencies. Yet not every enunciation need produce narration. That said, whenever there is a narration as causality, it has been produced through enunciation.

5.6 Olmi's *Genesi*

In cinema, narrative causality is not found in the causal elements of language relating two other elements: 'this therefore that.' Legisign is not necessarily linguistic Legisign, so the teleological Legisign for cinema requires a definition more general than language. It need only be ascertained that the initial sign is one determined by a Law (this is Peirce's definition, one that is broader in scope than a linguistic description).

The attitude of narrating as such – as a thought-sign – suffices for a First Correlate of the Legisign type of the Sign teleology or narrative purpose.[28] In this Sign the usage itself is the first event. This sign then has its Object which it Interprets in a second (now diegetic) event as difference together with teleology as its Third. Teleology means neither acceleration nor duration, which are two forms of time that are not Law. In film, teleology is only rarely excluded as a logic to organize time – and there remain scant alternatives to it (cf. *supra* concerning aesthetic and documentary organizations of time). This exclusion happens most radically when there is no second event for comparison. Strictly speaking, whatever comes after the 'incipit' is the second event of enunciation. Within the diegetic imitation of events, however, there can be a *non sequitur*, in both the temporal and the logical sense of the term. This is, for instance, not the case with Warhol's *Empire*; it would be inadequate to interpret this film from a narrative attitude. If it ever were viewed as such, its infinite delay of a second event would make it extremely boring.

Yet it is possible to continue narrating that is, from within narration to interpret teleology non-teleologically. To achieve this, an image must be as 'eternal' as those at the beginning of Olmi's *Genesi*. As counter-proof: such an 'eternal' image would immediately be destroyed by a moving camera or by any other aiming or purposive movement. This would be sufficient for a typically cinematic Legisign. As we shall see, precisely this imagery is, however, the beginning of an altogether different type of enunciation: Aesthetic Interpretation. We need not fear linguistic patterning, because Legisign is a logical definition and not a linguistic feature. As we discussed earlier with regard to the classification of Signs, inferential arguments require Symbols, which require Legisigns. Cinema also requires the initial logical status of a Legisign, which is the act of narrating as such, in order to become narrative. If this attitude (i.e., this sign usage) were not there, film would be merely a row of photographic frames in a physical, existential order. The intention of using a filmic event as a temporal Sign is what transforms it into a sequence under the Interpretant of a narrative purpose.

It is self-contradictory to speak of narrating (i.e., through temporal ordering) the before and the birth of time. The difference in the kind of Legisign makes it reasonable to assume that this is not to be adopted from literature; rather, it is specific to cinema. Consider, for instance, Ermanno Olmi's *Genesi: dalla creazione al diluvio* (1994). Olmi succeeds brilliantly in showing two intrinsically different times (timeless and teleological time) in one film. Unlike – for instance – Annaud's *La guerre du feu* (1981) – also a 'foundational' subject – Olmi refrains from narrativizing the origins. The difference lies not in their literary basis – Rosny Aîné (with Anthony Burgess and Desmond Morris) for the one, Genesis for the other – but in the narrative set-up.

Annaud's is a thoroughly novelistic vision that resorts to a primitive psychology of characters (in other words, what the *Poetic* calls ἦθη and διάνοια). Genesis, in contrast, does not psychologize at all (which is generally uncommon in biblical literature); it also uses an archaic language (common to sapiential treatises). The narrative turning point and basic astonishment (θαυμαστόν) are different in both texts: in the one it is a novelistic curiosity as to how we humans started to behave in a human way; in the other it is a cosmological interest in the order of things. Order is eternal, a-temporal, and time is introduced into this order after the original, pure state has been forfeited. *Genesi* starts time with a strong event, a killing. Before it is lost, paradise is timeless and just, a perfect order of how God wanted things to be and 'remain' (this postlapsarian word is of course 'before the fall'). It is therefore as close as it is possible for us to come to a necessary metaphysical law (if we could think of such a law as other than one of before-time-began). Consequently, in theological discourse, paradise with regard to time can be collapsed with the 'end of times,' when the disturbed order is perfectly restored. In between is time, and longing. As a sign of generality, the before and the after of time can thus only be a negation (of something general): a 'natural order,' 'ordered chaos,' '*tohu-bohu* as order' (cf. Gen 1: 2).

Linguistically, this timeless state is difficult to convey without forms of negation. It requires a sort of past present 'of definition' tense. In Semitic languages this is not so difficult to convey, since there are no tenses to be selected. In other languages a strong adverbial construction is required in order to undo the temporal positioning of tenses: 'in the beginning was,' ἐν ἀρχῇ ἦν ὁ Λόγος. The real meaning of this, however, is 'before there was any beginning' – which is a contradiction in terms and the limit of the usual, non-lyrical sign type of language. A Semiotic prefiguration of pragmatic logic would create a complete aimlessness, which is a contradiction of the verb in propositions.

Olmi, of course, could not film adverbs; he had to disconnect 'the beginnings' and their before in a different way. He achieved this effect through his editing. The montage of the first part of *Genesi* contains no causal connectors – it is aimless, as it were. Everything could be at the same time, and what comes first is of no relevance. This method is common enough in essayist films (which are held together by rhetorical means) and is also found in certain passages of Godard's *Je vous salue, Marie*, which prise open the causal context of narration through obvious symbolization. In *Genesi* the first event (corresponding to Aristotle's θαυμαστόν) is Cain raising his hands against his brother Abel. The situation of this sequence (starting with God's 'unjust' acceptance of Abel's sacrifice) perfectly meets Aristotle's definition of a narrative beginning. Of course, this does not mean that before the narrative event there is no history. Aristotle merely excludes all causes, which might lead to the situation of origin (ἀρχή δ' ἐστὶν ὅ αὐτό μὲν μὴ ἐξ ἀνάγκης μετ' ἄλλο ἐστί, μετ' ἐκεῖνο δ' ἕτερον πέφυκεν εἶναι ἤ γίνεσθαι 50b27f). This event is the cause of all and yet is caused by nothing.

Olmi introduced remarkable formal changes in order to set off the first event logically as event. Glances *now* (Noah's, for instance) become deictic temporal elements, interpreted psychologically as apprehensive outlooks. Glances *then* ('before ... and then') are contemplations of the celestial order. After the first event the film has its one and overwhelming telos, which has the power to reduce pragmatic logic into one action (Aristotle's ἐν αἷς ἀνάγκη ... μιᾶς πράξεως ποιεῖσθαι δήλωσιν ἀλλ' ἑνὸς χρόνους 59a22f). With teleology there is desire, apprehension, and hope – in a word, *time*. Now Olmi's film can repeat the logical course of teleology, this time transformed into time (psychologically from within time). The prelapsarian state (not time) is temporally comprehensible as the general potentiality of all. If we had not followed the teleological constraints of that first event and the beginning of history, we would be able to remain. Thus, however, we must 'repeat' in poor, tense-ridden words the original order and beauty. Now, though, we must narrate in a generalized past tense as the irremediably lost. It is still there, however, as the potential that can give hope. Noah and humanity see a sign of hope in the dove, its olive branch, its final absence. Thus hope becomes utopian and placeless and has no place in time. Olmi must show this through the meaningfully empty 'absence of.' The absent dove matches the absent, lost paradise: both are the absence of time. Yet after the lapse, the absence of time can no longer be imagined and shown. It can be narrated, however, as it was meant ἐν ἀρχῇ (which is the contrary of 'what used to be').

The precausal state has consequences for the usage of signs, because the merely possible can only be Iconic. The prelapse part of Olmi's film is an Iconic semiosis inasmuch as it obfuscates or restricts pragmatic logic. In short, it cannot be a narration. The murder of the just Abel also kills the Possible and begins Determination (literally, the process of introducing a term to everything). The child's gazing eyes (in the first half of *Genesi*) can see the astonishing quality of novelty in everything; they must take nothing for granted, and nothing must be explained,[29] because everything is beautiful. It can only be present aesthetically, which almost means not re-presenting. There can be no more beautiful and fitting illustration of the unifying logical effect of causality (as one mode of being temporal).

This meaning depends entirely on time and on the transformation of time into a non-teleological mode (within the narrative imitation of events). Although this non-episode could still be meaningfully interpreted in hermeneutic narratologies, the crudest contrast of the entire gamut of narration theories is with regard to timeless theorizing. How would such a particular meaning be treated in *fabula*-narratologies *sans* time? When capabilities are limited to the production of universes (obfuscating the pragmatic origin of such universes), and either their defamiliarized rendering or their (extensional and intensional) ambiguation and disambiguation for basically the same reasons, these *Genesi* sequences must be flat. Their narrative information value is next to nil; they would not serve even to set the ambience for a romantic narrative. If any meaning could be assigned at all, it might pass as a 'stylistic device,' but this (still narrative) meaning is imperceptible in constructivist-formalist accounts.

Enunciation need not be a temporal event, and it can play a pivotal role for entirely different reasons, as in Eco. It refers strictly to the tactic order of sentences, especially the hypotactic modification of meaning.

Here 'spectator activity' and 'cueing film' would be the special conditions of a general pragmatic framework. Notwithstanding its name, there is no pragmatic institution of teleological purpose and time as an essentially distinct principle of unification. It merely stands for increased freedom (compared to standard hypotaxis in propositions) in the 'disambiguation' of an otherwise rigid system of meaning. If the temporal origin of narrative configuration is obfuscated, as in Eco's narratology, *sujet* becomes a task of intensional semantic and *fabula* of extensional semantic (this is on the basis of Petőfy's TeSWeST – ('*Text-Struktur Welt-Struktur Theorie'*) (Eco (1979: 14).

Again there is a division of labour such that communication (enunciation) must give meaning (purpose) to the plot, and the construction of an extensional universe/world of narration is left to the semantic system. The communication frame is necessary. Applying autonomous schemata (narrated by nobody, to nobody) is not enough and does not help us decide how and with which 'schema' to fill the many (extensional) lacunae of a narrative. A text of any interest must be ambivalent and not merely deficient in its lacunae. Semantic needs 'pragmatics' – according to the premisses of both Morris and Eco. Just as iconicity played the role of a communicational extension of the binary system in the case of representation, so has the pragmatic of enunciation here. The basic challenge is always a coherent unity of meaning, which remains inexplicable in rigid systems of binary differences. Under identical premises, Eco's solution is radically different from Greimas's semionarratological generativism (which is deduced from propositional structures, v. *supra*).

Thus any work of representational art that consists of semantic and syntactic units requires communication extensions into its 'before whom?' and 'toward whom?' Now Greimas assigns this function to the roles of the enunciational process: a 'faire persuasif' equal to 'faire faire interpréter' on the side of the 'enunciator,' and a 'faire interprétatif' on the side of the 'enunciated' (spectator, reader). Readers, as implied by textual meaning, are indeed 'positioned' or directed in their reading process. Solitary 'cue'-based constructions of textual meaning with home-grown hypotheses or schemata[30] are not the same. With his invocation of a 'deus absconditis [*sic!*],' Bordwell (1985: 62) seems to be suggesting anthropomorphic narration techniques. This, however, is a misunderstanding. An 'implied author' is not the physical[31] author ('sujet de l'énonciation' in Jakobson). There remain narration devices that must be attributed to a textual source other than characters: precisely a 'sujet de l'énoncé' (cf. Eco 1979: 10). Narration as structure,[32] at best a substrate of its discursive usage, eliminates time. It is not a law of time that creates narrative order, but 'eternal' rules of syntax. However, combinational possibilities increase enormously and are too many to be univocal. Now if meaning is defined by its systemic position any ambivalence at this point must destroy meaning. Through communication – this is the general idea, as with iconicity – *ad hoc* agreements on meaning can be established as 'inferential walks.'

Semantic disambiguation has as its result a 'macro-proposition' of a coherent narrative universe, not a teleology of a closed world of pragmatic logic. A schematic representation of TeSWeST (Eco 1979: 14) displays ten factors that contribute to the final outcome of readings enabled by the text or 'syntactic-semantico-pragmatic device' (ibid.: 3). As a general frame, three basic factors determine the correct reading: manifest linear text, vehicled language plus cultural codes and over-codes, and circumstances of utterance.[33] The constitution of narrative meaning is divided into extensional and intensional acts. On the side of extension we find the world construed (inferred) by the reader. Intensions comprise interior structures of the narrative. Extensional inferences go from first assumptions about a narrative 'site' to world structures. On the intension side of the narrative we find discursive structures (semantic disclosures: Speech Acts and isotopies), narrative functions, and actantial structures as well as ideology. So far this is more or less Eco's encyclopaedia, applied to narrative texts. The insistence on the pragmatic cooperation of the reader – even for the semantic disclosure – is worth a closer look. The same – 'upstream' – for the contribution of enunciative textual and concrete narrator instances guiding the reader discursively (rhetorically). For both sides the concrete meaning of a narration is an open negotiation or 'cooperative activity' (ibid.: 15). TeSWeST comprises Formalism, and – if understood as extensional and intensional disambiguation – *fabula* and *sujet* are more complex than in Bordwell. Here *sujet* comprises the three variables of 'communicativeness,' 'self-consciousness of the narration,' and 'depth of information.' As intension, pragmatic creates the communicational frame around the pure 'linear text manifestation.' Furthermore, by identifying all discursive factors, we understand 'the text' when it determines through rhetoric – and thus cooperatively – pathways of possible comprehension. It can be narrowed down or ambivalently enlarged. All of this is the extension of a narrative, or *fabula*.

The primary narrative construction allows us to infer exactly one *fab-*

ula, as Bordwell demonstrated with classical Hollywood narratives. Speaking in 'Ecoese,' the spectator in an 'inferential walk' can construct one 'macro-proposition' – a sort of cinema TV guide précis. This macro-proposition can also be rather complex, as indicated by the careful analyses by Bordwell and Thompson of seemingly simple films.[34] In Formalist speech (actually, musical metaphors), 'dominant' is equivalent to the principal macro-proposition. Following the metaphoric lead, however, also implies 'subdominants' and 'tonica.'[35] Such a 'hidden agenda' for a narrative macro-proposition in fact adds to its ambiguity. The 'adding up' of strangeness is accomplished relatively effortlessly through Greimas's 'isotopies,' which are only global rhetorical denominators or 'discursive structures' of 'semantic disclosures' (cf. Eco (1979: 14, box 4 in figure 0.3 and passim). Very prominently in 'misleading plots,' and indispensably in comic effects, a secondary inferential walk is performed by the spectator, which creates a parallel narrative macro-proposition. That second isotopy can be – or can become – probably as equal to the primary isotopy. Eco (1979: 200–56) provides and example of this for a simultaneously comic and misleading plot: 'Un drame bien parisien' by Alphonse Allais (1854–1905). The plot offers two isotopies, both suggested by 'intertextual frames' (Bordwell's 'motivation'): one of 'adultery,' the other of 'misunderstanding.' We would add to these two macro-propositions another, which is the point of comparison for the 'abnormal' comic side: the 'normal life' (cf. Jauss 1977), a presupposition furnished by the exhilarated reader and by the 'tongue in cheek' author of the 'drama' (which it is not, unless by *contradictio in adjectu*: '*drame parisien*'). The workings of the enigmatic reading involve the first two macro-propositions; the comic compares either one with the implied macro-proposition 'normality.'

Apparently Eco believes that narrative closure is explained through the nature of propositions. However, this is not so (or it would need a deduction, as in Greimas's generativism). Strictly speaking, there is no proposition in the narrative macro-proposition, in either the linguistic or the logical sense. Also, it is somewhat misleading to introduce unlimited interpretability to ambivalent dramas. Before all of these interpretations can take place, we need to explain the primary closure of narration as such, for without this, there would be no narrative comprehension. Narrations are not open, for the same reasons that world cognition is open. They are open merely because of their lacunae (if these are kept open by one or more teleologies operating alternative narrative paths). Narration cannot be explained without temporality. It is already tacit that narration is there merely on the basis of negotiated meaning with an enunciation instance. Once it is there, its closed universe can certainly be ambiguated or disambiguated. *Why* it is there remains obscure, however.

An 'author's role' of enunciation is also practical for other reasons. Narration is a quite peculiar Sign usage of a law of time. It is only practical for it to commence as a determinate Interpretation process. Spectators must have this 'logical' guarantee when embarking on the fictional contract. If they didn't, they would have to reckon with a mere stream of unorganized recounting of objects, states, or actions, one without confines and leading nowhere. Thus, the fiduciary contract promising an understanding of something would have been broken.

What Bordwell sets out to abolish in the name of cinematic specificity becomes a practical loss. He is really abolishing the logical preconditions of narration itself whereby a process of transformation must take place through time. Only after that can Neoformalism set in as aesthetic transformation (namely, already presupposing what has now been abolished). Bordwell (1985: 49) maintains: 'We have seen theories of narration founder upon superficial analogies between film and other media – literature or theater (the mimetic approach); literature, speech, or writing (the diegetic approach).' That abolished instance, in lieu of the supposedly too linguistic enunciation, comes back in disguise when he continues: 'The theory I propose sees narration as a formal activity, a notion comparable to Eisenstein's rhetoric of form. In keeping with a perceptual-cognitive approach to the spectator's work, this theory treats narration as a process which is not in its basic aims specific to any medium. As a dynamic process, narration deploys the materials and procedures of each medium for its ends.' He should have written 'for its *end*,' because narrating deploys a pragmatic purpose and thus closes its universe.

It seems that Neoformalism does not explain transformation at all, not even in the guise of a constructed εἰκός, transformed or 'inferentially walked' by *ostranenie*. Cinema is not an automatic (i.e., 'familiarized') means of representing a universe of human action (which is meaningful only as teleology): сюжет[36] techniques (inevitably with 'style') to allow for the reconstruction of a 'normal' '*fabula*,' the hypothetical *ob-jet* of the *su-jet*, the 'world' as represented. This, of course, needs no enunciation (and not much of the transforming agency of film cueing either, except for the application of schemata). In the decision to narrate, the ignition spark for a certain kind of logic has already taken place. This exact logic with its temporal ordering must remain operant, in a text-founding role, in the narration and film. It is not left to the will of an appropriately cued spectator to give birth to an author as a role in a narrative (as Bordwell polemically suggests: but auctorial roles are time generators). Neoformalist narratology is a less powerful theory than Narrative Grammar. It lacks narrative, pragmatic logic, let alone temporal totality and perspectivism (which would allow an anchor in the 'real world' of human acting).

Explaining how pragmatic logic functions is not a trivial exercise. Moreover, it is almost impossible without an awareness of time. In Ricoeur's narratology, this is because of temporality in Dasein. For Greimas, this logic functions in the manner of linguistic universal laws. Ricoeur's critique of this claim concerns the logical force of those laws, which is not independent, but rather derived from acting: Greimas defies his own statement Il n'y a que le texte' by admitting *thymie*. Linguistic universals have indeed a limited purchase when they are derived from the propositional form. We have seen that this cannot attain true Generality. Ricoeur does not need such a narrative Generality, which he finds elsewhere. For his own philosophy, he really needs only the narrative form. There is not merely a practical inclusion of a technique. Narrative form must remain the Other, strange and alien to authentic *Dasein*. Narration is a merely borrowed Being-a-whole. Furthermore, it is important that it stay so, to vouchsafe the integrity of temporality. Pragmatic logic, the driving force of narration, need not even be totalizing as death. Being-toward-the-end is achieved by another force. Narration is only – and need not be more than – the repetition of a deeper reality of unity. Once we have made these assumptions, the appropriate question cannot concern the development of a pragmatic logic from a basis of human acting. In Ricoeur's eyes, this question is answered in the caring *Dasein*.

Whether Ricoeur's critique of Greimas is pertinent depends on whether we admit to transcendental reasoning. The strength of the logic in Narrative Grammar and especially in the Semiotic Square depends entirely on the generativist mechanism; the passage from virtuality to realization by way of actualization can be and has been read as a new transcendentalism. Then it is no longer a chronological development, but a special kind of serialization, in the sense of Deleuze (1973: 318). Time becomes an effect of a series of sense effects, and not primarily a travesty of action time. In Greimas (1976), this is made quite clear. The Square in its fourth 'leg' – the implicational, deictic reference from non-S_2 to S_1 – would be an identity. In the example given, there it is '*non-non*,' not-no to '*oui*,' yes. If it is a taxonomy of negations, not-no implies yes, but syntagmatically it becomes a '*si*,' 'yes indeed.' Thus it is at a new level of the same, and not a chronological progress. This indi- cates that it is the transcendental, *a priori* form of sense that holds it all together. It 'pro-duces' sense in a non-chronological sense of 'pro,' even if Ricoeur rightly does not admit a logical force proper as agent.

A Semiotic theory of narration has neither the transcendental nor the solitary-testimony inconveniences. Nevertheless, it attains a strong unity and totality, which is part of experience, however. As such it can dispense with a primordial experience of Being-toward-an-end. Semi- otic experience is fundamentally conceived as experience of a next. There can be no end to semiosis, but there is no known end to all semi- oses. There 'is' only Continuity, in the signs relating to a next, and also in other aspects of evolutionary metaphysic. Totality in Semiotic is not like any other reality. Its mode of being is that of Possibility. Genuine time is therefore not the vicious alternative between subjective and physical time. Continuity, Possibility, is real, but it is not existent. Ricoeur's narratology requires the existent existence of caring *Dasein* in order to attain the whole. The whole in Semiotic is a real Possible. It is part of the sign relation, however, and therefore subjective as much as objective, 'cosmological.' What counts is the genuine and very special unity and totality that can be attained in the Sign relation as cognitive effort. Conduct, or habits of acting, is possible through the Sign rela- tion in its fullness. Unlike human acting in all its necessary dimen- sions, narratives do not unfold *ad libitum*. Narration is not shaped after the model of a concrete human action, which is continuous, amor- phous, multilayered, and unending. Only when we impose time as a logical order onto concrete empirical action, (i.e., when we are narrat- ing) are salient points and their causalities sharply identified. At that point they can be understood *as* unities and then communicated. How- ever, even after we have established narration as a temporal law, the other two necessary Correlates remain. Used as a degenerate Sign rela- tion, there is even a Firstness in action, as the analysis of *Ordet* has shown. The narration of this film has not undone the pragmatic of action, nor has it placed this pragmatic under the absolute sway of Thirdness. Instead it has widened its time horizon into the Possible. This temporality and its contrast with normal, semantic pragmatic time is constitutive for precise aesthetic effects. A 'presemantic' tempo- rality is also before human action. This is not an anti-intuitive claim, but a 'real-life' experience of contemplation and its time experience. Dreyer has shown how cinematic narration contemplates. Also, Cavalier shows in a different 'lifting' of the curfew of narration how contemplation is attained by film.

Evolutionary metaphysics and Semiotic capture with Continuity a glimpse of another dimension of human time. Time of human action is not time-before-death, but a Pragmaticistic Being-toward, evolution, becoming, modal being, being-*in-statu-fieri*, discovery. Furthermore – and this is the important point here – this time becomes a Sign and is communicable. The problem of narrative totality is a question of both time and truth, in a Semiotic perspective. However, what exactly do we mean by 'becoming Sign'? Enunciation will answer this question.

6 Enunciation in Cinema

Enunciation has not much meaning in itself, yet it has an enormous practical meaning (to put it a little paronomastically). It is a necessary part of the semiosic process, considered in isolation. All theories of meaning must comprehend enunciation in some form and under some name, even though we might declare it evasive and unanalysable[1] or simply take it for granted.[2] Semiotic has accounted for 'utterance' from the start; no other theory attributes so much importance to the use or occurrence of Signs, the event of cognition.

For entirely different reasons, however, 'enunciation' has also become a cherished 'pragmatic' addendum to semiological film theory, thus filling an intrinsic lacuna in that theory. If it is more than a stopgap, it is also acknowledged as a necessary insight by another theoretical approach. Here, the profit from enunciation does not originate in a lacuna but in fact constitutes a core theorem. For hermeneutic film theories, the *via regia* to cinematic meaning has materially become a certain kind of behaviour, which linguists and logicians have called enunciation.

One of the earliest instances of this was Bettetini, who attempted to marry hermeneutic with semiological theories. This is an instructive case that illustrates how enunciation can bear fruit for both approaches. The appeal for hermeneutic film theory is that it can personalize with ease certain cinematic techniques. The *suppositum* of such a metaphoric transfer is that existential analysis also be applicable to cinematic machines. This application alone gives those theories their breath of life or meaning. Phenomenological and hermeneutic theories cannot dispense with consciousness (and psychology and existence) for the production of meaning. Interiority is the source of all meaning, which means that if there is no interior, as in a camera, it must be metaphorically exported. Of course, beyond the immediate metaphor, this export is ultimately founded – as in Ricoeur's narratology – on the existence of both the reader and the author. The purpose of enunciation is precisely to tie the 'text' or 'technique' to consciousness or existence. It is not by chance that Ricoeur's preferred term for enunciation is 'vox narrativa.' Analogously, Albert Laffay's enigmatic notion of 'grand imagier' serves the same purpose in film theory (cf Casetti 1993: 74).

Bordwell has an aversion to such 'positioning' theories, which might be argued against from a fundamentally antihermeneutic stance; But he has no 'better argument' against a psychologizing consciousness philosophy. At any rate, this is certainly not the 'better fit' in cinematic data. Carroll's polemic against all essentialisms, then, would be better directed against the hermeneutic equation of lens with eye. More than an essentialist ampliation this is the spiritualization or psychologization of a technical device.

It seems that the later Metz – who also came to find enunciation useful – seems to have acknowledged implicitly that syntax alone is not enough. The key to the fullness[3] of real meaning is to profit from the use of a grammatical fact recognized since antiquity (thus following closely most of modern literary theory, starting from Émile Benveniste): the *dictum* triple modalized as *tempus, modus, persona*. The dual nature of enunciation as behaviour (which is rejected by Metz) and as linguistic 'mark' (which is acceptable and useful) not only facilitates its integration into intrinsically divergent theories, but also creates a certain ambiguity in both. As always with linguistic characteristics, it is very difficult to separate the contingent features of natural languages from linguistic universals. Greimas attempted a deduction of universals from the propositional form. However, he merely exploited the copula, which is a feature of Indo-European languages although not of many others. Peirce, for his part, distrusted in principle any reliance on features of natural languages. Even if we could establish as a fact that all known languages share one feature, we would gain no logical force of necessity by this. This reflection induced Peirce to base his logical theory on Rhemata, and not on the copula between a subject and a predicate (cf. *supra*).

What enunciation is, in a Peircean framework, cannot be determined by language or by a pattern of social interaction, even though it may also manifest itself as such. The root of enunciation must be sought in meaning, not in trivial circumstances. It is not a matter of explaining the obvious fact that narrations do not narrate themselves, that their igniting spark must come from outside. Hyperbolically speaking, the theoretical problem would start this way: Why can narrations not tell themselves? Far from being a *sottise*, theory must be aware of the improbability of narrative meaning. Once we realize how impossible it is to arrive at one correct interpretation to a narration, we face a practical problem with narrative meaning. Because of its inherent vagueness, it defies all attempts to describe its argumentation so that it can be reproduced validly and universally. This, even though all narrating is intent on producing one meaning. Despite all this, theories of narration restrict themselves to supposed constants.

Against the interpretational flood we seek a remedy in the invariable functions of narration. In the previous chapter a temporal constant, teleology, was emphasized, yet it was concluded that this sign of time only comes-into-being through an act of enunciation. Time itself owes its being to a comparison of 'two events in their difference.' The act constitutes the first event. If a comparison is to be made, a second event is required that is a point on the axis of narrative teleology. Enunciation must also establish that there are representations, which can then be constructed into one order by temporality. In narratives, therefore, enunciation plays a doubly constitutive role with regard to time and to representation.

What, then, 'is' enunciation? Where, in Semiotic framework, does the problem of enunciation arise? It is not overly counterintuitive to relate time to a constitutive act. Regarding representation, however, why should reality owe itself to an enunciational constitution? A commonsensical truism would put it that data are the 'real' real and that doubt and ambiguity are only a matter of cognition (hypothesis). This is not only too simple but also epistemologically wrong. In a more sophisticated theory of cognition we will be confronted in various ways with changes or progress in cognition (i.e., changing and growing reality). Pragmaticism is therefore a very realistic theory (and history) of cognition; so a Semiotically framed enunciation makes sense in this Pragmaticistic context of evolving cognition. Here, time and representation are intrinsically related and must be treated as one problem.

A reduction to a taxonomy of some linguistic marks of enunciation misses the explanatory power of the Pragmatic Maxim. Unfortunately, a number of debates in film theory have evolved around the taxonomic question of how communication interferes with the otherwise pure linguistic object. All taxonomies describe a great deal but cannot explain what they describe. The paradigms of enunciation are hypotactic sentences – that is, sentences in which the dependent clause contains all of the marks of the enunciation of its upper clause. A broader Semiotic context is required in order for us to understand that these are the normal and necessary constitution of reality.[4]

6.1 Enunciation: From Vagueness to Generality

Enunciation – it will be argued – is generally speaking a process for setting in motion the Pragmatistic process of 'all possible consequences.' This type of process is not limited to narration, rhetoric, and aesthetic. These are – our second argument – merely condensed habitual forms of what is taking place in the history of science. The problem is of the same nature – that is, of theorizing on an unlimited object, where the *terminus ad quem* of the cognitive process cannot be given. Nevertheless, the cognitive process cannot be arbitrary. We have seen already what such a constitution of reality means for two-valued logic. Modes of being are an immediate consequence. We will see that this applies equally to narration, rhetoric, and aesthetic, whose bounds of Interpretation also cannot be determined. For any concrete object of cognition, this means that it 'is' not there; instead, it is a growing focus of meaning (seen from the perspective of the present cognition) or a vague contour of something (seen from the perspective of the final cognition).

The fundamental features of a Semiotic 'epistemology,' comprehended as a semiosic process, need not be repeated here. On the basis of this principle of an open cognitive process enunciation acquires its unique relevance. We might characterize it as an 'off-the-shelf' inventive form. On the one hand, this oxymoron reflects the habitual form, even as a literary genre, which guides the cognition of the open-ended: through rules to invention. Our discussion of Peirce's peculiar use of the term 'aesthetic' has shown that he situates it in the context of percepts, which fulfil the purpose of the cognition of mere Qualities. This is the vastest imaginable cognitive domain, since everything passes through this stage: *nihil est in intellectu quin prius fuit in sensibus*. On the other hand, enunciation forms raise a problem that is specific to the realist nature of Semiotic. Nothing indicates the event nature of a contingent cultural form of cognitive habit dealing with exactly this sort of cognition, which is then enshrined as art or aesthetic object. The habit of art is the enunciation cognizing Qualities in an emphatic manner. However, this seems to run counter to the general Categorical insight that any true cognition originates from a genuine doubt (v. *supra*). Cognition must have its corrective in the brute force of an 'outward reality.' Enunciation habits seem to isolate cognition from such a force and transpose it to the realm of the fictitious, the rhetorical illusion (or Formalist trick/priem[5]), the imaginary and useful. Briefly, it is either *homo mensura* or reality constraint. So later we will need to address how enunciation relates to outward reality.

Aesthetic is not the only cognitive openness. Theoretically, facts of outward reality force themselves onto a cognizing mind. Concretely, however, too many facts vie for our attention. So a rhetorical habit such as figuration must bring the right facts to bear on our cognition. The elaborate techniques of ancient discourse – starting always with the establishment of a *status questionis*, as a *quaestio elenchi, juris, facti*, and so on – serve precisely to focus attention on some desired aspects of certain facts. Instead of speaking about 'referential illusion' (R. Barthes), insinuating a fantasy product, rhetorical devices can indeed establish a brute fact relation – to the facts of their choice. Documentary style in cinema uses rhetorical devices for the clear purpose of establishing facts and truth values. We have already discussed Godard's peculiar cinematic rhetoric. Godard's very difficult aim – which he achieved brilliantly – was to establish certain truths, such as Marie's virginal motherhood.

The third cognitive openness to be harnessed by enunciation involves the establishment of a necessity (always for factual qualities). Certain types of causal relationships must be constituted through laws. However, temporal causes are among the most difficult to establish. One reason why is that it is so difficult to identify the non-identical, changing subject and the order of first and second states. This identification does not relate to the simple, physical persistence of an object. It is merely semantically convenient to speak of a changing object, because the change of something in reality means that it ceases to exist and something else takes its place. So it is the soberness of Philip that ceases to exist and drunkenness that takes its place, and only a law that comprehends alcoholic intoxication can create a sameness of subject (the subject is not the physical body of Philip, but nerve reaction). Enunciational habits such as narrative causality clearly aid and hasten identifications of different states of the same subject. Conversely, the absence of such – habits as is the case in scientific experimentation – reminds us of the cognitive support afforded by enunciation.

Enunciations exist not as cognitive laws but as cultural contingencies; this fact determines their logical nature. Their logical effect is a fact: they generate belief where cognition, without their help, would not easily have succeeded. This should not be surprising from the perspective of Critical Common-sensism. It merely constitutes an explicit common sense. In rare borderline cases it can even construe an appearance of a cognitive object, which cannot be sustained as Critical Common-sensism evolves further. So narrative fiction, as clearly stated in Peirce's Scheherazade illustration, has its sole – but ineluctable – real cognitive object in the narratrix's existence and the act of her narrating and 'fabulation.' Much then, is sustainable also 'in the long run,' but the 'temporary suspension of disbelief' only survives as her enunciational effect.[6]

Enunciation is the habitual practical form of a vague, growing cognition of three different kinds. These cognitive objects may eventually appear on the radar screen of our cognition; however, even without enunciational assistance, cognition cannot ordinarily bear this problematic situation. There is a necessity inherent in enunciational habits that transcends purely logical necessity (i.e., how usage itself must determine the meaning of the sign). This consequence of Secondness, it has already been noted, manifests itself as real doubt, which must be present as a precondition for cognition or Interpretation. Even mental experimentation with pure possibilities presupposes that we are imagining an unsatisfactory previous possible quality.

In the case of enunciational habits, however, the usage of the sign is standardized. There are quasi-rules (such as good taste) that regulate what is recognized as an aesthetic sign. Thus the real doubt requirement does not seem to apply. In narrative fiction, the doubt in the constitution of the sign is derived even more (and exclusively) from the teleological rule for narrative closure. In *North by Northwest*, 'suspense' is produced by the rules that Hitchcock applies when narrating to us, and not by any event, except for the event of his narration act. As cognitive determination, this is not much and is not in itself sufficient to sustain the subsequent Interpretations.

However, enunciational rules behave like any other rules or logical laws. Categorically they are Thirdness, but for this reason they ordinally comprehend Seconds and Firsts. Thus narrative 'suspense' is a Second Correlate of a strong teleological constraint. It can strictly be expected – but only on this premise – as a quasi-event, as a cognitive Object. It is an event of an instance of the narrative rule that a final outcome of a plot must be reached through dramatic reversals ($\mu\varepsilon\tau\alpha\beta o\lambda\acute{\eta}$). Evidently this is not the result of scientific research into human reality; rather, it is an instance of the drama idea. Drama is a culturally contingent enunciational habit that exists in some cultures. There is no universal form of dramaticity. It is not a cognitive necessity but simple fact that the ideal drama has been canonically enshrined as tragedy in the Greco-Latin tradition. Even though the tragic effect with guilt (ἁμαρτία) and its tragic consequences-beyond-any-measure presuppose a certain sort of pagan world view, it is still effective today in Europe (albeit probably not in the same way in other places).[7]

Enunciational rules must be between cognition and its object, from which place they bring the cognitive process to a state of common sense or commonplace (topos). They form and disintegrate like every other common sense, though usually not under the pressure of outward reality. *L'art pour l'art* is a slogan which advocates that the realm of art be isolated from the constraints of reality; this is sometimes understood even as the loss of the seriousness of art. Peirce's silence on aesthetics has become a truism; in this vein, he did not treat poetics either. However, apart from his oft quoted 'admission' (in which he cast himself as an unaesthetic ignoramus), we can deduce the reasons why, insofar as they have not been explicitly stated, from his system architecture. As a philosophical discipline, 'aesthetic' in Peirce's sense is not an art theory that reflects the rules of a practice. His sole interest is the cognitive aspect of aesthetic signs. However, neither does he reflect on the purport of factual habits of art form in their cultural contingency. We can understand this, though, as a special instance of the Common-sensism of all cognition. Thus we comprehend aesthetic, rhetorical, and poetic forms as relatively fixed states of cognition, without considering evolutionary aspects of cognizing.

6.1.1 Why Does Enunciation Operate?

Forms exist as conventional rules. This fact, however, does not yet tell us why they do. It is also a fact that we do not need an enunciation form for every cognition, but only for certain types. For instance, not all of our cognitions are or need to be organized finalistically as leading toward a narrative end. On the contrary, it would be an obstacle to the Pragmaticistic progress of true cognition if the ultimate adequate opinion of the unlimited community of researchers could be identified in a concrete knowledge. For true progress, it is crucial that, in spite of its finality, this remains indeterminate.

Where the enunciation effect prevails, however, a commonsense determination is desirable. Such a closure, relative as it may be, is justified only by the peculiar openness it creates. As a social habit, which can then be used as meaning determination or as determinate meaning, its purpose should not be to fix cognition, but to open up new potential. Thus, while art may be a commonsensical presumption of a meaningful object of value, under the umbrella of its formal rule it opens the potential for aesthetic attention. Aesthetic qualities are transformed into art objects, but this is compensated for by the facility through which genuine aesthetic meaning can still be produced. Nobody can deny that aesthetic qualities abound even outside the art form. Even Kant's Third Critique made provision for the *Naturschönheit*,[8] an aesthetic object already upstream of any decorative play of imagination.

When we introduce of enunciation this is not an acknowledgment of Kant's subtle distinction between 'beauty' as accessible through *Verstand* (understanding) and 'sublime' as accessible through *Vernunft* (reason). Semiotic does not in principle need to deny that aesthetic judgments are capable of object cognition. So there is no need to differentiate playful imagination with objects, from another variant of noncognitive admiration – based on the reason category of quantity – in the sublime. Enunciation does not take the place of playful imagination with objects, supplying them with the supposition of the appearance of an end. Enunciation does not create an appearance at all. With the demise of transcendentalism, every Sign is constituted by a certain kind of cognition, and this includes Signs of aesthetic experience. Art form, then, does not have the purpose of creating an appearance of finality (*Zweckmäßigkeit*) in an object; rather, it retains all the cognitive characteristics of aesthetic cognition. Only if this cognition is seen as a cognitive process of Interpretation can we make a distinction between a commonsensical state and an open process. It must retain the cognitive characteristics of its underlying process, however, even as a state, and this is only possible if it attains an internal openness of its own.

Introducing enunciation does not reintroduce (i.e., surreptitiously) art form as appearance of cognition, then; rather it fulfils a genuine Semiotic function. A state of common sense is still cognition, and this cognition is not always limited (discounting intellectual progress), as the term seems to suggest. On the contrary, as art form it launches ordinary cognition into uncharted territory. Yet it is still a form, and thus created by rules and habit or controlled behaviour. Instead of appearance and surrogation of veritable cognition, it is a cognitive promise that, by assuming a certain kind of controlled behaviour, brings within reach a certain kind of cognition.

Semiotic sees no problem in aesthetic truth claims as appearances (which is Kant's legacy to some contemporary epistemologies). Art form is no exception and as enunciation remains within the normal Semiotic realm of Pragmaticistic cognition.

6.1.2 Enunciation as a Sign Process

Enunciation Semiotic[9] is concerned with the nucleus of meaning determination in the Sign. In view of the form artifact of common sense, a question arises:[10] Which logical force can produce the enunciational Sign? This form is determinate meaning as a form, vague at the commencement and general at the conclusion of its Interpretation. Concretely, we recognize at once something as narration or piece of art, we are vaguely aware that there is a particular meaning attached to this object, and we only grasp it once 'it makes sense.' It is enunciational form, initially open meaning (failing this, it would become kitsch), and finally determinate meaning (failing this, would be enigmatic or nonsense).

In every single Sign – as next Interpretation – a true or truer cognition must take place. Seen from the perspective of artistic Vagueness, a Sign increases in generality. This constitutes a radical commitment to artistic cognitive experience (in Thompson's words – 'trouvailles adding up') as well as a stance against formalism of all sorts and attempts to close the openness of Interpretation. More precisely, then, the question concerns the Semiosic process within enunciation: What produces an increase in generality here? In normal cognition, in normal abduction, it is ultimately the corrective constraint of 'outward reality' that corrects or amplifies generality (down to perceptual judgment). Does enunciation provide such an anchor in experience? Narration, rhetoric, and aesthetic enunciation distinguish themselves from other Signs in that normally there is no direct 'outward reality' determining the Sign. Instead, this necessary function of the Second Correlate is assumed by the enunciation instance. In the Pragmaticistic line, this occasioning of the Interpretation must bring about the change from doubt to belief. This enunciational occasioning would also qualify for the (necessary) external Object of the Sign process.

Now this effect is a social habit of behaviour. Enunciation, just like any other cognition, produces a habit; this explains the quasi-automatism of narrative meaning. Enunciation is not a singular, isolated act of producing meaning. It is especially relevant to aesthetic enunciation that it can rely on a conduct – perhaps in contrast to aesthetic feeling. Its cognitive effects are not the result of a communicative negotiation of meaning; instead they can avail themselves of rules of conduct, which are (logically) Thirds. For all the free play of imagination involved in these enunciational representations, it is important that they be framed by rules of conduct. As with every habit of behaviour, this restricts Possibility (the chaotic aspect of vague cognition). However, from a Pragmaticistic perspective, habit is not a final meaning, the end of Interpretation, but merely a rule. Thus habit turns into potentiality to produce this kind of meaning through this rule. Narrative habits restrict the Possibility in meaning through temporal logic, and rhetorical habits do the same through propositional logic; aesthetic habits enjoy the least restriction vis-à-vis the possible through a logic whose norm is the admirable in itself (cf. *supra*). Here is the common nature of enunciation – together with a specific difference: Only the social habit[11] of behaviour justifies us in joining such distinct meanings as narrative universes, rhetorical persuasion, and production of aesthetic admiration. A logical approach to enunciation has two distinct areas: Possibility and Potentialities, vague and general rule, the chaotic resources of meaning and rules restricting the Possible.

Certainly, every cognition (i.e., consisting of a rule or law that allows the production of all conceivable meanings) confines possible or imaginable states of affairs into an arbitrary number of Occurrences (i.e., which fall under this rule), and all Occurrences into one Law. Yet the metaphysically Possible in General (which is of course more than this possible world) is not the same as the Possible in these habits of enunciation. They produce meaning in an enunciationally extended frame that does not exhibit the same necessities as normal common sense. This is especially relevant for art forms as extensions of the aesthetic judgment. Their Sign processes must be the freed from the normal cognitive range of aesthetic judgments, which typically cover percepts (v. *supra*). We do not think with Signs of art; rather, we 'feel.' The result is a judgment not of a perceived Quality but of another artistic Quality. In all Signs there is a Third Correlate, and for art this Third Correlate must reflect the norms of art. As aesthetic law, it cannot concern itself only with perception. We can conceptualize this vague law nature, as in our earlier attempt, as the power of law as a norm as such – as admirability in itself. This is vague enough to accommodate all judgments of art. However, it can also admit arbitrary standards of taste (*de gusti-bus [non] est disputandum*), which in their open contingency convey merely the admirable as such – in such-and-such a manner.

Art, the Interpretation of an artistic Sign, has a meaning that either is quite precarious when compared to more 'arguable' Signs, or is scant because it is applied to this unique, present art experience. This meaning can be reduced to a feeling that (a) it is good (b) for this real experiential conduct in this world. This does not provide much logical traction for generalizing all of this into something of stricter generality, but there can be nothing that has a more universal validity than admirability as such.[12] However, with all its frailty, it guarantees the aesthetic Sign of art.

Gadamer's aesthetic distinguishes 'ästhetische Unterscheidung' from 'ästhetische Nichtunterscheidung.' What he is naming – or better, hinting at – as 'Urbild' of a general Human Nature is not only the third point of comparison for that distinction. It could also be reframed as the origin of all admirability and this kind of Thirdness of the aesthetic Sign. This is the only way to re-establish a cognitive potential for art and the aesthetic experience.

The Possibility restricted through rhetoric is also broader than that can be (i.e., is determined in) thought – otherwise there would be no need for persuasion. The objects of rhetorical enunciation are existents, states of affairs. Yet it is never enough to proffer the purest possible proposition, such as 'Look here!' (whose informative value depends entirely on an existential relation). It is always of the sort 'This oven here is [a case of] black[ness].' Rhetoric achieves a new Subject that is not yet thinkable. Its technique consists in showing me here its new Subject, which then becomes existent for me. This means that it is related to a new Third.

The enunciation of narration, then – the poetical form – restricts in principle the Possibility of temporal cognition in its unique way through a relatively strong teleological determination. Even here we must not presume that its Possibility reduction coincides with non-enunciational world universes. Here narration can also imaginatively exhaust a broader realm of Possibility, even when compared to Laws of Time, which do not rely on enunciation. The latter are cosmological laws, whereas narrative temporality is determined through pragmatic purposes (cf. *supra*).

Other questions concern the potentialities opened up by the forms of enunciation. A rule is as powerful as its capacity to enable potential meaning. Enunciation being a 'mere' rule, it is a vague rather than a concrete meaning. Properly speaking, it 'is' not, but 'is' the rule, which produces every single one of its instantiations. We carry the rules for narration in our heads, as it were – that is, in the social practice narration. An abstract concept or definition of narration (i.e., order through temporality) is less than the practice narration. The former is actually meaningful; the latter, because of its vagueness, produces more meaning without being itself a meaning. In other words, enunciation is neither a concept nor a Sign; it is a pragmatic rule of conduct.

6.2 Narrative Enunciation

> I have so many tales to tell, so much forgiveness to ask.
>> Lord Hidetora, the dying prodigal father to his dead son
>> Saburo who had found him again, in Kurosawa's *Ran*

In film theory there are basically two approaches to narrative enunciation:[13] (A) through marks of enunciation (*marques d'énonciation*), or (B) through identity parameters. Although film narratology displays a general preference for identities, this does not always relegate marks to linguistics. Amalgamations of convenience are quite common.[14]

In both, Semiotic sees variations of the same Sign process, which produces traces of vagueness and then imposes a lawlike logic (cf. *supra*). Interpretation of the Vague is a prerequisite of enunciation as such; only then can the fragile narrative order of teleology be created, one that is not based on outside events. Furthermore, narration represents objects vaguely as probable objects (the poetic *narratio probabilis* or εἰκός). Narrative probability is in principle not a question of a likely object world (Greimas's and Barthes's *illusion référentielle*); instead, it stems from temporal arrangement. Narrative causality originates in the construction of a probable teleology as a logic of some credible necessity of temporal sequence.

6.2.1 Cinematic Marks of Enunciation Theories (A)

6.2.1.1 What Are Linguistic Marks of Enunciation?
Understood as traces of Vagueness, these modifiers of meaning are made/make dependent from a communicational origin. Enunciation in its marks determines the mode of that which depends on it. Modification takes place through the manipulation of the enunciated. Since this

manipulation is linguistically operated by verbs, it subjects the manipulated to three conditions: (a) person, (b) tense, and (c) mood (compared to Branigan's 'at least six' psychological shifters; cf. *infra*). Therefore, such meaning dimensions originate from propositional hypotaxis, constituted through the dimensionally regulated contrast between a hypotactic phrase and a hypertactic proposition. The first plane determines in three respects what it conveys on a second plane, its 'about-ness,' which in turn contains the marks of enunciation. For this function, language[15] must provide linguistic elements, which are inherently deictic. If they cannot be referred to an *origo*, they are incomprehensible. If this hypotaxis is understood as a communicational device, it is about something and by the same token defines our attitude toward it (*modus*), our position in time with respect to that object (*tempus*): Finally, *persona* defines other roles of the discourse in their relation to the speaker.

Linguistic elements can clearly be attributed to one of these modifiers, but in film they are of course not unavailable. However, based on the communicational parlance of enunciation, it is simple enough to find equivalents in cinema. After an anthropomorphic transformation of the technical apparatus as the role of origin and the source of dependency, by definition everything else falls into place following its dependency type. A comprehensive list of audiovisual parameters based on this dependency has been investigated by Carontini (1986). For instance, a character directly gazing into the camera must be interpreted as present tense, which breaks the narrative attitude and creates an attitude of commentary (except in the case of a present of irruption). The diatribe against Casetti's psychologizing in Metz (1991) – justified in itself – is without object because there can be no serious objection to Carontini's translation of enunciation into pragmatic logic, as far as it goes. If dependency as such is not in question, the understanding of it as an action amounts to saying that it is a Sign relation in the Pragmaticistic sense. By making use of proxemics and kinesics, which are the most 'pragmatic' of all communication means, he succeeds in classifying attitudes into non-dependent ('comment') ones and dependent narration ones.

The choice of classifier concepts along the 'shifter' line should not obscure the fact that the explanation itself is pragmatic. For example, the combination of significant variations of all (relevant) audiovisual elements produces the 'cinematic pluperfect effect.'[16] Each element in different variants and combinations constitutes all other tense effects as well. This is remarkable for several reasons. First, taken in itself, each element is technically a pragmatic program. Second, this pragmatic is based on the anthropomorphism of the camera, which 'mimics' human social behaviours and situations. Of course, there is no logic that can precisely attribute this global tense effect to these film operations. Only the pragmatic operation enunciation rendered probable the camera pragmatic operation, not the linguistic operation of 'shifting.' If this pragmatic act succeeds, we can describe its dependent universe as the manipulation of its time, mode of being, and personal relation. But in order to avoid reductionism, we should retain the complexity of enunciation dependency for meaning other than narrative teleology. Carontini's anthropomorphic or communicational Interpretations are taxonomically ordered by grammatical categories. Their explanatory power comes from enunciation as device and dependency. When we take a look at the three linguistic modifying dimensions themselves, their introduction of Vagueness becomes more obvious.

The *'Modifier' persona* offers, as degrees of Vagueness, a minimum in the neutral third person, singular and plural. It can be used in definitions and hardly refers in a deixis to any particular person. The couple I–thou (we–you) is definitely vaguer, which makes any meaning dependent on an instance of enunciation. An interesting case in point – one that combines temporal and modal dependency – is the enunciation of a lie. This presupposes a dependency of the first persona from all other persons, suggesting degrees of knowledge. 'I' (without enunciation) cannot lie, because 'I' always know myself. (Only in a temporalized tense dependency can I have been wrong. As a sign, this is the case when the former knowledge becomes a First of a better Interpretation.) If the first starts enunciating the 'less true' of another, non-first person, it presupposes that there is one who knows. This last state of verity is the enunciation instance. This effect is avoided in dependent, in other than genuine first-person accounts; however, omniscience is typical in that state of a sign relation which claims generality. Its preferential grammatical form is therefore the impersonal 'it' combined with the present of definition. Thus the epistemic dependency effect of enunciation can also be avoided. In a psychological context this person dependency can easily be interpreted as personal 'motivation.' Although a definition in a dictionary does not need to be motivated, texts that depend on an enunciation in the fiduciary narrative contract assume a basic meaning dependency. This is the premise of the δυνατά of the *Poetic* (cf. 51b32): possible as the possibility of someone's acting. Narrative enunciation is the dependent creation of a probable action space for another human being; the independent action of the enunciation instance is unquestioned and firm. Within the realm of this dependency, the role of the reader can also become a Vague meaning. In the hermeneutic tradition, this has been described as the aesthetic effect (identification and difference). The meaning is produced as a new Generality in a Sign relation, which discovers norms and values for human conduct in general. Person as dependent meaning is not so different from Branigan (1984), who framed the subject as cinematic space production through 'vision with.' Similarly, Casetti (1986), who has a more generally linguistic framework (i.e., is less dependent on literary theories).

Enunciation also creates dependencies through *tense modification*. In literary theory, especially in Weinrich's tense theory, tense has been a crucial topic. It has been adopted in Bettetini's film theory. Appropriate tense creates its own Vagueness. When compared to a present of definition, for instance, all other tenses are relatively Vague. Past tense has less Generality and thus is only comprehensible if the point of reference is clear. Evidently, this requires a considerable effort for further Interpretation. Such a Sign is quite remote from a final Interpretant, which constitutes its entire meaning. If tense creates the 'interruption of communication' (constitutive of the narrative universe, in Weinrich's sense), its narrative enunciation produces dependent Vagueness of a special kind. Such is, for instance, the difference between a present tense ('philosophical' or TV-Guide) statement, 'Life is a comedy of human errors,' and the past tense, 'and this was his last error.' The latter is Vague because its meaning as the final point of a sequence is meaningless without that sequence itself. Enunciation through its Vagueness creates space for teleological Interpretation. However, the latter mode 'knows less' because epistemologically it is not a concept. It has not (yet) made a general law of its Sign relation. At this enunciational habit stage it remains a hypothetic *propter hoc* causality; it is still a merely Actual *post hoc* 'and then.'

Modal dependencies are devices for creating Vagueness. It is striking how much Interpretation is necessary to make the meaning of a conditional clause clearer. Regarding cinema, it may seem almost impossible to reproduce the meaning of verbal moods in temporal images.[17] For this, Carontini (1986) relies on various parameters of gaze. Yet his list is merely an anthropomorphic version of the sort of Interpretation rules that is required in order to give meaning to intrinsically Vague concepts. It is important for narrative enunciation to qualify the various representational universes it produces with regard to existential modes, thus unrealizing (e.g., through use of conditional mood) or realizing the dependent existence. Moreover, the requested credibility in the *Poetic* (always οἷα ἄν εἰκὸς γενέσθαι καὶ δυνατὰ γενέσθαι, 1451b31f; cf. *supra*) can also be reversed into more doubt. A standard film example that comes to mind is 'vision with' modified in the optative, conditional, or other unrealizing mood (of strictly narrative enunciation). This is even a case of enunciation within an enunciation. In enunciations other than narrative – but often amalgamated with narration – other modes of Possibility operate in tropes or figures. In the cinematic field, the figure irony is certainly one of the most powerful and customary unrealizing moods. Modal, figurative, metaphoric probability is very difficult to pin down to the objects on which it is exercised. However, we have seen a number of examples in Godard that could be interpreted in this sense. It is the non-bracketed, the non-other (contrary to the bracketing of narrative enunciation and its other universe), but it is at the same time the other as not yet, as possibility. Figuration is the domain of rhetoric enunciation. The Vague potentiality of enunciation is – at any rate – the feasible, a possibility of conduct. Through this Pragmaticistic extension it becomes available to narrative, ethical, or aesthetic habits of action.

Enunciating produces in its dependent parts modes of being. These can be attached to linguistic modalization in verbs, or to psychologizing modalization, or to other systems of modalization.[18]

6.2.1.2 How Are Marks Used in Narratives?

Enunciation marks are at the core of many narratologies, especially in the various schools around Benveniste. One of the most prominent, which has been broadly accepted in film studies, is Weinrich's classical narration theory based on the analysis of narrative tense dynamics. Notwithstanding its hermeneutic armour, the backdrop of this theory remains crucially enunciation as an operation of logical necessity for the non-necessary probable. This logical habit narration was created long ago with a limited set of devices and customs to signal the logical production of the probable. One of the more conspicuous and intuitive of this devices is the 'narrative contract,' whereby enunciation as it were assumes responsibility for the credibility of a narration. Text-immanent interpretative judgments are attributed to enunciation. 'Marks of enunciation' are just that.

Weinrich defines narration as 'between two interruptions of communication'[19] (i.e., told in the real world and time of narrators and their audience, but not taking place there). This amounts to a complex interplay between temporal and rhetorical enunciation. In between the linguistic metaphor of shifting, and theories based on psychological identity such as Branigan's, hermeneutical narratology explains enunciation through communication metaphors. In the hermeneutic tradition, communication holds deeper assumptions than commonsense 'all-must-be-said-by-someone-to-someone.' We have seen in our discussion of Ricoeur how a narrative link between two solitary existences can be conceived hermeneutically, and how difficult this is. Literary theorists such as Weinrich (1964) address problems such as enunciation instead of philosophical questions; that said, the linguistic features that constitute enunciation do not explain it ultimately; rather, they explain communication in the hermeneutical sense of identity.[20]

The idea behind Weinrich's *Textlinguistik*[21] (8ff) is the dialectical suture of communication and text. To achieve this, the enunciator must 'bracket' the text – that is, separate the text from what is before and after it. In this way it is possible to create three enunciation dependency effects: (1) locutory attitudes, (2) relief effect, and (3) perspective, which are communicational descriptions. Enunciation – this is the premise – cannot be deleted from texts. Their origin and finality (i.e., the pragmatic setting of their production) are inscribed in various linguistic traces. Speaking in identity ('role') metaphors, it is the enunciation and the spectator roles that leave their respective textual traces. Apollonios Dyskolos, Karl Bühler, and Weinrich (1964: 32) identify enunciation as *origo*, the 'I-here-now,' the coordinates for any further signification. In another nice metaphor, Greimas calls this step 'uncoupling' ('*débrayage*') – that is, from the I-here-now into a Not-I-here-now (i.e., Greimas casts definitions only through the three kinds of logical negation). If the true explanation of enunciation lies not in its linguistic features but in a communication dependency, and if an anthropomorphic role is assigned to the camera, this is analogous to the *origo* of enunciation, 'speaking' translated into the equivalent communicational role of 'showing.'

Regarding point (1): The two correlated locutory attitudes (*Sprechhaltungen*) – commentary (*Besprechen*) and narration (*Erzählung*) – stand for what we called the construction of probability. Weinrich's is functionally equivalent to Benveniste's *discours-histoire*[22] dichotomy. Now hermeneutic has no difficulties comprehending communication as occurring between *ego* and *alter ego*. Understanding *alter* is never the same as being *ego*; furthermore, it is always in degrees of probability and is never perfect or beyond further efforts at interpretation. Obviously, then, there is a big difference between the lossless 'communication' of encoded messages and coming to an agreement communicating with an irreducibly other identity. Weinrich seems to think of locutory attitudes as differing in the type of their probability. Commenting, then, produces a hermeneutic identification on the grounds of a common intentional projection ('object'), whereas narrating communicates on the grounds of (common displaced: v. *infra*, 'perspective') temporality or a teleological aim. As long as the normal case of identifying understanding is regarded as agreement on objects, narration seems to be the exception. Narrators therefore must efface themselves from the enunciated.

But how does the camera efface itself? In grammatical texts there is a surer way. The pragmatic marks of commencing the narrative world are the perfect tense (in English), together with 'once upon a time,' *incipit*, and so on.[23] Also, what Hamburger (1968) called the narrative past tense ('erzählerisches Präteritum') constantly keeps us within the narrative universe. Film must use different pragmatic markers. These are normally already given with the viewing situation of cinemas, television program openings, announcers, and recognizable program types. The conspicuous absence of the pragmatic instance establishes the *incipit* and provokes the viewer into a narrative Interpretation and attitude. Once this kind of Interpretation has gained a firm foothold, the vision of the camera can be subjectivized again, and in much the same way as any other grammatical person. This other subject has a beginning that is contrary to the time of enunciation. One might even say that it is constituted temporally as a subject by the fact that as a story it begins. Then the subject is its story, seen by subjects without duration (at this moment).

Regarding point (2): Weinrich's relief ('Reliefgebung') creates a difference of weight, or narrative foregrounding and backgrounding.[24] Parts that have narrative importance are contrasted with mere settings, which are precisely 'background information.' This comes close to Branigan's idea of levels, without 'nominal subjects,' however, 'High' and 'low' relief is a thoroughly temporal operation. Important is what leads a narrative to its end; what does *not* contribute to this teleo-logic is retardation or digression.

Cinematic teleology employs the metaphorical foreground/background literally as spatial arrangement. Montage as a logical operation

apportions spatial images into paratactic or hypotactic, equally important or subordinated respectively.[25] For example, consecutive close-
ups do not subordinate and thus serve no purpose, whereas 'establishing shots' explain subsequent detail shots as leading to a purpose.

But this is where the explanatory power of linguistic, phrasal-order
features ends. Once again, cinema is left to its own means to establish
teleological aims. Subordination only functions in a teleology of action.
Through this, one action becomes logically and temporally a first, and
another a second, and the whole becomes development toward an end.
In themselves all shots are equal and without any natural sequentiality;
shot sequences can be reassembled at random. An obviously (alarm-
ing?) case in point: Eisenstein reported that in Sweden, his *Potjemkin*
was entirely recut to reflect a counter-revolutionary and 'system-con-
servative' narrative teleology.

Relief[26] as a linguistic feature is inherent in grammar itself and taxis is
the result of every use of shifters: syntax involves taxis. This is obvious
enough regarding phrasal construal; it is less evident when it comes to
textual dependency. Spatial imagery of hyper-, hypo-, and para-taxis
must not obscure the fact that as a logical dependency, Relief is one
part's Interpretation of the other part in a very specific temporal logic. If
– as in Peirce's Letter to Lady Welby (8.332) – 'a sign is something by
knowing which we know something more,' relief dependency needs to
know more about teleological purpose.

In connection with Relief are two linguistic observations that have
some bearing on cinema. One is that foregrounding can become so
absolute that even enunciation itself almost seems to retrocede behind
the maximum weight and direct presence of the narrative purpose.[27]
Cinematic means for its achievement include fast and slow motion,
still frames, and speed manipulations, and the most basic measure to
freeze the narrative flow, stop-frame. Not surprisingly, these narrative
stases are resorted to most often in thrillers and suspense films. Only if
the teleological development assumes an absolute weight, the standard-setting instance loses all incidence. This can obliterate for a certain time the anchor and source of teleological meaning. However, this
effect 'works' only after teleology has been put in place.

The second observation is that narrative weight logically consists in
understanding the purpose of a narrative subject. Thus, it will translate
into the reason for the importance of something to someone, as if this
subject engaged in a narration of its own and for itself.[28] The history of
literature has produced very sophisticated ways of narrating, from the

most direct immediate I, through Me-narratives, down to the ultrarealist 'He'-narratives. This differentiation owes its comprehensibility to the one teleology of the narrator and to all derivations of further teleologies from the original standard instituting act. Therefore, this strategy reaches its limits where narration loses its coherence when looking-with cannot be traced back to a unique source, on which the inference converges. Spectators must know at any moment with whom they see (feel, look, etc.). If it is not a diegetic character it can only be the *vox narrativa*. In this way a multiplicity of subjects[29] are held together by the enunciating instance. Its effacement into character point of view is potentially disturbing because it is contradictory, especially when spectators are unsure with which to look. This disorientation can only be sought for aesthetic effect.

In cinema, whose meaning a look represents (i.e., a character's or an enunciator's) can remain logically indeterminate. In linguistic narratives this is impossible to efface, because language requires personal pronouns.[30] In cinema this sort of ambiguity is eventually remedied – for instance, through a narrative automatism to investigate 'possible actions.' It is not necessary to psychologize the camera into a person as long as the primordial logical construction of temporality is ascertained. Cinema substitutes personal pronouns and suggests subjectivity by representing a new teleological standard setting. Yet nothing prevents cinema from creating an Ideal Spectator, as in explicitly ironic comments (e.g., Woody Allen's direct address to his imagined audience in the *Purple Rose of Cairo* and *Mighty Aphrodite*).

Regarding point (3): *Perspektive* is a meaning of incongruity of two temporalities. In this case, narrating and narrated time are not the difference between a teleological temporality and the experience of time. When a narration disposes its three states of possible temporal dislocation, it refers to the time of narrating not as 'real time' but as the zero point of the other teleology. This can have three results: (a) Asynchrony, when the time and place of narrating are different from what is being represented. Narrative cinema often goes immediately *in medias res* without the further anchor of a fictitious act of telling. If enunciation and enunciated are synchronic, (b) they can coincide with the act of showing itself (televised, transmitted reportage style), (c) or with a framing of the narrated in a visible narrating source. This is often used in the 'diary' sort of film. The last two pretend not to be dislocated, that is, to be co-located with the spectator present and space, from which they distance another time and space. Without any dislocation, we have a zero point (*Nullpunkt*); which is typically the prerogative of present tense in commentary, or *imparfait* and *passé simple* in literary narratives. From a zero point we can refer backward or forward, either in a text (e.g., cross-referencing in scholarly texts) or in the dual universe of narration (where referring backward or forward applies to the represented world, thus assuming a zero point from which everything is either before or after).

This communicational explanation considers temporal means of enunciation. This perhaps explains why it has been considered most congenial to cinematic narration. The underlying effect is a teleological probability (non-existent outside the enunciational bracket). In Weinrich it is unclear precisely how a narrating subject communicates dependency, as logic or existential analysis was not within his purview. That said, it is clear enough how communication is interrupted.

Cinematic narration theories based on the *explanans* of linguistic marks have been subject to some harsh critiques (mentioned earlier, and some of them throw the baby out with the bathwater). This debate, however, should not be reduced to the long familiar argument that cinematic narration does not operate through linguistic means. Instead, the critique must be carried into the realm of narrative meaning itself – and from there into cinema. As an explanation, it is not enough that it be based on facts (i.e., on linguistic features). Nor need we deny the fact that in many (but not all) languages, various elements vary when phrasal construal produces hypotactic and hypertactic clauses. This observation is at the core of the text grammatical theories of Weinrich and others. Besides the inability of any fact, or any number of facts, to construct a law, these theories share a basic and mostly tacit[31] assumption: the explanatory power of the linguistic fact is that it is a linguistic universal or 'quasi-universal.' However, regardless of the factual linguistic features that are relevant for narration, a relevance for narrative meaning can be achieved only by the means of meaning – logic. So narration is not a *consecutio temporum* or any other means of 'shifting' and 'unshifting'; rather, it is the representation of an action from its beginning to its end. This definition in the *Poetic* has not been superseded by any 'turn' in philosophy, be it linguistic or cognitivist. Thus the problem described by this definition has still to be addressed.

From a meaning perspective, the logic of enunciation seems to be the only meaning-relevant approach. It merely adds one crucial perspective to a strictly logical consideration: the determination of meaning is contingent on the use of its Signs. Through Sign use, time as meaning enters into meaning; only with time as meaning can the particular teleological time meaning become a form of meaning. Enunciating this form, then, I enunciate now and here that then and there another action starts toward its end. This is more than a dependent meaning; in the strict sense of the word, it is a consecutive meaning. In the logical and ordinal sense, it follows my setting of the zero point as the standard for the determination of a first, and a different second, state. Thus, text grammar is strictly an ordered set of events, understood as temporal events but also as 'logical' steps.

Yet, narratologies that are aware of enunciation offer a wealth of practical insights, even from a linguistic or hermeneutic perspective. Their principal differentiation between commenting and narrating agrees with what is also at the basis of a Semiotic theory of temporality. As a strict consequence of the ordinality of the Categories, we must cognize existence and quality before the cognition of temporality. Commenting can be understood as object representations, typical of propositions. It is a rhetorical enunciation, logically upstream of narrative enunciation of temporality.

For the narrative contract, the hermeneutic deduction of temporal enunciation is coherent – that is, assuming immediate consciousness and its phenomenological analysis. However, its direct application to film is fraught with difficulties. How can the immediate consciousness of a camera be analyzed and theorized? Either it becomes a *ceteris paribus* argument, or the specific meaning contribution of the camera is again suppressed as a transitory transparent stage between two communicating subjects. For a phenomenological method, such suppression is not impossible, as its language theory shows. The argumentation – which we will not repeat – is of the same kind as Ricoeur's confrontation with Greimas's formalism (in Greimas 1989: cf. *supra*, 369, 614n12) and can be reduced to the priority problem of *explanans* and *explanandum*.

Outside of phenomenological thought, we cannot abstract temporal enunciation from the medium or the nature of the sign. Narration is not so much an operation of interrupted communication, but it is perfectly understandable as a logical operation. There is a logical difference between experience-in-signs leading to teleology and experience-in-signs leading to time before teleology. Weinrich's locutionary attitudes, as logical difference, are as follows: (1) The act ('comment') of indicating an aim, from which vantage point pieces of film change nature and become episodes ('narration'). (2) Pieces of film as pure events of 'then and then' (not problematic in film with its permanent change) are in a state of moving images before being polarized by enunciation. In principle, this movement is in the same logical universe as the utterer and the receiver, so we can perhaps call it commenting (which really only states a hither-of the other universe). Weinrich's idea goes further, however, understanding it rather as 'logical patches' in a different universe, patches into which the logic of that universe is emptied. Since these empty patches are not exemptions or contradictions of narrative logic, they must be treated in a relation of logical anteriority.

Extreme examples in the history of cinema illustrate the practical problem of how and where enunciation can insert itself into the flux of events of moving images. A film would have to create patches empty of narrativity in order to reduce episodes to events. Some of Aki Kaurismäki's films sometimes reach the outer limits of narrativity, where images seem to flow without any purpose: we are not allowed to understand the goal of those changes and events – they simply happen. The exact opposite is found in Bresson's *Un Condamné à mort s'est échappé ou Le vent souffle où il veut*. Here the exact teleology is exhaustively given in the title itself, which enables Bresson to keep it out of the enunciated (according to his film theory). One of Bresson's strategies for conveying a deeper meaning-beyond-teleology, together with teleology, can be seen in *L'Argent*, where the actors themselves comment and explain their acts. Rohmer in *Conte d'hiver* brought this approach to its zenith with his explanation of chance. Moving pictures cannot produce teleological enunciation in themselves, but the use of language for this varies considerably. With Godard a quite complex example in this respect was analyzed earlier, but are there 'run of the mill' techniques? At the very least there seem to be teleological highways in two non-iconic modes: 'epos' and clear narrative 'task.' Tavernier in *Un Dimanche à la campagne*, for example, pokes fun at epos by stating as it were: 'now it begins' (i.e., and will end in death). We see much the same thing in many films that start literally with 'this is the epos, story of ...' (e.g., Jean Becker's *Les Enfants du Marais*). Since Propp, the narrative task as a beginning has been recognized as the quintessence of fairy tales, and the lack of a Proppian «*réparation d'un manque*» is almost a trademark of shunning the stuff of tales: Marguerite Duras's *India Song* succeeds in protracting such a task almost interminably.

Clearly, then, a theoretical grasp of narrative enunciation, achieved in a Semiotic and logical way, need not fall back on an analogy with linguistic marks or customs of social conduct. Semiotic awareness of the cinematic Sign itself must in this case consider its usage/enunciation, since moving images in themselves do not constitute narrative change. So such a logic is brought into, and becomes the premise of, the narrative movement of images. There it can be discovered in teleologically empty patches of narration (which may or may not be related to a communication interruption). However, enunciation remains the logical *conditio sine qua non* of all narration, including cinema.

There are those who do not recognize the logical function of enunciation. By tacitly relying on its logical operation, we are conceptually suppressing it. Sometimes this sacrifice is made – improperly – in favour of 'diegesis'–'mimesis' and other similar dichotomies. Hermeneutic narratologies such as Ricoeur's may exaggerate enunciation in the sense of the primordiality of an existential anchor. At the opposite end, there is the Formalist polemic (cf. *supra*: Beaugrand's remark) purism of 'sole narration,' which apparently is oblivious to enunciation. Such demise cannot long remain in its self-elected autarky. Surreptitiously, the preconditions of narration are recycled with other labels. The commencement of an Interpretation as narration is not just a logical change; it needs to be marked, otherwise, when would spectators know they must apply narrative schemata (i.e., pragmatic logic) and not normal perceptual ones? They are helped, for instance, by evaluative adjectives and cinematic equivalents,[32] or by rhetorical figures.

As long as it is clear that enunciation is a precise and logical sign process, personifying metaphors are convenient. Calling it Ideal Author's Voice (or with Ricoeur, *vox narrativa*) does not change its nature. It is also crucial to keep the context of different questions apart. The *vox*, and so on, is not required by narration as temporal order, but enunciating the probable (including narrative) requires a special Interpretational instigation. This special dependency is addressed in various dichotomies. The difference between *fabula–syuzhet* (i.e. *sujet*) and narrative *énoncé–enunciation* marks (and all equivalents) relates only the explanatory depth and the perspective, text to author or author to text (artist to world). Neither explains the special logical dependency that operates in narrative, rhetorical, and aesthetic enunciation; both presuppose it, however.[33]

That being said, Bordwell's narratological *fabula/syuzhet* constructs contain in themselves nothing cognitive. *Fabula* is not a chain of causal inferences, and *syuzhet/sujet* is not a subjectively motivated interpretation of the former chain (for a specific purpose). It is not even a narrative theory, because it cannot theorize causality as teleological temporality. It is an aesthetic theory in the narrower sense, which in its core operates with psychologizing metaphors such as 'trick' (on the author's side) and 'familiarity' (on the reader's side). His negative definition that 'the fabula is not an unmarked enunciative act; it is not a speech act at all' is possibly pertinent. The positive claim 'but a set of inferences' relying 'upon more supple principles basic to all narrative representation' (Bordwell 1985: 51), however, is not warranted at all – not even etymologically. Only if *fabula* and *sujet* were schemata-operated perceptions could we dispense with enunciation, but temporal logic is never perceived or a schema. By rejecting enunciation (or its material equivalent), however, we are foregoing the sole instrument of setting the temporal standard to a narrative.

Are there functional substitutes for the logic of enunciation?[34] In particular, is there an explanatory power in Metz's extremely linguistic version of textual marks? This topic was debated in film theory even before Metz (1991). By now it is a canonical problem: What is the apparatus of cinematic means that is used to enunciate something other than itself? Behind Metz's reductive definition of that apparatus as non-anthropomorphic instance we encounter his linguistic persistence. His theory would indeed be invalidated if such instances were explained as human existences and interpersonal modes of communication (whereas film does not communicate in this sense). If enunciation is upheld, it is because of its linguistic origin, *'ce qui pour certains lui communique le choléra'* (ibid.: 175). Gaudreault (1988) goes one step beyond this by reducing enunciation (admitted as a framework instance) to linguistic shifters proper (the narrator instead is supposedly not connected with these means).

What are we explaining, however, when we distinguish between narration as such and its mode of representation? What is meant by such terms as 'récit,' 'histoire,' 'discours,' 'narration,' 'enunciation,' 'narrator,' 'enunciator,' 'énonciataire,' *vox narrativa,* diverse 'instances,' and the increasingly diverse 'roles' of spectators, authors, and readers? How do they 'mean,' if they are meaning? Is there a meaning in shifting, or is it simply a fact that is observable in some languages? The meaning problem is as old as the diegesis/mimesis distinction in Plato's Republic and Aristotle's Poetic. Unavoidably, then, enunciation is the 'principle basic to all narrative representation'; it is also crucial to film theory. Narration is the imitation of actions through teleology, not (properly speaking) shifting, but it means creating logical dependency. Dependency, once it is understood, can be described in linguistic terms (or as a role psychology). Plato and Aristotle, at any rate, are not antagonists between cognitivism and linguistic. Diegesis and mimesis have an altogether different meaning as degrees of the same and not opposites.

Mimesis was the founding idea; it is of Platonic origin and had to be impregnated with his ontology. The first major reorientation of mimetism came from Aristotle. The object, which mimesis was imitating,[35] now became mythos as the imitation of human action, while Plato concerned himself with artistic truth. Correspondence with facticity was not his concern. His truth is the 'truer' side of the real, the essence, and Gadamer's idea of play is still indebted to this sort of theatrical *raison d'être*. Through Aristotle's transformation into mimesis of action, Plato's truth was thus without object, as human action in its interlacing follows other truth constraints. It is pointless to renege on this mimetic heritage, and to misconceive it by opposing it to diegesis. Aristotle had already distinguished three modes of imitation: one where the author presents characters 'as living and moving before us'; one by telling in his own person; and one by telling in the disguise of another personality. The distinction between showing and telling merely has regard to one of the 'necessarily six parts' of *Poetic*: $\lambda \acute{\epsilon} \xi \iota \varsigma$.

Another inheritance from mimetism, however, should not lead as easily to false debates in film theory. The finality of imitating, admitted by Aristotle, is a cathartic effect of $\mu \acute{\iota} \mu \eta \sigma \iota \varsigma \ \pi \rho \acute{\alpha} \xi \epsilon \omega \varsigma$. This must also strengthen the corresponding part of an enunciating instance, the Ideal Reader. We might speculate on why human beings want to imitate the action of others. It must be mimetic 'mi(a)'[36]-ness, the one-ness that enables apprehension of, and interest in, the one guiding principle of all action. Being one with all mankind and all possible action, we understand also the justice (of punishment) or the injustice (of persecution) in a represented action. This comprehension hinges on the fact that we understand a narrative turning point ($\mu \epsilon \tau \alpha \beta o \lambda \acute{\eta}$) for better or worse ($\epsilon \dot{v} \delta \alpha \iota \mu o \nu \acute{\iota} \alpha, \kappa \alpha \kappa o \delta \alpha \iota \mu o \nu \acute{\iota} \alpha$). Aristotle in the Poetic did not reflect explicitly on who is the ultimate judgmental instance, who holds and pronounces values of better and worse. Yet these are the true 'deictic' elements in narration, without which its logic would cease to operate. By the very enthymemic nature of how the probable of narration ($\tau \grave{o}$ $\epsilon \grave{\iota} \kappa \grave{o} \varsigma$) is argued, an enunciation instance is an appeal to an unquestionably larger instance. To lose this philosophical context of narration would be to reduce 'deixis' to Metz's deictic 'marques d'énonciation.' Clearly, it would be inadequate to have these refer to a human narrator (or the camera, or the author, or even the cinema apparatus). Mimesis need not be the metaphysical truth of Plato, but even in Aristotle it is more than a technical question. Through the notion of probability, it concerns the functioning of narration itself.

Before we reject these classical notions of mimesis and diegesis in the name of cinematic specificity, we should be aware of their function, both then and now. In all three versions (i.e., diegetic, or through vicarious acting, or the mixed δι' ἀμφοτέρων), theories of mimesis are concerned with the composition of actions (ἡ τῶν πραγματῶν σύστασις). Thus, they conceptualize the task of producing pragmatic logic in drama. It is possible to do so using various poetic techniques involving anything from sung declamation to acting; that said, all techniques use the same logic of composing action teleologically. Contrary to Bordwell, then, no narratological options are involved.

No functional substitute for enunciation can be derived from marks, yet the ancient poetics had a conception of time in which enunciation served no function. Teleology is ontology, the becoming of being (τό ὄν, not the εἶναι, which is eternal), and the time of movement is only apparent (the countable of the moved). If the reference point of time is not outside but rather inside the experienced, we must set its standard reference zero so that it will be cognitively effective; and this is enunciation. There is only one film theory that has a cogent approach and that can dispense with enunciation, and this is Deleuze's. Here, however, we again enter ontological territory.

6.2.2 Theories Using Metaphors of Identity (B)

A final conceptualization of narrative enunciation involves the idea of a 'role,' which is actually a psychological description of dependency (exactly what Metz tried to banish from film theory). Role identity (with its derivatives) is the metaphor of choice here, but what is its explanatory power?

Linguistic marks of enunciation are meaningful for communicational ('functionalist') linguistic theories. To derive similar cinematic marks, we must use the communicational effects as a basis for anthropomorphic derivations of modifiers. The step to psychology is not big, since the same communication makes identities and roles plausible as the principal descriptors of enunciation.

The role or identity metaphor seems rather fecund, but *un train peut cacher un autre* – that is, it conceals quite different explanatory theories. At least in some cases,[37] identity is understood as a cognitive centre of consciousness. How do boundaries of consciousness understand narrative enunciation ('e-speculation' might be more to the point)? Does dropping language properties as explanatory tools in favour of consciousness lead to a better grasp of the cognitive processes involved in producing dependency? In the psychological parlance of stock literary theory, this is a question of 'knowing the motivation of characters.' Such a 'knowledge' is dependent on a superior, omniscient 'knowledge.' Materially, this amounts to Interpreting (a cognitive practice) another Interpretation (the pragmatic purpose of a character). Speaking of 'seeing or knowing with' is more convenient and intuitive than speaking of Interpreting, but one does not see with someone (e.g., I do not see with you) unless one interprets accordingly. Evidently film theory is strongly tempted by visual metaphors of this sort. It also offers an advantage by suggesting 'naturally' available space. Space is visual in the life world, yet we cannot really speak in the same manner of cinematic or even narrative space. Doing so would obscure the fact that we see actions and that space is there only through and for actions (i.e., it is pragmatic space).

Perspectivism (or 'seeing with') constitutes figures of action. Figuration produces and specifies meaning. Perspectives, then, are in the first place mindsets of characters. Aristotle placed these characters ($\mathring{\eta}\theta\eta$) immediately after the mythos and before the psychological understanding of a character's action ($\delta\iota\acute{\alpha}\nu o\iota\alpha$, cf. 1450a 7–9). In an act of identification with characters as focal points of acts, a reader or spectator 'sees with' someone else's eyes. However, the picture does not change and neither does the language. Thus, within the same image, it is merely a shift in logic: all perspectives uncouple[38] a not-'I-here-now' from an 'I-here-now.'

A cinematic narratology that explains how film uncouples is therefore of great interest. Branigan (1984) claims precisely this, on the basis of perspectivism. Interestingly enough, classical literary theories use almost cinematic metaphors to describe narration as an ordered interlacement of points of view.[39] Branigan's theory, which in Bordwell's words is 'the most detailed mimetic theory of filmic narration that we have' (1984: XI), first defined 'narration in the visual arts as a positioning of the viewer with respect to a production of space, and subjectivity as a production of space attributed to a character' (ibid.: 177); so it was impossible to preserve a coherent 'perspective' metaphor. Eight years later, he redefined narration in cognitivist[40] terms. In the first version he did not have simply one enunciator and its story, but a Chinese box–like building up of character and referred character spaces (e.g., a character telling about another character, and so forth) up to the ultimate space of the narrator and the reader of the film as a whole.

'Space' consists of everything that is necessary for a visual identity – that is, 'six elements of representation: origin, vision, time, frame, object, and mind.' The first element, *origin*, is the camera, which is sometimes identified with the gaze of a character (in which case it is a 'subjective camera'; cf. ibid.: 61f). *Vision* is, on occasion, the reverse of origin – in other words it is scenic space created by viewing, glances, and so on. Space created in this way can happen in a direction other than camera axes. Next is the *time* of narration, one of telling and one of the told. Furthermore, the *frame* must be taken quite literally as the visual field cut out by the camera, creating both the seen and «*hors champ*» (and the dialectic between them). The *object* is of representation, in that it has a narrative value (cf. ibid.: 65). Mind is the mental origin of something. Objects, for example, refer to a character's will (cf. ibid.: 66f).

The result of this insight into an acting identity is one narrative level. Explaining a psyche as a level is likened by Branigan to linguistic shifters: 'The analysis of linguistic shifters shows that literary narration comprises not just "person" but also "time" and "place" indices; and pictorial narration, I argue, comprises at least five elements' (1984: 178). However, are there in cinema – in more than a metaphoric sense – strictly deictic elements (or, more precisely, morphemes or their adverbial equivalents)? Metz (1991) attempted to deflate the use of 'deictic elements' in cinema; he objected to the metaphoric use of deixis. Branigan's enlargement of the list of cinematic shifters can be approached in light of that critique. He claims that his six narration elements are textual features accessed through textual analysis. Yet what he really obtains is different when he relies implicitly on the mimetism of action logic. All of his elements 'understand' human action and identify with another centre of action that allows the perception of changes in mind, time, and vision. It is difficult to concur with Branigan that there is a differential system of cinematic signification devices.[41] His own are not differential examples; they are action-based.

It is patent, then, that the true explanation of levels is to be gleaned not from shifting but from psychology or consciousness. Levels are 'epistemological boundaries within the text – associated in the reading with such labels as character, narrator, effaced narrator, author' (Branigan 1984: 180). Branigan (1992) overhauls his narratology in a cognitivist key, emphasizing and expanding level theory. Levels are now hierarchies of eight distinct mental operations[42] that build on one another. The (cognitivist archi-concept) 'perception' – suggesting a perceiving identity – constitutes each level; however, 'reader activity' must be what accounts for passing from one perception to the next one down. Compared to linguistic shifting, this certainly explains less. When readers get active they operate cognitively by 'data organizing.' Their epistemic result consists in narrative comprehension.

In light of these cognitive operations, we must logically (*de jure*) justify the existence of separate levels. Furthermore, do these eight constitute a comprehensive list? Separations occur along 'consciousness boundaries.' A level is 'thinking with another consciousness,' and each level has a different object of thought (text, fiction, story world, event, etc.). But are these objects construed in different ways, thus imposing a logical difference? 'Focalized chains of causality' evidently refer to agents and not to different cognitive operations. Thus eight levels are eight agents, which merely differ in their action programs, which are aimed at eight intentional objects. Thus they appear more as 'positions on a continuum rather than sharply exclusive alternatives' (Branigan 1992: 86f). If the operation is the same for all, a question arises. What do levels contribute, and what makes their hierarchical order necessary?

At the same time, however, levels 'describe typical ways that a reader participates in a literary text' (Branigan 1992: 86). Now, does the reader provide the logic? Or, instead, is the fictional agent's pragmatic causality constituting meaning? As reader one can only logically comprehend in fictional agents what one constitutes in them, since they have no other life than the pragmatic purpose of their narrative action. Levels being simultaneously a stage of cognition and a psychological intentionality, it must be agreed what-explains-what. 'Egg-hen' circularity is only avoidable when there is a clear order of *explanans* and *explanandum*. In reality, we escape this circularity only at the zero level, where narration is part of the cognitive constraints of the real (even in a Pragmaticist plurimodal reality). Here is exactly the origin of enunciation, even though seen from within the narration it appears as ultimate textual instance. Only at the ultimate level of narration – which is also the first entry point into the cognitive real world – do psychological categories apply. In Branigan's version of cognitivism, at this point universe-representational schematisms are substituted with 'causal chains' of psychological origin. Only a catch-all definition of cognition, or 'perception,' such as 'description of data,' admits this ambiguous illogical substitution, where psychological causation (*causa finalis*) organizes data in the same manner as representational causation (*causa efficiens*).

Branigan's cognitivist schematism prevents him from recognizing fully the fundamental logical difference at the origin of narration. The distinction between reader activity on the one hand and intentionalities on the other is already an important one. However, if their crucial difference were taken into account, the Russian dolls of levels could become a house of cards. It is impossible to imitate logically the enunciation level at a deeper level of narrative identity. At that stage we are already caught up in the logic of teleology and cannot surface to cognitive constraints of outside reality (i.e., without destroying the narrative). The parallel universe of a narrative is not at all a replica of the real world universe; instead, in its entirety, in its nature, and in its very existence, it is a creature of a particular logical act.

This difference in nature is obfuscated by the sameness of object 'schematisms' of supposed cognitive subjects. To each level – as one of the 'positions on a continuum' (Branigan 1992: 86f) – an implied nominal subject is supposed to correspond; but this is really the case only for the enunciation subject. Conversely, when nominal subjects 'focalize' as agents, 'causal chains' should be constructed. The fallacious focalization semantic suggests identities of agents, which connect, however, only through their pragmatic purpose. It can only be called 'cause' in a finalistic sense (and not in the common sense of the word; v. *infra*). In reality, identity in narratives is a reader operation – that is, they make or construe identity, not agents. This is a logical procedure that is quite different from acting. Readers interpret. If they (1) Interpret the Generality of a conduct of action as a motivation of another person, the result is an identity and a shared Generality (v. *supra* regarding the Pragmatic Maxim).

If they (2) Interpret the temporal sequence of actions as teleological, by supplying a purpose of action, the result is narrative time of a 'finious process' (as Peirce called it). Time is a thought and as such quasi-necessary; even so, it is not a necessary law that produces this cognition. Therefore its causal necessity is not at all deductive, following the type of analyzable concept suggested by Branigan's term 'procedural knowledge' (ibid.: 116). Meaning-as-procedure is not a simple process; it is a complex one that involves the idea of habit of behaviour. This also fulfils the maxim in the *Poetic* that narration is an imitation of conduct (μίμησις πράξεως) and not an imitation of men. Habits, through their teleology, are easy to narrate (that said, there are certainly still other, non-action teleologies, even other forms of time, differentiated by a more or less of Law: v. *supra*).

In the former case (1), the cognition and representation of a motivational Generality must concern itself with the conditions of communicating '(interior) motivation.' It can only acknowledge that thought (both mine and other persons') is communicable as a sign. Cognizable is not the action of other persons as such but its Generality – which, however, is available only in a Symbol (v. *supra*). We have already discussed that purpose is the only communicable Generality of action. Branigan's levels turned into nominal subjects are not nearly as complex as is necessary for the cognition of motivation. Identification in narration is being-dependent; in prenarrative human interaction we can achieve an understanding of alter's identity in a hermeneutic way, by being vicariously another subject by 'divination,' but this is irrelevant here. We understand narrative characters only if they are Interpreted for us in this way by the narration. They must partake in a determinate way in the Interpretation purpose of the narration. Therefore it does not matter how many dependencies we can Interpret. All are in any case predetermined by the basic dependency, and this dependency instrumentally uses the laws of time. Their constraints are specific (i.e., their causal relation is 'finious' or *causa finalis*), whereas common usage restricts causality to *causa efficiens*.

However, it is crucial not to mix this instrument of dependency with the logic of the act that produces it. In other words, enunciation itself does not operate with final causality in its sign relation. The probability of narration is created through an act that creates an occurrence for a sign, its specific Second: 'because I tell it so ...' (cf. *supra*, Peirce's Scheherazade illustration). This representational universe of my narration exists: 'I attempt through the offer of my Sign (as First Correlate) here and now to make an Interpretation necessary and for this purpose offer determinate logical constraints (which are not I-here-now).' Instead of speaking of a 'continuum' (Branigan bridging representation and teleology of conduct), it is better to account for the radical diversity and precariousness of the two moments of the constitution of temporality and the constitution of probability. Psychological identifications are superfluous regarding the former and are not helpful regarding the latter.

Also intrinsically connected with narrative enunciation is what Branigan (1992: 117) calls the 'illusion of occurrence.' The essence of producing narrative teleology is not grasped through illusion (i.e., we do not grasp it as psychological error); rather, it is produced by a determinate meaning. Occurrence, therefore, is unlike any other cognitive object. It always needs a second in comparison to which it is a change. This is with regard to time experience; but in a narrative it runs into nothing (cf. *supra* the discussion of narrative and physical occurrence). In a narrative there is no occurrence of an outward reality that 'contingent laws of time' can 'causally' relate to a previous occurrence (at least it is not the occurring pronunciation of a narrative that counts as a point on the vector of teleological narration temporality). A sign of temporality must be substituted for occurrences lacking in narratives. This sign does not relate two occurrences; instead it produces time conceptually – that is, it is a deductive process from a cognitive concept of temporality. Such a sign starts a causal chain of its own, which must be related to other causalities through a different sign relation. 'Illusions of occurrence' do not, therefore, simply blend into occurrences as such.

The result of this diversity of involved causalities is that it is not advisable to equate narrative time with the experience of change. The act of producing narration uses time in a highly restricted manner; as a consequence it suppresses constitutively crucial parts of experiential time (cf. *supra*, the description of the irreplaceable First and Second Correlate of the time Sign process). Narrative temporality, in contrast, cannot be experienced; it can only be understood, not experienced. As a Sign of time, it functions only through its First Iconic Correlate, which connects it remotely with the experience through enunciation. This is the condition under which it can be used in its specific teleological form as a concept by enunciation while still being a temporal Sign process. The concept 'teleology' thus Interprets as its First a Sign other than the experience time (which, as we know, Interprets the diversity of two events to which it is directly connected). In other words, we do not come to a conclusion of, say, 'development,' 'movement,' 'acceleration,' or other Signs of time experience, on the grounds of two events in their diversity. Instead, we experience an act of enunciation. This enunciation must succeed in producing a meaningful Interpretation by means of a logical suggestion: either pragmatic-teleological, or pragmatic-opposed, or pragmatic-normative.

Seen from the perspective of this 'division of labour,' only some of Branigan's eight levels correspond materially to narrative enunciation – and not even in its pure form. However, although there is no doubt that a narrative on the whole is a cognitive object, 'levels' claim to be analytical instruments,[43] which appear to be haunted by psychological 'visions' at their core. They are defined not by a cognitive operation but by a supposed psychological identity. Here, however, the analogy between narrative and real pragmatic identities is exhausted. In a 'nominal subject' of narration, there is no special comprehension of alter's motivation. This remains the sole competence of the narrative enunciation instance.

The *punctum saliens* of Branigan's theory is in the 'level' paradigm. As an original reframing of what is materially narrative enunciation, it is midway between a linguistic and a hermeneutic explanation. From the former it claims the 'feature'-like or clearly recognizable textual traits (or in its later 'schemata' avatar), which afford an either/or meaning as in grammar. Closer to the latter is an operation of ego's identification with alter ego, which affords a literally 'intuitive' understanding of the alterity of the other. However, the profound philosophical problems of cognizing another identity are not addressed. Instead there are simple 'boundaries' of consciousness, as if another consciousness were a crossing into foreign territory on a map. Yet this does not falsify Branigan's theory, because his 'consciousness' is not a consciousness, just as his 'nominal subject' is not a subject. Only if the narrative universe were the real world universe would identities also be a real problem. Thus they are merely epistemic 'boundaries' or – more precisely – cognitive operations. Inexorably, this leads us again to the operation itself, named but not described, in the level metaphor. Which cognitive operation, then, produces the meaning that we see in an acting person or an action centre? This is not the same as *being* an action centre. Instead, the operation consists in a determinate way of representing an action centre in/as a logic and causal chain.

Branigan has a good argument against Bordwell when he persists in the 'perspectival' metaphor, because this is precisely the effect of the logical operation at the basis of narration.[44] Indeed, what narrative enunciation creates is (in the following order) (1) the pragmatic temporality of action as teleological constraint, (2) action space, but (0) all of this on the basis of rhetorical object representation (often forgotten).

The narratologies of Weinrich and Branigan raise the general question of which types of Generalities produce which types of narrative meaning. Both linguistic marks and motivational identities seemed to be of limited scope, explaining only certain aspects of narrative meaning. They could, however, be considered as special cases of logical dependency in narrative enunciation. However, neither features of contingent languages used for communicational switches, nor the identity behind a motivational pragmatic force, can ultimately explain the logic of narration. When we avoid psychological and linguistic explanatory models, we can comprehend narration as a strictly logical and cognitive procedure. Only in this way can we grasp the really possible complexity of narrative meaning. Once the teleological probability is instituted, narration can function on all its registers. We cannot expect to adequately understand a fairly sophisticated cinematic work unless we can account for the full range of narrative complexity.

Referring to the discussion of narrative logic (v. *supra*), this complexity has three sites where variations with relevance for meaning can take place: First, an important but difficult meaning produced narratively is the raw 'perception of passing.' Since it usually has no significance for the plot, it is often forgotten (except when film critics complain about excruciating long-windedness). A memorable example of a film offering the feeling of the raw passage of time is the interior sequences of the first part of Akerman's *Je, tu, il, elle*. Second, the standard-setting act of enunciating can become an object of meaning variation. This is most crucial for meaning in newscasts and reportage; it can also be increasingly effaced. Where one initial act of telling is the only vestige of the zero point in narrative temporality, the outcome can only be a fairy tale meaning. Third, teleology itself can be manipulated; this evidently has far-reaching effects on meaning. In this regard, compare Chantal Akerman's *Lettres d'Amérique* with Truffaut's *L'Histoire d'Adèle H*. Doing so should reveal a meaningful range in the variation of teleology, from quasi-aimlessness to a strict, inexorable biographical vector.

Narrative enunciation, then, needs to be reinstated in its full rights. Otherwise there can be no grasp of complex narrative meaning. A better point of reference for enunciational temporality in cinema would be Deleuze's bipolarism of movement-derived time (for an extensive discussion, cf. *supra*). The cinematic fate of movement – its time and the whole – can only be contained in a subtle and complex narrative process into which all the variations of meaning have been woven. This was the case in our Godard example.

For instance, with the biology class sequence in *Je vous salue, Marie* (##27–39), Branigan's 'six elements' and 'eight levels' must fail. There is nobody's vision for the music and other extradiegetic elements, even though these are nevertheless primordial to the meaning.

27 III C   Eva with a   MARIE: *le grand événement pour moi est là*   M: Bach, *St John Passion*,
              Rubik's cube   FILM-VOICE: [off and over]: *Et le soleil, enfin*   Chor: 'Herr unser
                                                                                      Herrscher'
                             visible, se met à appliquer sur les océans primitifs.   D: laughter
                             Alors, la vie est apparue, dit-on, [music starts]
                             tout-à-fait par hasard. Il y avait de l'hydrogène, de
                             l'azote.

28   TITLE: EN CE TEMPS-LÀ   M: ends
                             MALE VOICE: [off] *et s'il n'y avait pas de hasard?*

29 II C   Eva 50 cm   EVA: *sans foi (cent fois) celle de l'univers*
                             PROFESSOR: *Ça signifie quoi? Qu'il n'y a jamais*
                             eu le temps. Le hasard n'a pas eu le temps.
                             Puisque la vie n'a pas eu le temps d'apparaître,
         IV C   'voice'   UNKNOWN VOICE: [over] [N] [whispering] *sur*
                             la terre!

This example is Semiotically interesting because of its complexity. This does not prevent it from producing narrative probability, also – but not only – in terms of action space and rhetoric, all in one. Godard's enunciation means are variegate. They involve linguistic ambiguity ('sans foi' or 'cent fois,' which appears only in transcription, but whose ambiguity creates a significant *double entendre*) and a strange play with music (which is not a sentimental aside but has a commenting function similar to that of the chorus in the ancient theatre).

Every sign relation requires two elements of comparison; here, however, we have many more from which to choose. First there is the teleological meaning, referring to a standard, which is responsible for the overall impression of story development. Into this, elements in an ambiguous relationship are added, which in themselves have no natural relation with one another (Bach's 'Herr unser Herrscher' and the 'appearance of life' in the dialogue, the linguistic ambiguity of #29, the clearly audible but unattributable voice: 'on earth!'). Yet positioned together by enunciation, they compel interpretation. This is also narrative comprehension, because it sheds light on the narrative purpose in a strict sense. Only through this intellectual understanding do we comprehend how drama evolves. The result is a probable meaning (in the double sense that the meaning itself is uncertain and that the object is only a probable one). Here it is also the action space for Eve and Eva (in her double role): she acts as the great seductress at the beginning of all (this line continues with her seemingly gratuitous blinding of Pascal) and as the pupil seducing her teacher. Her vision, with which we see, is epitomized in her counterpoint glance, which provides motivation to both of her seductive enterprises. Suppressing or overseeing one of them, however, deprives the other of its deeper meaning and reduces the action to a banal pattern.

Without the help of pragmatic and rhetorical logic, identifying shifters in this sequence would be a hopeless analytical task. Here almost everything shifts everything else ('shifting' taken in Branigan's metaphoric extension). There is no base level at all, and the 'Chinese boxes' are actional brackets of brackets, and ambiguous ones at that. One bracket might be motivationally probable: seduction. The same 'object,' however, might also be probable as a rhetorical statement about our universe on-this-side-of/before narration (thus it would unbracket narratively and rebracket metaphysically). It becomes then a sequence about our accessing this world in the manner of Pascal's calculation and wager. In addition to this, the chorale in the *St John Passion* points to an alternative rhetoric of adoration, in the second grammatical person and vocative mood. Certainly, it also sets the stage for a common sexual seduction, which actually takes place (not, however, before the biting of the apple #130, in a place called *Le Paradis*; ##115, 114–32). Then, however, it is The Seduction at large.

Fortunately, this film consists mainly of Symbolic Signs, which are easy to describe. Such Signs are relations with order and rules, and there is little of identities that relate to other identities. Such a relation is explained as a probability of either a narrative or a rhetorical enunciation. This can also incorporate more subtle Sign relations, such as Iconic time which as pure passing is not teleological. This temporal Iconicity can also be found in Godard's arsenal, although it is not as obvious as in other films (consider here the subtle Signs of eternal temporality in *Ordet*).

It is undeniable that narratives make us see motivations and subjectivity. However, this is the appearance of an enunciation product, which has succeeded in making a temporality probable. We can understand this temporality as the motivation or purpose of action (once it is established), and thus as instrumental in making subjects of action appear (equally probable). On this basis alone, it is possible to conceive psychological states or personifications in film, which necessarily pass through the (construct of) subjectivization of 'vision,' the anthropomorphism of a camera identity. Grammatical 'person' can thus be replaced entirely by subjectivization. It is instead incisive for the cinematic mode that it is impossible to indicate with the same neatness as in grammatical persons how subjective a vision is, if it is subjective at all. The relative indecisiveness of cinematic subjectivity opens up the potential for creative ambivalence. This is shown in the above example of *Je vous salue, Marie*. The same shot often is (or can be) both the first-person singular of the vision of Éve and third-person singular of the sight/vision of Eva, as a *prototype* of something in the literal sense of the term. There must not be much subjectivity in the latter – the proto-typical image must impose itself, as it were. Consequently, its effect is to close action spaces and the narration effect of a teleological time. If it is Eva as The Seduction of Humanity, this creates the rhetorical effect of a force of Law, making its existence (more) probable. However, if the camera makes us look with Éve upon her victim, the Professor, the question immediately arises: How does she do it, what comes next (probably)? This is more than an indeterminacy with regard to the person Eva or Éve; it is also an Interpretation play with the enunciation type. The third grammatical person is often used rhetorically as non-person – as if convincing someone of the unquestionability of an exis-tent, in the manner of 'one' or 'it' (French *on* or German *man*). Follow-ing Benveniste, this is tantamount to a maximal non-opposition and is often combined with the present tense of definition. It stands for a real-ity enunciating itself: a sign relation dominated by a Third.

Personification unites shifter and identity models. As this example shows, however, the concretely complex meaning creates a state of undecidability in which neither person nor identity shows a path to meaning. Interpretation, then, must help itself by other means. It must find a meaning that agrees with a vague temporality and a vague assertion of an existent state of a Generality, both possible simulta-neously and not alternatively. Enunciating the probable is both.

6.3 Rhetorical Enunciation in Cinema: Meaning in Figures

Truth is an argument.[45] Cinema can argue truth. What is true is not a simple question of what is covered by a concept, of whether the fit is perfect. Otherwise, if the 'data' do fit imperfectly into the 'theory' or hypothetical concept, there can be only a presumption of truth. Neces-sary only in the first case, 'non-necessary' truth seems to become an oxymoron; 'rhetorical argumentation' has been considered as such a make-believe. 'An incomplete argumentation is properly called an enthymeme, which is often carelessly defined as a syllogism with a suppressed premiss ... The ancient definition of an enthymeme was "a rhetorical argumentation" ... By a rhetorical argumentation was meant one not depending upon logical necessity, but upon common knowledge as defining a sphere of possibility. Such an argument is rendered logical by adding as a premiss that which it assumes as a leading principle' (Peirce 1893 [2.249], 'Grand Logic'). However, the distinction between necessary and non-necessary thought cannot withstand the reality of inquiry. Real cognitive progress is not grasped in the alternative between deductive and inductive reasoning.

Those who think only in deductions would assume that they know a world formula from which they can conclude every cognizable object. Thinking only inductively would entail that no cognitive act ever arrives at a conclusion as long as we cannot be certain that the number of cases is exhaustive. This latter certainty, however, is deduced from knowing that cases are exhausted by some necessity. As soon as real inquiry comes into play, we require a new kind of inference in order to arrive at cognitive conclusions without exhausting the totality of cases.

Rhetorical arguments are such non-exhaustive but conclusive inferences. This being so, the normal inquiring cognition is indeed rhetorical and not simply a form of non-necessary thought – implying the usual deficiency or uncertainty. Everything, then, becomes rhetorical (i.e., an abductive inference) in the sense that all cognition is owed to practical thought. Inquiry – thought that seeks truth – can only start from a problem, and it can only consist in the achievement to 'recommend a course of action' (MS637:5).

This is the realist framework for an investigation of cinematic rhetoric. There can be no false debate, then, about the supposed 'illusionisms' of cinema (v. Currie [1995] for a debate about such a film-theoretical bogeyman). But how does cinema cognize what is – that is, what is true? Cinema says 'is,' but certainly without copula; nevertheless it claims truth or falseness. How can this be shown? If this were not the case, cinema could only show what is and could never show what is not. 'What is' – this is the deeper reason – can perhaps be camouflaged as a question of quality, but what-is-not always involves truth or falseness. Denying that cinema cognizes truly, amounts to saying that cinema in its essence can never be false. It cannot even be an illusion, because then it would offer no purchase for discerning false illusions from true perceptions. What-is must be asserted as either existent or not. Assertion has often been confused with proposition; especially in film theory, this problem becomes a question of how film can imitate propositional language. However, film does not need to assert by means of a linguistic intermediary, because as a Sign it has its own power of argumentation.

The real is a film theory problem in a much more decisive way than that in which 'realist' film theoreticians conceive it. Reality is argued for, in language as in cinema. Thus film theory should treat cinema as an argument proper and not so much as a question of cinematic essence.[46] Cinema itself is realist as long as it is capable of arguing for a (yes or) no. If it is argument, however, then enunciation – and not technology – is the key to cinematic rhetoric. By asserting, by enunciating and by using a Sign as an inquiry into a genuine and real problem we can achieve true cognition. However, this is not grasped in the alternative of deductive/inductive thought.

What is a logical dependency? What is an argumentative dependency? In abductional inference, the problem of origin is not simply an unavoidable starting point; it also generates the correct hypothesis. Abduction embodies research economy because it does not need to go through the series of all inductive conclusions; it selects the 'right' general conclusion for the real problem more quickly and with more confidence. In this context counts again the realist metaphysic of Pragmaticism. It is unsustainable if the cognitive efforts are not matched by a real universe that 'allows' itself to be cognized (v. *supra*). In cinema, in keeping with the Sign's particular relation to an outward reality (v. *supra*), it is the enunciation's competence to engage in abductive argumentation for reality. The neat dichotomy of 'documentary' and 'narrative art' cinema – a dichotomy so often resorted to – somewhat obscures the Semiotic commonalities and specific differences in their probability construction, which are based respectively on truth and temporality arguments. However, given the Categorical ordinality of the real, we encounter no difficulty in arguing truth narratively (and in convincing someone of something through narrative efforts). The 'intrusions' of strictly rhetorical meaning into narration have already been observed and described.

With rhetorical enunciation, 'reader response' is not an afterthought in film theory; in fact, it is another instance of abduction. Only genuine doubt enables ampliative reasoning, and the cognitive situation of the 'reader' is constitutive. Thus additional 'pragmatics' of cinema (or even – to some degree – 'emotional response'[47]) is superfluous, since it necessarily arrives with the cinematic constitution of the real. It fades away once it is admitted that the truth of a reality in cinema results from arguing for it rhetorically. What are rhetorical arguments, then? In terms of social practice, Perelman (1970: 22–59) aptly describes rhetorical argumentation as that sort of logic which takes the audience into account. Strict logic (in the wake of Aristotle's distinction between syllogism and enthymema) assumes a universal audience; in contrast, rhetorical figures and 'common places' are aimed at reduced and less-than-universal communities of communication. This may not serve as an adequate logical distinction between patterns of reasoning,[48] but it is a practical description of probability that is used in cinema. Also, narration proper – let alone truth claims – cannot claim universal validity[49] by telling a temporal order of things.

Which logical force allows the typical 'augmentation of meaning' (in rhetoric, the technical term for this was αὔξησις)? We should no longer be concerned with the ideology of 'true philosophers' differentiating their truth seeking from mere 'bigger-than' effects, blowing up meaning, of sophists (v. *supra*). Today, the middle ground between ontology and the *homo misura* lies in the recognition that reasoning is also ampliative. This involves not only a time dimension but also an imperfection that is intrinsic to cognition. In the broader rhetorical tradition, argumentation has always been understood as greater in scope – and more true to life and to the actual cognitive appropriation of the world – than the mere application of syllogisms (necessary deductive inference). When we argue, we take our audience into account. The terminology may be one of identities with perceptible role differences, one role (audience) dependent on another (orator). However, the probable 'is' not (as truth is, simple and eternal); rather it is (made) probable to 'us' (if 'I' succeed in convincing 'you'). This could also be expressed in logical quantification: probability depends on both roles playing their part; however, all- and some-quantifiers distribute the onus of proof asymmetrically between proponent and opponent (v. *supra*).

Rhetorical enunciation usually counts as non-necessary argumentation. Its difference from the logically necessary lies in the numerical composition of the enunciational roles and communication. Deduction communicates to a universal audience, which a probabilistic argument delimits to a present (or even a mono- or dialogic) public. Within those limits we use conviction techniques consisting of an appeal to a generality that is 'general' only to this communicational community. This delimitation must seem a logical deficiency if verity is seen as in force only as non-contingent, general, and eternal. Topoi – places common to the envisaged audience – should replace generality, aided by the art of producing argumentative effects by figuration.

Perelman's communicational conceptualization of rhetoric is not far from Pragmaticism. We have seen that Peirce conceives every thought as dialogic and fallible. The other side of this is that a true and final Generality, also in the pragmatic form of the perfect unity of opinion (i.e. cognition) in a *consensus catholicus*, must also be real. Not existent, but real. As existence, a final state is a limit case because it will never exist perfectly. Its reality, as much as the reality of Possibility (which is even less 'existent'), is a prerequisite of every successful thought. No thought is finally true, but (in the long run) it must be truer than the previous one. Thus the usual description of rhetorical practice as logically defective deductive syllogism is tinged with an inadequate model of thought. Really productive ampliative thought is never deductive. Every cognition appeals ('recommends itself') to an Interpretant, and it does not matter whether that appeal comes from another person or from the previous thought.

What is special about rhetorical argumentation is not so much that it is different from 'certain' cognition. Its most outstanding feature, instead, is a cognition that is not 'finished' but occasions a new Interpretation. In this sense it is most prolific in meaning, which is more than deduction, because of the argumentative procedure of abduction. As a mirror of the research economy of scientific cognition, enunciation can make use of the transitory character of the inferential process. It can pass from an invention of a still hypothetical general rule to testing by concrete instances (inductive step), and from there (the deductive step) to corrections and refinements of the rule, and so on. The logical force of such a Sign Relation is not a rule alone (as in deduction); rather, it requires intuition and is not yet necessary. Enunciation's only role is to provide an occasion for interpretation. Rhetorical arguments, then, produce what Peirce calls 'musement' – an abductional play with thoughts. As long as it has not solidified into a final opinion, it constitutes a sort of experimentation, which is interesting only because it produces the one unexpected result. This starts another 'experimentation' in the mind, which plays with more or less probable Generalities for all the results.

In principle, rhetorical practice is no different from experimentation.[50] Having proceeded carefully in the topoi or rhetorical commonplaces through the construction of the known and familiar (this reproduces the series of expected experimental results), we introduce its point, or, as it was called, *'punctum saliens'* ('jump spot'[51]). Before this point everything is (presented as) common (i.e., shared between orator and audience). The point itself – which is no longer common or shared – becomes a conviction only in the end. It must first be a puzzle, digested in abductive inference with tentative Generalities.

Although not as common as narration, rhetoric in film is not rare either. In fact, the boundary between narrative and 'documentary' films is indistinct. Many examples that we investigated in Godard (v. *supra*) could not be explained narratively. The constitutive difference with rhetoric enunciation is that it concerns itself with facts (and not the causal context of temporality). Certainly, everything that we cognize because it is, in a certain way is necessarily; as pure chance, we cannot cognize it, not even as pure fantasy. Every cognition adds something to pure facts, which only then become either necessary or chance facts or something in between. The function of the Third Correlate in the Sign is to propose a stronger or weaker logical necessity. Rhetorical enunciation, therefore, constitutes objects (makes-be) by producing (i.e., abducing) a relative necessity from the possible. For singular, factual being there is no need for rhetorical convincing, since its 'logical force' consists merely in being opposite to a subject: you would not doubt a signpost when you hit your head on it. Also, if the object constituted by rhetoric is meant to convince as factual, its factual existence is derived from a particular necessity (rhetorically instituted Law) and not from Opposition. This also explains the peculiar nature of rhetoric: it cannot leave evidence to an only factual being-there, nor (as in a deduction) does a universal Law show its occurrences abundantly and at any moment.

We cannot expect the assertion of truth in cinema to be a simple operation. Like oratory art, it requires many rhetorical instruments and communicational prerequisites. Following Perelman's felicitous conceptualization, the 'audience in mind' must be constructed cinematically. Now, there is no reason why audience presence cannot be achieved visually as well as linguistically. In fact, the arsenal is vast, ranging from an already discussed sequence in *Purple Rose of Cairo* and the opening sequence of Juzo Itami's *Tampopo*, for example, to the viewer-addressing devices in newscasts and television reporting. In between, there is documentary film. According to this argument, the audience is a logical rather than a physical presence. Linguistic techniques for constructing this presence are culture dependent. Historically, tropes have developed, but merely as a heuristic classification, not a logical one.[52] Not all classical tropes are of use for cinema, of course. Yet among the many tools, some are especially useful to film. For instance, it is highly presence-creating to present one's matter all of a sudden in great detail – a tool often referred to as 'accumulation' or 'insistence.' This produces a strongly emotional presence (cf. Perelman

1970: 195f); in contrast, short, concise presentations have no more charm than military reports. There can be no doubt that cinema has a very special way of dwelling on things in a leisurely manner.[53]

The crucial operation, once the audience has its role, relates to the leap of meaning itself. At that point the creation of plausible probabilities becomes a matter of apt exposition and technique. Trope,[54] or shifter of meaning, is the technical term, but what is the technique? 'Trope' is itself a trope; without explaining, it designates meaning as being augmented in certain ways. What is the tropical technique, then? Generally speaking, tropes can be defined as preset hypotheses that give rise to abductive inferences. It does not say much that 'parts of speech' enter into a tropical relation so that any part tropically changes the meaning of other parts. The synecdoche 'at the threshold of the century' does not change the meaning of 'threshold,' but does augment its meaning.

Tropes, which have (or not) received their name by tradition, are really distinct only in the manner and in the extent to which they contribute to the construction of the probable fact. It does not matter whether the result is a classification in the manner of a treatise, since augmentation ($a\ddot{v}\xi\eta\sigma\iota\varsigma$) is the very definition of the sign 'knowing which we know something more' (8.332). Its greater concern is methods of investigation or Speculative Rhetoric; however, as 'practical thought' it also 'recommends a course of action' (MS637:5), as a social practice, of object constitution.

Rhetorical enunciation is the *pronuntiatio actio* of the classical treatise of Quintilian.[55] Its meaning parts (i.e., *elocutio*) – in particular its *exordium* and *peroratio* – are subordinated to the project of making a state of affairs probable. Rhetorical art in the cinematic text directly addresses its spectators, using forms that are different for serious matters (*oratio*) than for light conversation (*sermo*). Because the probability effect depends on the 'well said,' the *ars bene dicendi*, it is greatly helped by a *consuetudo* to do so. So rhetoricians respect (besides *latinitas* or strong command of language) customs of speech (*consuetudo*), even as they manipulate them. When we enunciate probable facts, we must ensure a staying power for the source, which is exercising – and making itself felt through – its *ars bene dicendi*.

Cinema must make an identical choice: bland, unobtrusive, unexciting imagery, or artful, refined, 'well-said,' meaningful, augmented meaning production. When tropes are overused, they become boring or they find themselves adopted by normal language. In this view, some of the stock tools of cinema have lost their significance. The absence of a source of meaning (i.e., of enunciational presence) prevents any further meaning. It has been suggested that with the evaporation of the frame – the most important tool of enunciation presence – the nature of the image in Godard's films has changed. When there is no frame, there can be no composition; and no composition means no *historia*, no perspective, no transcendental subject, no bourgeois ideology, and so on. However, although this is fundamentally the television image, the consequent 'ob-scenity'[56] can then be broken by a fragmentation of the narrative and the other meaning-bearing elements that show meaning *in fieri*, as it were. Now this is enunciation intervening in a *consuetudo*. Rhetorical augmentation of meaning can never be accounted for without such an effort and without the presence of an explicit social practice.

How does cinema assert (with truth value), then? If we do not indulge in a naive realism, first, this truth originates from an enunciational augmentation rather than a factual event. What rhetoric asserts cannot be shown in a simply dyadic relation of fact; but once the abductive inference is understood instances can appear in objects.[57] Second, this tropical meaning must then appear as existent, true or false. Irony, for instance – one of the most frequently used tropes – seems to say 'this here exists (= is) differently from that which it wants to be.' This comprises the augmentation of being both 'more' and an Index. So irony differs from the same cognitive content (in, say, black humour, sarcasm, or as a police investigation) by confining itself customarily as a trope to human objects and by judging them benevolently (v. *infra*, Jauss's theory of the comic effect). The critical judgment contains as its truth normativity – a general idea of being-human and not of true states of world. There is no irony in physical states (except by means of anthropomorphism).

These features (and perhaps a few others) characterize this trope sufficiently to become a social practice. The practice is neither the trope alone (it does not function) nor a mere enunciation event (which would probably lead to serious misunderstandings); rather, it is a custom dependent on enunciation.[58] In the absence of customs, rhetorical augmentation is rather difficult. A case in point is the parallel between customary tropes and unheard-of relations among elements, with the clear enunciational intention of augmenting meaning, in Godard's *Je vous salue, Marie*. While sometimes facile irony is at hand (in the seduction sequence between Eva and the Professor), the augmented meaning of other parts (of the water lilies, or of the moon and the lamp) is not covered by any known figuration (metaphor, metonymy? v. *supra*). Through his effort of enunciation, Godard produces augmentation by offering – away from known tropes – a General idea that could induce us to see it here and now. Such discoveries may be lengthy processes, tropes, however, offer practical shortcuts.

The outer limit of the power of rhetorical augmentation is encountered where tropes are lacking. At this point it begins to share some of the delicate nature of aesthetic cognition, contrary to which rhetoric does not benefit from the non-mundane nature of aesthetic norms (as we will discuss later). As long as this Sign process is produced as a social practice of rhetorical enunciation, we insist on seeing a probable object, an εἰκὸς, a mundane object that has its place in the rest of the objective things. An aesthetic attitude does not need to attain the probability of an object. It is the Possibility of a Norm of conduct, which in its non-opposition, non-concrete nature is sheer openness of meaning. For this reason, aesthetic insight is much more unlikely and more difficult to produce and sustain.

For cinema the relative importance of customary tropes is limited by these boundaries of general rhetoric. Classical inventories lump together quite heterogeneous processes, though, with little heuristic value regarding their meaning purpose.[59] At this stage of complexity it becomes an open question how far we can channel types of augmented meaning into customary tropes without the aid of its typical means (which are lacking in film). Cinematic rhetoric should be considered in a more general way. Rhetorical tropes are logical inferences of the enthymematic type (cf. Aristotle's *Rhetorica* I, 1).

Just how complex meaning and its manifold and variegate augmentations can become is shown in Wulff's painstaking analysis (1994) of a true icon of film art, the 131 shots of the cornfield chase sequence in Hitchcock's *North by Northwest*. In this sequence we encounter an enormous complexity of actorial motivations; a single sequence sometimes can contain three distinguishable motivations for the same character. Although in order to interpret this sequence as 'suspense,' it is crucial to keep those three motivational logics apart. Only with regard to this feature does the respective 'off-screen' have a different meaning in each of these logics. Off-screen space is thus the rhetorical standpoint from which to augment the meaning on-screen, but in different customary ways. Wulff lists: I. (shots 1–68): 'Where is George Kaplan?' For Thornhill, any glance *hors cadre* creates space for the expected location of a non-person, Kaplan. For spectators, instead, it creates probabilistic space for likely enemies: classical suspense. II. (shots 65-124): another off-screen, same technique. The aeroplane diving in from off-screen can be located clearly in a circumscribed universe. Yet through the passive persecution motivation of Thornhill, the meaning of that space changes into an annihilation of action space from all outside directions. III. (shots 125–131): Wulff describes how this part resumes the general topic of escape. The meaning of all invisible space outside the frame is that of a *grand large*, a space of freedom for a fugitive. The three off-screens are materially the same yet constitute different meanings. They noticeably create all narrative spaces where meaning is unified into universe constraints.

Wulff also identifies a clear ironic impression (a classical trope). As we know from *Je vous salue, Marie*, rhetorical relations do not always carry classical names, nor are they always even identifiable. The meaning here is a space transverse to all other spaces. Usually, we would call this symbolic space, but what is it that is not similarly symbolic in the three previous spaces? The comic effect, however, is space extending into the spectatorial life-world (cf. *infra*, where we will come back to this effect in the context of aesthetics). Thus, it is of a completely different kind and genesis.[60] Sheer rhetorical meaning has brought it into being; its probability hinges on the irony trope. We owe this space to the comfortable path of meaning contained in this figure of speech, irony, which helps reduce all plausible explanations for this character into this meaningful one. Yet what figuration in general achieves is a mode of cognition more on the side of *res* than of *verba*.

How does the augmentation of meaning take place in tropes? In principle, *translatio*, or transfer into a plus of meaning, occurs when one part is an Interpretation of another part – in traditional terms, when a word 'substitutes' another (*verbum translatum*). In the case of cinema, such substitutions – of image with image, image with sound, or image with music – are not in themselves meaning-generating. They still require a rhetorical enunciation effort. Besides relating pictorial elements, cinema can avail itself of the power of language. A shown dog becomes a proverbial 'dog' (in Godard's Feuerbach sequence in *Je vous salue, Marie*) if the rhetoric makes it possible, with the aid of a national idiom (*une vie de chien* may not have the same meaning in all languages; for instance, Lars von Trier's *Dogville* is speaking about other 'dogs'). Besides language there is pictorial metaphor generation – for example, where the *translatio* is made, by way of character traits and an animal (in the same film, #282, Joseph as donkey is a double synecdoche compared).

Cinematic tropes are not the entire inventory of meaning produced by film. Tropes are much too contingent on cultures, idioms, and history, whereas meaning is universal. Although they are far from being linguistic universals, it would be foolish to overlook habits of social practice in the production of meaning. Cinematic consuetudes, too, are of undoubted consequence for meaning. Even though most of this meaning is produced in the same cultural context, it is not evident that the quintessence of classical rhetoric in the inventory of *ornatus* applies equally to film. Ornate, artistic speech, however, is not an invention of one moment, but – as Quintilian's definitive treatise (cf. Ueding 1986: 264–303) suggests – fruit of some eight hundred years of practice of the highest education in that culture. Tropes cannot be deduced or invented; that said, meaning in all its universality relies on the customary figuration of augmented meaning.

Tropes are not tied to language or lexicality. The main work is in the τρέπειν itself, whose task it is to produce as an abduction an existent true reality that is not directly perceptible through senses. If the rhetorical consuetude or custom is a cognitive rule, then the use of the trope is the entire circle of abductive inferential process. In its inductive part, it invents suitable cases of the rule. The abductive process becomes much too complicated for a prompt and useful functioning in the short length of time; however, the support from familiar figures accelerates hypothesis-formation. Abduction requires a choice of hypotheses, all of which have a certain probability of fitting. These hypotheses, being nothing but tentative rules or Thirds, exist only in the arsenal of cultural conventions. There is no deeper reason why one uses 'threshold' as synecdoche but not 'lintel' or 'frame' (which is a different synecdoche), except that it is a cultural fact. Dictionaries are full of *trans-lationes* – that is, translations from one synecdoche or metaphor into a completely different one, or, lacking one, into literal meaning.

At the end of their abductional inference, all tropes claim a reality not seen before. Reality and truth should be different for every type of trope, but this classification can only follow that of Signs in general. Thus tropes can be divided into three kinds, which more or less coincide with the subdivisions of classical treatises. According to the number of parts involved, the first kind uses one element for the transfer, the second uses conjunctions, and the third involves the entirety. Elements of meaning are always correlations and need not coincide with linguistic, acoustic, or cinematic units. Types of tropical operation hinge on the type of relation afforded by that trope, which constitutes its precise meaning.

One class of meaning augmentation operates with logical terms – that is, with monadic relations.[61] How can this type of figure transform a single element into a new meaning? The designation 'ornate' means not embellishment but augmentation of meaning beyond the normal, which without the tropical sustainment collapses into normalcy. A trope argues the plus of meaning by implying more. This more, or ampliation, can only consist of a greater generality, as suggested by the term itself. For example, let us consider the metaphor 'freshness' in two strikingly different instances: A *faccia fresca* (Italian, fresh in the sense of 'getting fresh,' related to German *frech*[62]) is not a 'fresh face.' It has an utterly different metaphorical meaning, which relies entirely on firm cultural customs. Also interesting here is the way metaphors generalize. Strictly speaking, there is nothing fresh about a face. Freshness, in this example, must become more than it is usually generalized – it must, in other words cease to be a quality (perceptible); it must become a law. This law then makes freshness, for instance, a case of a surprisingly good conservation state of a rule of an aging process which is understood to be ineluctable. With this rhetorical abductional rule, and an established trope in this sense, we see this face as aging but fresh. However, in the Italian metaphor the rule is entirely different. A *faccia fresca* suggests a knowledge of the irreverence of the not-yet-mature, it cognizes the moral maturation process as something desirable. Thus the difference between the percept and the rhetorically enunciated reflects the exchange of abductive rules. To cognize a quality of 'something' in a perceptual judgment (v. *infra*), we require a simple rule for the simple idea of that something, whereas cognizing a metaphoric quality involves a difficult rule arising from an insight into a law, of which we see an instance in an object. This object's quality is therefore instilled by a law and against a percept.

This logical description also prescribes the necessary procedure. If cinema, in which there are no 'ornate single words,' wants to make tropical what it shows, it must first dwell on an element. This tends to decontextualize that element: 'emphasis,' therefore, is a base figure for making single objects meaningful. However, tropes must exist in their culture in order to work quickly. Thus all that a film can do is explicitly construct cognitions based on a law and then relate this law to a quality in a shown object. This makes the same door no longer a door: it is either a symbol of freedom (in prison) or a metaphor of separation (in, say, a divorce).[63]

Tropus, or *verbum translatum*, has nine traditional labels for tropes. In cinema this grouping is not very helpful, since it must translate into a particular vision of an object – of a *single* object – rather than into montage (*composita*). That said, certain cinematic techniques for emphasizing single objects can often remind us of certain classical tropes. One of the simplest tropes is to name X as Y – for example, someone as something, 'lie' as 'untruth,' Ève as Éva, and Pascal as (Blaise) Pascal (in *Je vous salue, Marie*). This procedure is known as *synonymia*, or more literally, 'the same having two names.' Yet this approach in cinema cannot be as blatant as in the linguistic equivalents, because the composition of images is not a Legisign. How can we picture something in its 'proper' way? When is a picture a picture 'as' picture? The synonymous procedure is quintessentially that 'as.' Thus, a non-spectacular way in Cavalier's *Thérèse*, women are also 'shown as' nuns, and provincial doctors 'as' inhibited, and so on. This is achieved mainly by props and behaviour (nuns' habits and boorish conduct). However, there are also cinematic means of expressing 'as' – for instance, certain camera angles convey certain personal characteristics such as power or insignificance.

When it comes to *onomatopoeia*, a qualitative similitude in cinema abandons the pictorial representation level in favour of a pure sensory stimulus connected to an object. Often this is done by means of velocity, colour: out-of-focus ('rack focus'), warmth, hue, and so on, or by means of pure geometric or other non-representational forms. The vertigo in *Vertigo* is an onomatopoeia more powerful than any words can describe. For a similar effect, American westerns often resort not to sound but to light: the merciless sun of deserts is 'imitated' by the mercilessly overexposed picture of direct sunlight picture in the darkened cinema. In sound, this is often the brutal loudness, rumble (or whatever) that communicates directly without representing an object as its source. In music, imitation is less rare. Then music assumes a representational function – for example, of the animals it imitates. If the argumentative purpose is clear, we can differentiate onomatopoetic figuration from simple representational showing. The Interpretative augment is an impression of immediacy and thus of unaltered authenticity.

Can images deny? This power operates behind the *litotes* trope as negation of some unnamed part, as euphemism or other *periphrasis*. Can cinema succeed rhetorically in not-showing what it shows? A *litotes* such as 'not bad' could be considered a typical linguistic feature of the logical indeterminacy of negation with 'not.' Greimas's Semiotic Square is one example of such a play on the differences between varieties of negation (v. *supra*). 'Not bad,' then, is a complete loop-back to an imaginary logical origin ('good' > 'not-good' > 'bad' > 'not-bad' > 'good, scil. indeed'), but as a reaffirmation. As a procedure of negating, this hints at how cinema can indeed deny. A sequence of images can be brought into a relation of negation. Some of the object transformations in Tati's *Les Vacances de Monsieur Hulot* are rhetorical renegotiations of their real meaning; things are not simply negated, however, it is more that their comical countersense consists sometimes of a 'not not' (his spectacular car is not-not-a-car, for instance). Yet how cumbersome it is to convey meaning cinematographically by euphemism or *litotes*. Things are understood perfectly, but how they were produced is hard to explain. Tati's *Mon Oncle* is full of objects (including cars) that seem not to be what they are. This 'modern world' is full of euphemistic non-objects that through irony become no-non-objects. Especially in cinema, double negation is only apparently a simple trope, suggested by substituting words. In reality, it hides a complex argumentation – at least two acts of negating something different. As a developed form, it is no longer 'ornate of a single word,' but a composition order, and it is used in that way cinematically (cf. Tati).

The next group is based on the common principle of metaphorical analogy between a 'phore' and a 'theme.' Thus it is always a comparison that presupposes a ground for comparison. *Synekdoché* basically involves speaking only of parts while meaning the whole. Images as such are intrinsically synecdoche insofar as every single pictured object can stand for its *genus*. Some famous sequences from Murnau's *Der letzte Mann* and the early Soviet cinema (*Potjemkin*) need no further description. What is part and what is *genus* is not a question of ontology. Argumentative purposes alone determine entirely whether something can stand for something greater than itself. Showing the lion or the lorgnon-wearing Admiral and meaning Tsarist power (among other things), or showing toilets and meaning the debasement of a human being, are merely two examples of the type of fusion this trope operates. Why this is an amplification and not 'literal meaning' cannot be clear, except with the hindsight of argumentation. When a film has no point to make, all tropical readings are suspect. Once this second level of meaning is in place, tropes are practically automatic.

When the tropical relation of parts yields to one part which conveys only a certain quality, this would be something like the *antonomasia* trope. It is so typical in cinema that people are revealed as police types, sissies, teachers, donkeys, and so on, that we can hardly consider this an important cinematic trope. Images can also create new concepts in less specific ways, by singling out objects to stand for something else. Technically a *catachresis*, this is so similar to metaphor that there is little point in explaining the difference. Examples include full ashtray for a long night; in Godard's *Je vous salue, Marie*, the petrol station for Marie ('toujours dans l'essence,' which, of course, works only in French). A still lesser degree of tropicality in cinema comes about through lighting, camera angles, sound perspective, and all the many other tools for reproducing accentuating adjectives or *epitheton ornans*. From some images of the 'abusive chief' in Welles's *A Touch of Evil* to Dreyer's *Jeanne d'Arc* (the moving images of *la Pucelle*), cinema proves that even an entire arsenal of adjectives is less powerful than a single image. A still further reduction of tropical means is *emphasis* – a short pause in the speech flow, or something similar. This can suggest an additional meaning that for some reason cannot be directly named. Often in cinema an unusual 'resting upon' a certain object, or a particular (high-)lighting, can suggest something further (e.g., Bresson's insistence on closed doors in *L'Argent*, where the camera dwells too long by Hollywood standards). The point is to make an innocent thing look ambiguous, simply because it stands out.

When tropes must resort entirely to convention, and when there no longer are 'physical' relations between the object and the *translatio*, the level of *hyperbole, metonymia, metaphora, allegoria, ironia* has been reached. These have considerable meaning potential for cinema and are often used. If from the context we expect to see one thing, but instead are shown another, the operation is always an implied 'is like.' A simile like this can serve various purposes, which, however, must be supplied by the spectator. In *hyperbole* the shown object appears exaggerated (e.g., the shoes of Charlot); in a *metonym*, the object stands for a broader context (threshold for house, key for a car); in a *metaphor* an expected object quality is replaced by that same supposed quality but in another object (lamb fleece for softness). An *allegoria* makes the object stand for a more philosophical idea (the tulip blossoms in Godard's *Je vous salue, Marie* [symbol #10] stand for Marie's virginal body). *Ironia* shows the opposite of what is meant. Nowhere is the fluidity of figuration more apparent. It all depends on the purpose of the non-proper in the usage. Common to all of these is the dependence on context; this constitutes the sole difference between a context-free symbol and an allegory. It is clear, however, that not all objects shown in film are what they are; the frequent use of irony in cinema proves this.

This sort of figuration in cinema has been discussed by many film theorists, for instance, by Carroll (1996a), who refers to it as 'verbal image.' What is surprising in Carroll's treatment, however, is the central role accorded to language. Without language (in the sense of a natural *langue*), Carroll sees no meaning in cinematic figures. Indeed, many of his examples presuppose an English-speaking interpreter, but in those examples this is owing to the prolific interpretation effort, be it the director's or the film theorist's. Such direct language/image links undoubtedly exist in abundance, as has been shown in Godard (v. *supra*). But this does not explain the meaning itself. Moreover, instances of figuration in the absence of language are not covered by this theory, and such pure image tropes also exist. Tati's elaborate irony would be completely lost (to non-French-speakers at least) if cinema were incapable of language-independent figuration.

But the real problem with Carroll's explanation is that he reduces cinematic tropes to 'verbal images.' To think along the gravity lines of language and *a fortiori* in terms of speech acts is to deny cinema its proper capabilities. Tropes must be accounted for as genuine cinematic meaning. A derivative of illocution, epiphytic on the limitations of propositions, cannot explain cinema's astounding capacity to show more than it shows, to make visible the invisible. This involves showing a reality with truth value. Only when this capacity is obviously out of cinema's reach should language be allowed to take over. At that point, however, film theory might as well become a branch of the philosophy of language. Carroll indeed contemplates film as language. His true *explanans* of the cinematic *explanadum* becomes sufficiently clear when he identifies the copula and reduces predication (v. *supra*) to 'identity relation,' with 'visual devices that portend identity' (213) in this sense. However, not even in language (except in tautologies) is predication identity; rather, it is a relationship of a general predicate to a singular subject. It becomes abstruse when figuration is cast into propositions, because the illocution approach itself suggests a meaning that is more than propositional. ('Physical noncompossibility' is *contradictio in adjecto*; it is actually a contradiction in existence propositions and bears no relation to logical possibility.)

What figuration actually is cannot be grasped in either/or propositions. The Moloch in Lang's *Metropolis* is not either machine or Moloch, but machine-as-Moloch. This reflects a logical process of generalization up to the point where two generals become the same quality. Generality by definition does not exist and is logically not subject to the principle of the excluded middle. Carroll's two 'decisive structures for film metaphor ... homospatiality and physical incompossibility' (221) do not require concreteness, asymmetry, or essentialist objectors; a simple logical objection suffices. The Semiotic figuration theory is much more comprehensive and includes also tropical meaning based on music, or sound, and images (of which we have considered Godard's rich arsenal). It is clearly meaningful that Dvořák's Cello Concerto is related to seduction and passion, even without a verbalization of passionate music and passionate love (in 'inner speech' or not). The cello makes us see the 'destructive fire' (allegory) of 'seduction' (literally a metaphor) under the cool image in the Villa Hermès at Lac Léman; this is a trope even for not-French-speaking dyslexics.

Yet another source of figurative meaning for cinema is the meaningful juxtaposition that is not narrative logic. Here speech and film are in a very different position. A study of the rhetoric of *ornatus in coniunctis*, does little to help us understand what in cinema is evidently the domain of montage. This is compounded by the virtually unlimited variations in 'montage within the shot.' The problem in cinema is not how to bring elements into relation with other elements; it is how to find meaning-bearing relational paths in the general relatedness of everything with everything else. Apart from temporal order governed by the relation of temporality, and apart from the sequential arrangement of tropes of single elements (see above), is there a meaning that is intrinsic to the sequential position? The obvious answer is yes, in the case of bare quality (i.e., mostly sensory meaning). Thus rhythm, colour harmonies, and contrasts between shots are noticeable and therefore meaningful. It is also obvious that the answer is yes for general concepts such as temporality; this, however, leads us back to the narrative problem. We are concerned here with meaning having truth claims that are 'about something here.'

It is obvious enough that there is a rhetorical meaning when a film shows something twice, perhaps in a simple close-up. The object might be the same as in a middle shot, but this sequence makes a point by drawing attention to a particular aspect. Even when exactly the same shot scale is used, a second showing of the same shot bears meaning. If this is done more often, it becomes clear that a sequence is being rhythmed according to a point of view, which the spectator must identify in order to understand the statement's structure. Speaking of rhythm is metaphoric. Quite contrary to musical form, it is not dance (or other), but a logical aspect that must be warranted since it is being structured. If it is true that most shot-to-shot logic is simply a temporal and spatial order ('and then ...' and 'and there'), most such sequences could also have been shot in one single shot, pan, or the like, without damage to the meaning. Yet as soon as some meaning can be lost, it becomes a clear case of rhetorical figuration.

Rhetorical figuration based on order can have three possible constellations in language, which are not directly replicable in cinema: adjective[64] (posing together), detractive[65] (taking away), and transmutative[66] (interweaving). There is no well-formed syntax in film, therefore there are no rules to stretch, manipulate, flaunt, or disregard. And yet ... We have analyzed the cadenza of Godard's intertitles *en ce temps-là*, which always precedes the same kind of imagery. This redundancy cannot fail to create very meaningful meaning, because in cinema we cannot ostensibly repeat the identical without suggesting the different (thus augmenting meaning of the identical). So it should not surprise us that the rhetorical skills in *figurae verborum* read like very sophisticated instructions for manipulating elements in order to augment some base meaning. A formal explanation is, however, difficult in argumentation theoretical terms, as to why the repetition of the same (in whichever order) is Interpretation and therefore ampliative reasoning. We must postulate an intervening new fact (and find it, as accession from outside) in order to make this serve as a new Interpretation.

In practical terms, the 'adjection' group could serve as a textbook for film editing *ante litteram*. Duplication of identical pieces, in different order and frequency, serves the general purpose of making a part of the sentence stand out – a part that might otherwise have gone unnoticed. Through this sort of highlighting we can give a particular structure to our thoughts, suggesting climaxes or conclusiveness or something else. In short, a second appearance always has a more or less different meaning from the first, and this can be augmented through further repetition. For example, an analytical shot sequence of the form a-b, a-c, a-d, could be the cinematic form of a climax. There are also cyclic movements that make their point by returning to the initializing shot and 'concluding' something by doing so. Yet the forms are manifold, and I am not suggesting here that cinematic forms can always replicate verbal counterparts. Often the logic between shots is too subtle to be expressed clearly in words (the same can be said of verbal figures). Also, the felt effect is then often not so different in the various figures.

The difference – even in one and the same technique – comes through its argumentative use.

6.3.1 Figuration of Sequence

If meaning in cinema could be reduced to propositions – as has been suggested by some [67] – this would be quite easy to grasp. However, complexity and subtlety reign also in moving pictures, which can only be grasped as figuration. The rhetorical figures discussed earlier related mainly to images or parts of sequences; yet sequence itself can also become meaningful. This corresponds to the domain of *figurae sententiae*.[68] Although most of these figures presuppose language, which has certain sentence construction rules, cinema cannot be specifically excluded from that meaning. This will be clear enough when we examine the mode of functioning in these figures. There are changes in sentence mode or order (*interrogatio, subiectio, dubitatio, communicatio, sustentatio, exclamatio, hysteron proteron*); there is the precision or elimination of meaning (*antitheton, oxymoron, correctio, permissio, licentia, commemoratio una in re – repetitio cerebra sententiae, subnexio, ironia, praeteritio, prolepsis*); finally there are scenic enlargement and direct audience address (*evidentia, fictio personae* or *prosopopoeia, mimesis* or *sermocinatio, apostrophe, aposiopese* or *reticentia*).

All of this can function as a truly communicational event only in a constructed community of a less-than-universal audience. Figurative form clearly has the communicative effect of manipulating a film's spectator address; the names of these traditional figures merely describe this addressing effect. What is not addressed, however, is the figurative logic of the form. Public discourse is not oriented toward any individual as an individual. When addressing their public, orators use figuration to mimic other communication situations. Of pivotal importance is the specificity in the presence of the audience. This means that the less likely the argument, the more intimate the community. One can mimic speaking only to oneself (*dubitatio*) so that one's rhetorical doubt is overcome by convincing one's alter ego. Also, one can speak directly to one's public in the second person, singular and plural (*interrogatio, communicatio*). One can speak to an absent imaginary public (*prosopopoiia*), or one can turn away from the public (*apostrophe*) and address someone singly. Other devices include apparent interruptions of the speech (*aposiopesis*), apparent changing of the topic (*aversio rei*), and insidiously omitting something that is announced (*praeteritio*), promising 'not to speak about the fact that so and so,' or 'I won't mention his inclinations for ...'

Can cinema pretend to achieve a *dubitatio*, for instance? Most of these tropical forms cannot be replicated technically in cinema. However, this figuration has not only communicational but also formal equivalents in cinema. Logically, the figurative form of *figurae sententiae* is identical to figuration based on single elements. In fact, it is the same abductive form, based also on an enunciative point of reference. The only thing that is special about this figuration is that the openness of Interpretation is derived from a sequential order, and that enunciation refers to a communication situation. (Thus without that 'community of understanding,' no meaningful sign can be produced. In the case of *dubitatio*, for example, a real doubt is presupposed expressly and is then interpreted in the figuration. This indicates that sequentiality in this type of figuration is not a grammatical feature (of sentences, etc.), but must be a logical one in order to appear as meaning. It is, therefore, clear that there is more to sequentiality than narration. Cinema is not essentially narrative; its essential sequentiality does more than produce final causality in the form of time. It can also be used to assert the existence of its object. Logically it is enough that the meaningful juxtaposition in sequence refers to a determinate enunciative communication.

Coarse compartmentalizations into 'fictional' and 'documentary' have no relevance for figuration. In specifically different ways, both deal with an invisible spectatorship, and nothing prevents a work from being syncretistic with narrative and rhetorical logic. Thus narrative cinema could represent all of these rhetorical events by way of having a narrative character address the spectatorship rhetorically. For example, many of Woody Allen's films 'wink' at the viewer but even so are very directly convincing. Usual practice, however, relegates to television some of the more conspicuous rhetorical techniques for addressing audiences. Here some direct address is always necessary. Often television is a verbal event and a medium for conversation and discourse. With regard to images, the communicational address can only be 'monstration.' Even in that 'monstration' context, however, there are genuine communicational aspects. A film, for example, can want a spectator to look, or it can mimic a voyeuristic visibility '*malgré elle.*' Pornographic conventions mimic *apostrophe*, turning their back deliberately on the supposedly male spectator, allowing him to peep over the shoulder as it were (cf. Kuhn 1985).

'Ownership of the look' has been an extensively debated topic – not as trope, though, but mainly with regard to psychoanalytic connotations. The communicational settings of oratory practice and cinema are too dissimilar to make the classic classification reasonable in the context of cinema. The main reason for retaining them is that there are usages which achieve forcefully selected spectatorships. The dosage of closeness and community can be manipulated. In the strictly cinematic context, manifestly rhetorical devices that mimic communicational settings are restricted. In a broader audiovisual context, from direct addresses to the spectators (rather rare), to a total *apostrophe*, everything is possible. For example, educational films demonstrate in an outright manner: they presuppose that someone is looking. So does Brecht's 'episches Theater' and those films which were inspired by this theory (e.g., Godard's *Made in U.S.A.*). The spectators are called on to decide for themselves what must happen. At the opposite end of the continuum are self-reflective films, which are so hermetic that they resemble speakers mumbling to themselves. They do not suppose (or want) spectators to ask what they are seeing. For example, Chantal Akerman's *News from Home* does not contain any spectator presence (cf. Ishaghpour 1986: 261–3). In between is narrative cinema, which usually provides the implied spectator with a vantage point on the shown universe; however, because of the differences of universe, the fiction requires the spectator to stay outside. Most communicational restrictions, though, are imposed by narrative conventions and not by cinema as such.

Cinema asserts truth and falseness but in a non-propositional and figuratively rhetorical way. Rhetoric augments meaning – that is, it produces new, real cognitive objects. *Ornatus*, 'meaning-added' ornate speech, in order to enunciate reality uses everything from the manipulation of expression to outright communication. Tropes (and figuration generally) are not cognitive exceptions to the rule; instead they are instances of the normal situation of cognition. Thus the rule of cognition of the real is not a (dyadic) propositional correspondence of sentence and fact (predication always involves particularity and generality, cf. *supra*), but a reference to a real doubt. This is an abductive inference from the enunciational situation of the usage of a sign. It is the task of the enunciation to produce the specific doubt. The figure or trope itself often contains syncretistically the basal doubt as well as the prefigured answer or Interpretation of that doubt (or the presupposed doubt). This means, for instance, that a metaphor must be used in a precise way and does not in itself produce the meaning outside of the proper enunciation. Having a 'fresh face' (v. *supra*) is not obvious, but it is meaningful from a presupposed enunciational appreciation.

In spite of the canonical problem of cinematic metaphors, the issue is not so much the traditional name and recognizable inventory of tropes, but the logic of figuration in images. Only a logical grasp of tropical signification processes can cope with the complexity of cinematic meaning, which cannot be explained by typologies of tropes, even if they could ever be comprehensive. It is not only part of a cultural practice when cinema participates in the subtle argumentative assertion of the real. From a general philosophical perspective, there is also a cognitive requirement to understand assertions of reality as an argumentative process with a rhetorical nature. This is no longer a mere tropical turnaround.

The point of film rhetoric is that cinema is not perception (which is without appeal) but assertion. What we see in a film is not what we *can* see but what we believe to be probable. Unless we inflate the concept of perception to cover all forms of cognition, it is more reasonable to account for the elaborate effort that makes an object seem probable using different terms. Enunciation in the Pragmaticistic understanding is complex enough to explain this special kind of meaning that is not deduced from anything pre-existing. To make something that is produced in this manner appear as existing is an intricate process. It involves establishing a living community with an audience (not for the sake of what 'we all' know already, but for the leap of faith into something unknown) and even all the customary scaffolding to augment meaning beyond the known. The price to pay is the meddling in the contingencies of meaning. However, cinema is also a place of subtle, delicate creativity. It is too crude to theorize on the fragile but convincing real objects of meaning in *Je vous salue, Marie,* for instance, as 'cinematic illusionism' (cf. Currie and Branigan *supra*).

Yet it must be conceded that rhetorical subtleties, as they exist concretely, are not (or at least are not hopeless) cases for schema-driven cognitive theories. There are no schemata for an εἰκὸς. Perhaps this is simply a new casting of a very old animosity. It is as old as philosophy and rhetoric, it dates back to when enthymemic and true reason were distinguished. Rhetorical practice was equated with the wilful distortion of truth. Quintilian, in *Institutio oratoria* (8,3,89) described it succinctly as belittling or inflating (*vis oratoris omnis in augendo minuendoque consistit*). The orator's tool of choice was *dilatatio*, filling in or passing over all the details and all fitting topoi. A true philosopher would not use rhetorical tricks, but instead would choose a way of life (cf. Rahn 1989: 18f); he had to prove the truth of his discourse with his life as φιλόσοφος βίος. Despising sophists was one thing, living in splendid philosophical isolation quite another (even in a 'bios theoreticos'). Evidently, a Speculative (= theoretical) Rhetoric such as Peirce's can reconcile Logic and Contingency, making truth historical.

In film theory the advantage of a rhetorical perspective would be clearer if the nomothetic temptation were less endemic. Indeed there is a profound insecurity regarding what film theory should be about. Metz (1991: 199ff), for instance, has a rather resigned attitude with regard to its scope, in view of the impossibility of comprehending of what spectators actually understand in a film. It is only logical to limit the scope of theory to the lawlike elements in cinema, to *langue*, because discourse (*parole*) is mostly unattainable through laws. The really interesting question – how is a film really understood? – must then be bracketed for theory's sake, and the film analyst as a human spectator must make abstraction of the effective understanding. In philosophical terms, this is a stark version of nominalism. It does not intrinsically take account of the modern status of truth as negotiated and negotiable common sense (as does Peirce's Critical Common-Sensism).

6.4 Aesthetic Enunciation in Film

In the broad stream of cinematic aesthetic, approaching film aesthetic as aesthetic enunciation is so unusual that it needs to be explained. It must, however, be made clear from the start that there is no natural aesthetic object. Everything that any aesthetic theory might claim is an object of that theory, and this theory can therefore never be a 'regional' theory. Every aesthetic theory is derived from a 'grand theory,' from which it takes its very object.[69] It always answers a question that is handed down from its parent theory, and it is a meaningful answer only in that context. For instance, formalism as aesthetic theory answers which question? Upstream of its descriptions of the poetic or 'literatureness' form is the Hume-Kantian antinomy (v. *infra*), which Kant resolves by denying all cognitive potential to aesthetic appearances. Correspondingly, Formalist devices *in se* do not cognize – that is, they never add up to a cognition. As an aesthetic, Formalism is reduced to a cognition of mere forms, without any explanation of how the form generates experience. (We are left to surmise, though, that form aesthetic could be thought, under the aegis of a 'schematism,' in the manner of Kant's synthesis of 'concept' and the 'manifold of senses,' even though this does precisely not apply to aesthetic judgments.)

So it is crucial to determine what aesthetic is about. As a discipline aesthetic is relatively new, whereas rhetoric as an episteme is thousands of years old. Also, aesthetic's origins in transcendental philosophy explain why it is inexorably linked to sensory apperception, to psychological feeling, why it is radically severed from true cognition.[70] A Kantian approach reduces it to the perception underpinning cognition (even as Transcendental Aesthetic). Without liberating itself from the Kantian heritage, one strand has followed the path of psychologically conceived interiority (at its most extreme point is perhaps Habermas's aesthetic validity claim, which can only be 'authentic' in order to fulfil all necessary discursive conditions). The other strand continued along the path of the aesthetic experience's resemblance to judgment. Judgments of taste can never be true, but they reflect the subjective appearance of 'something.' Even in recent times, analytical philosophy has emphasized the reasonableness of aesthetic judgment (cf. *infra*), but it is still assumed that there is no cognitive truth.

Aesthetic after Kant also meant some liberating breaks, some of which included attempts to restore the cognitive potential to aesthetic experience at a different level. This philosophical struggle being only partially relevant for our present purposes, we will concentrate on Semiotic, which is also a grand theory that is capable of a different kind of aesthetic – both as problem and as answer. In short, what 'aesthetic' means, achieves, and reflects is still far from obvious and must first be constructed.

Three questions will need to be addressed, then. (I) How are we to redefine aesthetic in its essence and purpose? (II) What are the concrete aesthetic processes in signs, which (of course) comprise cognition, intuition, and pragmatic? (III) How does film become art? The answers to these will lead to an aesthetic film theory.

6.4.1 The Aesthetic Questions

The aesthetic question is the (type of) question answered by aesthetic. While with certain philosophies aesthetic is a necessary part of their architecture, for most it has no genuine function. We will now reconstruct three problems and answers as they are encountered in Analytical, in Hermeneutic, and in Semiotic aesthetic. How well the 'eggshells' of aesthetic as a Kantian problem can be cracked is certainly one of the interesting questions concerning our three approaches. This struggle with Kant is also encountered in Peirce, but his aesthetic no longer fits into the Procrustean bed of Kant's aesthetic. As we have seen, in dismissing apriorism Peirce was compelled to reproblematize aesthetic in Semiotic, which, as true alternative, is the recognition of the aesthetic part of every cognition and discovery. The dominating currents of philosophical aesthetic, however, remained under Kant's influence, with psychological and subjectivist[71] approaches predominating. Another ramification is Analytical aesthetic (cf. *infra*).

Philosophical aesthetic is a recent discipline, one in which ancient conceptions[72] of the materially aesthetic problem have always been ignored, with the notable exception of Gadamer. Modernity, with its doubts about the subjective grasp of the objective (including the transcendental solution), had no place for art in cognizing the world. It is a commonplace in post-Kantian aesthetics that nothing object-immanent differentiates an aesthetic object from a normal one. Beauty is not a thing, nor is it a transcendental idea. The aestheticizing process always involves an apprehending subject that is the condition of its possibility. In art the subject confers on the object an 'aura' (in Walter Benjamin's sense) of uniqueness, which is easily lost in an epoch of technical reproducibility. Yet aura is not an object; it is something inherent in an object.

Kant's aesthetic is inseparable from transcendentalism, and as a form of judgment it is object of the Third Critique. The difference between the *a priori* form of judgment and judgments of taste is that the latter are 'freies Spiel der Einbildungskraft und des Verstandes' – that is, the free imagination play of the mind – and therefore do not constitute cognitive 'processing' of apperceptions. Notwithstanding that aesthetic is intimately connected to idiosyncratic conditions of stimulus and arousal, in judgments it can be abstracted from these conditions. What these judgments generalize is the feeling of subjective pleasure, which in spite of its subjectivity must be presupposed as being shared generally. This feeling is to be expected *a priori*, and only in the subject, and is therefore general but completely indeterminate in its content; Communication is possible in its formal determination as subjective pleasure, not in its judgmental content[73] (in the sense of the adage *de gustibus non est disputandum*). Only with Lyotard's postmodern aesthetics was such a general aesthetic subjectivity roundly dismissed.

Aesthetic as a function of transcendentalism becomes a philosophical problem of non-empirical judgments of the beautiful and the sublime (*Kritik der Urteilskraft*). For each of the three faculties – cognition, volition, and sensation – there had to be different *a priori* conditions of their possibility. Theoretical cognition had its form in schematism, practical cognition in the categorical imperative. Sensation could no longer be theoretical and logical, nor could it follow pragmatical-logical rules for action. What was required as an *a priori* condition for the possibility of (the faculty of) such judgments was a table of quasi-categories (analogous to synthetic judgments of experience). The force that produces the unity of aesthetic judgments is pleasure (*Gefühl der Lust* or *Unlust*), therefore it is not the synthesizing power of the theoretical mind that follows other *a priori* conditions of its possibility.

A certain precognitive role is assigned to Transcendental Aesthetic, which concerns the apperception of sensory data before they are unified by a theoretical judgment. Apperception cannot be free of form. This formal determination of apperception is similar to geometrical forms. Space and time resemble the formal idea of a triangle instantiated in any concrete triangle. Forms of apperception already reduce the 'manifold of senses' to something that cognition and theoretical judgment can digest. But in a strictly aprioristic system, where do these forms come from? This is no longer a problem for Peirce, for whom the *a priori/a posteriori* distinction makes no sense. This means that any kind of Transcendental Aesthetic has no function. Since everything is already experienced, it is meaningless to question pure data and pure *a priori* forms. When we say that everything is Categorically determined, this is just another way of stating that everything is experienced. Thus, Categories have completely absorbed the function of the Transcendental Aesthetic.

Analytical aesthetic shares this problem that any non-necessary kind of judgment is indeed difficult to communicate. For Kant, there was neither orientation in empirical cognition and in its *a priori* forms nor in any ought-judgment. It cannot be relevant that taste be identical among subjects and their form of mental free play of imagination; so their communicable identity consists only in their common transcendental form. Once it is clear that Ego means being able to imagine both playfully and freely, what can Alter's communication possibly consist of? The communicating of material as tasteful certainly requires both an appeal to perform a mental act of this kind and simultaneously the presentation of this material.

Analytical aesthetic philosophy, still as problem of communicability, understands judgments of taste in contrast to Kant's idea, not in terms of forms of faculties of mind *a priori*. Hume's antinomy that matters of taste are not decidable must be reduced to hypothetical general principles leading to subjective pleasure. There is, however, no point in trying to comprehend why certain properties in art should cause pleasure. The essential point is that any truth claims are inappropriate. The escape offered by the three-worlds theory of Popper as exploited by Habermas (1981) cannot really be accepted. If aesthetic is a matter of the inner world – or, for Habermas, an instance of the veracity validity claims – the result can only be a truth status reduced to authenticity (of a dramaturgically self-representing subject). Aesthetic propositions cannot be compared with existent objective states; we can salvage them from arbitrariness only by comparing the individual with a hypostasized general interiority. Ultimately, it does not matter whether we glean this insight from analyses of ordinary language or from forms of the judgments (which will also always have propositional forms). Even as a historically contingent form of rationality, such a categorization of validity is still a tributary of Kant's transcendentalism.

Consequently, an Analytic aesthetic such as that of Mothersill (1984) in principle denies the possibility of an aesthetic theory of taste. Yet even without generalizing on taste, it cannot be denied that there are reasoned general statements such as her own. She understands the term theory as having 'a well-defined scope, must provide a systematic way for organizing A[art]-related generalizations and principles, and must have testable consequences. A theory of beauty or artistic merit must provide some account of the predicate or predicates that it takes as generic' (135). This accounting, however, is a form of valid reasoning that must exhibit its causal links. It would be unreasonable to expect the experience of a general law of taste (which would have to be *a priori* and *a posteriori*). Thus a sufficiently qualified subjectivity is assigned the status of generality. A law of taste is defined as follows: 'For all S (S being a qualified subject), any x (where x is a work of art, a poem, a sonata, etc.) that has property phi will be *pro tanto* a cause of pleasure to S.' Mothersill's own theory consists of three theses: 'The judgment of taste is singular, categorical, and affirmative' (75). Based on Kant's Third Critique (*KdU*), she denies the possibility of general principles of taste. Notwithstanding this, aesthetic judgments must be contingently true or false, and therefore must be based on qualities.

The form of the aesthetic judgment, though, is rather dubious. The major premise is a kind of generalized notion of subjectivity and its pleasures. Only if this can be taken as a general cognition can the minor premise relate to it. Otherwise it relates unrelated states. Qualities of works of art should cause pleasure, but this is a 'singular' causation. One cannot understand *why* it causes pleasure, because there is no general law permitting this cognition. This is evidently very close to arbitrariness, and calling it 'categorical' can only be reasonable if the form of the judgment is meant. This certainly does not have the quality of 'ultimate necessary forms of being or perceiving.' What causes pleasure? What *is* pleasure? Why is a quality pleasant? The answers to these questions remain evanescent, so it is much wiser to limit our efforts at understanding to the communicability of aesthetic propositions of taste.

With Mothersill, a debate in analytical philosophy comes to a clear end – an end already proclaimed by Bittner (1977: 251). The end is surprising, since it seems to draw the analytical approach beyond its limitations (cf. Pfaff, in Bittner 1977). The result is thus Thomas Aquinas's *pulchrum dicatur id cuius apprehensio ipsa placet* (S.th. Ia IIae, 27, I, ad IIIm). A familiarity with the individual object of pleasure, which cannot be further generalized in laws, is then 'taking something to be beautiful,' 'finding something beautiful' (Mothersill 1984: 365 and passim), which can be assessed through reflection and which thus makes this a true statement. The contradiction between the form and the matter of aesthetic judgments in analytical aesthetic will become clearer when we compare it to a Semiotic aesthetic. Mothersill's argumentation almost leaps to a Peirceish conclusion. However, without the benefit of modality she lacks the tools for coming to grips with the particular kinds of norms in aesthetic experience.

It is highly indicative that analytical aesthetics, as soon as they try to be coherent and comprehensive, tend to reduce the aesthetic object to propositions. In this, they stay within the framework established by Goodman (1968). The price exacted for the maximal dismissal of subjective interiority is the predominance of meaningful sentences. Thus, Goodman requires – even for figurative meaning in art – that at least in principle it can be stated as a paraphrasis in an extensional form.[74] What cannot be stated is meaningless. Whether this is an extensional or an intensional amplification (as A. Danto claims) is of secondary significance, as long as the question is one of propositional truth. Only the point of comparison with a generality changes from a purely 'mental context' to an extensional context. In these last and vague recollections of Kantian Critique we can perhaps see a remote, if central, coming to terms with the cognitive power of aesthetic insight. At the same time there is a concession to the form that its truth value is compromised, with the effect that (1) the non-law essence is a stressed as much as (2) an experiential generalized interiority that nevertheless must be (3) communicatively validated. What the truth and the nature of such interior experience might be remains quite obscure, except inasmuch as it causes pleasure. Perhaps as an attempt to avoid the onus of the transcendental explication of a 'free play of the imaginative faculty,' pleasure seems to be an observable matter of fact and is, for the rest of us, inexplicable.

In HERMENEUTIC AESTHETIC, a clear rupture with Kant's aesthetic apriorism has brought a new approach to subjectivity. Hermeneutic has developed a truly novel aesthetic theory based on phenomenology and on the immediate givenness of consciousness. Provided that one is prepared to cede to psychologisms, the understanding and communication of taste (aesthetic experience) becomes a matter of identification with another mind ('divinatorisch,' as Schleiermacher has called it). Aesthetic fruition (including pleasure) becomes at once a dialogical event and not a proposition about the artistic properties of an object. It is not meant to yield a definitive judgment. The background of a parallel, oblique, and frail 'cognition' about a Non-Object, the Self, is however definitive. This, too, is a typical hermeneutic agenda. In hermeneutic analysis there are three aspects to the aesthetic experience: (1) the pragmatic context, (2) the aesthetic difference, and (3) aesthetic openness. These three moments epitomize hermeneutical aesthetic: *poiesis, aisthesis, katharsis*. They are dimensions of the classical concept of aesthetic fruition (Jauss 1977, again from Aristotelian *Poetic* 1448b8ff).

It is central to hermeneutic aesthetic that it is action which produces beauty. Acting is, thus, the true locus of these moments, their true setting, their genesis, and the condition of their possibility. Aesthetic is a pragmatic attitude. No longer is it a theory of perception, or a code, or infringement on a code that bears aesthetic significance. Nor is it a matter of aesthetic propositions. The term 'aesthetic attitude' used to refer to *l'art pour l'art*,[75] but it now has an importance vis-à-vis the deconfinement (*Entgrenzung*) of the modern work of art (cf. Jauss 1968). Not only has the canonicity of beauty foundered; the concept of beauty itself has been transcended by the inclusion of the 'ugly' in artistic signification. So the aesthetic object itself can no longer account for aesthetic effects. Yet, can pure interiority do so, as the logic of *l'art pour l'art* suggests? Gadamer introduced the complementary term/couple aesthetic non-differentiation (*ästhetische Nichtunterscheidung*) and aesthetic differentiation (*ästhetische Unterscheidung*; cf. Gadamer 1990: 91ff). The former is the non-difference, as is so manifest in rites – which are the origin of art.

The latter is the difference between museum artworks and the banality of everything else. When Benjamin identified the traditional relationship to art as 'aura,' as the quasi-sacralized non-profane *fanum*, he had something similar in mind. All of this is to say that the identity and integrity of a work of art today is far from taken for granted. We cannot determine beforehand what exactly a work of art is and what it is not. Artistic practice and its results are no longer confined by established institutions or by the canonicity of judgments of taste.

The auroral aesthetic moment is an 'attitude' (*ästhetische Haltung*). The pragmatic definition of this attitude is play. Play – the quintessence of aesthetic – has a central role in hermeneutic, not just in aesthetic. Gadamer gleaned this insight descriptively from phenomena ranging from cult rituals to children's totally absorbed playing. Important hermeneutical principles of human understanding and communication are less strange once we acknowledge that of which they are a phenomenological description. Play and cult – which is play's intensive form – are especially intense forms of communication. In this respect they compare with the fundamental phenomenological concept in communication: 'Life-world' (Husserl's *Lebenswelt*,' however, is functionally different from Schütz's version). Neither concept functions without the phenomenological consciousness/identity model that constructs the difference between two identities. Life-world could be reread hermeneutically as the rite most universal to human coexistence. However, that some general identity (as 'horizon of unquestionable validities') presides over individual identities is made much more explicit.

Cultic role differences merely postulate a general third identity of comparison. This third is neither independent from nor destructive of its constituent identity subjects. Schütz's Life-world shares with Gadamer's ritual or theatrical play the central act of being an autarkic Subject: in the same way that a play plays itself, as it were, and is not born of the intentional aims of its players (cf. Gadamer 1990: 107–39), thus society cannot be 'willed.' Both are as if they were their proper subjects. In Gadamer's description, play is this sort of pragmatic, which no longer sets out to achieve ends. It is serious on its own account, outside the 'earnestness of life.' Those who play (e.g., children) are committed to the earnestness of a world of sense in its own right, which is the ever evanescent and yet so present '*Urbild*' (image-origin) of the '*Bild*' (image, of my portrait, or whatever representation of my identity). This sense is broader than in the world of the teleological means/end rational pragmatic. In this means/end world, a countersense can also be located that pierces by comic force (*vis comica*, cf. Jauss). The point – crucial to both play and the Life-world – is the comparative: a sense greater than that prevailing, albeit a sense that is not readily available. Comic, play, aesthetic, and so on must all happen felicitously. They do not happen outside a subject, who by this means becomes more than a mere individual.

The distance from Kant's aesthetic (and to all other nominalistic aesthetics) could not be greater. From a transcendentalist perspective, aesthetic judgments can never be empirical. They can add nothing to cognition. Not so from a hermeneutical aesthetic, which constitutes emphatically an amplification of cognition. This, however, remains within the realm of subjectivity and identity, albeit on its transempirical side. Art, then, contributes something irreplaceable to cognition – its enlargement. Kantian aesthetic has lost its faith in the power of art. Kant's nominalistic scepticism reduces the aesthetic event to *Spieltrieb*, as Peirce complains (cf. *infra*), and this has had devastating consequences for aesthetic. In hermeneutic thought, as in Semiotic thought, the object of cognition in aesthetic is the comparative degree of sense, or the enlargement of meaning (αὔξησις), growing discovery. 'Aesthetic attitude' is essentially a particular type of openness to a presence. Gadamer's 'ontology of art' assigns the representational being not to qualities in an object (as does Mothersill), but to the pragmatic of an aesthetic conduct of a subject.

The mode of being of art is play, a pragmatic attitude contained in two classes of ritual, dramatic and theatrical roles. The players very literally 'represent' a closed world 'with four walls.' This is most visible in cult and in children's play, since neither of these is performed for somebody else. All participants are sufficient unto themselves and are absorbed by the play or rite. But as soon as the fourth wall falls, another role enters the play: that of the spectator. The play absorbs both roles, but in a significantly different way. Players or performers assume their new identity through the play; meanwhile, spectators must grasp the play through the form of sense in its wholeness ('Gesamt des Sinngehalts' in Gadamer) and not from the perspective of the participant role.

Gadamer's method can best be illustrated in films such as Souleyman Cissé's *Yeelen* and Landis's *The Blues Brothers*. Both are cult films (in the double sense of the term), but from radically different cultures. For European viewers the performance of Mali Bambara cults is such a strange phenomenon that comprehension of its genuine meaning is impossible. We can only comprehend cults by participating from within – that is, by being part of their pragmatics. We will never really understand the roles (competences and performances) in *Yeelen*; that said, the film also makes minor concessions to its European viewers. All of the non-cult elements can easily be grasped as mother/son and father/son dramas, as rivalries, and also as adultery conflicts (with the king's wife). Yet the film resists the temptation to make witchcraft cults accessible to Europeans. It could have used our patterns of 'haunting,' 'spirits,' or 'exorcisms,' or it could have allowed an ethnographical viewing. Yet it did not. It leaves us confronted with the strangeness of an African cult. This does not mean exclusion as a spectator (as would have been the case in ethnographic cinema). After all, the 'fourth wall' has fallen. But we can hardly cope with the universe of sense, which is visibly there.

The Blues Brothers, in contrast, allows us to become part of a Western cult. We understand the 'bigger than life' play of a rite, or at least a ritual. There are clear, repetitive, and regulated performances that create their own world. This world is, like *Yeelen*'s witchcraft, inaccessible to conceptual thinking; furthermore, it transforms all of the elements of its environment into elements of its play. In terms of Aristotelian rhetoric, everything is transformed into a sign ($\tau\epsilon\kappa\mu\dot{\eta}\rho\iota\upsilon\nu$). Because of the lack of conceptual access, the cult effect (i.e., the aesthetic) thrives on participation rather than on an object quality. Also, in contrast to theatre, its wholeness of sense is not 'Gebilde,' which is Gadamer's term for holistic representation of a sense universe. Play organizes itself around its unified sense universe, but only to a spectator does enactment become representation. *Gebilde* is the truth or essence of representation. The 'bigger than life' feeling is the fascination of the playful absorption into the true meaning of something, be it the cult and mystique of Chicago (life)style or the Bambara cult of Komo in Mali. Both transform their environment equally through the pragmatic of their participant players.

In the lesser instances of cult – art and theatre – the spectator role gains importance. The presence and truth of the play world becomes, in Jauss, connected to the Life-world of the spectator within the person herself and her 'better identity' (through the process described below). In keeping with Husserl's phenomenology, hermeneutic is intrinsically psychological. Jauss, who at this level can stand for all aesthetic inspired by Gadamer's hermeneutic, describes the elements present in the origin of aesthetic in this way:

The common background of all aesthetic reality is a *Doppelung* or doubling. There is an implication that it is possible for beholders (and producers) to distance themselves from their immediate goal-oriented action (which Jauss called *aisthesis*). By doing so we do not simply perceive the Other (the aesthetic object, for instance) – we perceive instead implicitly our own Self, as the presence of its truth. In Jauss's analysis this is the entry point into the aesthetic attitude, whose lower limit is the Comical phenomenon. The Comic is already an aesthetic phenomenon, whereas Ridicule is not (it is merely a pragmatic act). Comedy is the art form that relies on this. 'Implicitly perceiving one's Self' involves a special mode of self-cognition, because the Self is merely oblique to what is directly perceived. In between the extreme limits of loathing (*odium*) and pity (*misericordia*; cf. Jauss 1977: 182), the Other is perceived directly. Comic perception is 'bracketed' by becoming oblivious to oneself, or concretely, by an openness to and expectancy of laughter. The comical effect, however, is brought about by the free comparison of the Other's behaviour with the behaviour expected of him according to a valid norm. It is the aesthetic discovery of a countersense (*Gegensinn* in Jauss). Only the aesthetic attitude can instantaneously compare of what the 'I' recognizes as normatively valid for me, but dares not admit directly and therefore must see in the Other, and the risibly observed, non-sense. The aesthetic distance takes away the menacing earnestness of ridicule, which attacks only the Other. Aesthetic *vis comica*, then, is liberating in the sense that it allows me to see the ridicule in another. The Other, however, is the double of myself, but is such as to be free from being menaced by its/my ridicule.

The particular interest in Jauss's description of the comic effect is that it is the precise lower limit of a broader pragmatic aesthetic attitude. It reveals aesthetic to be constituted of oblique self-cognition while doubling myself into an object. Jauss' blends with Gadamer's 'ontology of art,' in which play (*Spiel*) is seminal (cf. Gadamer 1990: 107–39). The very heart of play is the roles that participants assume, again in a non-differentiating doubling of their Self. They are, simultaneously, their *personae dramatis* and themselves. Changeability of roles is a particular cognitive achievement. Neither part is forgotten, and neither is merely obliviously present. The upper limit of the very same aesthetic attitude consists of a lessening of the Self's oblivion – always within an aesthetic attitude of obliquely distanced cognition. For Jauss a prime example of such an oblivious consciousness is St Augustine. Masterfully, his *memoria*, in his Confessiones,[76] is the realm and the unique achievement of self-conscious Self-oblivion. Here the Self comes to itself, but is always doubled in the much deeper and comprehensive cognition (i.e., 'being-comprehended-by') of God.

In its comprehension of roles, such as hermeneutical narratology, hermeneutical aesthetic is concentrated on the question of identity, most prominently in Ricoeur (1990). Aesthetic still offers a better and a more direct way to answer the Modern Cartesian question of the Subject insecure of itself (its Self). This answer can no longer be provided in a solipsist way, only mediating an Other, as has become apparent in the temporal form of being-a-whole. Selfhood/Otherness is the seminal difference in hermeneutic. The cognition of the other is 'divinatory' identification, an enlargement of and the totality of one's Self. Thus it indirectly addresses the modern subjectivity question as question. Yet it offers as a solution to the Cartesian doubt the antecedent assurance of the subject through its other. Evidently, if the totality of Kant's transcendentalism lies in the *a priori* forms of the synthesis, in the *Ding an sich* and in the Transcendental Subject, there is no real totalizing function for aesthetics. An aesthetic judgment is not synthetic, and even the 'totality' of its judgment is only an appearance that does not reduce the manifold to a unity. The manifold, the disparate of judgments of taste, remains.

On the whole hermeneutic aesthetic has already progressed enormously from reified, essentialist conceptions of objects of beauty. This is especially important for cinema; media essentialism is still endemic in film aesthetic.[77] 'Iconic qualities,' 'ontologies of the realist art,' and similar concepts still suffer from a static, reified object definition of art. In this they follow a multitude of past theories of art. Schrader (1972), for one, inspired by H. Wölfflin's history of art (1915), was led to apply the object qualities of paintings to cinema. Approaches of this sort are no longer convincing – not since the hermeneutic-phenomenological overcoming of Kant's aesthetic. In this regard, Carroll's polemic against this substantial corpus of essentialism in film theory (cf. Carroll 1996b: 3–77) seems to be a rearguard battle. This does not make his arguments wrong, although it does create a strong expectation for an alternative that is better than hermeneutic aesthetic. There is no hint in Carroll of how such an expectation could be fulfilled, however. Hermeneutics has no use for aesthetic objects, which is in agreement with Carroll's and many others' postulates. Media essentialisms, instead, are falling back behind phenomenalisms into thinking in substances.

In hermeneutic aesthetic, the firm anchor for the phenomenal world of the aesthetic now lies in the subject itself. Undoubtedly, this is an advance over essentialism, including in cinema aesthetics. In film theory, Mitry is the foremost advocate of phenomenology. However, as we have seen, even he has incorporated essentialist elements of 'film language,' and he has not taken up the radicalness of the hermeneutic approach. This is now seen in certain currents in literary theory, such as Reception Aesthetic and the poetic of Reader Response, but it is still lacking in cinema aesthetics and film theory. Phenomenology as a theory of representation has established itself in film studies, but in the aesthetic domain it has not been taken up as a serious alternative to neoformalist or semiological aesthetic.

A phenomenological aesthetic in film theory is difficult, and as an analytical method it is not a facile, self-evident psychology of role switching. Unfortunately, this is how Reader Response theory has been reduced in certain 'television theories.' Small wonder that all relation to the original problem has been severed – its solution had required such a painstaking method. Phenomenology 'eidetically' reduced (all content and questions of existence from) consciousness in order to analyze the phenomenon itself as it is 'given' in consciousness. How this reduction functions was noted earlier with Husserl's analysis of immediate time consciousness. A careful analysis of the aesthetic consciousness or attitude follows the same painstaking reduction and is as much a method as a phenomenology of cognition. Robbed of its purpose, it must become a vulgar and commonsensical role psychologism. However, it then loses all its truth claims. Anchoring aesthetic experience in the subject itself – done properly and strictly – is therefore no easier procedure. Phenomenological aesthetic is, then, not another psychology of perception.

On the horizon of aesthetic theories there is a clear and distinct place for Semiotic Aesthetic. In principle, there are only a handful of options for treating the aesthetic phenomenon (of all of which there are still vague traces in aesthetic film theories): the substantial, the formal, the material, and the egological.

(1) Aesthetic (or what is today so called) has been addressed though such an ineffable concept as 'beauty.' For Plato, beauty is eternally the same (μονοειδές ἀεὶ), spiritual and absolute, for all visible beautiful objects partake in it (for instance, in *Symposium* 211b1–3: καθ' αὐτὸ μεθ' αὑτοῦ μονοειδές ἀεί· τὰ δὲ ἄλλα πάντα καλὰ ἐκείνου μετέχοντα τρόπον τινὰ τοιοῦτον). In Aristotle, even though beauty no longer imitates an eternal idea, it still imitates action as typical and better (than the real-

life action; v. *supra*). The very idea of imitation (mimesis) has metaphysical implications. Once metaphysical thinking is no longer possible, 'beauty' as such is unattainable.

(2) With Kant we must confine ourselves to the limits of the mental faculty of judgment. Here 'beauty' becomes a function of subjectivity. It has become a post-Kantian commonplace that beauty is neither the application of a general law[78] nor a substance. Its meaning must to be communicated without the benefit of logical constraints. Mothersill (1984) only brings this Kantian figure of thought to an end. Judgments of taste are mere *subjektiver Schein*, subtracting empirical truth. If, nevertheless, something can ascertain the communicability of taste, it is a mere function of transcendental subjectivity.

(3) What remains in analytical philosophy are subjective propositions without truth value. In a certain sense, investigations of aesthetic qualities of the object are diametrically opposed to Kant's aesthetic faculty. However, even this attempt in analytical philosophy really concerns itself with a rational description of such aesthetic qualities of an aesthetic object. This is not genuinely a realist aesthetic, as Mothersill's invocation of Thomas Aquinas's '*pulchra enim dicuntur quae visa placent*' (Sth I, 5, 4, ad 1) would suggest.

(4) Yet another possibility is a phenomenological hermeneutic aesthetic. Its true difference lies in the egological approach (v. *supra*). A derivative is aesthetic psychologism, which sees itself through a key of psychic interiority and consequently treats aesthetic as the problem of access to interiority[79] (as if it were a parallel universe).

(5) In the Neoformalist and cognitivist current, it is difficult to see the possibility of any aesthetic theory proper. This difficulty stems in part from philosophical foundations that are inconsistent among themselves. A further hindrance is their thematic restriction to narrow questions of cognitive representation and literary form. Cognitivism is marred by its obsession with existence ('fictional' in opposition to 'real'), which prevents it from picking up the aesthetic problem even in Kant's reduction to 'non-cognitive' judgments.[80] A purported lineage to Aristotelian *Poetic* is – at best – confined to certain formal aspects of some of the six elements of drama. Although drama as such was deduced from the two principles of mimesis and praxis, Cognitivist Neoformalism offers no developed equivalent to these two poetological origins. Neither is there an alternative (to a) theory of action, and neither is there a non-ontological (and thus possibly mimesis-free) theory of representation (except perhaps for propositional, existential relations). Thus, its contribution to aesthetic proper (as cognitive faculty, as object

character, or other) is scant; its greatest interest perhaps is still the rule theory of a form guiding artistic strategy as conduct. In a fully developed system, this might have required a certain theory of action in a formalist key (G. Simmel's, perhaps). This, however, was thwarted by the antitheoretical attitude of the original Formalists,[81] and could not be supplied by their contemporary successors in film theory. Later on, the aesthetical claims of this current will be investigated more thoroughly.

With Pragmaticistic aesthetic, a further option appears on this horizon – the normative idea. Every fundamental change in how we can think of the cognitive relation to the real also entails a total revision of aesthetic theory. Aesthetic remains a daughter of epistemology, and sometimes even a repudiated one. There can be no surprise, then, that abandoning the aprioristic approach to faculties of mind has consequences. The entire role assigned to Aesthetic in the architectonic structure of Pragmaticism is different when there is no function for a Transcendental Aesthetic or for non-cognitive aesthetic judgments.

In principle, there are two main contexts in which Peirce concerns himself with aesthetic: Aesthetic as a Normative Science and as Feeling (as a cognitive operation and not as a psychological state). As we shall see, these are not heterogeneous blocks of theory, but alternative ends on the same continuum. In both contexts, aesthetic is seen logically. In the former it is from a perspective ('from above') of cognitive processes in their entirety as pragmatic conduct, whereas from the latter perspective it is investigated as a Semiotic operation.

6.4.2 Aesthetic as a Normative Science

The nature of *Semiotic aesthetic* clearly suggests that there is a decisive difference between phenomenology and Phaneroscopy as foundation. An aesthetic based ultimately on categories, rather than on egology and subjectivism (as with phenomenology) is different from the ground up. Peirce's interest in this field started very early with Schiller and led him, in his maturity, to treat aesthetic as a Normative Science. He never understood it as a theory of art (even as a rationality of the subjective). Peirce insists that aesthetic is 'purely theoretical,' has its own value, and should not be confused with 'practical sciences' (cf. Peirce 1997: 209) such as, for instance, the appreciation or production of works of art. In short, he assigns to this theory the task of reflecting on the norm that directs conduct to what is 'in itself admirable.' His philosophy as a whole prevents aesthetic from being a purposeless exercise: it is absolutely necessary to have this norm if the Real is really a conduct of action (v. *supra*). Furthermore, Peirce in his later years succeeded more and more in clarifying his ideas on perception. Through relating critically to the Kant/Baumgarten tradition of sensation in aesthetics, the disconnection between sensation and cognition could be resolved and sentiment could be reintroduced to the broader realm of cognitive action.[82]

Peirce cut himself off from a number of possibilities for conceiving aesthetic. Two of the possibilities he ruled out were that subjectivity is meaningless if it is not intrinsically related to objective reality; and that the faculty of sensation and the judgments of taste, even though not claiming any cognitive meaning, are aprioristic abstractions and exist only as such. This latter assumption is analogous to the non-experienceable *Ding an sich*, which exacts the same price for apriorism – that something unknowable must be assumed with that faculty and shared as the same by every human being. Both these avenues having been blocked, Peirce was compelled to redefine the problem for which aesthetic is an answer; furthermore, this redefinition would have to be based on his realist system architecture. Now, what is a realist aesthetic? Oxymoron, *contradictio in adjecto*, insensitivity to the peculiarities of art? If the beautiful were reduced to something mundane, it might be real but it might, as well, no longer have this strange 'more-than-real' character. Thus it is commonly understood that any aesthetic must grasp this dematerialized and more than factual nature of its object. Is it an object, after all? And if not, is it necessarily the opposite of an object, subjectivity? This is, experienceable but not factual, not mundane but real? Peirce's thoroughly realist solution is based again on the recognition that 'being' is not *simpliciter*, but *juxta modum*. Before we experience something as real, we make a choice about the nature of its reality. In practical terms this means we follow a different rule of cognitive conduct. As discussed earlier, the Normative Sciences investigate the different values of those rules. It follows that the only way to develop a Semiotic aesthetic hinges on conduct that is ruled by a specific kind of value and that is expressed in a specific kind of Sign process.

The general idea of aesthetic as Normative Science shines brightly only in the context of Pragmaticism. Realist aesthetic, then, first concerns action (and not mental or psychological states), and second, concerns a certain determinate action that is (distinct from others) determined by one of three values. Clearly, this contrasts sharply with the approach of hermeneutic aesthetic, which holds that action means the expression of a subject. That immediately implies either a role as ideal 'type of action' or its absence in the authentic subjective meaning of an action project (in the manner of Schütz's 'understanding sociology'). For Semiotic and Pragmaticism, however, the very idea of an action does not hinge on the expression of a subject. From its very inception, the triadic element of a generality has a place in action itself; only through this does it become conduct (i.e., self-controlled behaviour). A single action is as inconceivable as would be a singular judgment/proposition or concept or experience. Despite the emphasis on the unique, non-repeatable 'kiss of the muse' in the rhetoric of geniality aesthetic, aesthetic experience is human conduct. Thus action intended as a 'project of a solitary subject with temporal reach' is concretely impossible. It is merely an egological reduction (which can become a methodological necessity only in an effort to construct a transcendental subject). Conduct, instead, always and irreducibly, comprises three elements: generality, 'brute facts,' and Qualitative 'quiddity.' Yet this still does not explain the novelty of the idea of Aesthetic as a Normative Science.

An aesthetic conduct must receive its guidance from a value. If it is essentially different from other types of conduct, it must be guided by a different value. If law and truth are the cognitive values of conduct seeking general understanding and factual reality, a value of Quality controls aesthetic conduct. However, quality excludes nothing because it is pure possibility. We can hardly label this kind of value a rational principle. Such an undue expansion of the term value smacks of complete instinct and is thus rendered a worthless term. Aesthetic conduct guided by instinct-as-value can only be considered as rule-based if a rule – which cannot become a negative rule by excluding its Other – is still comprehensible as a norm. This comprehension can be achieved only through, the differentiation as an architectonic requirement of Pragmaticistic guidance as a whole (i.e., as a precise logical necessity[83]). This has already been analysed (v. §1.4.1).

Based on our investigation of the science of the aesthetic norm, aesthetic conduct stands out clearly as a completely deconfined behaviour. It is not bound by truth and generality constraints. Also, it is not limited to art. Its closest realization is play, or the freedom of imagination. Yet it is still conduct, since even play is based on a minimal purpose[84] in the most indeterminate sense of that term. Thus even essential subjectivity (Gadamer's Urbild) must be considered too confining for this kind of conduct. The rule of play, however, cannot offer durative guidance. Play reverts to indetermination inasmuch as it remains a pure possibility. Aesthetic actions can therefore not become true, nor can they become generalized (i.e., communicated) with regard to their essence.

One intriguing problem that arises from these premises is whether purely aesthetic actions are possible. As conduct such actions can hardly be communicated, since this would be self-defeating. For art, then, this task must be assumed by aesthetic enunciation. Aesthetic experience as play being instinctual conduct, we cannot presuppose that this conduct can be identical for any two people. Nevertheless, it must become a Sign – that is, it must involve communication and critique. Therefore, an enunciation that is aesthetic must contrive to reconcile two distinct conducts.

For conduct – including the cognitive conduct of enunciation through the production of Signs – it is fundamentally important that the aesthetic norm relate to the admirable *in se* (which is not to be misconceived as a substantial concept), and not as ethical conduct to the *summum bonum* and to truth as existential goodness, and not as logical (i.e., cognitive) conduct to logical goodness. There are also metaphysical implications regarding Possibility as such, the reality to which aesthetic conduct relates.[85] These were discussed (v. §§2.3.1, 1.7).

However, the Normative Science aesthetic concerns itself with norms and not with conduct itself. It has to converge on a practical conduct through which such a relation is done. How does one conduct oneself (and not merely act, or perceive) aesthetically, then? If aesthetic values can lead no farther than to a universal appetite for and attraction toward everything (i.e., affording no more than perceptions), how can they become relevant to art?[86] In the 'cognitive association of feelings' theory, we must – as the next step – to concern ourselves with aesthetic conduct. The final step, after the aesthetic norm, and after aesthetic conduct itself as aesthetic feeling, will be the cognitive result of this conduct. This result is the aesthetic sign relation, which is produced in the aesthetic enunciation. Every sign's meaning being dependent on its concrete use, *a fortiori* this is true for the aesthetic sign. It can benefit little from 'eternal' generalities, and it takes all its meaning from the concrete moment. Thus practical conduct and its norm become all the more crucial for the operation of the aesthetic sign relation.

6.4.3 Aesthetic as Feeling and Association of Mind

6.4.3.1 From Where Does the Capacity for Aesthetic Conduct Come?
In a Pragmaticist approach, it is typical that the solution is sought (and thought) not as judgment but as conduct. This conception leads upstream of Kant to the older problem of an aesthetic rightness (ὀρθότης) proper; on par with: do we establish correct ways of reasoning? In recov-

ering aesthetic as conduct (i.e., freeing it from being reduced to aesthetic geniality), we are implying that some behavioural regularity is being followed. However, it must be a regularity of its own.

Aesthetic emphatically conceived as behaviour – without, however, a differentiating rule – would lead to Nietzsche (*Die Geburt der Tragödie aus dem Geiste der Musik* §1, 16f), who opposes the Dionysian ritual as quintessential aesthetic to the quintessentially theoretical, reproductive Apollonian world representation. Even then, there is still a ritual rule. We probably would not be too far off the mark if, in this early work of Nietzsche, we found that Schopenhauer's pragmatism was still determinant. Any will – including the aesthetic form's will – cannot be completely arbitrary. This is despite Nietzsche's profound aversion to 'aesthetic Socratism' (§12), which protests against the adage 'all must be reasonable to be beautiful.'

Peirce's conception of aesthetic conduct is clearly 'Apollonian.' As a pragmatic entity, it obeys a logical rule, yet it remains essentially different from other (e.g., theoretical) rules. Clearly, this dismisses two other options that have arisen in aesthetic pragmatic: one is aesthetic behaviour explained as subjectivity and the expression of it (v. *supra*); the other is its negation, through Nietzsche's Dionysian dissolution of subjectivities. This attempts to be conduct beyond the reach of control and rationality. The 'movement of life,' then, is kept in motion by a higher principle than action, which can perhaps be called life *per se*, a sort of cyclical vitalism. These two avenues being closed off, and assuming that any 'deliberate conduct is self-controlled conduct' (Peirce 1998: 348), aesthetic is also habit formation through a rule.

Control through a rule implies critical review, be it through others or through one's own correction. Aesthetic conduct, in its most general aim, follows 'attractive and repulsive ideas' (Peirce 1998: 378); this is its rule, but obviously such a rule is not terribly discriminating. Therefore this sort of subjective liking ('a physiological function') is not enough.[87] According to Peirce, arguing with subjectivity yields to the argument that the goodness of a judgment can be appraised only at a second judgment, and so on. Thus he contends that critical appraisal that does not result in infinite regress is in fact possible. His proposal is inherently complex, much more so than a transcendentalist solution. It has various stages,[88] but what concerns aesthetic immediately is the direct confidence of someone reasoning: 'A reasoner, as such, does not care whether such be the metaphysical constitution of the universe or not. Precisely what he is intent upon is that the facts shall not disappoint the promises of his argumentations' (2.159). So aesthetic reasoners or experiencers must feel the rightness of their conduct not as their interiority but as an outside value of their behaviour. Interiority has no promise at all and cannot control itself by itself.

Peirce argues for a logic and cognition without 'aesthetic'-subjective travesty. Yet this opens the way for an aesthetic Aesthetic, which is essentially different from both argumentative and factual cognition. Although it is an arduous task to provide a proper foundation to the 'promises of argumentation,' this is certainly not so in a feeling of 'right reasoning.' 'Promises of factual cognition' are easier to justify because the metaphysical foundation of propositional truth values is simply the existence of an outward world. There, something is or is not, and it is thus logically a dyadic state of affairs. But what are the 'promises of feelings,' of aesthetic cognition? Following Peirce's argument, there is no reason to conclude that this type of cognition is devoid of appraisal. So the practical consequence is that feelings cannot be 'just there.' If it weren't possible to accept or reject feelings, those feelings would be – and *a fortiori* Aesthetic – mindless, and this is unacceptable for an anti-transcendentalist Pragmaticism. Peirce treats this problem in the 'Minute Logic' not only polemically; this opposition is founded on some basic theory design options that distance Peirce from Kant and probably also from Husserl's Transcendental Logic.

Peirce argues (polemically against the 'German method') that there are aesthetic judgments. Once this is admitted, the next question concerns the rule. Is there an aesthetic rule governing 'physiological functions'? What immediately sounds absurd, is countered by the fact that there are indeed aesthetic judgments and that they are evidently based on physiology. Yet they cannot just be physiological. So we must conclude that Aesthetic is part and parcel of the same endeavour and principle and thus subject to critique (and rejection if need be). Taste is indeed a matter of debate, but it should not be a moot one, as Hume's antinomy implies. Only in this manner can aesthetic become a proven, responsible habit of behaviour, thus becoming 'the singular phenomenon of a physiological function which is open to approval and disapproval' (2.152) Furthermore, 'in the case of taste, it is recognized that the excellence of the norm consists exclusively in its accordance with the deliberate and natural judgment of the cultured mind'[89] (2.156).

The procedure for attaining aesthetic norms is typical of Peirce. The primacy of logic being beyond question (cf. 'When our logic shall have paid its devoirs to Esthetics and the Ethics' [2.200]), it next becomes evident that sound reasoning requires the determination of outward reality. 'The fundamental problem of ethics is not, therefore, What is right, but, What am I prepared deliberately to accept as the statement of what I want to do, what am I to aim at, what am I after? To what is the force of my will to be directed? Now logic is a study of the means of attaining the end of thought. It cannot solve that problem until it clearly knows what that end is' (2.198). Responsible conduct therefore consists in letting one's thought be determined by its other, 'brute factual' relation between an ego and a non-ego. In the case of cognition, ego's effort is guided by – or directed toward – truth.

That it is directed toward this value, however, does not stem from the logical cognitive operation itself but must be presupposed by it. Now in this directedness by ends there is another presupposition that is the concern of aesthetic: 'the one quality' (cf. 2.199), which is *beau* or καλὸς (Peirce deliberately avoids the term 'beautiful' because aesthetic is not the theory of beauty). Where does the need for such a quality arise? Do ends not suffice for the conduct of behaviour? Why does this question of 'what it would be that, independently of the effort, we should like to experience' arise (2.199)?

In another formulation of the same problem, the reason why direction of action cannot be blind and is reduced to 'activism' becomes clearer: 'We cannot know how we are deliberately prepared to aim to behave until we know what we deliberately admire' (L75, version D, 9). Either the fair or the ugly, as experience, is the basis of cognitive acts: 'Indeed, it is only the connection of logic with esthetics through ethics which causes it to be a normative science, at all' (L75, D, 19). Peirce, in his Second Lowell lectures (1903, No. 1, 1.614) expands in some detail on how we can think of this aesthetic ultimate good: 'The explanation of the circumstance that the only result that is satisfied with itself is a quality of feeling is that reason always looks forward to an endless future and expects endlessly to improve its results.' Only Reason is 'admirable in itself,' for no purpose (as in logic and ethic). Reason is seen no longer as a human faculty (as in Kant), but as developing and unfolding. This is all a necessary science of the 'admirable' can, and must, provide.

Not only is forward-looking reason in absolute need of an aim 'satisfied with itself,' but so also is any action. Deliberate, self-controlled conduct has not its opposite alone, its resistance in the real – but this is almost a truism. Under control of reason, it must go on to an endless future. However, only if acting has a What? or a 'something,' as it were, as its third component, can we understand conduct as being immediately satisfied with itself. Action is satisfied (the doubt/belief cycle completed) not in obtaining aims, not in attaining the real, but in containing whatness, a quality.

How can the guidance of such a conduct of behaviour be understood? Would it not drive such conduct to further aims, again and again? If any action is self-controlled conduct, aesthetic conduct can become only a problem of liking and pleasure (although beauty is only the product of aesthetic). However, pleasure *per se* as a result is not part of its own cause, which must be an 'immediate presence': 'What is the one quality that is, in its immediate presence, καλὸς?' (2.199). Pleasure is directed toward a second, and is in itself no more than pure attraction and repulsion; whereas the καλὸς is immediate and one (*Selbst-Zweck* – in its self-contradiction – might be the oxymoron rendering the idea).

Aesthetic experience, not as an actual event but – regardless of events – as a mere possibility, is such that it qualifies as one and immediate. Now it seems that these qualifications express the same idea with different nuances. Oneness (i.e., not a dyadic opposition) is the same as immediate or present because it would otherwise be distinguishable from a non-present. Furthermore, this is only possible when existential considerations play no role; this is a negative way of stating that what is possible suffices. Note here that 'possible' is much more than 'potential.' It is the vastest Real of all, omni-comprehensive to such a degree that the thought of an impossible cannot be thought of (because it is a possible thought).

In a certain way, aesthetic is always (a) Same without (an) Other. It is Reason in temporal form, but not as the perfect cognition of the ultimate opinion – that ideality of cognition having integrated all cognitive objects (v. *supra*). Upstream of this form of being temporal, the Same is 'experienced eternity' (which can only be expressed in such an oxymoron). It is an empty eternity of reason with itself, reason feeling itself as its own admirable quality of possibility, but without knowing itself.

It must be admitted that this account of aesthetic feeling is essentially different from psychological accounts of subjectivity and interiority. It still is the feeling of a pragmatic norm of self-controlled cognitive behaviour. Therefore, it remains subject to critique and is not an aprioristic treatment of a mental faculty. This mode of explanation must abstain from certain customary aesthetic discourses. Some might perceive in the Pragmaticist account of feeling a glaring absence of inner feeling, of feeling containing one's self or another deeper form of one's identity. Content is indeed absent from this formal, non-substantial Pragmaticist aesthetic. However, this is largely compensated for by the comprehension of the aesthetic feeling in a completely different relational form, the Sign. That aesthetic feeling is a Same does not imply that it is hermetically closed and is, therefore, incapable of becoming a Sign. However, aesthetic Signs must be very special and can never function in the same manner as run-of-the-mill Signs. The founding idea of the Sign, however, fully present with the aesthetic feeling, is a triadic relation of three essentially different correlates. Only in this relation is aesthetic feeling self-controlled and communicable. Aesthetic thus becomes an Interpreted external quality, although in such a manner that it need not subsist as a general or even a singular fact. Aesthetic feeling as enunciation involves meeting unusually high demands for the Sign quality.

6.4.4 The Pragmatic of the Aesthetic Sign

The general aspect of the aesthetic feeling is the aesthetic Sign, through which feeling must become conduct and communication. Before we turn to the specifics of cinema as a practice and aesthetic sign process, the aesthetic Sign's general nature needs to be clarified. The aesthetic conduct itself cannot be more than a Sign of presence, which is a quality of feeling. In view of the Categorical determination of any being, aesthetic Signs essentially are below ampliative reasoning and must convey no more than a quality of feeling. The ideally pure presence of feeling reduces maximally the power of cognition, which advances only when it can bind time and differences into a general idea above time. Aesthetic instead reduces the differences (even of pleasure and repulsion) into a pure presence beneath time. Later on we will see this aesthetic process with crystalline clarity by focusing almost exclusively on time in *Ordet*. The feeling produced by this Sign before it produces pleasure or pain is similar to the halting of time, to *stasis* – at least in its aesthetic essence. Kitsch, in contrast, searches pleasure; it 'knows' the pleasure it searches and thus consists in repetitiveness. Presence, therefore, calls for Signs that are not really repeatable, and aesthetic feeling or experience becomes fortuitous and felicitous.

Having established this, our primary interest is in investigating a particular Sign process. Signs are co-determined by all three universal

Categories. It is impossible to state that the aesthetic experience is pure Firstness, even though Peirce assigned the name Presence to the first Category and even used an artist's experience to describe it. This is merely a necessity of the language of description, not of the Categories themselves. In describing them we lose all differences from the procedure of abstraction ('prescission') to which they owe their phanero-scopical distinctness. In its concreteness as Categorically determined Sign, the Aesthetic Sign of Presence also shares the habit taking of Signs at large. As noted earlier, habits are principles of conduct. Signs, then, are more than the result of such principles; they are also their formation. So it is in the principled, self-controlled formation of conduct that we must investigate the action of the aesthetic Sign of pure presence. The result of the aesthetic Sign is pleasure, but this does not explain its action, which is logically First.

Aesthetic Signs do only one thing as a sensation: they attract or repel. Since Sign processes do not appear from nowhere, the feeling is usually attributed to the object, as its attributed quality. It could just as easily be attributed to the aesthetic subject – la belle âme, as it were. In this case the subject enjoys itself as enjoying. That said, by its very nature, the aesthetic feeling possesses no ego or non-ego considerations. It operates in the same manner as every Sign, that is, by association. In order to acquire the status of Sign, it is not enough that is be a singular psychic event, something that just happens to cross one's mind. The aesthetic moment has often been described as a flash, it does not follow that it is any arbitrary mental event. It already stands out, it is no longer an arbitrary particle in a psychic stream. This means that no Sign – including the Aesthetic Sign – can be a totally vague Sign. It must be at least minimally determined, and determinations take place when singularities are unified to form some general idea.[90] Now, the Aesthetic Sign cannot demand much help from a general idea. Generality here is extremely weak but cannot be totally absent. For example, when listening to a piece of music, we hear melodies, harmonies, and so on. This is more than just a perception of tones in a sequence. Although the general idea is not even a concept, a unification has taken place. Unified, it becomes a quality of feeling by forming a habit – in this case, of listening as a meaningful action. Conversely, there is no realm of being, marked 'aesthetic,' that is exempt from Categorical determination, as if it were 'pure sensation.'

A weak general idea does not make habit formation in the aesthetic field easy. For instance, compare a strong Sign with a weak Sign from the perspective of a general idea. Although a strong concept such as narrative teleology (Propp's narrative function 'rescue of the king's daughter') forms an almost inescapable habit of interpretation, there is no equivalent in a melody. We can sometimes encounter both habits in the same object (as we shall later see in *Ordet*). Moreover, both Sign processes produce time, which is even the same time of the story of the manifestation of the Word. In these circumstances it is quite easy in analysis to overlook the weaker Sign, which here is merely of the nature of melodies.

In film, there are a number of weak general ideas (always within the sole realm of time), such as the rhythm of montage, camera movement, and music. The quandary of film criticism is usually that it observes and labels these features but then cannot grasp their independent meaning. It is not satisfactory to channel them into tributaries of 'The Meaning,' which is usually the narrative goal. To avoid this finally becoming meaningless, we could try to collect those features as residuals of meaning. This is the basic idea behind 'style' as the Formalists abstracted it from the *fabula* and the *sujet*. However, there is still no meaning in style itself. When we restrict meaning to representation in the broadest sense (perhaps because an adequately subtle sign theory is lacking), such an understanding of style is unavoidable and is possibly the best solution.

However, meaning conceived as 'habit taking' is more subtle and can account for qualities of feeling. Aesthetic meaning thus would consist of a certain kind of habit taking – with the resultant pleasure or pain. Now, where is the habit in a feeling – that is, without the strong guidance of a general idea?

In principle, in any action there is always a distinction to be made between a resolution (which is a mental formula or image of a plan), and its execution. This is plain enough when we apply it to deliberate conduct of actions attaining their conscious goals. In the case of Aesthetic conduct, however, it is impossible to say that we know what we want to do in given circumstances (the formula). On the contrary, there is no specific goal at all. The habit here seems to consist of the non-specification of action goals. The artist's conduct (in Peirce's example) is a non-specific awareness of the shades of colour in a snowfield, not the practical use of it to determine whether it is safe to cross the snowfield without falling into the crevasses of a glacier. The maximum non-specification of a goal is admirability in itself,[91] which is not, of course, to be interpreted as the summit of pleasure. For pleasure is not simply secondary to the feeling itself; in Peirce's understanding, it need not even be conscious immediately.

Under general Pragmaticistic assumptions about conduct (including the pragmatic constitution of every being) there is a goal (a general idea) for feelings, since – and to the degree that – there is meaning. This gives aesthetic its necessary position in the architectonic of Pragmaticism, where the concern is with the goal as such, before it becomes determined. Furthermore, as a consequence of the ordinal nature of Categories, this goal subsists in every cognitive conduct. This feeling as a necessary part of thinking is a consequence of Pragmaticism. Aesthetic, then, is not merely a passing stage of logical argumentation, an embryonic stage before it finally becomes determined. Just as argumentation requires 'outward reality,' it requires a feeling of direction.

From the vantage point of argumentation, this feeling is the logical Possibility of thought (which is certainly much vaster than actual thought and also right thought). As a concept it is a Vague concept. However, from a metaphysical vantage point the feeling of direction is no less than the confidence embodied in every concrete thought that in the long run the spreading process of thought will lead to an ultimate final and adequate opinion of the real. By its very nature it is precisely no guarantee, because that would fall within the unique competence of logical argumentation. As long as the world is not (yet) 'God's grand argument[92]' (which would mean interpreting Peirce as an Objective Idealist), it can be, or can subsist as, only a feeling of direction and of Possibility. The metaphysical nature of Firstness (cf. Peirce 1997: 195–201) is Quality as a possibility; its concrete form is an Aesthetic Sign, a feeling.

The direction of thought must therefore already be in the feeling. Feelings must have an inbuilt tendency to connect with one another in such a way that this connection eventually gives rise to a unifying thought. There are many ways in which feelings could possibly connect. However, the origin of Aesthetic is not this openness; it is that feelings can and do connect. Through such connections the next feelings become similar to the previous ones. This is not the same as experiencing two different feelings, which are then compared in their distinctness and thereby united within a general conception. Aesthetic experience, if it cannot consist in an individual singular feeling, nevertheless is not a generalization that is produced by a Symbol. The similarity between feelings is certainly a habit, but only of feelings that are habitually excited. This can be thought of as a sort of memory in feelings, as a being disposed to readily come to mind, without an intervening thought to excite them. Only in its final result is the Aesthetic habit the foundation of a cognitive habit, which might eventually be expressed as an abstract concept. The Aesthetic experience itself, before it gives rise to pleasure and pain,[93] is an association of feelings and is no longer perceived as a single arbitrary feeling. Its pre-thought-induced pleasure is grounded in this mental association alone. Any art strategy (which is the technical knowledge around the Aesthetic experience) must possess feelings that assimilate themselves and (negatively) hinder thoughts of mediating such feelings.

There may be some doubts regarding this Aesthetic association. This aesthetic generalization is no less certain[94] than cognitive generaliza- tion or the generalization of the physical world (which Peirce dis- cussed as the problem of evolution). Only apparently does the process of thought 'automatically' generalize. In fact, the tendency of thoughts to spread to ever more general conclusions has no guarantee in itself. In spite of what might appear to be Peirce's 'metaphysical thinking,' this exactly is not the kind of ontological hedge that gives certainty to cognition in being. Peircean fallibilism is thorough. This means that no generalization of thought is by and in itself certain; it is no more than a habit of conduct. What such a thorough temporalization entails for cognition and its metaphysical grounding was discussed earlier.

For aesthetic generalizations – which because their lack of difference are not yet temporal – no 'automatism' recommends itself. Only as a fallacy does the universe of facts seem 'naturally' as compact and gen- eral as we could wish. That there is one causal chain in the physical uni- verse seems beyond doubt, yet there is still no conclusive proof of this. Therefore, Aesthetic generalization should not be considered a minor certainty compared to the 'really certain' modes of factual and concep- tual cognition. All modes of cognition are no more than habits. They may be somewhat entrenched and reliable but none of them is pro- tected from correction – all are simply a self-controlled conduct of present and future behaviour, a mental 'formula,' no more.

The Sign is the habit. The different kinds of Signhood are the different ways of 'taking habit' or cognizing the Real. If Aesthetic is an architec- tonic requirement from any perspective – Pragmaticistic, metaphysical, the classification of sciences (witness Peirce's 1891–3 Monist articles [6.7- 6.317]) – it is fully developed in Semiotic and Speculative Grammar. The logical understanding of aesthetic as a class of Signs – of feelings) if seen psychologically – is extremely helpful for investigating the special aes- thetic of cinema. This is, however, already an art practice,[95] which needs to be established through an enunciation. How art is practised is not irrelevant, but it follows another type of norm, one that cannot be confused with the normative science of Aesthetic. As a consciously reflected practice, it would fall into thought operation. The result of this practice is thus double. On the one hand there is the conscious operation or technique of producing a certain Sign; on the other, there is an art object, which is the appearance of characteristics of an object which is in reality the non-determined goal of a certain conduct (cf. *supra*). It follows that the technique of producing an Aesthetic Sign is not in itself a Sign of this type. We are justified in calling this technique again enunciation, because it enables us to differentiate the enunciated aesthetic as art.

Art is a determinate technique of enunciating the aesthetic, as object, as conduct, or as experience. Aesthetic itself is logically the possibility of a type of thought and pragmatically a conduct guided by a certain kind of goodness, distinctively different from truth and general cognition. The width of Aesthetic inversely relates to cognitive width (and thus cognitive narrowness). Aesthetic cognition is only cognition in the broadest possible meaning of cognition. Conversely, however, we must say: 'Vague Aesthetic – maximally controlled Generality.' In this cognitive mode, Aesthetic has no discriminatory power.[96] This is the least that a 'normal' intentional act of cognition requires. If Aesthetic is nevertheless cognitive, then it is so only as a 'shifting of attention,' which logically is a process of mere pre[s]cision. Thus it is extremely broad in scope and excludes nothing from standing before one's mind. This 'general admittance' offsets the existential Sheriff's desire to produce a factual basis for any cognition. Such an instance's duty is to reject what does not even pretend to be a fact.

A factually existing work of art is not a fact inasmuch as it is taken aesthetically. Conversely, everything possible (it need not even exist!) can be (aesthetically cognized as) art.

6.4.5 Aesthetic Enunciation or the Semiotic Practice of Cinema Art

As a specific act of aesthetic cognition, art – that is, concrete art – must be defined as a production technique achieved by a pragmatic act of enunciation. Thus, aesthetic Semiosis seems to contradict Aesthetic as logic. This contradiction does not arise from the Semiotic or Pragmaticist approach; rather, it appears in various forms in various aesthetic theories. Different ways of addressing this problem include, for instance, the dislevelment in hermeneutic aesthetic between an image and its essential origin (*Bild* and *Urbild* in Gadamer; v. *supra*). This difficulty can also be dodged by simply sticking to art theory in a narrow sense – by accepting art as a 'natural' given without reflecting on the conditions of its possibility. An art theory that is immune to these doubts simply presupposes the possibility of Aesthetic. The circumstances of production are then a matter of simple common sense, with no principles involved. All of this being noted, where does art come from? Defining the 'essence' of art through certain material or subjective characteristics – which at the very least must inhere to the art object – does not explain the reasons for these characteristics and not other ones (cf. the vicious circularity in Analytic aesthetic, v. *supra*). The problem simply rears its ugly head again in another form. It is fought but not vanquished as 'media essentialism,'[97] or it is passed on to positive sciences in the name of 'naturalism' and so on. But it is not solved.

A Semiotic perspective on art can never disregard the nature of the Sign (the question of Iconic Signs will be taken up shortly), but neither can it skip the difficulty inherent in producing art. Icons do not appear out of nowhere; they have to originate from a rule-based, rational conduct. Aesthetic, as a type of cognition that is confined to associating feelings, would thus appear to be incommunicable. Art – more precisely, the object of Aesthetic enunciation – therefore, is strictly speaking a *contradictio in adjecto*. This becomes a practical problem as a strategy of artistic practices: an object of art cannot be produced unless particular conditions in the aesthetic enunciation itself are met. In theory, communicating can obstruct the aesthetic experience unless it is done in a non-destructive way. For instance, the auratic atmosphere of a performance of one of Wagner' operas – which are sometimes compared to and celebrated as religious experiences (one of these is very well rendered in Syberberg's *Parsifal*) – is not a contingent or even undesirable pragmatic effect. It is vital for the production of the art effect itself. For certain objects of art, it would be lethal not to produce them (i.e., enunciate them) in the proper way.

So it must be expected that this precarious condition of production has as much an effect on aesthetic meaning, as narrative meaning depended on certain conditions for its temporality. Furthermore, enunciation is always a particularly cinematic enunciation. Again, as in narration, the nature of the first trichotomy, the representamen, conditions meaning.

Cinematic art consists precisely in the production of the Aesthetic sign under the conditions of cinema and as a problem of enunciation. This is necessarily a delicate matter, for enunciation in itself is the communication of a General idea, whereas the Aesthetic object in itself is a conduct with scant determination. Aesthetic signs, to succeed, cannot remain a blend of heterogeneous parts. How they can succeed, if they can succeed at all, becomes a practical question relative to this sign process.

The aesthetic enunciation, which I will argue here is a Semiotic process, will show five important and perhaps unexpected results: (1) Aesthetic enunciation is negative; it consists in destroying cognition of a higher logical order. (2) Aesthetic enunciation can thus be conceived as a normal Sign Degeneration (i.e., a relation of lower adicity in certain respects; v. *supra*); this process is completely described in the Classification of Signs and can be pegged to the First Correlate's change into an Iconic Sign relation. (3) Aesthetic enunciation is a 'secondary' enunciation, as the pragmatic consequence of this particular Sign degeneration. (4) As enunciated meaning, aesthetic is defined Categorially by a lower ordinality in the Iconic Sign relation. As enunciated meaning, aesthetic is also (5) felt as reduction of meaning. We will now have to develop each of these thesis individually.

In cinema, aesthetic enunciation must always deal with time. This is a constant, but it is not yet a predilection for a certain kind of meaning. In the fullest Semiotic sense of the term, time is meaning. Therefore it involves also the fact of events, physical change, as has already been discussed in the context of narrative time (v. *supra*). Cinema is intrinsically temporal in nature, but this does not mean that this logic focus cinema *in se* to become abstract knowledge – of a teleological purpose, for instance. However, the interesting point for aesthetic cognition is that cinema can 'use' such knowledge. This is, then, exactly sign degeneration, which does not invalidate or abolish the 'used' (i.e., interpreted) Sign, but switches the logic of the Interpretant by integrating the used Sign as a different First Correlate into a new Sign relation (interpretation).

The knowledge of, say, evolution, or life, will then become the Third of a sign relation of a sequence of images (of bubbles, algae, sun). However, this must remain quite uncertain. In our analysis of Godard's sequences in *Je vous salue, Marie*, we found that in the absence of linguistic signs – which he carefully avoid in these places – these images are extremely loosely connected by a vague general idea. This might be 'life' as well as any other related concept – 'evolution,' 'growth,' 'nature' literally as 'to-be-born.' It happens, though, that in a different part of this film the topic has been the evolution of life. This can be used to give more precision to these vague signs. If it is not used, however, then we must take a sequence such as this as Aesthetic sign. This exemplifies the precariousness of aesthetic enunciation in cinema.

When we approach cinematic enunciation from the practical side, the chief problem we encounter is the almost automatic reduction of temporal qualities into types of temporality. This tendency cognizes[98] and reduces the manifold (i.e., of subsequent states) into teleological knowledge. If there is a shortage of something that prevents cinema *in se* from a cognition of generality, it is certainly not time, but the abstract Representamen – that is, the Legisign. If this comes from elsewhere (as we have seen for narration), the teleological cognition is no problem – it can be grafted onto cinema through language, for instance. Even if this cognitive potential is a 'borrowed' one, it is still pervasive not only in everyday cognition, but also in cinema. For aesthetic it is imperative to escape by means of enunciation from this logical snare.

Cinema has two options if it wants to be aesthetic: it can prevent the accession of outside abstract ideas with their Representamina, or it can opt for 'de-existentializing.'[99] In the latter case, what is and was a fact must lose all the coordinates of its localization and become 'u-topian.' Non-factual facts in this way lose all truth value and become images, possible facts – that is, imagination. For cinematic images it is not always easy to sever the link with factualness. The main thing here is that the image is of a fact, or a probable fact. With regard to the former, credible images as a requirement are not restricted to documentary film. Even narration in film could not function without the 'narrative contract' that is embodied in the imagery. An existential relation between the image and its object is, however, not intrinsic, it is not built into the sign process of cinematographic images. The previous example from Godard proves that it is possible to cut the existential link.

Now aesthetic enunciation has these two negative tasks. By default, then, there is only one possibility left for sign relation – one guided by Aesthetic conduct. This is the lowest degree of meaning, but it is still meaning, because fortunately it is also the most basic, the one that cannot be avoided even in the most general modes of cognition: 'The only way of directly communicating an idea is by means of an icon; and every indirect method of communicating an idea must depend for its establishment upon the use of an icon' (2.278, 1899 [?]). In other words, when a film is prevented from becoming narrative and documentary, it becomes an Aesthetic film – although not necessarily art cinema, where it is strictly the product of an aesthetic enunciation. As always, enunciation is not itself aesthetic conduct, an Iconic sign relation.

This Semiotic solution can be understood as in clear contrast with cinema aesthetics, or film poetics, which derive the aesthetic side of their theory also from a destructiveness of some kind. 'Defamiliariza-tion' or estrangement, as used in Neoformalism, is negative – a nega-tion of the positivity of 'normal,' prosaic perception. We can confirm this only from a Sign relational perspective. However, there is still meaning in the resulting interpretation, and not 'no-adding-up.' This meaning can be described precisely and formally, as our discussion of the cognitive nature of the Iconic Sign (v. *infra*) will indicate. The aes-thetic question, then, can be placed in the context either of narration or of 'documentarism' (because aesthetic can also transform the real world, of course). The cognitive result for aesthetic must be the same.

Aesthetic enunciation, then, is a conduct within the context of narra-tive enunciation, which in Aristotle's classical definition of poetic pro-duces the probable and possible (cf. *supra*). The *Poetic*'s range, however, was limited to pragmatic mimetic arts, with tragedy as the quintessen-tial art form. With a Pragmaticistic understanding of Aesthetic as con-duct, then, we should find it possible to imagine narrative conduct from a perspective whereby we see it as an extreme form such that its teleological nature dissolves into something else. This extreme is at the outer limit of narration – an oxymoronic 'purposeless narrative,' as it were – where narrative conduct melts into conduct-before-conduct, or value. This aestheticizing of narration extends the range of *Poetic* into realms that Aristotle did not foresee (albeit not into subjectivism). When aesthetic becomes enunciation, one conduct produces another, and (Semiotic adds) both conducts are embodied as Signs. What aes-thetic does to narration can be expressed in terms of the latter's defini-tion: the probable ($\varepsilon i\kappa \acute{o}\varsigma$) always refers to a type;[100] the possible ($\delta v v a \tau \acute{o} v$) refers in the poetic to mores ($\mathring{\eta}\theta\eta$) of a given society, an *imag-inaire social*, but in aesthetic it extends further, to the imaginable. Then it has become an Iconic Sign.

Through the formal conception as Sign relations, it should be easier now to unravel the process of enunciation. In fact, when two Signs relate to each other, we can say that one Sign interprets the second. These Signs need not be of the same class, of course. If the first Sign is a Symbol, the second can be an Icon by way of Sign degeneration, or specification (v. *supra*). The very peculiar case of Aesthetic enunciation is thus a second Sign specifying the first. As 'next thought,' aesthetic experience reduces its 'previous thought' enunciation, and effectively deprives it of its two characters of dyadic, factual relation and triadic relation to a General concept.

Let us return to the example from Godard. These water lily images may indeed be framed by a narration and also by a theoretical discourse on the evolution laws of probability calculus; however, this frame is completely re-Interpreted Aesthetically by the Iconic Signs of images. Such an Interpretation certainly does not advance science, nor does it contribute to a truthful comprehension of life. It may not even be an advance toward the Final opinion of the 'community of researchers.' It does, however, regress into a wider space of mere Possibility.

Narrative enunciation must satisfy its own needs for temporal configuration within the uncoupled narrative universe. The task for Aesthetic is easier. It is not so much the active production of a certain logical constraint (such as teleology); rather, it entails a negative, non-production of constraints and a positive permission for all kinds of thought under the guidance of sheer instinct. If there is an intellectual instinct – and Peirce himself was convinced of this in the form of economy of research – then it is also Aesthetic. It may also be accompanied by pleasure and pain. But it will always depend on a Symbol, the storehouse of previous knowledge, which it reduces to an Icon of its present instinct of cognitive pursuit. This openness is shared by the aesthetic experience.

In cognition, every advance is anyway through abduction.[101] As such it relies on Iconicity on its way of 'mellonization' (8.284, 1904). It falls also under the economy of research that in hindsight instinctive insights must be justified in a full Symbolic Sign relation. For most Aesthetic experiences of art, this Symbolic Interpretation will remain spurious or even futile. Here Aesthetic enunciation remains instinct, and an Iconic Sign.

The fragile particularities of the aesthetic sign relation are the ultimate crucial point of a Semiotic Aesthetic. As was explained earlier, conceiving the aesthetic enunciation as Sign condenses all of the advantages of a non-transcendental, non-subjective, non-formalist aesthetic. Enunciation usually means any dependency of meaning modelled linguistically after dependent phrases. Our investigation of narrative and rhetorical enunciation has shown enough reasons to enlarge and generalize this model considerably into a general Sign dependency (i.e., Interpretation). This is even more relevant to aesthetic enunciation, which is not even conceivable in a phrase dependency model (*dictum,* with its unobliterable traces in mode, tense, and person). Sign Interpretation, however, is comprehensive enough to accommodate aesthetic experiences within a framework of non-aesthetic text.

Enunciation theories remain pegged at two levels; in contrast, Interpretation is unified, as one new Sign Interpreting previous Signs. This final Aesthetic result of a sign process bears no 'traces' ('marks of enunciation') of the previous Signs; it Interprets their Object as its Object. This new sign Relation comprises the entire new determination of thought.

6.4.6   The Aesthetic Icon and the 'Iconism' of Cinema

Aesthetic as conduct is radically different from media aesthetic, which explores certain qualities of the signifying material in cinema. Any treatment of the aesthetic question either in terms of subjective qualities (v. Analytical aesthetics), or in terms of objective qualities that are manipulated with an artistic intention, is not a logical perspective (in spite of contrary cognitivist claims). The 'objective' option has formed, after Arnheim, a film theoretical tradition concerned with 'iconism' of cinema as explanation of media-inherent expression possibilities. This iconism is, however, quite different from Iconic Signs. As a kind of aesthetic iconism, it is not identical with the iconism of cinematic representation (which was discussed in the context of the 'cinematic object' in §2), even though sometimes the two problems are blended into one supposedly common construct.[102] For the purpose of our discussion, it is better to keep the problem of aesthetic material conditions separate from problems of cinematic relations to factual reality.

'Media specificity' in Semiotic becomes an inquiry into the logical nature of the First Correlate in the Sign relation. This has no relation to supposed material 'essences' of some thing, because the 'thing' in question is not a thing at all, but always and only a Correlate. Its essence consists, if at all, in a relational rather than a material form. Once the aesthetic conduct or Feeling is functional in sign relations, aesthetic becomes a question of sign properties in relation to determinate media, inasmuch as meaning (Third Correlate) is determined through them. Needless to say, the first Correlate of a sign is different in each medium. Language as the standard medium may be the most important Sign relation for cognition, and in lyricism it has its own Iconicity, but it not the measure of sign property as such. For cinema, the property question rises independently from its own triad Sign relation, within which its own First Correlate has its own function.

What, then, is the point of cinematic aesthetic Iconicity? For every medium there must be a different answer where something begins to be taken not as itself, but as a sign or Representamen (of something else). The 'something else' is not automatically a physical thing,[103] and the Representamen is not a physical characteristic of something-taken-for-sign. The Representamen is something 'mental' or logical that can transform anything into sign (and not 'expression material' in the Hjelmslev–Eco sense of the term). Representamina (v. *supra*) can be constituted by a rule, a reference, or a single quality. In the class of rules (Legisigns), the prime example is linguistic. Sinsigns function in the presence of their other and are exemplified by deictic contexts. Qualisigns, in contrast, embody anything that affords distinct qualities. This is the minimal condition for signhood – that one quality can be taken to stand in relation to the same quality in something greater than the sign. For example, a piercing sound can stand in relation to the whistle of a steam engine; however, it is now only relevant to have a piercing sound and not the mechanics of the steam conduits and the colour of the brass. Everything can be a Representamen of at least the Qualisign sort, then, provided there is a relation to something else. This is both dependent on and independent of media. As logical process, the (logically) same can be embodied in anything, provided it allows for differences (of at least the distinction type; cf. p. 64)[104].

In most theoretical contexts, the very concept of an Icon is not self-evident. It offers no answer at all to the prevailing sign problem of the reference and representation of its other. For compelling relational reasons, Peirce split up the sign into more than the usual two parts of sign and that for which it stands (*vulgo:* 'signified'). So we must first relinquish this 'stand-in' idea of a sign so that we can grasp the concept of Iconicity. Although Peirce's foundation concept is as old as his work that led to the New List, his nomenclature of relationality – including sign relations – underwent some change. He moved from an understanding of categorical relationality to signs as a necessity of any thought, but signs are not another name for categories. It is not phenomenality but the categorical derivation that yields Iconicity and justifies it completely: there must be Icons.

The function of Icons is to be the Form of thought, and this can never be substituted. This holds true for all three sorts of Icons. Conversely, a thought is not its form, as is clearly stated in the Syllabus: 'But most strictly speaking, even an idea, except in the sense of a possibility, or Firstness, cannot be an Icon' (2.276). One of the *loci classici* in matters of

Iconicity, the Syllabus, specifies three sorts of Iconic Firsts or Forms of thought: image, diagrams, and metaphors. It is in the logical context of diagrams as irreplaceable forms of thought that Peirce illustrates the need for Icons: 'Nor are Symbols and Indices together generally enough. The arrangement of the words in the sentence, for instance, must serve as Icons, in order that the sentence may be understood. The chief need for the Icons is in order to show the Forms of the synthesis of the elements of thought' (4.544, *Monist*, October 1906).

A pure Icon is therefore a pure Form of reasoning. However, it is clear that this can only be found through a 'precision of speech' (4.544), a logical abstractive operation.[105] This is why Peirce calls this trichotomy 'hypoicons' in the Syllabus (2.276), which are otherwise full signs representing their objects iconically 'by their similarity.' If the sentence arrangement already counts as an Icon – which is quite evident in the case of metaphors – what is the lowest limit of Iconicity? Is removing the purpose of Iconic arrangements admissible, or is it feasible for a thought not to compare two elements? 'Pure Forms' are still forms of thought (and a thought can never be reduced to a monadic relation), but it is true that the Aesthetic thought needs its proper form, its Icon. Of all possible Icons (hypoicons) not all are eligible. However, the specifically Aesthetic in this is not exclusivity – what is *not* eligible, then – but 'inclusivity': except for Legisigns and Sinsigns, all other Icons are eligible. Aesthetic specificity means that almost nothing is excluded, and what it effectively excludes it has its own means of recuperating. A rule is less than a possibility. If the Form of thought in its normal usage is ordered by rules or by context, it becomes eligible for Aesthetic thought once it is used against its purpose for aesthetic purposes. Linguistic Representamina thus become onomatopoetic. In this way they use Qualities again and no longer use rules.

Icons are the forms of thoughts, and therefore not a Formalist reduction. If we take a step backward to try to get the bigger picture of aesthetic, we must rid aesthetic theory first of a certain illusion about thinking, certain remnants of Cartesianism. Thinking does not function in the way that some abstract representations of it imagine. Thus it is neither 'I have a thought' (in the same way as I have a body or as I have a physical object in my possession); nor is it 'I am my thought,' which is the Cartesian *cogito*. Applied to aesthetic thought, 'I experience an aesthetic feeling' fails to render the quality of that feeling. On the other hand, 'I am emphatically my aesthetic feeling' or 'In feeling aesthetically I am my essential I' amounts merely to a hypostasis of a

Transcendental Subject. Instead, the realist comprehension of thinking recognizes first that there is a form of (my) thought, second that there is an occasion for my thought, and third that there is a result of my thought as interpretation of the occasion by means of the form. These three elements taken together can realistically render this impression 'I have a thought' (i.e., of something).

The interesting point in aesthetic is not the result (interpretation), nor is it the occasion; rather, it is the form of thought. The Categorical nature of the aesthetic form of thought has an important practical consequence for its theoretical description: only by naming the result can we describe the form in an intuitive way. As a mere indicator of the form, this one result is placeholder for the many other equally possible results. The aesthetic form of thought, then, seen from the perspective of the resulting thought, is anything that produces a 'feeling-of ...' Seen in itself, it is (no more than) a quality. However, this says nothing because it says everything: all there is (possibly, really, necessarily), 'is-something.' The immensity of this information, which thus becomes useless, is only meaningful through an enunciation. The unlimited of the aesthetic form of thought is subject to a purpose – the purpose of enunciation. Through this, quality – possibly any quality – receives an aesthetic purpose of pragmatic value. This description is feasible only in the context of a theory of thought as such (i.e., of a Pragmaticist theory of cognitive conduct). It cannot be used as a prescription (this value does not differentiate; v. *supra*), not even for a theory of good or bad art. But it can describe art as a process of thought, and do so without sacrificing the crucial role of the form of thought.

For Aesthetic (enunciation) purposes, Iconic signs (forms of thought) have unique chances. They are indeed special: they are especially apt for discovery, but they cannot assert anything, nor can they cognize any General. 'Something-is' not because 'it' exists (contrary to positivist assumptions), but because it is a sign relation. It becomes sign because the auroral moment is the feeling of a form, giving form to a thought – for instance, by discovering two elements as similar. Similarity is not in the elements themselves; it is already directionally beyond them. It determines a third, which thereby comes into being albeit in a fragile state of feeling. As such it can remain a vague, which has being, but is not fully determined (v. *supra*). In experience and in cognition (in terms of the type described above), such signs are truly aesthetic. The Aesthetic form is Iconic Quality, the discovery of valid purpose, the validity Aesthetic.

What, then, is special about cinema? When we use cinema to give Form to thought (analogous to the arrangement of a sentence), does this arrange thought in a special way? Remaining aware of the cumulating, perhaps even syncretistic usage of film, it is still worthwhile to concern ourselves only with its unique features. If they take the lead in the Interpretation, these features can confine also those Representamina which they comprise. No part, then, will be of greater complexity than its dominant Representamen (provided the parts form a whole).

The reason for this is, again, the Interpretation model of sign processes. If Signs interpret Signs, 'dominance' technically means that the last Interpretation is, for instance, Aesthetic. It is perhaps also General, but not with a dominance of moving images. If moving images are taken over by some other Interpretant – for instance, narrative probability originating in social practice – then narrative teleology becomes the dominant in the syncretism of Signs. With the possibility of Sign relations to degenerate, the presence of genuine Generality need not really be decisive for Aesthetic Signs. 'Cinematic specificity' thus raises a question not of principle but of usage, of enunciation customs. Cinema is capable of representing a General Idea, and such representation is an exception, but there is no contradiction in stating at the same time that as an Aesthetic Sign cinema rescinds that capacity. Cinema of this kind can be called 'dys-narrative' (i.e., it leaves spectators guessing as to the tentative General of an author's implied communicative intention).

In serving the purpose of discovery, an Aesthetic film uses moving images as polyvalent. Such moving images come with or without legend, as it were. If they come without, everything is possible: Iconic forms of thought that have Images or Qualities of feeling in the First Correlate are also trans-Formed at any moment. They merely need to be similar to another element in thought, which may or may not be in the cinematic text. Not only is this a minimum requirement for a sign relation, it can also remain at that stage of a Feeling, or form all sorts of Symbols below the level of a narrative or an auctorial intention. Furthermore, even linguistic parts in cinema can be 'reiconized,' although cinema is not predominantly linguistic. For instance, language, which is so intrinsically Thirdness, must 'degenerate' in order to become lyric. Even though Symbols constitute communicability, in their aesthetic use they can be transmitted as Symbols *in statu fieri*.

Aesthetic conduct through enunciation follows a purpose of discovery in Iconic Signs.[106] Iconicity is so simple and so all-pervasive that such Sign relations acquire their interest only from an antecedent purpose, in the context of a value-guided conduct. Aesthetic discovery in art must open the path to the merely possible. This is not an intuition; rather, it must form a habit. The process of associating ideas into habits can also be described from a psychological perspective, as Peirce did in his 1898 Cambridge conferences (7.498). The starting point for associating Aesthetic feelings cannot be contiguity with an Object, because that would constrain the free association to factual presence. Nor can Aesthetic feeling be in associations of habit (this would require a rule). Aesthetic feelings form habits only through resemblances among feelings. This corresponds to the idea of an Iconic Sign (which is its logical expression) and to the conduct guided by the Aesthetic norm (which is its pragmatic expression).

In a continuation of the psychological approach to Aesthetic feelings, Kevelson (1993: 293 and passim[107]) describes this association of resemblance. As an initial stage, a feeling of rising curiosity, she attributes the function of emergence ('Fragment' as metaphor). Once something is experienced as fragmented, the 'rest' toward wholeness is in the mind as a feeling of telos. Here the model can be Peirce's account of 'inventing a type-writer' in a free association of ideas, which in a 'flash' resemble one another with respect to the invention problem (7.498). It is within the competence of the Second of aesthetic semiosis to focus on something on which to inquire (metaphor 'Focus'). The Third must consist of a General of aesthetic perception (metaphor [!] 'Form'), which is already a little more abstract, but is still resemblance and not a mental rule.[108] Peirce called this resemblance the 'mental formula' (v. *supra*).

From the logical perspective of Sign processes, this psychology of feeling association is chiefly a question of the Third Correlate. What is the 'form' of resemblance? Certainly, this is not something in the feelings themselves; rather, it is in the mind that brings such feelings together. There would thus be an endless range of possibilities for how two different feelings could resemble each other. The mind must therefore choose the quality, but in such a way that a rule does not guide the choice. Resemblance is much vaguer than knowing – it is a knowing-not-why, as it were.

Now the faintest rulelike general in a Sign is called Rhema, or Term. This resembling quality among feelings can be addressed – it already means something in, for instance, a flash of insight. Looking at the First Correlate – the 'sign in itself' or Representamen – such a flash cannot be a Legisign, since this type of Sign renders something in respect to that it *ought* to be as it is. This is impossible with mere qualities of feelings.[109]

Feelings (including Aesthetic), however, share their qualities, not a common rule, and not a common contiguous space. For instance, a sound is a vowel under a rule; it is a noise in the contiguous presence of its source; but it is a mere timbre, warmth, vibration as a feeling. As to the Third, the General idea, the question arises as to how in a mere quality of feelings – for instance, in the warmth of a voice as long as it is still felt – there could possibly be anything General. It is not a laryngologist's reflection on the human voice (which is knowledge), but the association of two different feelings under the influence of the perception of (what later might be called) 'warmth.' If feelings tend to spread, as Peirce noted in the 'Minute Logic,' then this is a case of it. This spreading just happens to have a fortuitous denominator in the word 'warmth,' but this is certainly not the most frequent case. Leibniz called this 'petite perception' very appropriately the 'je-ne-sais-quoi' (cf. Barnouw 1994: 157). It is not 'warmth' that creates this general idea but the association of the feeling of a stove and the feeling of a voice. No cognition could dictate their sharing a common law, nor would it be possible to link them existentially, creating one event joining the two feelings. Yet they can still have in common what a free play of musement happens to connect felicitously. This is the quality of feeling (but there is no limit to the number of qualities in a feeling, which is always created by a comparison with another feeling).

Interpretation also takes place through an association of feelings. Third Correlates can never be in an arbitrary or unordered relation to their two Correlates. Thus 'Quality' is not just any chance collection of sensory bits, or similar. It is already one (i.e., under one regard). As a rule of a higher form, this regard also compares an object's Iconic elements. Similarity (e.g., of 'images'; cf. 2.277) is the lowest possible limit for General ideas. The analogy of Diagrams (e.g., maps with their landscape) involves as a Third the physical sharing or spatiotemporal presence of the respective other. 'Metaphors' (2.277), in Peirce's technical meaning, do not amount to literary metaphors, although the latter are certainly an interesting illustration of the former. The figure of speech finds the rule of the parallelism neither in the subject-term of the compared nor in the compared-with. It is beyond the linguistic domain (v. *supra*). A virtual formal order beyond language is thereby created, and this gives its literary tokens this metaphoric Type form. 'Metaphor' or Legisign is more than its current linguistic usage suggests, even though Peirce himself exemplified it with words. Thus, &, 'and,' 'et,' +, 'y,' 'und,' 'καὶ,' and 'и' are one concept. Similarly, the use of frames in cinematic composition may be the same for each and every frame, but the notion of 'good framing' and 'bad framing' (i.e., amateurish) implicitly stipulates a rule for good framing.

The aesthetic 'sign itself' (first trichotomy) will only be Legisign when it is no longer experienced in a purely aesthetic feeling. Then the aesthetic Form has become at least a rudimentary rule of thought – for instance, as an acquired artistic knowledge or aesthetic expertise. This is no longer a 'petite perception,' on which, however, it is still based. The emergence of aesthetic rules (i.e., taste) does not contradict the iconic resemblance form of thought – that is, as long as it is not claimed that resemblance is a sufficient condition for the emergence of rules. If the rule can enter from outside, as in figurative enunciation (v. *supra*), it can make use of the aesthetic qualities which through this are transformed into a new type of cognition. Cinematic metaphors, then, are not strictly aesthetic 'devices'; they are keys to an Interpretation of the existing reality. Conversely, no one would use a metaphor (and call it so) for a mere imaginative play of thought. 'Fantasizing' is freed from all constraints of assertion; it says nothing about any object, but it could say all about anything (if it ever would care to come to an end with it).

The point is that 'cinematic metaphors' cannot be seen as a subject of cinema aesthetic. Metaphors must be known figures (knowing the rule for constructing those figures), yet without a reference to a real, a poem could not function. However, the quality used in such metaphor – for instance, a poem's onomatopoeia – functions only through an association of feelings. Unrepeatable aesthetic experiences of awe must, at the Iconic level of Qualisigns, remain associations of feelings. Beyond that point, any admixture of rules is no longer purely aesthetic.[110] The Metaphor as Third First becomes a precondition for increasing the valency of the Sign Relation to a logical Third Third (i.e., of an Argument, for instance of art standards). Then, when the aesthetic feeling is transformed into a planned (i.e., artistic) expression with its own set of canonicity, it is capable of conveying good taste, 'art meaning.'[111]

6.4.7 Aesthetic and Aestheticization of Cinematic Narration

As departments of cinematic meaning narrative, rhetorical, and aesthetic enunciation are far too neatly distinguished to reflect the entire gamut of cinematic meaning. By defining as 'pure' the aesthetic Sign relation, and enunciation negatively as prevention of general and existential cognition, we have grasped only the principle of cinema aesthetic. It is evident, however, that many pieces of cinematic narration and rhetoric are not devoid of aesthetic meaning. The same was found to be true for narration, which also had to comprehend some existential cognition (v. *supra*) as the basis of the 'narrative contract.' So an aesthetic Interpretation of narrative and documentary cinema is not surprising from a Semiotic perspective. In most cases of film art, we can expect to encounter aesthetic not 'from below' as it were, but mainly as an additional dimension. In Dadaist films, direct aesthetic cognition is the main purpose of the exercise of the 'absurd' – that is, the intrinsic non-narrativity and non-referentiality. In mainstream narrative cinema, aesthetic is just another possible Interpretation, much as it would be an additional dimension in a 'contemplative' documentary film. Here aesthetic cannot prevent narrative cognition; it can only dissolve it regionally into a Sign relation of lesser complexity.

When, as in most films, aesthetic must be enunciated through narrative or rhetorical enunciations, this obviously raises the impulse question of cinematic enunciation. Only through a change in enunciation (i.e., Interpretation) can cognitive conduct leading to general ideas reacquire the immediacy of aesthetic cognition. The relation of different enunciations, then, cannot be one of parallelism, mutual exclusivity, or contradiction. What, then, is the internal, logical relationship? Owing to the constructive and degenerative nature of Sign relations, aesthetic Interpretation follows the same principle as 'complexity-downward' Interpretations, which we have already investigated.

At the basis of every enunciation we find its proper Interpretational object, which is always a different relation for each object. Thus, aesthetic conduct is in the same relation to Aesthetic enunciation, as the true or false representational 'cinematic object' is to rhetorical enunciation, and as narrative teleology is to narrative enunciation. As a consequence, there is more than just the one canonical problem – treated as 'illusionism vs realism of cinema' – of how cinema succeeds in relating to a real world. Cinematic meaning is too complex and subtle for that false alternative. In cinema we see real things as much as plot outcomes and the imaginable, the true and the false, the purposeful and the accidental, and the possible. None of these things is seen directly; rather, it is wrapped in and produced by a communicational effort. Cinema does not let me see *simpliciter*; rather, it convinces me that it is true, or makes me expect what it is good for, or lets me imagine freely what is possible. Whatever is the kind of reality at the moment is therefore dependent on a further (and also rather complex) Interpretation.

Aesthetic enunciation, however, is in a Categorically determined relation to other enunciations: higher enunciations must rely on lower ones, but the reverse is not the case. All of this is not a matter of the enunciation as such, but of the respective objects and their Categorical nature. This enables the Reality of rhetorical probability to be also seen-as-aesthetical possibility. Regarding narrative enunciation, we have already seen that time is (literally unthinkable outside) a Third. This reality must again give rise to a different Aesthetic Interpretation, time-seen-aesthetically. Both re-Interpretations become cinematic practices that strive for Aesthetic experience, which we might call composition[112] and drama.

One kind of Aesthetic experience in cinema re-Interprets dramatic time. As art, drama is no longer just a meaningful pragmatic teleology, but a time-less truth. It is the target of the comparison direction of the comparative 'better and more virtuous than contemporaries' action of the *Poetic* (1448a12). As a difference in temporal Signs, this is the difference between conduct and drama. While drama is unthinkable without knowing 'conduct' first, its Aesthetic Interpretation transforms it into more than conduct by reducing Semiotically its temporality. Strict narrative logic can keep to the pragmatic time of 'purpose'; dramatic logic does not. There is no purpose (understood as type of temporality) to drama, only an Aesthetic possibility that is wider than what can be done.

How does drama transform time?[113] This does not preclude the possibility of the auroral moment of contemplation, which is directly Aesthetic without passing through the Sign degeneration of enunciations. Aesthetic Interpretation of narrative, Drama, seems a contradiction in terms: narrative stands for textual order, and Aesthetic stands for chaos, paradox, confusion, yet as a conduct with a view to a certain type of value.

Drama as aestheticization of narrative time must struggle against narrative constraints of probability. Even in its most absurd form, theatre must always be the representation of human action with the minimal requirements of pragmatic logic (v. *supra*). Once we take this for granted, the Pirandellos and Becketts of this world can disrupt the added orders of human action and social interaction, thus creating the impression of absurdity (relative to these orders). If we take this hint from theatrical practice, we can achieve an impressive dilution of order by ignoring or leaving out pragmatic values. Cinema as representation of human actions presents Ideas and concepts, which are translated into pragmatic temporality much in the model of the Pragmatic Maxim, and which can present an empty place replacing the pragmatic telos. Negatively stated, the aesthetic result in this case is incomprehensibility. A concept of meaning is lacking that would unify this set of acts into the one comprehensible action. Under the aegis of a *Kunstwollen*, however, spectators would not perceive 'foolish behaviour' on the screen or stage, but an absurd (curious, strange, mysterious, etc.) action.

Framed by narrative enunciation, its Aesthetic Interpretation must have consequences for time (which are already intrinsic to pragmatic logic as such). The Aesthetic process in film drama is initiated by feelings of bewilderment. Drama first puzzles; it fractures temporal directions, it serves no purpose and has no aim, but it aspires to engender possible aims-beyond-action. We perceive a 'fragment' (to take up Kevelson's term), yet we miss the whole to which 'it' is supposed to lead. When we characterize this first step as feeling, we are describing not a 'something' but a moment in a process.

What needs to be explained is not a spurious feeling, but drama as an Aesthetic degeneration of narration logic. First is logically first, and feeling gives rise to a Sign through an idea that associates similar qualities of time. Now narrative time is a teleological law based on the diversity of two different states of one subject (v. *supra* p. 305–10). The Icon of this time is certainly different from the Icon of drama time. Teleology demands an order of prior and posterior in one subject ('a subject existentially receives contrary attributes'; 1.495); drama merely requires the common Quality of feelings. In the case of drama, however, this Quality is made from the spoils of narrative teleology. In this situation, the 'fragment' metaphor can literally mean the product of fracture.

If we were to take this Aesthetic time in itself, however, the result would be similar to music. There are various characteristics of time, such as rhythm, *tempi*, and movements, but we would never speak of a time of music. In executing a piece of music, we are not creating a teleology. Although that music would exhibit many qualities of time, to such an extent that Husserl used music as a paradigm for immediate time consciousness. Dramatic time-*instar-musicae* is no longer a fragment of another time, but the beginning of a new synthesis. Logically only the first, it also calls for the second and third Correlates that correspond to its nature. Only as a triad is it an experience of Aesthetic time.

Only with respect to dramatic First ('monadic clause') is the quality of feeling different from music. Musical qualities are Aesthetic yet they do not achieve dramatic effects. It is interesting, however, that we can speak metaphorically about the 'dramatic effects' of a piece of music. Without a semantic denominator, this signifies a common quality of feeling between drama and music.

The 'dramatic effect' – a little awkwardly – translates into 'movement,' 'change,' 'decay,' 'passing,' 'transitoriness,' 'eternity.' These are teleological terms and thus quite inadequate for the non-teleological time of drama. As a Sign of an Aesthetic experience, however, drama has neither need nor use for Symbols and logical Generals. So drama *is* not transitoriness, although resembling it in some quality. It also resembles in the same quality the transition from vile to pure that gave rise to Aristotle's catharsis metaphor. For the Aesthetic experience of drama itself, this is of no consequence. These semantic difficulties merely signal that an Aesthetic Third is quite unlike a cognitive, logical Third, that it is based on Symbols and not on Icons. Drama is rather similar to music in another respect as well – it is impossible to clearly identify any content. Program music is no exception, because the lyric text is not the content of its music.

The example of music illustrates another central feature of Aesthetic time. This concerns the 'same subject' requirement of the 'dyadic clause' of the law of time. How can we identify a musical subject if all that changes is rhythmic emphasis, pitch, and so on? It is only a convention of notation to give an identity to what changes and call it a note. Yet a note is not defined except by what changes. So if there is an analogy, what changes in the time of drama? The only requirement so far is that we discover a simile of quality. Since in the Aesthetic Sign the Object must be no more than a possibility, the dramatic time just as much as the Aesthetic cannot be an event. The only aspect that is of the nature of an event is the flash of the Aesthetic moment. In this sense it is an inner event of sentiment. There is no need to surmise an auctorial instance – at least not so much as is the case with narrative enunciation, which is helped by such an imaginary focus. In narration we take up the gauntlet of the author ('focus'), we agree to be taken by the hand from event to event along a chain of credible causality; whereas Aesthetically, in the freedom to advance from hint to hint or from aesthetic sensation to sensation, the imagination of an auctorial intention would only be an obstacle.

There is no reason to deny that the sum of aesthetic sensations can also be added up with a different result. Once the Aesthetic experience concludes in an image of the aesthetic form, we can Interpret the same form as a logical General. Then we have two versions of the Aesthetic form: as instantiation and as artistic knowledge. In the hindsight of artistic knowledge, an Aesthetic object seems to be the instantiation of The Form – not, however, along the trajectory of Aesthetic experience.[114] As to the Aesthetic process, the recognition of a formal unity is tied only to the actual impression of an aesthetic object.

The Aesthetic time of drama will not be complete without its third Correlate, which makes it a Sign. The problematic semantics of the Aesthetic 'insight' of drama were noted earlier. Certainly, the Aesthetic form of drama cannot be teleological expectation. Aesthetic Interpretation of the narrative enunciation underaccentuates the expectable in narration. Only that which can no longer be foreseen – even in the form of 'suspense' or peripety – will and must be felt. Now there might be insurmountable obstacles to arriving at clear concepts, but in cinema excellent examples abound.

There are aesthetic feelings around all three dimensions of time. For example, the future in the form of 'restlessness' (which also suffers from semantic inadequacy). An exquisite example is Valerio Zurlini and Dino Buzzati's Il deserto dei tartari. Similarly, in Franz Kafka's 'Law.' The past, too, can be an aesthetic Iconicity once it is 'heavy,' present, but not graspable. Even after we dismiss films based on explicit knowledge of culpability, there is still Tengis Abuladse's Покаяние (Monanieba), there is still Luchino Visconti's Il Gattopardo, his Morte a Venezia. All of these aesthetic time effects operate through an opening of possibilities (or negatively as constrictions of the irremediable loss of possibilities). Death is, not the least, a metaphor of complete and final openness, which cannot be foreseen. 'Life before death' can easily become a feeling of the growing limitation of the time horizon, the end of pragmatic plans, similar to Heidegger's concept of Care. However, it can also become the opening of an unlimited open horizon, where 'action' is no longer a working concept of comprehension.

So there are many aesthetical situations involving direct feelings of time. All of them build on the debris of action, its stalling indirection, its unforeseeable momentousness. Perhaps it is also a new possibility owed to the Aesthetic experience of drama to 'have' time as directionless, continuity. The drama 'form' of this Quality of feeling is exploited by certain kinds of modern cinema, which need not even be post-Beckett. A case in point is the cinematography of Ulrike Ottinger's *Freak Orlando* or *Madame X – eine absolute Herrscherin*, her *bateau fou* (on Lake Constance) film, which is narrative and not experimental but nevertheless inconclusive. Its length is a mere section, not a whole. Here the aesthetic Interpretation of narration is that the end is not a cognition but only a feeling. Narration is thus a particular Iconic feeling of transition toward some end, if Aristotle's requirement 'of a certain length' is suppressed and the freedom of fabulation seems to be unbounded. All of this is Aesthetic 'form,' not a logical form of reasoning, and therefore not determined but vague. Likewise, interpretations of film drama from an Aesthetic perspective will always fail to be cogent. However, neither is such an exercise the purpose of the Aesthetic experience, which finds its own conclusions.

6.4.8 Aestheticization of Existential Reality in Cinema and Some Theories of Iconism

The Aesthetic of composition derealizes the Object of rhetorical enunciation in cinema.[115] The 'aesthetic of the real' has a long tradition in cinema and film theory, and one of its privileged *loci* is a certain aspect of the documentary genre. This is the artistic practice of documenting the real, and somehow not only the emphatically real, but also the real as 'symphony,' or 'harmonious' beauty of the real, and its contemporary opposite, the 'ugly real.' In short, a clearly artistic *Kunstwollen* is at work and not a mere forensic statement of facts. In our context, composition designates the formal (not intentional) characteristics of these efforts. It is understood as aesthetic re-Interpretation of enunciated facts. Whether or not this art is quintessentially cinematic (*pace* Bazin and all his opponents) is not a relevant question. A Semiotic approach can deal with all the subtle intermediate genres, or types of cinematic meaning. To describe types of cinematic enunciations is not to imply that there are only three genres of film: aesthetic, narrative, and documentary. Even though these genres illustrate the respective essence of enunciation types, real cinematic practice is full of *genera mixta*.

The theory (or ideology) of documentary film will always emphasize the production of the true reality effect, or 'claim the real,' as Winston (1995) has documented extensively. In our analysis of *Je vous salue, Marie*, we found that narration can be invaded by documentary procedures. The same is true for documentary film as dramatization of facts, as Winston (1995: 99–103) describes. In *Je vous salue, Marie*, the blending of narrative and documentary procedures can be called rhetoric enunciation – although it is not documentary (i.e., Godard is doing this within a narrative). He creates a real that is neither part of the universe of facts nor a real of the causal chain of narrative teleology. This sort of reality is a rhetorical construction of probable objects, which we would not normally expect in a teleology.

An aesthetic real is based on the rhetoric of the real (i.e., the really probable); it is an Interpretation of this enunciation through pictorial composition. By cannibalizing the reality effect – as drama does with pragmatic logic – it achieves analogous results (i.e., it is another instance of the Aesthetic Sign process). Aesthetic means that the existent must become a possible. Every vis-à-vis, dyadic, ego–non-ego relation is in the first place there, existent, so that it seems almost impossible to relate these to any 'possibly existent.' Even thinking about it is difficult because to think of something as being possible means mostly negating that it 'exists-as-that.'

The logical venture of Aesthetic is a positive production. It attains a positive possibility but does not propose it (which forces it again into a propositional relation). In contrast, rhetorical enunciation proposes. What it takes from (a range of) possibilities, it proposes as existent. Aesthetic grafted onto rhetoric follows the inverse procedure of enlarging existent truth into the wider possibility. In a certain sense this is a cinematic feature, as rhetorical enunciation is necessary for reality effects in film.

Aesthetic of paintings, outside cinema, might for instance be in the main directly contemplative, as can be seen when paintings become cinema. Such is the case in well-known art films, some of which refer either to an artist's biography, as in Derek Jarman's *Caravaggio* (1986), or to a fictional artist's life, as in Greenaway's *The Draughtman's Contract*, or to the idea of painting as such, as in Godard's *Passion*. In cases of cinematic recreation like these, paintings typically become re-enactments. Thus the composition becomes quite literally a posing-with, an establishment of vectors becomes literally 'veho' or driving-to, and the weight of areas in the painting comes to weigh on something else. Contemplation-as-painting is a Sign process that emphasizes the first Correlate, but not as a degenerative dyadic relation of true Opposition. Such paintings have no meaning relation to a real fact. Monet's water lilies are logically different from a biological illustration of water lilies (which may even look the same). If the same painting were to be re-enacted in a film – the painting Monet, for instance – it would have to show the events of 'becoming colour impression.'

How does aesthetic function in cinema if the framework is a rhetorical enunciation of facts? The most important tool for degenerating the rhetorical Sign is literally composition, posing-with, positing-with, or positioning-with. The logical operation taking place through this can be understood as an association. Associations are a common characteristic of the Icon in its three classes, but are very different according to the associated cognition. 'Association by similarity is related to association by contiguity somewhat as our inward consciousness is related to outward experience; the one association is due to a connection in outward experience, the other to a connection in our feelings' (7.452).

A pictorial composition is not a spatial accident, it is no *objets trouvés* next to one another; rather, it is an ad-sociation that is assembled through a unifying idea. What counts in aesthetic composition is not the spatial vicinity, which is the cause of an outward experience. Peirce's example of the weathercock is a perfect illustration of a unifying idea of existentiality. If events related to one another through spatial (existential) connection are perceived, the mind connects them into an idea of one acting upon another; this is the root of the idea of efficient causality. This is association by contiguity. In pictorial compositions (and other instances of spatially composed artefacts), this usage of an outward experience is not intended, as it would be if it were an image of a real event. Police photographs (with all the paraphernalia of scales, metres, dates, etc.) are typically used for this empirical association.

Aesthetic composition can take its unifying idea only from a non-causal relationship. There can only be a qualitative relation, which is an association of resemblance. This constitutes no more than one Quality of feelings, which brings about the associative relation. Contiguous association aims at a dependency that it can establish between opposing elements. In contrast Quality is completely free to elect anything that comes before a mind as the principle of associating ideas: as in a frame, two areas are associated by the same colour, or complementary colours, or tone-in-tone colours, or vectors, or lines, or dynamics (any kind of camera operation and also the dynamics of montage).

These logical possibilities of association by resemblance bear their fruit in the artistic practice of composition. It is not by chance that this term is used in both painting and music. More precise statements cannot be made about artistic practice. Composing is the most general term for an Aesthetic logical operation, provided that one does not intend it to refer to oppositional determinations. Through composition, for instance, colours relate to one another as weights relate to one another, and then we speak of the weights of colours in a painting. There is a common quality among notes in a chord, among colours, and among spaces; in all of these, harmony is a common term. The same can be said of similar/dissimilar warmth, clarity, and so on. The reverse is also possible (i.e., that painting borrows its qualities from music, as with 'coloratura' singers). Now this illustrates only those Aesthetic processes that associate similarities across different feelings that enjoy the convenience of metaphoric labels. Probably there was a need for labels in certain art practices, which could then be mastered as artistic techniques. Most of the other qualities thrive on composition alone. They cannot be catalogued, but they certainly can be positioned together. Composition is, then, a mental operation, completely free in its relational control.

Aesthetic Interpretation becomes complicated (i.e., an orgy of unwarranted interpretation) only when we interpret *contra naturam*. Aesthetic signs cannot produce more meaning, or meaning on a different level from that meaning which they contain. Interpreting music illustrates this restriction perfectly, because such a higher meaning cannot be found anywhere. Yet its impact on listeners is foremost among the arts. Usual art practice, however, shows another facet of Aesthetic Interpretation (and in music it is clearer than in other arts) – that the Aesthetic can become part and parcel of another meaning in no time. Conversely, this shows that there is already meaning of one kind in composition, and any meaning can always be Interpreted into other meanings. In cinematic usage, musical meaning often becomes a first Correlate of narrative meaning, 'background music' (and this is not a metaphor of space proper, but of an antecedent of this Interpretation now). In the worst case, music is simply incidental to something else, such as the dramatic highlights in Hollywood serials, the euphoria of consumption in a shopping mall, and so on. Even if narrative action is not the mother of music as music, the two have a common mother in meaningful conduct. This makes cohabitation possible. It is also capable of showing music as 'life before living,' or 'living (= acting) in general,' pure value. To undergo musical experience can mean feeling the impact of pleasure and repulsion on one's conduct. Even before it becomes cognitively aware or narratively effective, music has a truly pragmatic meaning.

The compositional force of music also becomes operative. Aesthetic conduct is not an unduly virtual extension of the meaning of 'conduct,' although it is difficult to imagine any guidance through something that is not determinate. The pure compositional 'form' of music is an illustration of value-guided conduct without any determination. Then it becomes immediate movement. It comes to resemble gestures, not only those of the orchestra's director, but also those whose physical movement produces the sounds. Real gestures, however, would be determined by some purpose. So here is a non-determinate conduct, immediate as a musician's body movement, more mediated as a dancer's. Examples abound, beginning with singers, dancers (even less able pianists than Glenn Gould jump, hum, and mimic at the keyboard; cf. Girard's *Thirty-two Short Films about Glenn Gould*). What happens semiosically in all these instances is an immediate 'translation' into pragmatic. Yet dancing is not jumping around. It is apparently guided by a value that transcends its movements into a real act of living, without doing something (pursuing a purpose or performing a useful action). Further interpretations of music, dance, mime, and singing can easily follow (e.g., opera), any *ars saltatoria*, and (why not?) cinema, in which music has an unfortunate tendency to be incidental to narration.

The Aesthetic process of composition becomes a little clearer if we use again the three-step metaphor of Kevelson. As a 'fragment,' then, compositional Aesthetic signs fracture the existential link to a vis-à-vis. How this functions on the debris of rhetorical enunciation was discussed earlier. The 'focus' part is particular to cinema and other pictorial arts. It is not necessary to focus the Aesthetic attention through an auctorial instance, as has proved convenient in the case of narrative enunciation. This function has been completely usurped by the frame. Only framing holds together those elements which can be composed mentally. The frame has a different function for representation, where it serves as a window on the world. As a second Correlate of a pictorial representation sign, there is a demonstrative function in the frame, which establishes an existential link between the observer and the object. A different kind of Sign relation transforms this demonstrative function of the frame into composition. The former is only dyadic, but the latter relation is almost unlimited regarding what it is possible to discover. Although it relates any number of qualities of feeling, it counts as a Relation of the monadic kind, with no other consideration in it than this Quality with which it is concerned at the moment. Bazin's double metaphor of the frame as the window and the masque or *passe-partout* is perhaps close to the difference between representing and composing.[116] Cinema focuses attention minimally through the frame, which must be seen as a logical device rather than as a technological constraint of camera construction.

It might seem a little pretentious to call the effect of composition 'meaning,' albeit aesthetic meaning. It would be difficult to describe the 'form' of composition, in terms of aesthetic conduct, as value *in se*, as was the case for narrative aesthetic. Seen in itself, composition is the non-existential Reality (reminding us that the Possible is a Reality). Unlike the 'form' of time in its Aesthetic Interpretation, we do not here have a truly descriptive metaphor for this really Possible. The 'beauty of the world' says nothing, and Peirce's term for the value of Aesthetic conduct, the 'admirable in itself,' is the vaguest possible maxim for any possible conduct.

At this point we might venture, in a Peircean spirit, to a designation of that ideal which also takes into account the type of Sign degeneration of which it is the repercussion. Aesthetic conduct, being under the guidance of the value of admirability, does not yet make a difference between good and bad (which is properly ethical conduct). However, when it is the result of a degeneration of Signs of facts, which are true or false, the aesthetic quality in question can also bear traces of that origin. This would be the aesthetic idea of 'truth-as-such,' as it were: this feels that there is an Opposition (and not a uniform quasi-Cartesian *res cogitans*), that being-opposite is the condition of the possibility of being true or false. In short, it is a feeling of the quality of the 'ob' in being ob-positum, pos(it[ion])ed against, of difference-as-such. This value is still a pragmatic factor, and therefore meaning, but it is not itself the meaning of a difference-between.

In a factual relation, there is the one difference between true and false, good and bad; all kinds of aesthetic relations are only an attraction or pleasure (of which repulsion is only the theoretical negation). If it is the καλός that is the object of Aesthetic conduct, then such 'form' is the only thing that can be said without determining Possibility more than is necessary. Further determination is indeed in danger of falling into the trap of substantial thinking; however, with metaphoric caution we might still speak of the 'beauty of reality' and see in it the cinematic specificity. This caution is warranted when this is only one step from giving existence to 'beauty,' which contradicts the very principle of the Aesthetic sign. However, 'form' as the third Correlate is absolutely necessary to the Sign process, for Interpretation. Again there is this embarrassment when it comes to demonstrating an Aesthetic sign in cinema. A conclusive proof that an Aesthetic Interpretation of some quality in cinema has taken place is not possible. Because everything is possible, nothing can be excluded from the realm of Qualities of feeling, and therefore nothing is left that could falsify Aesthetic claims. As always in such cases, there is only one possibility left – namely, illustration. Both types of Aesthetic Interpretation, degenerating Sign relations of narrative and rhetorical enunciation, will be illustrated below.

6.4.9 Aesthetics of Levels: Lotman and Formalism

Film theory finds itself in a kind of double bind when it is charged with grasping 'subjective' (intuitive, taste, art). It cannot ignore the fluid and murky matter of film's aesthetic aspects, because this is so obviously central to the phenomenon, but neither can it give up its status as a theory. The effortlessness of aesthetic fruition seems inversely reciprocal to the difficulty and effort of theory. We have already discussed Kant's radical reframing of the aesthetic problem in transcendentalist key, as well as the phenomenological-hermeneutic response in a subjectivist key. How difficult it is to escape the Scylla and Charybdis of these two was shown in the discussion of 'cognitivist' aesthetics. The most decisive and difficult labour in any film aesthetic, then, arises when we set out to define the object, problem, and frame of a theory of meaning within which a solution is offered.

Regarding the diversity of film aesthetics, the central point is not that they are diverse, because from our Semiotic perspective the object is such (i.e., a simple thought) that it can be neither true/false nor a logically correct general idea. On the contrary, the nature of the object stretches theories to the other extreme, where they must grasp cognition below the threshold of truth, but not as a negation of cognitive potential as such, in the manner of Kant. Yet the contrary conclusion – either that aesthetic is not completely accessible to theory or that any theory will do equally well – is not satisfactory since this would mean the end of all serious debate. We can at least gauge or compare the potential of different aesthetic theories, as has been done with subjectivist aesthetics.

The problem with the following two difference-based aesthetic theories is that they lack the framework of a comprehensive general theory of meaning, one that would allow us to critically appraise what they can achieve in the aesthetic domain. As a consequence, what they reconstruct as meaning in aesthetic is left in an undecidable state, unless we seriously entertain the notion that aesthetic is a meaning totally *sui generis*, with no comparison to meaning at large. Otherwise, we have to accept that aesthetic meaning comes from outside aesthetic itself: founded on a heterogeneous theory of meaning, aesthetic theory cannot itself provide the framework for meaning. In our context, this is of no further relevance, since these latter theories of meaning have already been debated (v. *supra*). If an aesthetic theory functions at the 'aesthetic' drop-in-level between two (Formalism) or recursive (Lotman) stages of descriptions of the same, then we must attribute their noticeable differences to an intention to express a surplus meaning of the same. Our next task is to investigate this figure of thought, not only because it exists, but also because it is a theory of meaning that claims a purchase on the aesthetic phenomenon.

In Lotman's film aesthetic, the salient point relates to the levels of Saussurean articulation turned into aesthetic, and not to how he contrived a particular iconism for cinema (which is more or less known from other semiological theories of 'motivated' signs). In spite of other distinct features, this makes Lotman's aesthetic comparable with Formalism. From here it might be tempting to merge articulation (or level difference, standing for the entire Tartu–St Petersburg figure of thought) into enunciation on the basis of levels (an idea that has been followed by the Milan School). The consequence is always a new order or taxis, in a hypertactical or hypotactical perspective, with the aesthetic meaning situated not at the higher level but at the difference between levels. At the emergent level, then – which is really a violation of the lower-level rules – a new order must be found. It follows that the invention of rules is the gist of these aesthetics. Once they are invented they can take on various names: trope, syntax, style, language levels (prose or poetic).

How do rules emerge?[117] This is the central problem in these aesthetics. What is their measure, against which the correctness or the applicability of the rule is determined? It would clearly be deviant for such a rule to regulate a comparison with 'mentality' (*horribile dictu!*) or with extra-mental reality, so that the only choice open is an internal complexification, whose complexity is then reduced through rules. This kind of rule determination amounts to a circular (or tautological) argument.[118] In Lotman, the order of rule is designated at any level, and this amounts to a system-theoretical media theory for cinema. In Neoformalism that designation ('style' etc.) is essentially vague and inevitably leads to a historical investigation of stylistic facts. Now, being a *quaestio facti*, it blocks the path to raising meaningful questions of justification or logical necessity. Therefore, and from this perspective, Neoformalism is a profoundly non-cognitive aesthetic, although it is supposedly a valuable historiography of styles.

Lotman's aesthetic of cinema attempts to transpose aesthetic problems onto a mold of differentiation. In the genealogy of the St Petersburg–Moscow–Prague Formalism, a feasible approach was long held to be Jakobson's 'poetic function,' which had ramifications through Bühler's Organon-theory of language down to Arnheim. Lotman, one of the key representatives of the Tartu School, opted instead for the two semiological natures of either coded[119] or 'analogical' material, with 'analogical' material the foundation of cinema aesthetic. This is then combined with elements of Formalist narratology. The pivot is 'iconism,' which, as a means of avoiding the intricacies of code theory in cinema, almost assumes the status of self-evidence. What is different is that 'icons' have 'one unique, naturally inherent expression.'[120] This becomes usable for aesthetics once differences are introduced.[121] What is not different in the original material must be introduced artificially, with two conditions: first, there must be an alternative, whose use or non-use is significant; and second, there must be order in use and non-use (cf. Lotman 1973: 34). This is very close to the old Formalist idea of the 'rhythm' in poetry (cf. Erlich 1955: 212–29). Such closeness is evident when this two-step procedure is given core aesthetic relevance. Creating a difference only with non-use presupposes an automatic use. By means of lighting, colour, motion, camera angles, and even 'natural sequences of events' (Lotman 1973: 32), their non-use is offset. This becomes significant as a cinematic trope within the order of a rhythm.

'Rhythm' constitutes the quintessence of artistic strategy, as it dissolves any 'normal' semantic units of signification. Once this second level is reached, we can dispense with the underlying analogical material except for the contrast. It seems, on the contrary, to be rhythm that transforms analogical material into signs. At least for text production, the only crucial element is the syntaxlike trope. A text of tropes is also the sole pictorial means for producing pictorial narration. Now cinema is 'a synthesis of *two* narrational tendencies: pictorial ('moving pictures') and verbal' (ibid.: 37). As an occasion of another, higher differentiation, this 'interpenetration' is not left barren. Now one system can mimic the other, which further alleviates the burden of iconic signs forming units. This third level of Interpenetration is itself again an iconic sign for a 'third concept' (cf. 42), which becomes the basic unit of the cinematic sign system. This three-stage cinematic sign-beyond-language finally delivers discreteness, albeit derived from a second order. From this stage another aesthetic transformation occurs by roughly the same principles as those of the lower-level units. At this level, meaningful omissions (e.g., in a drawing compared to the drawn object) abstract representation from all that is not essential to it. This reminds us of Arnheim's old idea of a specific cinematic aesthetic.

Lotman's film aesthetic continues with the same principles. The paradigm montage is a 'juxtaposition of heterogeneous elements' (Lotman 1973: 48), and already goes beyond a simple sign order in sentences or linguistic syntax. As syntagmatic device, montage has an aesthetic relevance that is quite different from normal syntactic 'rules,' which generate predictability and redundancy. This regularity is broken by unexpected juxtapositions that violate syntax. Another differentiation principle is found – the third, which gives rise to another meaning-beyond-tropes. Texts that signify differently at each level ('language') become ambivalent. Whichever level we choose, it excludes the other. The result is not simply a breach of rules, as in a 'monoplane' system that is made inconsistent. It is compensated for by the collateral system, which supplies its meaning instead of allowing redundancy.

What are the two 'languages' in film? Because there is no direct cinematic equivalent to what in language is the arsenal of articulations, layers of style, language levels, and so on, 'modality' and 'object' are the two contrasting juxtaposed cinematic systems. There is, at last, double articulation. Modalities such as lighting and camera parameters change the representation of objects. When we compare two elements that are not at the level of one language (syntax), but are between the 'same,' the result is a rhetorical device. The identity of an object with itself but in another modality means that a *tertium comparationis* need not be found outside in a third sememe that is common to both. What the *tertium comparationis* exactly is can be left open, because the shift is visible. Shifts are possible either from one object to the next with modality remaining the same, or from modality to modality with the same object.

Modality, which reminds us both of 'style' in Formalism and of mode dependency in enunciation, is not limited to narration. It is rather vague and 'analogical' (i.e., analogous to verbal modifiers). A zero grade of modification, similar to an indicative, leaves an unmodified 'object,' which makes it easy to switch to a modified object. The 'walking lion' in *Potjemkin*, for instance, if it is a statue, in the same modality is perceived as three different objects. Is it a living lion? Then one object in three modalities is perceived. This same principle extends to narration. Again, tropes are constructed through the juxtaposition of heterogeneous elements 'when one frame is conjoined to another' (Lotman

1973: 59); and again, tropical meaning is built on the 'normality' of temporal sequencing, which is supposedly unavoidable in film.[122] Temporal tropes create new (artistic) meaning, which through montage narration is more than the sum of its sequential parts. The aesthetics of narratological modalities follow the usual pattern (ibid.: 62–93). This adds another level of differentiation, narrative, after object, and cinematic tropes, thus construing comprehensively the syntax of cinema on four tiers (ibid.: 70). Text syntax creates its own units through differences created by rules.

Once these tiers and levels of tropical differentiation have been established, one further complexity is added, for these rules apply to elements of either identical functions (same level) or different functions. In the first case we have the simple 'contiguity' of a potentially unlimited series (Jakobson?). In the second case there is already a subordination of series, which are (by domination) necessarily limited. On this basic difference rests the capacity of texts to construct registers. If there were just identical functions, the result would be an even combination. Supposing that there are a certain number of modules of that even type, delimited but of different functionality, they must be joined by yet another function at a higher level. Now in cinema, text syntax is equal to linguistic grammar. There are parallels between (1) phonemes and shots (at the lowest syntactic level), (2) sentence and 'cinematographic phrase,'[123] (3) superphrasal units and sequences, and (4) plot ('second-degree phrase') and cinematic plot. Levels 1 and 3 both consist of equal elements; levels 2 and 4 are hierarchized according to the model of phrases ('the plot is always constructed on the same principle as the phrase' [ibid.: 71]). Applied to cinema, levels 1 and 3 'carry the fundamental burden of strictly cinematographic narrativeness' (ibid.: 72). The rest is generally narrative.

Lotman's film aesthetic pivots on the principle of difference, on the basis of iconic analogy. How many levels and registers there are in cinema is ultimately irrelevant. The operating principle, called 'aesthetic' or rhetorical, always remains the same, and serves to mimic linguistic double articulation. The lower of the two different levels is non-differential ('analogous') and becomes differential – and thus meaning – at the higher level.

As a general theory of meaning this is a well-known pattern. Upstream of it and from outside, the question arises whether this should count as aesthetic. Aesthetic should not just provide a general theory of meaning, but a theory of a very simple and particular meaning. What

Lotman provides as narratology is of no concern in this context, but what is left, apart from that, is apparently no more than a rhetoric of cinema (in the sense of the term as used in our Peircean context).

There is no question that art can make extensive use of rhetoric, and it is certainly not limited to cinematic art. This is emphatically so even for music, which is not usually perceived as a representational art. The work of Johann Sebastian Bach can be fathomed only if we grasp the enormous complexity of his 'musical commonplaces.' Musicology is only now investigating Bach's[124] pervasive use and mastery of standing musical 'figures of speech.' In this vein, his *Notenbüchlein* is considered to be the vocabulary of his musical language. It is so complex, however, that even the most careful listener cannot grasp that language by listening. Only a musicological analysis can reveal all of Bach's hidden numeric relations[125] and proportions, whose theological meaning is taken from Lutheran orthodoxy and Alexandrinian theology (Bach was a profound theological scholar and was well versed in musical mathematics and even kabbalah). The fact that such complexity can never be grasped by hearing does not signify that it is without meaning. Bach expressed his theology with these means, not only with feelings of pietistic affection and raptus; but his piety is enunciated in his extended tropical vocabulary. Clearly, this amounts to statements of realities, through musical means, but on the basis of defined tropes and other rational orders. This allows us to determine with exactitude what he meant, and what not (for instance, with three voices, which always 'mean' Trinity, or eighty-four bars, in certain parts of the Credo of the Mass in B-Minor; cf. Ehrat 2003).

Very much like Bach, Godard loves to 'hide' complex meanings. We saw this in our analysis (v. *supra*), which might be best explained by resorting to *loci tropici* and figuration generally. Our analysis of Godard's rhetoric and figuration clearly shows his artistry, or his cinematic art, but also that the resulting meaning is not aesthetical.

Bordwell's Neoformalism, it must be conceded, claims to be poetic and not aesthetic. In contrast, Russian *Ur*-Formalism clearly shows an explicitly aesthetic direction. Lotman's, instead, is Kino-aesthetic. But as should be clear by now, this cannot be intended in the Peircean sense of the term. There is no point in criticizing theories for what they do not claim to explain. Conversely, however, this shows how awareness of a problem, as a problem, is heavily dependent on a corresponding theory. The combination of nominalism (ontology) and difference (meaning theory) simply does not allow us to cognize simple thoughts.

'Simple' can be no meaning, because meaning becomes meaning only through the difference from an other(ness).[126] Difference aesthetics would certainly be capable of grasping the rhetoric of music, as was illustrated earlier with Bach's music, but there seems to be a lacuna in these aesthetics for simple cognitive processes that is fundamental even for Bach's music. Similar objections could be made with regard to aesthetic qualities of painting. The sign of that lacuna – and of the total dissimilarity of principles with Semiotic – is that this aesthetic meaning directly (in fact, necessarily) becomes representation as soon as it becomes meaningful. Semiotic aesthetic, as degeneration of the Sign relation, un-determines the triadic relation, and it does so without having to sacrifice meaning. Lotman's is basically a semiological meaning theory, in spite of 'iconic rhetoric' and – at this level – a non-differential analogical meaning.

6.4.9.1 Neoformalism as Film Aesthetic

On the side of rhetorical tropes, in Lotman there is a much greater resemblance to Russian Formalism. There are many historical links between the Tartu School and the Late Formalist Schools in Moscow and in Petrograd/Leningrad. 'Rhythm' defamiliarizes also the iconic image. This effect supposedly only recurs when deviation from a normal state is produced by the 'quality of divergence,' as Šklovskij called it in his Theory of Prose, following Christiansen's *Differenzqualität* (cf. Erlich 1955: 178, 252). From 'deviation,' it is only one more step to 'estrangement,' which is again one of the core principles of the aesthetics of Šklovskij and the Prague Linguistic Circle.

As Beaugrande (1988) (v. *supra*) noted, the Formalist approach has in principle been a polemical distancing, down to the distancing from the 'normal,' the automatic, the prosaic, and the un-poetical. To what extent this has a continuation at the core of the aesthetic of Bordwell and the Neoformalist group, must be seen. There is a concern for a proper aesthetic approach to cinema, but with the avowed aim of leaving behind the mainstream of 'SLAB theories' (de Saussure–Lacan–Althusser–Barthes). If it were not for the constructivist extensions, the 'Wisconsin project' (Barry King's term) of Neoformalism would reveal an astonishing affinity for Tartu–Leningrad Formalism. We will not concern ourselves here with what exactly inspired the anti-semiological and anti-enunciational stance of Neoformalism, nor with what exactly was the object of its critique. Under the linguistic model, 'flat' differentiation is rejected, but then there are a number of constitutive differences of levels (albeit not under the label 'articulation'). We can accept this as the differentiating characteristic; practically speaking, this gives Neoformalism a different identity from Lotman's.

Since there is no intrinsic connection between the Formalist and Constructivist blocs[127] in Neoformalism, both must be judged on their own merits. As an aesthetic theory, the Formalist approach does not benefit from Constructivism – perception is supposedly more congenial to film – not even as the cinematic equivalent to Šklovskij's pre-literary 'automatism.'

The aesthetic originates in estrangement, at the point when the automatically given has become strange. In Formalist aesthetics, analyses of art hinge on a change in levels, called estrangement. The vivid language used in the Formalist accounts of estrangement should not obfuscate the logical operations behind this 'becoming strange.' It is neither a psychological operation nor a practical performance when Formalists write about an artist who 'knows the trick' (Приём) of estrangement. What they had in mind with this was really levels of linguistic form, which in their contrast produce a logical effect, whose psychological description is estrangement. In the Russian Formalist context this is still closely linked to rhythm and to other prose operations. Had the Wisconsin scholars wanted to transpose the aesthetic theory from prose[128] to film, they would only have had to replace the object of the operation of estrangement. As we shall see, this project would have been snared by the same tautology as the Russians'. For it was not enough to simply replace linguistic with specifically cinematic features.

Being-feature is defined in a circular way, that is, as a device capable of 'tricking' (not just by any grammatical or lexical characteristic). If it is not used for estrangement, the same element is 'normal,' it recedes into the general pool of linguistic means for producing meaning. Formalism is therefore an aesthetic functionalism that uses language as its functional basis. Functionally pertinent elements are defined as those which have a function. There is as yet no trace of 'double articulation,' in either the Russian or the Neoformalist theory (which was first introduced by the Prague Linguistic Circle). Nor is there a higher-level order that is equivalent to double articulation. Constructivist 'bottom-up' and 'top-down' processes and applicable schemata do not constitute functions of estrangement or deviation.

Neoformalism constructs an opposition in much the same way as Formalism stood to its rival Symbolism, only here the intent seems to be to stand outside the sphere of influence of semiology. For such a purpose, one option is to remount the lineage from semiology, structuralist narratology, Propp, Jakobson, the Prague Linguistic Circle, and Moscow Formalists to the Leningrad *Opojaz*-Circle. This leap is basically the one that Bordwell took in his film aesthetic. This meant he did not have to commit himself implicitly to the orgies of codes. However, he still has to supply what the Leningrad group did not yet have at its disposal (and which Mukařovský critically requested from Šklovskij). The glaring lacuna was and is a theory of signs that is powerful enough to be completed with aesthetic additions and that is capable of substituting language with equivalences. One strategic option is to return to prestructuralist theory; an entirely different option is to take aboard a heterogeneous theory element.

A central intuition of the whole tradition starting with Formalism was given up when Neoformalism introduced 'spectator activity' as a factor in aesthetic theory. What seems to be a sensible theory extension on closer reflection appears to menace the very idea of pure form. The metaphoric bridge that links constructivism with formalism is 'schema.' Tacitly it becomes a mental schema, which 'forms' the cognition of a judging subject. As a 'cue' to this subject, such form is actually a logical *a priori* norm for a certain kind of adequate cognitive act. Conversely, an 'automatism' of language was Šklovskij's hallmark – everything else was rooted in it. 'Defamiliarization' was not meant to bring the aesthetic subject back into play, either as the genius of the author or as the refinement of the spectator. Instead it was supposed to create another quasi-automatism of a higher form, giving rise to genres and to poetic devices such as measure and rhythm. There is no 'cueing' in a form, there are no mental operations for reconstructing the *fabula* from a *sujet*. The formal perspective does not need that, just as the origin of forms, language, does not need speakers or any other subject. Already in opposition to Symbolism, subjective pleasure – taste as the subjective mode of apprehension – is excluded (cf. Striedter 1969: xviii). The price exacted for this is usually some kind of formalism, where 'form' has to account for the difference between an aesthetic and a normal object of cognition. Aesthetic perception is a 'stilted' perception, unfamiliar with its object because it is broken through an aesthetic form. The designation 'formalist' provoked by this was originally coined by its detractors and was intended to be pejorative.

In its essence Formalism is a thoroughly non-subjective aesthetic. It is far remote from the Kantian taste judgment and from the phenomenological apperception.[129] All of this presupposes a (transcendental or existential) subject as a unifying principle, otherwise there can be no meaning. Not so in the Formalist intuition (even though the Russian Formalists admitted their philosophical *nonchalance* just as they did their disagreement). It is their common ground, however, that it is precisely the form that functions and not a reader; it is the form that must be analyzed and not the aesthetic subject. Resubjectivizing betrays the idea of the form. It is not a contingency of theory development that the Russian Formalism sired only theories with a glaringly absent subject – most prominently semiology, structuralism, and Propp's Formalism.

Whatever other merits it may have, the 'Wisconsin project' polemic against SLAB theories contradicts this most crucial premise of Formalism. Cognition without subject is fundamentally SLAB, but only in Foucault's genealogy of knowledge have these formal genetical predispositions of Formalism been developed to their extreme. Foucault's antisubjectivity is more faithful to the vanquishing of the subject through the form. His scope is beyond mere literariness; however, nobody has more defamiliarized the view of all sorts of human causality, be it history, social interaction, knowledge, or institutions. His procedure for taking a 'non-practical' view of everything that seems to be causally connected and automatic starts with the 'rare space' (cf. Foucault 1969) of meaning without connections – with the topological positions of singularities, not causalities, in this rarefied space. The intuition behind his 'pensée du dehors' (i.e., outside the causally connected homely world of the subject) is a program of thinking stories and history without a subject. There are two autonomous parts of this 'thinking outside': what was made visible in a culture, and what organization of knowledge there is. (A certain Formalist prefiguration of this can be seen in the still undistinguished 'automatism' of everyday language. 'Defamiliarization' corresponds to a new power relation.) Subjects have been eliminated from the 'visibilités' (such as prisons, schools, clinics, but also theatres and – why not? – the camera 'appareil de base' of Baudry). Visibilities assign differential places to subjects and objects; it is not that subjects organize 'their' visibilities. A similar elimination took place for the 'énoncé' (e.g., the penal code, the *lèse-majesté*, *lex talionis*, 'offender correction' discourse), which does not need a thinker to organize itself. Even the 'diagramme,' the contingent relation of power between the two, is not operated by a subject of history, producing a causality through its act.

For Foucault the 'rapport des forces' has its immanent causality, not the mind, not operations of thought, and of course not ontological relations of physical beings. Here the premises of thinking without subjects have been brought to a logical conclusion. It is clear, however, that Foucault's visibility strikingly resembles the 'apperception' in Kant, that his 'énoncé' resembles the forms of mind, and that the power relations are matched by the judgment. It is Kant-without-subject. Only against this background does it follow that technologies, the 'rare spaces,' create subjects as topological positions. Only then is Baudry's now classical cinéthique article on the *appareil de base* not misunderstood as a theory of the subject of cinematic apperception. The subject-free formal approach – already crucial to Russian Formalism – has many realizations, however. It is so central to this aesthetic theory that it is much more astonishing that it could be reimported. However, at the price of structural damage?

Is it the antiposition of polemic, or the power of common sense and the self-evidence,[130] when the synthesizing power of the 'active subject' emerges as the one motor that drives everything? Evidently, Bordwell does not feel at ease with this empty place of the subject-free Formalist aesthetic theory. This is perhaps what drove him to graft it *contra naturam* onto 'spectator activity'[131] (or was this a radical correction of a model that was felt inadequate or lacking?). Formalism does not only not require spectators, it has – almost obsessively – eliminated them. The far-reaching ripple effect of this obsession with antisubjectivism can still be felt in Metz's 'impersonal enunciation' (cf. Metz 1991).

There are three principal ways to conceive of the Formalist Idea. (1) as the description of devices; (2) as a functional interpretation; and (3) as pragmatic or communicative. It seems that Neoformalism has restricted itself in the main to the first of these. All, however, including (3), have in common that antisubjectivity cannot be severed from Formalist aesthetic theory without maiming its explanatory power as far as it goes. However, a number of authors (v. *infra*) seem to agree that the core theory of Formalism is imprecise and murky; as far as we can see, this has not changed with Neoformalism and its Cognitivist superaddition or appendix. Our reconstruction cannot bring more light into it than it has. We can take stock of the lasting legacy of Formalism, in the following even-handed judgment: 'All this seems to indicate that Formalism had no clear-cut esthetics; it failed to solve, indeed to face squarely, such crucial problems as the mode of existence of the literary work or critical standards' (Erlich 1955: 283). Deviation (i.e., Christiansen's 'Differenzqualität,' the most significant category of this aesthetic theory) is ultimately tautological. More important is that, on the positive side, Formalism 'provided the students of literature with some immensely helpful definitions' (284).

(1) The same could be said for Bordwell's film aesthetic. The rigour is striking with which it describes cinematic 'devices.' These are shown to be more useful than impressionistic metaphors such as 'rhythm,' Balázs's 'point-of-view,' and so on. As artistic devices they tend, however, to be close to producing 'cookbook' wisdom. If Bordwell's devices are more than recipes – more than 'what one must do' as a film production professional or as an expert spectator – it is because they are mitigated by structural and functional insights. But function depends on knowledge of purpose. In Formalism this is not far from deviation, which does not 'add up' (Thompson) to some meaning. Thus Bordwell's pride in concerning himself only with 'middle range inquiry' (1996: xiii) perhaps proves to be the sad truth. Real theory (of whatever *grandeur*) requires more than inquiry, and indeed there is nothing in sight that lends itself as a principle of aesthetic theory. He might wish to put an 'end to Theory' (scil. Grand Theory), but the function of devices itself demands a theoretical knowledge. Then the question is only whether there is enough theory available to endow 'cookbook' devices with meaning.

Is there enough explanatory power in the Formalist idea for it to be applied to cinema? The answer to this hinges on its capacity to produce deviation, or the 'Differenzqualität.' This must also be the basis of devices in film. Deviation leaves us with a difference from something normal, because this is the sole purpose of devices. The crux of Neoformalism is no longer when it reaches the levels of the narrative universe, the *fabula*, *sujet* and style. It is situated at the very core of the aestheticizing operation itself. In film theory this cannot be a linguistic operation of deviation. So it is logical for Bordwell to look at perception as the cinematic core operation of an aesthetic of difference. How can a perception be strange, deviant, or different? Is it not a characteristic of any perception that it is normal? Conversely, what would be an 'un-normal' perception? Every felicitous perception (i.e., that could be performed or resolved from perhaps puzzling confused impressions) is normal. For this reason, perceptions count as unquestionable bases for any further operations.[132] What matters aesthetically is only deviation. To perceive something aesthetically is to perceive something differently, and this can only mean changing one's perception. We change a felicitous perception into another felicitous perception, not into a 'confusing' one, so the aesthetic perception must be a successful, meaningful perception as well. Assuming that aesthetic is some sort of meaning, a non-language-based cinematic aesthetic theory that is upstream of, and constitutive of, cinematic 'literariness,' 'cinematicity,' is a strictly required link in the chain.

Being a two-tiered differential, at the lower level, the 'special normal' perception of cinema art is part of 'bottom-up' processes insofar as physical stimuli are used. 'Prior knowledge and experience' in art perception, in the (presumably acquired) stylistic and narrative system, allows for ordinary 'top-down' processes. But where is the out-of-ordinary, aesthetic tier? 'What, then, distinguishes aesthetic perception and cognition from the nonaesthetic variety? In our culture, aesthetic activity deploys such skills for nonpractical ends. In experiencing art, instead of focusing on the pragmatic results of perception, we turn our attention to the very process itself' (Bordwell 1985: 32). The purpose of focusing on our attention – which would be a source of meaning – is not indicated. Non-practical 'artistic intention' begs the question at a different level. So the (empty) form of aesthetic translates into a perception, shaped through artistic intervention, which renders it less than 'normal.' Every successful perception applies schemata, otherwise perception cannot be achieved. Thus the aesthetic of Form can only be explained with schemata concepts and the substitution of one (strange) concept with another (*trouvaille*).[133] *Sujet* is a thematic interest; 'style' is the intention to manipulate material in a coherent, unidirectional sense for one's communicational, artistic purpose. Yet this still does not explain how artistic style is conducive to the new concept of an artistic *sujet*? At this point, the most interesting aesthetic explanation has become a psychological operation. Only the 'labour of forms,' not the transformation of form itself, can be described; the rest 'does not add up.' 'What is nonconscious in everyday mental life becomes consciously attended to. Our schemata get shaped, stretched, and transgressed; a delay in hypothesis-confirmation can be prolonged for its own sake. And like all psychological activities, aesthetic activity has long-range effects. Art may reinforce, or modify, or even assault our normal perceptual-cognitive repertoire' (Bordwell 1985: 32).

The difference between 'usual' and 'unusual' percepts – as required by Formalism – cannot be established at the form-percept level, then, but only downstream of it, at the level of a narrative universe (which is clearly a very complex 'perception' of a world with an action in mind[134]). In linguistic works deviations from grammatical and semantic standards indicate an unusual use of language –that is, the 'poetizing' of language. For an 'unusual percept,' however, Constructivism can only provide schemata, which either work or don't. In the first case there is a cognition, in the second case a cognitive act cannot succeed. It follows that there must even be (familiar) schemata for defamiliarization. Otherwise the aesthetic cognitive act would fail. As the composite theory it is, there remains a fundamental problem with the collapsing of perception (as 'usual,' conventional) and deviational meaningful defamiliarizations (cf. Thompson 1988: 7–21); indeed, how do these *perceptive* conventions fall into place *as aesthetic* ones, if not by a tautological operation? Is there a special pragmatic of 'non-practical' perceiving? What do non-practical – as opposed to practical – percepts consist of cognitively? What kind of different meaning is it? What is 'normal' perceptive expectation as it relates to art?

(2) As an alternative, we could leave in suspense the problem of an aesthetic core operation perception and take the more general approach to deviation. Then (Neo-)Formalism does not strictly require psychological explanation but merely a function – which in Bordwell becomes 'spectator activity' – in order to deautomatize the production of 'poetical' quality. This solution would take the functional interpretation of formalism into account. Language is not covered by its explanatory power (as in the Formalism before Jakobson and Mukařovský); rather, it is presupposed. If poetic functionalism is to be seen in the spirit of литерарност, this activity must function without a subject. When Šklovskij waxes lyrical, he sees the reinvigorating capacity of defamiliarized perception.[135] Such perception is not in nature, however, but through (literary) language, which, as always, is already taken for granted in Formalism. It is a perception of literariness, so to speak.

Jakobson, after his departure from Formalism, and when he was already a member of the Prague Circle, supplied the lacking linguistic foundation to formalist poetics. He chose a clear 'poetical functionalism,' thus expanding Bühler's three language functions (cf. Jakobson 1963: 220). The poetic function is defined as the paradigmatic projection on the syntagmatic axis. The results are the poetical principles of contiguity and similarity, metonymy and metaphoric. Obviously, with the 'poetic function' we can describe with some linguistic exactitude what is non-automatic in poetic language (and why). Defamiliarization becomes a linguistic function and less a matter of a subject, of its activity and intentionality.

Bordwell's own practice of also counting narration as a perceptional deviation clearly favours a purely functional interpretation of poetic deviation. Narration is in any case the *representation* of something (imaginary or state of world) that is already as such a defamiliarization of the referred object (= sign). The distinctly poetical deviation becomes a special restriction of the expectations and selection of schemata based on the genre (!) of narration (cf. Bordwell 1992: 7). Although Russian Formalism was not preoccupied with the 'languagedness' of representation (cf. Striedter 1969: xixf), Neoformalist poetics does not need more 'cinematicity' either – a functional approach suffices. Even here, the cinematic production of a narrative universe does not happen automatically (as we have previously analyzed). 'Prose' supposedly occurs automatically through language. But what is cinematic prose, if it is not a functional absence of deviation? A psychological theory of perception can grasp only the cognitive process of 'normal' perception. If its result is some different meaning of 'Differenzqualität,' 'Poetic perception' is not plain cognition but an aesthetic synthesis. An interesting test case is an abstract painting (the closest pictorial equivalent of Hermetic or 'Concrete Poetry'). There is no possible means to construct a 'normal' as opposed to a 'deviant' perception. No one, however, would deny the aesthetic quality of certain poems of Eugenio Montale, for instance. Nor is there any question that the Suprematist paintings of Malevich and the abstract paintings of Kandinsky and Klee are aesthetic. So how would the Formalist 'trick of estrangement' (приём отстраненя) function here?[136] The same holds for avant-garde cinema and certain types of 'narration.' In all of these cases, it must more than just practicality that makes the difference.

(3) Comprehension of the aesthetic operation proper in Formalism, then, is limited by the extent of aesthetic theory. 'Estranged perception' is impossible, and a functional interpretation is difficult; yet there is a third option, which is the one followed by Jakobson. When he shunned his brainchild Formalism,[137] he did so by effectively expanding it. The very act of aesthetic estrangement thus became pragmatic. Bühler's organon theory of language lent itself to being integrated into an enlarged understanding of language in its poetical *and* its prosaic usage. This led Jakobson to understand that the appellative function is also a necessary part of language. The 'trick of estrangement,' enriched with appellative functionality, thus becomes a linguistic act for somebody by somebody, intentionally producing effects. These certainly include the new vision of 'life' (cf. Erlich 1955), which Šklovskij was so lyrical about. This is how Brecht adopted the idea, and this can be seen also in Thompson's interpretation. 'Neoformalism jettisons a communications model of art' (1988: 7).

That version of pragmatic aesthetics reduces the aesthetic operation to a rhetorical act of convincing. This theory makes no heavy demands and does not try to explain much. This is rather remote from the formal analysis of formal, linguistic, poetical features such as rhythm and verse. What is left, the 'plus of art,' is constructed by the spectator actively, not contemplatively. Aesthetics is a 'made' hypothesis, but we know neither where this meaning comes from nor on what it is founded. In this new pragmatic key important Neoformalist concepts take on new, intentionalistic meaning. Style *flaunted* together with artistic *motivation* can only explain otherwise nondescript spectator *activity*. Everything aesthetic is cast into a formal concept 'style' and a pragmatic concept such as 'non-practical attitude.'[138] Both concepts suggest that the viewer must apply a unifying form that explains all of those 'excess' features which exceed the *sujet*.[139] This is an altogether different problem from what was discussed earlier. Here it is only the aesthetic dimension in a narrative, which (it is supposed) adds another dimension of meaning that shows transparently through the narrative, but without attracting conscious attention to itself.

The pragmatic understanding of aesthetic is far from wrong. It is also much more complex, and more promising in that complexity. The sense in which we can reasonably conceive of an aesthetic enunciation (as distinct from the other two enunciations) was discussed earlier. If aesthetic can be enunciated, the encounter with logical questions such as those relating to 'hypothesis making' is inevitable. Our Semiotic analysis of the Aesthetic problem evinced that this is merely the starting point of the question. The next question must be, of what would such meaning consist? The answer given by Neoformalism: it is a pattern proper of a work or author (not exclusive of epochal styles). But this begs the question: Of what is it a pattern?

It must surprise us, though, that the Neoformalist pragmatic, besides, shies away from enunciation,[140] understood as an extra instance beyond the *sujet*. Narrative style is either the banal need to express the media-neutral plot with media-specific devices or 'techniques'; or it leads necessarily to the assumption of an additional 'system' (cf. Bordwell 1985: 52) of additional sources of meaning. However, 'the *trouvailles* will never add up.' Nevertheless, as Thompson (quoted approvingly in Bordwell) says, they 'can allow us to look further into a film, renewing its ability to intrigue us by its strangeness' (both Bordwell 1985: 53).[141]

This lays bare the fundamental question of aesthetic meaning. Whatever the protestations of the inherently hypothetical, 'never adding up' result, there must be meaning to it (else it would be meaningless, or a mere appearance of meaning in the manner of Kant's aesthetic). We can concur with Formalism on the nature of aesthetic as non-conclusive (in the logical and metaphoric sense of the term). This is confirmed in our analysis of Peircean Aesthetic conduct. Even so, meaning cannot be described in a negative manner. Now the question is the same as with deviation-form: How can style be transformed into meaning? It is not meaningful in itself, not even if it stands for a hypothesis-making activity of a spectator or of an author gifted with 'tricks.' Action derives its intelligibility from purpose (as is the case with the 'purpose' of a sign). It would again be a false pretense for Aesthetic conduct to expect a determinate purpose, let alone one of the teleological kind. Although purpose without determination must sound self-contradictory to those who can think only in existential and general determinations. 'Activity,' conduct as such, is not necessarily determined by these two determinations; there can also be an abstract determination.

Perhaps it is best to content ourselves with this much, as can be gleaned from the aesthetic core operation in the Formalist Idea: a difference, as two complementary levels (in a spatial metaphor). The rest, such as the concept of style, is best left *in situ*: a middle ground theory of literariness (bracketing fundamental theories of representation and grand theories of meaning, for which Neoformalism has no real answers). Apparently 'device' is in practical terms not so much a general aesthetic form; rather, it has no other use than the one connected with the *sujet* parameters (namely, the twists of event presentation). This limits the scope of this aesthetic theory considerably to the 'middle ground,' which cannot gain purchase on perception as such (not even in the sense earlier described as 'com-position'). It cannot be expected to explain the aesthetic transformation of time. It only claims narrative as being capable of aesthetic treatment. The *sujet* is the aesthetically transformed (no longer familiar) *fabula* (and not the perception of something that is in itself aesthetic). Šklovskij had already emphasized the all-important *sujet* as the lion's share of artistic effort. An aesthetic, in *sujet* terms alone, means that plot is differentiated into its ordinary and artistic varieties, prose and poetic. Only 'practicality' indicates where this starts. All *sujet* is *fabula* defamiliarized, and style is the defamiliarization of *sujet* but is not essentially, logically different from that lower level. The result in both cases remains a teleologically determinate order for the presentation of narrative information. The aesthetic order is not motivated by a different meaning; it only makes the teleological meaning less secure, less familiar. If the active spectator decides to explain the more tentative teleological arrangement of narrative events as art, one presupposes a purpose[142] of 'Kunstwollen,' of an artistic intention.

What is the theory status of Neoformalist aesthetic? The quest for forms corresponds directly to a theory status as 'a systematic propositional explanation of the nature and functions of cinema' (Bordwell 1989a: 250) – that is, as opposed to all sorts of aesthetic interpretation licensed by current practices of film criticism. The nicety of this divide reflects the true theoretical nature of Formalist aesthetics. In fact, the Formalist Idea does not allow the discovery of strictly aesthetic meaning; any aesthetic interpretation must therefore appear as abusive, unwarranted, and wild. Theory then becomes the opposite of interpretation. As schemata and concepts are applied to data in Constructivism, and style forms to representational data, theory is a 'schematic' or 'heuristic' 'account' (ibid.: 253) for functions, 'possessing degrees of generality.' We need not 'share a devotion to interpretation' (loc. cit.) in order to transform a lack into a virtue. What is the meaning in accounting for aesthetic forms without meaning? What is the general insight of aesthetic theory that can be 'falsified empirically' (loc. cit.)? In fact, in its practice this is a historiographical knowledge of historical facts (from genres to devices). No general laws, which could be falsified, are involved. How we retrieve the object itself, the form, without interpreting it, is another mystery (which is but the theoretical manifestation of the tautological definition of 'device,' as discussed earlier). An interpretation[143] must at least help us distinguish a form from that which is not a form.

Semiology has de-aestheticised 'Poetics' as 'discours littéraire en tant que *principe d'engendrement* d'une infinité de textes' (Todorov, in Ducrot (1972: 107). Neoformalism proposed a new poetics of cinema, but apparently its congenial telos is a history of cinema as a development of style conventions. Thompson (1994), in her introductory rationale, identifies as a history-generating principle this question: 'How have uses of the film medium changed or become normalized over time?' (xxvii and 797). This would include 'form, style, and genres' (797). Since Aristotle, poetics has been related to the arts of the representation of the typical in human action, from tragedy to narration. Bordwell and Thompson inherited the theoretical weakness of Formalist aesthetics. Deviations do not yet make for aesthetic theory.

It happens that the Formalist Idea (in its Tartu, Russian, or Wisconsin avatar) can engage in various convenient ad hoc marriages. Formalism can accommodate *salva veritate* code or enunciation theories as directly as Constructivism and Cognitivism. What counts is the aesthetic 'struggle between some order ... and its destruction' (Lotman 1973: 65), which can become all-comprehensive, and 'various extra-textual associations – social, political, historical and cultural – in the form of allusions' (69). The aesthetic form remains empty and simple and tends to become all-pervasive. Schmid (1984: 478) justifiably criticizes the Formal concept of aesthetic (referring to the reduction to 'normalcy' of the *fabula*): 'Insofern die Formalisten dazu tendierten, den Begriff der *Form* mit dem Begriff des *ästhetisch Wirksamen* gleichzusetzen, reduzierten sie die – für sie ästhetisch indifferente – Geformtheit der Fabel zu einer passiven Komponente des Materials.'

Yet as an idea, there is more to Formalism than may have appeared in this discussion. The glaring absence of an aesthetic theory proper, which was discovered early in Formalism (cf. Erlich 1955: 283–6), also makes much sense if it is explained through the aesthetic tradition that brought it to light. There is a broad cultural presence of Schelling in Russian philosophy (cf. Paetzold 1987); moreover, but it has been claimed that the very Formalist aesthetic principle was historically influenced by Schelling's aesthetic. The Rule and its opposite, the homogeneous and the heterogeneous, encounter each other at an empty third point. Unless the two keys of homogeneity and heterogeneity are reflected, this third must remain empty. Language (in the broadest sense) is the homogeneous – it is the known world *in toto*. Because it is cognizable owing to its systemic nature, an opposite can be thought of as heterogeneous. This is the Formalist idea of the aesthetic process as deviation, 'life,' 'objects,' can be other than that which they are. Certainly it is astonishing that something can be opposite to the *totum* or Universal. If the Whole and its opposite can be thought of, it is only in an abstract or formal way. Lotman's 'functional difference' needs to be seen in this light. The Whole and its opposite cannot be separated into two different Universes, because they must meet in one aesthetic effect. Universes that cannot meet (e.g., a bilingual story for unilingual readers) do not become aesthetically relevant. Aesthetics thrives on the uni-Verse of the di-Verse, on the synopsis of the invisible.

Now, how can the meeting of opposites in One-ness be achieved? The key to that oneness is to understand the difference as modality. Lotman's modality refers to the *intensio–extensio* of a concept (not to modes of being), and limits the *intensio* (comprehension or *denotatio*) of the term and extends its *extensio* or connotation (in cinema by lighting and so on, but the achievement is a common cognitive one). 'Clean' is thus used for a kitchen and a conscience. When we place these operations in the aesthetic realm, a figure of thought is created that is more than just modality. Modality in opposition to 'normality,' or rule, indicates that this something, which is achieved, is simultaneously Universal and Concrete. Their mediation creates a 'third meaning.' In all its vagueness, it is close to Schelling's universal Particular, *Allgemeine Besondere*. Schelling's influence, or merely the closeness to the Formalists' central aesthetic principle, is certainly not one that can be proven as a school of thought. (cf. 588n23). Yet in view of his general influence on Formalism, we are now able to reflect the merely unnamed in the idea of estrangement and deviation. Then there is a cogent impression of an ultimately Platonic aesthetic theory in scanty Formalist dress: 'Die Schönheit ist weder bloß das Allgemeine oder Ideale (dieß = Wahrheit) noch das Reale (dieß im Handeln), also ist sie nur die vollkommene Durchdringung oder Ineinsbildung beider. Schönheit ist da gesetzt, wo das Besondere (Reale) seinem Begriff so angemessen ist, daß dieser selbst, als Unendliches, eintritt in das Endliche und in concreto angeschaut wird. Hierdurch wird das Reale, in dem er (der Begriff) erscheint, dem Urbild, der Idee wahrhaft ähnlich und gleich, wo eben dieses Allgemeine und Besondere in absoluter Identität ist. Das Rationale wird als Rationales zugleich ein Erscheinendes, Sinnliches' (Schelling Werke V,382).

Before these reflections on Aesthetica come to their close, there is no better way to collect the fruits of our theory inspired by Peirce's Semiotic than to apply it. Aesthetic theory is no end in itself. It is a cognition, it should lead to cognition, it must aver itself as meaning.

Epilogue: Two Aesthetic Processes in Cinema

Our Pragmatic and Semiotic analysis of the Aesthetic in film concluded with our identifying two distinct processes. Both are inscribed within the general framework of Aesthetic logic, but differ with regard to the enunciation on which they depend. One Aesthetic process is a Sign degeneration of the temporal enunciation of narration in film. The Aesthetic Interpretation creates a novel kind of temporality over the evanescent teleology of the narration. The other Aesthetic process is a Sign degeneration of the rhetorical enunciation of representation in film. The Aesthetic Interpretation creates a novel kind of real possibility over the evanescent reality constraints of existential objects. The epitomic *ut pictura poiesis* of pictorial composition is echoed in *ut musica drama* for the effect that Aesthetic has on narration.

Another result of our comprehension of Aesthetic as Sign process is that we can grasp precisely the theoretical status of any Aesthetic Interpretation. Owing to the logical nature of Aesthetic sign relations, there are only illustrations and no proofs. The illustrative 'proof' that an object is Aesthetic is certainly not the existence of this object, but simply that it is possible to see it Aesthetically. A proof of the contrary is impossible. We cannot prove that the following Aesthetic Interpretations of some features of cinema are correct or adequate, because this is not a criterion. These Interpretations illustrate a process, which other Interpretants might construct on the basis of different associations of different Qualities. No Aesthetic Interpretation is alternative to any of the others, and they are certainly not mutually exclusive. Furthermore, since almost anything can degenerate into an Aesthetic sign relation, there is a certain artificiality in choosing the two enunciations of cinema. Here we are merely focusing the field so as to concentrate on those parts which are inherent to the medium itself. To look beyond this would extend us into an immense field of sheer imagination, one that is undoubtedly replete with Aesthetic processes. Even the economy of research relies on initial guesses, imagination, logical processes of abductional inferences. Such a field would be too vast to be meaningfully described. As a proviso for the following illustrations within the confines of cinema, we must bear in mind the ubiquity of Aesthetic Interpretation.

Our analyses have indicated that everything is a Representation in Signs. For cinema, the representational function of Signs is a special kind of labour of rhetorical enunciation. We encounter this special character when we compare a film with normal cognition. The Pragmatic difference between the two is that only film 'is not what it is' – that is, it is treated as a Symbol even though it consists of Icons. We see shapes and colours, not letters, yet we construct meaning from film as if we saw letters. This is not an illusion or an abuse; indeed, it is warranted by the rhetorical efforts of the medium. There is no question that the foundation of that effort is the photographic process. Someone who ignores this – who takes film as a coloured celluloid stripe, for instance – would be unreachable through any rhetorical effort (albeit such ignorance is unimaginable today). Then, however, faith in a probable reality is based on the laborious process described earlier. The

Aesthetic of composition in film is grafted onto exactly this process. How we achieve this non-representation, which is constitutive of Aesthetic signs, is illustrated in Cavalier's film *Thérèse*. At the same time a dramatic aestheticization of time is taking place (such synaesthesia is quite common in the practice of cinema).

From its opening sequences, our first and strongest impression of this film is its slow rhythm. This is clearly a matter of time management; that said, this slow rhythm has strong repercussions for how reality is being represented. The particular reality of this film is mainly a consequence of the film's composition, but it is also the result of Cavalier showing one thing at a time, as it were. At various places in this film he not only isolates completely rarefied objects through visual and compositional means, but also uses the 'time' of rhythm to the same effect. Clearly, this is making a double Aesthetic use of time. As dramatic time, rhythm renders time directionless, and in this way it is quite unlike narrative teleology. When rhythmic time is applied to object representation, however, it has an effect on rhetorical representation. The coherence of the universe of the probable is broken up into lacunae and ilots, into nothing and yet emphatically something. Incoherent 'somethings' have a peculiar effect on reality as we normally experience it. Every cognitive act, every pragmatic conduct, assumes and relies on the chain of outside reality, temporally and spatially and – in various causal relationships – as a combination of the two. Aesthetic conduct produces the derealization of the existentially real also in the form of the rupture of the chains of causes and of spatiality. Spatial connections are severed quite visibly in *Thérèse*, through the use of black-outs and panning-outs. Causal connections, however, are always temporal relations. So for their rupture to be achieved, the flux of time must be broken. Here it is rhythm that ruptures time, and rhythm itself is first of all a spatial rhythm of the blacked out lacunae and ilots of autonomous objects. There is no general recipe for rupturing reality chains. In *Thérèse* this is done in a very particular way that is quite different from the aesthetic approaches followed in *Passion* and in *Ordet*. In these two films we are in the presence of a clear rhetorical (*Passion*) or narrative (*Ordet*) enunciational effort, against which the Aesthetic effort must impose itself. Godard's means are much alike in all his films; for instance, the water lily sequence of *Je vous salue, Marie*, which I have used repeatedly as an illustration, is quite typical of his method. Having carefully precluded any possibility of linking the ilot of image to any diegetic universe, he can use the resultant meaning as a rhetorical assertion (water lilies) or as much less. This is the case when he does not even provide a rhetorical universe of meaning, as we shall see in the analysis of the opening shots of *Passion*.

To rupture the chain of a narrative universe seems a self-defeating exercise. In *Ordet*, this effort presupposes a delicate and careful trans-formation of time from the teleological kind into an Aesthetic time of Presence. But, the second kind of time can only be grafted onto the first as an alternative Interpretation. Thus the Aesthetic Interpretation can-not impose itself as the only possible one, as in the case of *Passion's* opening sequence; rather, it must remain in competition with a per-fectly intelligible narration. There are only a handful of elements in *Ordet* for which there is no account in the narrative. Again, rhythm plays the crucial role in the concluding sequences here, where it evolves into a mood carried principally by the music. This rhythm is picked up by the imagery and camera movement. Once the meaning effect has set in and the causal chain has been relegated to the universe before death, we are not surprised by the derealizing effect of the over-exposed resurrection sequence.

An Aesthetic Interpretation in film must always struggle with the representational nature of the images themselves and not just with rhetorical enunciation. Even if a film has succeeded in Aesthetically reducing an image to an Icon with ruptured links to any useful Gen-eral idea, the problem remains that such a Sign relation is transitory. If it is not grasped firmly by an Aesthetic Interpretant, the first Correlate will be interpreted as Icon of a representational Sign process. When this happens, the Iconic surplus of an artistic cinematic image is reduced immediately to what it stands for. This tendency to represent can be thwarted only if the nature of the Representamen itself is such as to forfeit any potential for representing a General idea in an Object. With cinematic images, though, this is usually not the case. Thus a causal or existential link suggests itself if it is not impeded. Com-posi-tion – consisting of shadows, lighting, its arrangement in the frame, its compositional value, its colour qualities, and so on – is treated as if it would have it's only function in the rendering of one token of this type (of idea). For instance, the passages of Rembrandt-like intimist scenes through the dark into the next scene – the remarkable stylistic trait of *Thérèse* – can simply 'stand for' the local displacement of the narrative into an adjacent chamber. However, this dissolve of the Aesthetic Icon is unnecessary if the spectator can tolerate not knowing what it 'means.' As a causally meaningless passage, it might become (an 'association of feeling' of the) passage of time, or a physically felt *rite de passage* into the dark of the spectator experience, as in the narrative. We might feel the same anxious expectancy, or insecurity, or something else without name or meaning. Here *Thérèse* would have become an auroral moment of an Aesthetic process. In view of its unrestricted unfolding this process may come to an end with the film in its entirety or even in life after the film, as an aesthetic effect often mentioned by poets in the wake of Aristotle's cathartic effect. The extension of Aesthetic Interpretation in such a way, however, is no longer under analytical control. Although it is certainly possible, just as anything is possible in Aesthetic conduct.

Another instance of virtually unlimited Interpretation possibility can be seen in the opening sequence of *Passion*. This sequence has become so famous in film studies that probably no detail of it has not been noted. Although there are certainly more on record, nine descriptions have been rendered in Paech (1989: 57ff). This camera's pan over a blue sky with a white vapour trail illustrates the two dangers that arise from the need to produce sense in descriptions. Some of the critiques follow the approach of 'narrative scaffolding'; others construe meaning through rhetorical means. In any event this shot must mean 'something.' Yet this meaning is not warranted by the film itself, since there is no linkage at all with any strand of narrative. Nor is it easy to construe any link to this shot from the general 'philosophical' statement of this film. In fact, however we look at it, not enough is said to support any determinate meaning. So on the one hand all of these meaning proposals say too much, and on the other they do not say what could be said.

Here it is a second strategy to treat this shot by declaring it to be a 'reflection of itself.' Then its meaning is self-referential, but at least it is a meaning. We can still doubt that this shot is about 'something' when – regardless of what it could be – the real meaning is identified in its being a shot of a certain kind. Auto-referential meaning, however, is not new meaning at all. As a Sign, it has exchanged its object; in other words, it is 'about' something else. Now it is one aspect of a semiotic object, not a sign-about an object. In a loose sense of the term, it is the Representamen nature that is being examined here. While it is certainly necessary to investigate this all-important formal aspect, the cinematic Aesthetic sign itself has a meaning. Otherwise it would not be a Sign, and this kind of investigation would not concern a Representamen, but would perhaps concern a quasi-physical object in a metaphoric key. This suspicion gathers more weight in view of the term 'pencil,' the object of Paech's analysis. In fact, he explicates Bonitzer's felicitous metaphor of a *caméra pinceau* and is interested in how this functions. Now it is clear that a pencil is an instrument. Thus it is easy to connect with artistic intention, and Godard, when he describes his endeavours, makes extensive use of the entire semantic field of this metaphor. It is an instrumental metaphor, however, and as such abstains from making any pronouncements on the (clearly aesthetic) meaning produced by this tool, the camera pencil. Godard's vivid metaphors do not simply make him a painter with a camera. They also complete the picture with a film canvas, upon which the painting manifests itself. Furthermore, this metaphor can be transcended in the literal sense. Then the film artist goes behind the canvas, first literally and then again metaphorically, when the image of the painting is behind the canvas, 'under the painting.' Now it describes a generative process of imagination, which is imaginary, not visible. At this stage, applying the metaphor to cinema would be impossible if in itself it did not have a poetic meaning. The 'image behind the image' can be grasped in a painter; the *cinéaste* 'time painter' creates images in an analogous manner, bringing time to a halt so that the images can manifest themselves on the canvas (cf. many references in Paech 1989: 61ff).

The 'pencil' remains a tool of meaning, for the 'time painter' as well. With this specification of its usefulness, however, the metaphor itself indicates the essence of the procedure. Pencils com-pose, they compose something, they compose on a surface of spatial relations. A pencil composes relations, something that produces sense in a mind, relations that are produced through this sense alone. Godard uses this metaphor also to express the 'dynamic of the image' to come out from 'behind the canvas,' yet it is not the image that comes out. In reality, it is meaning, but in a much broader sense than in the usual one of determinate meaning. We are justified in rejecting this sort of meaning for cinema, both as images and as aesthetic. Thus, in speaking of cinematic meaning against the intentions of the metaphor chosen by Godard we must respect the limitations that are inherent in this meaning. It would be a mistake to expect too much determined sense, and we must be prepared to discover sense beyond determination, assuming we have the means with which to discover it. These means can only originate in a theory of signs that does not depend on the principle of differentiation (which would again introduce determination into meaning).

In our case, insisting on 'painting' means desisting from narration and from rhetorical constructions of reality (all commentaries about the opening shots of *Passion* agree on this). Conversely, no one denies that this composition 'makes sense' of some sort: the 'image behind the image' can be conceived of at the very least as a Quality of an association of feelings. This association cannot be described in language, but it can be 'painted.' Now this would open an unlimited space of freedom, because feelings cannot be constrained by concepts. Reduced to language, but without its inherent conceptual logical constraint, there is the feeling of the vastness of a sky extending beyond all limits. What makes this different from a rhetorical device is that, here at least, Godard has not pictured a trope, or even a proverb, as he so often does in *Je vous salue, Marie* (v. *supra*). For instance, when we compare the two quite similar images of airplanes soaring in the blue sky in the opening sequence of *Passion* and shots ##39 and 40 (soundtrack only) in *Je vous salue, Marie*, the difference we find is not so much in the image-Representamen itself. In fact, both could be stock images for almost any usage. In the latter there is a rhetorical linkage to the context of meaning that is an incarnation of the classical iconography of a dove hovering over the Virgin (cf. El Greco's famous Annunciation painting). This causes the airplane to mean something and to become a sign for something else. In contrast, the former is not explained by any rhetorical or narrative intention, and thus remains isolated. Now it can mean anything – for instance, the metaphorical vastness of freedom ('the sky is the limit'). Such a meaning is rooted in a Quality, which originates in a spectator who follows the diagonal vapour trail into the heavens.

Pure relation involves more than spatially positioning a composition as a procedure of meaning. Composition is what is left when the Sign itself, or Representamen, is such that it has excluded all questions of existential truth and of Generality (i.e., 'Is it?' and 'What is it?'). Yet there is still something left. This is proven when such a remnant becomes the target of a conduct of behaviour. Aesthetic conduct aims at compositional meaning proposing as the value of its action only the *summum bonum*. Ultimately, this is the only difference between this opening sequence and an experience of nature (at the same time, around Geneva airport, the same view). Composing degenerates the Sign relation in such a way that it is impossible to ask, 'Where does this airplane go?' (Michel Celemski asked instead, 'Is it a military airplane?' cf. Paech 1989: 58). Composing poses qualities of feeling into a relation, but the action of posing is guided by the vastest undetermined possibility. It makes sense. 'Composing,' however, is a transitive verb, and no more can be said or experienced without destroying this sense as Aesthetic sense through determination. Thus the airplane has become a 'comet announcing a Diluvial catastrophe' (Celemenski), without diegetic connection; or it has become the exordium of Isabelle Huppert toiling away in the factory in the next sequence (Raymond Lefèvre), with diegetic connection; or it has become the 'scream or signature' of Godard (Jean-Claude Bonnet), with biographic connection; or it has become 'commencement, easiness, liberty, emptiness' (Bonitzer), 'primaeval chaos' (Bergala). It is part of the Possibility of Aesthetic Sign relations that all of these interpretations are possible without contradicting one another.

Strictly speaking, Quality and *summum bonum* cannot be described further (thought in Symbols). They can only be thought in Icons. This means that what we see here is not really the blue sky, the white vapour trail; and it is not the white diagonal before a spatial depth with a field of whiteness in the upper left corner. For Aesthetic conduct this is not yet meaningful. In the first case, sky, it would still be existential meaning and in the second case an abstract meaning of abstract pictorial forms. No description can function without one of the two linguistic portraits, but this is not the concrete reasonableness of an association of feelings. As a project of action it is reasonable conduct; more than this we cannot determine. Only thus far is this value determined: that this association is feasible as conduct. This is disappointingly scanty, it must be admitted, for an interpretation of a film. There is, however, a point in placing this opening shot as the commencement of the film. In this way the Aesthetic image is not experienced in itself (as is insinuated by describing it). Now it has the capacity to extend the association. This is still no causal link of any sort, and it still does not partake in an auroral metaphysical or practical philosophical discourse (as may be almost unavoidable in film criticism). Instead, it salvages its lineage of association to the rest of the film by 'ad-sociating' what follows. For what follows this presupposes, implies, posits, that exactly this Quality is also found here. But it must remain a Quality if its meaning is to remain Aesthetic. By linking it to its narrative threads or rhetorical conviction, a film could choose to destroy the Aesthetic meaning at any time. However, the reverse is also possible. As our illustrations of the water lily sequences in *Je vous salue, Marie* have shown, rhetorical achievements can suddenly be re-aestheticized. This is shown as well in the final sequences (#292: 'Ascension,') where discursive and strong tropical allusions (the bleating sheep of the biblical

Shepherd) suddenly dissolve into purely pictorial images without diegetic or rhetorical linkages to the context.

These illustrations of the derealizing effect of Aesthetic meaning in the absence of causalities could certainly be extended to other descriptions. As descriptions, however, they would be able to tell their object. Part of the Aesthetic effect is that it must remain elusive. It is not by chance that all of these descriptions must be negative. For meaning, they must rely on the experience itself. This is a clear – albeit extreme – case where the actual meaning of a Sign rests entirely in its actual usage. As a concept of Speculative Grammar, this is not an impossibility. On the contrary, it is so common as to be the basis of every Sign relation, so that it is difficult to discover. It has no alternatives that can be noted.

Dramatic Aesthetic

Another, entirely different path of Aesthetic effect is meaning over the causal debris of narrative enunciation. The artistic strategy of narrative enunciation in *Ordet* was analysed earlier. A parallelism of two strands, of two alternative unities of action, brings to the fore an alternation of latency and visibility. These two strands are not equal, however, for only the visible one displays a causal chain of narrative teleology. The latent strand has its own temporality, which is of a different essence and is not a simple instance of 'parallel montage' or a precursor of *nouveau cinéma*. Here we are concerned only with what is 'latent' or, in fact, inaccessible through the narrative chain of causality. This is, in this respect, a remarkable example of how the same images can have double usage. Degeneration of the narrative enunciation translates, then, into switching to the second usage, which is Interpretation as an Aesthetic conduct. The double usage is intimately connected with the Johannes figure, whose Interpretation is both crucial and problematic. There can be little doubt about the unsatisfactory and functionally ambiguous narrative status of this figure. That said, what kind of meaningful relation exists between Johannes and the narrative is not at all clear. It might be a rhetorical commentary disguised as a narrative, or it might be an Aesthetic Interpretation of the narrative. The rhetorical solution is certainly easier to sustain. In Aristotle's *Poetic*, poets must represent in a necessary way ($\dot{\alpha}\nu\dot{\alpha}\gamma\kappa\eta$) what is probable ($\varepsilon\dot{\iota}\kappa\dot{o}s$) and what is possible ($\delta\upsilon\nu\alpha\tau\dot{o}\nu$) [51b31f]. In a more or less overt way, rhetorical probability is always part of narration, which in itself is the possibility of an action (which exceeds the probable). For Aristotle, both are based on one common type of argumentation, enthymemes (ἐνθυμήματα), dialectical syllogisms, which affect either as rhetor or poet the passions (πάθος) of the hearer. Representational arts contain figuration, the production of tropes.[144] Although figures are necessary as functions of rhetoric, strictly speaking they are not logically compelling. Narration is based not on an experiential reality but on a rhetorical negotiation. Therefore it is not unexpected if it transgresses into outright rhetoric. *Narratio* is an integral part of every rhetorical *expositio* with, as the principal purpose for arranging, the material for the following *demonstratio*. This creates a framework around the narrative, where rhetorical figuration (such as irony and metaphors) has affected the narrative itself. From a Semiotic perspective, figuration degenerates narrative teleology into an existential true or false Sign; it transforms narration into a forensic exhibit.

If the Johannes character is to be a rhetorical figure, this must be understood as a conviction device. Certainly, we can never conclusively deny that such an Interpretation is possible. If the forensic demonstration were to call for a proof of the dogma of the resurrection, it might use Johannes as its figure. Yet this use is perhaps not the main intent of *Ordet*. I argued earlier against Drouzy's rhetoric of femininity that there is plenty of evidence that this narration should not be interpreted rhetorically. However, there is also plenty of evidence that the evident narrative non-functionality of Johannes can be interpreted Aesthetically. What this Interpretation needs to show is nothing short of a new kind of temporality, the time of drama (in the sense of the Semiotic Aesthetic outlined earlier). Consequently, in the sense of this theory, and in distinguishing Aesthetic from rhetoric, a Formalist analysis of this film can only be a rhetorical account. *Sujet* is the rhetorical meaning of the *fabula* by means of devices of style. Rhetorical figuration is easier to demonstrate in language, where unusual semantic elements point to a metaphoric reading. With images, a rhetorical interpretation has no conclusive semantic or syntactic constraint. The rhetorical process as such is comprehensible but difficult to analyze, as is evident in the account of a deceiving flashback in Hitchcock's *Stage Fright* (in Thompson 1988: 142–61). By what means can a film signify 'lie,' or figures such as 'irony' and 'sarcasm'? The telling of truths or their opposites (which can be lies or their variants, such as irony) is indeed the purpose of rhetoric. Thompson can describe flashbacks as rhetorical conventions of truth telling, of rememberings of what was the case. If we could understand the point at which cinema establishes the rhetorical device of veridiction, it would not be impossible for us to detect at the same juncture irony or falsidiction (i.e., falsification). In *Ordet*, for instance, Bordwell (1981), too, sees that the construction of the narrative universe is neither straightforward nor free of ambivalence. In particular, the independence of the camera movements serves no real purpose if the only point of them is to advance the narrative. The camera as Dreyer uses it has no pragmatic motivation (i.e., interpreted psychologically as a standard emotional reaction to a standard situation of a possible action). But is Dreyer employing the camera as a rhetorical tool? If the answer is 'yes,' he is creating a tropical meaning – that is, using it as his stock device for giving a metaphorical interpretation to different situations. But this is not obvious. When we compare Dreyer's independent camera work with that of others (Tati's in *Playtime*, for example, or in *Mon Oncle's* remarkable 'staircase orgies'), we find that tropes of irony and the like are too conspicuously produced to be overlooked. There are no such obvious tropes in *Ordet*, and subtle tropes are more a matter of intentional interpretation.

Thus all indications speak for an Aesthetic Interpretation. This means that this film has the potential as a Sign process to degenerate further than the rhetorical stage. A strong indication of this comes from Dreyer himself, when – in his article on abstraction (Dreyer 1973) – he lists as his style: 'effect of rhythm and composition, the mutual tension of colour, interaction of light and shadow, the gliding rhythm of the camera.' However, this is hardly exhaustive. Among the more conspicuous means, there are also the following: extremely long takes; the tracking of characters one after another without psychological motivation and with an independent camera; the famous 180° shot around Johannes and the two children. The rhythmic and compositional qualities of the closing sequence of *Ordet* deserve particular attention. In Petric's detailed formal description, they achieve the 'transformation of an idea into a symbol' (1975: 109). Just taking up some of the key words (110f) renders the idea of the building up of the Aesthetic sign: 'strong visual parallelism'; 'visual simplification of components'; 'white tone of the dead side and black tone of the living side'; camera angle, on the dead side, from the position of Inger's corpse, and the slow gliding of the camera in this position. He summarizes the narrative quintessence correctly: 'The fact that Johannes' behaviour at the end seems more 'normal' than at the beginning of the film is designed to establish ... the spiritual mood of the finale' (111). Thus it is an excellent judgment when, as Petric writes, 'On the level of film analysis, abstraction can be delineated and appreciated only by a close, detailed examination of the cinematic values in a film' (112). Still, we would like to understand what happened in the 'ideation' itself. The most detailed description of the film's texture is not the description of the 'abstraction,' 'spiritual mood,' or 'overtone' (which is only a metaphor, exactly like Dreyer's own speaking of a 'fourth and fifth dimension').

All of these observations indicate only one clear fact: there is a conspicuous presence of something, and thus something is not functional to the narration, nor does it state anything (it does not even comment on the narrative). This 'something' could be called 'style' or 'device' if it had a narrative or rhetorical purpose, but it is not evident that it does. If it did, the meaning would be a determination of narration or of statement. It could be described clearly as this meaning (and not any other). Now all descriptions agree that they hesitate: What meaning can be assigned to this 'something'? Nobody treats these as meaningless, merely formal surfaces.

Still, it is possible to offer an Aesthetic description of this spurious meaning in the closing sequences of *Ordet*. The com-positional association was outlined above, but apparently the more important Aesthetic Interpretation here relates to the dramatic transformation of the narrative. If this Interpretation has some grounds in the sequence, it proves its worth by presentating of a transnarrative temporality of Presence. We take it from our analysis of narrative temporality that every 'time' as Sign of ordered sequentiality contains continuous supra-temporality (i.e., the non-discrete). If we Interpret this final sequence Aesthetically, we see in the narrative of *Ordet* from a transition strict sequential order to Continuity, which is pure Presence (i.e., not the absence of time as past and future). In Olmi's *Genesi*, instead, the transition is from Continuity *sans* causality to strict temporality. Such a Continuous, 'eternal time' is not the time of our experience as long as it remains causal experience; thus it can only be grasped through an exceptional relation. In normal circumstances this time is not unreal, it is only co-experienced in everything temporal. For an Aesthetic use, we must isolate a co-present element of whatever is being experienced temporally. A similar isolation, but for the use of metaphysical accounts of experience in time, takes place in the diagrammatic play of thoughts, which obtains concepts such as 'evolution.' Evolution in the Peircean sense cannot mean that we can indicate actually existent beings as being 'eternal,' infinite, evolutionary steps, and so on. However, the Aesthetic reduction of causal time is different; in a sense, it is the opposite of metaphysical extension. As metaphysic, time is the thought (i.e., not thinking) in abstract anticipation of the temporal process in thinking. As Aesthetic, time is the quality of feeling (but 'feeling' here is not verb). If as a beholder one feels, and associates what one feels, the thesis is that one can associate a temporal quality. The only quality of time that is no more than an association of feeling is Presence, since any future or past time necessarily involves comparison. For an Aesthetic Interpretation of cinematic time, danger looms over Presence in that it so easily becomes the present of a future. The Presence of the resurrection sequence in *Ordet* merely requires a little reflection, ideological justification, explanation, or something similar, for it to be built up into 'a new beginning after a crisis.' This is the end of Aesthetic perception, however. In *Genesi*, instead, the poetic quality of time must be brought to an end – an end that coincides with the first murder.

Aesthetic Interpretation makes immense demands on film images; it detaches them from object representation and attaches them to the merely possible. The resurrection sequence achieves this compositionally through the use of rarefied images. Rarefaction entails a rarefied time (i.e., rare in causal links such as 'rhythm,' gliding dissolve, and gliding camera). In this form, images yield too little information to be meaningful as representations. The puzzling aspect is that nothing can be defined conclusively, yet we are assisting in the advent of something not yet seen. This creates the shadow of indeterminate expectation, not of waiting. All of this takes place after the principal narrative strand has already been closed, foreseeable in every detail as an ordinary village funeral with a certain consoling mood. Yet somehow we step out of this dire sequentiality (which passes so painfully slowly) into a non-sequential mood. This is the temporal 'Quality of feeling' of Presence, an Aesthetic presence, not a metaphysical thought. A presence that can only be felt presently, and not stored in a repeatable thought.

The Aesthetic particularity of *Ordet* is that the Time of Presence is conveyed by means of an altogether different, teleological time. The hinge is the strange teleology of a fool. As a figure of thought, this genre follows the premodern pattern of the plausibility of the fool (also exploited in Bergman's *Det sjunde inseglet*, and by Kierkegaard in his famous parable of the fool and the fire alarm). Modernity has reduced fools to psychiatric 'cases,'[145] for whom the difference is chiefly one of the intelligibility of the teleological aspect of narrative action. As a counter-episteme, premodern culture assigned to fools a place on this side of the boundary of truth, which was lost when 'mental disease' reduced the actions of fools to inaccessible behaviour. Dreyer had a cultural warrant to offer a particular treatment to Johannes, the fool in *Ordet*. He used this warrant to reduce action to a non-teleological, non-logical meaning that could no longer make use of causal time. The dissolving of action into its possibility is far more difficult to achieve than a rhetorical, non-narrative representation. Since narration consists of (teleo)logical connection, dissolving it destroys the very object. Dreyer stated that his aesthetic strategy was to transcend the 'actual rooms of a film' into 'what the artist's eyes can see into a vision' (cf. Petric 1975: 109, quoting Dreyer 1973).

Dissolving without destroying teleology can perhaps mean rhetorical figuration, with rhetorical figures commenting on narrative characters. However, it can perhaps also consist in an Aesthetic reduction. In *Ordet*'s central character Johannes, figuration involves that as a trope, he would comment on the narrative that is evolving in parallel with his own rhetorical construction. An Aesthetic Interpretation, in contrast, does not compare with something else and has no parallel meaning. Johannes is still within the narrative universe of Borgensgård, but he is not linked to it as a necessary element. Conversely, the plausibility of 'Johannes' as an Aesthetic sign necessitates an association of feeling, and this erases the possibility of arriving at a judgment on him. In narrative terms, the efforts of those surrounding him to make sense of him all fail. Neither old Borgen, nor the Pastor, nor the Doctor, nor Mikkel judge him in ways that turn out to be relevant. But this is only a diegetic indication that the other characters of this universe cannot establish causal, psychological links. It still might be that the narration itself has a function for Johannes that is hidden from the characters. It would have to be a function either of rhetorical comment or of a 'hidden agenda.' In the latter case, a narrative constructs a veritable teleology of a 'real' event occurring beyond the grasp of any of the diegetic characters. This option cannot be discarded offhand, but it must be comprehensible to the spectators that the 'real' story is the one of Johannes and not the Borgen epos. What would be the teleology of that other, 'real' narrative? Clearly, there is nothing that can independently be told of Johannes (except as a precarious non-linking parallel strand of the Borgen narrative). If the Johannes theme is to be a rhetorical commentary on the Borgen narrative, it must be possible for us to elucidate meaning in such a way as to shed light on the narrative. What is the true meaning of the Borgen epos that the Johannes figure proclaims? What is the interpretation of the immanent film critic, Johannes? Is there any proposition of meaning that is clearer than the epos itself?[146]

In light of all the difficulties with possible alternatives, an Aesthetic Interpretation – which is always possible – here seems the *only* possible one. Other alternative Interpretations are apparently not reasonable; they would also counteract Dreyer's artistic intent of 'abstraction.' The rarified images he creates would have no meaning, except perhaps as artistic mannerisms. It seems much more important than any propositional meaning that this film wants to provoke a new kind of experience. If it is indeed experience, it must be noticeable as a transformation of the experience of time. That which can only be experienced is nothing that can be told over and over again (i.e., only a certain time logic is capable of such repetition). For compelling reasons, the proof of such an experience can never be furnished except by excluding its alternatives. It remains no more than an experience, and as such it can furnish only details, hints, which are in themselves without meaning, but which become meaningful once they are experienced. All of this hints at an Aesthetic Interpretation connected with the Johannes figure that can fall into place. Two indications of this meaning are his hieratic acting, movements, and parlance, manner of speaking, which are supported and fostered by camera angles and by distance; and the particular way in which (only) Johannes is panned (tracked). The experiential coherence is brought about by the rise of a new kind of temporality (which must be described differently from the way in which it is experienced). If there is a figure among all the characters in *Ordet* who is likely to undergo what Dreyer calls 'symbol'-ization, then it is certainly Johannes. The 'fourth and fifth dimension' would be projected onto him.

Now to the decisive question: How is this Presentic quality of time built up from within an altogether teleological narration? The treatment of the Johannes figure starts from a teleological void. For in the beginning was an Absence. (1) The first glimpse we get of Johannes is significant. His very narrative coming into existence is notably as an absence, namely, as his empty bed (#2). Before we are allowed to see him, he begins to cause turmoil in his family by his absence (note here that only Inger stays calm [#7]). Meanwhile, the family members are introduced one after another, but indoors (at the same time, the house is described visually, as a farmhouse with low ceilings and small windows). An empty time does not move towards a telos; in a teleological logic it is stasis. Things grow 'worse,' however, in the next Johannes event, when we see him leaving this world. (2) Johannes comes into view (#3) outdoors in the dunes, hieratically walking away upwards.[147] This is on the z-axis, which interrupts the incessant lateral panning for the first time (i.e., the family was introduced using lateral panning). The tone for that 'symbolic' dimension is thereby set, both literally and figuratively. Clearly, the scene is overflowing with more than the meaning that is needed narratively at this point. It is certainly no coincidence that the (invisible and extradiegetic) sheep are bleating when the unrecognized Good Shepherd goes out into the world. There is no need for this in the narrative context of the recapturing of the fugitive fool.

The narrative presence of the figure 'Johannes' turns immediately into a veiled transnarrative presence of a rhetorical now, but as a prophetic accusation. (3) This involves a visually impressive 'non-meeting' meeting between Johannes and his family. Here, Johannes never shares the frame with other family members. Not only that, but Dreyer flaunts the falseness of an eye-line match, which symbolically and narratively is nevertheless right. After Johannes's 'Woe unto you, ye hypocrites, thee ... and thee ... and thee ...[148]' we see – and this as reaction shots (!) – each one of the Borgens. As Bordwell (1981: 155) has noted, the non-communication between Johannes and the others is expressed visually. This is not simply a separation, as he suggests,[149] but more like a quite complex relationship. First, it is rather ambivalent, in that it is not clear whether Johannes is really addressing anyone. Visually, this ambivalence is expressed in the false eye-line match, on which the meaning of his words 'you ...' is based (v. *infra*). Second, however, Johannes is responding very precisely to his family's appellations, but in a symbolic way. Even more, all of his family, not just the two girls, are clearly responding to his messages, albeit with apparently awkward feelings. His symbolic messages are understood as being meant for them, but the resulting communication is bent off-track by their reinterpretation as symptoms. Their tropical foolish truth is reduced to the literal meaning of madness. Johannes, therefore, is clearly not just an 'absence,' as Bordwell (loc. cit.) sees it, but more of an undefined presence, the beginning of a Presence. Where this figure is heading becomes more and more unclear. All the other figures either develop their aims or lose them; in contrast, there is no imaginable direction in which Johannes can develop. Is this the narrative beginning of an aesthetic interpretation, of conduct either undefined or only 'defined' by the possible? The space of Possibility is kept open for the rest of the film. Such an ambivalent presence is visually supported by spatial indefiniteness. This is seen very clearly in this first meeting, yet from here onwards it is also seen by means of the eerie presence of Johannes. He can never be precisely located in the house; instead he drifts in and out almost all the time.[150] Both universes share the same space, yet they are visually kept apart and are absently present to each other. An inattentive analysis would perhaps conclude of madness, or a complete lack of communication between the normal and the madman. Yet this is supported neither visually nor through dialogue. On the other hand, the two universes do not converse directly before the resurrection scene. We might conclude, then, that there is a symbolic 'space' and a parallel time. There, communication takes place exactly in the same way as between people who speak in images (i.e., in the non-said of the said, in the non-causal co-presence of meaning).

Still in this first key sequence, Dreyer establishes crucial visual elements. Johannes is shown from an extremely low angle standing against the sky, whereas the Borgens are seen from a high angle. How these characters are shown is highly significant. Johannes's introduction ends with him looking down from heaven, as the last 'judgment' after his words. Thus it is the only place before the resurrection where heaven ('*himmilen*' is both 'sky' and 'heaven': the word is used twice in Johannes's speech) visually plays a role. Nowhere else can we catch a glimpse of the sky/heaven. Only during the resurrection scene does the light, flooding inside for the first time, play such an important role. Whereas in the dunes it is only the moon, and in the next scene with Johannes it becomes candlelight ('I am the light of the world'). So we are carefully prepared and sensitized to catch the importance when the chamber where Inger is laid out is lit (overexposed), in sharp contrast, with light[151] in the strong sense of the word. Dreyer clearly is providing visual closure from the initial prophecy to the laying-out chamber, but as a crescendo.

In the next decisive sequence (4), Johannes returns to preach repentance. In #11 he makes his first appearance inside the house ('I came unto my own, and my own received me not'[152]). Symbolically, he makes his mission known by lighting candles, which he places in front of the dark windows. What is narratively madness, is – ambivalently – made visible as a claim. Dreyer dwells with other eyes on this scene, through the attentive gazes, off-screen but felt, and 'their' reaction of 'amazement.'[153] This scene gives the narrative the occasion to test three different visions of Johannes, three principles of Interpretation. The first two ways of making sense of his behaviour resort to teleology. (a)

In the negative key of a deadend teleology is Mikkel's voice of reason. In fact, Johannes gives veiled but symbolically reasonable answers to practical questions of life, which his brother does not wish to interpret in an Aesthetic way. This renders Johannes's behaviour unintelligible. It starts a dispute when Mikkel accuses his father, who uses his own teleology in a positive but disappointed way. (b) Borgen responds with deep sorrow, describing how he foresaw and planned Johannes's mission as 'the man with the voice of a prophet,' 'the spark that should once more set Christianity ablaze.' Although this is closer to Johannes self-understanding, the teleological Interpretation – a paternal 'success story' – essentially misses the point. In the narrative, the failure of his Interpretation is named as Johannes concludes that Borgen's 'darkness comprehendeth it not' (i.e., what was expressed in his claims shortly before). (c) The third, essentially different Interpretation, sparked by the candle-lighting scene, comes from Inger. Later this is repeated by Maren and is also expressed narratively as the hope for a miracle. Dreyer makes it clear through a number of visual hints that this is not misunderstood as a pep talk, as optimism, or as empty despair in an upbeat travesty. Even before Johannes's entrance, a first symbolic hint is given by way of a Grundtvig picture: Jesus raising the son of the widow in Naim.[154] Inger's prophetic statement is not used as an *incipit* of an arc of narrative expectation; it remains as obscurely grounded as Maren's. What she starts to see is impossible to foresee. This obscure feeling has an equally obscure echo in the bleating of the sheep, when Johannes wakes from his fainting spell (or was it a catatonic state?). This dense web of allusions lends credibility to the seemingly irrational vision of Inger, but offers no ground that is narratively prepared. This is far from being a narrative counteraction to the heroization of Johannes (as Bordwell suggests); rather, Inger seems to be experiencing something that is not warranted by anything within the narrative. The intra-narrative breaking point of the expectation logic of teleology happens here. Her faith that Johannes will be 'his old self again' (but what is 'old' in connection with his 'self'?) is not a wish for a happy ending as announced by a narrative logic. Her statement remains ambiguous in remonstration of Mikkel's rationality, which declares Johannes 'mad as a hatter.' Although there is nothing from which we can deduce that Inger considers Johannes mad, we see no reason why Mikkel should be considered wrong.

There is a latent war of Interpretation in these three possibilities of meaning. All three echoes are types of sense making. If meaning is determination, Interpretations confine the space of possibility for Johannes either to be resigned (madness as the non-linkage of a teleologically determined probability chain), or to be dreaming (causal linkage is established, but on a horizon of paternal expectation), or to be presaging belief (as undetermined possibility). Only the latter corresponds to Aesthetic conduct and to its guidance through an undetermined value of *summum bonum*. These differences also reflect on their interpreters in the narrative consequences. Through their reactions to Johannes, these characters (and their narrative doubles[155]) are differentially defined and receive their narrative action plans. This includes Inger as a narrative character (and her doubles, her daughters). After the Grundtvig picture and Inger's faith, Maren's hope for her mother's resurrection becomes almost natural, and she certainly represents Inger herself in this. As Johannes becomes the pivot of the narrative character differentiation, he can then become the hinge of events, though on another 'non-event' plane. The climactic event of the main epic plot takes place: the family contracted contended between Peter and Borgen, around – but not caused through – Johannes's symbolic death (fainting and disappearance for three days) and 'second coming.' Dreyer's strategy contrives the increasing irrelevance of that plot, however. Although Inger's premature death is also seen as a family tragedy (the bitter remarks of Borgen and Mikkel go in this direction), Dreyer's treatment of the final sequences steers clear of solving this tragedy. Yet it is solved by accident, when all the teleological threads are summarily knitted together. In between, however, a new experience occurs, involving some narrative characters as if they were outside the narration. The narration is not destroyed, only suspended, as is made obvious when teleology is resumed and Dreyer rushes to now irrelevant conclusions.

What seems to be a narrative causal link is in fact much more subtle. If Dreyer had chosen to treat it as a miracle, the conventions of this genre of admiration would have called for a decisive transformation of a (witnessed) before and (astonishing; cf. Aristotle's θαυμαστὸν) after. Now there is no test. The final sequence does not function as a confutation of those sceptics who do not believe in miracles (doctor, pastor), even though this is also an accidental result. But, there is no way to show through narrative logic that this logic is suspended. There are only a number of strategies that make use of this logic but that prepare a different logic. Our earlier discussions showed that since this logic is different in nature and not different in a differently determined constraint, less determined Aesthetic logic does not eliminate narrative logic, and even impedes narrative to exercise its incidence upon Aesthetic signs. Thus the augmentation of possibilities in Aesthetic signs, although comprehensive of teleological determination, is merely indicated by an augmentation in the narratively unnecessary elements. What use we make of this augmentation is beyond narration but is otherwise left open. One such instance is Dreyer's treatment of the second disappearance of Johannes (5), which precedes his second coming. What seems to be a replica of his first disappearance (#2) is in fact already an Absence. While the first search was remarkably silent,[156] this one has an urgent tone. Father, brothers, and neighbours all shout the Absent One name. But the derealization is not an effect of temporal ellipse; rather, it works through a strange mixture of off and/or over voices, which is carried out in no place. Dreyer produces an eerie impression through the acoustic quality he gives to these shouts: he varies acoustic perspective (from so near that it is an acoustic close-up!), from all directions (even though the sound is monophonic, this is noticeable), with an echo reverberation far too prominent to be credible as that of the dunes. All of this adds up to an evident temporal ellipsis from shout to shout, rendering these shouts as an anxious rhythm of voices with different pitches, distances, directions. In comparison with the first instance – when Johannes disappeared only from his family – an 'abstraction' is evidently at work.[157]

In his final appearance (6) – indeed, if it were a narrative climax, we would say in his almost apotheosis-like re-appearance – Johannes is shown for the first time without a 'prophet's coat,' unconcealed and unveiled, as it were. This is only a minor hint at a far more important change (which is a cinematic technique): the manner in which he is framed. For the first time, Dreyer frames him with other people, in a significant manner. So far in *Ordet*, there have been only two notable exceptions to his visual separation from 'this world.' The first involved Maren, who believes in him without reserve. The second involved the pastor, but only partially – just until the latter expressed his scepticism after which point the frame excluded either him or Johannes. That this spatial severance and inclusion is strategic for Dreyer is confirmed when we encounter it again in this final scene. Here separation and unification are meaningful both humanly and spatially, as unity in faith as much as unity in frame. Inclusion and separation framings are systematic. Thus the frame unites Johannes with his father after the father's reconciliation with Peter. Then it unites him with his brother

Mikkel in his deep sorrow, until Mikkel loses his temper and refuses to believe; from that point on the framing separates them again. Most strikingly, Johannes – isolated from all, even the physical world, which becomes a white background – is united with Maren alone. These images have undergone rarefaction, to which Dreyer attributes the most abstracting effect.

Once his narrative function has bottomed out, the aesthetic nature of the Johannes-figure ends in the fulfilment of the long series of intimations. It cannot be a conclusion, however; an Aesthetic Interpretation prevents this logical operation except as the most general 'admirable in itself' (v. *supra*). The inconclusive openness of logical Possibility is there as a carefully constructed kind of temporality. The Presence of this time is prepared by the Absence in narrative time (i.e., in this type of time, presence is opposed not to future and past but to absence). Once the stage is reached where what comes next sequentially no longer counts, what follows remains undefined and possible without any direction. The representation of Johannes is complex and simple at the same time, but on the condition that we change the register of time differences. Dreyer's negation strategy of narrative fulfilment lets the Johannes figure go into dimensions beyond narrative information. *Ordet* is an example of how a narrative, without ever being broken up, can become the bearer of sublime meaning. It is really as Dreyer said: he adds indeed a 'fourth and fifth dimension' to the closed narrative universe (which in itself has only three, as does every other spatiotemporality). What those superadditional dimensions 'really' are must remain open to pragmatic conduct. Only actual Aesthetic conduct determines its aims. There is no strict requirement to determine these dimensions – as the dimension of the Self as in Gadamer (1990) and Jauss (1977), for instance. Yet there is no compelling reason to study aesthetics in a psychological key. It suffices that the norm of pure Possibility is a norm of conduct, which would in a further step also lead to an ethical norm. As such it finds its fulfilment and its complete understanding (of all possible practical consequences) in the seriousness of human action. On the basis of this film, we could indeed also write an ethics of cinema, a natural consequence of the aesthetics of cinema.

The global effect of Dreyer's treatment of the Johannes figure is his relative derealization, even as a narrative character, after a careful preparation culminating in the resurrection sequence. In order to achieve this effect, causal linkage must be severed. Dreyer's technique for this – as we observed it – remains, however, psychological, and this allows him to keep Johannes in the space of the narrative universe. Johannes behaves as if he belongs to another universe. Thus, psychological means lead to the psychological result, that neither spectators nor other narrative characters are able to identify with him. This strategy defeats the very core of hermeneutic aesthetic: identification based on divination. Once all the crucial links to narrative comprehension have been cut, is there any access to this figure other than the psychological? The Aesthetic alternative cannot be the construction of a different universe, which as such again becomes comprehensible. If artistic means make access possible only on a path of 'Quality of feeling,' then a second ('eerie') universe is obstructed; not only that, but a non-causal realm of possibility is opened. When we experiment mentally and imagine ourselves only in the 'world' of Johannes – as if the normal world of Borgengård does not exist – it is evident that that world cannot subsist. There is not even the causal scaffolding to keep it up as an appearance. This world is not only strange but 'impossible' (within the causal reality). It is a possible 'world' (in the loosest sense of the term); In the resurrection sequence, this is a manifest Reality. That Dreyer succeeds in manifesting this Reality is tangible in that he does not make us suffer through an intellectually unreasonable demand when he makes us see this scene. In fact, he deintellectualizes it when he derealizes Johannes's realm of Possibility.

In stark contrast are, for instance, the utterly un-Aesthetic solutions of some current products of the film industry. An early – and since then often rehashed – anti-*Ordet* pattern is instanced in the many *Frankensteins*, in *Dr Caligari*, in the *Nosferatus*, and even in Dreyer's own *Vampyr*. This pattern uses all means to make such a second (usually psychopathological) universe credible. Usually, its means are also psychological. In *Ordet*, Dreyer instead rejected the option of representing the credible in alter's (Johannes's) action; he also rejected identification with alter's action project. The Frankenstein pattern is not even against the fundamental rule of Aristotle's *Poetic* – that 'psychological identification' is the only Type that enables the mimesis of action. Which makes Dreyer's strategy in *Ordet* all the more striking.

The only serious contender for an alternative Interpretation key to the Johannes figure is its figurative rhetorical relation to the narrative universe, in spite of the difficulties with a rhetorical meaning of this figure in this narrative (v. *supra*). There is no real narrative function for this figure, as we have seen. There may, however, be a different kind of meaning that can – through this difference – shed light on its narration.

In this case Johannes amounts to a rhetorical argumentation of the type of *exemplum* or *paradigma* (v.p. 645n146). If this is the intended function of Johannes, we are arguing with something unknown for something that is already known and clear. The purpose of an example argument, however, is to transfer the clarity of the example to the doubts of the case in order to clarify them. Dreyer's Aesthetic treatment of Johannes achieves an opposite effect. Comparing the well-known epic world with Johannes does not explain it but does make it more inexplicable. Only if the inexplicable of Inger's resurrection were to become more comprehensible through the *auctoritas* of a renowned thaumaturgy of the Johannes-figure, would the paradigmatic argumentation work. As it stands, it does not contribute to a clearer understanding; it even disavows comprehension itself. This can also be conceptualized through psychological identification with Johannes as a figure who cannot be comprehended in a causal-narrative type manner, as an inaccessible alter ego. If it were not an oxymoron, we could say that the result is an 'Aesthetic action.' Under normal circumstances – and in terms of Aristotelian *Poetic* – an action without a Type cannot be imagined. Only in a Pragmaticistic Aesthetic does the oxymoron dissolve, when 'acting aesthetically' means acting without determination from values other than the highest. Here the *summum bonum*, the highest value of an action, is taken as a poetic paradigm, a type before the type. In the Johannes figure it is manifest that this is not 'something,' and is nothing substantial anyway, and is neither true nor general. Against the differentiating interpretation of *Ordet* as a 'religious film,' we must also insist, that such an interpretation is in any case not warranted by the Johannes figure. His (Aesthetic) action is not guided by a 'god,' understood as a distinguishable substance or existence, which in any case the Borgensgård doctor has no problem in explaining away conclusively. The doctor, however, uses his own healing powers as a paradigmatic argument for the non-god!. This contrasts with the 'religious film' genre, where a god has become a distinguishable force, either effective or lacking, enhancing or weakening, a character's action (a number of Buñuel's films – *Nazarin*, for instance, and *Simon en el desierto* – make this the topic of an entire film). As a concretely visible action under the guidance of an Aesthetic *summum bonum*, the distinctive feature of Johannes's conduct is that there is nothing left that is distinguishably valuable. As a condition of the possibility of comprehending others' actions, we depends on recognizing not just what they are doing, but more what they are aiming at and what seems to be desirable to them. For Aesthetic conduct this means that only value as such can be identified. Johannes is clearly acting – and quite intensely so – but what his purpose is, is not perceptible.

The labour of Interpreting this non-determinate value is what makes it so difficult to comprehend the Johannes figure. Probably it is this that Dreyer means by 'abstraction.' The purpose of the earlier narrative description of the Johannes figure was to illustrate how such an Interpretation – still of an action – is made possible by experiencing a different temporality. The *summum bonum* can be comprehended as another time, resulting from an action for which no aim is to be found. It is not comprehensible as a negation of aims, however – for instance, as despair, the Sisyphus subject, or *la nausée* of Sartre. As a negation, it still depends on the same time. Whereas the Johannes figure has an intentional relation to nothing. He cannot be justified or glorified after a failed appreciation (as Propp's narrative functions require). Other than with Peter the tailor, the pastor, the doctor, and old Borgen, Johannes is not intended to prove dogmas. In all these instances a narrative program would come to its end. *Ordet* does not conceive Johannes's action as leading toward a narrative ending. Inger's return to life comes at the end of this film, but this is not the end of this film (in the sense of a reversal of a preceding narrative program). Dreyer formed this sequence so abstractly that it greatly transcends the concrete plot. As an 'abstract plot' (if this is not a contradiction in terms), it is perhaps the 'plot of being human,' or (abstractly) any possible human conduct guided by the *summum bonum*.

Perhaps it seems to be working against an understanding of film to give an Aesthetic Interpretation or to propose 'abstraction.' Such an Interpretation must content itself with a less defined meaning than a 'normal' understanding would elicit from a film. Yet from a different perspective, this seems much less problematic. Undeniably, the first impulse of spectators is to construct a meaningful universe (as soon as cinema is prejudiced as a medium of representation, which no one would expect from music, for instance). We have taken account of this customary urge by locating the origin of cinema in different types of enunciation. After all, this is exactly what customary film criticism furthers. For a critic it might indeed be problematic to come up with less meaning than the spectators themselves understand. However, this is precisely our thesis here. Aesthetic enunciation contrives to offer less meaning in cinema, because it is parasitical on the narrative and on rhetorical enunciations. Compared with them, Aesthetic enunciation offers less. However, we might see the relation between the three types of enunciation in analogy to the relation of different kinds of Terms to one another. Terms vary with respect to their connotation and denotation – also called breadth and depth (v. *supra*) – but every term has its own area of breadth and depth (i.e., width; 2.419). The broader a term is (i.e., the more general it is), the less deep it is. A very general concept such as 'being' can apply to everything and is infinitely broad but has almost no depth ('what' is being?). Now, Aesthetic is the least broad and extremely deep. It has almost no general cognitive claims, and it conveys its one Quality of feeling in a very specific and exclusive way. For this logical reason, music is still the best illustration of the Aesthetic Sign or term. It is such a thin term (with almost no breadth) that in a proposition (even a mental one) there is almost no subject that can be joined to such a predicate. 'What does this piece of music mean?' is an irrelevant question because it is understood that there can be no answer to this question. The Semiotic answer, however, is an extension of the meaning of 'meaning,' which in this sense of the term must be all-comprehensive. This includes the lowest threshold of meaning. As a consequence, it must be claimed that even Aesthetic is already an Interpretation, and not just a Quality (which is merely a Category).

Aesthetic enunciation in cinema, therefore, should be meaning of a much lesser extent (breadth) than rhetorical and narrative enunciation, but also of a much larger (deeper) intent. For instance, narration is 'about' much more but 'of' much less. The point of Aesthetic Interpretation as a fully meaningful Sign is, that there is always a particular temporality in every type of Sign. As General cognition must comprise the totality of past and future, as true cognition must intend a present now, thus Aesthetic cognition has its time in an 'eternal' Presence. Also, this temporality is strictly consequential from the triadic Sign nature of the Aesthetic sign. Music is a perfect instance of such a time, so what counts is not where it leads, nor what is now; what does count is that the melody, harmony, rhythm, dynamic, and tempi are non-sequentially present. The sign 'music' through its usage, is therefore an instance of conduct guided by the *summum bonum*, since there is no broader meaning to it. As presence, it is a time that does not change, as the time of indexical Signs that need the difference in order to cognize the truth. In *Ordet*, Dreyer shows how much of the temporality of music can be preserved in a narrative, as time after its completion and beyond its telos. It is not by chance that he makes intensive use of music especially in the final sequence. This must have contributed to a synaesthesis of the temporalities, but in the temporal direction normally not found in film music. Music is customarily 'utilized' to give impetus to the intended psychological effects of narration (and certainly some films would have less of a sense of 'cliff hanging' if there were not the invisible orchestra to orchestrate the metaphorical sus-'pense').

Dreyer's example shows that musical temporality in cinema is not what has been metaphorically referred to as the 'rhythm of cinema' (at least in Lotman's sense; v. *supra*). This trans-narrative infra-narrative time is not unique to *Ordet*, however, although it is an important thread in many other films. While unavoidable in all such instances, the effect is very difficult to grasp and even more difficult to describe. Even so, this too can almost serve as a heuristic tool where the narrative meaning alone is clearly unsatisfactory. Tarkovskij's *Nostalghia* is such an instance. Here the difference between precis and experience will never be bridged. Clearly, the decisive meaning of this film, as also in *Offret*, does not lie in the rudiments of 'plot information.' The viewing experience, on the other hand, is a strange way of seeing a time imposed on oneself. (We should note in passing that teleological time is also the imposition of a logic that is by no means self-explanatory – that is, supposedly caused by the real events. Evidently, there are never events in narrative cinema; rather, there are logical constructions that can be interpreted as events. This is precisely not the case in these two films. Instead, we see without being bothered by teleology.) What we see is less constraining, it is initially no more than the pace of time. The opening shot of *Offret* immediately sets the tone. In one single take of almost sixteen minutes, it is not a case of a 'montage within the frame.' This would require there be narrative functions at work. Yet no event seems to happen (except of the most banal sort, for example, the invitation of the postman to a birthday party). There is however a slow and constant lateral panning, back and forth, repeatedly. This alone changes the pictorial composition of the frame dramatically. Mostly there is a very flat land and sea scape, flat meandering streets (a strong indication of spatial depth). The camera pans along these visual lines, when all of a sudden there is the lone verticality of a Nordic tree.

The camera movement is never psychologically motivated; it does not even satisfy spectators' curiosity. For any information demand, the panning takes too long and is as directionless as if it were aimlessly wandering about. The most extreme form of non-psychological panning is perhaps in Akerman's *Je, tu, il, elle*, but there are also remarkable instances in Tarkovskij's oeuvre. In *Stalker* we see a very long vertical upward travelling of a downward shot hovering over still and dirty water ending on the stalker's hand dipped in the water. Shots such as these create a time that is directionless – that cannot be interpreted as if something or someone was aiming at something. The loose content framework of *Offret* is a banal birthday party, which serves also as the occasion to bring it to its narrative end. The appropriate time, however, is the end of time, time after its ending. In this regard its temporality is a variation of narrative end-of-time cinema such as Pasolini's *Salò* and Ferreri's *La grande abbuffata*, or is even more as directionless and as non-narrative as the opening and closing sequences of *Teorema*. Here as in *Offret*'s opening, temporality without causality is constructed through the decisive support of visual composition. Especially the light, which is at the antipode of the desire-loaded *Out of Africa*-like sunsets. Here we see the pale Nordic light. The painter Hundertwasser – emphatically, by titling his paintings with the most vivid colours 'Regentage' (rainy days) – observed that colours start to shine ('glow') only when in the absence of sunshine they have lost contrasts. The same effect is shown in the Nordic colouration in *Offret*.

To conclude, the three different cinematic enunciations could also differentiate between three times. While the narrative time of teleology is usually not difficult to grasp, it already differs from the 'deictic' time of the rhetorical reality effect. Aesthetic is usually not associated with time, much less with a time of its own, yet the aesthetic experience has often been described in temporal metaphors, as the intuition of the 'moment,' of the felicity of a Presentic happening. The logical conception of Semiotic allows us to grasp this experience more precisely as a Possibility. It is by no means necessary that possibility be understood as the abstraction of facticity. The possible is not abstract, it has a time. Because Aesthetic experience is 'only' possible, no proof can show it, either as a fact or as a necessity. One might say, inverting a classical logical principle (*ex esse sequitur posse*), that 'it follows from its possibility that it is' (*ex posse sequitur esse*). This comes as no surprise in a classification of Signs, as we have seen that there are Sign classes where the principles of the excluded third and of contradiction do not apply.

Conclusion

At the end of this investigation one can ask: What has been achieved? What is still in need of further investigation? The objective was to develop a theory – as comprehensive a theory as possible – of the entire phenomenon of cinema. This aim differs from the purpose of many current film studies, which are concerned with particular aspects of cinema, for instance, cinematic narration, and which show scant interest in and awareness of the problems of meaning as a whole in cinema. I do not deny the usefulness of specialized, 'middle ground' theories. However, the many assumptions these specialized theories make about the phenomenon itself often are neither warranted nor critically reflected. These assumptions are always present, if only in the premises of argumentation or explanation. To subject them systematically to a critical reflection must therefore also support 'middle ground' theories. A general theory, in contrast, has different criteria (i.e., 'values' of cognitive conduct in the Peircean sense) than do theories that concern themselves only with particular features.

One of the principal requirements of a general theory is that there be no feature of the cinematic meaning that cannot be explained by it. In order to avoid misconceptions, this does not mean that a general theory has mutated into a 'grand theory' of sweeping statements. Such theories, in the sense of Bordwell's criticism (cf. *supra*), treat cinema as an object (of *prima intentio*, as it was traditionally called). A Semiotic theory, in contrast, treats cinema as a Sign, which is a concept/'object'-without-difference (i.e., there are not not-Signs). This 'object' can only be reflected on in *secunda intentio*, and whatever is said about cinema in a Semiotic context makes no claims about a physical state of affairs, but is about meaning.

This discourse type is controlled not by facts (true/false states) but by function – that is, by a successful Sign relation. The common and usual parts of cinematic meaning can apparently be explained quite easily, and there seems to be no need for a comprehensive theory of meaning. There has been general agreement that cinema thus represents some reality as the core of cinematic meaning, and only on this basis is it meaningful to develop theories of documentary film or to debate the reality illusion of cinema. Yet, many theories are unable to address, for instance, the aesthetic aspect of film. This is not always obvious, because an incapacity to address aesthetic aspects proper is sometimes concealed by negative treatment as the dissolution of something (representation, code, perception, etc.) Any question not content with an answer what aesthetic is not, must thus be seen as meaningless, as essentialist, or as a vestige of substantial thinking. Thus a camouflage may serve a rhetorical function (as in Eco's metaphor of the strategy of 'narcotizing'), but we have still moved no further in the direction of discovering what aesthetic actually is, and we still cannot differentiate between what is not aesthetic and what we do not know.

If the result of our Semiotic approach is a comprehension of aesthetic in line with our understanding of other types of meaning, this can be considered an asset rather than a limitation of a general theory, and the adage tells us that 'we see what we know.' The possibility of distinguishing the nature of narration from the representation of reality is another point where Semiotic is fruitful. It proved to be the source of much confusion when the nature of these two distinct meanings could not be separated. The worst confusion here involves the different causalities pertaining to each meaning. A narrative illusion of reality – which is, however, a reserve of representation – has been surmised by some. The temporal connection of narration operates as final causality, whereas efficient causality makes meaning from differences in representations. To comprehend this difference we must grasp what distinguishes 'suspense' from an intriguing image of interesting objects requiring explanation in a film. We could certainly not exclude that moving images fulfil a double function for two types of causality. A clock, for example, becomes the object 'clock' once the causes that make it function are understood, but at the same time, over and above being a clock, it can have a meaning that is specific to the narrative purpose, and this creates a teleological vector (for instance, in a suspense sequence, using the image of a clock with the intention of showing the prevention of the explosion of a bomb).

Fundamental comprehensiveness does not force a theory to develop each new avenue in a substantial way. Our interest focuses on three areas: narration, representation (especially through rhetorical means), and aesthetic meaning. Other interesting avenues require future investigations. One such avenue might be more relevant to television than to film studies – the production of truth claims by moving images. This is the quintessence of the identity of documentary film; it is also a component of every cinematic sign. Certainly, this is ultimately due to the Second universal Category, but in the documentary sign it must have found its proper Representamen, without which it could not function. 'True images' as meaning are very important and could be investigated on a broader basis than our rhetorical analysis. Rhetoric 'keeps an eye on the audience,' it is said, for the construction of its probability. This creates a context of action, including the values of conduct. In the case of 'true images' this must become a very general context, cognitive conduct of truth investigation, with a general and total audience in mind. Obviously this also makes demands on the Representamen, and this would be more general than the rhetorical figures we observed in Godard.

Another promising avenue rooted in the Semiotic approach concerns the cognition of Generality. As we have said, a General is never true but is necessarily vague, which is a different type of logical constraint. The only Generality we were interested in was narrative teleology, which is 'true' only when every state of affairs corresponds to the narrative purpose. But we are already at the sunset of this type of logic when it becomes a matter of dyadic 'verification.' As long as it is narration, it cannot be verified but only fulfilled in the future. Teleology is merely a special case of Generality; arguably, it is also the one most common in cinema. This leaves the question about a broader theory of Generality in film. We are already in the realm of Generality when film manages to produce vague Signs. Of course, 'vague' is not tantamount to ambiguous; only fully functional Signs (i.e., the bases of a successful Interpretation) are considered. Vagueness is a cognitive achievement over Oppositionally determined Signs, which are only true or false and are not of the nature of a genuine cognition. The question that must thus be explored is this: To what extent is cinema capable of producing General Sign relations beyond teleology? From Peirce's sign theory, we know that such Signs require a Representamen of the nature of a Legisign. So the next question is: Are there rules in the cinematic Representamen that amount to more than the fixed optical relation to its object of representation? These are some of the investigations waiting to be continued.

What has been treated extensively in this investigation? First, the basic question of the 'nature' of film. At this theory stage, substantial differences among film theories already can be noticed. Subsequent skirmishes may expose starker disagreements, but their root is most often in a certain understanding of the capabilities of cinema (and this is thus an area which cannot be avoided). Compared to merely axiomatic assumptions, or to media essentialism, or to solutions based on codes and so on, a thorough analysis of cinema as a Sign process has clear advantages. It is based entirely on relational logic without becoming trapped in psychological speculations, for instance, and without making ontological assumptions about matter and time.

Second, this investigation has pursued the intricacies of time insofar as it is captured by films and has become the core of their nature. It is helpful to be able to separate temporal reality from existential reality. This avoids any confusion – in many film narration theories – between spatial and temporal being, as if they were of the same type of reality and of the same causal relation. Logically, such an assumption is wrong. Film theory must treat time in an entirely different way than 'oppositional' perceptive representation (often called 'space,' which it becomes in film through narration, as space of action – that is, after the imposition of temporal logic).

Third and this is still closer to the cinematic phenomenon, is the problem of the threefold enunciation in cinema. In our analysis of time we found that every teleological Sign must be constructed through the setting of a zero point. While this is common to all time experience, in cinematic texts this task is performed not by the reader's living experience, but by textual rules. We have discovered the three types of enunciation in film: the narrative, the rhetorical, and the aesthetic. These three differ in the rules a text must establish in order to produce those meanings as specifically different ones. Certainly, as modes of cognition they are not limited to texts. Texts merely ascertain through rules that certain types of cognition are facilitated and other types are impeded (which are covered by other enunciations). We could say that there is a certain gradation in the genesis of meaning. The universal, relational Categories are the basis of phenomena as such. This must become Sign to be a cognition. On the basis of Signs, textual organizations produce further rules, and these are also a further determination of meaning. However, in all three grades meaning is always the same process.

The method, then, in Semiotic investigations is a true formalism. This combination is usually an oxymoron, but in Semiotic both qualities are necessary. Formalism alone does not allow us to account for a concrete cognitive act, but only for formal cognition. The consequences have been visible in formal aesthetics, which are incapable of rendering the cognitive result of a formal aesthetic operation. What codes produce, and what styles yield as resultant meaning is a mystery. If, however, formal theory comprises various types of truths, and if Signs always are forms of truth, the result is meaning (when such Signs are used). This formalism not only knows that the aim of forms is meaning, but also reflects how this meaning is produced by the form. This is the essence of the Pragmaticistic conception of cognition as conduct.

Such a method goes far beyond a mere philological theory of cinema. Cinema as the development of styles cannot be the object of a theory of film. This is a strictly historical reasoning. A Semiotic film theory does not offer an easy purchase for performing a substantial historiography of stylistic developments in film. The reason for this, however, is not a limitation of Semiotic, but that the result must be a very complex cognition. A concretely used Sign is already complex enough in the meaning it produces. Historical reasoning confines the various meanings (in their differences over time) to a further Interpretation, 'progress' or teleology of a development. This is a different meaning than the cinematic Sign itself, but it presupposes that the various instantiations of cinematic Signs are understood as meanings. A pure history of forms is illusory, since the meaning of such a form has already been understood. A historiography must filter out from such meanings what is different between them, but among the myriad differences, only those count that yield a teleological consideration of a certain feature (usually of the mode of representation, not of content). Once this development is understood, it can be recounted as a special kind of narrative, as the history of film style. As such it can follow a number of modes of constructing historical causality, beginning with a sociology of knowledge method or with a history of literature. This no longer concerns the meaning of a cinematic Sign; rather, it is an independent causal construction.

Finally, with regard to the practical value, it is clear that a Semiotic film theory must be of use for Interpretation. Such a theory cannot be an exercise in meta-theorizing the nature of film. Our premise has to be that films are something to be understood that they are meaning, therefore Signs – and not cosmological objects. Thus the value of a Semiotic film theory is to be measured in terms of how useful it is for an Interpretation and not as a new insight about the nature of film. If the result of this Semiotic of film has been to show that there are many more possibilities in Interpretation than current practice suggests, this is more than enough justification for its existence and its procedures.

'Some people seem to love to argue a point after all the world is fully convinced of it. But no further advance can be made. When doubt ceases, mental action on the subject comes to an end; and, if it did go on, it would be without a purpose' (Peirce 1998: 115, 'The Fixation of Belief').

Thank you, Peirce!

Notes

Introduction

1 Film interpretation has recently been described as a kind of potlatch; that may be the pleasurable side of the 'interpretative rage,' but it hardly contributes to an understanding of cinema. Unfortunately, it cannot be denied that Bordwell and Carroll are right in their sometimes scathing remarks on the arbitrariness and licence of certain theorizing film interpretations (cf. Bordwell 1989a, and 1996, Carroll 1988a, and Currie 1995. They propose, as a remedy, the ditching of 'grand theory' and the taking up of observable data and rules. This throws out more than the baby's bathwater. It merely relocates grandly theoretical assumptions into preliminaries and common-sense knowledge of the (supposedly familiar) object. There is little advance in film scholarship when we turn an out-of-context sentence into utter gibberish, as for instance Currie (xviii) does with Deleuze. His philosophical approach *in toto* should measure up to Deleuze's new vision of the time nature of cinema, not to a different intellectual style of presentation (a matter of taste). Apparently, it was as plain to semiological film theories that cinema is a sort of language, as it is today to constructivists that it is perception. It might be something else, though. This makes it worthwhile to listen to Deleuze, to phenomenology, and to other strands of narratology. As Peirce contends, genuine cognition always starts with a surprise.

2 NB: 'semiology' and 'Semiotic' (Peirce himself proposed 'Semeiotic') will consistently be referred to as quite different systems; their meaning is never going to be interchangeable. The reasons will be shown below. For convenience's sake, terms in the narrower Peircean sense will always be capitalized: categories are not identical with Categories, for instance. This seems to be a necessary precaution, not only because Peirce insists forcefully on

the precise meaning of his term (having suffered an 'abduction' of pragmatism, which let him rebaptize it Pragmaticism), but also because, where a deceptive vicinity to common language usage might be suspected, capitalization (which was, besides, Peirce's own habit) indicates a Peircean acceptation. Peirce's works are quoted in the usual way:

- MS Peirce, Charles S. Unpublished Papers, Microfilm. Numbers follow: Robin, Richard. 1967. Annotated Catalogue of the papers of Charles S. Peirce. Amherst: University of Massachusetts Press.
- NEM [volume, page] Peirce, Charles Sanders. 1976. *The New Elements of Mathematics.* The Hague: Mouton.
- SS [page] Peirce, Charles S., and Victoria Welby. 1977. *Semiotics and Significs.* Bloomington: Indiana University Press.
- W [volume, page] Peirce, Charles S. 1981–. *Writings of Charles S. Peirce: A Chronological Edition.* Bloomington: Indiana University Press.
- [volume. paragraph] Peirce, Charles S. 1960 & 1958. *Collected Papers.* Vols. 1–8. Cambridge, MA: Belknap.

3 'Film' and 'cinema' are used interchangeably, since these terms have an identical 'informational breadth.'

4 Substituting this investigation with an appeal to cinematic specificity can be suspected to be a mere smoke screen – that is, a refusal to reflect the basic 'mechanisms' of film properly. It comes close to decisionism, if in such circumstances one specific method is declared the most appropriate to film.

5 Film aesthetics and semiological methods have a long tradition in film theory of warring with one another (cf. Casetti 1993: 12ff). One limits serious reflection about film to lawlike features in film, whereas the more traditional film aesthetics take an essentialist approach. Aesthetics and law need not be in real opposition, though; this contradiction can be sustained only on the basis of certain implicit premises, which can be traced back to Kant. Implicitly, the double articulation of natural languages has modelled semiological film theories (despite their ritual claim that film cannot be considered a language proper). Film aesthetics has hitherto been conceived implicitly as a psychological awareness of means of expression (even though it is much less congruent). Two 'school heads,' Metz and Mitry, in their 'testament' books, epitomize the conflict between two implications. Metz, keen to fend off all inclinations to take anthropomorphic enunciation theories into film theory as a trace of personal presence, owes this to the methodological purity of the linguistic conceptualization of film. Mitry launched a fierce attack on all sorts of semiologists, valorizing his own more aesthetic 'phenomenological' approach. There are philosophical rea-

sons for both positions, and losing one of these intents for lack of reflection is a loss for film theory.

6 The latter two questions, for instance, relate also to Currie 1995: 19–75, 92–103. Currie 1997 also manifested his vision of a philosophically informed film theory, which contains a *tractanda* catalogue in the analytic tradition: 'In addition to the disambiguation of terms, typical strategies for authors in the analytic tradition in pursuit of logical precision would be the discrimination of strict, logical implication from implicature (the implied or indirect assertion of a proposition) and of deductive from inductive and abductive reasoning' (5). In the sense of this description, Peirce, discoverer of abduction, would be a quintessential analytical philosopher. Here we will argue that Peirce has seen more and deeper than analytical philosophy, not to the least when it comes to signs.

7 Following Kevelson 1993: 294, cf. Ketner 1981: 58: 'Observing that Peirce scholarship is just now beginning ... Much past scholarship then, can be seen as an instructive prelude, although most often in a negative sense.'

8 This reduction is especially critical in areas that fall under the competence of the other two relations. If 'reference' is addressed by means of codes, an 'Outward Clash' (8.43), as Peirce notes in his review of Josiah Royce's 'The Religious Aspect of Philosophy' (1885), there is no opportunity to take note of it. Furthermore, if signs are not even representations (but 'monadically degenerated', cf. *infra*), then arbitrariness, & convention theories have no purchase at all. This, however, is exactly the Semiotic mode of being of all things aesthetic. As also of temporality. Even narrativity is grounded in such a sign relation of the first kind (because it 'is' time, cf. *infra*).

9 The reason is to avoid as much as possible a prejudgmental definition and by this hurting sensibilities in this area.

10 There is sympathy for Bordwell's demise of unaccountable interpretations of cinematic works of art and his call for a genuine film theory (cf. Bordwell 1989a: 253). In fact, Signs of cinematic aesthetic do not contain Interpretations. In Semiotic strictness, Iconicity is a relation without an Interpretant, with a degenerative exclusion of any determinate Interpretant.

1. On Signs, Categories, and Reality and How They Relate to Cinema

1 Marie-Claire Ropars-Wuilleumier 1991: 19f. Attributing infinite regression to Peirce's philosophical basis, his theory of categories, and his sign theory inasmuch as it depends on the former, reveals a profound misunderstanding. Categories have their function in producing a 'state of affairs,' a Real, by relating Being to Substance. Their 'secret' is not that they provide the

564 Notes to pages 10–21

most general concepts to guide the unification of the manifold; rather, it lies in their power to relate. A Category is therefore a certain kind of relation (and Peirce showed that there are exactly three such kinds). Only analytically, *post factum*, can one proceed to further relations, which indeed are inherent to Firsts and Thirds; yet within the actual relation there is no regression, either to the perceptual judgment level or to the ultimate level of a perfectly cognized Real.

2 For instance, there is a materialist basis in structuralism, if meaning is determined by positional structure, and neither by any mind nor by empirical material. The transcendental character of 'Structure' is not tied to laws of thought or synthesis; rather, it is a realm in itself. Its materialist nature is not, however, dialectical.

3 For instance, in Branigan 1984: 39.

4 Taken in itself, of course. After the discovery of the Logic of Relatives, it must be clear that the third element is itself a complex one, mediating the other two.

5 NB: Usage of 'sign,' a preliminary terminological remark. Signs 'are' nothing; 'this is a sign' – implying 'and this is not' – would be an utterly nonsensical statement in the framework of Peircean Semiotic, because every-thing 'is' sign. We must be careful, then, to use the term without discriminatory power. Linguistically, this is impossible, so we should make a mental reservation when speaking about signs. This is by Peirce's own admission (cf. *infra*) stretching language usage to its extreme. But at this stage it is too early to indicate his very far-reaching arguments, consequences, and thoughts connected with this term. Suffice it to say that some customary ways of speaking about signs are excluded: For one, one cannot talk about psychic events and then about signs as their exterior expressions; or, about upper and lower 'thresholds' of signs (Eco), meaning the pre-sign reality and, separated from it, the sphere of meaning regulated by signs. This note on terminology is all the more necessary in view of popular misunderstandings of Peirce's concept. Ogden's triangle, notoriously standing for Peirce's sign concept, often has to serve as the argument of authority for separating sign from object and meaning. In this, sign tends to become the *'flatus vocis'*; object becomes reference to something physical, non-sign; meaning becomes the convention of an attribution. Unfortunately, discussing Peircean Semiotic today still involves clearing the heap of dust gathered through the ages. To not do so, however, would be to obscure the geniality of his insights; moreover, it would bring nothing new to the film-theoretical debate.

6 The use of these terms is specific: 'action' means the oppositive impulse, to

act against a resistant reality, whereas 'conduct' and 'behaviour' always means the reason- or self-controlled, rule-based way of relating to the world or states of affairs, or in short, Pragmatic acting; cf. Peirce 1998: 147.

7 This is supposed to thwart the danger of begging the principle in an open recursiveness. It does not afford any criterion, such as realism or mental laws, against which a cognitive theory can be measured. It merely offers a reflexiveness of the foundational paradox and an infinite number of perspectives on the 'real,' which are different for every closed, 'autopoietic' system.

8 Which is recognized by Dewey when he treats primary and secondary experience as two different categories that never agree. 'End results' (i.e., of acting) and 'ends-in-view' (i.e., of desire), because it needs reflection-after-doubt as a secondary experience to produce desirable objects. How Dewey describes those ends, though, bespeaks a motivational model of action: ends are produced when 'an experienced whole [is] treated as composites of parts made by sequential differentiations and integrations' (Waks (1999: 599f, quoting Dewey LW1:115), which whole decays through this treatment. This is such a common thought, found in Wundt (passed on to Mead and Dewey) and Bergson (passed on to Husserl and Schütz), that its psychological presuppositions are easily forgotten. For Peirce, however, behaviours/interpretations/signs are not parts of a whole, but stand in a rather particular relation to a general, as we shall see.

9 Peirce uses both 'Pragmaticist' and (in his later works) 'Pragmaticistic' – purposefully an ugly, not easily abducted terminology.

10 All further details v. *infra*.

11 Cf. Carroll (1988b), who has criticized extensively the inconclusiveness of both myths in classical film theory, without, however, appreciating sufficiently their adequacy from their respective points of view.

12 Peirce discovered his formal theory of relations independently from DeMorgan, and did so rather early in his life (cf. Whelden 2000). It grew out of Boole's calculus of logic. In its earlier denomination as 'logic of relatives,' which he reneged on later in favour of DeMorgan's 'logic of relations,' it is clearer that the immediate subject matter is relative terms and predicates. These can either be openly comparative ('greater than'), or in a semantic shroud (parent [...of], son [... of]), or in a maximally comprehensive understanding of the relative nature of every predicate. Peirce's basis for such comprehensiveness is the relational nature of cognition. To *understand* means to relate a concept to other concepts. From there it is a far way to develop a calculus of relations, including an adequate notation, into a relational sign theory.

13 Peirce was aware that his Categories answered the same question as the

one behind the Aristotelian categories (cf. Pape 1982:53 and Carls 1974: esp. 203–7). Peirce's would constitute as much of a logical as of an ontological interpretation of Aristotle's theory of categories (cf. Oehler in Ketner 1981a: 335–42]. Today there seems to be general agreement that Kant misinterpreted Aristotle's categories (cf. Carls 201).

14   There is an apparent contradiction with what Phenomenology calls the 'immediate time consciousness'. It will be evidenced in our discussion that this is not one perception; it is a comparison of passing perceptions, even though Phenomenology claims that there are two levels in this comparing the 'now-moment' ('*Jetzt-Punkt*') and the 'immediate past.'

15   Cf. Watzlawick (1976), as well as his reader on the fundamental texts of Constructivism (Watzlawick (1981).

16   Used against its original purpose by Eco (1976), who comes to remarkable conclusions.

17   Although Peirce (1998) clearly states 'that pragmatism is, in itself, no doctrine of metaphysics, no attempt to determine any truth of things' (400), he leaves open – after its chief purpose of 'ascertaining meaning of words and concepts' – what could be said of its presuppositions and consequences: 'As to the ulterior and indirect effects of practicing [sic!] the pragmatistic method, this is quite another affair.' (400).

18   Assumption is absolutely the proper term because there is no possibility of proving a Phaneron, as Peirce has stated clearly. We will see that it becomes important that this is not possible. If it were, there would really be *a priori* cognitions. Yet, as with the Categories, one needs in every mental operation what should be cognized *a priori*. The genius of Peirce is precisely that he avoids that trap. Instead, the proof of a Phaneron lies in action, as it does with the universal Categories. A 'practical consequence' can also be one that must be ever practised without ever accessing a true generality. Since Thirdness is another Phaneron as epistemological status, the proof – that all thoughts are connected (this is what Thirdness means) – is also one in mere action i.e., by thinking we discover that we are 'in thought' as an uninterruptable chain of single but not isolated mental states).

19   This can also be its past self. Mead, as the pupil of Dewey and thus in the tradition of Peirce, would much later make extensive use of the dialogic nature of the mind. Perhaps it is found in a deceptively psychological context in Morris's edition of *Mind, Self, and Society*. From its Peircean origin, it would certainly be read more favourably with a logical and Pragmaticistic key.

20   Thus Pragmaticism reveals itself as precisely the opposite of a naive understanding of pragmatism as resembling 'self-evidence.' Pragmaticism

demands not 'a' practical consequence but 'all' practical consequences. The difference is enormous.

21 Contrary to Toulmin's and Habermas's contemporary pragmatic argumentation theory, there is no need for a societal pragmatic project that yields rationality from outside argumentation itself. The founder of Pragmaticism would not admit to such a vicious circularity.

22 Cf. Pape 1990: 53–65 and Esposito 1980: 211–29.

23 Others prefer to leave this question open: for instance Gadamer, who is not sure whether one ever reaches a perfect 'fusing of horizons' (*Horizontverschmelzung* in Barden's and Cumming's English translation), particularly with the past, which is actually a 'projecting of a historical horizon' from our present. This is a problem of past and cross-cultural cognition; it also applies to what we must anticipate as cognitive projects.

24 Peirce (1998: 148f) mentions sixteen points that must be addressed in order to recommend the Categories (because, of course, they can no longer be proven). The theory core is – after a thorough description and 'rational form' of each Category in its characteristic difference – a proof 'that it is an element of the phenomenon that must by no means be ignored' (149). Proving, then, each one's irreducibility is the converse argument of the former; together, they show that each Category is necessary. Completeness is shown when, fifth, no fourth Category can be added to a comprehensive list. What we called universality is the task incumbent on Categories, (i.e., to deliver a '*Weltanschauung*' (146) to the other positive sciences. What follows is 'the moral of the whole story' (149), namely the variances in metaphysics resulting from a neglect of one or two of the Categories.

25 Deleuze (1973) identifies eight distinctive traits in structuralism; however, these are meant to be converging, building on one another. In the systemic differentiation principle, they have one common vanishing point.

26 This idea, that what 'is' cannot be said in one mode, but only in different modes, is a rather old one, as we see in Aristotle, *Metaphysica* 1028a.10–13: Τὸ ὂν λέγεται πολλαχῶς, καθάπερ διειλόμεθα πρότερον ἐν τοῖς περὶ τοῦ ποσαχῶς· σημαίνει γὰρ τὸ μέν τί ἐστι καὶ τόδε τι, τὸ δὲ ποιὸν ἢ ποσὸν ἢ τῶν ἄλλων ἕκαστον τῶν οὕτω κατηγορουμένων.

27 Cf. Sala 1982 and Apel 1975, passim. Sala 218f: 'Die Vermittlung zwischen deutschem Rationalismus und englischem Empirismus, die Kant mit seiner KrV herbeiführen wollte (A 760 f, 856; ...), war in der Tat ein bloßes Aneinanderfügen zweier heterogener Komponenten. Das Auffallendste und Folgenschwerste, das sich aus dieser heterogenen Dualität ergibt, ist die bekannte Aporie zwischen dem eindeutig realistischen Ansatz der KrV, demgemäß die die Sinnlichkeit affizierenden Gegenstände Dinge an sich

sind, und ihrem idealistischen Ausgang, demgemäß die Gegenstände der Erkenntnis überhaupt aus der Organisation des Subjektes hervorgehen. Diese Spannung, die dem ganzen Werk zugrundeliegt, nimmt an den verschiedenen Stellen verschiedene, oft schwer durchschaubare Formen an, ohne jemals eine endgültige Lösung zu finden. Ohne sie aber wäre die KrV nicht das rätselhafte Buch, das jedes konsequente "Zu-Ende-Denken" von Epigonen und Interpreten verblüfft.' Peirce seems to have achieved a mediation between rationalism and empiricism in his own way, and this precisely as Semiotic.

28　There seems to be a prejudice that Peirce's system was never coherent. A Janus-faced system at the best. As so often, the hermeneutic key of questions sometimes shapes the object domain, often in a manner that makes it unrecognizable to other hermeneutics, the author's included. So Peirce quite soon found himself in the position of having to defend himself against a certain acceptance of his own theories – an acceptance, by the way, that made his belated fame as the Father of Pragmatism. H. James, who was instrumental bringing fame to his teacher (and in whose honour Peirce changed his baptismal name Sanders in Santiago = St Jacobus = James), found Peirce's later intellectual developments so confusing and incomprehensible that he advised strongly (and successfully) against their publication: they did not fit with his concept of Pragmatism. As we know, Peirce chose to call *his* system from then on Pragmaticism. James was not the only one who placed Peirce in a tight framework of his own thought; so, one might suggest, did Bertrand Russell and Charles Morris, and perhaps even the editors of Peirce's Collected Papers. Among the exegetic efforts, all of those which disregard Peirce's stance in the philosophical debate at large tend to extract or highlight only some of his characteristics. We expand below on Eco's exegesis. The quasi-transcendentalism of Peirce was indeed the greatest stumbling block for many interpreters. Fitzgerald (1966: 9, 51, and passim) mentions Thomas A. Goudge (1950) as maintaining that irreducible duality of Peirce's, and J. Feibleman (1946) as thinking of Peirce's as a coherent system of thought. One might add K.O. Apel (1975), who attempts to see the historical development of Peirce in its major phases. He concludes that Peirce's development covered the entire spectrum between Rationalism and Empiricism.

29　Esposito (1980), on whose reconstruction we draw for the following, has the merit of demonstrating how fruitful this early five-year pre–New List period was in the development of Peirce's metaphysics. Contrary to Murphey (1961), who strived to show the inconsistencies and failures of Peirce's attempts to systemize his thought, Esposito shows the growth of it and its consistencies. Peirce very seldom felt he had to rectify past positions; even in his later evolutionary metaphysics he could accept his New List. It is true, though, that Peirce admitted to his early nominalism.

30 A 'photographic realism' is on the side of the infinite, whereas the feeling subject with its imagination is certainly a process which makes worldliness finite. Both are unprescindable, and the entire debate is based on incorrect epistemological premises. When it is resuscitated in contemporary discussions, it leads to such misconceptions of aesthetics as the pure effluence of psychodynamics; whereupon it merges with psychoanalysis and its dream processes. Any realism is out of place then – usually epistemologically on nominalist assumptions.

31 In MS 891 (1857: XIX, cf. Esposito 1980), we find there is one of Peirce's earliest attempts to reorder Kant's (Long) List of categories, taking into account his early inspiration of triadicity:

Faculty	I	Reason Faith	Goodness	Love of Order	Unity	Reality	Permanence
The Impulse THOU Soul		Affection Love	Beauty	Love of Man	Totality	Limitation	Causality
	IT	Sensation Hope	Truth	Love of World	Plurality	Negation	Community

Peirce's plan was to establish a regular system of relations dialectically on the basis of his Short List of three Categories.

32 Phaneroscopy as prescientific investigation of the 'method for the discovery of methods' (W5, 166) is itself a fine example of how discovery functions (cf. Kevelson 1987). Its cognitive purview is limited to a quasi-aesthetic process because 'we are no gods,' – that is, we cannot know, in the strict sense of the term, how we discover. Any pretension to know is ontology in the bad sense of the term. The theory of discovery is the same as the method itself – it must be discovered by everyone because it cannot be known.

33 Therefore his investigations were based on the form of propositions that assert, for empirical judgments, that subject and predicate are united under a more general concept than is contained in either. Thus 'Socrates dies because he is mortal' is meaningful and possible as empirical judgment only if there is an immediately more general concept such as 'mortality'

and the most general concept of 'causality.' These are no longer grades in
ontological being – that ontological categories (cf. Carls 1974: 199–238 for a
description of their Aristotelian function); rather, they are within the faculties of mind those principles which guide experience through judgment.
Now that which determines the experienceable is supposed to be no longer
an order of being with its principles of nature, but rather a subjective activity with its principles of judgment. Kant's gradation of more and less general concepts may be unavoidable (traces of that hierarchy survive in
Bordwell's 'constructivist' top-down and bottom-up metaphors; cf. Bordwell 1985 v. *infra*). The crucial question concerning generality was its
underlying rule. In Kant, its result was rather unclear to Peirce. His investigation on the Kantian path was arduous, and he could not free himself easily from transcendentalism; cf. Esposito 1980.

34 Propositions achieve the unity of a predicate and a subject always under a
'higher,' more general concept. When we come to the most general concepts, a question arises: Where does this generality come from? For Kant,
grades of categories are mental grades. For Peirce's 'representational turn'
they were immediately grades of reality. Grades of perfection in the Categories assume increasingly general propositions, for the most perfect must
be the most general. Peirce's ideas about the Perfect are not merely of historical interest. The real question behind them relates to the regulating
principle of thought, which must have ultimate premises. What *are* these
perfect grades? While he was still ordering Kant's categories and coming to
a gradation different than Kant's, Peirce took Kant's four principal categories (Quantity, Quality, Relation, Modality) and distinguished in each one
of them three grades. The first grade, simple or null grade, is a null state of
absolute indifference; the second, the human, a state of more/less; and the
third and perfect grade is a unification of the first two. The grades of Relation, for example, are 'community', 'causality', 'influx.' (The latter is such a
strong, infinite dependency that it is impossible to predicate partially or
negatively. It does not add something specific to the predicated, but it cannot be thought of independently from that which it qualifies). The principle
of gradation is rather obvious, intuitive in particular in the middle term for
human grade; perfect grades are extrapolations of the human grades.
Which purpose do perfect grades serve for human cognition (on the second
grade)? One example is infinity (e.g. predicated as a quality of lines). Infinity is not the negation of limits, but an infinite quality. Now infinity is at
once 'thought-of' (and thus exists) and nothing the human mind can realize
immediately, because the mind is incapable of realizing any quality, immediately, infinitely (thus, not everything in consciousness is immediate). Per-

fect grades are necessary even though the mind can never realize them immediately: 'The idea may be infinite and the thought finite' (MS 921).

35 The term 'metaphysic' is used here and in the rest of this chapter in concordance with the young Peirce's own neutral terminology. It does not reflect a prejudice for or against any philosophical option. Although his approach from the very beginning was not open for ontology in the precritical sense of the term, Peirce returned to metaphysical concerns in his later works.

36 Cf. Potter (1967: 180–8) on the terminology and the philosophical basis of it (6.302, January 1893). Tychasm (τύχη, being chance), Anankasm (from ἀνάγκη, force, necessity, being constraint by facticity), and Agapasm (from ἀγάπη, love, being in the ordered, reasonable openness of love) are Peirce's terms for the three evolutionary modes of being; they correspond to purely spontaneous being, to the brute, 'blind interaction of objects,' and to being reasonable (cf. Potter 1967: 186). While cinema 'is' all three, it is especially important that it 'is' (in the mode of) Possible. Otherwise, everything would just be as it is: the order of being/signs/system reigns absolutely, merely mitigated by the free arbitrariness of interpretation. Being, temporally, in three modes, defies the common impression that the problem is 'only' one of cognition, understood as the appropriation of its Other. Cognition, however, is not *with* being, but rather *part of* being, as Possibility is also part of it.

37 However, Peirce came to grasp the Categories also through an analysis of the appearance – phaneron – itself. What started as an analysis of consciousness (v. *supra*) became a phenomenological awareness of what stood in different ways before one's mind (e.g., in his 1903 Lectures on Pragmatism, the quality of a colour in a different way than the comprehension of a rule). A further alternative, which Peirce held in high esteem, was his quite complex algebraic logic.

38 Those accustomed to difference, differential place values, the idea that everything is different from all other things, and so on, might find this example and the logical operations Peirce illustrated in this a little outlandish. The operations will be explained below, but everything is based on the insight that not all differences are equal. These are not the kinds of differences that Greimas used in his Semiotic Square (v. *infra*): negation in its various forms. Space is not the contrary negation of colour; rather, it stands in a relation to colour. When we think of colour, we can think of it in such a way that we do not have to think of space. When we look at this colour, we also have to look at the space it occupies. When we see this colour, we see only the colour we see/imagine, and not other possible colours. Even though we use the word *colour* in all three cases, in one case it is a tone, in

the second a speck, in the third a knowledge. Furthermore, Peirce's operations reveal that higher cognitions comprehend the lower ones, so there cannot even be a negation. Clearly, our cognized world consists of such relations and not of simple negations of one affirmation.

39 Duns Scotus's term, used by Peirce (cf. Apel 1975: 49).

40 In reality, there is a foundational 'ontology of structuralism' and *a fortiori* of semiology, as Deleuze has shown in the essay with this title (which will be discussed below). The key term is 'homology,' but there is no way to prove this belief in a non-recursive way.

41 The decisive claim is 17b.26–28: ὅσαι μὲν οὖν ἀντιφάσεις τῶν καθόλου εἰσὶ καθόλου, ἀνάγκη τὴν ἑτέραν ἀληθῆ εἶναι ἢ ψευδῆ, καὶ ὅσαι ἐπὶ τῶν καθ' ἕκαστα, However, cf. 17a.38-39: Ἐπεὶ δέ ἐστι τὰ μὲν καθόλου τῶν πραγμάτων τὰ δὲ καθ' ἕκαστον, and 17b.1-3: ἀνάγκη δ'ἀποφαίνεσθαι ὡς ὑπάρχει τι ἢ μή, ὀτὲ μὲν τῶν καθόλου τινί, ὀτὲ δὲ τῶν καθ' ἕκαστον.

42 Objections to the theoretical treatment of colours in film can be made, (e.g., in Wulff 1999: 146–202), which for most cinematic perception/cognition would be largely a Category mistake. It is patent that colour is present in higher signification processes. Wulff's *'Farbmodalitäten'* are mostly narrative (i.e., manipulations of narrative enunciation applied to its temporality and universe, of which Wulff mentions the modal bracketing of narrative space, dream, flash, b&w past made present though colour) or figurative–narrative–discursive [emphasis] functions), even in conventions of cinematic renderings of dream universes as either black and white or in pale blueish or other colour. Whereas what Wulff calls *'Filmfarben ohne Darstellungsfunktion'* is indeed the genuine meaning of colour as such. Analogically, maps and semaphores also use colours for indexical meaning, and Peirce's own logical graphs use colours for entirely logical purposes; but all of this is not based on the quality of colour. For cinema, it can practically be assumed that colour is used in everything. We can subject all of this to logical differentiation, in order to discover the Categorial nature of any one meaning. Thus if we can discriminate such meaning from its other meanings, it is not the typical colour meaning of a quality. However, if we can only dissociate what we perceive – namely from other percepts – then we are on a logical level of meaning that is no longer relational. We perceive the red of the desert (in Antonioni's *Deserto rosso*), and then (only temporally then, not causally) we perceive the coolness of shadow or blue. Or perceive the greenish everything in Kieślowski's *Krótki film o zabijaniu* throughout the film. These latter examples evince quality (of colours, or shrieking sounds as in Fosse's *All That Jazz*) as meaning, in itself, without referring to a place or space of its occurrence. This space, however, can use

it to attract its meaning indexically to something of that space, as for instance the greenish neon light of the execution sequence in *Krótki film o zabijaniu*, when green becomes (!) the quality of killing.

43 This all important method – subtle and at the same time not destructive of the thought itself – is reflected in its result, the Categories. Two aspects are noteworthy: Categories owe their description to a rigorous and logical method and not to an intuitive invention, 'phenomenological' in a sense different from Peirce's acceptation. Then it is also clear that Categories are universal (i.e., there are only three and they are simultaneous and they are in everything there is$_{\text{Ist,IInd,IIIrd}}$). However, this is an extremely simple method of invention and does not presuppose what it wants to prove. By using it, one discovers different relations at the basis of all being, which can then be described in another method.

44 The practical import of the three modes of abstraction yielding the Categories may not be sufficiently patent, considering that for most people there is only 'reality' – in the singular and unmodified. In film scholarship this ingenuously unimodal 'real' is often dissimulated as the unquestioned assumption of the 'film illusionism' debate. The origin of such confusion – Aristotle estimated – is the trap of language, that we use 'is' for whatever can be said. A closer analysis soon reveals that there are various modes of using the predication 'is.' On the most universal level, before predicating something of something, one must choose between three modes – following Peirce's relation logical analysis – of relating to reality. No mode is the 'natural manner' of reality appropriation (relegating the other modes to merely a derived, 'hypothetical' knowledge of what 'is'). This is the real practical import of Peirce's three abstractions, – namely, that the reverse process is the concrete use of the Categories in everyday cognition: *because* one is precising something, one uses the Second Category and is therefore logically capable of making a proposition. In this instance, one's 'red' is$_{\text{IInd}}$ here in a semaphore, but not there. Completely different is an instance where one has an intuition. By doing so, one uses the First Category, *because* one uses the torchlight function of the mind flying over any possible thought irrespective of any consideration for facts. In this instance, one is$_{\text{Ist}}$ (happens to be) with red and not at the same time with blue or any other sensory impression. This can certainly be so while looking at the semaphore red and minding it – in difference to yellow (which one does not mind). Only when one is forced to cognise something, one distinguish one's cognitive object through discrimination from other cognitions. In order to accomplish that, one makes use of the Third Category, through which red is$_{\text{IIIrd}}$ thought in such a way that one thinks of it as a case of

colour – the way a colour theory treats it, for instance. In that context it is absolutely irrelevant that these colours have to be painted on some surface. However, when one makes use of colours in a geometry book, one is not representing colours but rather whatever law of spatial relation.

45 Here, one has to resist the temptation to psychologize. There are no mental states corresponding to any Category, because every feeling or sensation is already such only by being fully triadic semiosis. As Peirce calls such a feeling 'thought-sign,' its non-psychological meaning is very clear. There is a considerable difference between the Semiotic process of perception and how Constructivism reconstructs perception (in principle, taking into account the contradictions within this non-unified theory). Firstness, as Secondness, has a quite specific function in those fresh starts of the 'train of thought' that we call perception. It is very instructive how Nesher characterizes this: 'The naturalist (not physicalist) conception of the evolution of knowledge, the method of ascertaining the truth by repeating the *trio* of logical operations, the fallibility and relative certainty of human knowledge, hold for every human knowledge, for everyday experience, for experimental science, and for philosophy as well." (1997: 252).

46 As has already been said, that for Peirce every sign can become the Icon of the next semiosis ('sign or icon') can be interpreted in this way: the semiosic use is its determinant, not objective criteria.

47 These vary enormously between languages. For instance, in Chinese graph – (but not in spoken) signs, there are the so-called meaning-meaning compounds. This is a very common feature, and one of six ways of forming graphs. The six are the pictural; the symbolic; the phonetically similar; the phonetic-meaning relation, where the graph contains one part for the phonetic and one for the meaning; and, then, the meaning-meaning relation. This last involves reclarifying graphs that could be confused among objects they designate. By the addition of a further component they are made to refer to a more definite object. All of this is logically interesting because, for instance, the graph composed of the three graphs 'wife' (phonetic: nü), 'right hand' (phonetic: yòu), and 'heart' (phonetic: xīn) stands as compound graph for 'anger, passion, rage' (phonetic: nù). Here the Chinese script creates a logical relation among three correlates. 'Heart' – as often in similar cases – stands for a general idea, for a sort of *animus*. It seems to combine two ideas that in themselves might be general but that here are reactional (i.e., 'this wife' and this 'right hand' enter into an antagonistic concept). This is – notably – not a strictly logical analysis; it is merely another, non-propositional way of creating relations of meaning in script-language (of which in this case there is no trace in the phonetics – which is

another interesting case, when sound similarities have to produce a similarity of ideas).

48 There is, however, the postulate of a 'three-valued logic' in the Luhmann
school, which assimilates a number of tenets of Prior's modal 'tense logics'
(cf. Esposito 1987).

49 Burch's reconstruction of Peirce's proof merely adds four further derived
relational operations (the Comma operator, the Quantification operator,
the Hook-identity operator, and the Product operator). Without going into
details, these serve mainly to translate Peirce's teridentical relations into
well-formed formulae of first-order predicate logic and from there to the
application of hypostatic abstraction.

50 Although we still see the Structuralist belief that the seriality of one system
applies *homologically* to all others, because they find their quasi-transcendental unifier in the zero degree of structure, in an unnameable something
(cf. *infra*).

51 In this sense, Peirce can deny God's existence (= 'react with the other like
things in the environment' [ibid.]), but not his reality (cf. also 6.349, 1902).

52 We will come back to this comparison when discussing Deleuze's diagno-
sis of semiological film theories.

53 One remarkable exception is Petitot-Cocorda's (cf. *infra*), who brings out the
intrinsic extreme idealism of semiology. Criticism of such extremism is easily
instigated from many theoretical perspectives; furthermore, a number of
critics find it opportune to resort to Peirce-ish sign classes without taking
even minimally into account the implications of a Categorical, trimodal Reality. Such a semiotic critique of semiological film theories is often no more
than a meaningless and gratuitous play with classifications. Speaking of
'indexical' documentaries or 'iconic' drama films is as meaningless as label-
ling certain cinematic procedures – or even entire films – with these terms.
They simply lose their Semiotic meaning (e.g., Mitry 1987, cf. *infra*), which
makes it inappropriate to refer this to Peirce's Semiotic sign division. It is difficult to defend Semiotic terminology film theories against the enemies of 'all
such' theories, especially when they come as packages of 'psychoanalytic-
critical-feminist' discourse. The misery of 'semiotic film theory' is fully
accounted for by the lack of a grounding in anything upstream of sign
classes. Weak analyses and poor analytical insights can be the only result.

54 Even in the early Peirce there was germinal Realism, as the New List
evinces. His early development culminated in the article 'On a New List of
Categories' in the *Proceedings of the American Academy of Arts and Sciences* 7
(1868: 261–87), which concerns more than just Categories. He prepared this
article after conducting intense studies up to 1866, in particular in (what the

editors named) 'Searching for the Categories' (W1, 515–28). The importance
of these writings is, first, he clarified his doubts about a purely relational
conception of the Categories; and second, he stated clearly the ultimate
consequences of anti-apriorism. Having dismissed the necessity for incognizable *a prioris*, he then had to explain why cognition of the concrete world
is not just possible but also true. A naively realist option would have led to
either a complete epistemological relativism, or otherwise would have
necessitated a complete and ultimate knowledge of all ('if we were Gods').
Either option is unacceptable. Only an embrace of both the preliminary
nature of cognition and the 'eternal' aspiration for truth can be called a
truly ingenious solution. Semiosis had already won over transcendentalism
in the early Peirce (cf. Apel 1981: 54–83). Antifoundationalism is the other
important radical consequence of representation. There is no way to prove
thinking before or beyond thinking. Peirce's achievement at the crossroads
of Empiricism and Rationalism is remarkable. A general post-Kantianism
leading to Heidegger and beyond – without exaggerating similarities –
brought some strikingly parallel solutions (cf. Leventhal 1988). Small wonder that Peirce's pragmatism could so easily be adopted by Apel (1975) and
Habermas (1968), notwithstanding Habermas's criticism of Peirce from an
antitranscendental perspective (cf. however Apel 1975: 256 Anm.). Cognition, in general, is linked to behaviour; this is possible only because it is
questionable fact that human beings are acting. To that purpose, the real
existence of reality is needed (and logically presupposed). Even if Heidegger deduced this transcendent horizon from the temporal *conditio humana*,
trimodal Realism meant a much broader horizon of cognition than merely
the Reality of the Real in principle. He, too, comprised a diachronic dimension to truth, even though not the existential one 'towards-death.'

55 No one *is*, of course, this general soul, as he would then be eternally true in
his cognition. It is merely a consequence of logic that there must be the
symbol of everything, in which one participates gradually symbolizing. As
early as 1866, long before agapism, Peirce identified this Symbol of symbols
with God. In any case, Peirce is remote from any form of solipsism, as Descartes had proposed it; Wittgenstein was more radical (cf. *Tractatus* 5.632
'Das Subjekt gehört nicht zur Welt, sondern es ist eine Grenze der Welt,'
dissolving the subject into worldly states (cf. Wittgenstein 1961, Tractatus
5.64). Peirce strongly maintained the opposition between ego and non-ego
(cf. Nesher (1997). Generally, cf. Kolenda in Ketner et al. (1981: esp. 229f).

56 The reason is that every single, individual act of abductive inference – even
the intellectual effort of discovery of an individual person – points beyond
itself. Therefore, Peirce is very insistent on the 'proper method' to be fol-

lowed in thought, because the approximation to truth is in a very 'long run' and because an ever-increasing, comprehensive 'community' (5.354) is exceedingly interesting in this regard. 'Each of us is an insurance company, in short. But, now, suppose that an insurance company, among its risks, should take one exceeding in amount the sum of all the others. Plainly, it would have no security whatever. Now, has not every single man such a risk?' (cf. Apel 1975: 103). Without such an overarching guarantee no single induction is true, or partakes in truth. 'That logic rigidly requires, before all else, that no determinate fact, nothing which can happen to a man's self, should be of more consequence to him than everything else. He who would not sacrifice his own soul to save the whole world, is illogical in all his inferences, collectively. So the social principle is rooted intrinsically in logic.' (104).

57 This appears to be contradicted when we totally separate signs from Categories (cf. Baltzer 1994). However, even if relations are a matter of logic, and cognition (in signs) is another thing, applying relations to cognition is not secondary. Categories are meaningful only as forms of cognition (i.e., thinking) and thus become logic (i.e., thought in general). Although valencies of relations stand in themselves, it would be an inconsequential banality if it could not be proven that they play a role as necessary forms of thought. Therefore, it is necessary for thought to relate in a dyadic two-valency relation to its other. Perhaps Baltzer underestimated this point (cf. Ehrat 1995). He analyses relations as if they were self-sufficient forms of operation, whereas as logic they mirror thought in its necessary forms. This is how Peirce could conclude that one thinks only in signs.

58 This is not like the historiographical imagination game, which involves considering what would have been and how the course of history would have been different had a certain event not taken place (cf. Veyne 1979; Currie 1995).

59 In contemporary concepts of complexity, within the framework of systems theory and other scientific philosophies based on chance, Peirce's basic intuition lives again. Yet Peirce would take exception to automatic complexity reductions. Models of 'natural' chance reduction through chance itself, with an unfathomable 'selection risk,' contradict the inventive force of the mind, which reduces Firsts or qualities in a Third.

60 Cf. Potter (1977), who corrects the presentation (albeit pioneering) of Continuity in Murphey (1961) in the central point of contention with Cantor's theory of transfinite sets.

61 In his first pre-Cantorian period, Peirce himself misinterpreted continuity as infinite divisibility (cf. Potter 1977: 21).

62 Interestingly enough, he finds it again in a mathematical element, a pure topology of the structural form. Matter by this procedure becomes an amorphous entity, in keeping with Hjelmslev's hylomorphist double substances and matters (to expression and content). Form alone gives shape literally to the shapeless, and pure form is topological. Furthermore, topology is best described in terms of a mathematical catastrophe theory. Now, what remains as a difficulty is caused by the structural keeping form and formed separate. This either inevitably makes it arbitrary to apply the form on a formed, or necessitates an outright idealist, neoplatonist form-in-itself. This is not so in Peirce.

2 Semiotic and Its Practical Use for Cinema

1 For example, in Husserl (1921: 25–31), who is the original source of all phenomenological theorizing on signs, then Heidegger (1927: §17), Gadamer (1990: 149–65, esp. 156ff [1960: 137–52, esp. 144ff) and Schütz (1981: 165–86 [§§24–6]).
2 The difference between semiotic and semiology, between Peirce and (let us say) Eco, becomes more than apparent, when Eco reinterprets these terms for his purposes: *denotatio, connotatio*, and, in addition, a term quite alien for Peirce: referent. Peirce adopts these terms explicitly from the once commonly available and widely used *Tractatus de proprietatibus terminorum* (cf. Apel 1975: 82). For Eco, a denotation is the immediate designation of an object, or the connection of an expression material with a content material: 'una marca denotativa è una delle posizioni entro un campo semantico a cui il codice fa corrispondere un significante *senza previa mediazione*; una marca connotativa è una delle posizioni entro un campo semantico a cui il codice fa corrispondere un significante *attraverso la mediazione di una precedente marca denotativa*, stabilendo la correlazione tra una funzione segnica e una nuova entità semantica,' Eco 1975: 123). As soon as experience (in Peirce's sense) is abandoned, an object of cognition can only be an arbitrary systemic (cultural) totality of semantic fields and universes, consisting of interrelated 'interpretants' and codified existence conditions of signifieds, as Eco (1975: 120) notes.
3 This film pragmatic is not based on the obvious fact that, as human beings, we find ourselves constantly acting. For a full Semiotic-aware pragmatic, it is much more to the point when we find that we have an inexhaustible pool of possible, not potential, actions. Thus, the concrete situation of our behaviour is not adequately rendered in an abstraction that relates an intentional agent subject with a worldly object. The truly intriguing part of behaviour –

that nothing seems to exhaust its possibility – must be accounted for with other concepts. The same is true for the evolution of thought, which is based on experience. It is unimaginable to claim that everything which can be thought is available or even conceivable. However, every thought being the next thought of a previous thought, it is part of the phenomenon that thought goes on without a conceivable termination. Even in the absence of its totality, thought is directed.

4 'Logic is the science of the general necessary laws of Signs and especially of Symbols. As such, it has three departments. Obsistent logic, logic in the narrow sense, or Critical Logic, is the theory of the general conditions of the reference of Symbols and other Signs to their professed Objects, that is, it is the theory of the conditions of truth. Originalian logic, or Speculative Grammar, is the doctrine of the general conditions of symbols and other signs having the significant character ... Transuasional logic, which I term Speculative Rhetoric, is substantially what goes by the name of methodology, or better, of methodeutic. It is the doctrine of the general conditions of the reference of Symbols and other Signs to the Interpretants which they aim to determine '(2.93 1902, Minute Logic. This would be Peirce's complete idea of Semiotic, which is not taken sufficiently into account by some, too superficial, 'semiotics.'

5 It may be easier to ask: What is it not? This by no means leads to the arbitrariness of a cultural contingency, organized in a system of meaning (Saussure's *arbitraire du signe*). Neither is logic as sign, in a naive realistic sense, a mirror of the physis. Such a stance pretends that there are at least two universes, of physis and of mind, 'data' and mental 'models.' It is known, for instance, that Popper felt the need to distinguish three worlds and that Habermas made a similar distinction of three types of validity claims. Each world follows its own mind data rules. A number of subsequent problems from any division of 'worlds' follows. Not the least is that all those worlds need to use the same language and signs.

6 That is, unified, one world of mind and matter and possibility, overcoming Kant's dichotomy of theoretical and pragmatic cognition.

7 There are a plethora of further, less well known classification attempts in Peirce, as the translations of Pape (1986; 1993) indicate. This is not surprising if we believe Ransdell (1977: 158) that more than 90 per cent of Peirce's work concerned Semiotic. Short (1982: 288) is much less confident in the coherence of Peirce's sign theory, because of changes in the understanding of the Interpretant.

8 For instance, everything that Habermas (1981) lists under (validity claim of) self-representation falls under a class of Signs that offers no possibility

of factual cognition. Self-representation in Habermas's sense is feeling of one's and the other's self; this, however, on closer examination does indeed need the fact of being affirmed in factual circumstances (cf. *supra*). A Sign that truly involves no factual component, and that therefore is not even liable to 'aesthetic critique' (Habermas), must remain a pure feeling.

9 Cf. Müller (1994: 144f). Müller also speaks of Walther's attempt at a reclassification as a view oblivious to relations (cf. Walther 1976).

10 cf. Ducrot (1972: 142), who, however, writes: 'Étant donné que les rapports syntagmatiques semblent, dans une large mesure, spécifiques à chaque langue particulière, on en est venu à fonder sur eux les paradigmes linguistiques: en ce sens, étroit, deux unités *u* et *u'* appartiennent à un même paradigme si, et seulement si, elles sont susceptibles de se remplacer l'une l'autre dans un même syntagme, autrement dit s'il existe deux syntagmes *vuw* et *vu'w*. D'où l'image devenue classique de deux bandes sécantes, l'horizontale représentant l'ordre syntagmatique des unités, la verticale, le paradigme du *u*, c'est-à-dire l'ensemble des unités qui auraient pu apparaître à sa place.' The fact remains that those unities represent things or states-of-world, whereas the other syntagmata below that level referentially represent nothing. Paradigmata in this sense are the smallest referential units. It is only in a strictly semiological (and analytic) context that signification can be severed completely from reference (or denotation) (cf. op. cit. 133). The next stage of syntagmatic units after paradigmata could be the level of sentence, text, or narrative, all of them understood as *combinatoires* as well, with a limited number of alternative choices. Regarding this sense, consult Chabrol (1973: 8–28).

11 Cf. Chauviré (1995) on this kind of 'vagueness.'

12 In disagreement with Wollen (1969), there is no symbolic cinema as such. This would entail a level of generality that obliterates any actual relations. It is possible to see three apples and to generalize the number aspect with the cypher '3.' This is not possible in cinema, except in some scenes of Godard's propaedeutic films, such as *Tout va bien* and *Masculin–Féminine*. Yet this is achieved by means of Legisigns, letters (i.e., not by pictorial representation). Peirce gives a moving example to Lady Welby (8.357) that is, in this respect, comparable to cinema. He writes to her of the ugly statues in so many North American cities that are memorials of the Civil War. For most, these provide actual relations to sons, husbands, fathers, who were killed in the war. As a Symbol, or Continuant (8.352), these status constitute abstract ideas of abstract duty to an abstract state. Relatives will hardly get rid of the actual, just as film spectators can rarely dispense with their actual viewing. Even so, 'there is life after film,' and abstract reasoning –

for instance, about the meaning of that film – can go on at any length. We shall see later that Godard experiments with a 'narrative' rhetoric, one that attains Symbol status even for some rare images.

13 The *pointe* of the Neoformalist sujet-fabula distinction has its Semiotic-logical foundation here. Indeed, it distinguishes two types of object relation, one more determined by a general idea, and a 'raw' one. It is clear from this trichotomy that two different cognitions (with further consequences at the level of the next trichotomy of 'ideas') are at work here. Moreover, while *sujet* and *fabula* concern artistic motivation and intentions, there is nothing tangible beyond intention, that would allow for their differentiation. If we understand them as signs, the difference is shown as Semiosic classes; this even allows predictions for further cognitive paths.

14 The exceptions to this rule are entirely analytical inferences, where the meaning of something is already fully contained in its antecedent proposition. Syllogisms of this sort are pure deductions and add nothing new to cognition.

15 For film, this has consequences so devastating that the main thrust of critique of linguistically based film theories in Deleuze is based on this intrinsic limitation. Capturing the time dimension of film fails in these theories because in the cinematic picture there are no morphemes of tense, or textual equivalents of syntactical formants, that combine sememe-like differential units of cinematic language (videmes, cademes, edemes) through quasi-grammatical (or semi-grammatical) rules (i.e., through combination into larger units, referential rules, and so on). The problem with these rules is that they are intrinsically static (or even 'innate'!), despite their purported 'generativity.'

16 Just to prevent any fear of extending this term into the realm of political theory, which seems to preoccupy Bordwell to some extent: Representation is not representation (lower case). As a strictly formal description with many explicit philosophical presuppositions, it seems to be sufficiently distinct from Subjectivity, and its construction as a visibility in a given historical episteme or similar connotations.

17 These quotes are from a draft of the Monist articles, (1905), in which Peirce must have seen his last chance of bringing his philosophy to bear. However, if we follow the speculative explanation in Pape (1989), the publications and public appearances of Peirce in these last years suffer from the much too narrow perspective in which he had to be perceived. He had to sail under the banner of the 'father of pragmatism,' and he seems to have felt like Laocoon in his struggle to get some breathing space for his much broader Semiotic system. Thus, in the reformulation of the Pragmatic

Maxim we certainly find the repercussions of his advances in the logic of Relations and in Semiotic. In particular, his insistent emphasis on Real Possibility is a sign of this influence.

18 Gadamer's (1960) description of it is certainly to the point, but there is no need to reduce the wonder to a higher, original level (*Urbild*) of a normative image of the holistic wholeness of being-human. Explained in this way, tragedy is no longer tragic, but a genre.

19 To Lady Welby: 'Imagine yourself to be seated alone at night in the basket of a balloon, far above earth, calmly enjoying the absolute calm and stillness. Suddenly the piercing shriek of a steam-whistle breaks upon you, and continues for a good while. The impression of stillness was an idea of Firstness, a quality of feeling. The piercing whistle does not allow you to think or do anything but suffer. So that too is absolutely simple. Another Firstness. But the breaking of the silence by the noise was an experience. The person in his inertness identifies himself with the precedent state of feeling, and the new feeling which comes in spite of him is the non-ego. He has a two-sided consciousness of an ego and a non-ego. That consciousness of the action of a new feeling in destroying the old feeling is what I call an experience. Experience generally is what the course of life has compelled me to think' (8.330). On a similar note: 'A man walking with a child points his arm up into the air and says, "There is a balloon." The pointing arm is an essential part of the symbol without which the latter would convey no information. But if the child asks, "What is a balloon," and the man replies, "It is something like a great big soap bubble," he makes the image a part of the symbol. Thus, while the complete object of a symbol, that is to say, its meaning, is of the nature of a law, it must denote an individual, and must signify a character. A genuine symbol is a symbol that has a general meaning. There are two kinds of degenerate symbols, the Singular Symbol whose Object is an existent individual, and which signifies only such characters as that individual may realize; and the Abstract Symbol, whose only Object is a character' (2.293)

20 Of which he writes: 'which I never ceased, myself, to loathe and abominate, and surely was as little adapted by nature to practice as anybody could be.' (MS649, 18). However, he takes it as an example – just as his prowess in weight-lifting – of acquiring a facility to do something through habitual experience.

21 Only in a system ontology (such as semiology and systems theory) is chaos threatening to meaning.

22 The 'greatest difficulty of acquiring either [scil. also the attentiveness to sensations] is that one does not for a long time have any notion of what

kind of effort is requisite. One has to go on trying one mode of effort after another, while closely watching the efforts one makes, until at last one comes upon one that is remarkably successful. Then one must make an endeavour to repeat the same kind of effort, and often one will find that he has suddenly acquired a new power.' (MS649: 15). 'I myself acquired the ability to lift twelve hundred pounds of dead weight; and in order to keep myself in practice, I got a pan cast and purchased enough old iron to make up, with the pan and the chain, a half a ton. There was considerable difficulty in disposing my irregularly shaped and too large pieces of old iron upon a circular pan, or disk rather, so that, when I lifted it by a chain attached to its centre, it should remain closely level; and after I had lifted a good many times, and the four stalwart negroes who were aiding me had, after each lift, made such shifts of the masses, as another assistant had directed (I being unable, while holding up the weight, to see how the pan was tilted,) I began, after a half hour of this work, to think I had done as much of it as was good for me, for one day, – although the weight lacked 200 lb of the limit of my power. So I asked the strongest of the negroes, whose muscular strength was, I suppose, double my own, if he did not think he could do the lifting for a while. He was very confident he could; but after a long struggle gave up the attempt without having been able so much as to stir the pan, which , owing to its imperfect balance, cannot have required much more than half the force needed to lift it. Now it was not strength that was lacking, but acquaintance with the particular kind of effort required.' (MS649: 16–18).

23 Interpretants 'contain' even behaviour to which they were applied *actu* never before (5.313, 1868). Words are 'enriched' with experience and enrich actual experience. Peirce, in explaining this process of the influence of knowledge on the actual formation of a true opinion about the Real, offers the simile of a triangle immersed in water: At the horizontal borderline is the actual insight. Pulling the triangle out of the water one would find an unlimited number of water lines, which all correspond to previous inferences even though they are at that moment unconscious. Every one of these conclusions is virtually a true opinion of the Real (which in Critical Commonsensism could be retranslated into a behaviour).

24 An 'ultimate opinion' beyond the present Commonsense in an 'unlimited community of investigators' can only be thought of meaningfully in Pragmaticism, not in semiology. Thus, *Privatsprachen* in Wittgenstein's sense will inevitably arise when one abandons experience as the ultimate criterion for truth. In Eco, for example, cultural codification is the absolute and ultimate horizon. The problem of prior knowledge and its incidence in con-

crete cognition need not even be posed as such. The price to be paid is a blind spot for the problem of new cognition, new experience, which does not really exist (in a Peircean sense) in a global code system.

3 What 'Is' Cinema?

1 In view of Bordwell's anti-semiological polemic, the scientific project of structuralism can only be measured by an explicit discussion of alternative theories of 'cinematic being'. There is nothing to recommend cognitivism as a natural attitude toward cinema.

2 Cf. Ducrot (1972: 36, 42) and Albrecht (1988) for an overview of the succession of Saussure.

3 To avoid confusion with Peirce's Icons, Eco's concept is either left as 'iconismo' or made lower case 'iconism.' 'Iconicity' is used in Peircean contexts.

4 Metz (1973: 136), concurred with by Chateau (1986: 53).

5 For example, Andrew (1985: 626) notes some *effritements* of semiology, partly because semiotic approaches eventually grew beyond their own stacked fields of theory, seeing themselves forced to include somehow the 'murky areas of psyche where art, novelty, and interpretation reign,' partly also because of concomitant different approaches such as phenomenology, hermeneutics, and the 'Reader Response School' (probably the *Rezeptionsästhetik* of Jauss, Iser, and Warning et al., which can also be seen as one version of genuine classic hermeneutics). Certainly among the most radical and serious attacks on semiology – on Metz and his '*émules*' (Mitry 1987: 8) in particular – are Mitry (1987) and Deleuze (1985: 38–50 *et passim*). Both critics have the advantage of offering an alternative to semiology for coming to terms with the cinematic phenomenon. '*Just*' a critique – especially of the 'founding texts' of film semiology – is Henderson (1980). He attempts no more than to show the inherent contradictions of theoretical texts; he does so without offering explicit alternatives of theory. In his view, all those theories are mutually critical of one another, and none achieves a coherent solution to the problem of the cinematic phenomenon ('... posits film theory as a single structure capable of various investments rather than a group of opposing whole theories,' xiii).

6 Deleuze claims the title *sémiotique* for his system (cf. 342ff). However, his Bergsonist inspiration prevents him from reverting to common sense or to non-cinematic perception theories. Behind this claim we might see Deledalle, who has been instrumental in the quite determinate reception of Peirce's philosophy in France as well as quite critical of the semiological

current: 'Il va de soi que la notion de signe restreinte au signe linguistique qui peut à la limite convenir pour une sémiologie du texte est impropre ou, à tout le moins, n'est pas la plus propre à décrire un système de signes non linguistiques comme un film ou tout autre système à dominante iconique.' Deledalle (1979: 196f) and Mitry (1987: 30).

7 Cf. his invective against Eco's (1970) invective against Pasolini: Deleuze (1985: 42).

8 Cf. what Mitry (1987: 31) quotes Deleuze as having said: 'Les essais d'appliquer la linguistique au cinéma sont catastrophiques.'

9 Metz (1971: 155f), where he justifies his rejection of the concept of Peircean and de Saussurean (!) sign in favour of the apparently more precise one of 'code.' Peirce, read through the spectacles of Morris, is indeed conveniently paraphrased by this substitution, but at the cost of suppressing an important aspect of Peirce's work cf. Apel 1975, cf. *supra*, 785).

10 Cf. Metz (1968): 'Contrairement à ce que nous pensions il y a quatre ans, il ne nous paraît nullement impossible, aujourd'hui, de supposer que l'analogie est elle-même codée sans cesser néanmoins de fonctionner authentiquement comme analogie par rapport aux codes de niveau supérieur, lesquels ne commencent à entrer en jeu que sur la base de ce premier acquis.' The eminent usefulness of such a codification was not only with regard to reference or denotation, but also with regard to pictorial representations of everything that can be perceived. The strategic importance of such codification appears clearly: cinema can be understood as an *ensemble* of different codes, which all have their proper smallest units. Yet Metz also remarks: 'Dans chaque film les codes sont présents et absents à la fois: présents parce que le système se construit sur eux, absents parce que le système n'est tel que pour autant qu'il est autre chose que le message d'un code, parce qu'il ne commence à exister que lorsque ces codes commencent à ne plus exister sous forme de codes, parce qu'il est ce moment même de repoussement, de construction-destruction.'

11 It is noteworthy that Bergson is already vehemently opposed to the concept of representation as something entirely idealistic. Deleuze is very consistent with Bergson's anti-idealism: Idealism that must place all causality into the thinking mind is similar to the semiological substitute of mind (namely, language). Language, however, is easier to analyse in a lawlike manner than the transcendental mind, which lends its grammar to a more objective aspect. Again: Bergson could refute idealism only on the basis of his own metaphysic, which would make better sense of what he perceived as antinomies.

12 Eco thoroughly misunderstood this alternative, or did not perceive it as an

alternative, as a footnote concerning Peirce's sign classification ('a complete failure') in his 'semiotic treatise' demonstrates: Eco (1975: 283n 30).

13 Eco (1975: 258) quotes *Signs, Language, and Behavior* (1.7, 7.2), among the scarce remarks on Iconicity in this work.

14 '*Behavior*. This term is presupposed by semiotic and not defined within it,' writes Morris (1946: Glossary), describing it as goal-seeking of an organism.

15 Morris 1946: 7.2. This quote should be seen as an expression of Morris's sign theory, which is so distinct from Peirce's. 'Every sign involves behavior, for a sign must have an interpretant, and an interpretant is a disposition to a response' (1946: 7.1). Or else: 'something that directs behavior with respect to something that is not at the moment a stimulus. .a preparatory stimulus' ... (glossary, s.v. 'sign'). It is quite clear that Morris means only concrete interpretants, not Peirce's Category of Thirdness. A sign is thus a required, standard behaviour (if adequately interpreted), toward some concrete other. Quality is the same other, but merely as aspect or sensory selection. Otherwise, Quality can only be included as a determinant of behaviour toward the object. Iconicity then allows one aspect of the object to determine behaviour directly. It effectively bridges the sign relatively, which is normally only a preparatory stimulus, to the extent in which it is direct behavioural stimulus. Morris's example – that of onomatopoeic signs – is thus quite indicative. Having taken over sensory data from their object, they allow it to respond as if it were the object (denotatum) itself, 'similar in some respects to what it denotes.'

16 Eco abandoned behavioural traces of differed responses to preparatory stimuli. Yet he strongly adopted the societal regulation of signs. A sign is that which is convened upon. The fracture is visible in their respective treatment of iconicity. Eco cannot treat sensory stimuli as origins of cognition. On the contrary it is the other way around: conventions regulate which contents can correctly be connected with which percepts. Eco's adaptation of Morris is indeed antibehaviourist; however, the reduction of the concept sign into just one relation is maintained. Behaviour becomes convention, code beyond all negotiation. This provides the necessary stability for communication, even if it is now more of a cultural availability of things than a prescription of behavioural responses.

17 For a more detailed discussion of Eco's reception of Peircean sign theory, cf. Ehrat (1991: 175–87).

18 Cf. Esposito (1977), who objects on similar grounds to Eco (1975).

19 In the following, where the difference might have a bearing, as a cautionary measure, upper case refers to Bordwell's, Currie's, Carroll's, and

other variants and lower case refers to constructivism or cognitivism generally.

20 This is not the place to evaluate critically Bordwell's representation of constructivist cognition. His bibliography is impressive (cf. Bordwell 1989b: 34–40). Gibson, Hochberg, and Brooks are direct points of reference. Yet the picture of the theoretical concepts guiding these psychological experiments is much larger. The strain of experimental psychology, which is mentioned, is mainly interesting for one reason: it reintroduces meaning as a variable that cannot be substituted into experimental set-ups and hypotheses. Clearly, the theoretical model applied to experimental 'data' is that of logical inference. Its purpose is to establish the difference between 'low-level' (automatic perception) and 'higher-level' applications of meaning to 'data.' Hypotheses concerning the low level of perceptual systems have no overarching scope. The concluding remarks of Hochberg (1989: 54) are instructive: 'These two-dimensional patterns trigger the early responses that the visual system makes to changing images' would relate to Bordwell's 'automatism.' The point of this research narrative is only that these system responses to stimuli need no mental, conscious, inferential *explanans*. In this experimental set-up, the 'early responses' (moving images), possibly leading to perceptual errors, are overlaid by 'more meaningful factors,' which are mental (slide show), because the subject is given time to reflect. The task is 'to ensure the desired perceptual integration of successive views.' It is thus research narrative that introduces a teleology, and *by this* thought and meaning. The epistemological problem of the mind–brain–body relation and of the different kinds of causality and explanation are indeed immense and are not to be debated here. There is in no way an easy solution to this problem. One should, however, be aware of the artefact introduced by the research narrative, which suggests a 'truth' that is not there. Moreover, constructivism as a theory is more than experimental psychology. It is capable of solving this causality dilemma with its system-environment difference. Gibson was certainly an early discoverer of the environment in the context of perception. Yet the major theoretical developments in constructivism have taken place outside experimental psychology. Representative as a collection of theoretical texts from von Glasersfeld to Varela are Watzlawick (1981), Schmidt (1988), and Willke (1989). What counts for Bordwell's Constructivism, though, is the basic explanatory model, which makes such experimental set-ups as Hochberg's possible. Thus, the foundational difference of environment and system really explains 'meaningful factor' psychology. Constructivism severs the causal link between meaning (representation inside the system) and stimuli (envi-

ronment). Automatic processes would still belong to the outside environment, explained in the causal chain prevailing in the physical world.

21 So far Constructivism has caught up with Kant. Let us assume that experiential cognition is cognition of the world. Kant said that apperception cannot but have two *'Anschauungsweisen'* in Time and Space. The world, inasmuch as perceivable, *is* (apprehended in) Time and Space, but cognition itself consists of judgments (applying concepts to *'Anschauungen'*). By this, Kant went a step beyond the receptacle concept of a mind, where thoughts consist of stable associations among ideas. Here, percepts are only the most primitive ideas. Judgments, then, are possible according to the categories, which are somehow contained in every natural language or are universal to human knowledge.

22 And we might add – whenever we have learned to – we will always see an 'a' as a letter and not as an ornamental drawing. Yet this is not certain in a 'bottom-up' hypothesis, since a letter is never a mental conclusion; it is always but a cultural form. Nevertheless, its recognition is undoubtedly automatic. Apparently, Constructivist axiomata do not account for something that must have been a 'top-down' apperception while it was being learned, but eventually became fully 'bottom-up' (provided these terms still make sense in such a case). Again, Peirce could offer a reasonable solution to this.

23 Cf. Bordwell (1985: 32n14), in which he acknowledges that he is aware of the Kantian ring to that term. He claims, however, that the original site of his concept of 'schema,' is in Gombrich (1959: 31n7). It is probable that the commonness of schema helped Bordwell underpin Formalism with Constructivism. The Constructivist account of cognitive perception is all too close to a stripped down Kantianism; furthermore, Formalism shares in this strange separation of percept and concept. This is exactly what Lotman criticized in Šklovsky (cf. Stacy 1977: 45–7, and also 35–6 about Schelling's or Kant's influence on Šklovsky's concept of art).

24 Or one must share the belief in scientism, 'philosophischer Wissenschaftsimperialismus,' as Pape (1989: 23f) very pertinently remarks.

25 It is not permissible to answer a *de jure* question with a *de facto* answer. The logic of truth is not explained by organism and brain physiology, or by biological evolution (cf. Currie 1995: 85f). Doing so is a category mistake, which cannot be concealed by 'level' metaphors. The real *explanandum* is how 'recognition' becomes 'judgment'. This is what Semiosis explains. 'Automatism' merely stands for a refusal to explain. However, the real intent behind cognitivism remains cognition, not brain processes. Thus it must be in its interest to understand those automatic cognitions on its own premisses.

26 There are good reasons to compare the schemata of Kant and Bordwell. Both are epistemological principles which, in a quite determinate way, explain apperception as guided hypothesis making or possible judgment. Constructivism is arguably pre-Kantian. Let 'empiricism' be called theories stating that knowledge of the world is limited to pure experience. One can further determine such an experiential object subject relationship as one that anti-idealistically denies that mental knowledge structures influence experience. This basic Humeian concept of experience subsists in contemporary theory in this form: a theoretic, synthetic construct outside the construction itself is placed in relation with an experience that is immediately certain (à la association). Two directions can be imagined: one that leads from an array of data to theory (inductive) and its opposite, which allows the retranslation of the synthetic process into data. Experience, therefore, is not understood as being itself synthetic, but rather as an immediate 'pure datum'. This version of empiricism presupposes the stable identity of the datum, notwithstanding its being a theoretical, methodical, or experimental approach. This is not the case, however (what Heisenberg called *Unschärferelation*). So the 'pure datum' is not pure. A datum always subsists in linguistic descriptive sentences. Data are not 'mute' things, in the way the Vienna Circle took the physical demonstration of a datum as being the basis of understandability as much as the truth of sentences. Their program consisted in the 'Überprüfung was der Fall ist,' up to Ayer and replaced only when Popper consummated a turnaround with his falsification thesis.

27 We would be quite mistaken, then, if we would take the Immediate Object as less real than the Dynamic one (as we have seen it in Eco). It just stands before the mind differently, neither true nor false (which is Dynamic) nor necessary (Normal). The Dynamic Object is not the 'raw, physical' entity, but always an Object of a Triadic Representation.

28 Unfortunately, manuscript MS318 (which consists of five different drafts of letters to the editors of the *Nation*, etc., all incomplete, but three with Peirce's signature [i.e., with an end]) has been published in pieces and at times in a disfigured form, in the Collected Papers (5.11–5.13, 5.464–5.466, 1.560–1.562, 5.467–5.496). However, 5.481 continues with the last sentence from a completely different draft and from a different context.

29 In his letters to James, Peirce again takes up the subject of connection types to Reality. James is characterized in MS318.9: 'The most prominent of all our school and the most respected, William James, defines pragmatism as the doctrine that the whole 'meaning' of a concept expresses itself either in the shape of conduct to be recommended or of experience to be expected.'

Then he notes that *his own* Pragmatism does not regard mere feelings, but rather concepts involving what became known as a would-be-conditional habit of behaviour. In that letter (8.315) from 1909, he goes carefully through the problem of how an outward Reality impresses itself on sign activity. 'Experience to be expected' refers evidently to the logic (or merely statistical probability) of such an expectation. The constancy of the world as cognized for Peirce is a result of the concept (i.e., the Interpretant, or even more precisely the Final Interpretant). Its object differs from the merely dyadic Objects, even from the more mental of the two: the Immediate Object or 'Image.' Peirce is very careful to abstract from Quality considerations, even though some Quality will always be part of the concrete semiosis. This is because of the hierarchical nature of Categories, which comprise their respectively lower correlates. This is stated thus: 'The Immediate Interpretant consists in the *quality* of the Impression that a sign is fit to produce, not to any actual reaction. Thus the Immediate and Final Interpretants seem to be absolutely distinct from the Dynamical Interpretant and from each other' (8.315).

30 In 1.533 (Lowell lectures, 1903) he sets out to 'express the Firstness of Thirdness, the peculiar flavor or color of mediation.'

31 Peirce divides cognition, volition, and perception or feeling (1.332 from 1905), as respectively the psychological end of an argument or Thirdness, an Index or Secondness, and a percept, which is Iconic.

32 In Peirce, 'signification' is not 'meaning,' whereas in Eco both tend to become 'signification.' Only Peirce's meaning qualifies for what is so important to Eco – namely, the translation from one sign into another, where one equals the other (4.127, 1893; 4.132, 1893; also 5.179, 1903). This idea is hardly contained in 'signification,' in contrast to 'supposition' (5.320n; W2.243, 1869). *Significatio* is defined as "rei per vocem secundum placitum representatio" ... It is a mere affair of lexicography, and depends on a special convention (*secundum placitum*), and not on a general principle. *Suppositio* belongs, not directly to the *vox*, but to the *vox* as having this or that *significatio* ... Thus, the word *table* has different *significationes* in the expressions "table of logarithms" and "writing-table"; but the word *man* has one and the same *significatio*, and only different *suppositiones*, in the following sentences: "A man is an animal," "a butcher is a man," "man cooks his food"' (ibid.). This traditional usage can be translated partly into semantic intension (or *acceptio*) as equivalent to *suppositio*. Semantic extension corresponds to *significatio*, although the angle of view is somewhat different (cf. W2.76, 1867 = 2.399, where Peirce gives at least twelve acceptations of the term 'extension,' (cf. W2.72, 1867 = 2.393): '"intension' is now

frequently used for comprehension; but it is liable to be confused with intensity, and therefore is an objectionable word.' It seems, however, that Peirce can without contradiction write, 'It was there [scil. in an anterior part] shown that real things are of a cognitive and therefore significative nature, so that the real is that which signifies something real' (ibid). Now when Eco quotes Peirce concerning signification, Peirce's term is 'meaning,' not signification (even in 1.339, which is a brief definition of the sign). Meaning indeed acquires a sense close to Firstness or Quality, in 1.339, especially when Peirce writes that 'meaning is nothing but representation ... stripped of irrelevant clothing.' Here, too, is an 'infinite regression,' a regression that changes clothes for more diaphanous ones, though never stripping them off. In other words, there is always a Quality involved in semiosis, even of the most abstract ideas. Eco (1976: 54f) tries to make it a translation from one sign into another, despite Peirce's attempt to describe that translation, that infinite regression, as one which operates on all three sign Categories simultaneously and concomitantly. As an abstract object ultimately ends in a concrete and simple one, so do Interpretants, which 'hand along ... the torch of truth' (ibid.), as well as Qualities or meanings. No question of stripping off *haecceitas* or Quality.

33 Narrated time, estranged or not, confers a suggestion of easy availability, as we will see in the context of cinematic narratology. Seen as asset, this seems to be the only way of communicating time as public (Heidegger: 'vulgar') time. Seen as a liability of an artefact, it is a false consciousness compared with the immediate time consciousness in Husserl's sense. The kind of verdict Foucault has for this taming construction of historical Otherness need not be mentioned.

34 This is the sort of time experienced in music, for instance. It has no meaning – that is, it cannot be grasped through a meaning assigned to it; yet it is 'there', so to speak ('there' meaning a particular mode of presence).

35 This, by the way, places him solidly into the Aristotelian, Kantian conception of cosmological time of movement.

36 If the Iconic sign Time-of-enunciation is to stand for something (is representing something), this can only be the real time of projection, reading, seeing, and so on. It is not plain reality, but a sign (a distinction important to Bettetini), because it is reduced compared to reality. A second sign, diegetic, textual time, is in a Symbolic (and in chunks, Iconic) semiosic relationship to the first sign. The difference relative to linguistic time representations is the Iconic part of this second semiosis, which prevents such linguistic tricks as 'iteratives,' different tenses in their interplay (*consecutio temporum*), and suchlike. The problem with Bettetini's argument is only his

contention that 'cinema produces time,' the first semiosis. Interpreted as epistemological statement, its simple truth is that viewers must experience their own time, starting from the time of reading. However, Bettetini fails (as he could have within the hermeneutic tradition) to go as far as Ricoeur, wrongly attributing this time to cinematic creation. One can argue that there is really an Iconic time experience (as Ricoeur's mimesis I) at the basis of all narrative configuration. It might be misleading to describe cinematic time creation as semiosis of a 'real time.' This argument shows the danger of explaining with 'iconism.' It is surely not just the onto-semantic logic of Russell that is behind a separation of 'real' and 'sign' (nonsensical, as it pre-supposes that we know about such a 'real' before we know it). That a communication event such as enunciation is temporal, and that temporality is an integral part of the 'reality' (= sign) of enunciation, is evident. How social and chronometrical Interpretants and the like capture that aspect is more complex than just Iconic. Mitry's 'logica dei fatti' (i.e., Russell's biunivocal relationship) and 'logica delle implicazioni' would not have to be differentiated if we did not assume Iconicity as a degenerate Thirdness.

37 This logic in Mitry is really a narrative one, configuring 'epochs' of action, orders among various future or various past events, and so on. Bettetini distinguishes between a base time and a higher organization of it looking for a 'logica della rappresentazione temporale' beyond a 'logica dell'organizzazione temporale del discorso televisivo, della diegesi filmica' (Bettetini 1979: 53).

38 Cf. Mitry (1965: 450), in Bettetini (1979: 49).

39 Bettetini sees his task as: 'ricerca di una logica del cinema ,.. : non tanto una logica del tempo cinematografico ..., quanto di una logica di una rappresentazione audiovisiva che si struttura in un tempo forte e rigido, elemento cooccorrente a definirne la forma espressiva, l'organizzazione significante' (Bettetini (1979: 54).

40 That is, when the act of (1) enunciating creates (2) an enunciated, producing thus a dependent object (cf. Greimas 1979; also 1986 s.v. 'énonciation'), in detail v. *supra*, 414.

41 In the literal sense of the word *re-cordare* (*cor* = heart), re-member contains *memoria*.

42 'La production d'un énoncé dit modal, surdéterminant un énoncé descriptif' (Greimas 1979 s.v. 'Modalisation').

43 But Greimas succeeds in creating an astonishingly complex system of negation types, and on this basis of layered modalities creates a very efficient narratology.

44 Which is but part of modal logic (cf. Prior 1967: V, 12). He states that in

propositions (p) about future (Fp) and past (Pp) events, and permanent ('always') events (Gp)(Hp), there is a natural direction of higher (implying preceding) forms: 'that p' is implied by 'it will have always been the case that p' (FHp).

45 As Bettetini remarks, linguistic native grammars are very imprecise in how they deal with time. Therefore they were rejected by some logicians: 'In the quasi-modal areas the tightest logical structure is perhaps to be found among the tenses, although some logicians believe that a logically accurate language would dispense with tenses altogether (handling only dated sentences and sentences about the temporal order of events, which are timelessly true, rather than the ones like 'I have eaten my breakfast,' which are false at one time and true at another)' Prior (1967: V, 12). Cinema is by nature much more precise, because its enunciation creates time immediately.

46 Cf. Deleuze (1985: 365), where he offers an explicit rationale of his theoretical practice about cinema.

47 Due to his counterintuitive usage, one is well advised to take all those deceptively familiar concepts as having a distinct meaning. In their Deleuzian acceptation they are meaningful only in the context of Bergson's philosophy.

48 Even in film theory, image is treated – *mutatis mutandis* – the same way as the perception of 'reality.' Conversely, affirming emphatically its closeness to symbolic universes, as in film 'linguistics,' is merely exchanging 'language' with 'reality.' In this murky zone between image and reality, every film theory must come to terms with some patent facts. The image is without any doubt somewhere in between the subject and its objective real. Philosophically, the most radical reduction of this distance is the Platonic solution. Image ($\varepsilon\tilde{\iota}\delta o\varsigma$) comes to stand between the philosopher's mind and the Idea; it has an irreducible tendency to falsify truth. Therefore it must be eliminated by a pure $\theta\varepsilon\omega\rho\iota\alpha$. At the Platonic antipode is the vast Humian, Berkleyan tradition of objectivism. The outside world leaves its impressions on the mind through sensation. Now the philosopher's chore is to eliminate the artefacts of the mind in order to take hold of the truth of the real. Constructivism is clearly also an objectivist theory, as resulted from the discussion above. The status of the image can only be that of a placeholder of the outside, and the beginning of its mental treatment. If the collective treatment, taken in itself and abstractly, is the focus, then the linguistic solution alleges itself as the answer to the image problem. Is the segmentation of the world of physical appearances coinciding with the sense produced by language segmentation? Metz (1968) is not far from that

position when, for the extra-cinematic codes of the 'choses filmées,' he assumes them to be referential of perceptual segmentations: (v. *supra*, 585n70). The question of images is dissolved, since it makes no sense to speak of 'reality' as something that can be separate from language. Again on a middle ground, a preconstructivist onto-epistemology of images tries to re-conduce the cinematic proper into a kind of perception, or even its Gestalt. Arnheim (1932: ch. II and *passim*) characterizes film as (just normal) perception particular through certain sensory limitations inherent in the material. This indicates that cinema is not reality – and excludes notions of Arnheim's earlier passive mechanical reproduction theories. Nevertheless, he still accessed it in the same way as reality. Arnheim certainly was inspired by Formalism (or he had the same roots as Formalism) in that the missing characteristics can be employed artistically as a means of conveying aspectualities or ideas. When meaning is created through conspicuous privations – always compared to 'normal' reality – the meaning construction process nevertheless remains the same. Despite providing an impressive list of artistic means of sensory manipulation, Arnheim does not ask why they work or why this is not particular to film. It would require an epistemological inquiry into Gestalt theory to evaluate its ontological assumptions. As Andrew (1984) remarks, Gestalt principles, though often disguised, found their way into many other film theories. Perceptual forms (acquired or innate) tend to be taken as facts that require no further explanation.

49 And which is not merely its epistemology, as Deleuze (1983: 89) also remarks. The far-reaching consequences for film theory will be seen: Here is both *grandeur et misère* of film ontology.

50 Deleuze is clearly aware of the Heideggerian ring of this term. '*Ganzsein*,' Being-a-whole is a quality of originary temporality before it becomes derivate as vulgar time. Most prominently, this aspect is at the centre of Deleuze's 1986 book on Foucault. In this book the vitalist background of 'Wholeness,' in its Nietzschean (seen through Heidegger's eyes) acceptation, is more than apparent.

51 This term was invented in Sellars (1968: 140).

52 Despite affirmations to the contrary in Leutrat (1988), which betray only a semiological frame of reference. The organic system of Deleuze is not based on differences; and it is impossible that this escapes his attention. After all, he authored a quite lucid description of the implicit ontology of structural principles in precisely 'À quoi reconnaît-on le structuralisme?' (Deleuze 1973). Thus, the opening declaration of Deleuze (1983: 7) has to be interpreted *juxta modum*: 'C'est une taxonomic, un essai de classification des

images et des signes.' It is very literally the law of the order (taxis), which constitutes this theory, as we will see.

53 That this could be a consequence of Bergson's thought is doubtful. The very *raison d'être* of Bergson's system is now void.

54 Everything is three-step: heuristically, maieutically, and by essence. The general structure of the two volumes is the symmetry movement – time. Excluding the preparatory and concluding chapters, each volume has three times three chapters, each with three paragraphs. two *volets* (= volumes), each with three 'books' of three chapters of three paragraphs (and sometimes of three subparagraphs).

55 An example of 'reification' of this metaphysical concept: 'dans "L'homme que j'ai tué," est une image-perception exemplaire: la foule vue de dos, à hauteur de mi-homme, laisse un intervalle qui correspond à la jambe manquante d'un mutilé; c'est par cet intervalle qu'un autre mutilé, cul-de-jatte, verra le défilé qui passe.' (Deleuze 1983: 102). Seen from Deleuze's deliberate distance from 'natural perception' as seminal theory, which on the contrary is situated in an entirely different site (cf. *supra*, 200–3).

56 Deleuze succeeds in associating Expressionist film and the French School with subjective perception images, offering as an introduction Pasolini's 'free indirect speech' concept. There is certainly great merit to the very pertinent observations and reflections on concepts of cinema in Deleuze. Here, however, the question is only classification, which is also – and not least – an explanatory tool. Not all the explanatory power of Deleuze's reflections comes from his metaphysical classification, of course, but certainly a great amount does.

57 Example: 'Quant à l'image-affection, on en trouvera des cas illustres dans les visage de Jeanne d'Arc de Dreyer, et dans la plupart des gros plans de visage en général.' (Deleuze 1983: 102).

58 Example: 'Fritz Lang fournit un exemple célèbre d'image-action dans "Mabuse le joueur": une action organisée, segmentée dans l'espace et dans le temps, avec les montres synchronisées qui scandent le meurtre dans le train, la voiture qui emporte le document volé, le téléphone qui prévient Mabuse' (Deleuze 1983: 102).

59 Represented in Bergson's famous memory cone of infinite layers (cf. Deleuze 1985: 108n21; also Bergson 1959: 302/181).

60 Cf. Deleuze (1985: 54): 'Ce que le mouvement aberrant révèle, c'est le temps comme tout, comme "ouverture infinie," comme antériorité sur tout mouvement normale défini par la motoricité: il faut que le temps soit antérieur au déroulement réglé de toute action, qu'il y ait "une naissance du monde qui ne soit pas liée parfaitement à l'expérience de notre motoricité" et que

"le plus lointain souvenir d'image soit séparé de tout mouvement de corps."' It is evident that strong resonances of Bergson's understanding of pure memory are present, especially in the line of argumentation of its necessary anteriority to all concrete remembering (without language).

61 Deleuze never really followed up the Peircean inspiration present in parts of his film theory. It might be significant that his intellectual interests lead him to Foucault. There he takes up the thread of thinking on the Outside ('*la pensée du dehors*'). This figure of thought is foreshadowed in his film theory, as various stages of Outside, but in its purest form it is also pure thought. The hope connected with this aesthetic and historical development is fully present only in Deleuze 1986). Clearly, this defies totally the Realist nature of Peirce's thought; but it should not be denied that this is an interesting form of nihilist–vitalist (Nietzschean) nominalism.

62 Cf. Bergson (1959: 220/76f): 'De là l'importance capitale du problème de la mémoire. Si la mémoire est ce qui communique surtout à la perception son caractère subjectif, c'est, disions-nous, à en éliminer l'apport que devra viser d'abord la philosophie de la matière. Nous ajouterons maintenant: puisque la perception pure nous donne le tout ou au moins l'essentiel de la matière, il faut que la mémoire soit, en principe, une puissance absolument indépendante de la matière. Si donc l'esprit est une réalité, c'est ici, dans le phénomène de la mémoire, que nous devons le toucher expérimentalement. Et dès lors toute tentative pour dériver le souvenir pur d'une opération du cerveau devra révéler à l'analyse une illusion fondamentale.'

63 A term not employed by Bergson (cf. Deleuze 1985: 106n17).

64 From the description of Deleuze (1985: 105ff), there seems to exist a certain nearness to Husserl's concept of the immediate past in his *inneres Zeitbewußtsein* (cf. Ricoeur 1985: 37ff). Also the distinction that Husserl and Bergson both make between the immediate past of a present and the remembered ('*ressouvenir*') or dreamed past, which creates its own present – in Husserl, by imagination.

65 Again one can observe a depsychologization and an ontologization in B/D's idea of time, (cf. Deleuze 1985: 110), the same as space. Taking as point of comparison Kant's Transcendental Aesthetic, the situation is reversed: We exist in time, not time in us. Kant's Critical Question applies: How does he know? Does he possess an *eidos* of time that need no synthesis of judgment?

66 'Étendu' (ibid.: 364/263). 'Entre l'affection sentie et l'image perçue, il y a cette différence que l'affection est dans notre corps, l'image hors notre corps. Et c'est pourquoi la surface de notre corps, limite commune de ce corps et des autres corps, nous est donnée à la fois sous forme de sensations et sous forme d'image.'

67 Which is two-tiered: the first has more connection with the sympathetic nervous system, or at least the primitive brain stem, the second is situated in the cortex and comprehends non-automatic, free reactions within the limits of the brain's choices. Even animals and plants have memory of the first sort, albeit sometimes quite restricted.

68 It has been mentioned that Constructivism is based on the ontology of systems theory, without which it quickly becomes mere methodology. As an account of the real, it passes through the ultimate reality of systems, which alone 'are' emphatically.

69 Cf. Bergson (1959: 161) defines 'La matière, pour nous, est un ensemble d'"images." Et par "image" nous entendons une certaine existence qui est plus que l'idéaliste appelle une représentation, mais moins que ce que le réaliste appelle une chose, – une existence située à mi-chemin entre la "chose" et la "représentation."'

70 Bergson in particular is describing the alternative as follows: 'Espace homogène et temps homogène ne sont donc ni des propriétés de choses, ni des conditions essentielles de notre faculté de les connaître: ils expriment, sous une forme abstraite, le double travail de solidification et de division que nous faisons subir à la continuité mouvante du réel pour nous y assurer des points d'appui, pour nous y fixer des centres d'opération, pour y introduire enfin des changements véritables; ce sont les schèmes de notre *action* sur la matière. La première erreur, celle qui consiste à faire de ce temps et de cet espace homogènes des propriétés des choses, conduit aux insurmontables difficultés du dogmatisme métaphysique, – mécanisme ou dynamisme, – le dynamisme érigeant en autant d'absolus les coupes successives que nous pratiquons le long de l'univers qui s'écoule et s'efforçant vainement alors de les relier entre elles par une espèce de déduction qualitative, le mécanisme s'attachant plutôt, dans une quelconque des coupes, aux divisions pratiquées dans le sens de la largeur, c'est-à-dire aux différences instantanées de grandeur et de position, et s'efforçant non moins vainement d'engendrer avec la variation de ces différences, la succession des qualités sensibles. Se rallie-t-on, au contraire, à l'autre hypothèse? veut-on, avec Kant, que l'espace et le temps soient des formes de notre sensibilité? On aboutit à déclarer matière et esprit également inconnaissables. Maintenant, si l'on compare les deux hypothèses opposées, on leur découvre un fond commun: en faisant du temps homogène et de l'espace homogène ou des réalités contemplées ou des formes de la contemplation, elles attribuent l'une et l'autre à l'espace et au temps un intérêt plutôt *spéculatif* que *vital*. Il y aurait dès lors place ... pour une doctrine qui verrait dans l'espace et le temps homogènes des principes de division et de solidifica-

tion introduits dans le réel en vue de l'action, et non de la connaissance, qui attribuerait aux choses une durée réelle et une étendue réelle, et verrait enfin l'origine de toutes les difficultés non plus dans cette durée et cette étendue qui appartiennent effectivement aux choses et se manifestent immédiatement à notre esprit, mais dans l'espace et le temps homogènes que nous tendons au-dessous d'elles pour diviser le continu, fixer le devenir, et fournis à notre activité des points d'application' (Bergson 1959: 345f/ 237f.).

71 Deleuze does recognize, though, the 'realism' of semiotic which he takes pain to distinguish from semiology on that account: 'On appelle sémiotique au contraire la discipline qui ne considère le langage que par rapport à cette matière spécifique, images et signes.' (Deleuze 1985: 343). The two latter terms must be read in their strictly Deleuzeian or Bergsonian sense, however. Deleuze defines and describes sign entirely differently to Peirce or even to Deledalle (his source).

72 Proof of this could be the very formulation of his critique of semiology: 'Mais précisément, dès qu'on a substitué un énoncé à l'image, on a donné à l'image une fausse apparence, on lui a retiré son caractère apparent le plus authentique, le mouvement' (Deleuze 1985: 41). In this apparently innocent statement we can see implied Bergson's Anti-realism and Anti-idealism. Not assuming with intuition an ontological attitude means falling back into Zenon's paradox, which is – as implied by Deleuze's assertion – the case with semiology because it relates to a 'coupure' 'on immobilise le mouvement' and not to the entirety of movement. Deleuze consequently interprets digitalization as slicing up the whole of movement. When digitalization is menaced, however, the whole concept of code falls, because code can only be thought of as difference. From a purely differential system to action upon matter itself is an enormous abyss.

73 Cf. Deleuze (1985: 46); also there we find Deleuze's very short summary of Peirce's philosophy.

74 As long as the cinematic Sign is involved as determinant. How other Sign logics can 'take over,' was discussed earlier.

75 The transcript of the entire film in found in Ehrat (1991: Annex, Shots ## 4, 6, 8, 10, 24, 26, 42, 81, 85, 89, 146, 168, 178, 232.

76 Cf. James Peterson's non-explanatory explanation of avant-garde irrationality, or surrealist style, in Bordwell (1996: 117–18).

77 Publications on Godard tend to overlook this film. To date there apparently has been only one substantial and serious critique, by Ishaghpour (1986: 285–97). Generally speaking, most other studies of this film are too short or too impressionistic to be of great value in the present context. In most of

these critiques any indication as to how an argument presented as evidence can be comprehended on the basis of grounds is entirely lacking. Instead of wild interpretations that make sense only in their own right, theory must seek a more controlled understanding of the work and the processes it engenders. In Ishaghpour is a valuable interpretation; even so, it tends to apply uniformly a certain aesthetic theory that is not explicitly outlined. We comprehend only that it relies strongly on Benjamin's lost aura aesthetic and that it is especially open to the Frankfurt School's comprehension of form. Thus his hermeneutic circulation seems to be somewhat like Nietzsche's 'Ewige Wiederkehr des Gleichen." Some films, like Wenders's *Paris, Texas*, fall completely through the grid because there are only inadequate instruments in this aesthetic other than by dealing with it as an expression of the production system. Apparently, the more philosophical a film aesthetic becomes, the less attention it can give to the process character of signification: all things become an expression of something else.

78 All numbering and other symbols refer to a tentative transcription of the entire film in Ehrat (1991: Annex). Transcribing *Je vous salue, Marie* is difficult and unsatisfactory from whatever angle one looks at it. An attempt is made in the following, after the shot number, to render in the next column with (Roman) numbers the Number of Universe. Since many of Godard's images do not refer to an extensional universe, they can be grouped as symbolic universes into some undefined space and time coherence. As will be seen, their existence depends on narrative universes, to which they are rhetorically connected.

79 Extracts from the transcript of *Je vous salue, Marie* in Ehrat (1991) mostly (where reasonably informative) follow this scheme: 1. Shot number (defined as uninterrupted filming). 2. Number of narrative universe of the imagery (if diverse from sound track). Either 3., number of sequence in the narration(s), or 4., number of recurring symbolism. 5. Semantic content of the image, plus significant camera parameters. 6. Approximative spoken (!) dialogue. 7. Sound track.

80 Reflected in the logical archi-principles of Excluded Middle and Non Contradiction (cf. *supra*).

81 Cf. in particular Weinrich's (1964) 'Erzählen –Besprechen' dichotomy, which in their inter-wovenness and contrast yield the most interesting text effects.

82 The Feuerbachian figure Joseph, in addition, is fighting with the anti-Bourbonic Revolutionary Gabriel. In terms of certainty, the revolutionary certainty is much more adapted to the mission he is charged with, than the interior fight of a no-longer and simultaneously becoming Idealist (of another sort, though!) like Joseph.

83 Godard seems to be wrong on this. What he refers to is the last verse of the
   next to last stanza from Georg Trakl's poem 'Herbstseele':
   Bald entgleitet Fisch und Wild
   Blaue Seel, dunkles Wandern
   Schied uns bald von Lieben, Andern
   Abend wechselt Sinn und Bild
   Heidegger commented on it not in a lecture of the Bayerische Akademie
   der Schönen Künste 1959, which is published as 'Der Weg zur Sprache,' but
   in what was published as 'Die Sprache im Gedicht' from a lecture on the
   Bühlerhöhe, 4 October 1952. Both are contained in 'Unterwegs zur Sprache'
   Heidegger (1985: Abt.I, Bd 12). The context of Trakl's verse in Heidegger's
   lecture is nevertheless crucial to our understanding of Godard's *Je vous
   salue, Marie*: The departure ('Schied') from beloved one, who are others
   ('Lieben, Andern') is due to something that grounds in a 'Schlag' (blow,
   Greek πλήγη = curse) from where 'Ge-Schlecht,' in the sense of both sexuality and generation (genus). Sexuality contains division ('Entzweiung') into
   the two-ness of other-ness in sex. Therefore it produces strangeness ('Frem-
   dling'), which leads to the falling in blue-ness (Trakl's 'Blaue Seele'). It is
   the evening, which is blue, because it changes all things in a spiritual dawn
   ('geistliche Dämmerung') and contains also the beginnings of new being.
   'Das Scheinende, dessen Anblicke (Bilder) die Dichter sagen, erscheint
   durch den Abend anders' (op. cit. 45–7, all quotes).
84 Which is crudely made even more clear by subtitling in the English version
   of *Je vous salue Marie*: Hail Mary.
85 These two terms must be taken in their original rhetoric meaning, not
   στοχασμός or *status conjecturalis* but already ποιότης *status generalis*, in the
   context of 'stasis theory' as it came from down to us from Hermagoras, cf.
   Enos (1996: s.v. 'Stasis theory').
86 Cf. donkey intercut with Joseph in ##282, 284.
87 Unfortunately, in dubbed versions (e.g., the German version) no care has
   been taken to reproduce the very exact coincidence of this image with this
   text, as in the original version. Evidently, when we contemplate Eve's
   naked female body and at the same moment hear an inexplicable comment
   about it, the demonstration is even more complete.
88 'La force de la bible, c'est que c'est un beau scénario,' said Godard (in
   Ishaghpour 1986: 287). Luke's annunciation narrative has left many traces
   in *Je vous salue, Marie*. There are the names Marie, Joseph, Eva, and Gabriel.
   There is the basic respect for all the important stages in Luke. There is
   Jacob's-wrestling-with-God style (Gen 32: 23ff) between Joseph and Gabriel. There is Eve is biting the apple and giving her classmates a 'ver de

terre' (death) instead of ants. Toward the end, Marie's son is quoting and re-enacting the gospels. Godard had planned to have more of this in his film (cf. Plan 23 in Godard [1985: 597]).

89 N = acoustic perspective is 'near'; G = audibility is 'good' (compared to the usual).

90 Le sacré dans le film de Godard n'a d'autre lieu que le paysage comme résurrection: la "Pâques des yeux," qu'on a du mal à distinguer, pourtant, du prospectus publicitaire' (290).

91 *pneuma* = breath in Greek. ἅγιον πνεῦμα is the Holy Spirit.

92 Cf., among others, Ishaghpour (1982: 13–80).

4 Narration in Film and Film Theory

1 It will not surprise us that narratology and film theory sometimes seem to coincide. In the case of Metz's semiological 'grande syntagmatique,' film theory has rather exclusively been a theory of film narration. Bordwell's Neoformalism is actually no less than a film narratology, poetic, or 'narration theory.' Yet others are in the same boat, albeit less explicitly. Instead of concerning themselves with narration as a whole, they take an interest in some aspects of cinematic narration. There are some good grounds for holding on to such a special relationship between cinema and narration.

2 There should be no confusion of terms here. One first has to deal with represented action, and not with actual human behaviour. Contrary to commonsensical appearances perhaps, speaking about action already conceives of a representation and not an actual behaviour. On the other hand, the representation is not unrelated to the represented; action represents behaviour. The question must remain open, how transformation operates, on which premises, and by which agent. Only the difference is of interest here.

3 Since antiquity, the dramatic (really the tragical) representation of events has intrigued philosophers. Aristotle in the *Poetic* and Plato in the *Republic*, Book III, formulated the problems as they are still being debated today. Aristotle's thought rose out of the aesthetic questioning of drama. Another thread of theory developed from a practical knowledge of civic life. Interestingly, both philosophers emphasized narration as something quite central. The debate around Sophism produced its own theory – namely, Rhetoric, which was later adopted into modern literary studies, linguistics, *Textlinguistik*, and so on. Modern scholars in narratology – for example, Booth, Lubbock, Propp, Benveniste, Genette, Weinrich, and Ricoeur – created a corpus of theory that owed much to antiquity. Given the great potential of these theories of textual and narrative organization, they were

soon applied to cinema. Almost all of the important authors and schools have found followers among film theorists.

4 Some have resisted the temptation to enlarge their rather technical theories to the next higher level of reflection, namely, action theory. Ricoeur (1984), in particular, criticizes the semiological *École de Paris* for its narrow limitations. Even though mostly concerned with actantial schemes, functions, rules, and squares, that method seems to be opening itself more toward a general theory of human action. This also happens at the discursive level.

5 Neither is evident in itself. Narratological comprehension of the text mechanics makes us not immediately see there the production of a new kind of time. Neither it is obvious that the pragmatic result of acting in the world is the production of time, not just the manipulation of objects. By the same token, both practices are connected when storytelling founds societies. Almost every society, both past and present, needs and has its foundation myths. Since Thucydides, historiography has been laying the foundations of societal cohesion. This explicit use of narrative cohesion to create societal wholes has been thematized by the hermeneutics of Dilthey and Gadamer. Structuralism, even though a temporal, also takes mythical order as the homology for social order.

6 The strategic reason why the question of cinematic representation has been treated before narration is here. Even though narration makes use of Object representation, itself it represents events and not objects. Therefore in itself it is a Sign process of Time. We will see that there is an enormous logical difference that is fully revealed in the type of Signs used.

7 If we were to check this principle mentioned earlier – the Generality of purpose and the relative irrelevance of Facticity in narration – against narrative examples, we would argue against it, supported by genres such as documentary and history. Indeed, it does not seem plausible to deny Secondness to these. After all, they are 'about' something concrete. However, as narratives they are not concrete. Narrative causality is finality. Such a 'cognitive instrument' has rightly been criticized by eminent historiographers – Veyne (1979), for one. Historical facticity is, however 'rare,' not naturally connected with anything higher. In particular, to hold the history of something is not the same as to 'act' it. Only action brings the mental model of 'pragmatic logic' into events. Therefore, when we treat history (taking the word literally) as narration, we are referring to the typical in the factual, not to the factual. This is not difficult to think about semiotically. It can be regarded as sign degeneracy. Aristotelian Poetics had already emphasized this point (cf. *infra*), which reflects clearly in the graduation of 'poeticity' from tragedy downwards. The Formalist insight, taken up by Bordwell, is

not after all so new. Every narration is by its very nature a typos. Any 'defamiliarizing' deviation only places more emphasis on the typical, from which it deviates.

8 This was outlined earlier, in §1.3ff, in the epistemological implications of Pragmaticism.

9 'The statistical ratio of the number of experiential occurrences of a specific kind to the number of experiential occurrences of a generic kind, in the long run.' (Peirce 1998: 137).

10 Thus it is no longer an absolute truth to say that action (as behaviour) is either goal-oriented or communicative (the central watershed in Habermas's theory of action). In these two concepts of conduct the category 'object manipulation' (also a central category of Habermas's action theory) is not relevant; it is more than equivalent to conduce acting into the future of a not-yet-realized, now present as a general idea (the Pragmatic Maxim).

11 'The idea of time must be employed in arriving at the conception of logical consecution; but the idea once obtained, the time-element may be omitted, thus leaving the logical sequence free from time. That done, time appears as an existential analogue of the logical flow. '(1.491) The Logic of Mathematics (1896).

12 This means that Time is neither logically true, nor materially true, nor is it comprehended as a quality of contemplation.

13 Apparently, this is still a prevailing understanding of time, for instance, in general systems theory. For Luhmann (1984: esp. 116ff), temporalized systems build up sequences of moments. Their discreteness is the presupposition that the actual state disappears and is followed by a necessary different other state. The reflexivity of any one moment into its own past and future creates a supra-numerable set of discrete elements, or an enormous complexity. Only an emergent new order such as finality reduces this complexity to a form of temporality, which can be handled by the system. This is precisely the problem, which time theories based on abnumerable quantities incur. The only fundamental difference from Kant's Schematisms (also reductions of the multiple) is that not even the stability of a priori forms is admitted. These forms emerge eventually, though, in systems of sense. Compared to this, Peircean time as true Continuity is truly novel.

14 Which among some of Peirce's 'heirs' (certainly, with one of Peirce's more illustrious pupils, James, who was in great part responsible for spreading – together with Dewey – what was to be known as American Pragmatism), risked becoming (empirically) 'feasible' as a political social community acting according to certain principles. It is interesting that these were serious attempts to use Pragmaticism for a theory of public (not just general)

action. In a similar vein, Apel (1975) saw Peirce as lacking the capacity of *Verständigung* (agreement: v. *supra*. To recapitulate: If the teleology of scientific discovery can no longer be presupposed, and if the truth of true adequate opinions no longer results from the unquestioned relationship of the cognizing subject – as an acting – with the universe. Or does the mere capacity to act at all [i.e., have habits and 'behave'] guarantee truth?) Reaching an agreement is a public affair, pure communication. Agreement is that mode of cognition which is proper to purely communicationally constituted and relevant 'facts' (i.e., not [objective] facts [in Peirce's sense, because they have no basis in existence]). After the loss of factual constraints, the adequacy of the opinion of the community would be arbitrary and merely conventional. For example, speaking of 'our history,' or public time in general, is fully meaningful only if it determines actions teleologically for all and the whole unlimited community of past, present, and future persons.

15 Moreover, Continuity is so ubiquitous that it also shows up in other, more derived contexts, which are at the other limit of our present field of interest, in the Legal Semiotics of Kevelson. She translates the Continuity into a science of invention of norms, which is literally creative by discovering what was previously only in the mode of Possibility or the possible Real. Possibility means Firstness, wherefore agreement is an aesthetic process, aesthetics being a normative science. This, although Legal Semiotics is merely an outermost application of Pragmaticism, which the mature Peirce himself was very keen to make known only upon the foundations of Categories and Sign theory.

16 Which is also a metaphor for expressing the τί, the mathematical, or – Aristotle sees it – the 'number of the movement, according to the before and the after' (*Physics*, VI,2,219 b 2).

17 If the entirety of Continuous time could become cognition, it would indeed remind us of a Hegelian concrete general of sorts. However, no temptation can emanate from Peirce to develop such an idealist philosophy of history in a meaningful way. This would involve an impossible vantage point from a concrete generality. However, time is something to be lived pragmatically.

18 This takes away the pressure to establish communicable time as a public derivate of the authentic – but solipsist – time: Peirce's equivalent of Ricoeur's *temps humain*, Heidegger's derived temporality, or historicality (*Geschichtlichkeit*), is the Sign itself in its temporal dimension. There is a fundamental difference between this and existential temporality, then. For Peirce, time is unlimited openness, inexhaustible Possibility. For Heideg-

ger, temporality is limited closure. Only as non-authentic time is it forgetful of its being-toward-an-end, and therefore open and without any boundary. We shall see Ricoeur's attempt to correct this (by various accounts) awkward conception in mimetic time (cf. *infra*). Yet Heidegger (1927: 432n30) is indeed right when he sees a major difference between his conception of time and those of Aristotle, Kant, Bergson (with some nuances), and Hegel. They share the primordiality of the Now, whereas his is the 'Zu-künftigkeit' (future as coming toward). Peirce instead transcends this difference with his non-discrete, non abnumerable pure Possibility.

19 Continuity is indeed the key in Peirce and also leads to evolutionary metaphysics. That truth can come out in a Continuous chain of Interpretation in Signs depends as much on the Continuity of being-in-evolution, since the Continuous object constancy of an existent thing depends on the Continuity of number theory. Only if the chain of causalities is Continuous, and is efficient on all, it is possible to assert true propositions on existent objects. This a-temporal truth is connected through Continuity with the temporal truth of Continuous Interpretation. The latter will lead 'in the long run' to a final adequate opinion. Causality here is not of the efficient kind; rather, it is final causality and therefore of a completely different nature, though at the same time sharing Continuity. Moreover, not just the Existent and the tendency to a Final state is Continuous; it is also crucial that Possibility be real and therefore Continuous. Pure Possibility is at the same time pure Time. If pure chance were no more than disconnected singularities, of course there would be no Time involved in it. A world of that absolute chance sort is not one we could join together in numbers, in a calculus of chance. If chance is indeed the total openness to all Possibilities, the implication is that the space of the Possible is coherent, that one possible element relates to other possible elements. This implication (whose Reality is beyond proof) is the basis of 'Musement' (Peirce 1998: 436), diagrammatic thought, or mental experimentation: 'In fact, it is Pure Play. Now, Play, we all know, is a lively exercise of one's powers. Pure Play has no rules, except this very law of liberty. It bloweth where it listeth. It has no purpose, unless recreation. The particular occupation I mean – a petite bouchée with the Universes – may take either the form of aesthetic contemplation, or that of distant castle-building (whether in Spain or within one's own moral training), or that of considering some wonder in one of the Universes, or some connection between two of the three, with speculation concerning its cause '(ibid.). Therefore, the only Reality whose existence to prove was crucial to Peirce's architectonic thought was Continuity itself. If there is real Continuity – which however appears/'is' never a phenomenon – then all of the

implications and assumptions outlined above are admissible. Otherwise, this is only bad ontology.

20 'Real is that which is such as it is regardless of how it is, at any time, thought to be' (5.547).

21 Cf. 5.454; Peirce again uses the example of the cottonwool-diamond (5.547): 'The unsophisticated conception is that everything in the Future is either destined, i.e., necessitated already, or is undecided, the contingent future of Aristotle. In other words, it is not Actual, since it does not act except through the idea of it, that is, as a law acts; but is either Necessary or Possible, which are of the same mode since ... Negation being outside the category of modality cannot produce a variation in Modality' (5.459).

22 1.492: 'Time is said to be the form of inward intuition. But this is an error.' Here Peirce is referring to Hegel's evolution of thought. He has been criticized for too narrowly tying time into the conceptualization process (*auf den Begriff bringen*). Certainly – he admits – 'conception is framed according to a certain precept, [Then] we proceed to notice features of it which, though necessarily involved in the precept, did not need to be taken into account in order to construct the conception ... It is thus that thought is urged on in a predestined path. This is the true evolution of thought.' The idea of time is evidently involved in that process, only in the course of cognition 'the time-element may be omitted, thus leaving the logical sequence free from time' (1.491). In this notable distancing from Hegel's dialectic of the Spirit, Peirce gives Time a different essence. Time is contingent to logic, not a necessary law as in Hegel.

23 1.487: 'Metaphysics consists in the results of the absolute acceptance of logical principles not merely as regulatively valid, but as truths of being. Accordingly, it is to be assumed that the universe has an explanation, the function of which, like that of every logical explanation, is to unify its observed variety.'

24 Obviously, our graduation here is done in view of lesser or greater distance from logical reasoning or laws of thought (which is Peirce's definition of Semiotic, after all).

25 1.494: In view of the title of Peirce's writing, we can relate Time to the third trichotomy of signs dealing with the logic in the sign relation. Inasmuch as every sign is cognition, containing logic, and this monadically as Term, dyadically as Dicent, and triadically as argument (arguments being in turn a triad of induction, abduction and deduction); now, Time is inherent in every Real, which is necessarily event. Although it is not part of the Real as in Hegel's dialectic, as a contingent metaphysical law it is cognized and cognizable. As such it can be Quality, Fact, and Law in any semiosis.

26 Besides, such a default has found an outspoken and sharp critique, as epit-
    omized in Foucault's philosophy of history. His approach to historiogra-
    phy levelled the accusation of too facile a construction of narrative
    causality in the classical tradition of writing history (à la Ranke). This
    overly facile one causal chain reveals itself easily as a projection of a con-
    temporary consciousness onto past facts. However, it comes disguised as
    'reality itself.' Such a critique is not feasible except against the background
    of some alternative Oneness of time (in the 'dehors du dehors' as 'pensée
    du dehors'). However, Foucault's unity of time and of history cannot be
    experienced (by virtue of being 'outside'). Any narrative connection is
    therefore nominalistic, the result of a discursive practice of power relation.
    A functional equivalent to such an 'outside' of narrative unity is the way
    code-based film theories make sense of cinematic narration. Everything
    must be kept together through an act of enunciation. In a basically a-tem-
    poral theory such as semiology, this is the best we can achieve in imitation
    of a temporal unity. Pseudo-pragmatic orders made an ultimately uncon-
    vincing attempt to order 'actions' after the unifying model of phrase syntax
    (less stringent, and therefore merely syntagmatic). We have already seen
    Deleuze's scathing remarks about this sort of constructed unity of time.
27 Even though the narrative universe in *Ordet* is the same sectarian world
    that gave birth to evangelism and televangelism.
28 As Ricoeur (1985: 356ff passim), shows masterfully.
29 But there are also certain conditions for this; cf. Habermas (1981) on the
    veracity (indeed, felicity) conditions of such a communicative action.
30 Cf. Habermas (1981), in the sense of the third of his validity claims, which
    presupposes privileged access to one's interiority.
31 As we often find in Buñuel, Fellini, and Bergman, to name but three. Per-
    haps *auteur* cinema in general tends to be dominated by the restricted range
    of subjects a director is interested in.
32 Sic! Drouzy seems unaware of the theological mutual exclusion of his two
    claims. All extracts from Drouzy (1982: 327).
33 Dreyer's published script reveals itself as an *abrégé* of the biblical narrative.
    It quotes (exactly, the King James Version) passages in the dialogues and
    reflects quite precisely the handful of 'scene directions' in the New Testa-
    ment. Dreyer took great pains to expand the latter with his carefully gath-
    ered archaeological knowledge. Dreyer's interest is matched by historical
    theological interest – for example, the *ipsissima verba Jesu* research begun by
    J. Jeremias and E. Käsemann and continued by many others. Compared to
    that corpus of historical knowledge about Jesus, Dreyer's version is much
    closer to the biblical text and farther from the historical reconstruction of

the Aramaic rabbi Ben-Yoshua. An illustration of this influence can easily be seen in Arcand's *Jésus de Montréal*.

34   145. In Lc 9,35 it is the voice coming 'out of the cloud.' Dreyer then changed this scene in order to make Israel (= Moses!) recognize that Jesus is the Son of God. It must be noted, further, that Dreyer has retained all the attributes of divinity, modelled after the apparition on the Sinai.

35   At least Drouzy cannot name a single proof for his interpretation in *Ordet* (or even in Munk's play). It is merely an excerpt from an interview, in which Dreyer argues with Einstein for 'une approche plus profonde de la compréhension du divin' (Drouzy (1982: 341), which would consist of a science capable of explaining the super-natural by way of the natural. This is understandable as Dreyer's hope for a new science that is truly comprehensive – much more so than the mechanistic one preceding it. In particular, he hopes to see all of the psychic dimension included; this would truly be a comprehensive world model, in complete contrast, as Drouzy recognizes, to the one of the doctor and the pastor in *Ordet*.

36   'Comme on le sait toute l'action tourne autour du personnage du vieux Borgen ... sectaire et un tyran domestique' is an astonishing statement, in particular if confronted with the dramatic trajectory and climax of the film, where Borgen becomes an increasingly overwhelmed bystander. His presence is almost inversely reciprocal to Johannes's, which is especially strong in the resurrection scene, where he becomes increasingly abstracted, first with little Inger (who is the only one who believes) and then when completely alone with Inger's corpse.

37   'C'est aux valeurs du coeur et de l'imagination plus qu'à celles de la foi installée que vont ses [sc. Dreyer's] préférences. Ordet est un hymne à la femme, et donc à la vie, plus forte que les croyance et que les théories' (Drouzy 1982: 343).

38   There is a clear narrative *and* spatial closure in this film. Although there is indeed an escape route to heaven, Drouzy is right in saying there is no escape route into the vastness of open, unlimited horizons, as would fit with this Jutland landscape. The dunes are the limits of both the narrative and the universe. However, Dreyer uses this limit as a condition of the possibility of finding the vast openness within, in faith. Narrative narrow enclosure of space instead becomes concentration. This same aesthetic strategy was followed by Vilsmaier in *Schlafes Bruder*. The extreme, almost obsessive closure of an Alpine valley, dramatically emphasized by the enormous quantity and weight of the snow that cuts off the valley from the outside world, is the equivalent of the dunes. No help can come from outside: the village burns and Inger dies (the doctor is out). The difference

from the obsession of horror movies is that this dramatic and spatial closure gives rise to an inner horizon, which in both cases transgresses death.

39 50a16f: μίμησίς ἐστιν οὐκ ἀνθρώπων ἀλλὰ πράξεως καὶ βίου καὶ εὐδαιμονίας καὶ κακοδαιμονίας.

40 If Bordwell (1981) counts merely I. Night (of Johannes's adventure in the dunes) II. Day (Anders's episodes) III. Night (of Inger's struggle with death) IV. Day (of the funeral), he is clearly suppressing a very important and exactly defined ellipsis. The customary traditional visitation interval between decease and funeral three days; moreover, that tradition certainly arises from the religious symbolism contained in the three days following Christ's death. Even more, in *Ordet* the three-days disappearance of Johannes is especially significant, since it is precisely he who represents Christ. Only through his own victory over death does he himself become the victor over death. Certainly, none of this could have escaped *Ordet*'s original playwright, Pastor Kaj Munk. Dreyer maintained this narrative information explicitly and then but supported it audiovisually even more through a confused temporal orientation between Inger's decease and the funeral scene. It is impossible to situate the release of the death certificate and also the newspaper announcement of Inger's death, other than somewhere in between. That timelessness is faithful to the same sort of empty time in the Gospel narratives after Jesus' deposition from the cross and the first resurrection narratives. Except, of course, for the explicitly stated three days' interval.

41 A transcript of *Ordet*, in support of arguments, is not necessary, as Dreyer published the script in Dreyer (1970) and Storm (1964). Numbers in the text (#) refer to the numeration in the former. It must be noted, however, that the dialogue in the English translation is not exactly identical with the English subtitles. Furthermore, mise-en-scène directions are not merely descriptive; they also contain rudimentary interpretations of the narrative (e.g. the psychological motives of the characters). Although there is no universally valid method for transcription, it must be admitted that this one is not especially made for critical analysis purposes.

42 Bordwell (1981) doubts whether Johannes is a real narrative character. The main difficulty with his comprehension of this figure is that he fails to acknowledge that Johannes lives in a parallel narrative universe. Although his is not extensionally a parallel universe – it remains Borgensgård – we must follow a different 'inferential walk' to disclose its coherency. Only on a closer look can we discover that Johannes is by no means the only character in this universe. From the very beginning, he relates to other characters, for instance, to Borgen and Mikkel ('Woe unto you and you and you'), who

relate to him by not being able to relate. A non-communication is very much a communication. In psychology (in which Dreyer was especially interested), Bateson and Watzlawick described the function of non-communication as a double-bind. Since extensionally the two universes coincide, it is deceptively easy not to recognize the action plan of Johannes as coherent. Inevitably, one faces the problem of how all of a sudden he becomes a character with the two girls when Inger is dying. However, we should note that for them he has always been a character. Bordwell considers it especially problematic that Dreyer could find narrative closure with the final miracle; he does not understand that in Johannes's narrative plan, this was always a solution. Dreyer's finesse is precisely in having counterpoised two alternative universes, whose initial mutual incomprehension gradually and finally yields to a perfect embrace after Inger's resurrection. However, this unification does not take place on Borgen's (or normality's) terms, but on Johannes's.

43 It is again Bordwell (1981: 148) who must see in Maren (and little Inger?) agents whose narrative task is to check the unlimited power of Johannes. However, there is really no need to do this. In the eyes of everyone in possession of full reason, he is simply mad – and therefore at best awkward and bothersome – and not at all powerful. Only within his own auto-mandate has he the power of faith, which is set forth from the beginning. Yet that is precisely a power is not among the usual boundless divine attributes of omniscience and so on. Johannes is not a wizard, nor is he Superman or some other fairytale figure. His power and powerlessness are closely modelled after the earthly Jesus, that the faith of another agent is not *"checking"* it, or making it operant like a catalyst. Here the explanatory model of fairytale narrative fails completely; because the narrative clash of wills is not antagonistic, with one of the two prevailing (i.e., Peter *or* Borgen). Its power is more a conjunctive one, more like a gift that does not make the donor a hero. Johannes is not the great star outshining everyone in the end. That is Inger, but not as the accomplished hero, as fairytale logic would have it.

44 Implying perhaps that if he had not done so the result would have been a mediocre *deus ex machina* – style glorification of a hero, or something worse. The understanding is that there is a trajectory in the arrangement of the narrative disequilibrium.

45 Dreyer's film is a rather faithful adaptation of Munk's homonymous theatre play. That said, it has not been the only film made of that play. The same plot structure has been and can be used in more than one film, but it doesn't necessarily follow that the meaning will be the same. In fact, the

differences can be profound. Dreyer does more than simply render narrative information and its artistic, formal transformation through Munk.

46 So as not to be unnecessarily confusing, we must distinguish some terms: We could, with some justification, collapse the entirety of meaning into narration; but in our context we extensionally restrict the term narrative to the ordered rendering of human action by a narrator. We take it from Ricoeur that as such, narrative minimally follows certain laws that make it recognizable as a particular epistemological operation. Everything beyond the rendering of human action will be treated as aesthetic operation with its own epistemology – albeit with its subterranean connections to the former.

47 Though not limited to narration, and not even to Representamen. Dreyer left us an example of how an unpretentious documentary about a bridge (*Storstrømsbrøen*), far from being a 'conventional "bridge film"' (Bordwell 1981: 223), can aestheticize indexical semioses. There is a clear rhythm in every respect, and compositional techniques add to the overall aesthetic impression of that short film.

48 This is certainly not doing justice to Bordwell's admirable analytical description of *Ordet*, which does much more than simply construct a narrative macroproposition. It is just that his conclusions regarding the Christian narrative closure as a formal device seem unconvincing. As we have seen, this closure is not problematic from within the plot, and it needs no aesthetic intervention. An entirely different problem is the aesthetic impact of Ordet, and it is the convincing which in turn depends strongly on aesthetics.

49 A Neoformalist reading of Dreyer is not generally accepted. Carney (1989: 35–53) is strongly critical of 'Professor Bordwell's' formalist interpretation of *Ordet*. One can concur with Carney that much more might be gleaned from a thorough narrative compactness than Bordwell admits. There is a Formalist need to 'parametrize' elements. He does not go so far as to call them codes in the semiological sense of the term, but in functional terms, 'devices' are the same for restricted use in poetics.

50 Bordwell's arguing with the 'conspicuous' absence of such means is arguing in a vicious circle. Nothing can prove the contrary, because the reference point normality is also a mere practice. Nothing dictated to Dreyer the use of certain cinematic means (as does the grammatical and lexical correctness in language); he just happened to use what he used. A quite different investigation would be one into the quasi-necessity of a logic of action (as Danto's basic actions, cf. *infra*). Yet this is not Bordwell's point. What he describes in Dreyer's film would fit perfectly for other films. If one compares two of Chantal Akerman's films, *Je, tu, il, elle* and *The Golden Eighties*, for instance, the 'normality' and usualness of a Form become obvious. The

extreme scarcity of all sorts of means in the former film are exactly what it means: this is the universe it wants to represent. In the latter film, loud, showy, spectacular, this is the represented world and pragmatic. Is the 'real' world different? From which film? Who cares, however, if both produce their own *narratio probabilis*? 'Restriction in means' is only explanatory if it adds temporary semantic meaning to an otherwise 'normal' – because adequate – representation of their worlds.

51 This has been seen in film criticism as well. *Revault d'Allonnes* (1988: 63), for one, speaks of 'l'infilmable' of the resurrection sequence: 'gommant l'espace, Dreyer concentre a fortiori sur le temps.' One should, though, have argued the other way round, but he, too, sees Dreyer's mastery 'à retenir le flux inexorable du temps.'

5 Narration, Time, and Narratologies

1 There are historical reasons for the embedding of literature and aesthetic in the broad stream of post-kantian, historicist *Geisteswissenschaften*, from Droysen-Dilthey to Gadamer. Perhaps the strongest stimulus was the problem of identity, of ego and alter. One obvious consequence was a social science, which proved to be the first and most fruitful encounter with the pragmatist tradition, in the lineage of Peirce. This place of encounter, however, is accessed from two opposite directions. It was the social nature of cognition and Interpretation in Signs that led to the pragmatic interest in sociality.

2 Heidegger in English might sound rather clumsy (more than in German, perhaps). Therefore, for the key concepts, I have adopted throughout the usage of Macquarrie and Robinson's translation (Heidegger 1962).

3 This virtually untranslatable term – 'preoccupation' would be Heidegger's *'Be-sorgen'* – finds an etymological affinity in the Old English word 'sorg,' which eventually became 'sorrow' (cf. Oxford English Dictionary q.v.). Ricoeur translates it as souci, therefore *Sorge*, Care (cognate with the German *kar* [e.g., in *Karfreitag* = Good Friday], grief) might also be rendered weaker as 'concern.'

4 Barthes's catchy remark in his opening lecture at the Collège de France, that language is fascist (cf. Greimas 1989: 555), goes in the same direction. Every kind of structural or ontological fixation tends to become nostalgically repressive if enacted. An anthropology without a perspective of human change, be it forgiveness or the Principle Hope, is limiting as a system of thought.

5 The already mentioned general systems theory is a case in point. If systems

are defined functionally as reductions of complexity (i.e., chance), and if 'there are systems' (Luhmann 1984: 30), asymmetrical systems through temporalization constitute one of the most effective reductions of complexity to order. However, the order achievement of the system does not come without a price. If everything is system, there must be an ultimate environment proper to the ultimate system. This is extremely difficult to think of, because any system is selective, selecting its own environment, and the ultimate difference cannot comprehend all. Thus it is not a totality but an ultimate selection. If Luhmann needs God to reduce the risk of an ultimate selection into a 'chiffre,' this is just one way to escape the ultimate tautology (paradox) created by this very approach.

6 This is a fundamental difference between an existential-phenomenological approach such as Ricoeur's, and Habermas's communicative 'liquidification' of 'being.' The latter admits only to validity claims based on agreement, 'Verständigung.' Any existential foundations are suspected as being metaphysical evidence (i.e. they cannot be argued). The discrepancies are so enormous that it would seem almost impossible to uncover Habermas's implicit assumption of a similar transcendental horizon. Peirce's concept of evolutionary love shows how 'Reason' (which figures also in Habermas's system) comes very close to a 'transcendental.'

7 By suppressing this primordial distinction, Bordwell's Neo-Formalism never overcomes a certain ambiguity. A deed (i.e., a narrated action) is not the estranged version of a concrete action, but a self-standing creation. As product, it is intrinsically a cultural entity and it differs fundamentally from behavioural forms given to human interaction. Acting is a constant flow; it has no beginning or end as Deeds have.

8 Ricoeur (1983: 106): by quoting Kant on Schematism, KrV A145 (B184) – 'Die Schemate sind daher nichts als Zeitbestimmungen a priori nach Regeln, und diese gehen nach der Ordnung der Kategorien, auf die Zeitreihe, den Zeitinhalt, die Zeitordnung, endlich den Zeitbegriff in Ansehung aller möglichen Gegenstände.' – he postulates the same automatism for narrative comprehension.

9 Northrop Frye (1957) investigates these transhistorical schemes or mythoi (tragedy, romance, comedy and irony) as subsisting in three parameters: Archetype (the form of human desire, in the literary form of myth or other holy Writ), Mode (the hero's power compared with ours: five modes), using basic Symbols of the 'hypothetical' and converging ultimately in the One symbol of the Logos (cf. op. cit.: 121).

10 Ricoeur's interpretation of Heidegger focuses on time. The perspective must change when the problem becomes one of theoretically founding the

conditions of the possibility of human action. In a reverse process, one would go from the 'vulgar time' constituent of social acting to the existential roots. Or not, perhaps, so far as that. In the 'theoretical reconstructive pragmatic' in Habermas (1981), such a procedure is used to found communicative action: every manipulative act needs social coordination. Objects are defined in common by agreeing on their social usage. In this way reality becomes the societal point of reference, defining the definers, providing also legitimacy as the order of things to the Order over things and subjects. Heidegger in particular, however, already sites genesis of society at the level of experience of Social Time; objects (of action-in-time) are certainly connected with concern, 'Besorgen,' and are therefore *a fortiori* social. Although Habermas restricts himself to communicational processes as the last instance of truth finding, the process of agreement itself is guided by Reason, not by existential *conditio humana*.

11 Poetics is the question of genres, but not all cultures have the same genre logics. Tragedy, drama, literature, comedy, historiography, modern media, novels, are converted today homogeneously into 'entertainment.' That signals that in being entertained we intend an object to be unobtrusive in our everyday lives. This strategy contrasts deliberately with 'weighty' conspicuous objects of questioning as, concerning justice, war and peace, and so on. A theory of entertainment drama calls for a poetic other than tragedy because the way of questioning a cultural state or object has another purpose. Neither cognitive truth nor cathartic pathos can grasp the narrativity of plots introduced unobtrusively into everyday life for entertainment purposes. Yet tragedy and entertainment are narrative constructs, provided that they have a general frame within which they can become the problem 'narrativity.'

12 For example, Greimas (1990: 540) Also, a debate between Ricoeur and Greimas on deep structure (ibid: 551–62). Ricoeur: 'My claim here is that surface is more than a kind of reflection of deep structure, it is more than the instantiation of narrative rules that can be construed at the deeper level. Something happens at the level of figuration that makes the dynamism of the processes described possible' (552). Greimas: When we speak about semio-narrative structures we are in fact dealing with kinds of universals of language, or rather with narrative universals. If we were not afraid of metaphysics we could say that these are properties of the human mind. The collective actant possesses these narrative universals and so does humanity' (555). Evidently, hermeneutic circularity and methodological layers may coexist uneasily. Their respective 'transcendentalia' are at variance (namely, existential condition and mental structure [logic]).

13 Language is undeniably important in Gadamer's hermeneutics, though. Its status vis-à-vis divinatory identification of subjectivities is to put 'World' as object before a community of speakers. 'Language reveals world' by virtue of its spokenness: 'Sprachliche Verständigung stellt das, worüber sie stattfindet, vor die sich Verständigenden hin, wie einen Streitgegenstand, der zwischen den Parteien in der Mitte niedergelegt wird. Die Welt ist derart der gemeinsame, von keinem betretene und von allen anerkannte Boden, der alle verbindet, die miteinander sprechen' (Gadamer 1990: 450). Language is each speaker's perspective on a world. We can, however, step over it into the language and world of another subject.

14 Ricoeur is fully aware of the questions that arise from this claim, in terms of philosophical methodology as well as in terms of the limitations this methodology imposes. In fact, to his mind the price to be paid for phenomenological epochè is extremely high, because in the reflection of time experience it repeats the Augustinian–Aristotelian aporia in a higher-level aporia of unreconciled perspectives.

15 First proposed in Greimas (1966) and then elaborated on in Greimas (1970), with amplifications in Greimas (1979) and corrections in Greimas (1986). In the 1970 book, he affirms the parental relationship to the Klein group in mathematics and to Piaget's group in psychology.

16 Wolde's attempts (1986; 1996: 340f), and those of many others, to reconcile Greimas with Peirce shatter against this fundamental obstacle.

17 Cf. the strong critique of Greimas in Ricoeur (1984) – in particular, the methodological exclusion of what he called 're-figuration' or mimesis III. Moreover, some film studies were influenced by Greimas (1970) and Bremond (1973), as well as by generally linguistically oriented narratologies. For a general overview, see Bertrand (1984), Everaert-Desmedt (1981), Hénault (1983). Regarding audiovisual publicity, see Everaert-Desmedt (1984). Ricoeur's echoes in film theory were much weaker; with one notable exception (Gaudreault 1988), Ricoeur has not stimulated any important film studies.

18 This name, given by Coquet (1982), comprises a group that to varying degrees followed Greimas.

19 Greimas (1968), as quoted in Bertrand (1984: 30). Such methodological limitation reduces language in the broadest sense of the word to language as a closed system (at least as an object of analysis). This certainly facilitates its description as a structure.

20 In Ricoeur's rendering and discussion of Greimas's narrative grammar, this question is clearly highlighted (cf. Greimas 1989: 595ff).

21 This is, of course, an inadequate because far too brief rendering of a rather

technical narratology. With the taxonomy of V. Propp (1968), we distinguish thirty-one functions, which can be roles, situations, or deeds (six prepare the dramatic problem, twenty-five others are needed to resolve it).
Once these functions have been brought into binary oppositions or into the
Greimassian square, they lose their fortuitous empirical appearance and
are understood as non-arbitrary logical functions.

22 To the extent of its reception in film theory, complete expositions of either
'Formalism' (Bordwell versus 'Russian Formalism') or Neoformalism
(Thompson versus 'Formalism') can be found in Bordwell (1985: 48–62;
1981: 3–8) and Thompson (1988: 3–44).

23 On Bordwell's Neoformalist methodological incapacity to find a critical
vantage point see p. 644n134. However, Frederic Jameson emphasizes a
genuinely critical potential also in Šklovskij's Formalism (cf. Beaugrande
1988: 385–415). 'Defamiliarization is always polemic and depends on the
negation of existing habits of thought' (408) – an idea taken up by Thompson for film theory. Now a topos in aesthetic theory, it serves to think about
artistic creativity when culture is understood as a system with all the implications of fixedness. Instead of a real theoretical explanation, it seems more
of a necessity to overcome essential methodological limitations of
approaches which have the premise of arbitrariness. Only a system incapable of thinking of cognition historically – truth-*in-fieri*, as it were, instead of
structure – needs theorems that soften the structural rigidity to allow for
change and tradition. There are more convincing ways of thinking about
historicity of cognition, truth, and cultural form. Peirce for one, without
being Hegelian, succeeded thoroughly in thinking of cognition, in all its
aspects, as a process of unlimited semiosis.

24 The method followed by Bordwell (1985) for coming to terms with these
two approaches in film theory is not quite convincing: 'mimetic theories
assign few *mental* properties to the spectator ... Diegetic theories, for all
their apparent concern with narrational effects, also tend to downplay the
viewer's role. In keeping with the revision of Benveniste whereby *énonciation* gets reduced to marks of the speaker, enunciation theorists have notably ignored the spectator' (29). In Bordwell's eyes, this spectator is 'cued' to
perform 'a definable variety of operations' (ibid). We might surmise that
such a backward-projected (Aristotelian versus Platonic) classification
serves primarily as background transparencies for Bordwell's own discourse. This is apart from their somewhat tendentious rendering and their
subsumption under one heading of Bordwell's choice: 'Owning the view'
(Bellour, Metz, Browne, Ropars), as the consequence of 'diegetic' narrational effects, is certainly a spectator activity. The spectator must reconsti-

tute the vision of textual roles, a task that also involves their temporalities and spatialities. After all, what is the use of raising artificial frontiers in narratology when the differences – including those from Bordwell's own Formalism – are really not so clear? Besides, the terminological mimesis / diegesis dichotomy alone does not explain anything. Gaudreault (1988: 53–70) shows how both terms had a different meaning in Plato's and Aristotle's poetics. To base a theoretical alternative on these terms seems rather arbitrary, since both classics use both terms.

25 This reproach may be pertinent and correct exclusively regarding the passages from the authors whom Bordwell quotes. Evidently Bordwell needs a reason to distance his own approach (based on the 'metalanguage' of Constructivist psychology) from approaches that compare with theatrical ('perspectivist') or linguistic ('diegetic') models. In all fairness, however, these theories are complex. It is unclear what allows us to label them cumulatively. In recent developments in particular, there has been a very notable recuperation of the reader's / viewer's activity in text- and author-oriented theories. Semiology – especially the second wave – is open to phenomenological aspects, (e.g., Barthes's 'second semiology,' as quoted by Bordwell [1985: 17]). This does not constitute an argument against Bordwell's theory; but it must be said that almost all of Bordwell's theory can be found in semiological ('linguistic' or 'diegetic') theories, generally under different labels. We will have to see which theory has the greater explanatory power, since both are limited by axiomatic exclusions. Probably Constructivism should thwart any notion of sign from cinema by supplying it with a 'virgin' perception theory. This leads to the polemical context around the (supposedly redundant) concept of the 'author's role' in enunciation theories of cinema. To be suspected of 'diegesis' is unnecessary. No text tells itself, because the reason behind its being told will always exhibit marks of its author, as an instance of the text. For Bordwell this is not so – in cinematic perception this presents itself by itself.

26 As, incidentally, the etymology of *fa<bula* (from φημί = speak) already implies.

27 Cf. Bordwell (1985: 62), where the textual auctorial instance is declared unnecessary: 'As for the implied author of a film, this construct adds nothing to our understanding of filmic narration ... could not more simply be ascribed to narration itself.' He refuses the communicational sender receiver model, which he suspects behind the 'implied author.' With his model of cues, he thinks that narration can even mimic a narrator figure. 'Far better, I think, to give the narrational process the power to signal under certain circumstances that the spectator should construct a narrator.'

28 This is not begging the question, because narration can be known as the Symbol (logos) of a certain kind of telos. It is not the discovery of teleology, which presupposes behaviour; however, once self-controlled conduct is known, it can become a Symbol, which is then used as the Law in the time it produces narratively.

29 In the sense of logical necessity, Abraham's 'explanations' are really showing what literally stares one into the eye. He says what one sees, and we see what he says and also more (i.e., that it is good so). In exactly this sense, these sequences are a perfect illustration for Peirce's 'in itself admirable' (cf. *supra*).

30 Even with the help of 'schemata of transtextual, compositional, realistic, and artistic motivation' (cf. Bordwell 1985: 36).

31 How much 'real life' circumstances do indeed determine meaning is another question. Roger Odin's recent development of a semiological socio-pragmatics of film seems to address this explicitly. If we follow him, the social and historical conditions of film consumption determine the internal codes of cinema. In a similar vein, cf. Staiger (1992).

32 When Eco proposed that an author's assumption of a possible reader must be a constituent part in the construction of meaning, he reported that Lévi-Strauss criticized his concept of 'open work' ('opera aperta') as too vague and open to arbitrariness. He insisted on conceiving a work as having 'the stiffness – so to speak – of a crystal' – quoted by Eco (1979: 4), who objected to that objection precisely on the grounds that in concrete texts this conception of a text does not work. As a witness he quotes Lévi-Strauss himself, who tried to analyze Baudelaire's 'Les Chats.' Eco's conclusion: The reader as a co-operant cannot be eliminated from the text by any means. 'Stiffness' of a pure form as the methodological abstraction in Structuralism is not too remote from the ideal of the Formal method, the forebearer of structuralism (cf. *infra*).

33 In other words, everything that must be presupposed for the work of sign production, described in Eco (1975).

34 Cf. Thompson (1988: 56–8), for example, rendering the 'stairstep construction' of Terror by night. She summarizes: 'On the whole, however, the constant motivation of the stylistic devices de-emphasizes their manipulative functions. Classical style seems largely informative, straightforward, "helpful." In this way it succeeds in creating a sort of veneer which conceals the underlying plot manipulations from the spectator' (80). With regard to ideology: 'Holmes is depicted as superior to the official representatives of societal law, and hence he is able to name the criminal, not through logic, but simply because of his superiority.' (81).

35 Again, Thompson (1988: 89–109) provides us with the narrative usage of the interplay of these elements in her analysis of Tati's *Les Vacances de Monsieur Hulot*: it creates the 'vis comica' of narratives. How this can yield humorous effects remains a mystery, though. What is the 'tertium comparationis' of the hilarious comparison?

36 Bordwell throughout his book insists on using the Russian term, which is merely a Cyrillic rendering of the French *sujet*, in plain English: subject or topic. Yet apart from its painting connotation (but there is also a derogatory social connotation as in 'mauvais sujet'), it is difficult to discover additional meaning in the Russian term, apart from Šklovskij's insistence on it. In a rhetorical artifact, 'topoi or commonplaces are more exactly what constitutes a *narratio probabilis*.

6 Enunciation in Cinema

1 The *mise-en-discours* in semionarratology escapes the available methods of structural linguistics.

2 Formalism and Neoformalism take the 'normal' (i.e., non-poetic, prosaic) description/depiction of the world as basic effort, onto which artistic efforts of style can be grafted. 'Cueing' and 'spectator activity' are theatrical metaphors for the enunciation process, but it is not clear how far the result of meaning is determined by these factors.

3 At least a key that allows us to tackle more of it.

4 Ordinary Language Philosophy has generalized these findings to the various locutionary forces of speech acts.

5 Cf. 'Una nota dell'editore,' in Šklovskij (1966: 285–92), which describes the semantic ambiguity of this core term in Formalist aesthetics.

6 MSS314, 316. Peirce (1998: 209) provides this illustration: 'For every proposition whatsoever refers as to its subject to a singular actually reacting upon the utterer of it and actually reacting upon the interpreter of it. All propositions relate to the same ever-reacting singular; namely, to the totality of all real objects. It is true that when the Arabian romancer tells us that there was a lady named Scherherazade, he does not mean to be understood as speaking of the world of outward realities, and there is a great deal of fiction in what he is talking about. For the fictive is that whose characters depend upon what characters somebody attributes to it; and the story is, of course, the mere creation of the poet's thought. Nevertheless, once he has imagined Scherherazade and made her young, beautiful, and endowed with a gift of spinning stories, it becomes a real fact that so he has imagined her, which fact he cannot destroy by pretending or thinking that he imag-

ined her to be otherwise. What he wishes us to understand is what he might have expressed in plain prose by saying, "I have imagined a lady, Scherherazade by name, young, beautiful and a tireless teller of tales, and I am going on to imagine what tales she told." This would have been a plain expression of professed fact relating to the sum total of realities.'

7 Many films derive the core dramatic idea from this incongruity (e.g., with the Kalahari Bushmen's causal chain of events in Jamie Uys's *The Gods Must Be Crazy*).

8 Kant *KdU* §48 defines: 'Eine Naturschönheit ist ein schönes Ding; die Kunstschönheit ist eine schöne Vorstellung von einem Dinge.' This requires certain characters for the beautiful object: 'Um eine Naturschönheit als eine solche zu beurtheilen, brauche ich nicht vorher einen Begriff davon zu haben, was der Gegenstand für ein Ding sein solle; d.i. ich habe nicht nöthig, die materiale Zweckmäßigkeit (den Zweck) zu kennen, sondern die bloße Form ohne Kenntniß des Zwecks gefällt in der Beurtheilung für sich selbst.' Natural aesthetic objects do not need an idea of perfection (*Vollkommenheit*) on the basis of a knowledge of its end (*Zweck*). However, a teleological determination of nature can be assumed, beyond aesthetic judgment, as providing the basis for the judgment that nature is, and does not simply appear as, beautiful. This is illustrated with a 'beautiful wife': 'wenn z.B. gesagt wird: das ist ein schönes Weib, in der That nichts anders als: die Natur stellt in ihrer Gestalt die Zwecke im weiblichen Bau schön vor; denn man muß noch über die bloße Form auf einen Begriff hinaussehen, damit der Gegenstand auf solche Art durch ein logisch-bedingtes ästhetisches Urtheil gedacht werde.' Nature, however, is better admired as a sublime object, making it object of a negative pleasure. §23: 'Der wichtigste und innere Unterschied aber des Erhabenen vom Schönen ist wohl dieser: daß ... die Naturschönheit (die selbstständige) eine Zweckmäßigkeit in ihrer Form, wodurch der Gegenstand für unsere Urtheilskraft gleichsam vorherbestimmt zu sein scheint, bei sich führt und so an sich einen Gegenstand des Wohlgefallens ausmacht; hingegen das, was in uns, ohne zu vernünfteln, bloß in der Auffassung das Gefühl des Erhabenen erregt, der Form nach zwar zweckwidrig für unsere Urtheilskraft, unangemessen unserm Darstellungsvermögen und gleichsam gewaltthätig für die Einbildungskraft erscheinen mag, aber dennoch nur um desto erhabener zu sein geurtheilt wird.'

9 For the enunciation of narrative, rhetorical, and aesthetic representation, an apparently elegant solution is in sight. Customary usage speaks of mere fiction, as if merely truth-semblance, *le vrai-semblable*, is required. Yet here, too, cognitive processes take place inasmuch as they are determined. It

must also be possible here to determine what 'is,' even though Interpretation, (i.e., determination), is not final.

10 This plain question presupposes, of course, more than a two-valued propositional logic. In a triadic logic, Sign relations are always modal, never simple 'is' equations. It already contains the indetermination of Interpretation in its third Correlate. This describes the problem of enunciation better than linguistic marks. The explanatory task, however, is not mastered by declaring the general non-determination.

11 It is clear that these meanings are very distinct psychological states. The methodological consequence is that psychological approaches are not so adequate for an understanding of the different meaning processes evoked by enunciation. The Pragmaticistic advantage is again the independence of meaning from the mind. Metaphorically speaking, we dislocate Generality or 'the mind' in all being, existent or not. Thus, even between a river and enunciation there is something in common: both are habits and both can be thought of without consciousness. A riverbed is a habit of nature, enunciation is a social habit. In neither case is a psychological perspective adequate or necessary. This liberates enunciation from its chains to personal identity contexts and at the same time opens new avenues for its very useful integration into crucial film theory problems.

12 V. *supra* concerning desirability *in se* as presupposition of all normativity.

13 Enunciation as such, a term originating in logic, became exclusively narratological and was used as another term for the traditional *vox narrativa*. A Semiotic approach can re-extend it into rhetoric and aesthetic, which agrees with common insights of Speech Act philosophy, which in turn have been integrated into Semionarratology and into literary theory generally.

14 Bettetini's theory has been discussed in the context of temporal iconism (v. *supra*).

15 In most but not necessarily in all languages, the respects are the same. However, some Semitic languages, for instance, are without tenses proper, as is (after the Sapir-Whorf thesis) Hopi.

16 A verbal narrative using the pluperfect tense carries out the same function as does film performing the following operations. In Carontini's list (102f): 1. a look not directed toward the destinator; 2. a body and head posture of ¾, less preferred: back view, forbidden: absent; 3. camera distance intimate, less: social, less: public; 4. punctuation through blackout, less: white-out; 5. anaphor as flashback in a diegesis; 6. shots, in decreasing order: middle, medium-long, long; 7. focus depth should be 2nd and 3rd order; 8. hypotactically the sequence is subordinated; 9. with panning and dollying-back camera movements. In terms of Weinrich (1964), points 1 to 3 make it a nar-

rative dependency, points 4 and 5 a retrospective 'perspective,' points 6 to 9 a backgrounded 'relief.'

17 Cf. Guynn (1990: esp. 69–148), who describes in detail, along the lines of Metzian syntagmatics, what might be called the production of indicative mood in film.

18 Greimas's semionarratological system of modalisation – a possible, more abstract alternative to verbal modes – is construed after the proposition model. It needs a dose of anthropomorphic constants in order to organize the meaning generation into levels of human action. Both meaning and action are progressively 'realized' from levels of virtuality. Although it could be conceded that it is a mixed model of logical and pragmato-anthropomorphic elements, logically it does not really go beyond the verbal model (except for strata of abstraction). No real linguistic universals are found in this theory, as in our previous analysis.

19 Weinrich (1964: 11) defines: 'Ein Text ist eine sinnvolle (d.h. kohärente und konsistente) Abfolge sprachlicher Zeichen zwischen zwei auffälligen Kommunikationsunterbrechungen.'

20 It is not by chance that he can be counted among the *Rezeptionsästhetiker* (cf. Warning 1975: 157 and passim) and that Ricoeur also uses him to support his narratology.

21 there is of course a connection between the linguistic tradition coming from Benveniste, Genette, and colleagues on the one hand and the *Rezeptionsästhetik* current in Jauss, Weinrich, Iser, and colleagues, whose ancestors include Ingarden (1960) as much as they do Käte Hamburger and Gadamer. That being said, the considerable differences between the two traditions, and between the single theorists, must not be overestimated. As a historical aside, this does not hinder inspirations from apparently flowing in both directions: Metz describes his tortuous relation to Hamburger in a long interview in Metz (1990: 293f).

22 Ibid. (224ff), but he defines his terms more broadly than through the distinct use of tenses and grammatical persons associated with both dichotomies alone. In addition, the tense adverb combination proves to be especially relevant. Both attitudes are distinguished mainly by their respective use of tenses: All tenses can be used in commentary with the exception of *passé simple*, with a preponderance of *présent, futur*, and *parfait* (Weinrich is speaking about French literature). Whereas narration prefers *passé simple*, especially in combination with the third person, and excludes *présent, futur*, and *passé composé*. The employment of tenses differs in other European languages and dialects, and even in oral rather than written styles.

23 Ricoeur (1984: 103) lists various *incipitur*: *Il était une fois …, Érase que se era,*

vor Zeiten, and one might add the proverbial narrative release in Grimm's collection of fairy tales: *Es war einmal* ... Weinrich associates the present tense primarily with commentary, but it is also used in narrative summaries, which are normally preludes to subsequent communicational interventions. Narrative summaries use the present tense, as do film scripts (and dramaturgic indications in plays, newspaper captions, and the like). All, in common with film, want to show something with the present tense in the present time of the viewer. They establish a communicational attitude of vision as in cinematic enunciation.

24 Using *imparfait*, the past participle ('was singing'); foregrounding uses *passé simple*, preterite. It is, however, a fact that this is mainly proper to Roman languages, as Weinrich notes. German uses the preterite in both instances but achieves relief through adverbial means, whereas English makes the difference between participle constructions and straight tenses (he sang, he was singing). However, this is not limited to narratives, but exists *also* in commentary.

25 There is a similarity to a linguistic feature found in German, where relief is not given by the alternation of *passé simple* and *imparfait* (or equivalent tenses in other languages). The syntax of comparatively free German verb positions within the sentence allows us to make nuances of signification that equal the verbal tense syntagmata. *Imparfait* but also *passé simple* must be translated as *Imperfekt*. The difference is rendered only by the position of the personal pronoun: either meta- or protactic, *Endstelle* or *Zweitstelle* respectively (cf. Weinrich 1964: 157). For example: protactic *ich schreibe* as opposed to metatactic *schreibe ich*. When the pronoun is followed by the verb, this gives narrative foreground relief; in reverse it yields a background. Evidently, cinematic sequences cannot be described so easily. This would require the identification of syntactic units and functions in audiovisuals; furthermore, we would also need to weigh something by its position in the syntactic grid. Speaking (as Bettetini does) of paratactic and hypotactic is, however, effectively giving weight similar to the weight determined by the position of a word in a sentence. It is possible to see in the two audiovisual relief-giving modes equivalents to the signification potentials of French and German linguistic narrative relief. The German construction of narrative (or prose) relief entails, however, there being an exact syntactic or stylistic justification for positioning the pronoun in the metatactic manner. In point of fact, it can occur only in dependent sentences and must therefore be construed by relative pronouns or suchlike. This, by the way, gives rise to the possibility of composing *Zweitstelle* sentences virtually without limit, *Schachtelsätze* or involved sentences. Even though in many

instances not very elegant, these sentences are syntactically perfectly clear and ordered. This feature cannot be replicated in languages with a more rigid word position syntax.

26 Relief means the taxis-intratextual order – that some parts must be marked as being pragmatic-logically dependent on other parts. Weinrich claimed only this equation of grammatical and logical dependency of order. It is not that the metatactic part (*imparfait*) of a sentence is less noted than the protactic (*passé simple*) part. We would do better to think of it as syntactic and therefore as presentation- order dependency. It is as precisely because of this rule of syntax that cinematic means can never be determined with an accuracy as unmistakable as syntax. We should not overtax this spatial metaphor of over/under, whose precise grammatical *fundamentum in re* in some languages is sentence dependency expressed as tense dependency. After all, it is Relief*gebung* in Weinrich that very actively establishes an order (low and high). Weinrich stated clearly that this is not a time dependency of earlier/later, but simply an acknowledgment of the fact that not every tense usually follows upon another tense, and that if it does, it implies a dependency of order.

27 Literary narratives, which use *imparfait* and aequiv. for enunciation and *passé simple* and aequiv. for the narrative, bring the narrative to a 'halt' using a sequence of what Weinrich calls *imparfaits de rupture*. It brings the narrative, as it were, into the reader universe and so mediates an almost immediate expectancy. However, this tense – through a syntaxical identity of conjugation – merely imitates enunciation time (tense: *imparfait*), and does not close or terminate the logic of the narrative universe. Expectancy remains a teleological orientation, and is not life expectancy.

28 In other words, this resembles 'objective meaning' in A. Schütz (1981) as ego's reconstruction of alter ego's intentionality as source of alter's meaning.

29 According to Lintvelt (1981), the consciousness of the reader/spectator can have three *loci*: either identical with a character's consciousness, or with the narrator's consciousness, or non-identical, excluded from both. The narrator's consciousness can be greater than the character's ('vision "par derrière"'), or equal ('vision "avec"'), or less than the character's ('vision "du dehors"'). This play with points of view gains importance in Ricoeur's (1984: 131ff) theory of mimesis of action (= mythos); it becomes logical that every participant's actions can be imitated – both external ones and inner ones such as thought and feeling. Ricoeur credits Hamburger with the investigation of fictional consciousness focuses. She finds: 'Epic fiction is the only gnoseological place where subjectivity ('Ich-Originät') of the third grammatical person can be represented as third person' (quoted in Ricoeur

[1984: 133]). Dorrit Cohn (1978) identifies 'mimesis of consciousness' as either one of the other's mind or (in fictions of confessions) of the own mind. These can be directly narrated or 'quoted,' as it were ('quoted monologue,' or 'self-quoted monologue,' or *erlebte Rede* aka 'narrated monologue'). Lintvelt (1981) goes farther than this, providing an entire inventory of narrative classifications, which is a combinatory play with the mentioned parameters and degrees on the axes Spectator–narrator, narrator–character, auctorial– actorial fiction, narrative–commentary, and so on. What this classification really does, is testify to the fine-tuned signification potential of language when dealing with the 'other' universe of narrative in this enunciation universe. In audiovisuals this dichotomy must be construed through other means; the variability of the system is, therefore, certainly rather different.

30 Even in the case of actorial *Er-Erzählung*, where it is entirely unclear why and through which instance this narrative knowledge comes to My attention. Audiovisual tradition was established firmly on this track of narrativity by the Absence of the camera.

31 Except for Greimas and Rastier, who make it an explicit theorem: cf. 'Les jeux des contraintes sémiotiques' in Greimas (1970: 135–55), and all theoretical concerns around Greimas's categories and then 'sémantique fondamentale' passim in many places.

32 Through all kinds of cinematic means, starting with lighting, framing, and camera angles (let us call these cumulatively 'photographic means', even though they are moving pictures); then by all temporal, succession-based means ('montage'). Ad-jectives in themselves are voiceless; that said, their juxtaposition to nouns or even to the larger parts of text to which they refer creates a value judgment. The same is achieved rhetorically by figuration (linguistic as well as cinematic) to such an extent that Bettetini (1979) makes it one of his basic theoretical constructs.

33 Narratology is more than narration. As theory, narration is always explained by something else. Either we explain it by language (in which case the terms of description are linguistic, but not the theory that explains the functioning of language itself); or we explain it in a constructivist-cognitivist way (in which case narrations must appear as perceptions). The consequence is a terminology of cognition psychology. The explanatory framework of Bordwell must first provide a merger of an aesthetic with a narrative, the whole equated with mundane cognition. The fact that this cognitive theory has no use for the sign nature of cognition justifies its rejection of sign-aware theories (which tend to forgo cognition). In this light, Bordwell's protest is comprehensible as an anti-anti-cognitive attack.

34 If enunciation is only the opposite (in certain regards) to the 'enunciated,'
   there are a number of functional equivalents such as *discours-histoire, berich-
   ten-erzählen*, showing-telling(-talking-quoting: which Gaudreault [1988]
   adds to the catalogue). As mentioned earlier, these distinctions are made
   between a narrator inasmuch as they are different from the narration. Such
   distinctions are as old as *Poetic*; only their linguistic nomenclature is new in
   that it identifies parts of speech signalling the presence of one or the other
   logic. Story as sort of real course of events, differentiated from plot, is
   merely a narrator's effort and his art of presenting or withholding: *mise-en-
   intrigue*, Aristotle's mythos.

35 Whether a narrative is simple narration (ἅπλη διήγησις) or narration
   through 'similar' representation (διήγησις διὰ μιμήσεως) is not simply a
   question of theatrical genres; it also makes a practical difference. In the first
   case, the ordering of events comes directly from a narrative instance, a narrator. In the latter case this is not directly so – at least this is not visible.
   Here applies Gadamer's idea of play, which is not intended to keep up the
   difference between play and the universe outside the 'four walls' of representation ('ästhetische Nichtunterscheidung,' v. *infra*). The highest degree
   of theatrical representation therefore is not theatre. Owing to its historical
   roots in sacred practices cult representations of a ritualistic (dionysiac)
   nature have the maximum identity loss; this loss persists to a lesser degree
   in theatrical dramas. Not that an auctorial instance is lacking in cult performances, of course, but the 'maître du jeu' stays transcendent (and is of a
   divine nature), never entering the stage. The ritual enacts only itself. This
   requires from participants the highest degree of self-identification with the
   play, peculiarly in those holy trag-oidiai in honour of the god Dionysos and
   in all their historical descendants. After Aristotle's *Poetic*, tragedies consequently elicit most catharsis in the spectator through ἔλεος καὶ φόβος. The
   intermission of narrators does not really thwart this identification. Narrators, however, mediate considerably with comments and perspective; furthermore, they pace the possibility of identification with various
   characters. Apparently this difference is behind Genette's refusal to admit
   the parlance of a 'filmic narrative' (cf. Gaudreault 1988: 29n9 personal letter
   to Ga.), because it certainly deviates radically from ἅπλη διήγησις. Without
   a doubt, the technicality of a filmic narrator must differ from that of a transcendent δημίουργος of a drama. Since cinema is clearly and preponder-
   antly of the second Platonic type (its aesthetics and narrative thus being
   mimetic), we might be tempted to negate auctorial instances in cinema. As
   Jauss (and Gadamer and Ricoeur) tell us, however, a dichotomistic separation of the two ways of narrating is misleading.

36 After εἷς, μία, ἕν; this seems to be the etymological root of μιμεω. Menge-
    Güthling, in *Griechisches Wörterbuch* (Berlin, 1913), traces μιμεωμαι back to
    ἀμείβω, *tauschen, wechseln, vertauschen*. The root is cognate to *mei, lat.
    munus, communis, gemein.

37 In other cases it is grounded (loosely) in hermeneutic assumptions. Appar-
    ently irreconcilable, for instance, is a hermeneutic perspective observed in
    Ricoeur's approach to narration. Here he can even dispense with linguistic
    marks of enunciation, but only because he provides functional equivalents.
    In lieu of linguistic reference to a speech situation that disambiguates all
    deictic elements of speech, the *vox narrativa* for Ricoeur refers back to the
    existential authenticity. That there is no autarky of narration proves that
    narrative probability (the *Poetic's* εἰκὸς) does not emerge without a special
    Interpretation. Iser's hermeneutic parlance (in the 'Role of the Reader')
    describes this emergence as 'temporary dislocation' (in German, a word
    play with confusion or folly) – that is, of one subjectivity into another, built
    into an identity context. However, narrative identities are merely symp-
    toms of a fundamental logical operation. They are certainly not normal
    human identities (however these are explained). In the context of aesthetic
    enunciation, we will discover philosophical presuppositions, which make
    only the problem 'identity' meaningful.

38 Benveniste coined the metaphor (which was then taken up by Greimas).

39 Panofsky (1927) pointed out the link between pictorial representation form
    (the central perspective) and ideology. Comolli and colleagues extended
    this into the ideology of the cinematic apparatus. The broader intellectual
    framework of Foucaultian *visibilités* (cf. Deleuze 1986: 55ff), which perhaps
    inspired the subject-constituting 'apparatus,' need not preoccupy us here.
    Central perspective and the camera architecture, suture, and so on all have
    this point of view in common, as well as the important narrative conse-
    quences. Branigan focuses on the same subject, but as a narrative problem
    and not as an ideological one.

40 As with Bordwell, Carroll, and colleagues, 'cognitivism' designates their
    cognitivism, consisting of a common set of explanantia ('buzzwords'),
    which are all more or less plain nominalism (v. *supra*). We are not inter-
    ested here in how much of this can be traced back to cognitivist psychol-
    ogy, brain research, and philosophical cognitivism.

41 cf. Branigan (1984: 29ff): 'An important consequence of the belief that
    meaning is a play of difference is that there are no inherent meanings.'
    Whether or not there is something like a cinematic paradigmatic axis can be
    left open here; the question at hand relates to the narrative use of any such
    device placing it in the entirely different context of 'mise en intrigue.' That

cinematic features have no determined fixed meaning is true only abstractly. Insofar as the form has been defined by a tradition, films are made as from a recipe book of cinematic devices. To such a degree that gratuitous and redundant devices can be used in order to 'fabricate' types of meaning. Conversely, this uneconomical use would show how 'overcoded' or standardized these devices have become. See the analysis of Dreyer in Bordwell (1981); cf. *supra* 338ff.

42 There is a certain resemblance between such levels and Greimas's rigorous generative layers of meaning effects, but the principal difference is Branigan's total lack of generativism.

43 Branigan's concern for speaker/viewer levels in not a novelty in narratology. In many languages, verbal tenses are used to signify *oratio obliqua* (indirect speech) and 'free indirect speech.' Weinrich describes the latter as *innere Rede* – the inner monologue of a character – whereas the former is reporting another character's speech 'without quotation marks.' A detailed and complex usage of verbal marks, and the prohibition of certain other verbal marks, obtains the effect of having another person speak in one character's words. Free speech – linguistically conditioned as it is – is a determinate pragmatic way to represent action, not a way of composing sentences.

44 This is central focus of Poetics, since Aristotle defined genres in terms of heroes who are 'better or worse than their contemporaries' (v. *supra*). Being-better actually is a pragmatic comprehension – or 'seeing-with' – of an identity and its action program.

45 'An "Argument" is any process of thought reasonably tending to produce a definite belief. An "Argumentation" is an Argument proceeding upon definitely formulated premises' (6.456).

46 Essentialism is endemic in 'cognitivist' (aka 'Anglo-American,' 'analytical'; see Currie [1997: 42]) film theory despite claims to the contrary. Carroll's long-winded recusation of essentialism cannot obfuscate his 'definition' of cinema in its technological 'essence,' or characteristics (cf. Carroll [1996b: Part I]). Currie (1995) is realist in a more reflected way; he takes into account 'observer response capacities' (33).

47 Cf. Smith (1997) regarding the narrative text but *en lieu* of characters inside seeing their pragmatic reality. How is this logical abyss bridged in imagination as cognitive activity?

48 The distinction between enthymema and syllogism usually assumes that the difference is in the first premise, which in the case of the former is omitted (i.e., left to what everybody beliefs to be true). The latter instead can state its premise as based on a higher principle of being.

49 As this story, it is a singularity; but its being narrated conveys an implicit scope with a meaning broader than just the fate of single characters (this is already shown in the *Poetic*). Cathartic effects thus play on the comparative, of characters being 'better and of greater valour than the present men' (cf. *supra*). Telling the singular and meaning the universal is the entire purpose.

50 Peirce did not refer to the treatise wisdom of rhetorics, meaning the practical technique of convincing someone; rather, he had in mind, according to MS774:3, 'a art of universal rhetoric' that refers to everything in the physical universe (cf. Liszka 2000: 444).

51 Referring to the first trace of a beating heart in an embryo (since Aristotle).

52 Perelman (1970) is a rich quarry for all linguistic devices of this kind. One is the metaphorization of tenses. On page 216, he provides a beautiful example: Mauriac falls unexpectedly into the present tense in the midst of the historic tense: 'elle quitta sa couche, glissa ... sortit de la chambre. Elle descend l'escalier, suit ...' In cinema this can be reproduced only if the effect is clear – that of creating a common presence with the audience. Thus the present of rupture is equal to a direct look into the camera, provided that the cinematic context supports this effect of an otherwise anodyne device. For Weinrich (1964: 191), this is a case of *Tempus-Metaphorik*, recognized since before Quintilian as μετάστασις or *translatio temporum*, a common rhetoric device. Yet this is only one technique for creating of the rhetorical presence of a delimited audience. Also, arguments *ad hominem* and *ad personam* appear as much in this arsenal as the choice of semantic levels.

53 Cavalier's *Thérèse* has even made this its stylistic hallmark. In the forefront, the presence of the audience is emotional, a loving being-there-with. This can be contrasted with the hurry, the insolence of being-there, in some sequences of the errant aimlessness of the murderer in Kieślowski's *Krótki film o zabijaniu* (Thou Shalt Not kill). Also here, however, the long, almost interminable process of oiling the trapdoor of the gallows is emotionally insupportable only because the audience is emotionally there. 'Cinematic Quintilians' systematizing film tropes to some degree include Siegrist (1986) and especially Clifton (1983). The latter inventoried all known named tropes in their film equivalents, showing that many complex forms need a culture of rhetorical tradition and learning in order to be recognizable. Conversely, rhetorical devices from alien cultures are virtually incomprehensible. European conventions of irony would not be replicable in Japanese films, for instance, and Indian figures of speech would not be appreciated here (cf. Satyajit Ray's *Chess Players*, which is evidently full of humour, which to non-Indian viewers most probably will be lost).

54 It is interesting to observe that all the designations of this kind of sign relation are themselves what they design. If 'figures' are literally potters' work
('fig*') and if a trope is a 'turn-around' (τρέπειν), then strictly speaking the
terms explain nothing – they *demonstrate*. The fact is that figures were noted
as conspicuous within discourses and given names. Yet their number is
variable and extendible, and their names vary. Seemingly it depends on
who makes the classification. Their later forms were arrived at by grammar
teachers. Baroque rhetoricians were oriented more toward effect and orna-
ment, yet they had an intuitive grasp of modes of operation. Perelman
(1970: 229ff) classifies terms according to communication and not from the
perspective of oratory decoration.

55 This presentation of the *rhetorica ars* follows Ueding (1986), who in his systematic section follows Quintilian's nomenclature. Perelman (1970) chose
to classify from an argumentation perspective, which is no longer the classical manual type. As a crucial fifth stage of a rhetorician's work or
rhetorices partes, this *ars* deals with such things as gesture, mime, and action.
The latter is notably comprised of ocular demonstration, the effective display of witnesses, 'charts' *ante litteram*, and theatrical props such as the
preparation of the stage with posters, flags, and so on. (within the limits of
the *aptum*). Such a well-established social practice of meaning augmentation is on par with cinematic practice (when it is not avant-garde or video-
clip). The main thing is that the attitude of rhetorical demonstration of a
probable object can be grasped. If narrative meaning must be excluded,
and the application of aesthetic meaning would dematerialize too much,
then it must be assumed that the intended cognitive object is probably a
state of world.

56 Also literally: ob-σκηνή, a Latin-Greek compound, 'away from the tent,'
(i.e., synecdoche for stage, scene).

57 This point is made in Ricoeur (1975: *La métaphore vive*), who approaches the
question from a perspective that emphasizes the novelty in tropes as being
the creation of a new reality. Undoubtedly, 'customary tropes' seems a contradiction in terms, and language should be seen as a dust heap of used figuration (as Nietzsche opines). If there is not even a minimal refiguration
(i.e., not even a *verbum translatum*) in a trope, it can be considered as part of
the normal lexicon.

58 Woody Allen's *Purple Rose of Cairo*, for instance, already uses irony in the
title. Someone not in the enunciation community of a limited audience
might expect an archeological documentary. Yet it is not enough to drag an
audience to one's side. It must still understand that there is a custom of
laughing that is instigated by saying things one does not mean. The critical

comparison is between an observation (or an observable character such as the illusion-hungry, gray little wife) and a purely inferred otherness of the same object (the same woman as a glorious lover, albeit the sameness need not be in the person). The trope *ironia* 'is' a conspicuous absence, the non-said, yet it needs the enunciational context inviting here and now in order to fill the empty place with some ironic insight. The probability of this new content is vacillating and on ambiguous foundations. Here the enuncia-tional intentions are incisive. The literal can be replaced by the benign (as in Allen's film) or by hateful Interpretations (although difficult to imagine, some sequences could be seen as macho propaganda).

59 For instance, some tropes function on a phonological basis (such as the entire class of *figurae verborum per adjectionem*). Their meaning is at best of aesthetic relevance. Others are direct manipulations of the enunciational communication itself (such as the notorious *praeteritio*; v. *infra*). A depen-dency in order to signal the unique or the repetitive character of something (corresponding to the singulative and iterative moods respectively) is not even dependent on tropes, but is close to Weinrich's tense metaphors (v. *supra*). After Kinder (1990), following Genette, cinema uses a pseudo-itera-tive form. Kinder's example (quoting Henderson's) is rather unconvincing, however, because it is illustrated with voice-over only (which is certainly not one of the most cinematic of features). Iterative/singulative reliefs are bound up with *passé simple* (singulative) and *imparfait* (iterative) in speech. Regarding cinema, the real question is not whether 'some (as Henderson cautiously observes) might take an ultra-literal position and say that this makes the iterative impossible in cinema: its images and sounds are always singulative,' and it is not Kinder's contrary position. This considers means only, whereas the task is to understand object meaning as generated through enunciation and cultural forms. The iterative has a background function compared to the important and rich-in-detail matter of the singu-lative. In the combination of rhetoric and narrative, such a judgment desig-nates something (e.g., an event) as either typical or exceptional. *Translatio temporum* (i.e. μετάστασις) produces this effect for any object in speech. In film, the absence of cultural customs is certainly a hindrance, but it does not preclude cinematic rhetoric from 'singling out' and 'levelling out' objects. How is this done? Kinder suggests reasonably that 'the combina-tion of rich perceptual detail and strong emphasis on genre' (5) creates an identical sort of augmented meaning in cinema. As intuitive as this sugges-tion is, it is never the means alone that create a custom of augmentation. The enunciation effort itself must cooperate with a number of factors to actually augment this meaning through these means. In particular, if the

rhetorical effect is much more complex, which Kinder herself characterizes as 'realistic or truthful in the sense of being habitual, typical, or inevitable' (1990: 5). The Iteratives of her film examples are all constructed by verbal narration (of course, all of Genette's theory applies to films to the extent that they are verbal narratives). On this evidence, however, one would adduce Iterative as not a being cinematic but a literary feature, used in and by films.

60 It would no longer make sense to refer to it in terms of (narrative) off-screen. More appropriately, this space should be termed 'off-universe', which is more 'off' than even a 'voice' can be 'over.'

61 Corresponding more or less to Quintilian's *ornatus in verbis singulis*.

62 Oxford English Dictionary: '[Perhaps influenced by G. frech saucy, impudent.] Forward, impertinent, free in behaviour. orig. U.S.'

63 There are three obvious ways to choose 'choice words.' *Archaismus* and *fictio* (i.e., neologisms) are not irrelevant for cinema; tropes are important for truth claims. Perelman would count these tropes among those purposeful means which, by style choices, establish a community with a chosen audience. These first two *ornatus*, quite common in language, for film must presuppose iconographic *consuetudines*. A film uses archaisms as augmented meaning, as for instance when there are clearly classical tableau compositions. At times even accented framing suffices. Paramount examples of archaism abound in Greenaway's *The Draughtman's Contract*. Godard's artistic strategy strives, on the contrary, for neologisms, the opposite of archaism, as a televisionlike boundless (frameless) space (in early films of Godard). The amateur film sequence in Wim Wenders's Paris, Texas (Travis watching an old vacation film with his family) is also cinematic neologism and not artistic or technical ineptitude. Yet any 'funky,' frenetic cinematography can yield the same effect, as Fosse's *All That Jazz* showed magnificently and as 'video clips' and television advertising continue to show.

64 *Per adjectionem* can be *geminatio*: aa, aa, *anadiplosis*: ba, ac, *gradatio* or *climax*: ab, bc, cd, *redditio*: abcda, *anaphora*: ab, ac, *epiphora*: ab, cb, *epanalepsis*: a, ba, *epanodos*: abc, cba, *regressio*: ab, a, b, *polyptoton*: same word with change of grammatical case, *synonymia*: *veni, vidi, vici!*, *paronomasia*: same word, different meaning, *traductio*: repetition, but once in direct, then in figurative sense, *asyndeton*: omission of copulative conjunctions.

65 *Per detractionem* – that is, *ellipsis, zeugma*.

66 Per transmutationem, which is *hyperbaton, isokolon, antitheton, chiasmus*.

67 This is not the place to come back to the 'horse recognition capacity' of Currie, which relies on the model of a proposition (i.e., the predication 'this is a

horse'): 'when I see that the picture depicts a horse I must associate some visual feature of what I see, namely a picture, with the concept horse' (Currie 1995: 81).

68 Figuration beyond single elements and 'sentence' considers composition over an entirety (*compositio*). It consists of *ordo* (correct position in a series: stronger before weaker), *iunctura* (effects upon clash of two words: e.g., hiatus), and *numerus* (metric measure and rhythm in lyric). This takes place differently with different materials, (e.g., differently with sounds and syllables than with moving images). Speaking of rhythm in cinema is as metaphorical as speaking of it in language, however. The *princeps analogatum* should be music – or even better dance. Thus, metaphorically speaking there are certainly caesurae in films, and there are also temporal regularities in their sequence. Undeniably, superimpositions of fast rhythm – in cuts or in *mise-en-scène* cadenzas – bear meaning, although their contribution to argumentation cannot be predicted. It would be pointless to use such superimpositions autonomously, but their non-gratuitous presence can indicate a desire to convince.

69 Especially if this object constitution is transferred upstream to a grand psychological theory.

70 With this understanding, then, aesthetic can be expanded to corresponding social practices. It becomes a particular rationality in Weber's sociology of a society whose integral *Weltbild* has been shattered.

71 A case in point is Habermas's sole truly aesthetic validity claim: veracity as self-expression. This is meant subjectively; furthermore, only through subjectivity does it become meaningful to speak of aesthetic alienation and colonization. The subject is alienated from its subjective means of expression. Habermas therefore follows Adorno and Lukács (Simmel, really) in their critique of culture as alienating subjectivity.

72 Poetics and rhetoric – in particular theories of tropes – were non-subjectivist means of probing a cognition inherent to artistic *techne*. There was a philosophical canon of artistic quality, as earlier references to Aristotelian *Poetic* showed.

73 This *a priori* formalism has a less reflected match in certain strands of film theory. Accounts of cognition based in part on 'Constructivist' schematism look as if they are inappropriately applied to aesthetic – as aesthetic judgment. Thus, they are either not aesthetic (missing their epistemic object) or they are media-essentialist (but characteristically without a determination of aesthetic essence). In Kantian terms this leads to a wrong expectation of generality. 'Bottom-up' or 'top-down' schemata apply only to empirical, truth-capable cognition, not to aesthetic subjectivity and pleasure. A Kan-

tian schema gives generality to apperceptions through concepts in judgment. Everything not qualifying for this remains an appearance, an *a priori* form of imagination (*Schein*). On the basis of a strict separation of apperception (bottom-up) and concepts (top-down), a strong case can be made for Kant's affirmation of aesthetic non-generality. This contradicts Formalist premises, which pretend to capture the aesthetic attitude using general forms along and with deviations from these rules, which are typically grouped in a given artistic style. Observation of artistic canonicity does not imply that the aesthetic experience aimed at through these artistic means is also canonical (i.e., an application of rules). Subjective pleasure is not achieved through skill but through freedom and play.

74 This idea of semantic amplification was built on by Eco's theory of metaphors.

75 Originally an antibourgeois protest against treating art from a utilitarian perspective. The consequence of this refusal to submit differentiated rationalities, as Weber has it. Teleological, means end rationality was prohibited from infringing on the rationality of the expression of interiority. Effectively, this meant a reassignment of art, whose truth claims could now be subtracted from the all-pervasive object rationality. Art could no longer be true, and this became the undisputed realm of objective rationality. It could merely be authentic, as Habermas (1981) calls the propositional structure of the aesthetic rationality.

76 Or modern banal equivalents of it, as we can see in the multitude of imitations of *Confessiones*: feeble autobiographies, or even feebler, *mémoires*.

77 Cf. Casetti (1993: 23–45). Arnheim's film theory is paradigmatic in this regard. However, he has more contemporary epigones than what one might think, if one can believe the solemn antiessentialist protests.

78 There are abundant analytical *loci* of this Kantian topos in Bittner (1977). The laws of taste are not real laws. Their canonicity is only determined subjectively. Cf. Gadamer (1990) for Kant's reduction of substance to subjectivity (48–87), and on aesthetic normativity (87–106).

79 Veracity, one of Habermas's (1981) three validity claims, goes in this direction. All of his typification is based on historically contingent rationalities, including the aesthetic one. Although he recognizes norms as a different universe of discourse, as non-objective, as using other means to come to agreement, he fails to recognize aesthetics as a means for discovering such norms. He assigns aesthetics to the universe of interiority. This discourse, if it functions properly, can at best achieve a form of veracity, authentic to the true state of one's interior. Agreement in this matter hinges on a comparison with one's own interiority and the plausibility of the other's claimed

psychic state. As an Ideal of cognition, a telos or norm of investigation and debate, it is close to no longer being decidable. Thus aesthetics in Habermas do not reach far beyond Kant, despite – or even because of – orientation to the linguistic analysis of speech acts.

80 The consequences arise when philosophical film aesthetics restricts itself to sensible, observable judgments (i.e., those of knowledgeable people). Recent efforts of this kind have made considerable strides toward demolishing all sorts of speculative film theories but have made rather small contributions to our understanding of this peculiar aesthetic phenomenon in film. Cf. Carroll (1988a, 1988b) and Jarvie (1987), for example.

81 'Formalism is a thing of the past. All that has remained from the Formalist is terminology ... and a number of technological observations.' So says Šklovskij, in Erlich (1955: 132–6, 72ff, 97f, quote from 137).

82 It is, therefore, inconceivable that a Third Critique could be written from a Semiotic perspective, as much as it was impossible to sever pragmatic from cognition (v. *supra*).

83 Peirce's Syllabus of 1903 – terse *locus classicus* – in the Classification of Sciences, assigns to Aesthetic the first place among the Normative Sciences, before ethic and logic: 'Esthetics is the science of ideals, or of that which is objectively admirable without any ulterior reason ... it ought to repose on phenomenology. Ethics ... must appeal to Esthetics for aid in determining the *summum bonum*. It is the theory of self-controlled, or deliberate, conduct. Logic is the theory of self-controlled, or deliberate, thought; and as such, must appeal to ethics for its principles' (1998: 260).

84 'Normative science treats of the laws of the relation of phenomena to ends, that is, it treats of Phenomena in their Secondness' (Peirce 1997: 209).

85 Qualities are possible Reality. Thus we must ask how a possible comes to mind, what the adequate conduct is for the opening of such a mind to whatever is possible, without the aid of factual determination. Now the sum of all qualities (as correlate of aesthetic cognition) is a nonsensical abstraction, because it would have to pretend to state something about everything Possible. Furthermore, to state that whatever felicitously appears before a representing mind without further questions (of truth and generality) is the aesthetic relation, is likewise nonsensical, because it does not discriminate anything from anything else.

86 The distinctiveness of art is a pointless question, and a false problem from a Semiotic perspective. Everything has an intrinsic capacity to be aesthetic meaning, and it is incumbent on art to enunciate it in this sense/meaning – no more and no less. The mastery of enunciation techniques, which can reach levels of considerable sophistication, must not be mistaken for the

resulting meaning, which is emphatically simple. However, Semiotic being comprehensive, there is no need to attach a pragmatic point of view to the cognitive part of aesthetic, because aesthetic is already intrinsically pragmatic and also intrinsically cognitive. On the contrary, a disregard of these two parts collapses the aesthetic meaning into meaningless techniques or 'devices.'

87 As per Peirce's critique in a long diatribe against the subjectivism of German logicians in the 'Minute Logic' of 1902. An editors' footnote (2.152n2) suggests that Husserl and Wundt are being targeted here, but it seems from the course of the argument that the chief target is actually any sort of transcendental argumentation. Peirce's counterposition – which he calls the 'English method' – recommends something more subtle and complex and less surrendering to threads of infinite regress.

88 The ultimate stage was a metaphysical speculation on the reasonableness of being, and a reasonable confidence that the cognitive process (or in more fallibilistic terms, the process of the convergence of adequate opinions of the real in the long run) reaches the real and takes its logical goodness from there.

89 Besides, in this context it is indeed striking how the fundamental function that Peirce (in keeping with an old philosophical tradition) assigns to aesthetics is treated in other systems that concern themselves with the origin of meaning itself. Even in the semiological tradition – which is otherwise strictly differential in its method – there is a 'se sent' Greimas (1983: 93). There is a remnant of corporality in the generation of pragmatic meaning that is equivalent to Peirce's 'physiological function.' In order to become an action centre, a subject must feel itself to be 'un système d'attractions et de répulsions.' However, this dyadic theory has no means with which to account for reasonableness in feelings, let alone in aesthetic feelings. Attractions and repulsions remain 'blind' anthropological constants whose only purpose it is to provide an otherwise unavailable ground for transforming of taxonomies into axiologies. Perhaps this is even more liable to fall within the Peircean verdict on 'German method.' It is at best a 'pragmatic' science without being a normative one.

90 Noted that aesthetic Signs are not identical with art. They are closer to perceptual judgments in Peirce's sense (v. *supra*). This corresponds roughly to the common definition of 'perception,' without however, including very much of a general idea of whatness. Aesthetic perception does not want to find out a rule about its percept. It contents itself with holding fast to the quality it has in mind; and in doing so habitually, it is guided only by its behavioural value of attraction. As long as it keeps up that perceptive state,

it remains aesthetic; but as soon as it becomes a Sign concerned with a rule, it becomes ampliative reasoning. This is the difference between listening to music and understanding music, for instance.

91 Upstream of the (ethical) *summum bonum*, with the 'reign of evil,' (not 'axis of evil', because an axis already is polar) as its opposite.

92 Or as Peirce said in the context of his 1903 treatment of metaphysical systems: 'The universe is a vast representamen, a great symbol of God's purpose, working out its conclusions in living realities. Now every symbol must have, organically attached to it, its Indices of Reactions and its Icons of Qualities; and such part as these reactions and these qualities play in an argument that, they of course, play in the universe – that Universe being precisely an argument.' (1997: 201).

93 Rilke's famous and often quoted verse covers the entire range of aesthetic experience: denn das Schöne ist nichts / als des Schrecklichen Anfang (*Duineser Elegien* I, v4–5 'because the beautiful is but awe's commencement'). The non-ego of the ego is both terrible and pleasant, but in itself it is a conduct guided by what is in itself admirable and not by psychic reactions.

94 In the specific certainty of the Possible, of course, which follows a different value than truth or general cognition.

95 We have already solved the confusion surrounding aesthetic and art theory. In this Peircean and more traditional sense of philosophical Aesthetic, it concerns itself with a conduct that is different from the conduct of a practical knowledge of art.

96 Cf. *supra*, 63–4, regarding the Peircean methodological triplet of dissociation, discrimination, and precision.

97 Against Arnheim and early film theories, consider Carroll (1996a: 3–74), who, however, remains indebted to this same paradigm.

98 In the Pragmaticist account of cognition, the intrinsically temporal nature of cognition as such is recognized. Every general cognition has temporally mediated different states of an identical object. It follows that time is not alien to cognition; indeed, it is central to cognition.

99 Corresponding to a double and simple degeneration, respectively, of the Sign relation.

100 And is, at this end of a perfected custom formation, of no interest to aesthetic, whereas at its normative commencement it is emphatically so. Probability always has to do with expectation hinging on the past; this cannot be the case with aesthetic conduct. In this sense, aesthetic is an auroral moment of probability. As the limit case it is conceived of in the range of the Normative Sciences.

101 The connection between Aesthetics and positive reasoning as a whole is not fortuitous but is exactly what Peirce meant it to be. 'All positive reasoning depends upon probability. All probability depends upon the supposition that there is a "long run." But a long run is an endless course of experience. Now even if there be a future life, every man's course of experience with which his reasoning has to do, comes to a speedy end. Therefore, if his purposes are purely selfish he cannot be logical. That argument is open to some apparent objection; but the subsequent careful analysis of it has only shown that the argument has even more force than was supposed. Other considerations have also appeared which make the dependence of what we ought to think upon what we aim at still more close. Logic is, therefore, more or less dependent upon Ethics. Ethics, in its turn, or the question what we are deliberately prepared to aim at, depends in a similar way, upon esthetics, or what it is that we would deliberately, pronounce to be καλόν κ' ἀγαθόν. Indirectly, therefore, logic even depends upon Esthetics (L75, version D, 14f). The manuscript L75, Peirce's application to the Carnegie Institution for financial support (15 July 1902), comprises the final and five draft versions (A–E), transcribed by Joseph Ransdell (electronic archive).

102 On a nominalistic basis, this is not so much of a problem, since representational codes are as unreal as aesthetic codes and can therefore be treated as independent objects, without regard for reference or for subjects.

103 For the first point, it is enough to refer to what has been said about the Aesthetic object.

104 'Media' as a term already suggests the existence of physical bodies that are being mediated (i.e., signs). This makes conventional use of distinctions on the basis of artifacts. In a Semiotic context, however, it is not meaningful to speak of 'natural signs' when everything can be taken as sign. If, however, the opposite of natural is artificial, then such signs are merely at the upper Legisign scale of Representamina. Media tend to be identified with this area of the scale. So 'analogical' media engender an artificial problem, since that term seems to be self-contradictory. The photographic image of film had to exhibit some artifactual form – for instance, in Arnheim's film-specific aesthetic – in order to become apt to expression. This is unwarranted, however, and shows a lack of understanding of signification in general.

105 Cf. *supra*. In this regard, the quotations from Santaella Braga (1996: 207) give the impression that the pure Form is of a different degree of Iconicity than Diagrams, which are the Forms of reasoning that Peirce has in mind. In Santaella Braga's understanding, a pure Icon is close to an 'aesthetic

creation ... a quality of feeling which is engendered in a form' (207), albeit mitigated by its being an occurrence and therefore becoming Sinsign, and by its 'bearing traces of a legisign,' which gives it a formal unity.

106 Kevelson arrived at a description that resembles the practice of art. It is perhaps closer to the practical rules that Peirce kept outside Aesthetic as Normative Science.

107 Compare to Santaella Braga (1996), who attempts a logical description of the same as a Sign.

108 Kevelson's terms reflect the Sign relation in its entirety, not only the first trichotomy (Qualisign, Sinsign, Legisign), which would correspond to the form of thought mentioned earlier.

109 That the position of the Legisign (or Type, from the second classification of signs in the 1903 Harvard lectures [5.14–212]) is called 'metaphor' in the Syllabus (2.277) should not confuse us. Peirce is not investigating lyric as art practice. So in the non-lyrical technical meaning of this term, the 'resemblance of the sign in something else of the object' (Syllabus) involves a rule.

110 For instance, consider the difference between musical experience and musical exercises. The latter strive to find the Form of an ideal musical interpretation, whose only reality is that of a rule. Thus every single actual instance of musical practice is diagrammatical use, of musical Iconicity, with regard to a rule. Only this makes this singular instance also an instance of a general (i.e., of that nascent Form).

111 Even if not aesthetic, it is still artistic meaning, and there is still a great distance between the 'interpretation' of the latter meaning and the exuberant rage of meaning in the discourse of art criticism. As with every other Sign, there is no upper limit to Interpretation, as long as it is still in relation to the same object.

112 Aesthetic 'documentary' cinema – a decidedly rhetorical usage of cinema – constructs its images in such a manner that new existential claims can be drawn from it, or can be insinuated by it. Certain kinds of *soigné* composition of the cinematographic image (i.e., frame in movement) seem too gratuitous to have any existential implications. Thus they can be contemplated, (i.e., we can contemplate the represented real). The aesthetic of image composition inasmuch as it can open another dimension behind the factual, would draw us into the broad and deep discourse of painting and art pictures, which is not possible here. Here 'composition' concerns only the aesthetic degeneration of the factual in narrative cinema. The 'cinema of facts' – documentary film – follows its own aestheticization (v. *infra*).

113 A question of a lesser Sign degeneration, comprised in the narrative Sign: How does (pictorial) composition transform the object into an object of contemplation? The rhetoric of the convincing Real in cinema usually involves the ordering of a coherent universe of representation. In order to make sense, films are preoccupied with being credible as unaltered representations of the real. This can be achieved only through a strict internal order that builds up this illusion through coherence. A disregard of this coherence inevitably leads to a breakdown of reality illusions. Film aesthetics must cope practically with cinema, which cannot cease to be a tool of representation and which, furthermore, fosters expectations of a credible universe through its rhetorical enunciation. Aesthetic, even while cannibalizing it, would not want to disrupt this credible universe. Yet at the same time it must become free, and therefore to an important degree paradoxical.

114 A similar transition has been observed in narration from the causal chain to the author's intention. It can simplify the cognitive process if we can attribute the teleological form to an author who wanted to use it in these circumstances. This is no longer part of the original process, because once this vision is there, we have the starting point for a further Interpretation. Authorship must furnish the Interpretant, the concept, the pragmatic meaning we miss in the actors.

115 In Drama, pictorial composition merely has the function of matching the Aesthetic of drama, yet in this it has a distinct function. Drama *in se* is strictly speaking only the Sign degeneration of narrative enunciation.

116 Cf. Bazin (1985), but it is not seen in Carroll (1996b: 46f). Carroll's three levels of the photographic depiction in cinema – which he calls 'physical,' 'general,' and 'nominal' portrayal – concern only certain aspects of Representation. This has been discussed in the context of the 'cinematic object,' in which sense every thing-as-cognized is a triadic Sign relation. Carroll's general portrayal is the third Correlate, which recognizes that everything is a case of a General. 'Nominal portrayal,' as opposed to 'physical portrayal' is instead an affair of narration, or narrative roles. For this kind of depiction we need to understand an action, not a picture. Certainly there is a progressing Interpretation taking place between the two portrayals, but as such it brings about a change in logic, a different class of Sign. It adds teleology. Video footage of a crime scene in a police documentation illustrates the first kind of Representation; exactly the same scene in a crime film is a different Sign guided by a teleological logic. For our present context, however, we are concerned with a third kind of Sign, which Carroll does not take into account at all. Aesthetic Interpretation

unravels all three 'portrayals' – it (literally) 'protracts' nothing (from here to there) as it were, but snaps all existential links.

117 In Lotman's film aesthetic, the threshold of meaningfulness is reached only at the trope level (v. *infra*). What is the trope of something, and what is this something in itself? In order to be different from the something-in-itself, tropical meaning operates on two determinations. First, it 'names' its existential opposite; not much more than a presence is indicated, since 'telling' knows too much, including its quiddity. Second, tropes, set off the objects presented. Such an offset is not in itself meaningful (in keeping with the double articulation idea) except as pure difference. Being-other begs the question, 'Other than what?' At this juncture we would expect a solution similar to the idea of Peirce's Interpretation, but there is none. No third, of a nature different from the different qualities to be compared, offers a General meaning. In a Semiotic key, Lotman's quasi-double articulation could be interpreted as the production of a General meaning over the existential designation. (However, as we discussed in the context of the cinematic object, such a representation theory does not do justice to the image. Already images have meaning – that is, there is a General idea in Interpretation. So for the sake of Lotman's argument, let us assume that there are 'dumb' images). On considering of the function of composition, we notice an augmentation of meaning through more determination. Thus a reader must understand the finesse of rhythm in order to reach poetical comprehension. It would follow that spectators watching cinema as a plain representation of a real world could not grasp the aesthetic refinement of an art film.

118 This is not a danger for a theory if it is the kind of 'system re-entrant' theory that Luhmann's system theory is so centrally concerned with. Such theories are capable of treating their paradoxical or tautological circularity in a non-vicious way, as the condition of their possibility inasmuch as selective achievement (positive form) or blind spot (negative form).

119 Film as a complex of code systems is not a novelty, as it has already been discussed in the context of representation of the cinematic object. Nobody claims, though, that there is an aesthetic code proper. In such circumstances aesthetic has to be fitted into the three articulations of the film language and its codes at various levels: cinemes, edemes, cademes, videmes, kinemorphemes and the like. Approaching film following the Bauhaus tradition (Klee, Kandinskij) (cf. Colin 1985; Odin 1990) involves analyses of basic forms and colours. Why they produce aesthetic effects and why they serve as a means of artistic expression is not a question, because the traditional transcendental-subjectivist problem of aesthetics is not accepted.

120   So Lotman (1973: 5) is in good company in calling non-conceptual signifi-
      cation 'icons,', 'iconic signs,' and the like. Even if used in the Peirceish tri-
      ple icon, index, symbol, there is no influence from Peirce's classification of
      Signs. Such 'icons' play a role in Mitry (1987) and Monaco (1977: e.g., 132–
      4) – albeit merely taken from Wollen (1969), Peters (1981: 25ff), and Wol-
      len (1969: 122–4). For Nöth (1985: 472), this iconism is a variant of
      Horace's *ut pictura poiesis*, the non-linguistic aesthetic way of the imma-
      nent coupling of expression and content.

121   The reason for this is that under the aegis of Jakobson's 'poetic function,'
      only such differences can be exploited (and this, as a metaphor theory,
      makes it different from those of Black and Goodman).

122   However, movement (which is indeed intrinsic to film) does not amount
      to time, and *a fortiori* not to teleological temporality (v. *supra*).

123   Cf. ibid.: 71; defined as 'a complete syntagm having internal unity and
      bounded at each end by structural pauses' (l.c.). At this stage, this is a
      mere *petitio principii*, because the paradigm would attribute sentential
      parts to pieces of cinematic signification. If the paragon of the sentence is
      to be meaningfully applied, the equivalent of a logic of predication (syllo-
      gisms etc.) should be found.

124   The leading encyclopaedia of musicology characterizes: 'Es ist die
      musikalische Rhetorik, deren Kenntnis und Gebrauch Bach durch Birn-
      baum ausdrücklich bestätigt worden ist. Entsprechend den 'loci topici'
      der Redekunst werden musikalische 'Figuren' gebildet, Tonformeln, wie
      sie schon das ganze Barockzeitalter hindurch (und früher) entwickelt
      worden waren, und die konkrete Inhalte bedeuten (Schmitz: 'die Figur ist
      Trägerin der Bildlichkeit''' (*MGG I*, 1030 s.v. Bach, Johann Sebastian).

125   That is, 7 for creation, 12 for church, their products, and so on. This
      applies also to the number of the letters of the alphabet, not only with
      regard to the famous variations on the theme B A C H (in German nota-
      tion), but also to the number of bars, notes, canon starts, and son on: '...
      heiligen Zahlen der Bibel, ihre Summen, Produkte, Potenzen usw. durch
      musikalische Mittel ausgedrückt werden (z. B. 7 für Schöpfer und Schöp-
      fung, Anfang und Ende; 12 für Kirche, Jünger, Gemeinde; im Credo der
      Messe h erklingt das Wort "Credo" $7 \bullet 7 = 49$ mal, das "in unum Deum" 7
      $\bullet 12 = 84$ mal; am Ende der Fuge "Patrem omnipotentem" hat Bach die
      bedeutungsvolle Zahl der Takte (84) eigenhändig notiert; nach Smend)'
      (*MGG*, ibid).

126   It can be doubted that this combination allows for a genuine cognition of
      facts, lacking a true real opposite, but this is not the concern here.

127   The functional equivalent of language in Lotman, or semiology at large, is

the Neoformalist 'perception.' Thus the linguistic substratum of Formalist aesthetic is replaced with what is taken to be its analogue, perception, as accounted for (separately) in Constructivism. Constructivism and Formalism, this infelicitous amalgam, have been separated for good reasons, as we discussed earlier in connection with cinematic representation. Russian Formalism contented itself with 'automatism' and as a theory of 'literariness' did not venture into a theory of language and its grasp of states of affairs. There is no Formalist language philosophy. In a similar vein, Neoformalism as an aesthetic theory functions perfectly without any superaddition of perception theories.

128 The package of Neoformalism is further unpackaged, and some might consider this highly problematic, when the poetics are split into aesthetic and narration theory. That there are compelling reasons for this is a consequence of Semiotic, but it does not follow from the theory design of Neoformalism itself. Narration is cognitively distinct from aesthetic, which is based on the different logics of teleology and simple quality. However, it is still done justice by Neoformalism, because it takes the narrative configuration as such as an unproblematic given, as if teleological logic were already in place through the plot or *fabula*. So the real problem is instead essentially aesthetic. The origin of teleology, which is never an observable fact, is not treated in Neoformalism, but might be considered as explained by schematisms dealt with in Cognitivism (cf. our discussion in that context).

129 With neutrality modification, suspending judgments on existence (cf. Casebier 1991: 15), or as the 'Habitus der Realität' of an intentional subject in Ingarden (1962: 319–41).

130 However, neither antisubjectivity nor Constructivist subjectivity is self-evident. It is not within our scope to construct epistemologies of either position if their proponents failed to do so. Self-evidence, however, no longer works when inherent contradictions arise within the same theory. On that basis, we cannot engage in a meaningful dialogue with such completely different approaches as Bergson, phenomenology, and semiology. Cognitivist Neoformalism is merely one approach; it is not evidence. As should be clear by now, a Semiotic perspective can agree with the aims of constructivism: triadic Signs always considered thought as the pivot of cognition and world appropriation. The reasons for this non-psychological, logical 'subjectivism' are explained in the theory of Categories.

131 Which can also assume, like a Janus face, a 'passive' activity ('automatic', 'bottom-up'). Such a subject-on-automatic-pilot becomes aesthetical in the conscious use of artistic forms.

132 Hochberg's account of perception does not change this assumption; it merely inflates the concept of perception to virtually any cognitive operation. Common usage might be on his side, however – a popular version of the *esse est percipi* adage. But, this is not the question at hand.

133 As in Goodman's theory of metaphor (v. *supra*), exemplary substitution does not answer the question as to what happens in the aesthetic between.

134 This agrees with a Peircean understanding of perceptual judgments (v. *supra*), which are peculiar in that they are without appeal. A critique of percepts can only be a critical comparison of perceptual judgments. In Bordwell, however, 'perception' is used in a much more comprehensive sense.

135 In fact, the Šklovsky quotation in Thompson (1988: 10) is a little misleading. Speaking of 'general laws of perception,' he shifts into metaphor (or a different register?) when calling normal perception 'prose perception' whose habituation even 'devours one's wife.' Raw perception, then, is languaged perception, and it is the ability of language to show things differently to 'recover the sensation of life.'. Counterposing 'things as they are perceived' and 'as they are known' contradicts even Bordwell's Constructivist hypotheses.

136 It is instructive to observe that the Formalist Idea no longer plays a part in recent Cognitivist literature. In Bordwell and Carroll's collection of Wisconsin studies in film, Peterson (1996) analyzes avant-garde cinema from the perspective of problem-solving theory. Nothing needs to become deviant for an aesthetic effect; his avant-garde illustrations are already 'defamiliarized' in themselves. Instead, as the example of Baillie's Quixote shows, 'the viewer's problem solving' (122) concerns itself with the material organization and 'what it all means,' and with (as we might call it) the symbolism of single elements: tires mean white, birds mean Indian culture (126). Film art thus becomes a cognitive problem to be solved. Although we can only concur emphatically (the answer to Peterson's question is no) with the cognition approach, nothing indicates what could be the peculiarity of an aesthetic cognition.

137 In Jakobson's preface to a French anthology of Formalist texts (Todorov 1965: 11), where 'estrangement' is apostrophized as one of those 'platitudes galvaudées.'

138 This is clearly an inheritance from Jakubinskij's early distinction between practical (Šklovskij's prosa) and poetical language.

139 The kind of excess we are interested in here is exclusively an aesthetic one. It is not the result of a narrative operation that brings about teleological causality, translating 'event' into a *fabula* through the *sujet*.

140 Bordwell refutes theories of authorship. One might hear in this a distant echo of the old antisubject approach that is so crucial to Formalism. After all, it is literally the приём, 'trick of estrangement,' in a literary theory of 'литерарност'. To call this unifying principle 'style' or an author's personal style, or a genre used by an author, is all the same.

141 Certainly, Formalism will not be mistaken for a hermeneutic identity aesthetics of identification with an author's interiority and artistic intention (v. *supra*).

142 Style (of the presentational technique of one and the same *sujet* element) is not fortuitous and makes a meaningful difference for such presupposition, although without knowing what this meaning should be. Is it a better choice when (with Thompson) the systemic side of style is named 'defamiliarization'? *Sujet* and style must remain empty concepts when there is an 'artistic intention' that does not will anything.

143 Bordwell, besides, provides a marvellous example of 'real life' felicitous film theory by his titling. 'Ends/end [of interpretation]' (ibid.: 249, 254) is itself a trope *in conjunctis* (paronomasia, to be exact), which can hardly be 'falsified.' Nevertheless it is an interesting, open-ended way of interpreting theories.

144 It is for good reason that Aristotle in the *Poetic* (ch. 21) speaks of metaphors. This is common to both rhetorical and poetic style. In a deeper sense, the argumentative force of both appeals to a mimetic of action; thus the appealing force must use all sorts of necessity – even those of mere changes of letters and other 'suggestive' similarities.

145 Of which Hitchcock was so fascinated in a number of his films – *Psycho*, *Marnie*, *Spellbound*, and so on (cf. *KIM* [1994], a collective work surveying the vast corpus of the modern topos of psychiatric subjects in cinema). For a history of the discovery of psychiatric 'disease,' see Foucault (1972).

146 A serious rhetorical alternative Interpretation brings the Johannes figure into a paradigmatic relation to the narrative. A *paradigma*, or *exemplum*, is a well-known, traditional rhetorical trope, and as such is a quasi-syllogistic form. It stands between deductive (apodeictic) and inductive (epagogic) inference. Logically, it infers from one singularity and a new singular by maintaining the latter as similar. Thus it is a preliminary form of what Peirce called abduction. For transforming Johannes from a diegetic character into a *paradigma* of the epos universe, the narrative parallelism in *Ordet* is as important as the cinematic treatment of Johannes. Being a *paradigma* or example is in fact a division of roles, not simply a distribution of singularities: the epos is certainly singular (i.e. not a general cognition), and the Johannes parallel is also singular, but the relation

between the two compares the former with the latter, not the other way around. The paradigm serves as the reference point of the comparison. The rhetorical effect, however, comes about when the comparing relation is drawn into something third. In our case both singulars are narratives, but in this interpretation they enter into a rhetorical relationship with each other. The general cognition can also remain in the narrative mode, as long as it is in a third. As *dénouement* of both parallel lines, the climactic closing sequence would have to be the general conclusion. The trope *ironia* might serve as a contrasting model for the trope *paradigma*. Here, would the figure Johannes reverse the ironic thrust of the *vis comica*? (Obviously, he is seen ironically as 'the light of the world' when he places a candle under the window.) The camera work seems to prevent this kind of judgment. Johannes is a fool but not a joker or buffoon. He also stands out visually in that he receives a treatment that is different from any other character. This strengthens his declared (by his own declaration) and supposed (by the plot's cautious and open-ended questioning about his true characteristics) representation of Christ. If this were a sort of 'dogmatic' commentary' on the Borgen universe (which, however, remains conspicuously unnoticed), such a rhetorical relation would have to convince us of a truth. Seen from the closing sequence, however, this film is very unconvincing – although it is undeniably a strong experience.

147 This is made very clear by the white linen moving in the wind at the top of the dune. These are the only other moving elements, apart from Johannes; consequently, they catch the viewer's eye unmistakably.

148 Even though not a direct biblical quotation (it is actually a piecing together of many quotations, with significant 'editorial' additions from Johannes in the context of his masked communication with his family), the introduction is clearly a citation from Matthew 23: 13–39, the seven curses ('Woe unto you, hypocrites') on the Pharisees. Significantly, this pericope ends not only with the same apocalyptic words as in *Ordet*, but also with the same kind of promise ('they who have faith ...'): 'Amen, I say to you, you shall not see me henceforth till you say: Blessed is he that cometh in the name of the Lord' (Matthew 23: 39). Apparently, Dreyer is letting Johannes announce – in the form of a prophetic pseudo-quotation – the exact events to come, including the personal transformations of those he is addressing.

149 'In the first eleven shots, Johannes is completely separated from the family, locked within his own space by the editing.' (loc. cit.).

150 Cf. the excellent description in Bordwell (1981: 155), in particular his absent presence during Inger's dying.

151 This light is even more astonishing, considering what is shown outside of Borgensgård. The hearse is not shown in bright sunlight, although it is clearly spatiotemporally contiguous. The fact that light floods into the laying-out chamber, and not into the mourners' room (no windows), in this context is certainly not gratuitous, given the careful narrative and visual preparation.

152 Quotes from the St John prologue: John 1:11 resp. John 1:5 (light in darkness) but characteristically turned into the first person (originally in the third).

153 Direction given in Dreyer's published script (242).

154 Not Lazarus', as in Bordwell (1981: 147). The difference is not so trifling, since by giving her son back to the widow, the place of Inger is much more directly filled. But the foreshadowing is even more direct: the entire resurrection scene is a faithful rendering of Luke 6:11, where Jesus orders the dead to rise, 'and the dead sat up and began talking. Thereafter Jesus gave him to his mother.' A parallel pericope, which is quoted by Johannes in #49 – 'She is not dead, but sleepeth' (the healing of the daughter of Jairus, Luke 8: 52) – in particular with regard to the bystanders' doubts – provides the model for the scenes preceding Inger's resurrection.

155 Mikkel is matched by the pastor and doctor. Old Borgen's narrative function is replicated in Peter and the entire wedding subplot and its antagonists. This function is coherent only when Inger fails in this subplot for her specific reasons, while still keeping her irrational hope (which is only shared by the two girls).

156 Dreyer often uses acoustic perspective. At some very significant moments, a character is acoustically extremely close-up, even though his visual distance remains the same. Another clear marker in *Ordet* is the moment when (always extradiegetic) music sets in. This is most notably the case in the opening scene, and here in the second search for Johannes.

157 An attentive gospel reader cannot help but notice the biblical resonance. The public life of Jesus, after his baptism in the Jordan, began with his Sermon on the Mount. Johannes, conversely, after walking away, starts his own sermon on the dune, not with the beatitudes ('blessed are ...'), however, but with condemnations. This second disappearance is modelled even more clearly on the disorientation and fear that seized the disciples after the Passion. They could not find him, until he showed himself.

Bibliography

Albrecht, Jörn. 1988. *Europäischer Strukturalismus. Ein forschungsgeschichtlicher Überblick.* Tübingen: Francke.

Andrew, Dudley. 1984. *Film in the Aura of Art.* Princeton: Princeton University Press.

Andrew, Dudley. 1985. *Concepts in Film Theory.* Oxford: Oxford University Press.

Apel, Karl-Otto. 1973. *Transformation der Philosophie II. Das Apriori der Kommunikationsgemeinschaft.* Frankfurt: Suhrkamp.

– 1975. *Der Denkweg von Charles S. Peirce. Eine Einführung in den amerikanischen Pragmatismus.* Frankfurt: Suhrkamp.

– 1981. *Charles S. Peirce: From Pragmatism to Pragmaticism.* Amherst: (University of Massachusetts Press.

Aristarco, Guido. 1963. *Storia delle teoriche del film.* Turin: Einaudi.

Aristotle. *Analytica Prior*, Aristoteles graece Ex recensione Immanuelis Bekkeri. Edidit Academia Regia Borussica Berolinum (Reimer) 1831–70.

– *Metaphysica*, Aristoteles graece Ex recensione Immanuelis Bekkeri. Edidit Academia Regia Borussica Berolinum (Reimer) 1831–70.

– *Physica*, Aristoteles graece Ex recensione Immanuelis Bekkeri. Edidit Academia Regia Borussica Berolinum (Reimer) 1831–70.

– *Poetica*, Aristoteles graece Ex recensione Immanuelis Bekkeri. Edidit Academia Regia Borussica Berolinum (Reimer) 1831–70.

– *Rhetorica*, Aristoteles graece Ex recensione Immanuelis Bekkeri. Edidit Academia Regia Borussica Berolinum (Reimer) 1831–70.

– *Topica*, Aristoteles graece Ex recensione Immanuelis Bekkeri. Edidit Academia Regia Borussica Berolinum (Reimer) 1831–70.

– *de interpretatione*, Aristoteles graece Ex recensione Immanuelis Bekkeri. Edidit Academia Regia Borussica Berolinum (Reimer) 1831–70.

Arnheim, Rudolf. 1932. *Film als Kunst*. Berlin: Rowohlt.

Aumont, Jacques. 1990. *L'Image*. Paris: Nathan.

Baltzer, Ulrich. 1994. *Erkenntnis als Relationengeflecht: Kategorien bei Charles S. Peirce*. Paderborn: Schöningh.

Barnouw, Jeffrey. 1994. 'The Place of Peirce's "Esthetic" in His Thought and the Tradition of Aesthetics.' In Herman Parret, ed., *Parret, Herman. Peirce and Value Theory*. Amsterdam: Benjamins.

Bazin, André. 1985. *Qu'est-ce que le cinéma?* Paris: Cerf.

Beaugrande, Robert de. 1988. *Critical Discourse: A Survey of Literary Theorists*. Norwood, NJ: Ablex.

Beilenhoff, Wolfgang. 1978. 'Der sowjetische Revolutionsfilm als kultureller Text. Semiotische Grunddaten für eine Kulturtypologie der zwanziger Jahre in der Sowjetunion.' Diss., Ruhr-Universität Bochum.

Bergala. Alain. (n.d.) *Initiation à la sémiologie du récit en images*. Paris: (Ligue française de l'enseignement et de l'éducation permanente.

Bergson, Henri. *Oeuvres. Éditions du centenaire*. 3rd ed. Paris: PUF.

Bertrand, Denis. 1984. 'Narrativité et discursivité: points de repère et problématiques.' *Actes Sémiotiques- Documents, Paris, École des Hautes Études en Sciences Sociales* 6, 59: 1–38.

Bettetini, Gianfranco. 1979. *Tempo del senso. La logica temporale dei testi audiovisivi*. Milan: Bompiani.

Bittner, Rüdiger, and Peter Pfaff, eds. 1977. *Das ästhetische Urteil*. Cologne: Kiepenheuer & Witsch.

Bordwell, David. 1981. *The Films of Carl-Theodor Dreyer*. Berkeley: University of California Press.

– 1985. *Narration in Fiction Film*. Madison: University of Wisconsin Press.

– 1989a. *Making Meaning*. Cambridge, MA: Harvard University Press.

– 1989b. 'A Case for Cognitivism.' in: *Iris* 5(2). 11–40.

– 1990. 'A Case for Cognitivism: Further Reflections.' *Iris*. 5(2). 11–40.

– 1992. 'Kognition und Verstehen. Sehen und Vergessen in Mildred Pierce.' *av/montage* 1(1): 5–24.

Bordwell, David and Noel Carroll, eds. 1996. *Post-Theory: Reconstructing Film Studies*. Madison: University of Wisconsin Press.

Branigan, Edward. 1984. *Point of View in the Cinema: A Theory of Narration and Subjectivity in Classical Film*. Berlin: Mouton.

– 1992. *Narrative Comprehension and Film*. London: Routledge.

Bremond, Claude. 1973. *Logique du récit*. Paris: Seuil.

Brunning, Jacqueline. 1997. 'Genuine Triads and Teridentity.' In Nathan Houser, Don D. Roberts, and James Van Evra, eds., *Studies in the Logic of Charles Sanders Peirce*. Bloomington: Indiana University Press.

Bucher, Theodor G. 1998. *Einführung in die angewandte Logik*. Berlin: de Gruyter.

Budniakiewicz, Therese. 1992. *Fundamentals of Story Logic: Introduction to Greimassian Semiotics*. Amsterdam: Benjamins.

Burch, Robert W. 1991. *A Peircean Reduction Thesis*. Lubbock: Texas Technical University Press.

Burch, Robert W. 1997. 'Peirce's Reduction Thesis.' In: Nathan Houser, Don D. Roberts, and James Van Evra, eds., *Studies in the Logic of Charles Sanders Peirce*. Bloomington: (Indiana University Press.

Byrnes, John. 1998. 'Peirce's First-Order Logic of 1885.' *Transactions of the Charles S. Peirce Society* 34(4): 949–76.

Carls, Rainer. 1974. *Idee und Menge. Der Aufbau einer kategorialen Ontologie als Folge aus den Paradoxien des Begriffsrealismus in der griechischen Philosophie und in der modernen mathematischen Grundlagenforschung*. Munich: Berchmanskolleg Verlag.

Carney, Raymond. 1989. *Speaking the Language of Desire: The Films of Carl Dreyer*. Cambridge: Cambridge University Press.

Carontini, Enrico. 1986. *Faire l'image. Matériaux pour une sémiologie des énonciations visuelles*. Montréal: Presses de l'Université du Québec à Montréal.

Carroll, Noël E. 1988a. *Mystifying Movies: Fads and Fallacies in Contemporary Film Theory*. New York: Columbia University Press.

– 1988b. *Philosophical Problems of Classical Film Theory*. Princeton, NJ: Princeton University Press.

– 1996a. 'Prospects for Film Theory: A Personal Assessment.' In Bordwell and Carroll, eds., *Post-Theory: Reconstructing Film Studies*, pp. 37–68.

– 1996b. *Theorizing the Moving Image*. Cambridge: Cambridge University Press.

Casebier, Allan. 1991. *Film and Phenomenology: Toward a Realist Theory of Cinematic Representation*. Cambridge: Cambridge University Press.

Casetti, Francesco. 1986. *Dentro lo sguardo. Il film e il suo spettatore*. Milan: Bompiani.

– 1993. *Teorie del cinema: 1945–1990*. Milan: Bompiani.

Cavalier, Alain. 1987. 'Thérèse. Un film de Alain Cavalier.' *L'Avant-scène Cinéma* 364: 3–87.

Chabrol, C., S. Alexandrescu, R. Barthes, C. Bremond, A.J. Greimas, P. Maranda, S. Schmidt, and T. Van Dijk. 1973. *Sémiotique narrative et textuelle*. Paris: Larousse.

Chateau, Dominique. 1986. *Le Cinéma comme langage*. Paris: AISS-IASPA.

Chauviré, Christiane. 1995. *Peirce et la signification. Introduction à la logique du vague*. Paris: PUF.

Clifton, Roy. 1983. *The Figure in Film*. East Brunswick, NJ: Associated University Press.

Cohn, Dorrit. 1978. *Transparent Minds*. Princeton, NJ: Princeton University Press.

Colapietro, Vincent. 2000. 'Let's All Go to the Movies: Two Thumbs Up for Hugo Münsterberg's *The Photoplay* (1916).' In *Transactions of the Charles S. Peirce Society* 36(4): 477–501.

Colin, Michel. 1985. *Langue, Film, Discours. Prolégomènes à une sémiologie générative du film*. Paris: Klincksieck.

– 1989. 'La Grande syntagmatique revisitée.' In *Nouveaux actes sémiotiques* 1: 1–56.

Coquet, J.-Cl. 1982. *Sémiotique. L'École de Paris*. Paris: Hachette.

Currie, Gregory. 1995. *Image and Mind: Film, Philosophy and Cognitive Science*. Cambridge: Cambridge University Press.

– 1997. 'The Film Theory That Never Was: A Nervous Manifesto.' I Richard Allen and Murray Smith, eds., *Film Theory and Philosophy*. Oxford: Clarendon.

Deely, John. 1996. 'The Grand Vision.' In Vincent M. Colapietro and Thomas M. Olshewsky, eds., *Peirce's Doctrine of Signs: Theory, Applications, and Connections*. Berlin: Mouton,

Deledalle, Gérard. 1979. *Théorie et pratique du signe. Introduction à la sèmiotique de Charles S. Peirce*. Paris: Payot.

– 1987. *Charles S. Peirce, phénoménologue et sémioticien*. Amsterdam: Benjamins.

Deleuze, Gilles. 1966. *Le Bergsonisme*. Paris: Presses universitarres de France.

– 1973, 'À quoi reconnaît-on le structuralisme?' In: François Châtelet (ed.), *Histoire de la philosophie*. Paris: Hachette.

– 1983. *L'image-mouvement*. Paris: Minuit.

– 1985. *L'image-temps*. Paris: Minuit.

– 1986. *Foucault*. Paris: Minuit.

De Tienne, André. 1996. *L'Analytique de la représentation chez Peirce. La Genèse de la théorie des catégories*. Brussels: Publ. Fac. Université Saint-Louis.

Dreyer, Carl Theodor. 1970. *Four Screenplays*, trans. Oliver Stallybrass. London: Thames & Hudson.

– 1971. *Jesus*. New York: Dial Press.

– 1973. *Dreyer in Double Reflection*. New York: Dutton.

Drouzy, Maurice. 1982. *Carl Th. Dreyer né Nilsson*. Paris: Cerf.

Ducrot, Oswald, and Tzvetan Todorov. 1972. *Dictionnaire encyclopédique des sciences du langage*. Paris: Seuil.

Eco, Umberto. 1970. 'Sémiologie des messages visuels.' *Communications* 15: 42–56.

– 1975. *Trattato di semiotica generale*. Milan: Bompiani.

– 1976. 'Peirce and Contemporary Semantics.' *Versus* 15: 49–65.

– 1979. *The Role of the Reader*. Bloomington: University of Indiana Press.

– 1981. 'Peirce's Analysis of Meaning.' In: Kenneth Laine Ketner et al., eds. *Proceedings of the C.S. Peirce Bicentennial International Congress*, No. 23. Lubbock: (Texas Technical University Press.

– 1997. *Kant e l'ornitorinco*. Milan: Bompiani.

Ehrat, Johannes. 1991. 'Peirce's Iconicity and Meaning Processes in Audiovisual Communication: The Religious in Film and Television Aesthetics, Narratives and Social Form.' PhD dissertation, Université de Montréal.

– 1995. 'Rezension Baltzer, Ulrich, Erkenntnis als Relationengeflecht.' *Theologie und Philosophie* 70(3): 431–4.

– 2003. 'Emblematic and Emotional Treatment of Music: Godard's Interplay with both Variants and the Peculiar Meaning Derived from This.' Paper delivered at Laterna Magica Pécs, forthcoming.

Eley, Lothar. 1973. 'Faktum.' In Hermann Krings, ed., *Handbuch philosophischer Grundbegriffe*. Munich: Kösel.

Enos, Theresa. 1996. *Encyclopedia of Rhetoric and Composition: Communication from Ancient Times to the Information Age*. New York: Garland.

Erlich, Victor. 1955. *Russian Formalism: History – Doctrine*. 3rd ed. The Hague: Mouton.

Esposito, Elena. 1987. 'Negazione e modalità.' In Claudio Baraldi, Giancarlo Corsi, and Elena Esposito, *Semantica e comunicazione. L'evoluzione delle idee nella prospettiva di Niklas Luhmann*. Bologna: CLUEB.

Esposito, Joseph L. 1977. 'Is there a Semiocentric Predicament?' *Semiotica*. 19(3/4): 259–70.

– 1980. *Evolutionary Metaphysics: The Development of Perice's Theory of Categories*. Athens: Ohio University Press.

Everaert-Desmedt, Nicole. 1981. *Sémiotique du récit. Méthode et applications*. Louvain: Cabay.

– 1984. *La communication publicitaire. Etude sémio-pragmatique*. Louvain-La-Neuve: Cabay.

Fisch, Max. 1986. *Peirce, Semeiotic, and Pragmatism: Essays*. Bloomington: Indiana University Press.

Foucault, Michel. 1969. *L'archéologie du savoir*. Paris: Gallimard.

– 1972. *Histoire de la folie à l'âge classique*. Paris: Gallimard.

Frye, Northrop. 1957. *Anatomy of Criticism*. Princeton, NJ: Princeton University Press.

Fumagalli, Armando. 1995. *Il reale nel linguaggio. Indicalità e realismo nella semiotica di Peirce*. Milan: Vita e Pensiero.

Gadamer, Hans-Georg. 1990. *Gesammelte Werke. Hermeneutik I+II*. Tübingen: Mohr.

Gale, Richard. 1996. 'William James's Quest to Have It All.' *Transactions of the Charles S. Peirce Society* 32(4): 568–96.

Gaudreault, André (sous la dir.). 1988. *Ce que je vois de mon ciné ... La représentation du regard dans le cinéma des premiers temps.* Paris: Meridiens Klincksieck.

Godard, Jean-Luc. 1985. *Jean-Luc Godard par Jean-Luc Godard.* Paris: Cahiers du Cinéma / Éditions de l'Étoile.

Gombrich, E.H. 1959. *Art and Illusion. A Study in the Psychology of Pictorial Representation.* London: Phaidon.

Goodman, Nelson. 1968. *Languages of Art: An Approach to a Theory of Symbols.* Indianapolis: Indiana University Press.

Greimas, Algirdas Julien. 1966. *Sémantique structurale.* Paris: Larousse.

– 1970. *Du sens. Essais sémiotiques.* Paris: Seuil.

– 1976. 'Pour une théorie des modalités.' Langages 43: 90–107.

– 1983. *Du sens II. Essais sémiotiques.* Paris: Seuil.

– 1986. *Sémiotique. Dictionnaire raisonné de la théorie du langage. II (Compléments, débats, propositions).* Paris: Hachette.

– 1989. 'On Meaning.' In *New Literary History* 20(3): 539–50.

Greimas, Algirdas Julien, and Joseph Courtés. 1979. *Sémiotique. Dictionnaire raisonné de la théorie du langage.* Paris: Hachette.

Guynn, William. 1990. *A Cinema of Nonfiction.* Rutherford: Associated University Presses.

Habermas, Jürgen. 1968. *Erkenntnis und Interesse.* Frankfurt: Suhrkamp.

– 1981. *Theorie des kommunikativen Handelns. I & II.* Frankfurt: Suhrkamp.

Hamburger, Käte. 1968. *Die Logik der Dichtung.* Stuttgart: Klett.

Heidegger, Martin. 1927. *Sein und Zeit. 7. Ausgabe.* Tübingen: Niemeyer.

– 1962. *Being and Time.* New York: Harper and Row.

– 1985. *Gesammelte Werke.* Frankfurt: V. Klostermann.

Hénault, Anne. 1983. *Narratologie, sémiotique générale. Les enjeux de la sémiologie 2.* Paris: PUF.

Henderson, Brian. 1980. *A Critique of Film Theory.* New York: Dutton.

Hesse, Mary. 1978. 'Theory and Value in the Social Sciences.' In Christopher Hookway and Philip Pettit (eds.), *Action and Interpretation: Studies in the Philosophy of the Social Sciences.* Cambridge: Cambridge University Press.

Hintikka, Jaakko. 1997. 'The Place of C.S. Peirce in the History of Logical Theory.' In Jacqueline Brunning and Paul Forster (eds.), *The Rule of Reason: The Philosophy of Charles Sanders Peirce.* Toronto: University of Toronto Press.

Hochberg, Julian. 1989. 'The Perception of Moving Images.' *Iris* 9, (Spring): 41–68.

Husserl, Edmund. 1921. *Logische Untersuchungen.* Band II,1 (131,) Halle: Niemeyer.

– 1966. *Zur Phänomenologie des inneren Zeitbewußtseins: Husserliana X.* Den Haag: Nijhoff.

Ingarden, Roman. 1960. *Das literarische Kunstwerk. 2., verb. & erw. Auflage.* Tübingen: Niemeyer.

– 1962. *Untersuchungen zur Ontologie der Kunst.* Tübingen: Niemeyer.

Iser, Wolfgang. 1976. *Der Akt des Lesens. Theorie ästhetischer Wirkung.* Munich: Fink.

Ishaghpour, Youssef. 1982. *D'une image à l'autre. La Représentation dans le cinéma d'aujourd'hui.* Paris: Denoël/Gonthier.

– 1986. *Cinéma contemporain de ce côté du miroir.* Paris: Éditions de la Différence.

Itten, Johannes. 1970. *The Elements of Color.* New York: Von Nostrand.

Jakobson, Roman. 1963. *Essais de linguistique générale.* Paris: Minuit.

Jarvie, Ian. 1987. *Philosophy of the Film: Epistemology, Ontology, Aesthetics.* London: Routledge and Kegan Paul.

Jauss, Hans Robert, et al. 1968. 'Gibt es eine "christliche Ästhetik"?' In *Hans Robert Jauß, Die nicht mehr schönen Künste.* Munich: Fink.

– 1977. *Ästhetische Erfahrung und literarische Hermeneutik I.* Munich: Fink.

Joas, Hans. 1989. *Praktische Intersubjektivität. Die Entwicklung des Werkes von G.H. Mead.* Frankfurt: Suhrkamp.

– 1999. *Pragmatismus und Gesellschaftstheorie.* Frankfurt: Suhrkamp.

Kant, Immanuel. 1787 (2. hin und wieder verbesserte Auflage). *Kritik der reinen Vernunft.* Berlin: Preußische Akademie der Wissenschaften, Kants Gesammelte Schriften 1902–23.

– 1790. *Kritik der Urteilskraft.* Berlin: Preußische Akademie der Wissenschaften, Kants Gesammelte Schriften 1902–23.

Ketner, Kenneth Laine. 1981. 'Peirce as an Interesting failure?' In Kenneth Laine Ketner et al., eds. *Proceedings of the C.S. Peirce Bicentennial International Congress.* Lubbock: Texas Technical University Press.

Ketner, Kenneth Laine, et al., eds. 1981. *Proceedings of the C.S. Peirce Bicentennial International Congress.* Lubbock: Texas Technical University Press.

Kevelson, Roberta. 1987. *Charles S. Peirce's Method of Methods.* Amsterdam: Benjamins.

– 1993. *Peirce's Esthetics of Freedom: Possibility, Complexity, and Emergent Value.* New York: Peter Lang.

KIM. 1994. *Caligaris Erben. Der Katalog zum Thema "Psychiatrie im Film."* Bonn: Katholisches Institut für Medieninformation und Psychiatrie-Verlag (Hrsg.). Bonn: KIM.

Kinder, Marsha. 1990. 'The Subversive Potential of the Pseudo-Iterative.' *Film Quarterly* 43(2): 3–17.

Kuhn, Annette. 1985. *The Power of the Image. Essays of Representation and Sexuality.* London: Routledge and Kegan Paul.

Leutrat, Jean-Louis. 1988. *Kaleidoscope. Analyses de films.* Lyon: Presses Universitaires de Lyon.

Leventhal, Robert. 1988. 'Heidegger's Signs.' *Kodikas/Code* 11(1–2): 195–211.

Lintvelt, Jaap. 1981. *Essai de typologie narrative. Le 'point de vue'. Théorie et analyse.* Paris: Librairie José Corti.

Liszka, James Jakób. 1981. 'Peirce and Jakobson: Towards a Structuralist Reconstruction of Peirce.' *Transactions of the Charles S. Peirce Society* 17(1): 41–61.

– 1996. *A General Introduction to the Semeiotic of Charles Sanders Peirce.* Bloomington: Indiana University Press.

– 2000. 'Peirce's New Rhetoric.' *Transactions of the Charles S. Peirce Society* 36(4): 439–77.

Lotman, Jurij. 1973. *Semiotika kino i problemy kinoèstetiky.* (Семиотика кино и проблемыкиноэстетики). Translated as *Semiotics of Cinema.* 1976. Ann Arbor. University of Michigan.

Luhmann, Niklas. 1984. *Soziale Systeme. Grundriß einer allgemeinen Theorie.* Frankfurt. Suhrkamp.

– 1997. *Die Gesellschaft der Gesellschaft.* Frankfurt: Suhrkamp.

Marty, Robert. 1990. *L'algèbre des signes.* Amsterdam: Benjamin.

Merten, Klaus. 1977. *Kommunikation. Eine Begriffs- und Prozeßanalyse.* Opladen: Westdeutscher Verlag.

Metz Christian. 1968. *Essais sur la signification au cinéma. I.* Paris: Klincksieck.

– 1971. *Langage et Cinéma.* Paris: Klincksieck.

– 1978. 'L'Étude sémiologique du langage cinématographique: À quelle distance en somme-nous d'une possibilité réelle de formalisation?' In D. Noguez, ed. *Cinéma. Théorie, lectures:* Paris: Klincksieck.

– 1990. 'Michel Marie et Marc Vernet: Entretien avec Christan Metz.' In *Christian Metz et la théorie du cinéma.* Social issue of *Iris* 10 (April). 27–97.

– 1991. *L'Énonciation impersonnelle, ou le site du film.* Paris: Méridiens Klincksieck.

MGG. 1986. *Die Musik in Geschichte und Gegenwart.* Digitale Bibliothek Band 60: vgl. Die Musik in Geschichte und Gegenwart. Bärenreiter-Verlag.

Mitry, Jean. 1965. *Esthéthique et psychologie du cinéma. II Les formes.* Paris: Éditions Universitaires.

– 1987. Jean. *La sémiologie en question. Langage et cinéma.* Paris: Cerf.

Monaco, James. 1977. *How to Read a Film.* New York: Oxford University Press.

Morris, Charles. 1946. *Signs, Language and Behavior.* Englewood Cliffs, NJ: Prentice Hall.

Mothersill, Mary. 1984. *Beauty Restored.* Oxford: Oxford University Press.

Müller, Jürgen E., ed. 1994a. *Towards a Pragmatics of the Audiovisual: Theory and History.* Münster: Nodus.

Müller, Ralf. 1994 'On the Principles of Construction and the Order of Peirce's Trichotomies of Signs, *Transactions of the Charles S. Peirce Society* 30(1): 135–53.

Murphey, Murray. 1961. *The Development of Peirce's Philosophy*. Cambridge: Harvard University Press.

– 1993. Murray. *The Development of Peirce's Philosophy*. Indianapolis: Hackett.

Nesher, Dan. 1997. 'Peircean Realism: Truth as the Meaning of Cognitive Signs Representing External Reality.' In *Transactions of the Charles S. Peirce Society* 31(1): 201–57.

Nöth, Winfried. 1985. *Handbuch der Semiotik*. Stuttgart: Metzler.

Odin, Roger. 1990. *Cinéma et production de sens*. Paris: Colin.

– 1994. 'Sémio-pragmatique du cinéma et de l'audiovisuel.' In: Müller, ed., *Towards a Pragmatics of the Audiovisual: Theory and History*.

Oehler, Klaus. 1981a. 'Notes on the Reception of American Pragmatism in Germany, 1899–1952.' *Transactions of the Charles S. Peirce Society* 17(1): 25–35.

– 1981b. 'Peirce contra Aristotle: Two Forms of the Theory of Categories.' In: *Kenneth Laine Ketner et al., Proceedings of the C.S. Peirce Bicentennial International Congress*. Lubbock: Texas Technical University Press.

– 1993. *Charles Sanders Peirce*. Munich: Beck.

Opl, Eberhard. 1990. *Das filmische Zeichen als kommunikationswissenschaftliches Phänomen*. Munich: Ölschläger.

Paech, Joachim. 1989. *Passion oder die EinBildungen des Jean-Luc Godard*. Frankfurt: Deutsches Filmmuseum.

Paetzold, Heinz, ed. 1987. *Modelle für eine semiotische Rekonstruktion der Geschichte der Ästhetik*. Aachen: Rader.

Panofsky, Erwin. 1927. *Die Perspektive als symbolische Form*. Leipzig-Berlin: Bibliothek Warburg.

Pape, Helmut. 1982. *Phänomen und Logik der Zeichen. Peirces Syllabus*. Frankfurt: Suhrkamp.

– 1989. *Erfahrung und Wirklichkeit als Zeichenprozeß. Charles S. Peirces Entwurf einer Spekulativen Grammatik des Seins*. Frankfurt: Suhrkamp.

– 1990. *Charles S. Peirce. Semiotische Schriften. Band 2*. Frankfurt: Suhrkamp.

Pape, Helmut and Christian Kloesel (eds.). 1986. 'Einleitung' zu *Charles S. Peirce. Semiotische Schriften. Band 1*. Frankfurt: Suhrkamp.

– 1993. 'Einleitung' zu *Charles S. Peirce. Semiotische Schriften. Band 3*. Frankfurt: Suhrkamp.

Peirce, Charles Sanders. 1976. *The New Elements of Mathematics*. The Hague: Mouton (quoted by volume and page number).

– 1981. *Writings of Charles S. Peirce: A Chronological Edition*. Bloomington: Indiana University Press (quoted by volume and page number).

– 1992a. *Reasoning and the Logic of Things: The Cambridge Conferences Lectures of 1898*, ed. Kenneth Laine Ketner. Cambridge: Harvard University Press.

– 1992b. *The Essential Peirce: Selected Philosophical Writings, Vol. 1 (1867–93)*, ed.

Nathan Houser and Christian Kloesel. Indianapolis: Indiana University
Press.
– 1997. *Pragmatism as a Principle and Method of Right Thinking. The 1903 Harvard
'Lectures on Pragmatism.'* ed. Patricia Ann Turrisi. Albany: State University of
New York Press.
– 1998. *The Essential Peirce: Selected Philosophical Writings,* Vol. 2 *(1893–1913).*
ed. Peirce Edition Project. Indianapolis: Indiana University Press.
– Unpublished papers on microfilm, catalogue annotated (1967) by Richard
Robin. Amherst: University of Massachusetts Press.
– 1960 and 1958. Collected Papers. Vols. I–VIII. Cambridge: Belknap. (quoted
by volume and paragraph number).
Peirce, Charles S., and Virginia Welby. *Semiotics and Significs.* Bloomington:
Indiana University Press.
Perelman, Chaim, and Lucie Olbrechts-Tyteca. 1970. *Traité de l'argumentation.
La nouvelle rhétorique.* 3rd ed. Brussels: Éditions de l'Université de Bruxelles.
Peters, Jan-Marie. 1981. *Pictorial Signs and the language of Film.* Amsterdam:
Rodopi.
Peterson, James. 1996. 'Is a Cognitive Approach to the Avant-garde Cinema
Perverse?' In David Bordwell, ed., *Post-Theory: Reconstructing Film Studies.*
Madison: University of Wisconsin Press.
Petitot-Cocorda, Jean. 1985a. *Morphogenèse du Sens I. Pour un schématisme de la
structure.* Paris: PUF.
– 1985b. Jean. *Les catastrophes de la parole: de Roman Jakobson à René Thom.* Paris:
Maloine.
Petric, Vladimir. 1975. 'Dreyer's Concept of Abstraction.' In *Sight and Sound*
44(2): 108–12.
Platon, *Respublica.* Πλάτνος ἀπάντα τὰ σωζόμενα / Platonis Opera quae extant
omnia: Ex Nova Ioannis Serrani Interpretatione, perpetuis eiusde[m] notis
illustrata: quibus et methodus et doctrinae summa breviter et perspicue
indicatur. eiusdem annotationes in quosdam suae illius interpretationis
locos, Henr. Stephani ...(S.l.) 1578.
– *Sophistes.* Πλάτνος ἀπάντα τὰ σωζόμενα / Platonis Opera quae extant omnia:
Ex Nova Ioannis Serrani Interpretatione, perpetuis eiusde[m] notis illustrata:
quibus et methodus et doctrinae summa breviter et perspicue indicatur.
eiusdem annotationes in quosdam suae illius interpretationis locos, Henr.
Stephani ... (S.l.) 1578.
– *Symposium.* Πλάτνος ἀπάντα τὰ σωζόμενα / Platonis Opera quae extant
omnia: Ex Nova Ioannis Serrani Interpretatione, perpetuis eiusde[m] notis
illustrata: quibus et methodus et doctrinae summa breviter et perspicue
indicatur. eiusdem annotationes in quosdam suae illius interpretationis
locos, Henr. Stephani ... (S.l.) 1578.

Portis-Winner, Irene. 1994. 'Peirce, Saussure and Jakobson's Aesthetic Function: Towards a Synthetic View of the Aesthetic Function.' In Herman Parret, ed., *Peirce and Value Theory*. Amsterdam: Benjamins.

Potter, Vincent G. 1967. *Charles S. Peirce: On Norms and Ideals*. Worcester: University of Massachusetts Press.

Potter, Vincent G., and Paul B. Shields 1977. 'Peirce's Definition of Continuity.' *Transactions of the Charles S. Peirce Society* 13: 20–34.

Prior, A.N. 1967. s.v. 'Logic, Modal.' In Paul Edwards, ed., *Encyclopedia of Philosophy*. New York: Macmillan.

Propp, Vladimir. 1968. *Morphology of the Folktale*. Austin: University of Texas Press.

Quintilianus, Marcus Fabius. 1959. *Institutionis oratoriae Libri duodecim*. Edidit Ludwig Radermacher Lipsiae: Teubner.

Rahn, Helmut. 1989. 'Bemerkungen zur philosophischen Rhetorik in der Antike.' In Helmet Schanze, Hrsg. *Rhetorik und Philosophie*. München. Fink.

Ransdell, Joseph. 1977. 'Some Leading ideas of Peirce's Semiotic.' *Semiotica* 19: 157–78.

Revault d'Allonnes, Fabrice. 1988. '"L'esprit dans et derrière les choses": *Ordet*, Carl-Theodor Dreyer.' *Vertigo* 3: 63–6.

Richter, Ansgar. 1995. *Der Begriff der Abduktion bei Charles Sanders Peirce*. Frankfurt: Lang.

Ricoeur, Paul. 1975. *La Métaphore vive*. Paris: Seuil.

– 1983. *Temps et récit. I*. Paris: Seuil.

– 1984. Paul. *Temps et récit. II. La configuration du temps dans le récit de fiction*. Paris: Seuil.

– 1985. *Temps et récit. III. Le temps raconté*. Paris: Seuil.

– 1990. *Soi-même comme un autre*. Paris: Seuil.

Ropars-Wuilleumier, Marie-Claire. 1991. *Écraniques. Le Film du texte*. Lille: Presses Universitaires de Lille.

– 1994. 'The Cinema, Reader of Gilles Deleuze.' In Constantin Boundas and Dorothea Olkowski, eds., *Gilles Deleuze and the Theatre of Philosophy*. London: Routledge.

Rosensohn, William L. 1974. *The Phenomenology of Charles S. Peirce: From the Doctrine of Categories to Phaneroscopy*. Amsterdam: Grüner.

Sala, Giovanni. 1982. '*Kants Lehre von der menschlichen Erkenntnis: eine sensualistische Version des Intuitionismus*.' *Theologie und Philosophie* 57(2–3): 202–24, 321–47.

Sanders, Gary. 1970. 'Peirce's Sixty-six Signs?' *Transactions of the Charles S. Peirce Society* 7: 3–16.

Santaella Braga, Lucia. 1996. 'From Pure Icon to Metaphor: Six Degrees of Iconicity.' In Vincent Colapietro and Thomas Olshewsky, eds., *Peirce's Doctrine of Signs: Theory, Applications, and Connections*. Berlin: Mouton.

Schmid, Wolf. 1984. 'Der semiotische Status der narrativen Ebenen "Geschehen," "Geschichte," "Erzählung" und "Präsentation der Erzählung."' In Klaus Oèhler, ed., *Zeichen und Realität. Akten des 3. semiotischen Kolloquiums Hamburg. 3 Bde*. Tübingen: Stauffenburg.

Schmidt, Siegfried J., ed. 1988. *Der Diskurs des radikalen Konstruktivismus*. Frankfurt: Suhrkamp.

Schrader, Paul. 1972. *Transcendental Style in Film: Ozu, Bresson, Dreyer*. Los Angeles: University of California Press.

Schumm, Gerhard and Hans J. Wulff, eds. 1990. *Film und Psychologie I. Kognition–Rezeption–Perzeption*. Münster: MakS Publikationen.

Schütz Alfred. 1981. *Der sinnhafte Aufbau der sozialen Welt. Eine Einleitung in die verstehende Soziologie*. Frankfurt: Suhrkamp (orig. 1932, Wien: Julius Springer.

Sellars, Wilfrid. 1968. *Science and Metaphysics*. New York: Humanities Press.

Short, Thomas. 1981. 'Peirce's Concept of Final Causation.' in: *Transactions of the C.S. Peirce Society* 17: 369–82.

Short, T.L. 1982. 'Life among the Legisigns.' *Transactions of the Charles S. Peirce Society* 18(4): 289–310.

Siegrist, Hansmartin. 1986. *Textsemantik des Spielfilms. Zum Ausdruckspotential der kinematographischen Formen und Techniken*. Tübingen: Niemeyer.

Simon, Josef. 1989. *Philosophie des Zeichens*. Berlin: Gruyter.

Šklovskij, Viktor. 1966. *Una teoria della prosa*. Milan: Garzanti.

Skoller, Donald, ed. 1973. *Dreyer in Double Reflection*. New York: Dutton.

Smith, Murray. 1997. 'Imagining from the Inside.' In Richard Allen and Murray Smith, *Film Theory and Philosophy*. Oxford Clarendon.

Spinks, Cary W. 1991. *Peirce and Triadomania: A Walk in the Semiotic Wilderness*. Berlin: Mouton.

Stacy, Robert H. 1977. *Defamiliarization in Language and Literature*. Syracuse, NY: Syracuse University Press.

Staiger, Janet. 1992. *Interpreting Films: Studies in the Historical Reception of American Cinema*. Princeton, NJ: (Princeton University Press.

Storm, Ole, ed. 1964. *Fire Film af Carl Theodor Dreyer. Udgivet med indledning af Ole Storm*. Kopenhagen: Gyldendal.

Striedter, Jurij. 1969. *Russischer Formalismus. Texte zur allgemeinen Literaturtheorie und zur Theorie der Prosa*. Munich: Fink.

Tejera, Victorino. 1989. 'Has Eco Understood Peirce?' *The American Journal of Semiotics* 6(2–3): 251–64.

Thomas Aquinas, *Summa theologiae*. v.1 cura et studio Sac. Petri Caramello ...

v2-4: De Rubeis, Billuart, P. Faucher o.p. et aliorum notis selectis, ornata, cum textu ex recensione leonina. Taurini: Marietti (1948).

Thompson, Kristin. 1988. *Breaking the Glass Armor. Neoformalist Film Analysis.* Princeton, NJ: Princeton University Press.

Thompson, Kristin, and David Bordwell. 1994. *Film History: An Introduction.* New York: McGraw-Hill.

Tiercelin, Claudine. 1997. 'Peirce on Norms, Evolution and Knowledge.' *Transactions of the Charles S. Peirce Society* 33(1): 35–58.

Todorov, Tzvetan. 1965. *Théorie de la littérature. Textes des formalistes russes.* Paris: Seuil.

Ueding, Gert, and Bernd Steinbrink. 1986. *Grundriß der Rhetorik: Geschichte, Technik, Methode.* Stuttgart: Metzler.

Veyne, Paul. 1979. *Comment on écrit l'histoire; suivi de Foucault révolutionne l'histoire.* Paris: Seuil.

Wagner, Hans. 1973. s.v. 'Reflexion.' In Herman Krings, ed., *Handbuch philosophischer Grundbegriffe.* Munich: Kösel.

Waks, Leonard J. 1999. 'The Means-Ends Continuum and the Reconciliation of Science and Art in the Later Works of John Dewey.' *Transactions of the Charles S. Peirce Society* 35(3): 595–611.

Walther, Elisabeth. 1976. '*Die Haupteinteilung der Zeichen von C.S. Peirce.*' *Semiosis* 3: 32–41.

Warning, Rainer. 1975. *Rezeptionsästhetik.* Munich: UTB.

Wartenberg, Gerd. 1971. *Logischer Sozialismus. Die Transformation der Kantschen Transzendentalphilosophie durch Charles S. Peirce.* Frankfurt: Suhrkamp.

Watzlawick, Paul. 1976. *Wie wirklich ist die Wirklichkeit? Wahn Täuschung Verstehen.* Munich: Piper.

– 1981. *Die erfundene Wirklichkeit. Wie wissen wir, was wir zu wissen glauben? Beiträge zum Konstruktivismus.* Munich: Piper.

Weinrich, Harald. 1964. *Tempus. Besprochene und erzählte Welt. 2. Aufl. 1971.* Stuttgart: Kohlhammer.

Weiss, Paul, and Arthur Burks. 1945. 'Peirce's Sixty-Six Signs.' *Journal of Philosophy* 42: 383–8.

Werner, Carol M., and Lois M. Haggard. 1985. 'Temporal Qualities of Interpersonal Relationships.' In Mark L. Knapp, ed., *Handbook of Interpersonal Communication.* Beverly Hills: Sage.

Whelden, Roy. 2000. 'The Origins and Use of the Theory of Relations: Peirce, DeMorgan and Music Analysis.' *Transactions of the Charles S. Peirce Society* 36(1): 49–73.

Wiesing, Lambert. 1997. *Die Sichtbarkeit des Bildes. Geschichte und Perspektiven der formalen Ästhetik.* Reinbeck: Rowohlt.

Willke, Helmut. 1989. *Systemtheorie entwickelter Gesellschaften.* Weinheim: Juvenla.

Winston, Brian. 1995. *Claiming the Real: The Documentary Film Revisited.* London: British Film Institute.

Wittgenstein, Ludwig. 1961. *Tractatus logico-philosophicus* (the German text of Ludwig Wittgenstein's *Logisch-philosophische Abhandlung,* with a new translation by D.F. Pears and B.F. MacGuinness: and with the introduction by Bertrand Russell). London: Routledge and Kegan Paul.

Wolde, E.J. van. 1986. 'Greimas and Peirce: Greimas' Generative Semiotics and Elements from Peirce's Semiotics United into a Generative Explanatory Model.' *Kodikas/Code Ars Semeiotica* 9(3–4): 331–66.

– 1996. 'Relating European Structuralist Semiotics to American Peircean Semeiotic.' In Vincent Colapietro and Thomas M. Olshewsky, eds., *Peirce's Doctrine of Signs: Theory, Applications, and Connections.* Berlin: Mouton de Gruyter.

Wollen, Peter. 1969. *Signs and Meaning in the Cinema.* London: Secker & Warburg.

Wulff, Hans J. 1994. '*Die Maisfeld-Szene aus North by Northwest. Eine situationale Analyse.'* montage/av 3(1): 97–114.

– 1999. *Darstellen und Mitteilen. Elemente der Pragmasemiotik des Films.* Tübingen: Narr.

Wuss, Peter. 1993. *Filmanalyse und Psychologie. Strukturen des Films im Wahrnehmungsprozeß.* Berlin: Sigma.

Filmography, by Director

Index